Carl C. Chapman
1670 Bryn Mawr Dr
Newark O

By Bennett Cerf

LAUGH DAY

RIDDLE-DE-DEE

OUT ON A LIMERICK

THE LAUGH'S ON ME

READING FOR PLEASURE

THE LIFE OF THE PARTY

AN ENCYCLOPEDIA OF MODERN AMERICAN HUMOR

GOOD FOR A LAUGH

LAUGHTER, INCORPORATED

SHAKE WELL BEFORE USING

ANYTHING FOR A LAUGH

LAUGHING STOCK

TRY AND STOP ME

Edited by Leonora Hornblow and Bennett Cerf

BENNETT CERF'S TAKE ALONG TREASURY

LAUGH DAY

LAUGH DAY

*A New Treasury of Over 1000
Humorous Stories and
Anecdotes*

BENNETT CERF

With Illustrations by Michael K. Frith

DOUBLEDAY & COMPANY, INC., GARDEN CITY, NEW YORK

Library of Congress Catalog Card Number 65-19902
Copyright © 1965 by Bennett Cerf
Illustrations Copyright © 1965 by Michael K. Frith

Contents

Introduction

Two of my favorite girls in all the world are my diffident wife, Phyllis, and my sometime collaborator, Leonora (Zsa Zsa) Hornblow. Both of them are superb housekeepers, able to open a can of beans with the best of them, preside with assurance over the most difficult dinner party, almost balance a check book, and dress to the Queen's taste on not a cent more than a hundred thousand dollars a year. They have but one serious failing: a sadly deficient sense of humor. This failing manifests itself most clearly—and predictably—when my own sparkling sallies are unveiled before them—only to wither in the icy silence and exchange of "How-much-longer-can-we-endure-this?" looks that ensue.

Even I, with the patience of Job, have been known on rare occasions to protest mildly at this ludicrous lack of appreciation. The end result was not precisely what I had bargained for. The two ladies—sometimes known as "The Twitter Girls" because, when together, they communicate in a series of weird and continuous chirps that only they and a very few highly inbred, supersensitive dogs can decipher, came up with a semi-annual ceremony of which I do not entirely approve. The ceremony has been designated by them as "Laugh Day," when—Zsa Zsa installed as a guest—from the moment I sally forth for a day's labors at my usual hour of 7:00 A.M., the pair of them roll on the floor laughing hysterically at every remark that passes my lips. A "Good morning, girls" brings shrieks of girlish merriment. A "Who the hell has been messing up my copy of the morning *Times?*" sends them into obscene convulsions. By about 7:08 A.M. my justly acclaimed patience has been exhausted, and I am ready to murder them both in cold blood.

That my two sons have seen fit to join in this outrageous

Laugh Day conspiracy is a development that pains me even more deeply, but they are sturdy, fun-loving lads, and I cling to the hope that their appreciation of true wit, despite their stints on the editorial board of the Harvard *Lampoon*, will ripen and mature as they shake off the influences of the Beatles, James Bond, and the New York Rangers hockey team.

Meanwhile, there remained the problem of what name to affix to this compendium of tales and anecdotes—the ninth of my lifetime and my first in five long years. The imminence of 1965's first Laugh Day—duly heralded and savored by everybody concerned but myself—suddenly gave me an inspiration. *Laugh Day* would be the name of the book. And, in my dreams at any rate, it would go marching to glory, hoisting the originators of Laugh Day on their own diabolical petards.

I don't think Americans are laughing enough these days. We're worrying too much about our "image," and whether other people love us enough. The strongest country in the world needs respect from others more than love. And it needs the saving grace—and courage—to be able to laugh a little bit at *itself*. The country that can no longer chuckle sometimes at its own foibles is in trouble. We've become too thin-skinned—and, yes, too pompous.

Laughter is the greatest humanizer and medicine God has given us. It can relieve tension and hysteria faster than all of the newest pills rolled into one. There is no more beautiful, soul-satisfying sound in all the world than a solid, reverberating "belly laugh."

May *Laugh Day* provoke a few from you!

Cordially,

Bennett Cerf

Mount Kisco, New York
Summer, 1965

LAUGH DAY

1. *A Look at the Record*

SOME OF THIS, GENTLEMEN, WAS HISTORY!

To begin at the beginning, rumor has it that Father Adam got bored with life in the Garden of Eden in general, and his wife Eve in particular, and went on a bender one fine Saturday evening. When he returned home he fell into a deep, deep slumber. When he awoke Eve was bending solicitously over him—counting his ribs.

*   *   *

The most incontrovertible statement of the year 1965 was made by a fifteen-year-old on an essay submitted to a students' prize contest on the subject of "Prehistoric Times." "In prehistoric times," stated the fifteen-year-old boldly, "books were very scarce."

* * *

One of those researchers who doesn't care how he spends his time came up with a dubious bit of history concerning Alexander the Great. According to this researcher, Alexander whipped up a crude timepiece for his soldiers, consisting of a chemically treated cloth worn on the left forearm. Under the heat of the sun, the cloth changed colors every hour, providing the Macedonian warriors with the world's first wrist watch. Among historians, adds the researcher, the device is known as "Alexander's Rag Timeband."

* * *

Burt Shafer pictures the boy Nero practicing his violin lesson with obvious reluctance while his mother in the background confides to a neighbor, "I'm afraid my son will never set the world on fire."

* * *

After his conquest of Turkey, the legendary Tamerlane, it is told, found out that the local keeper of the exchequer had falsified his books and was getting rich on loot. Tamerlane ordered him to appear with his records, tore them into pieces, and made his terrified subordinate eat them on the spot.

The successor to this unfortunate grafter was a great deal wiser. When Tamerlane demanded that he appear with *his* financial reports, it turned out that they had all been neatly inscribed on a platterful of griddle cakes!

* * *

Mike Connolly relays a story about an Indian brave who glumly watched Christopher Columbus land and grumbled, "Well, there goes the neighborhood!"

* * *

Fellow who claims he was there quotes Christopher Columbus at a banquet honoring him for discovering the New World. Columbus, claiming he had not expected to be called on for a speech, smiled at Queen Isabella and began, "A funny thing happened to me on my way to India . . ."

* * *

Charles V of France was determined that everybody in his realm was going to subscribe to his own religious beliefs, and killed thousands who refused to conform. Finally, realizing he had failed, he abdicated and retired to a monastery, where he amused himself by trying to make a dozen clocks run absolutely together.

When he failed in this endeavor, he exclaimed, "How foolish I was to think that I could make all men think alike about religion when I cannot even make two clocks run together!"

* * *

"The principle of spending money to be paid by posterity, under the name of funding, is but swindling posterity on a large scale."

An anti-Administration blast by a conservative banker made

in Washington the other day? Not at all. It was said by Thomas Jefferson, almost two hundred years ago!

❅ ❅ ❅

At the height of the French Revolution, Robespierre, mainly responsible for the Reign of Terror, had his heart set on capturing a bold and elusive count who was the head of an effective resistance movement near Versailles. Finally the count was captured, but all efforts to persuade him to reveal the names of his lieutenants failed. He was led to the guillotine. At the very last moment, his nerve failed and he cried, "I'll talk! I'll tell all!" Alas! The blade had already been released, and it severed the count's head clean as a whistle.

Robespierre was outraged by the news, and gave the executioner a terrific dressing down. "How often have I cautioned you," he thundered, "NOT TO HATCHET YOUR COUNTS BEFORE THEY CHICKEN??"

❅ ❅ ❅

What was everyday life like in Paris during the French Revolution—"The Days of the Terror?" Reveals André Castelot in his engrossing book, *Paris 1783–1871*, "Chateaubriand's concierge enthused, 'Ah, those were the days! Every morning there went past my window little duchesses whose necks were white as snow when they were guillotined! Now it's all over. The people's pleasures have been taken from them!'"

❅ ❅ ❅

Judge Carl Friebolin insists that this note was found among the possessions of the Empress Josephine after her death: "Dear Josie: I seem to have misplaced one of my gloves, and since it's mighty cold here near Moscow, I wish you'd look in my top bureau drawer to see if I left it there. If you find it, please rush it to me by special courier, since I now have to keep one hand in my waistcoat—and the troops seem to find this amusing. Your devoted husband, Nappy."

❅ ❅ ❅

A familiar American legend—as rewritten by a Detroit wag:

A Chinese father summoned his four sons and addressed them thus: "Honorable sons, which one of you sullied the honor of our family by pushing outhouse in creek?" Number two son bowed ceremoniously, and admitted, "Honorable Father, I cannot tell a lie. I pushed outhouse in creek." Number two son thereupon received beating of his life.

At conclusion of whomping, bruised Number two son said, "Honorable Father, must point out that great President George Washington never beat son for telling truth. Is not so?"

"Is indeed so," agreed Honorable Father, "but big difference should be noted: great President George Washington not sitting in cherry tree."

*   *   *

Indefatigable researcher Norman Cousins has found out how electricity really was discovered. Benjamin Franklin tried to date a hoity-toity Colonial damsel—and she told him to "go fly a kite."

*   *   *

Little Olde New York (Statistics assembled by Sam Himmell): Broad Street in 1637 was called the "Heere Graft" and Wall Street was known as the "Cingle." . . . Peter Kock, who appears to have been the first houseowner—at No. 1 Broadway in 1633—also is credited with concocting the first Martini cocktail ever served in America. . . . In 1664, at the present Peck Slip and Pearl, intrepid voyagers wishing to be ferried across the East River to Brooklyn would blow a blast on a long metal horn suspended from a tree growing close to the water's edge. Upon hearing the blast, Commodore Rudo Kaplan, an imbiber, would saunter out of the beerstube, don his uniform, find his paddle, and propel them over to "Breukelen." . . . Gas was introduced into the city in 1825, and cabs were first launched on New York streets in 1840, with three in service in front of the old Astor House. . . . In July 1842, New York celebrated the opening of Croton Aqueduct, providing the city with an adequate water supply for the first time. . . . In 1845 the New York Knickerbockers, the first regular baseball club, was organized in New York City. . . . The first practicable passenger elevator was installed by the Otis Elevator Company in Haughwout's Store on Broadway in 1857; and the Tower Building, thirteen stories high at 50 Broadway, was the first steel-structure building in New York, erected in 1888. . . . In May 1883, the Brooklyn Bridge was finished by John A. Roebling & Sons. . . . In 1869–70, the first "El" was constructed in New York City. It ran on Greenwich Street from Battery Place to Thirtieth Street. . . . In June 1885, the French vessel S/S *Isère* arrived at Bedloe's Island with twenty-two tons of the Statue of Liberty in 210 wooden cases. A great celebration greeted her arrival.

* * *

Shortly before the outbreak of the Civil War, President Lincoln had a mild attack of smallpox (the doctors called it varioloid) to add to his troubles. Informed of the nature of his illness, Lincoln didn't lose his precious sense of humor. "It is too bad," he noted dryly, "that this one time while I have something to give everybody—no one comes near me!"

* * *

Another Abraham Lincoln anecdote: Lincoln had in his Cabinet one maverick who was against every move proposed, and automatically disputed every statement the President made. Lincoln, however, was adamant when advisers begged him to get rid of the dissenter. In explanation, Lincoln told about a farmer he once encountered who was trying to plow with a decrepit horse. Lincoln noticed a big horsefly on the flank of the animal and was about to brush it off when the farmer cried, "Don't you bother that fly, Abe! If it wasn't for that fly this danged old hoss wouldn't move an inch!"

* * *

One of those sick comedians swears that an earnest do-gooder was heard asking, "Wouldn't you like to contribute to Indian relief, Mrs. Custer?"

* * *

Only yesterday, it seems, schoolboys were learning that "the sun never sets on the British Empire." History is made so rapidly today, the day-to-day changes are so radical, that it's almost impossible to keep abreast of events. A member of the U. S. Foreign Service was saying the other evening that it was in what now seems like another era—shortly before the outbreak of World War II—that an English delegation visited then President Franklin D. Roosevelt to discuss a tiny uninhabited island which Britain, among other nations, was claiming as its own. "What is the basis for your claim?" asked F.D.R. The head of the English delegation thought for a moment, then explained frankly, "It's always been colored red in the Encyclopædia Britannica!"

* * *

They say that just three days before the final fall of Nazi Germany, Hitler summoned the heads of his disintegrating Air Force, Navy, and Army to the Berlin bunker in which he was holed up and demanded, "How are we doing?"

The Air Force head announced, "We have one plane left: a 1914 model." The top admiral reported, "Our only boat afloat is a flat-bottom rowboat in the park." And the ranking general mourned, "Our remaining troops are undisciplined, unequipped, and in panic."

Hitler brooded momentarily, then brought his hand down sharply on his desk. "That settles it, gentlemen," he cried. "NO MORE NICE GUY!"

* * *

Are there ghosts in the White House? If so, none seem to have manifested themselves to the Johnsons—as yet, at any rate. But former President Truman, Mrs. Coolidge, and Mrs. Theodore Roosevelt all reported apparitions of Abraham Lincoln, and other strange occurrences—never under oath, however. It is a matter of record that when Queen Wilhelmina of the Netherlands was a guest at the White House, she swore that she saw Mrs. Lincoln march straight into her drawing room—and fainted dead away. Mrs. Woodrow Wilson was convinced that the ghost of Dolly Madison dropped in one evening to pay her respects. Even Winston Churchill reported strange noises and visitations while he stayed at the White House during World War II (for top-secret conferences with F.D.R. and Harry Hopkins).

Maybe these are the very ghosts who are writing those so-called "inside stories" of doings in top Washington echelons?

* * *

Had the equivalent of modern-day draft boards been in existence in times gone by, many of the world's most famous military figures, pointed out Dr. Logan Clendenning, would have been turned down cold for the following reasons: George Washington had false teeth, U. S. Grant was a confirmed alcoholic, Bismarck was grossly overweight, the Duke of Wellington was underweight, Nelson had only one eye, Kaiser Wilhelm had a withered arm, Napoleon had ulcers of the stomach, and Julius Caesar was an epileptic!

* * *

An insensitive lady at a dinner party demanded of fellow guest Herbert Hoover, "What do retired U. S. Presidents do to pass the time?" The late President answered graciously, "Madam, we spend our time taking pills and dedicating libraries."

* * *

Bill Nichols has a few encouraging statistics for self-doubters who fear they may not be getting ahead quickly enough:

1. In 1882, a German couple worried that their three-year-old son had not yet learned to speak a word. At twenty, the son was a grubby little office worker—with a side interest in obscure mathematics. The side interest eventually paid off. The son's name was Albert Einstein.

2. A happy-go-lucky drifter was turned down by West Point, and got successive jobs as a soda-jerk and clerk in a haberdashery. The drifter's name: Harry S. Truman.

3. A French lad, born in 1841, got into so much trouble in Paris that his father exiled him to America where he taught French in a girls' finishing school until he paid too much attention to his pupils after hours. Back home in France, he finally settled down to serious business. His name: Georges Clemenceau.

The late starters often cross the finish line first!

✻ ✻ ✻

In light of the fact that the United States will soon be celebrating the two hundredth anniversary of the signing of the Declaration of Independence, an anonymous statistician points out that the average of former great civilizations was just about two hundred years—and that each of them passed through the following evolutions:

1. From bondage to spiritual faith.
2. From spiritual faith to great courage.
3. From courage to liberty.
4. From liberty to abundance.
5. From abundance to selfishness.
6. From selfishness to complacency.
7. From complacency to apathy.
8. From apathy to dependency.
9. From dependency right back to the bondage where it all started.

How far along this cycle will *we* have moved by 1976? And can we profit by the lessons of history?

POLITICS

A stanch Republican commuter had this complaint to register: "The Democrats have made it tough for me to get out of New York these days. I have to go out the Franklin D. Roosevelt Drive, past four Johnson restaurants, to Kennedy Airport, and pay my toll with a Kennedy half-dollar."

His companion, Jerry Beatty, advised him, "Why not save up enough Lincoln pennies, buy a ticket to Hoover Dam—and jump off!"

*　*　*

Fellow running for office in November against a popular incumbent was asked by a voter, "I'd like to know your views on what the main issues of this campaign are." "Main issues?" echoed the candidate. "There's just one, the way I see it. That so-and-so has the job—and I want it."

*　*　*

"Remember," the late Mayor Curley of Boston always advised his young political protégés, "that every time you do a favor for a constituent, you make nine enemies and one ingrate."

*　*　*

Somebody once remarked bitterly to Benjamin Franklin that the Constitution of the U.S. was a booby trap. "Where is all the happiness it is supposed to guarantee for us?" jeered the cynic. "Look at the bickering, the injustice, the poverty."

Franklin smiled tolerantly and replied, "All that the Constitution of the United States guarantees, my friend, is the *pursuit* of happiness. You have to catch up with it yourself."

*　*　*

Wonderful are the ways of Washington bureaucracy! Here's a story about a Californian who applied through regular channels for a job in Washington he knew he was qualified to fill. While cooling his heels awaiting a reply, he happened to meet in person in San Francisco, the head of the very agency to which he had applied, and was given the position on the spot.

The scene now shifts to Washington. Our Californian had been doing a fine job there for three months when a letter was forwarded to him from his old address telling him that, unfortunately, his application for the job he was now holding down had been denied because he lacked the necessary qualifications.

And here's the kicker. The letter had been signed by himself.

* * *

A candidate for Congress in Wisconsin was out drumming up support among his constituents when he spotted one of them milking a cow. Never the one to miss an opportunity, the candidate seized a pail and set out to help.

"That dumb opponent of mine," he began cheerfully. "Has he been around to talk to you yet?"

"He sure has," nodded the constituent. "Matter of fact, he's working the other side of this cow right now."

* * *

At New York's Dutch Treat Club, the late Frank Crowninshield was once obliged to introduce a politician who had just
been clobbered unmercifully in a bid for re-election to Congress. "Gentlemen," began Crowninshield in silky tones, "our
next speaker bears a strong resemblance to the earth. You will
recall that the earth is not a perfect spheroid, because it is
flattened at the poles. That's precisely what happened to our
next speaker."

* * *

Charlie Rice, no great admirer of committees, recalls the
definition somebody once coined for a camel: "a horse designed by a committee"; also William Sumner's warning, "If
you live in a town that is run by a committee, you had better
be on it yourself." Rice sums up:

> Committees of twenty deliberate plenty,
> Committees of ten act now and then,
> But most jobs are done by committees of one.

* * *

"City Hall," said the phone operator, answering a call. There
wasn't a sound at the other end of the wire. "City Hall," the
operator repeated. "With whom do you wish to speak, please?"
Finally the caller admitted sheepishly, "Nobody, I guess. I just
found this number in my husband's pocket."

* * *

Rex Stout was week-ending recently in a Southern town
where two prominent Democrats were seeking the nomination
for mayor. The town was split about fifty-fifty and feelings
were running high. "Who are you going to declare for?" Stout
asked the editor. "I haven't decided yet," admitted the editor,
"but when I do—I'm going to be mighty bitter!"

* * *

New Hampshire conservatives couldn't get over the fact
that the state legislature had approved a sweepstakes lottery.
"To think," marveled one, "that it wasn't until 1947 that they
legalized hand-holding up here!"

* * *

Overheard at the New York World's Fair:
Lady Number One: "What do you think of Cabot Lodge?"
Lady Number Two: "I prefer Grossinger's."

* * *

Don Maclean heard a congressman tell one of his secretaries, "You've been here two months now and I'm glad to note your typing has improved miraculously. However, it's not so good that you can stop wearing those tight sweaters yet!"

* * *

A town in South Dakota was in the process of electing a new mayor and board of advisers, and Mrs. Hubbard thought it would be educational to take her seven-year-old daughter with her to the polling booth. On the way home the daughter asked, "Mom, do you always vote for the men you love most?"

"Whatever put an idea like that in your mind?" wondered Mrs. Hubbard.

"Well," said the daughter, "I saw you put kisses next to their names."

* * *

Senator Borah of Idaho mailed out more letters to constituents than any of his colleagues—and the bulk of them went to his bitterest political enemies. "No point in sending copies of my speeches to friends who already agree with me," Borah explained. "My enemies, however, read every word I say—looking for mistakes."

* * *

A candidate for a high state office in Arkansas was accused by his opponent of merely posing as a "son of very poor parents." "As a matter of fact," thundered the opponent, "my adversary comes from the richest family in his county." The candidate answered calmly, "It's quite true I wasn't born in a log cabin. *But we moved to one as soon as we could afford it.*"

* * *

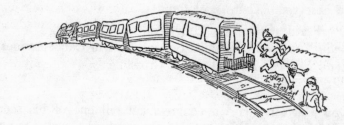

Eugene Field once told how a large group of Illinois legislators were vacation-bound on a train that was held up by bandits. "After relieving the bandits of their cash and watches," concluded Field, "the legislators proceeded on their journey with increased enthusiasm and *joie de vivre.*"

❖ ❖ ❖

A windy, unreconstructed Southern senator put in an unexpected appearance at a big country picnic one late summer afternoon and announced that if a platform could be provided, he happened to have a few words to say to his constituents.

Reluctantly, somebody pulled up a farm wagon which the senator mounted. He then whipped a long speech out of his pocket and began to read it, while some two hundred picnickers, slices of watermelon or ears of corn in their hands, gathered lackadaisically to hear.

When he reached the bottom of page twelve, the senator looked up for the first time. His audience had simply melted away—with the exception of one bedraggled, pop-eyed farmer who stood motionless before him. The outraged senator bellowed, "I thank you, my good friend, for being the one voter in this county who is sufficiently interested in world affairs to stay and listen to my comments. I am grateful to you, sir."

The farmer shook his head vehemently. "I don't care a hoot for your comments on international affairs," he admitted, "but you're standing on my wagon!"

❖ ❖ ❖

Philip Stern's controversial book, *The Great Treasury Raid,* points out the vast difference between illegal income tax *evasion* and entirely legal tax *avoidance.* Judge Learned Hand once observed, "There is nothing sinister in arranging one's affairs so as to keep taxes as low as possible. Nobody owes any public duty to pay more than the law demands. To ask for more in the name of morals is mere cant." Senator Pat Harrison summed it up with, "There's nothing that says a man has to take a toll bridge across a river when there's a free bridge nearby."

* * *

How much did Adlai Stevenson enjoy living in New York? Well, in 1964, he told a story in Washington—and with great relish, too—about a family about to move to Manhattan. The young daughter was saying her very last prayer in her old home. It went as follows: "Bless my daddy, bless my mommy, bless my brother Freddy. And now, dear Lord, I'll have to say goodbye to You. We are moving to New York. Amen."

* * *

John Straley tells about a lovely German fraulein in Washington who was suspected of some hanky-panky with government officials. So an investigator asked her if she'd ever been away on trips with senators. Indignantly, she replied, "Nein" —so she was deported.

* * *

Martin Levin predicts this airwave bulletin one hundred years from today: WASHINGTON: The President checked into the Walter Reed Army Hospital early this morning. Doctors say it may be twins. . . . NEW YORK: Traffic Commissioner Bargle has warned motorists that the city will crack down on litterbugs who fail to deposit their disposable automobiles in trash receptacles. . . . UN HEADQUARTERS: A visiting Dodger spokesman has denied a rumor that the team will move to Tangier. "We'll never leave Kuwait," he declared. . . . DETROIT: The Ford Foundation has granted $750,000 to an educational experiment which will investigate the use of books as possible visual aids. . . .

* * *

Leon Harris in *The Fine Art of Political Wit* has collected these telling observations by the late Adlai Stevenson:

1. An editor is one who separates the wheat from the chaff and prints the chaff.

2. Eggheads of the world, arise. You have nothing to lose but your yolks.

3. Someone must fill the gap between platitudes and bayonets.

4. Much of our foreign policy in the fifties was based on the power of positive brinking.

5. As scarce as truth is, the supply seems greater than the demand.

6. I understand that Mrs. Karl Marx, at the end of a long and bleak life, remarked, "How good it would have been if Karl had made some capital instead of writing so much about it."

*   *   *

Pierre Salinger recalls a day when George Reedy, then the two-hundred-pound Press Secretary at the White House, was ordered to a hospital to go on a strict diet and lose some weight. When his office staff sent him a big basket of flowers, Reedy acknowledged the gift with this wire: "Thank you for the flowers. They were delicious."

*   *   *

From an Indian on a New Mexico reservation came this bit of advice to Vice President Hubert Humphrey: "Dear V.P.: Be careful in revising those immigration laws of yours. We got careless with ours. (Signed) A Native American."

Our Vice President admits he's thoroughly fed up by this time with the story of the male camel with one hump who married a female camel with two humps. They had a baby with no humps, and named it, naturally, Humphrey.

LATTER-DAY PRESIDENTS

William Beebe, in *The Book of Naturalists*, tells about a little game he and President Teddy Roosevelt used to play in the latter's summer home at Sagamore Hill. After an evening of conversation, they would go out on the lawn and search the skies until they found a faint spot of light mist beyond the lower left-hand corner of the great square of Pegasus. Then T.R. would intone gravely, "There is the spiral galaxy of Andromeda. It is as large as our Milky Way. It is one of the hundred million galaxies. It consists of one hundred million suns, each larger than our own sun."

T.R. invariably would pause at this point, grin, and conclude, "Well, Will, I guess we realize again how small we are. Let's go to bed!"

* * *

President William Howard Taft was holding a reception one day when his tailor arrived to try on his new Prince Albert. The tailor was hustled into the reception line by zealous guards. When he reached the President, Taft remarked, "You look very familiar to me." "Naturally, Mr. President," chuckled the tailor. "I made your pants."

"Ah, yes," nodded the President. "How do you do, Major Pants."

* * *

Somebody once asked Woodrow Wilson how long it took him to prepare a ten-minute speech. "About two weeks," he estimated. "And a one-hour speech?" "That would take me a week," he said. "And a two-hour speech?" "Oh," laughed the President, "if you'll let me ramble on for two hours, I'm ready now."

* * *

When Woodrow Wilson was President, he often complimented author Oliver Herford, and, in fact, liked to repeat Herford's better quips in his political speeches. This didn't please Herford at all, because he considered Wilson a political accident and a piece of bad luck visited on a helpless populace. So the dedication in Herford's next book, *This Giddy Globe*, ran, "To President Wilson: with all his faults he quotes me still."

* * *

Woodrow Wilson's valiant fight for the League of Nations ruined his health to a point where rumors hinted that his mind had been affected. Senator Albert Fall, a bitter Republican foe of Wilson, called to see what truth there might be in these rumors. "Well, Mr. President," was Fall's greeting, "we all have been praying for you." Wilson answered, "Which way, Senator?"

* * *

When Calvin Coolidge occupied the White House, he ducked reporters so consistently that one day they formed a conspiracy against him. Before a conference to which he reluctantly agreed, each one wrote out precisely the same question: "Are you going to run again in 1928?" Coolidge read each slip carefully, without comment or change of expression, then threw them all in the trash basket.

"Gentlemen," he said, "the only question in this lot I care to answer today concerns public schools in Puerto Rico." He then delivered a fifteen-minute talk on the subject, full of statistics. The reporters never tried *that* trick on him again.

* * *

A story President Hoover loved to tell about his predecessor, Calvin Coolidge, concerned the day the Coolidges entertained a missionary at their Northampton home before the visitor delivered a scheduled address at the Congregational Church. Grace Coolidge cooked a special dinner, but the missionary wouldn't eat a bite of it—explaining that a meal would spoil his delivery.

Mrs. C. was so annoyed she stayed home, so Mr. Coolidge escorted the missionary alone to the church. When he came home, Mrs. Coolidge asked, "How did it go?" Cal's laconic reply was, "He might as well have et!"

* * *

A frequent caller at the White House during F.D.R.'s tenure of office was the self-satisfied Alexander Woollcott, who liked to tell the President just what books to read. At one dinner, he inquired testily whether or not F.D.R. had gotten around to a new detective story he had recommended. "I have not," said the President.

Later, F.D.R. told attorney Morris Ernst, "I did read it—and enjoyed it, too—but I was darned if I'd give Woollcott the satisfaction of telling him so."

* * *

Rear Admiral William Mott, who once worked in the White House Map Room, tells about the day President Franklin D. Roosevelt came in to inspect the map collection. "Somehow," recalls Admiral Mott, "I managed to get his wheelchair stuck between the map of North Africa and a filing cabinet. The more I tried to pull him loose, the more we seemed to get tangled up with the cabinet. Finally the President looked up and said with the hint of a smile, "Young man, are you trying to file me?""

* * *

"President Harry Truman," recalls H. Allen Smith, "always gloried in being a country boy, scornful of the pretensions of the stuck-up sassiety folks in the East. Back home, whenever someone got gussied up in a boiled shirt, Harry had a standard taunt: 'You look like a jackass peerin' over a whitewashed fence.'

"Once when he was being given an honorary degree, President Truman tripped over his academic gown. 'Whoops,' he muttered. 'I forgot to pull up my dress!'"

* * *

Truman likes to tell of the day, a year or so after he left the White House, that he went calling on a friend on Park Avenue and rang the wrong doorbell. The man who answered accepted his apology, then did a double take, and exclaimed:

"Say, did anybody ever tell you you're the spitting image of that old ———, Harry Truman?"

* * *

Former President Harry Truman revealed to Marianne Means for her book, *The Woman in the White House*, that he once discovered his good wife Bess on her knees in their Independence, Missouri residence, burning papers in the fireplace. He asked her what she was doing. "I'm burning your letters to me," she said, shoveling in the remainder. "Bess, you oughtn't do that," he reprimanded her. "Think of history!" "I have," said Mrs. Truman.

* * *

Robert Keith Gray tells in his book, *Eighteen Acres Under Glass*, about the time a little girl in the Midwest invited President and Mrs. Eisenhower to a surprise party she was cooking up for her mother. In a postscript she added, "I am also inviting the Queen of England and Lassie."

*　*　*

If you can believe Allen and Rossi, a country club attendant stepped up to former President Eisenhower in the locker room and asked, "Do you notice anything different since you left the White House?" "Yes," was the rueful answer. "A lot more golfers are beating me."

*　*　*

A young reporter in Wichita rode in an open car down the main street with Jack Kennedy during his 1960 campaign tour. While the onlookers cheered lustily, the reporter begged, "Won't you tell the driver he's going too fast?" "It's all right," the soon-to-be President assured him. "They all know who I am."

"I know," grinned the reporter, "but I'd like to give them a chance to see who's riding with you."

*　*　*

The difficulty of making good on expensive campaign promises was something John F. Kennedy understood thoroughly long before he even dreamed of being President of the United States. In his book *Profiles in Courage,* the late President quoted this letter, sent by a California congressman to one of his more persistent constituents:

"Sir: One of the countless drawbacks of being in Congress is that I am compelled to receive impertinent letters from a jackass like you in which you say I promised to have the Sierra Madre mountains reforested and I have been in Congress two months and haven't done it. Will you please take two running jumps and go to hell. (Signed) John Steven McGroarty."

*　*　*

Merriman Smith tells of one of the most unusual phone calls ever received at the White House. It came in via a pay telephone just off the lobby. A voice with a distinct Southern drawl announced, "I'd like mighty well to talk to Miss Mary, please." The Secret Service man who had answered chuckled, "There's no Miss Mary here. This is the White House!"

There was a moment of silence. Then the awed caller whispered, "Pardon me, Mr. President. I sure didn't mean to bother you!"

*　*　*

A certain governor who had the presidential bee buzzing furiously and conspicuously in his bonnet in 1964 was observed rushing out of his private office in a swivet one morning, shouting to his secretary, "Quick! Where's that list of people I call by their first names?"

*　*　*

An understandable reaction from G. Barker:

> The more I examine the world's sorry mess,
> The more I would like to be President less!

*　*　*

An enterprising New York youngster, with infinite faith in the Lord, wrote Him this note recently: "I would like to give my mother, who takes such good care of me and my four sisters, a nice birthday present but I have no money at all, so won't You please send me $100 right away." He addressed the envelope simply, "For God."

Somebody in the New York Post Office was intrigued by the note and impulsively readdressed it to the White House, where it duly reached the attention of President Johnson. The President promptly sent the youngster a check for five dollars with a cheery greeting clipped thereto.

Three days later the youngster wrote another note addressed to God. "It was wonderful of You," ran this one, "to send me the hundred dollars I asked for. But why did you send it through Washington? As usual those birds down there deducted 95 per cent of it!"

* * *

Some of the problems Harry Truman encountered as President of the United States are reflected in a comment he made just before turning over the reins to Dwight Eisenhower. "He'll sit there at the White House," predicted Truman, "and he'll say, 'Do this! Do that!'—and then absolutely nothing will happen!"

* * *

Some examples of the trigger-quick wit of the late President Kennedy:

1. Upon receiving an honorary degree at Yale in June 1962: "It might be said that I now have the best of both worlds: a Harvard education and a Yale degree."

2. An inscription on a copy of a photograph of the President, snapped by Senator Goldwater: "For Barry Goldwater, whom I urge to follow the career for which he has shown such outstanding talent—photography. From his friend, John Kennedy."

3. On appointing his brother, Bobby Kennedy, as Attorney General in 1961: "I see nothing wrong with giving Robert some legal experience as Attorney General before he goes out to practice law."

4. To a Los Angeles crowd, while campaigning in 1960, he began, "I appreciate your welcome. As the cow said to the Maine farmer, 'Thank you for a warm hand on a cold morning.'"

5. At SHAPE Headquarters in Paris, in June 1961: "I do not think it altogether inappropriate to introduce myself to this audience. I am the man who accompanied Jacqueline Kennedy to Paris—and I have enjoyed it."

6. Asked by a small boy at Cape Cod, "Mr. President, how did you become a war hero?" he replied, "It was absolutely involuntary. They sank my boat."

7. To a White House dinner for Nobel Prize winners, he

commented, "I think this is the most extraordinary collection
of talent and human knowledge that has ever been gathered
together at the White House—with the possible exception of
when Thomas Jefferson dined alone."

*   *   *

Dwight Eisenhower joins the growing list of people demanding shorter presidential campaigns. "By golly," he recalls, "I
sure got tired of all that clackety-clack!"

When Calvin Coolidge was campaigning, somebody asked
him why he didn't play up more to famous novelists and poets.
Answered Coolidge, "I knew a poet once, when I was in Amherst. Class poet, name of Smith. Never heard of him since."

*   *   *

The United States continues to subject incoming Presidents
to attacks of pneumonia and worse by insisting that they take
the oath of office outdoors in often foul midwinter weather in
Washington. Ed Newman, however, points out gradual evolutions in the inauguration ceremonies.

It was James Madison, for instance, who first resolved to
wear only American-made clothes at his inauguration. Martin
Van Buren introduced the ceremonial ride the length of Pennsylvania Avenue. William Henry Harrison spoke the longest
—a solid hour and forty minutes in sub-zero cold. It's a wonder
the crowd didn't demand his impeachment then and there!

McKinley's Inaugural Address, incidentally, was the first
covered by motion picture cameras; Coolidge's the first broadcast on radio, and Truman's in 1949 the first flashed on a TV
network.

*   *   *

President Lyndon Johnson received a letter at the White
House recently whose envelope was marked "Personal." The
letter began, "I'm sure you'll remember me. I sent you a get-
well card in 1953. . . ."

*   *   *

Loquacious V.P. Hubert Humphrey won the hearts of all the ladies at a Women's National Press dinner when, on the eve of Inauguration Day, he told them, tongue-in-cheek, "President Johnson has given me only two instructions for the next four years. Number one is that I must keep my eyes open. As for number two—well, I don't think I have to mention that!"

2. *Always in Good Humor*

A PAUSE WITH THE PROS

A hypocritical business pirate once told Mark Twain, "Before I die I mean to make a pilgrimage to the Holy Land. I will climb to the top of Mount Sinai and read the Ten Commandments aloud." "I have a better idea," said Twain. "Why don't you stay right at home in Boston and keep them?"

A reporter visiting Mark Twain's boyhood haunts in Hannibal, Missouri, some years back found one old gaffer who discounted the glory and fame of his erstwhile school chum. "Shucks," he said. "I knew as many stories as Sam Clemens. He just writ them down."

❖   ❖   ❖

From a letter written by Mark Twain in the twilight of his career: "Twenty-four years ago, madam, I was incredibly handsome. The remains of it are still visible through the rifts of time. I was so handsome that women became spellbound when I came in view. In San Francisco, in rainy season, I was frequently mistaken for a cloudless day. . . ."

✷ ✷ ✷

From the notebooks of the immortal Will Rogers:

"In the early days of the Indian Territory, there were no such things as birth certificates. You being there was certificate enough."

"I had just enough white man's blood in me to make my honesty questionable."

"Once you are a showman you are plum ruined for manual labor again."

"Being a front-page hero is about the shortest-lived profession on earth."

(Referring to Calvin Coolidge): "He was the first President to discover that what the American people want most is to be left alone."

(When he was named Honorary Mayor of Beverly Hills): "I've never seen a Mayor who wasn't funny—and when he puts on a silk hat, he's even funnier. What this country needs is more ex-mayors."

✷ ✷ ✷

The late George S. Kaufman once explained to the Dutch Treat Club why it took him over a year to write *Dinner at Eight* in collaboration with Edna Ferber. "Edna," he remarked with some bitterness, "worked from 8:00 A.M. until 3:10 P.M. I worked from 3:00 P.M. until 8:00 P.M. That gave us exactly ten minutes a day together."

✷ ✷ ✷

A group of Montreal nature lovers once invited the great Canadian humorist, Stephen Leacock, to accompany them on a pre-dawn bird-watching expedition. "Ladies," Mr. Leacock told them candidly, "I freely admit that I am the kind of man who would have absolutely no interest in an oriole building a nest unless it built it in my hat in the check room at my club."

* * *

Other memorable lines attributed to Stephen Leacock:

1. There is only one beautiful child in the world, and every mother has it.

2. Many a man in love with a dimple makes the mistake of marrying the whole girl.

3. A friend is a man who has the same enemies you have.

4. Many college graduates need that sheepskin they get to cover their intellectual nakedness.

* * *

A neglected humorous classic, says Frank Sullivan, is Stephen Leacock's *Gertrude the Governess.* Sullivan, a famous humorist himself, particularly likes Leacock's opening paragraph: "It was a wild and stormy night on the west coast of Scotland. This, however, is immaterial to the present story, as the scene is not laid in the west of Scotland. As a matter of fact, the weather was just as bad on the east coast of Ireland. But the scene of this narrative is laid in the south of England."

Later on in *Gertrude the Governess,* one will encounter the oft-quoted "Lord Ronald said nothing: he flung himself from the room, flung himself upon his horse, and rode madly off in all directions."

* * *

Moments of high comedy on the stage that are lovingly recalled by Frank Sullivan:

1. When Ed Wynn, telling another character in a musical about something frightening that had happened to a friend, said, "Why, he turned as white as your shirt." With this, Wynn took a closer look at the shirt, and added, "Whiter!"

MKF
AFTER THE GREAT
GW

2. When Bob Benchley reminisced in a monologue, "While rummaging through a bureau drawer in my youth, I came across some old snow."

3. When Bobby Clark, sampling a bowl of soup in a beanery, was asked by a solicitous waiter, "How's the soup, sir?" and answered pensively, "To tell you the truth, I'm kinda sorry I stirred it."

*   *   *

Many of the late Jim Thurber's finest humorous pieces were devoted to affectionate chronicles of the oddballs in his own family. Of his own mother, he wrote, "For some reason or other, during storms, she always took the telephone receiver off the hook and let it hang. And she lived the latter years of her life in the horrible suspicion that electricity was dripping invisibly all over the house. It leaked, she contended, out of empty sockets."

Thurber's great-uncle, maintained Jim, met with a unique fate: "He caught," noted Mr. Thurber, "the same disease that was killing off a lot of chestnut trees one year and passed away.

It was the only case in history where a tree doctor had to be called in to spray a person."

* * *

James Thurber once encountered a lady at a cocktail party who assured him that his books were even funnier in French. "Ah, yes," mused Mr. Thurber, "I lose something in the original."

* * *

In the last piece that James Thurber wrote, the greatest humorist America has produced in the past thirty years took a dim view of modern trends in his chosen field. "Comedy," he noted, "didn't die; it just went crazy. It has identified itself with the very tension and terror it once did so much to alleviate. The roost is ruled today by what has been called the comedy of menace: horror jokes, magazines known as Horror Comics, and sick comedians. . . . Life at the moment is a tale told in an idiom, full of unsoundness and fury, signifying nonism."

* * *

Meanwhile—back at the high schools—what are a few of the "sick jokes" our teenagers are now circulating?

1. "I guess I've lost another pupil," sighed the professor as his glass eye slid down the drain.

2. James McNeill Whistler came home one evening to find his mother sprawled out on the living room floor. "How come, ma?" he chided her. "You off your rocker?"

3. "Better hurry over here, Mom. Junior just ate the raisins off that sticky brown paper."

4. "But, Oswald, that isn't our baby." "Quiet, you fool; it's a better carriage."

THE PERENNIAL EAVESDROPPER

1. Driving instructor to confused student: "Lady, those steel objects you complain are keeping you from concentrating are the accelerator, the brake, and the clutch."

2. Door-to-door salesman to housewife: "Let me show you a little item your neighbors said you couldn't afford. . . ."

3. One rat in a laboratory cage to another: "I've finally got Dr. Skinner conditioned. Now every time I press the bar and stand on my head he gives me a piece of cheese."

4. In a golf course shelter during a thunderstorm: "When I met my wife, I got a lump in my throat. She was a judo expert."

5. At a hamburger stand: "Who was that cute little blonde I saw you outwit Tuesday night?"

6. Mother, tucking youngster into bed: "Honey child, if you want anything at all during the night, just call Mommy—and she'll send Daddy in."

7. Tulane senior to his girl: "I'll phone you tonight or dial in the attempt."

8. In a crowded department store elevator: "Take your hands off me, you cad! No, not you! YOU!"

9. Little boy leaving a movie: "I like television better. It's not so far to the bathroom."

10. Fight manager to his new heavyweight: "Don't be so terrified. Remember: if he was any good, he wouldn't be fighting you."

11. At Baylor University in Waco: "In my calculus exam this morning I was mighty close to the right answers. They were only two seats away."

12. In the garment district: "I'm truly sorry, Max, but if I let you take off two hours for lunch today, I'd have to do the same thing for every other cutter in the place whose wife gave birth to quintuplets!"

13. At a big cocktail party: "Every time I turned around, he was kissing my wife. So I stopped turning around."

14. In a barber shop: "Just give me a shave. I haven't got time to listen to a haircut."

15. Young lady in phone booth to impatient man waiting to replace her: "This won't take much longer. I just want to hang up on him."

16. Eight-year-old reporting to his favorite teacher: "Pop

came in very late last night and crashed into the garage doors. It's a lucky thing he didn't have the car!"

17. Visitor from outer space getting his first glimpse of a skating rink: "Well, well! People on the rocks!"

18. Darling old lady at an airline ticket counter: "How long a hangover will I have in St. Louis?"

19. Chiropractor giving patient a massage: "It's going to rain. I can feel it in your bones!"

20. Long-winded Rotarian at the microphone: "I will have to conclude this discourse because of my throat. Several members have threatened to cut it."

21. In a locker room: "There's only one way I can let the kids know when I'm home from the office. I walk in front of the television set."

22. At Aqueduct Race Track: "I haven't got a cent to bet today. My wife just blew our entire bankroll on the rent."

23. Dignified Harvardite resisting the advances of an ardent Radcliffe-Hanger: "Please, Miss Arbuthnot: you're steaming my glasses."

24. Golfer, yelling from the woods: "Never mind about my ball, caddy. Come find *me!*"

25. Newlywed to his bride: "Save the recipe for that tapioca pudding, darling. I have to mend a patch in the driveway."

26. Father to son asking for money: "Junior, have you ever considered being a professional fund-raiser?"

27. At Danny's Hideaway: "No wonder she's gushing. The fellow she's dining with owns two hundred oil wells."

28. Complaint by a member of a trio specializing in folk songs: "My son loosened one of the strings on my gee-tar and he won't tell me which one!"

29. On a Fifth Avenue bus: "Grandma can never find her glasses any more—so now she drinks from the can."

30. In an Eskimo igloo: "My wife is driving me nuts. She keeps asking me to buy her a *cloth* coat!"

31. At Schrafft's: "My fiancé likes the same thing I do—only he likes to save it and I like to spend it."

32. Near M.I.T.: "My wife doesn't understand me. I'm a nuclear physicist."

33. Off Broadway: "That man tosses money around like a boomerang."

34. At a party honoring a film star just back from a safari in Africa: "He's the first man the head shrinkers ever failed with."

35. In a big office: "A fresh goof tried to pick me up in his big convertible last night. Boy, what an apartment he's got!"

36. From a customer in a branch post office: "This package contains a very fragile vase—so please throw it underhand."

37. In St. Petersburg, Florida: "When I was a kid, ten cents was a lot of money. How dimes have changed!"

38. Mr. Meek to his domineering wife: "I will NOT take you to '21' this evening—and that's semi-final!"

39. At a commencement dance at a seaboard university: "I'll give you exactly forty-five minutes to get your hand off my knee."

40. At a shopping center: "You don't sell used cars? What kind of a drugstore is this?"

41. Man with a terrible hangover hollering at his cat: "Confound it! Stop stamping your bloody feet!"

42. At a bridge party: "My son's new girl friend is so hefty she could play fullback for Ohio State. You know what she wears on her charm bracelet? *Old license plates!*"

43. At Toots Shor's: "I come from a long line of boxers—except for an uncle who was a Doberman pinscher."

44. At a downtown lunch counter: "My boss is so incompetent this restaurant refused to serve him the businessman's lunch."

45. Disgusted drill sergeant, after marching a new lot of draftees around the parade ground: "I've seen better drilling by cans of beer on my TV screen!"

46. In a girls' dormitory on the University of Wisconsin campus: "The important thing in saying good night is to keep your feet on the ground."

47. Broadway star in Dr. Pullman's Dental Parlor: "It's the one in the first row, right, in the balcony."

48. A lady at a bank teller's window: "I want to make this withdrawal from my husband's half of our joint account."

49. Leader of a flock of geese to the birds following: "Stop that infernal honking! If you want to pass, pass!"

50. At a cannibal conclave: "Don't tell me you hate your mother-in-law's guts. Just push them to one side and eat the vegetables!"

QUICKIES

Brevity is a virtue appreciated today by practically everybody but political orators, burlesque show censors, perpetrators of TV deodorant commercials, and authors of current novels.

And whatever else you may say about the thirty-seven "short shorts" in this section, you'll have to admit they're brief. It won't take more than a few seconds to read—or retell—any one of them!

1. Two angels were enjoying an idle conversation aboard a cloud. Finally one asked the other, "Do you believe in the heretofore?"

2. A wife suggested to her husband, "Let's buy Junior a bicycle." "Do you think it might improve his behavior?" asked

the ever-hopeful husband. "I do not," admitted the wife, "but at least it will spread it over the neighborhood."

3. A bargain hunter went to a gigantic fire sale last week—and bought a gigantic fire.

4. Have you heard about the absent-minded Siamese twin? Everything went into one ear and out of his brother's.

5. A pert miss at a soda counter sighed wistfully, "What I really crave is one of those darling foreign sports cars—with the foreign sport still in it."

6. "Phew," sighed a relieved surgeon as he joined his colleague in the hospital's executive dining room. "I just got under the wire with that last emergency operation! Another hour and the patient would have recovered without it."

7. A movie star saw a fellow thespian enter a restaurant with a beautiful girl on his arm. "That's his wife," he was told. "His wife!" echoed the star. "What a publicity stunt!"

8. Eve Backer has discovered a snazzy new restaurant just off Park Avenue where the prices are so outrageous that when you find a pearl in your oyster you break even.

9. A sporting goods store in Duluth advertised a mammoth removal sale and had spectacular results within four hours. Burglars who read the papers removed the entire stock of the store that very evening.

10. There's at least one understanding wife in Las Cruces who lets her husband go out one night every week with the boys. He's a scoutmaster.

11. There's also a bridegroom there, however, who knew he was going to be henpecked right from the start. As he carried her over the threshold she warned him, "Wipe your shoes."

12. A grouchy boss kept rattling his box of pens and pen-points. "I wonder," whispered his secretary to the phone operator, "what's the matter with his nibs."

13. Two prominent figures in a nudist camp became involved in a bitter argument. The more temperate of the two finally laid a restraining hand on the other's shoulder and counseled, "Hector, Hector! Keep your shirt off!"

14. One thing you'll have to concede to a wolf: he whistles while he works.

15. A brokerage clerk admitted to his folks, "Since I'm married, I've really learned how to meet expenses. My wife introduces them to me."

16. In the Bronx Park Zoo a tipsy gentleman regarded a huge hippopotamus reproachfully and beseeched, "Don't look at me that way, my love! I can explain everything."

17. In a boardwalk auction parlor, a triumphant auctioneer clamped down the cover on a box of garish chinaware and declared, "Sold—to the stout lady with her husband's hand over her mouth."

18. A sailor went peacefully to sleep on a Riverside Drive bench, with this sign hung over his shoes: "Please do not disturb. The fleet's all in."

19. An octopus fell into a cement mixer. Just a crazy, mixed-up squid.

20. Larry Wolters knows a conservative teen-ager who drives a warm-rod.

21. A worker in a violin repair shop claims he restrings an average of fourteen instruments a day. "And that, gentlemen," he adds, "takes guts!"

22. Steve Allen has sent his wife Jayne to U.C.L.A. to improve her cooking. The name of the course she's signed up for is "advanced defrosting."

23. Sign in a Washington merchant's window: "You can fool some of the people some of the time, and generally speaking, that's enough to allow for a profit."

24. There are four things, insists Herb Caen, that every bona fide Hollywood star simply *must* have: a Japanese gardener, a Filipino houseboy, a French maid—and a Mexican divorce.

25. Ralph Henderson maintains that his golf game is looking up: he played a full round of eighteen holes the other day without falling off his golf cart once.

26. A harassed office manager was asked, "Who are you working for these days?" His answer: "Same old outfit: my wife and six kids."

27. A Vassar senior told a plastic surgeon she yearned for a "turned up" nose. The doctor turned it up a trifle too far. Now every time the poor girl sneezes she blows her hat off.

28. A Texas debutante returned her boy friend's friendship ring. She found out his definition of friendship.

29. A gangster's son spent four years learning how to be a successful safe-cracker. He was determined to follow in his father's fingerprints.

30. Two Indian fakirs discovered a tub of nails outside their tent. So they had a pillow fight.

31. There exists one bride who treats her husband like a Greek god. At every meal she places a burnt offering before him.

32. Bob Campbell reports the sad case of the nitwit who fell into a lens-grinding machine—and made a spectacle of himself.

33. Overheard in the Lonesome Pine country:
Door-to-door salesman: Madam, I represent the Stretchit Woolen Mills. Could I interest you in some coarse yarns?
Mrs. Hatfield McCoy: Sure. Tell me a couple.

34. Comic Joey Bishop spotted a midget friend exiting from a health spa steam room and told him, "I warned you, Sam! You can take only so much of that stuff and no more!"

35. A character parading about Fort Lauderdale, Florida,

insists that his name is Seven-and-One-Eighth Flannery. Explains that his parents picked his name out of a hat.

36. A tenderhearted big league baseball manager sought out his third baseman in the locker room. "Joe," he said, putting his arm around the player's shoulder, "it's okay for you to forget all those batting tips I gave you. We just traded you to Kansas City."

37. Robert Q. Lewis, TV philosopher, was in a butcher shop when a lady customer complained bitterly, "That chicken I bought here yesterday had no wishbone." The butcher answered earnestly: "Madam, the chickens we sell here are so happy, they have nothing to wish for."

SHAGGY DOGGEREL

To the surprise of everybody at a recent stupendous, all-star benefit performance, the hit of the evening was scored by a miniature talking poodle who brought down the house with a series of superb imitations and snappy new jokes. While the applause of the audience was at its height, however, a large dog shot out of the wings, grabbed the triumphant poodle by the scruff of the neck, and pulled him offstage.

"Sorry, folks," yelled the poodle as he disappeared into the wings. "It's my mother. She always wanted me to be a doctor."

❂   ❂   ❂

Two "at liberty" vaudevillians met at a bar one afternoon, and one demanded, "Say, whatever became of that talking dog of yours?" "I gave him away," admitted the other. "An actor has to have *some* pride." "But that dog was one in a million," said the first. "Yeah," nodded the other, "but he got too smart for me. First, he took more curtain calls than I did, then he demanded top billing. But the climax came when he started making out his own income tax returns—and tried to list me as a dependent!"

❂   ❂   ❂

Two flies met on top of a huckleberry cake. "How's the
world treating you, Mrs. Buzz?" asked one. "Not so good," was
the weary reply. "Junior's been in such a pet I've had to walk
the ceiling with him all week."

* * *

A man selling two-dollar tickets at the Aqueduct horse racing track registered considerable surprise when a horse stepped
up to the window and asked to bet on himself. "What's the
matter," snorted the horse. "Are you astonished that I can
talk?" "Not at all," said the man. "I'm astonished that you think
you can win."

* * *

Dolores Duck was the most seductive fowl that ever had
paraded on Lake Lookout, but proud, sullen Darwin Drake
remained impervious to her charms.

Dolores had just decided he wasn't worth any more of her
time when she spotted a hunter in the reeds drawing a bead
on the two. "Look out, Darwin," she quacked as she dove to
safety.

When she resurfaced the hunter was gone—but where the
handsome Drake had been there floated nothing but a bunch
of splinters.

"Ah, ha," nodded Dolores in a flash of understanding.
"Wooden duck, eh?"

* * *

A missionary and a very un-Elsa-like lion met head-on in an impenetrable jungle. Flight was out of the question; the missionary sank to his knees and prayed. To his astonishment, the lion did likewise.

"How miraculous," babbled the missionary, "to join you in prayer when just a moment ago I gave myself up for lost!"

"Quiet," ordered the lion severely. "I'm saying grace."

* * *

In a well-stocked clothes closet, a moth and his mate came upon a pair of all-woolen spats and had a feast for themselves. Later the moth flew about a bit to digest his dinner and bumped into a pal who caroled, "Hi boy! How ya doin'?" "Not so hot," admitted the moth, "I just had a spat with my wife."

* * *

Jerome Beatty tells about a doctor whose doorbell began ringing frantically in the middle of the night. He rushed to answer it and found on his doorstep a man on whose head a pelican was roosting.

"Say, Doc," begged the pelican, "can you get this thing off my feet?"

* * *

A family of bears, rummaging in a Yellowstone National Park garbage dump, looked up when a car crammed with eight tourists pulled up at the side of the road. "It's cruel," commented Papa Bear to his brood, "to keep them caged up like that!"

* * *

Hugh Downs submits the story of the leopard who visited his optometrist to complain, "Every time I look at my wife, I see spots before my eyes." "What do you expect?" scoffed the optometrist. "You're a leopard, aren't you?" "Of course I am," conceded the leopard, "but my wife is a zebra."

* * *

Gertrude Bayne avers that she heard two sharks talking off Sandy Hook Light recently. "Take my tip and stay clear of Coney Island," one shark was advising the other. "Irving was swimming down there last weekend and he got mugged."

* * *

A theatrical agent would have no part of an applicant who claimed he could do any kind of bird imitation.

"At least listen to my act," begged the applicant.

"Haven't got time," snapped the agent. "Bird imitators died with vaudeville."

"Okay, if that's the way you feel about it," concluded the offended artist—and flew out of the window.

* * *

According to Dick Rodgers, there was once a vacationing bartender who encountered a grasshopper in a field. "Do you know," inquired the bartender respectfully, "that a very popular new drink has been named after you?" "Golly," nodded the grasshopper, obviously impressed. "Who could have dreamed there'd be a drink named Leonard!"

* * *

According to the always-reliable Jack Lemmon, a lobster strolled into a restaurant and sat down at a table by the window. "What would you like, sir?" asked a waiter, and the lobster answered, "A little mayonnaise."

* * *

En route to the seashore for a weekend engagement, a trainer and his talking dog were speeding along in a new sports car when a motorcycle cop started closing in on them. The dog advised the trembling trainer, "Better pull up at that parking area, and remember—when he gets here, *let me do the talking.*"

3. *All the World's a Stage*

ACTRESSES AND ACTORS

Two grizzled acrobats who had been the opening act in countless dilapidated vaudeville houses throughout the country wound up one night in Boston lodged in jail, charged with assault and battery in the first degree. They summoned a local lawyer, who asked, "What happened?"

"Well, Bertie here and me," explained the elder acrobat, "had a night before our new show opened so we decided to spend it improving our minds. We hadn't been to a concert in twenty years and I said, 'Bertie, this Boston Symphony is supposed to be the cat's whiskers. So that's where we'll go.' We buy seats in Row A, and watch the conductor come out in white tie and tails. We're impressed. Then he raises his baton and what do you think that orchestra does? PLAYS OUR ENTIRE OPENING NUMBER!"

* * *

Another acrobatic duo finally got a chance to play a top Broadway showcase after long, weary years in the sticks. "If you make good in this house," their agent promised, "I'll get you a fifty-week contract playing the whole circuit. But keep your eyes on an owl the manager keeps on the balcony railing. The manager takes great stock in that owl. If he keeps his eyes open during the act, you're in like Sinatra. But if it blinks—good night, Charlie!"

The opening night arrived and the acrobats advanced to the footlights, their wives watching nervously from the wings. Suddenly one acrobat whispered to the other, "Do you see what I see, Joe? That ventriloquist has your wife in his arms and is kissing her madly."

"Never mind my wife," hissed the other. "Keep your eyes on that owl!"

* * *

No admirer of child actors was acidulous drama critic George Jean Nathan. When a more indulgent colleague declared, "In my opinion, 90 per cent of all children are natural actors," Nathan's sharp rejoinder was, "What a pity the other 10 per cent go on the stage!"

* * *

The late Sir Cedric Hardwicke, accomplished British actor, liked best of all his press notices on accolades bestowed upon him by George Bernard Shaw. "Hardwicke," wrote Shaw, "is my fifth favorite actor, the first four being the Marx Brothers."

* * *

King George had a little trouble the day he knighted Sir Cedric. As Hardwicke knelt before him, the Lord Chamberlain read his name. The King said sharply, "Who?" He didn't get it the second time, either, then demanded, "Spell it." "For an actor's name to be spelled out," confessed Hardwicke, "is his greatest humiliation."

It turns out that spelling didn't help King George a bit. He finally whacked Sir Cedric on the back with his jeweled sword, and dubbed him, rather testily, "Sir Samuel Pickwick."

NOW PLAYING CEDRIC HARDWICKE in MACBETH by W. Shakespeare OLD VIC Admission $1.50

* * *

Very early in their fabulous career, the Four Marx Brothers were booked for a vaudeville tour through the Middle West, and their father took a train from New York to Chicago to arrange the details of their itinerary. It was by far the longest train journey any Marx had undertaken to that date, and the entire family trooped over to the 125th Street station to see him off. There were speeches, cheers, and even a few tears as Papa Marx hopped aboard the train. Fifteen minutes later he hopped off again—at Grand Central Station. He had boarded an incoming train instead of an outgoing one.

* * *

During World War I, the immortal Will Rogers was delivering his monologue in the Ziegfeld Follies one evening when a hatchet-faced woman in the ninth row called out, "Why aren't you in the Army?" Rogers gave everybody in the audience time to turn around and look at his heckler, then drawled, "For the same reason, Madam, that you aren't in the Follies: *physical disabilities.*"

* * *

Peter Lind Hayes delights in reminiscing about his erratic old friend, stuttering Joe Frisco. Joe was in constant terror of being robbed, says Hayes. One night he checked into a fleabag in Altoona, and searched every corner of the room before retiring to make sure no robber was lying in wait for him.

Then he double-locked the door and dove into bed. He took one more precaution even then. In the darkness he called out, "Oh, Lord, here I am in Altoona again—dead broke!"

* * *

"There," said a diner at Sardi's, "is an actor who's going places." "Have they given him featured billing?" asked a companion. "No, no," answered the diner impatiently. "I mean his wife is out of town."

* * *

Several years after she had married Charlie MacArthur, great star Helen Hayes announced to him and their young son James that she had secretly been taking cooking lessons, and proposed to cook dinner for them that very evening. "If I spoil it," she ordered, "I don't want to hear a word from either of you. We'll just get up from the table, *without* comment, and go to a restaurant for dinner."

A short time later, she entered the dining room, bearing aloft the first steak she ever had cooked. Mr. MacArthur and Son Jamie were sitting in silence at the table—with their hats and coats on.

* * *

Radie Harris tells of a time Rosalind Russell was doing a series of one-night stands. She was resting for a performance after a 250-mile journey from her last engagement, and hung a "Do Not Disturb" sign very carefully outside her dressing room.

A half hour later she was awakened from a delicious doze by a persistent knock on the door. She jumped up to open the door and found a little girl with the "Do Not Disturb" sign in her hand. She thrust it at Miss Russell and said, "Please autograph this for me."

* * *

Gypsy Rose Lee would have you believe that this is how she embarked upon her career as a stripper: "I was trying out for a singing role in a musical comedy. I sang my heart out, in fact. When I had finished, a brute of a director said, "Well, don't just stand there, young lady. Un-do something!"

* * *

A ventriloquist told veteran showman Bill Kennedy he had developed the sock novelty act of the year. "I throw my mother-in-law's voice," he beamed. "What's so unusual about that?" scoffed Kennedy. "You don't dig this yet," the ventriloquist explained earnestly. "I throw her voice while it's still in her."

* * *

In the Players' Club, the death mask of Richard Sheridan invariably intrigues visiting celebrities. A hard-to-impress author once grumbled to a member, "Hmph! He looks mighty dour for a celebrated humorist." The member patiently pointed out, "You must remember he was not at his best when this mask was made."

* * *

Barbra Streisand, the new toast of Broadway and shining star of *Funny Girl*, was christened Barbara at birth, but later took an "a" out of it just to confuse everybody. Now she says, "I don't care what you write about me—so long as you spell my name wrong." Once she considered changing her name entirely—to Angella Scarangella for no particular reason—but desisted in the nick of time.

She told her first interviewer that she was born in Madagascar and grew up in Rangoon. Investigation proved, however, that she never left Brooklyn until she was fifteen and was an "A" student at Erasmus High there. Nothing ever has stopped her since and, obviously, nothing will. Miss Streisand is a law unto herself.

* * *

George Abbott advised a group studying acting for the experimental theater, "Always be extremely careful of the scenery. There's no telling who had it in his mouth just before you."

* * *

Billy Rose tells the story of a well-known ham actor who gave up Broadway and became a surgeon. He removed an appendix so skillfully one morning that several doctors watching him started to applaud. Whereupon he bowed gratefully and cut out the patient's gall bladder for an encore.

* * *

"My wallet," boasted an old Shakespearian ham, "is bursting with big bills." Then he added sadly, "If only some of them were paid!"

* * *

Oscar-award-winner Peter Ustinov submits to a great deal of kidding about his beard, but refuses to give it up. "People can hear me better," he explains, "when I speak above a whisker. Besides it gives babies something to hold on to when they're climbing into my lap."

Ustinov admits his beard got him into some difficulty when he was riding in a New York elevator. The operator gave it a playful yank (pulling out several hairs in the process) and exclaimed, "I know you! You're that crooked wrestler on TV!"

* * *

Off Broadway, they tell of a performer who tried to impress an agent with a brand new act. "I catch razor-sharp butcher knives with my teeth," he boasted, then, noting an incredulous look in the agent's eye, added, "I suppose you think I'm smiling!"

* * *

Carol Burnett is a great big star these days, but still likes to tell stories in which she figures as the patsy. One of her favorites concerns the out-of-towner who grabbed her arm in the

Waldorf lobby one morning and called loudly to his wife, "Hey, Mae, here's What's-her-name! And you know what? She ain't such a dog after all!"

* * *

Pat O'Brien tells of an old ham actor who was happy to secure a bit part in a new Broadway play, laid in an East Side saloon. He was to portray a customer in Act 1, and again in Act 3.

On the opening night, the director grabbed him when he made his exit in the first act and roared, "You dummy! You left your hat on the bar and the whole audience noticed it." The contrite actor made sure to retrieve the hat when he appeared in Act 3. When he placed it on his head, the audience surprised him by bursting into laughter and applause. "What did I do now?" asked the actor when he escaped to the wings. "Idiot!" bellowed the director. "This last scene is supposed to be fifteen years later!"

* * *

Deems Taylor tells a story to demonstrate that even the greatest stars suffer twinges of jealousy. He attended an audition of budding talent with Alfred Lunt and Lynn Fontanne. The participants—mostly female—groped their way through the sleepwalking scene in *Macbeth*.

Afterward, Miss Fontanne whispered to Deems Taylor, "Absolutely no talent in the whole group"—and added, "Thank God!"

CIRCUSES AND FAIRS

A beautiful and adventurous girl ran away from home and joined the circus. "I don't want to make the usual beginner's mistakes," she told the ringmaster. "Can you give me a few helpful hints?" "Well, for one thing," mused the ringmaster, "don't ever undress around the bearded lady."

* * *

At a convention in Chicago, a magician whispered to the toastmaster, "Boss, I've got a great act for you. Out of the air I pick two hundred lighted cigars, puff on them, and then swallow them." "You mean to say you swallow two hundred lighted cigars?" challenged the toastmaster. "Nothing to it," shrugged the magician. "I buy 'em wholesale."

* * *

George Kirgo, making a survey of new circus acts in Europe, came across one troupe that features a man diving two hundred feet into a sofa pillow. "Of course," amplifies Kirgo, "they use a different man every night."

* * *

For generations, one of the standard products offered for sale by circus hawkers has been "pink lemonade." The origin of this peculiar potation, according to John Ringling North, goes back to the day when one Peter Conklin was handling the refreshment concession for Mabie's Mighty Circus in the South.

One afternoon was such a scorcher that lemonade sales reached unprecedented heights, and Pete Conklin ran out of his principal ingredient: water. He rushed into the dressing room of Fannie Jamieson, the Fat Lady, and heedless of her protests, seized a tub of water in which she had been soaking her bespangled red dress. "Analine dye never hurt nobody," pronounced Pete.

To the reddened water he added a spot of tartaric acid and sugar, and promptly began shouting, "This way for the only lemonade in the world guaranteed PINK." The customers were enchanted, and when nobody came down with even a mild convulsion, pink lemonade became standard equipment in the refreshment tent.

* * *

When Billy Rose's Aquacade was turning them away at the 1939 World's Fair, the diminutive showman was enraged to hear that an unknown had opened a pet shop just outside the Fair grounds with a big sign outside proclaiming "BILLY

ROSE'S PET SHOP." Billy rushed over to tell the unknown, "If you haven't got that sign down by tomorrow morning, I'm going to get out an injunction to close you up permanently." The proprietor replied calmly, "I have a birth certificate handy to prove that Billy Rose is my real name. What's yours?" Showman Rose knew when he was licked. He bought a canary.

* * *

The star tightrope walker of the Ringling Brothers and Barnum & Bailey Circus one winter discovered that she was going to have a baby, but managed to conceal her condition from the management and fellow artists by adroit use of costume and parasol.

At the end of her seventh month, however, the artiste sought out a leading doctor in Boston and asked how much longer she could safely continue doing her act in the circus.

"The circus!" exclaimed the astonished doctor. "What do you do in the circus?"

"I walk the tightrope," she told him proudly.

"Holy smoke!" said the doctor. "You do your act tonight, because I have tickets. But *tomorrow morning,* you *quit!*"

* * *

A circus owner caught his trainer administering a merciless beating to the most valuable elephant in the troupe. "Stop!"

roared the owner. "What's the idea of beating that poor animal?"

The trainer explained grimly, "He tripped in the middle of his act this evening." The owner cried, "Do you mean to say you're beating him just because he tripped?" "Just because he tripped, my left eyebrow," said the trainer—or words to that effect. "He tore the tails out of all your eleven other elephants."

THE FLICKS

Lives there a writer with pockets so lined with gold he never once has succumbed to the siren songs of the movie and TV magnates in Hollywood? I doubt it.

Even James Thurber, one of America's greatest and most uncompromising humorists, hankered after some of that California gold on one occasion, and set out to do a screen version of his own story, "The Catbird Seat." He was assigned a secretary and started to dictate some dialogue. "I'm sorry," interrupted the secretary, "but I don't take dialogue. I only take letters."

Thurber proved equal to the occasion. He began the dictation of every scene with the salutation, "Dear Sam," and he and the secretary got along perfectly.

* * *

George Bernard Shaw was no lover of motion pictures. "Films bore me," he explained, "because they show interminably people getting in and out of limousines, trains, and buses. I am not interested in how people get to different places, but what they do when they get there."

* * *

That great comedian W. C. Fields was definitely antiauthor, particularly after he hit Hollywood. After one full day's shooting on a new script, Fields returned to his dressing room in an unusually jovial mood. "This was a day to remember," he explained happily. "I didn't say one word the so-and-so wrote for me!"

* * *

Gene Fowler once caught the irascible Fields violently kicking a rose bush in his garden. "Bloom, damn you," Fields was muttering.

* * *

When Dorothy Parker was writing screenplays in Hollywood, the bejeweled wife of an important producer named Pizitz bore down upon her in her cubicle in the executives' building and pinned her down for a dinner party eight weeks in advance. Thinking the wife had gone, Miss Parker instructed her secretary, "Remind me to write those illiterate, phony boors that I can't attend their confounded party because . . ."

At this point, Miss Parker looked up and saw to her dismay that the lady was listening, frozen, in the doorway. "Because," Miss Parker improvised hastily, "I am dining that evening with the Pizitzes!"

* * *

A world-famous director tried in vain to cajole a star into throwing himself down a mobile staircase. Finally he exploded, "You coward! I'll show you myself how easy it is."

After his demonstration, while still lying at the foot of the staircase, he sneered at the star, "Well, do you think you can do it now?" "I guess so," said the star reluctantly.

"Okay," said the director. "Go ahead. And while you're at it, tell somebody to call for an ambulance. I've broken a leg."

* * *

Jayne Mansfield recalls that when she was a sweet young co-ed at the University of Texas she once walked into a dress shop and inquired of the manager, "May I try on that bathing suit in the window?" The manager eyed her appreciatively and urged, "Go ahead. It might help business."

* * *

A Hollywood bit player who fancies himself as an irresistible Lothario was boasting about his conquests on location in the San Joaquin Valley. "My very first night there," he revealed, "I had dates with Sally, Irene, and Fido."

"Fido!" echoed a friend. "That sounds like a dog to me."

"If you think Fido was a dog," admitted the bit player reluctantly, "you should have seen Sally and Irene."

*   *   *

Anita Loos recalls a summer day in Hollywood when Aldous Huxley, Bertrand Russell, one of the top professors at U.C.L.A., Charlie Chaplin, and Greta Garbo joined her for a picnic. The dazzling group parked in a shady glen, and not one of them noticed the "No Trespassing" sign tacked to a sheltering tree. Just as they were unpacking the caviar and champagne, an angry sheriff hove into view and demanded, "Don't anybody in this gang know how to read?"

*   *   *

Kirk Douglas, dressed as a Roman soldier of Caesar's legions for a big historical picture, took advantage of a break in the day's shooting schedule to repair to a nearby bistro for a drink. He took with him two lesser actors in similar garb.

The bartender wasn't used to serving movie actors in costume, and his eyes popped when Douglas and his friends walked in. Douglas, noting his astonishment, asked casually, "What's the matter, pop? Don't you cater to servicemen here?"

* * *

Filming outdoor shots for a Western film, Director John Rich had to reshoot one scene seven times because of such extraneous noises as yelping canines and jets flying overhead. A passing lady motorist stopped to watch, and finally interrupted the director to ask, "Why do you persist in shooting the same scene so many times?" Rich answered patiently, "Madam, have you stopped to consider how many theaters there are in this country?"

The lady drove on—satisfied.

* * *

One of those new movie stars with extraordinary measurements is so candid and unpredictable that her studio has assigned two press agents to do her talking for her. An enterprising reporter, however, cornered her when the press agents were out to lunch and came back with an interview that was a sizzler. The star confessed, for instance, that she liked to "wear dresses so tight that the men can't breathe." She also suggested a sure-fire way to keep children from biting their fingernails. "Other mothers should just do what I did," she proposed cheerfully. "I knocked my little boy's teeth out!"

Asked why she was seen so frequently with a wealthy and publicity-mad octogenarian, she explained, "He possesses that rarest of masculine virtues—about fifteen million dollars."

* * *

A pretentious movie producer, always boasting about his rare books, became such a bore that his associates decided to cut him down a peg. They hired an actor from the East and introduced him as a country doctor from Ioway. Quickly, the conversation was brought around to rare books.

"Personally," asserted the good doctor, "I loathe very old books. They're moldy and I can't stand their smell. Only a couple of days ago I threw out an old German Bible that had been in the family, I reckon, for generations."

"Old German Bible?" repeated the producer hastily. "You don't happen to remember who printed it?"

"I think it was Guten-something or other," yawned the doctor.

"Not GUTENBERG!" shrieked the producer. "You fool, you have thrown away a great fortune. We must fly back to Iowa at once and try to retrieve that Bible before it is destroyed!"

"Hold your horses," counseled the doctor with elaborate unconcern. "This particular Bible couldn't be worth anything, no matter who printed it. Some character named Martin Luther had scribbled his name all over it!"

HOLLYWOOD SHORTS.

— Life in Hollywood is like this: a big bad man-about-town was having difficulty persuading a sweet thing to go home and hear his hi-fi set. "Look," he implored, "how long have I known you?" "About three-quarters of an hour," she estimated coyly. "All right then," he stormed, "have I ever lied to you?"

— Will Jones avers that the evening he visited a movie theater in the Middle East, he saw the man next to him tap the lady in front of him and ask her, "Would you mind removing your jug?"

— Envious whisper to a movie star who had had four husbands by a virtual novice who had had only two: "You're two chumps ahead of me!"

— Driving on one of California's jammed-up freeways, observes Matt Weinstock, you can watch a drive-in movie, follow a revolving searchlight in the sky, and wave at a blonde in a sports car—all in the same accident.

— A studio head summoned his assistant, embraced him warmly, and told him, "Mac, old boy, this new project of ours calls for ingenuity, imagination, clear thinking, and hard work. That's why I called you in on it! I want you to resign."

— Mike Connolly cites a Hollywood star who knew instinctively how to behave when invited to the Flower Show. He got potted. Mike has also discovered the one way to keep a couple of jumps ahead of his wife. He plays checkers with her.

— "Husbands," warns Zsa Zsa Gabor, "are like fires. They go out when unattended."

— An indignant chorus girl pointed to a friend, "Remember that fellow I told you about who got me by saying he makes Westerns? The phony cuts up the ham, onions, and green peppers for omelets at the Automat!"

— One of Hollywood's most famous word assassins was invited to a party recently. "I can't make it," he announced regretfully, "but I hope you'll give me a raincoat."

— "I looked too thin in my last rushes," complained a petulant film star to her cameraman. "Can't you do something to make me look round?" The cameraman did something and the star slapped him in the face.

— A reigning Hollywood movie queen told an interviewer earnestly, "I believe very firmly in early marriages. I always get married before noon."

— A movie starlet determined to have her nose fixed, but was appalled to discover that the surgeon demanded five hundred dollars for the operation. "Surely," she persisted, "there must be a less expensive way of doing it." "There is," agreed the surgeon (a mean one, as you shall see). "Why don't you try walking into a brick wall?"

— Two ladies in Atlantic City were watching the emoting of a current blonde favorite in a movie theatre on the Boardwalk.

"I wonder who made her dress," mused one.

"I imagine," replied the other, "it was the police."

*   *   *

Walter Slezak visited Hollywood for a brief chore and while there, called an old, old friend to ask, "How's it going with you?"

"I was in a bad auto crash recently," reported the friend, "but I can't kick."

"Tough break," sympathized Slezak. "And your wife?"

"She ran away with my agent last week, but I can't kick."

"I'm sorry to hear that, but at least you still have that soft job at Paramount."

"What job? They fired me three months ago—but I can't kick."

"With all that bad luck," marveled Slezak, "why do you keep telling me you can't kick?"

"Because," moaned the friend, "I'm in a cast from the waist down!"

*   *   *

Into a Hollywood restaurant walked an ill-matched couple who had already caught the attention of the gossip columnists: a middle-aged widow whose husband had left her millions and a handsome, but not too fastidious young leading man. The gifts the widow was showering on him proved more than the leading man's longtime sweetheart could counterbalance.

Said sweetheart saw him enter the restaurant this particular evening. So did her companion who said, "What on earth can those two find to talk about?" The sweetheart bared her fangs and explained, "It's very simple. She's giving him a complete course in *nouveau riche!*"

*   *   *

The late head of a big film studio in Hollywood was an ardent do-gooder who thought every picture should emphasize the rewards to be won by clean living and the American way. Unfortunately, most of his productions lacked box-office appeal and the fortunes of his studio declined sharply. "Poor Hugo," sighed one of his big stockholders. "He's selling out our company for a pot of message!"

* * *

A hopeful Manhattan bachelor read that Kim Novak was looking for a de luxe New York penthouse. "You can have mine for nothing," he wired her posthaste, "if you will put up with a few things. Me, for instance."

* * *

Here are just a few of the honest-to-goodness names of current movie heroes and heroines:

Kirk Douglas is really Issur Danielovitch; Rock Hudson: Roy Fitzgerald; Tab Hunter: Arthur Gelien; Red Buttons: Aaron Chwatt; Bill Holden: William Beedle. On the distaff side, Shelley Winters is really Shirley Schrift; Cyd Charisse: Tula Finklea; Doris Day: Doris Kappelhoff!

* * *

Doris Day was dining in Chicago's famous Pump Room one evening when a waiter hustled by with a serving of shish kebob (lamb held aloft on a flaming sword—a specialty of the house). "What the heck is *that?*" inquired Miss Day. Jimmy Durante, sitting next to her, explained, "A customer who left only a ten-dollar tip."

* * *

A heartwarming scene was enacted at the poolside of a Beverly Hills hotel the other day. A grandmother was explaining to two impatient youngsters that they simply could not go in the water until the lifeguard returned from lunch. A famous starlet arose from her deck chair and announced that she would be happy to take the kiddies in wading. "How thoughtful! How unselfish of this supposedly spoiled and beautiful girl," thought the grateful grandmother—until the starlet explained candidly when she returned the youngsters, "I had to have some excuse for staying at the shallow end. I can't swim."

* * *

Herb Stein tells of a Hollywood merchant whose wife fell so madly in love with Cary Grant (whom she never had met, of course) that she could talk of virtually nothing else. The merchant finally went to his barber, and pleaded for a haircut that would make him look as much like Cary Grant as possible.

"Leave it to me," said the barber confidently, and went to work with a will. Soon big clumps of hair were falling in all directions. Increasingly concerned, the merchant finally asked, "Are you quite sure you know what Cary Grant looks like?" "Of course I'm sure," asserted the barber. "I saw him four times in *The King and I.*"

NIGHT CLUBS

Before each of them became famous singly on Broadway, Judy Holliday, Betty Comden, and Adolph Green had a night club act that sent audiences into gales of laughter. They repeated their triumph when invited to perform for the Dutch Treat Club—but one famous gentleman at a table directly in front of them never smiled once. It was the late President Herbert Hoover, and Judy Holliday in particular was determined to break down his resistance.

"If this number doesn't get him," she whispered to me, "I give up." Alas, Mr. Hoover again watched impassively and his rather solemn expression never changed.

Directly after the meeting was adjourned, however, Mr. Hoover came up to the three young performers and told them warmly, "You kids have the jolliest, most original act I've seen in years. I don't remember when I've had a better time. You're going to go very far!" "But Mr. President," interrupted the delighted Judy Holliday, "we were watching you particularly, and you never smiled once!" "I know," nodded Mr. Hoover. "I never have learned to smile on the outside. But inside, I was smiling all over!"

* * *

Eyeing the scantily clad chorus girls at a popular night club recently, comedian Joe E. Lewis sighed, "They don't make them like they used to." Even more wistfully, he added, "At least I don't!"

* * *

A new girl in the check room of a popular night club whispered to a veteran employee, "What does it mean when a college student slips you a dollar tip?" "It means," answered the knowing veteran, "that you have given him the wrong coat."

* * *

Milton Berle once broke in a new routine in Sioux City. Late that night he wired his agent, "I won't say I died out here, but when I picked up my suitcase to check out, it had eight handles on it."

*　　*　　*

Herb Stein, in Las Vegas to cover the opening of Mitzi Gaynor's new night club act, overheard a fellow guest at the Sands Hotel complaining, "I'll never share a room again with the fellow I came down here with from San Francisco. At three this morning the desk clerk called to say, 'You'll have to get your friend to stop snoring. They're trying to have a party next door!'"

*　　*　　*

One of the best remembered of the wild parties staged during Prohibition days was the one hosted by producer Earl Carroll, in which he offered a chorus girl fifty dollars to take a bath for the entertainment and enlightenment of his fastidious guests. The gendarmes broke up the party, and Carroll never got around to paying the girl her fifty dollars. Several mothers of other girls in the same chorus line expressed deep concern —not at the bathtub routine, but at the non-payment. As one of them put it, "WHERE was her mother?"

*　　*　　*

George Burns acknowledges a debt of gratitude to one loyal fan named Feldman who came to see his night club act thirty-seven times in succession. Every evening at eight, Feldman's five sons deposited him in a seat in the orchestra, and every night at eleven one of the sons returned to take him home.

"You may ask," continues Burns, "why it took five sons to bring the old gentleman to the theatre and only one son to take him home. The answer is that Feldman fought like a steer."

*　　*　　*

Frank Gilchrist, top executive of a Southwestern oil combine, has a framed picture in his office that depicts a lightly clad night club dancer showing a snapshot to her sidekick. "This is my new fiancé," she is boasting. "He's a clumsy, funny-looking lout, I'll admit. That thing behind his house in the background is an oil well."

* * *

The proprietor of a small night club in Los Angeles has been featuring a singer who, he claims, has a soothing effect on the customers. She calls herself Tranquil Liza.

* * *

Overheard backstage at the Copacabana: "I go with him because he has a will of his own—and it's made out in my favor!"

* * *

Before he won fame and fortune as a night club entertainer and TV standby, Sam Levenson eked out a modest living as a teacher in a Brooklyn elementary school. In the corridor of this school one day, a brash pupil yelled, "Hey, Levenson!" Sam, enraged, grabbed the fresh student by the collar, shook him violently, then admonished him, "In the first place, boy, hay is for horses. In the second place, you owe your teacher a minimum of courtesy and consideration."

A look of utter mystification on the boy's face stopped Levenson short. "What's the matter," he asked in a much gentler tone. "Don't you know what the words 'a minimum of courtesy and consideration' mean?"

"Teacher," faltered the boy, "I didn't even know hay was for horses."

* * *

Alan King complains that his wife is such a compulsive shopper, every department store in town that is planning a sale phones her first to make sure she's available. King also confides that the town he hails from is so small the barbershop quartet consists of three people.

King says that his wife, incidentally, was working in the same office he did when they met. "I took to whispering sweet nothings in her ear," he recalls, "and she whispered back sweet nothing-doings."

* * *

Mrs. Housewife persuaded her overworked husband to take her to a night club—the first one he had tried, he proclaimed, since he had been a junior at Princeton. The doorman at the club, however, greeted him as an old and valued customer and the scantily clad cigarette girl cooed, "Back again, eh, cutie pie?" Mrs. Housewife, without batting an eye, extended a hand and murmured, "I don't believe we've met. I'm Mrs. Pie."

* * *

That talented crooner, Tony Bennett, is worried lest the telephone company's craving for code area numbers seeps over into the field of popular songs. Even now Tony can envisage the day when he will be requested to render a chorus or two of "Moon Over 305," "312, 312, That Wonderful Town," "Shuffle Off to 716," "Way Down Yonder in 504," or "I Left My Heart in 415."

Phone buffs will know that 305 is the code area number for Miami, 312 for Chicago, 716 for Buffalo, 504 for New Orleans, and 415 for San Francisco.

* * *

Vaughn Meader, who became famous for his uncanny impersonation of the late President Kennedy, had, of course, to revamp not only his entire act, but his personality as well, when the President was assassinated. That the new act was off to a big start immediately was a tribute to his skill and versatility. Now he conducts a seminar for pet owners in which he portrays the pipe-puffing Dr. Bow-Wow. To the typical question, "What can I do if my dog has ticks?" he answers imperturbably, "Don't wind him."

Reminiscing about his home town, Waterville, Maine, Meader observes that "It's so small, the local Howard Johnson branch has only one flavor."

TV AND RADIO

The late Fred Allen, one of the canniest and best-loved personalities in all show business, spotted the drift in television early in the game. "The only performers who will last in this medium," he predicted accurately, "will be the 'pointers.' Pointers never do anything themselves. They merely stand in the center of the stage, point to another performer, and announce, 'See that fellow? He's going to do the darndest trick you ever saw!' Then the other fellow comes out and does the trick. A week later, the pointer is back gesturing at somebody else, but the fellow who did the great trick has already given his all and is out in the cold. TV can eliminate pointers if times get tough enough. They can teach dogs to do the same routine simply by smearing meat on the actors!"

* * *

Almost every important official in television circles has a very definite opinion on the supreme value—or worthlessness —of ratings. The trouble is that practically none of the opinions coincide. Columnist George Frazier once wrote caustically that he knew of one show that actually registered a *minus* rating in the Greater Boston area. "Not only does nobody watch it," reported Frazier, "but there's one fellow in Swampscott who calls up every day to knock it."

* * *

Jack Paar, entertaining a glittering assemblage of television nabobs, assured them, "You fellows have made astonishing progress. I can remember the days when commercials were no louder than the rest of the show!"

* * *

James Reston, of the New York *Times*, is one man who has no fear that television ever will replace the newspapers. "One of the great things about a newspaper," Reston points out, "is that, especially on Sunday, you can split the thing up and let everybody in the family settle into a quiet trance with the section he likes best. TV makes you listen to all the news you don't want to hear in order to get around to the news you do want to hear. You can't split up Chet Huntley or throw away part of Dave Brinkley."

* * *

There's a motel on Route 1 in Maryland that reserves one of its units for newly marrieds. A little sign over the door says, "Welcome to Honeymoon Inn." A long-married visitor noticed the unit as he was checking out one morning, and said, "Your 'Honeymoon Inn' doesn't look a bit different to me than any of the other units." "It isn't," agreed the proprietor. "But the TV set inside it is busted. So far not one guest has noticed it!"

* * *

At a rehearsal of one of his big Sunday night shows, Ed Sullivan asked a visiting TV star if he knew whose face adorned a ten-thousand-dollar bill. "I'll give you three clues," volunteered Sullivan. (The face is that of Salmon P. Chase.) "His first name is a fish, his middle initial is a soup, and his last name is what college boys do after girls."

The TV star pondered momentarily, then reached for his wallet. "Mind if I take a peek?" he asked.

* * *

Professional comedians rarely appreciate each other's talents, but George Burns and Jack Benny are notable exceptions to the rule. Not only have they been fast friends for thirty-odd years, but Burns can break Benny up by merely sticking his tongue out at him. Benny calls Burns up from all corners of the globe just to gab with him, and keeps yakking so long that Burns usually ends up by hanging up on him.

Benny, in fact, now counts on this so that one day in Hollywood he told an agent named Rubin, "I'm calling George Burns in Chicago in ten minutes and I'll bet you twenty-five dollars he hangs up on me." Rubin accepted the bet. When Benny got George Burns on the wire, their usual kidding, desultory conversation ensued. Finally Benny, sounding puzzled, said, "Well, George, aren't you going to hang up on me in your usual insulting fashion?"

"I certainly am not," declared Burns, then added, "and by the way, Rubin called me and gave me half his bet."

* * *

A radio quiz show moderator told the contestants, "I'm going to ask you to name some famous episodes in history associated with animals. First, what animal do we associate with Lady Godiva?" An eager young lady contestant blurted out, "Bear."

* * *

There's a fellow at Random House whose face is full of cuts and slashes every morning. He insists on trying to shave himself as fast as they do it on television.

* * *

Abel Green saw the pilot of a new Western TV show, updated to appeal to 1965 audiences. In it, the outlaws beat the stagecoach holdup rap—but are convicted for income tax evasion.

* * *

The wife of the stingiest man in a Western TV station gave birth to twin boys, and the father, in a rare burst of generosity, announced, "If anybody has a cigar, I'll be happy to light it for him."

* * *

During the height of a blizzard in Philadelphia last winter, a local radio station went on the air with a list of events that faced cancellation unless the snowfall ceased. Caskie Stinnett swears he heard this announcement: "The Back-to-Nature Club still plans to hold its scheduled hike tomorrow—provided the Market Street subway is operating."

Televisionaries . . .

—Zsa Zsa Gabor once found time in her busy life to moderate a TV show devoted to husband-and-wife problems. The first guest on the show confessed, "I'm breaking my engagement to a very wealthy man who has already given me a beautiful home, a sable coat, diamonds, a stove, and a Rolls-Royce. Miss Gabor, what should I do?" Zsa Zsa counseled, "Give back the stove."

—Jack Leonard, the stylish stout comedian, squeezed himself laboriously into one of those horrible new miniature taxicabs and instructed the driver, "Take me to a larger cab."

— "TV cameras," frets Kitty Carlisle, "seem to add ten pounds to me. So I make it a policy never to eat TV cameras."

— "Sunday was always the noisiest day of the week in my family," confided Buddy Hackett. "Everybody sang at the top of his lungs in the bathtub." "You all must have been full of animal spirits," commented a friend. "What do you mean, animal spirits?" countered Hackett. "Our bathroom door had no lock."

— Tennessee Ernie Ford before the first broadcast of a new TV series: "I'm as nervous as a tomcat in a roomful of rocking chairs."

— One of Groucho Marx's most famous rejoinders was made when a friend stopped short on Sunset Boulevard and exclaimed, "I must find a Western Union office. I've got to wire my father." "What's the matter?" demanded Groucho. "Can't he stand up by himself?"

— Among Woody Allen's so-called autobiographical notes: "When I was born, my family was so poor my mother couldn't afford to use talcum powder on me. So she used to douse me with kitchen baking soda. The result was most unfortunate. About once every month I'd break out in a severe case of cookies." . . . "I had a terrible education. I attended a school for emotionally disturbed teachers." . . . "The Boy Scouts kicked me out because I tried to rub one stick together to make a fire. This is very Zen—but definitely not Boy Scout." . . . "My wife was an immature woman. I'd be in the bathroom taking a bath and she would walk right in—and sink my boats."

—"Who *says* I don't do my exercises regularly in the mornings?" demands an indignant Jackie Gleason. "Immediately after awakening, I always say sternly to myself, "Ready, now. Up. Down. Up. Down. And after three strenuous minutes I tell myself, 'Okay, Boy. Now we'll try the other eyelid.'"

✿ ✿ ✿

A stunt man was offered a hundred dollars for a one-day task of portraying a savage gorilla in a TV drama. It took him so long to perfect his makeup that he didn't bother to remove it at the lunchtime break. The bartender at the bistro next door was favored, therefore, by a visit from one mighty ferocious gorilla. He never batted an eyelash: simply handed the gorilla a price list of drinks for sale and called to his assistant, "Keep an eye on the peanuts."

✿ ✿ ✿

I've often been asked what contestant, of all the thousands I've encountered on the TV panel show, "What's My Line?" I remember most clearly. Without any question, it was a chap who worked at one of New York's summer recreation centers. No sooner had we guessed his occupation and shaken hands with him, than he walked into the arms of six cops who were waiting for him in the wings.

It developed that the misguided lad was wanted in six different states for stealing automobiles. The minute his face was reproduced on the TV screen every police station in New York was alerted and went into action!

✿ ✿ ✿

The people who dig up occupations to puzzle the panelists on "What's My Line?" have come up with some dillies in the past few seasons. For instance: a lady cow washer; a seller of paper panties for lamb chops; a lady who crocheted pockets for pool tables; a jelly bean polisher; a boxing glove stuffer; a painter of dots on dice; and a man who made false teeth for chickens—as an aid to their digestion!

* * *

"What's My Line?"'s famous moderator, John Charles Daly, has invested some of his hard-earned dollars in two interesting new business ventures: 1. A company producing toothpaste with particles of food mixed in for people who haven't time to eat between tooth brushings, and 2. A tobacco company's new cigarette package that includes plastic ear plugs for buyers who are tired of hearing why they should quit smoking.

* * *

A TV tour of New York City was scheduled for shooting early one midweek morning, with the first scenes penciled in from the very center of the George Washington Bridge, spanning the Hudson. The cameraman picked that very morning to oversleep. When he awakened, he took one look at the clock, threw a coat over his pajamas, climbed into a pair of bedroom slippers, and dashed out of the house. "Get me up to the George Washington Bridge as fast as you can make it," he implored a passing taxi driver. "New York end or Jersey end?" asked the driver. "Neither," said the cameraman. "I've got to get to the center of the bridge." The driver took a quick look at his prospective fare's anguished face and peculiar attire, and shoved him out of the cab. "You don't need a driver, buddy," he announced. "You need a good psychiatrist!"

* * *

At one of those infrequent periods when Bob Hope wasn't feeling up to the rigors of the incredible schedule he sets for himself, his regular doctors told him that among other things he'd have to give up for a time at least was his beloved game of golf. Outraged, Hope kept looking until he found a doctor who told him he could play eighteen holes any time he wanted to. "Thanks, Doctor," exulted Hope. "Just for that I'll remember you in my will." "In that case," the doctor assured him, "play thirty-six!"

Hope confesses that when he took Jayne Mansfield along with him to entertain Armed Forces personnel in the Pacific area, he made her wear a special dress for the tour. It was made of two hundred yards of barbed wire. . . . When the troupe entertained on the deck of a big cruiser, Jerry Colonna pretended to be one of the sailors on the vessel. "What's your job?" Hope demanded. "I polish the brass," explained Colonna. "I've got the shiniest captain in the fleet."

* * *

Touring Army bases one Christmas season, Hope found himself in South Korea, with an audience composed largely of native soldiers who didn't understand a word of English. Fortunately, a Korean major volunteered to translate the comedian's monologue.

The performance was a riotous success. When he left the stage, Hope enthused, "That old routine of mine never got half that many laughs before. Thanks for your wonderful translating job."

The major registered acute embarrassment. "You talked so fast," he admitted, "that I lost you completely after your first three sentences. I was telling the boys a few stories of my own."

* * *

How badly do they cut fine old films so they can be shown on TV with all the commercials intervening? Here's what Bing Crosby has to say on the subject: "I won't swear they're chopping the footage out of old movies on TV, but I saw *Road to Bali* the other night and Hope and I weren't even in it!"

* * *

An autograph hound buttonholed Milton Berle outside of Sardi's and gushed, "I haven't stopped crying, Uncle Miltie, since you quit your regular program on TV." "Confidentially," answered Berle, "neither have I."

* * *

A teenager came home from a party at 3 A.M. and woke up his parents. "Come clean," he demanded angrily. "Which one of you left the TV set turned off?"

* * *

Having problems with events, humanity-wise? Well, we hold these truths to be as plain as the nose on your face – everybody's equal and has got some rights. Try INDEPENDENCE, and you'll get, _absolutely free_, life, liberty, and more happiness than you can catch...

A thought for today proposed by an editor of *Changing Times*: "Without a den or place of refuge, a man can achieve neither tranquillity nor greatness. Jefferson wrote the Declaration of Independence in a serenely quiet room in Philadelphia. The soaring ideas that went into it evolved during hours of reading and contemplation in a secluded library where not a sound could be heard. Had it been a TV-guest-family room, the U.S. today might still be a colony!"

* * *

A television star told his regular barber he wanted a particularly good haircut one morning. "I'm flying to England tomorrow and I'm going to be introduced to the Queen!" The barber was unimpressed. "In the first place," he commented, "English weather is terrible at this time of the year. In the second place, flying across the Atlantic is no bargain with these winter storms raging. In the third place, you won't like the food over there. And in the fourth place, you won't really meet the Queen. There will be about five hundred people at the same time and she won't even know you're there!"

The television star made the trip, nevertheless, and in due course was back in the same barber's chair. "In the first place," he reported, "the weather in England was superb. In the second place, the plane rides both to and fro were so smooth I never felt a tremor. In the third place, I loved the food so much I gained fifteen pounds. And in the fourth place, there were only two other visitors at Buckingham Palace when I met the Queen. And do you know what she asked me? She asked me, 'Who on earth gave you that horrible haircut?'"

LEGIT

Eugene O'Neill, America's greatest dramatist, was the son of the famous matinee idol, James O'Neill. When Gene O'Neill was eleven, his father sat him down for a heart-to-heart talk. "Son," said James O'Neill, "I'm not going to tell you not to smoke, because I know you will. Nor will I tell you not to drink, because I know you'll do that, too. You'll also gamble and chase women, if you're a son of mine, so I'd be a fool to say 'Don't do that, either.' But now I want you to listen carefully to your father: one at a time, Gene, *one at a time.*"

* * *

A would-be dramatist, who had been pestering the great Flo Ziegfeld for weeks to read his new play, was struck by a hit-and-run driver one afternoon directly in front of the old Ziegfeld Theatre with the manuscript tucked tightly under his arm.

When the man was carried into the theatre, Ziegfeld reluctantly produced a bottle of brandy from his private stock. Then he suggested a headline for the newspaper account: "Foul Play Suspected."

* * *

A great star, now a grandmother but still beautiful, dropped into Sardi's West for a snack with a lovely young thing who just had graduated from Vassar. The star's manager, at another table, took one look at the youngster and sent over a note which read, "Who is that ravishing kid?" The star answered, "Me."

* * *

A summer stock company was doing *Springtime for Henry* one week, with *Arsenic and Old Lace*, featuring Boris Karloff, scheduled for the week following.

In the middle of Act 2 of *Springtime for Henry*, a bat suddenly whooshed out of the eaves and brushed the face of the male lead. Very calmly that resourceful gentleman waved the bat away and said very clearly, "No, no, you fool. *Next* week. *Next* week."

The bat flew away and the relieved audience applauded madly.

* * *

The visiting star at another summer theatre boasted to the local manager: "I'm so popular in New York, they're going to name a new cigar after me." "Yeah?" yawned the manager. "Well, I hope it draws better than you do!"

* * *

Play producer Max Gordon recalls in his nostalgic memoirs the time he was readying that famous revue, *The Band Wagon*, which starred Fred and Adele Astaire, Frank Morgan, and Tilli Losch. The score was written by Arthur Schwartz and Howard Dietz, who phoned Gordon in great excitement at 2 A.M. one night to tell him, "We've just written a sure hit song. It's called 'I Love Louisa.'" "Fine," chortled Gordon. "Let me hear it over the phone." Schwartz banged it out on the piano and Dietz warbled the lyrics. Gordon was delighted. "Boys," he told them, "you're wonderful. It will be a pleasure to go broke with you."

One morning Gordon instructed his secretary to locate a certain brash comedian who was working on the road. She returned to report, "You're too late. He died last night in Kansas City." To which Gordon sighed, "He always did!"

* * *

The author of one of Broadway's reigning hits is investing his royalties in Wyoming cattle. Asked why, he explained, "There are two reasons: one, it's a favorable tax setup, and two, cows don't ask for free tickets."

* * *

The late Sir Cedric Hardwicke liked to tell of an evening in Dublin's famous Abbey Theatre, where Irish playwright W. B. Yeats was trying to create the lighting effect for a glorious sunset. For hours he had the electricians trying all kinds of color slides and combinations. Suddenly he saw exactly what he wanted. "That's it," he cried. "Wonderful! Hold it, hold it!" "We can't hold it, sir," answered the chief electrician mournfully. "The bloody theatre's on fire!"

* * *

Playwright William Inge was interviewing a wistful girl who sought a part in his next play. "I've played the lead this season in an important production off-Broadway," she told him. "Whereabouts off-Broadway?" inquired Inge. "Peoria," explained the girl.

* * *

An ambitious Yale student got a job with a summer theatre and came home to report triumphantly, "I've snagged my first part! Next week I'm going to play a husband who's been married for thirty years!" "Good start," approved his father. "Just you stick to it, and you'll get a speaking part yet!"

* * *

Theatrical producer Jed Harris tells of a time when he and the late George S. Kaufman were seeking a young juvenile actor for a part in their Broadway production *The Royal Family*. Kaufman heard that there was a promising young actor named Guido Nadso trying out in a new play in New Haven,

and took a train there to look him over. Sadly he sent a telegram to Jed Harris at midnight. All he said was "Nadso Guido."

One of Kaufman's biggest hits was *The Cocoanuts*, which he
wrote for the Marx Brothers. Late in the run, Groucho tried
to insert a joke of his own, but Kaufman would have no part
of it. "I'll bet they'd laugh at it," insisted Groucho. "Don't forget they laughed at Bell and his telephone." Demurred Kaufman, "Not at matinees!"

A brazen, ill-mannered chorus girl once berated Kaufman for
"overlooking" her in casting his new play. Very properly annoyed, Kaufman asked, "How old are you?" "Eighteen," said
the girl. "Oh, no! You must be more than eighteen," countered
Kaufman coldly. "Nobody's neck could possibly get that dirty
in eighteen years."

Kaufman's lovely wife, Leueen MacGrath, persuaded him
one day in the twilight of his brilliant career to go with her to
a famous antique shop. While she was examining numerous
treasures, Kaufman stood by, so obviously bored to distraction
that an executive of the shop asked him, "Isn't there anything
we can show *you*, Mr. Kaufman?" The playwright responded
sourly, "Yes. What have you got in the way of second-act curtains?"

* * *

Harpo Marx's first professional stage appearance was in the
basement of his flat off Second Avenue in New York. The play
was *Quo Vadis Upside Down*, a travesty written by Harpo's
uncle, Al Shean (of Gallagher and Shean). The admission price
was one cat!

It appears that there was a mouse plague in the neighborhood, and store proprietors were paying a penny apiece for
cats. So Harpo (aged twelve) and an older brother named
Groucho decided to cash in on the demand. Harpo recalls that
the performance grossed seven cats at the box office, but that
the troupe netted only four cents in profits. Three cats got
away.

* * *

That superb playwright—and gentleman—Robert E. Sherwood once signed another theatre great—George M. Cohan—to star in a new play he was producing. To get his signature on the dotted line, Sherwood had to make a firm commitment with Cohan for ten weeks.

The play, unfortunately, proved to be a clinker, and folded after one dismal week on Broadway. Cohan took his check for ten weeks without a word. Many years later, however, Sherwood, out of a clear blue sky, received a check back from Cohan covering the nine weeks for which he had not played. Attached to the check was a note reading, "Dear Bob: I couldn't go out with this on my mind."

The next day George M. Cohan died.

* * *

Outside of business hours, old John D. Rockefeller occasionally betrayed flashes of a certain sly humor. There was the evening, for instance, in the twilight of his life, when he was taken for his first look at an edifice he had authorized: the then brand-new Radio City Music Hall.

Mr. Rockefeller was taken to the back of the very top balcony—a spot from which the mammoth stage looks something like a postage stamp. A herd of trained elephants was going through its paces when John D. focused his attention on the performance. He shook his head after a moment and chided his general manager: "What do you mean by putting mice on the stage of my beautiful new theatre?"

* * *

Happy Memories: When Ed Wynn played a waiter in *Manhattan Mary* and a customer demanded lamb chops au gratin. Wynn shouted to the kitchen, "Cheese it, the chops." . . . When Eddie Cantor told a pair of worn-out acrobats, who invariably closed the show in the old vaudeville houses, "Boys, if you ever expect to get anywhere in this profession, you'll have to dream up a new finish for your act." "New finish!" echoed one of the acrobats indignantly. "Nobody's ever waited to see the old one yet." . . . When Lou Holtz told about the law firm of Button, Button, Button, and Button taking in a new partner named Zipper. "Yes," explained Mr. Z., "I've replaced one of the Buttons." . . . When a druggist stopped Bobby Clark to ask, "Did that mudpack I suggested improve your wife's appearance?" Bobby's answer was, "It did for a couple of days, but then it wore off." . . . And when, in Frank Craven's *The First Year* the lady of the house, preparing dinner for an important guest, asked the new maid, "Did you seed the grapefruit?" The maid's answer was, "Oh yes, ma'am, I seed 'em."

* * *

There's a special niche in Hades reserved for oafs who rush onstage in the middle of somebody else's act to read special messages, but the house manager of a theatre in northern Michigan certainly was justified in interrupting a performance of *Annie Get Your Gun* to implore, "Will the owner of a car with license plate number M-3177 kindly go out and move it. It is parked over an open manhole, and the worker in it wants to go home for supper."

* * *

The man at the box office for the musical hit *Fiddler on the Roof* received an unusual phone call one morning. "I bought seats G-108, 110, and 112 yesterday for the Saturday matinee," he reported in an agitated voice, "and my cocker spaniel just ate G-110."

* * *

Jimmy Durante recalls the night his father first saw him acting behind the footlights. Jimmy rushed offstage to ask his father, standing in the wings, "Well, Pop, how'd ya like my work?" The father, whose name, incidentally, was Barthelmeo Durante, answered cautiously, "Lissen, boy, let's not get in an argument."

* * *

Play producer Josh Logan's mother Susan, who comes from the Deep South and reveres its every tradition, was taken aback a bit when, early in World War II, the son of a fine old family she knew was drafted. She rallied, however, when she heard that he was receiving his basic training at Fort Bragg, North Carolina. "How nice for him to be in that part of North Carolina," she nodded, "at rhododendron time!"

* * *

Never, insists Alexander King, have there been audiences quite so skeptical and hard-boiled as the lonely men who used to crowd into the old-fashioned, bawdy burlesque shows of the twenties. He remembers one night when the strip-tease queen at a theatre in St. Louis grew a trifle too animated, and lost what passed for her costume entirely. While the audience sat stunned for once, and the stripper stood momentarily frozen in her tracks, one beefy spectator in the twelfth row jumped to his feet and yelled derisively, "IT'S A FAKE!"

* * *

My Fair Lady, that incomparable musical, has now been played in over thirty different translations in as many different countries. One of the most intriguing is its translation into Papiamento, a polyglot language of Aruba. In those parts it goes by the name of *Laizo Porko Sushi*, a literal translation of which, any hep Aruban will tell you, is *Liza Dirty Pig*.

* * *

A Broadway agent, lunching at Sardi's, overheard a famous producer of musicals bemoaning the fact that he couldn't find a beautiful redhead to play the lead in an upcoming show. The agent rushed over to the producer and assured him, "I have the perfect girl for the part."

"Great!" enthused the producer. "Get her over to my office on the double."

"She won't be able to see you today," explained the agent. "First she'll have to get her hair dyed red."

* * *

A star of a new musical smash, assured that a three- or four-year run in New York was in the bag, leased a swank duplex apartment on Sutton Place, and had a complete repainting and redecorating job done on it. To give the very independent painter added incentive, the star slipped him a pair of tickets in the third row center—seats that were practically unobtainable even from speculators.

The first of the following month the star was staggered by this item in his bill from the painter: "Wednesday night: four hours' overtime watching customer sing and dance: $36."

* * *

A Broadway producer who has a genius for feuding with six critics, eight stars, and eleven authors and directors at the same time, insisted that one number in a new musical trying out in Boston be eliminated forthwith. "It's awful," he cried.

The author and composer disagreed. "We think," they dared say, "it's the funniest number in the show."

Finally, the producer allowed them to leave the number in when the show moved on to Philadelphia. "It's just to shut you up," he explained. "The audience won't laugh once."

But the audience *did* laugh. In fact, it all but fell in the aisles. The author rushed triumphantly to the producer and demanded, "Do you hear them howling?" The producer came up with the stopper of the month. He grumbled, "They don't mean it."

4. *Animals Galore*

DOGS AND CATS

Dog lovers will be interested in the story of a poodle in Connecticut who objects so violently to the telephone that each time it rings, he jumps up on the desk and bites through the wire. After replacing the wire several times—in places the supervisor foolishly figured the poodle wouldn't be able to get at it—a new strategem was called into play. The phone bell was replaced by a chime. Now, every time the phone chimes the poodle races to see who's at the door.

If we know poodles, however, this new trick will work out just so long. That pooch will have things figured out inside of another two weeks!

* * *

A city dog met an acquaintance at a friendly curbstone. "What's your name?" inquired the acquaintance. "I'm not quite sure," admitted the city dog, "but I think it's Down Boy."

*   *   *

Swift & Company is about to launch a new dog food called "Arf." The slogan, dreamed up by a young genius at the Earle Ludgen Ad Agency, is "The Only Food Dogs Can Ask For by Name."

*   *   *

Late December scene on Madison Avenue: a lady admonishing a cocker spaniel pulling desperately on his leash, "No, no, Stanley! Those are *Christmas* trees!"

*   *   *

Two poodles were watching a couple of exuberant teenagers doing one of the wild new dance routines. "Hmphh," sniffed one poodle, "when I act like that, they give me worm pills!"

*   *   *

A starlet sought to purchase a sweater for her poodle, but didn't know the exact size. "Bring him in and have him fitted," suggested a clerk. "I couldn't do that," protested the starlet. "It's for his birthday—and I want to surprise him."

*   *   *

A rabies scare in the suburbs prompted the town fathers to decree a special inoculation for all dogs in the neighborhood. Several society debutantes volunteered assistance. One of them looked up brightly when rare book expert Dave Randall led in his pedigreed boxer, Lord James Boswell. She opened her record book and inquired, "Name, please?" Randall answered, "Lord James Boswell." Visibly impressed, the debutante continued, "And the dog's name, M'lord?"

*   *   *

Congressman Mike Kirwan tells about a man who picked up his mongrel pup one day, brushed him carefully, tied a ribbon around his neck, and started down the street with him. "Where are you taking that mutt?" asked a friend. "I'm going to enter him in the dog show," said the man.

"You'll never win a prize with an animal like that," hooted the friend. "I know," nodded the man, "but think of the contacts he'll make!"

*   *   *

A sheepdog at Provincetown fell insanely in love with another sheepdog. Into her ear one night at Balliston Beach he whispered, "Mary, I cannot live another day without you. . . . You are Mary, aren't you?"

*   *   *

A lady's big Labrador dog refused to accompany her from the supermarket, and she had to drag him into her car. Back home, the dog refused all commands—and even failed to greet his master—whom he adored—when the latter returned from his office.

Just then a friend phoned the nonplused couple. "Do you

realize," asked the friend, "that your Labrador dog is still waiting for you at the supermarket?"

* * *

There's a student at Iowa State who figures he can make a
million dollars if he can teach his poodle to talk. "You're on
the wrong track," his roommate assured him. "Who'd pay a
million dollars for a talking dog?" "Nobody," admitted the student, "but I bet I could find a half dozen dog food outfits who'd
pay me a million just to keep him quiet!"

* * *

Actor director Romney Brent owns a cat whose nocturnal
adventures dictated an operation at the local vet's. Back home
to recuperate, the cat was steeped in gloom. Mr. Brent's maid
put her finger on the trouble. "Mr. Brent," she declared, "I'm
afraid that poor cat misses himself!"

* * *

Arlene Francis, my Mount Kisco neighbor, claims she was
visiting an authoress named Zsa Zsa Horntoot when a cat
strolled in and asked if anyone had seen the Sunday newspaper. He was handed the paper and left.

Arlene, for once, was almost speechless. "Incredible," she
managed to gasp. "A cat that reads!"

"Don't let him fool you," said Zsa Zsa Horntoot. "He only
looks at the comics."

* * *

A few words from cat-lovers:

"A cat can be trusted to purr when she is pleased, which is
more than can be said about human beings."—*William R.
Inge.*

"To keep their shape without getting muscle-bound from
exercises, women ought to try stretching like cats. You never
see a muscle-bound cat!"—*Corinne Calvet.*

"If a man could be crossed with a cat, it would improve man, but it would deteriorate the cat."—*Mark Twain.*

* * *

My own favorite cat story involves two intrepid young husbands whose wives traipsed off for a summer vacation and left them in the city to keep house together as best they might.

One evening they purchased a four-pound sirloin steak, and left it on the kitchen table while they repaired to the library for a few libations. What with an extra dividend or two, they were weaving a bit when they re-entered the kitchen, but not too discombobulated to overlook the fact that their four-pound steak had disappeared.

A frantic search proved unproductive, but then one of the men noticed that a cat under the sink was licking his whiskers with an uncommonly satisfied air. "I'll bet," he exclaimed, "that cat has eaten our four-pound steak."

"One way to find out," said the other grimly. He seized the cat by the scruff of the neck and deposited it on the bathroom scale. Sure enough, it weighed exactly four pounds.

"Well," he announced triumphantly, "there's our four-pound steak all right. Now where the hell's the cat?"

* * *

Many years ago, Westbrook Pegler, emphasizing the point that expectation of success is often more gratifying than realization of same, wrote about an elderly gentleman in a Gulf Coast resort who went about leading a soft-eyed, gentle old greyhound on a leash.

"Nice dog you have there," people would say. "Is he a racing dog?"

"He was," the man would reply. "He was a very fine, fast-racing dog, too—but one night he caught the rabbit. After that dogs like this lose interest. They discover that the thing they have been chasing so hard is just a phony, and they just lie down from then on and watch the other dogs run. If this dog could talk, he'd be saying, 'Go ahead, you fools: run yourselves ragged for just a mess of hair and sawdust!'"

* * *

Every Girl Scout in little Mary Higgins' Spokane troop was given ten dollars' worth of cookies and assigned the task of selling as many as possible by the following Friday. Results varied all the way from $1.15 to $7.70—until Mary bounced in and planked two five-dollar bills on the table.

"Girls," beamed the leader, "Mary has sold every last one of her cookies! Tell us how you did it, Mary. Did you sell a box apiece to everybody on your block?"

"I did not," said Mary. "I sold them all to the very first gentleman I called on. His dog bit me."

* * *

There is an imaginative couple up Roxbury way in Connecticut who have a cat and a dog. Nothing unusual in that, granted. But wait. The name of this particular cat is "Dog." And the name of the dog is "Cat." The animals answer to their names unfailingly. It's the neighbors who are confused!

* * *

A cat in Kansas City proudly exhibited a basket full of twelve new kittens. "Considering the fact that I didn't know a soul in this neighborhood four months ago," she purred smugly, "I don't think I've done too badly."

HORSES

Frances Parkinson Keyes tells about a Cajun horse-trading wizard west of New Orleans who gave a prospective customer a big buildup on a nag he wanted to sell and concluded, "That horse is not only the most beautiful and speediest in the whole parish, but he is one great actor as well. When you go down to the paddock to see him, just watch that old devil act like he's gone lame!"

* * *

Jack Benny has a story about a race track habitué who was down to his last two bucks. A sympathetic redhead said, "I know an old Irish trick to change your luck. I'll pull out one hair from my head. Wrap it around the two dollars before you place your bet and see what happens."

What happened is that the gent put the two dollars on a 100 to 1 shot—and won! When he repeated the process successfully on the next three races, he ecstatically proposed to the girl, "Love Boat, with your hair and my selections, we're an unbeatable combination. Let's get married!"

They were wed, and for the next five years the hair pulling and wagering were faithfully continued. So today she is totally bald and he's shining shoes outside of a Jamaica race track.

* * *

The sports editor of a crusading newspaper got a phone call just before the bulldog edition went to press. "What do you mean, you can't make a buck at the race track any more?" demanded the caller. "I made over ten thousand dollars at Belmont this afternoon." "Who are you?" countered the editor. The caller answered, "I'm a horse!"

* * *

Two married men were comparing notes on their respective wives. "I took mine out to the race track for the first time Saturday afternoon," boasted one, "and she won four races." "Remarkable," admitted his friend. "My wife gets winded after one watusi."

❖ ❖ ❖

Taken to a race track for the first time, a very conservative lady was persuaded to bet five dollars on the daily double—and she won! As she was raking in her loot at the pari-mutuel window she shook a warning finger at the payoff clerk, and said sternly, "Young man, I hope this will be a lesson to you!"

❖ ❖ ❖

An inveterate race track gambler died, and one of his pals called another devotee of the horses on the phone. "I've got to go to poor Al's funeral," he reported, "but I can't remember the name of the cemetery." "So who cares what the name is," shrugged the friend. "Take the Midtown Tunnel and it's the third one on the way to Aqueduct."

❖ ❖ ❖

Back from attending his first Kentucky Derby in Louisville, Art Buchwald estimated that he consumed about two hundred mint juleps, heard "My Old Kentucky Home" sung almost as often, and was made an honorary colonel of at least thirty impressive organizations. He didn't quite get to see the Derby itself, but just before he left, the greatest honor of all was bestowed upon him. They made him an honorary horse.

❖ ❖ ❖

Herman Levin, one of the shrewdest judges of horseflesh in Shubert Alley, came home from Aqueduct one evening with self-satisfaction written all over his face. "I licked them today, boys," he exulted. "I licked them in the first race, the second race, the third race, the fourth race, the fifth race, the sixth race, and if I'd had a nickel left, I'd have licked them in the seventh race, too."

❖ ❖ ❖

There was once a racehorse, avers Ira Gershwin, who in three years on the track had never finished better than sixth.

Finally the owner told him, "I've stabled and fed you long enough, you no-good palooka. Today I give you your last chance. I've signed a famous jockey to ride you. The other horses in the race are worthless. If you lose this time, I promise you that by five o'clock tomorrow morning you'll be pulling an ice wagon."

The race began. At the clubhouse turn, our poor horse was dead last. The jockey resorted to his whip. The aggrieved horse turned his head and snapped, "Cut that out, will you? I gotta be up tomorrow morning at five o'clock!"

* * *

Mourns comedian Joe E. Lewis, "Did I have a great Derby winner last year! But she wouldn't go to Louisville with me."

* * *

Martin Gabel, racing expert, was visiting the stable of Alfred Vanderbilt when he noticed one nag prancing around his stall with the arrogance of a Derby winner. "I notice," remarked Gabel, "that he's 70 to 1 in this afternoon's feature race. What's he got to be so high-hat about?" "Not so loud," cautioned Vanderbilt. "He thinks he's the favorite."

WHO'S ZOO

A Midwest zoo boasted a lion that was known far and wide for his fierce roars and majestic mien, but old age began to cramp his style, and the directors bought a very young lion as insurance.

The young lion was placed in a cage adjoining the old lion's. At five o'clock sharp a keeper appeared and tossed twenty pounds of fine, red beefsteak into the old lion's cage. All the new lion got, however, was a bunch of grapes and a banana.

The young lion was outraged. "I don't mean to hurt your feelings," he told the old lion, "but maybe you are responsible for my getting a raw deal instead of raw meat. How can an up-and-coming, self-respecting lion be expected to do his stuff on a diet of grapes and a banana?"

"You are the victim of a crisis in the city's finances," sighed the old lion. "The budget for this zoo now allows for only one beaten-up lion and that is I. They've had to inventory you as a monkey."

* * *

Books about lions, incidentally, are very much in fashion these days. One of the most fascinating is *Ibamba* by Wynant Hubbard, in which the reader will discover, for example, that:

1. Most lions have a definite sense of humor.

2. Female lions moan piteously with rage and grief when their mates are killed.

3. Male lions go for cheap perfume in a very big way.

4. Lions whistle like birds! (Mr. Hubbard swears to this.)

5. A lion bellowing on a misty night can be heard eight miles away.

* * *

In *A Midsummer Night's Dream* William Shakespeare observed, "A lion among ladies is a most dreadful thing"—and for centuries not even a horse could be found who would say him "Neigh." And yet, here in 1965, in a fashionable cocktail lounge, a very lusty lion sat lapping up the juice in obvious content with three very busty ladies, who also were feeling no pain.

"Gad," exclaimed a bedazzled barfly, "get a load of that lion. He's almost human!"

"You can say that again," nodded the bartender. "Wait till you see him laugh his way out of paying for the next round!"

* * *

An out-of-town member of one of the most exclusive and hoity-toity clubs on Fifth Avenue was glancing listlessly over the evening stock exchange tables when a remarkable sight met his eyes. Feebly clutching the arm of a passing attendant, he wheezed, "Do my old eyes deceive me, or do I perceive two penguins strutting up and down this supposedly sacred chamber?" "Of course they're penguins," nodded the unperturbed attendant. "Where else do you think they'd feel comfortable in tails at five-thirty in the afternoon?"

✿　✿　✿

Zoologist Rowland Taylor has discovered how penguins keep their feet warm—even when they're standing all day on a cake of solid ice. It seems that they just rear back on their well-padded tails and keep their tootsies off the ice entirely. Dr. Taylor adds that this is a hereditary instinct: penguins born and raised in the sun-bathed San Diego zoo still sleep with their toes in the air.

✿　✿　✿

A little boy brought a canary in a cage to the local chiropodist. "It hasn't sung or made a sound in a week," complained the boy. "But what do you expect me to do about it?" grumbled the chiropodist. "Well," said the boy, "mom says you're a good chiropodist. Make the canary chirop."

✿　✿　✿

Legend has it that lovebirds are so devoted that when one dies, the other soon dies, too, of a broken heart. Conscious of this, a pet owner resorted to a clever stratagem when one of his lovebirds gave up the ghost.

He propped a mirror inside the cage of the surviving lovebird, who, seeing his image, chirped happily, snuggled against the mirror, and lived happily for years.

Then one day a careless maid upset the cage, and it crashed on the floor.

The poor lovebird died—of a broken mirror.

✿　✿　✿

At a children's pet show this fall, a duck won the title "happiest pet." When the pets lined up for awards, said duck broke loose from his young mistress and in a trice ate up his competition: a frog, two worms, and a cricket. The judges thereupon awarded the "happiest pet" a second title: "most hungry."

* * *

A carnival performer was aboard an Ohio train when the conductor asked, "What are you carrying in that wicker basket?" "Pigeons," said the performer. "I thought so," said the conductor. "You can't ride with them in here. Rules specifically forbid pigeons in passenger cars."

The performer's plea that these were specially trained pigeons availed him naught, so he reluctantly pried open the car window—no mean feat by itself—and eased the pigeons out.

"Okay, I hope you're satisfied now," said the performer to the conductor, "but believe me, your superiors are going to hear about this when the train gets to Cleveland."

"Cleveland?" repeated the conductor. "This train goes to Cincinnati."

"Holy smoke," exclaimed the performer. Then he leaned out of the window and hollered to his vanishing pigeons, "Hey, fellows! Cincinnati. CINCINNATI!"

* * *

Newly elected public officials should bear in mind Hubert Humphrey's story about the customer in a pet shop who toyed with buying a parrot on display. The bird was absolutely quiet for several moments, and the customer finally asked a sales clerk, "Does this parrot ever talk?" "Indeed he does, ma'am," the clerk assured her, "but he doesn't wish to be quoted."

* * *

A vaudeville act that stumped the experts for years was called "Hans, the Educated Horse." Hans, a swaybacked fugitive from a glue factory, was billed as a "mathematical wizard." Let's say that a man in the audience called out "What's six times seven?" Hans would tap four times with his left forefoot, twice with his right: 42. If the problem was "Divide 96 by 3,"

Hans would tap three times with his left foot, twice with his right: 32.

The solution was simple, once it was discovered. Hans had been trained to tap each foot until signaled by a barely perceptible crooking of a finger by his master to stop.

* * *

Mrs. Gottrod, out to bag some big game in the jungle if it was the last thing she did, fired her rifle one day, turned to her guide with a satisfied air, and declared, "There! I just know I hit something that time. Run and find out the name of the animal I shot."

The guide was back in a few moments to report, "He says, ma'am, that his name is Sylvester."

* * *

Marston Bates, in his fascinating book, *Animal Worlds*, points out that periodically, even without man's interference, certain species have gone down to defeat, and become extinct. Man has hastened these processes immeasurably. Take the case of the musk-ox. Defending themselves against wolves—

their natural enemies—musk-oxen developed a technique of forming a tight circle with their calves in the center. This worked just fine against the wolves, but then man with his weapons came along—and the musk-oxen, in their tight circles, made a perfect target for the spear, and then the rifle.

* * *

An official of the Philadelphia Zoo should embarrass litter-bugs with his report that, when careless visitors drop paper cups and containers into the otters' pool, the praiseworthy animals gather up the trash and put it in a neat pile.

* * *

Bill Sutherland reminds us all that when two cows stand with their heads to each other's tails, switching flies offen each other, that's cow-operation. And when nags do it, that's horse-pitality.

* * *

Animals have their domestic troubles, too, it seems. Consider the case of the exasperated centipede who told her husband she was sick and tired of waiting on him hand and foot, hand and foot, etc. And there was the hen that observed the undisciplined behavior of her youngest chick with obvious disapproval. "If your father could see you now," she cackled disgustedly, "he'd turn over in his gravy."

* * *

Up in Connecticut there lives a retired film director who has realized a lifetime ambition: he's writing a novel and raising chickens on the side, and since he has been thus engaged for only a month or so the period of bitter disillusionment has not yet set in. To prove to himself he was through for good with his old Hollywood routine, he even threw out the can of film that had won him a cluster of Oscars back in the forties.

Among the other livestock acquired by the ex-director was a goat which he had named, over my vehement objections, "Mr. Cerf." Mr. Cerf saw the can of film come sailing out of the upstairs window, and promptly had it for dinner.

The next morning, another goat inquired wistfully, "How

was the prize-winning picture that you ate last night?" "It was nothing to write home about," admitted Mr. Cerf. "Frankly, I enjoyed the book a lot better."

* * *

Lorrain D'Essen has become famous for supplying animals of every description to capricious TV directors, fashion photographers, and advertising salons. Her pets include llamas, kangaroos, tiger cubs, pigs, and wombats. They all live peacefully together in Mrs. D'Essen's private home.

The largest semipermanent guest Lorrain D'Essen ever entertained was a miniature bull named Mortimer. Mortimer slipped often on the smooth floors, and became self-conscious and moody if anybody laughed at him.

There was a 300-pound baby elephant in the house one night, too. Jackie Gleason wanted him for a TV show. Lorrain bundled him into a taxicab (no Cadillac being available that night) and the driver became so intrigued with his unusual passenger that he ran right through a red light and almost bowled over an irate cop. "Whassa big idea?" snarled the cop. "You blind or sump-thing?" "Not at all, officer," pleaded the cabbie. "It's just that I got this here elephant in the back seat. . . ." The cop was too flabbergasted to give him a ticket.

Another time, Lorrain supplied a camel named Loomey for a promotion at Macy's Department Store. Loomey made a great big hit with the customers, but lost face (and a return engagement) by chewing up Chairman Jack Straus's new Panama straw hat.

For an Arthur Treacher TV show, she produced Bertha, a hoity-toity White Leghorn chicken who demanded her own dressing room, and broke up rehearsals by cackling continuously till she got it. Treacher referred to Bertha as "the most edible actress" he ever worked with.

There are tricks in every trade, and Lorrain D'Essen has had to learn a new one every day. A piece of shrimp, for instance, in an actor's ear will persuade a cat to kiss him there or "whisper" to him. A lion will roar angrily if talcum powder is shaken on his mane. Cooked liver cut into tiny chunks looks exactly like canned dog food on camera, and dogs never hesitate to gobble it down greedily.

Jordan, a pony in a Broadway musical, learned one trick all by himself. Jordan showed his teeth menacingly every time the show was running late.

* * *

The AOMC, which stands, of course, for the Animal-of-the-Month Club, announces the following irresistible selections:

1. A nearsighted whale who fell in love with a U.S. submarine and followed it clear around the world. Every time the sub fired a torpedo, the proud whale passed out cigars.

2. A tiger in the Central Park Zoo who abhorred captivity. "I've discovered a way to escape," he confided to his cage-mate, "and tonight's the night." "I'd think twice before I risked anything like that," warned the other tiger. "They say that at night this park is full of juvenile delinquents."

3. A taxidermist's pet monkey. He suffered from mounting apprehension.

4. An elephant who lumbered into a saloon. "We're not allowed to serve intoxicating liquids to pachyderms," announced the bartender. "Who wants intoxicating liquids?" countered the elephant. "I just came in for the peanuts."

5. An angleworm in Altoona, who was sunning herself in the grass one morning when a hoity-toity caterpillar inched by. "Hmph," sniffed the angleworm, "I'd give plenty to know how she got that fur coat!"

6. A father mosquito who supervised a trial flight of his two young sons over the beach at Elberon, New Jersey. "What a wonderful age we live in," he sighed happily. "When I was young, the only places you could sting those girls were on the hands and face!"

7. An otter in the London Zoo who took it upon herself to watch over a baby weasel and a newborn anteater. On her cage they've hung a sign reading: "Department of Otter Confusion."

8. A giraffe who had a wild affair with a swordfish. The result: the darndest looking tree surgeon you ever saw.

9. A preoccupied porcupine who backed into a cactus plant and mumbled, "Pardon me, darling."

10. A rooster in Ottumwa, Iowa, who is without doubt the laziest in America. He's never crowed once; he just waits for another rooster to crow—and then he nods his head.

* * *

A pig and a chicken, alleges W. R. Grady, were promenading down a Fort Worth thoroughfare when the chicken suddenly proposed, "Let's stop in at yonder beanery and eat some ham and eggs." "A thoughtless and repugnant suggestion," was the pig's reaction. "Kindly remember that for you a dish of that sort is a mere contribution. For me it means a total commitment."

* * *

A proud eagle, waxing romantic one moonlit spring evening, suggested to his mate, "I'd like to hug and kiss you while we're soaring through space." "Why not?" nodded his wife. So off they flew into the wide blue yonder, where the eagle's ardor knew no bounds. Back in their nest later, the male eagle asked, "Did you enjoy the trip?" His mate smoothed her wings and exclaimed happily, "IT'S THE ONLY WAY TO FLY!"

5. *Battle of the Sexes*

GIRLS

What is a girl? A discerning student at M.I.T. obliged with this "chemical analysis." "Thought to be a member of the human race. Seldom found in natural state. Surface coated with paint and other chemical compounds. Has low freezing point, but is also highly explosive. Extremely active when in vicinity of opposite sex. Chiefly ornamental. Probably the most powerful seducing agent known. Illegal to own more than one specimen."

❖ ❖ ❖

Richard Condon offers this explanation of the origin of kissing: "The cave man found that salt helped him survive the fierce summer heat, also that he could get the salt by licking a companion's cheek. Then he discovered that the process became more interesting if the companion belonged to the opposite sex. Next thing you know, everybody forgot all about the salt."

✿   ✿   ✿

Warning broadcast by Tom Poston: "Beware of the girl who runs her fingers through your hair. She's probably after your scalp!"

✿   ✿   ✿

Goody Ace was present in a beauty parlor in Beverly Hills when a very pretty girl refused to allow the operator to restore a blonde glow to her naturally dark hair. "Your hair really needs touching up," insisted the operator, "and I assure you we can do it every bit as well as they do it back East." "Impossible," sighed the pretty girl. "I may be here in Beverly Hills, but my roots are in New York."

✿   ✿   ✿

A young Southern belle asked her mother, "What do you give a man who has everything?" Her mother answered unhesitatingly, "Encouragement."

The Lass Roundup . . .

1. The Sioux City siren who treats her gentlemen callers like dirt. She hides them under her bed.

2. The Beverly Hills bride who made a slight change in the wedding ritual. She kept the bridal bouquet and threw the groom away.

3. The Syracuse strip-tease artiste whose manager propelled her on stage every evening with the same admonition: "Get out there, kid, and show them what you're made of!"

4. The Minneapolis minx who simpered to her friend: "You look like a million, my dear—and I mean every day of it."

5. The daughter of a country auctioneer who dazzled a hardened old city slicker. She would smile, wink, and nod to him, and he would smile, wink, and nod back. After the auction

he discovered he had purchased a pair of mules, a churn, and an electric milking machine.

6. The young lady who had been trying to land a cautious beau for three solid years. In a chop suey parlor she saw her opportunity. He asked her, "How would you like your rice, my dear, fried or boiled?" She answered, "Thrown."

7. The pretty airline stewardess who whispered to her assistant in flight, "Careful, Toots, if you have to carry anything up front. They've got the automatic pilot on."

8. The beautiful but nearsighted fashion model who spotted a many-legged black thing slithering across her bathroom floor and clobbered it with the heel of her shoe. Finally she summoned courage to look at the insect at close range—and discovered she had ruined one-half of a pair of ten-dollar false eyelashes.

9. The loser in a beauty contest who was coldly appraising the face and figure of the girl who just had been declared the winner. "I wonder where she got those looks?" pondered a chaperone. "From her father," stated the loser unhesitatingly. "He's a plastic surgeon."

10. The young co-ed from Kansas State who knows precisely what she wants. Her English professor was elaborating one day on the advantages of acquiring a large vocabulary. "Say a word out loud to yourself five times," he advised, "and it will be yours for life."

Our heroine closed her eyes and whispered, "Walter, Walter, Walter, Walter, Walter."

* * *

A beautiful young lady in the Park Avenue sector has been squired this season by a variety of eligible men-about-town. They bring her home to an exclusive apartment house, where she bids her dates farewell, and is then ushered inside by an obsequious doorman. Her date is no sooner out of sight, however, than the obsequious doorman kisses the young lady warmly and sends her off via the subway to her real home. He is her father.

* * *

"Why won't you buy me a mink coat?" pouted a luscious young thing at a hockey game. "I'm very, very cold."

"Since you know the answer," growled the hockey enthusiast, "why do you ask the question?"

* * *

Fashion tip from a Kansas weekly: "Girls will be wearing the same thing in brassieres this year that they wore last year."

* * *

Just before the opening of a new campaign, the coach of a Big Ten basketball team had a glorious dream. He dreamed that a beautiful, wealthy co-ed lured him to her dormitory—where he met her brother, who was seven feet tall.

* * *

The father of a teen-age daughter found her redheaded boy friend with a coke in one hand and a huge slab of apple pie in the other. "I'm mighty glad to meet you, Clifton," declared the father. "I've noticed you in our budget for some time."

* * *

A chorus girl friend of John Straley asked him if he could find a stage job for a beautiful friend. "What are her measurements?" asked the statistically minded Straley. "They're 26-32-85," replied the chorus girl. "Holy smoke," gasped Straley. "What is your friend doing now?" "She poses," said the girl, "for pyramids."

ROMANCE

Alaska seems to be one of the many places where the course of true love does not run too smoothly. A long way from Nome, a young gallant took his adored one for a ride on his dog sled. In due course he hollered "Mush," then she hollered "Mush," and while they were mushing somebody stole the dog sled.

* * *

Mr. Jones patted his daughter's hand fondly, and told her, "Your young man told me today he wanted you as his bride, and I gave my consent." "Oh, Papa," gushed the daughter, "it's going to be so hard leaving Mother." "I understand perfectly, my dear," beamed Mr. Jones. "You just take her with you."

* * *

In Pinsk, an ambitious young man called upon a marriage broker and allowed as how he would take unto himself a bride —if the dowry was big enough. "I've got just the girl for you," enthused the broker. "Her name is Olga, and she has a dowry of twenty-five thousand rubles. Unfortunately, she has only one leg." "No," said the young man.

"Aha," smiled the broker. "How about Natalie? A fifty-thousand-ruble dowry, but she can't see or hear." "No," said the young man. "Maybe you'll have Petrushka," urged the broker. "A hundred thousand rubles is her dowry—but I'm sorry to say she's insane." "Absolutely not," said the young man—but then, wistfully, he inquired, "Have you a client, maybe, who has only one leg, can't see or hear, and is insane all at one time?"

The marriage broker nodded sagely, and folded up his list of prospects. "I can't do business with you," he admitted. "You're too much of a dreamer."

*   *   *

Shirley MacLaine has figured out the Seven Lively Arts of Making a Man Say Yes: 1. Find him. 2. Fascinate him. 3. Flatter him. 4. Feed him. 5. Fuss over him. 6. Fondle him. 7. Frame him. And oh, yes—if none of these does the trick, adds Shirley, forget him!

*   *   *

"Did you follow my advice about kissing your girl when she least expects it?" asked a senior of a young fraternity pledger. "When?" echoed the pledgee, applying a piece of raw beefsteak to a very black eye, "I thought you said WHERE!"

It Must Be Love . . .

"The way women go about finding magnetism in impossible men is appalling."—*Michael Arlen.*

"If a woman wants to hold a man, she has merely to appeal to what is worst in him."—*Oscar Wilde.*

"There are no oaths that make so many perjurers as the vows of love."—*Rochebrune.*

"In love there is always one who kisses and one who offers the cheek."—*French Proverb*.

"The magic of first love is our ignorance that it can ever end."—*Disraeli*.

* * *

Don Lindsay tells of a young man who confided to his mother at an inopportune moment that he proposed taking unto himself a bride. "Wotsa dees?" screamed Mother. "Who's agon' love you like Mama? Who's agon' starch-a your socks? Who's agon' make-a you lasagna?"

"Wait a minute, mom," pleaded the son. "Why are you talking like that? You're not Italian!"

* * *

The last remaining "bachelor girl" in a big office appeared radiantly one morning and began to pass out cigars to all and sundry. "What's the big idea?" chorused her cohorts. Proudly she displayed a diamond ring and exulted, "It's a boy—six feet tall and weighs 190 pounds."

* * *

The fellow who makes exaggerated statements—a movie press agent, for example—is rarely taken seriously by anybody. Dean Leys, of Roosevelt University, cites the case, for instance, of a chronic exaggerator who lost his girl with this ill-advised note: "My Irreplaceable and Indispensable Treasure: I would climb the highest mountain for you, swim the widest river, battle the wildest animal barehanded. Nothing will ever keep me from your side. (Signed) Your adoring Charlie. P.S. I'll be over Saturday night if it doesn't rain."

* * *

Observes Jim Backus: Many a man owes his success to his first wife—and his second wife to his success.

* * *

And Bob Melvin pinpoints a girl who's broken every date she's had. She goes out with them.

* * *

An anxious young suitor inquired of the proverbial younger brother the whereabouts of his beloved. "Keep your shirt on," counseled said young brother. "She's upstairs working on her acceptance speech."

* * *

A short, short story from the University of Texas:
Oh, Brad, let's not park here.
Oh, Brad, let's not park.
Oh, Brad, let's not.
Oh, Brad, let's.
Oh, Brad.
Oh.

* * *

A wealthy but rather staid banker from Oklahoma brought a beautiful young bride home with him from New York. "She's the last word to me," enthused a friend. "How did you manage to meet her?"

"There was nothing to it," boasted the banker. "I just opened my wallet and there she was!"

* * *

Mary Lou's caller drove his own foreign sports car but his conversation left plenty to be desired. "Your new boy friend hasn't got much to him," grumbled Mary Lou's dad. "What does the lad do, anyhow?" Mary Lou explained, "He inherits."

* * *

The young foreman on a building job reported for work one morning sporting a magnificent black eye. "I gave my fiancée a beautiful diamond bracelet for her birthday," he explained sheepishly, "and now it turns out she wants to keep it."

* * *

In Anniston, Alabama, reports S. Himmell, a lass rummaging in an attic trunk came upon a yellowing letter her father had written to her mother in his courting days. Laboriously the daughter copied the letter word for word, signed a masculine name to it, and mailed it to herself. Then she showed it to her father.

The resultant explosion shook the house. "This lovesick loon," roared the father, "is the biggest idiot I ever heard of. Keep him out of this house or I'll break him in two. We're not going to have a simp like that in this family—and the sooner the ding-busted, fatheaded lunatic knows it, the happier I'll be."

When he discovered the trick, the father reacted the way all fathers do. "I knew what you were up to immediately," he insisted. "Your ma and you were hoping so obviously I'd fall for the gag, I decided to give you both a good time."

* * *

A pert Southern miss was outraged when she received a letter from her beau at Baylor with several X's at the bottom. "The skunk," she muttered darkly. "I'll teach him to double-cross me!"

* * *

Papa Shrecklich wasn't too impressed with the girl Junior brought home for dinner. "I thought you said your girl's legs were without equal," he jeered while she was out of the room. "Not at all," hedged Junior. "I said they were without parallel."

* * *

A sailor spotted a greeting card which expounded this sentiment: "Here's my heart and soul for the only girl I ever loved." "Just the card I'm looking for," the sailor enthused to the sales clerk. "Give me two dozen."

* * *

A local Romeo's face appeared in the window of his beloved's bedroom. "Get a move on," he whispered hoarsely, "and let's get this eloping business over with."

"Ssh," cautioned his Juliet. "Papa'll hear us and spoil all our plans."

"I wouldn't worry about that," smirked Romeo. "He's down on the ground holding up the ladder."

* * *

George Jessel remembers the time a prominent actor and a beautiful girl approached a hotel registration desk and signed in as Mr. and Mrs. The clerk inquired, "Double or twin beds?" The actor turned to his companion and asked, "Would a double be all right, dear?" She answered, "Yes, sir."

MATRIMONY

Very few people alive today seem to recall the evening Adam came stamping into Eve's kitchen to complain, "Confound it, you've put my pants in the salad again!"

* * *

When anybody asked the late Jim Thurber, "How's your wife?" he generally countered with, "Compared to what?"

* * *

Julius Pretzfeld, inveterate newspaper reader, usually perused two of them, from front page to last, at the breakfast table, thereby annoying Mrs. Pretzfeld very thoroughly. One evening she asked him casually, "Julius, did you notice anything unusual about me at the breakfast table this morning?" "Why, no, my dear," replied Mr. Pretzfeld. "Ah ha," cackled Mrs. Pretzfeld, "I wasn't there!"

* * *

A young bridegroom followed his gal into their shining new kitchenette. "What is my snookums doing in here so long?" he inquired. His worried bride explained, "I rinsed the ice cubes in this hot water and now I can't find them."

* * *

Overheard by Alfredo Macitado in a Rio de Janeiro hotel: "And just when I was able, finally, through my relentless logic, to convince her of the absurdity of her argument—she hauled off and socked me!"

* * *

"I accept your proposal of marriage," said a maiden coyly, "provided, of course, my pappy gives his consent. He loves me madly, and he's mighty tough and choosy, so be careful how you approach him."

Thus warned, the suitor charged into pappy's study and blurted out, "I want to marry your daughter." "Go ahead, and blessings upon you, young man," beamed pappy. "By the way, what did you say your name was?"

* * *

"The boss," reported Mr. Henpeque to his aggressive wife, "turned out to be a real lamb when, like you told me, I demanded a raise. . . . He said, 'Baaah.'"

* * *

Two college alumni who had roomed together for four years met for the first time since graduation at their fifteenth reunion. One of them sported a beard that made Mitch Miller look clean-shaven. "I'd never have known you with those whiskers," laughed his old pal. "Did you lose a bet or something?"

"I presume that you refer to my beard," said the hairy one loftily. "If you must know, I hate the darn thing."

"Then why don't you shave it off?" asked the friend.

"Because," was the logical reply, "my wife hates it even more than I do."

* * *

The bride kissed her husband warmly upon his return from the office and sympathized, "I can tell by your face that you've had one of those frustrating days where everything possible went wrong. What would you say to a round of vodka martinis, followed by a fine thick steak, French fries, a tossed salad, and some fresh peach cake?"

"Not tonight, darling," begged the bridegroom. "Let's just have dinner at home."

* * *

A wise word of caution from Vince Rivers: "That argument you won from your wife isn't over yet!"

* * *

Sign discovered by the milkman on the doorstep of a suburban ranch house: "Please leave two bottles of cream and my wife alone."

* * *

A young bride's face fell when she noticed twin beds in the bridal suite. "What's biting you?" inquired her solicitous bridegroom. "Nothing really," she assured him, "but I certainly thought we were going to get a room all to ourselves."

Ten Wives to Look Out for . . .

1. Mrs. Jones was jubilant. "I've finally cured my husband of biting his nails," she declared. "Land sakes," said her neighbor. "How?" "I hide his teeth."

2. From under the handsomely decorated Christmas tree a wife called to her husband, "Here's your most important present. It took me weeks to find just what I wanted." "I'll be right in to look at it," said the husband. "No, wait," cautioned the wife. "I've got to put it on first."

3. Mrs. Fraunces had a hard time locating her spouse at a big party, but finally spotted him, ecstatically festooned over a limb of a tree in the garden. "It's our signal to bid you adieu," she told her hostess. "My husband is beginning his imitation of Spanish moss."

4. Mrs. Ambruster was just picking out a neat, pearl-handled, six-barrel revolver when she saw her husband ambling into the store. "Don't bother wrapping that revolver," she instructed the clerk. "Here he comes now!"

5. A frowning doctor told Mrs. Gumbach, "Frankly, I don't

like the looks of your husband." "Neither do I," nodded Mrs. Gumbach, "but he's good to the children."

6. At a big Hollywood wing-ding, scribe Mike Connolly overheard a wife solicitously murmur to her spouse, "What did I say to annoy you, dear? It may come in useful again some time."

7. The coroner shot a sympathetic glance at the widow dressed in black, with tears streaming down her face. "Can you recall your husband's last words?" he asked gently. "Indeed I can," sobbed the distraught widow. "He said, 'Don't try to scare me with that shotgun. You couldn't hit the side of a barn.'"

8. It was a cruel, cruel wife who told her husband, "You sure made a prize fool of yourself tonight. It's a good thing those people don't realize you were sober!"

9. Mrs. Wimdinger watched silently as long as she could stand it while her middle-aged husband ogled a striking brunette in a tight-fitting, revealing cocktail dress. Then she hissed in his ear, "I'll bet the sink in her kitchen is well-stacked, too!"

10. A fantastically henpecked husband finally did something on his own initiative. He dropped dead. His nagging wife mourned her loss—and the fact that she had nobody left to badger. A visitor sympathized, "How you must miss dear Wilbur." "Yes," sighed the widow wistfully. "It seems but yesterday that he stood at that very door, holding it open until two flies got in."

And Ten Husbands . . .

1. A mousey little man was hailed into court for beating up his wife—a formidable, Amazonian creature. The judge, trying to conceal a certain amount of admiration, demanded, "What came over you?" The little man explained, "Well, Your Honor,

she had her back to me, the fire poker was handy, and the back door was open. So I took a chance!"

2. Somebody made the mistake of asking Joey Bishop how his wife could cook. Bishop grimaced, grabbed the inquirer by the arm, and implored, "Tell me: How can anyone burn lemonade?"

3. "My wife," boasted a well-to-do jeweler, "has only one extravagance. She just loves to spend money."

4. Complains the husband of curvaceous Zsa Zsa Horntoot: "My wife is like Noah. When she packs for a weekend she takes two of everything."

5. In Hollywood, a luncheon companion of Tony Randall's had this tale of woe to impart: "I thought I was set for life with a healthy bank balance, a beautiful home, and the love of a passionate and wealthy woman. Then, wham! One evening my wife walks in!"

6. At a Coney Island boardwalk cafe, a rather disheveled individual disclosed that he had been married eight times. "Are you married now?" he was asked. He answered angrily, "Do you think I'm a sucker?"

7. "Look at the shabby old frock I have to wear," grumbled Mrs. Black to her husband. "If one of your office friends came to call, he'd think I was the cook." Replied Mr. Black, unperturbed, "He'd change his mind if he stayed for dinner!"

8. A salesman in a swank leather goods store suggested to a male customer, "Can I interest you in a beautifully embossed letter opener?" "You cannot," responded the customer firmly. "I'm married to one."

9. "Why," Ardie Deutsch was asked, "did you send that brand new pressure cooker to the rummage sale?"

"It may look like a pressure cooker to you," explained Deutsch, "but in the hands of my wife, it's a secret weapon. Last Wednesday she shot a pot roast into outer space."

10. Peter Lind Hayes met an old gaffer at the Winged Foot Golf Club who boasted, "My wife and I were married fifty-five years ago today—and we still hold hands." Then he added, "If we didn't—we'd kill each other!"

* * *

The parents of two badly spoiled brats suddenly came to their senses and sneaked off to Florida for a genuine rest—by themselves. Sunning on the beach, the wife murmured happily, "It's wonderful to get away from the kids, much as I love them, for just a few days, isn't it?" "Sure is," agreed the husband, "but just to make me feel at home, darling, would you please throw a few handfuls of sand in my face?"

* * *

"Paw," said Mrs. Simpson over her knitting one evening, "it's time you spoke a piece to our son Wilbur. 'Pears to me he jest plain don't want to get hisself married." "Don't worry 'bout our Wilbur," soothed Mr. Simpson. "He'll marry fast enough when the wrong girl comes along."

* * *

Winter autoists will appreciate a cartoon from a Northwestern weekly that shows a weary husband who has just dug a fifty-yard patch through a six-foot snowdrift from his garage to the road. As he is about to open the garage door with a sigh of relief, his wife calls out from the kitchen, "Oh, I forgot to tell you, dear. I took the car over to mother's yesterday before the storm started."

* * *

One housewife was describing her troubles to another on the terrace of a Catskill resort. "It's impossible," she complained, "for me to satisfy my husband with my cooking. Take last week, for example. I buy him a fine twelve-pound rabbit. Monday I give him rabbit steak. Tuesday, rabbit's feet. Wednesday, barbecued rabbit spare ribs. Thursday, rabbit hamburger. Friday, rabbit goulash. And do you think all these delicacies satisfy him? No, ma'am! Saturday morning he just glares at me with those big, pink eyes!"

* * *

"It says in the paper," a wife reported to her husband, "that a man on the next block throttled his mother-in-law this morning." "Hm-m-m," mused the husband. "Sounds like a practical choker."

* * *

An inquisitive youngster asked his father one evening, "Dad, what was the most money you ever earned in one year?" "Ask your mother," replied Dad from behind his newspaper. "I forget what I told her."

* * *

As they stepped out into the bracing winter night, and left the noisy, overheated cocktail party within, a wife faced her husband squarely and demanded, "Elmer, did anybody tell you in there that you were ordained the life of the party—the greatest wit, the greatest raconteur, and the greatest lover boy in town?"

"No, dear," admitted the puzzled husband. "I can't say anybody did."

"Exactly," said the wife grimly. "Now tell me this: Just where did you get the idea?"

* * *

A prisoner serving a twenty-year sentence in a Wisconsin jail fell to reminiscing with a fellow inmate of the fun he and his wife used to enjoy at the seaside burying each other in the soft, white sand. "I suppose," he concluded whimsically, "the proper thing to do when I get out of here is to go back and dig her up."

* * *

Bill Feather clipped this out of a Chicago column: "Wouldn't it be wonderful to have a marriage license that expired every few years like a driver's license?"

* * *

Four staid, successful Minneapolis business moguls invested jointly in a hunting lodge deep in the Northern woods, and thither they were wont to repair for a fortnight twice a year. "Roughing it is what we want," they would tell their wives, "no hot water, no modern conveniences—and above all, no women!"

One September the four deserted ladies decided to surprise their husbands and followed them to their woodland lair. They were stopped at the gate, however, by a wizened old guide. "You gals better beat it quick if you know what's good for you," he advised. "This time these fellows brought their wives with them!"

* * *

Matrimonial bliss in Hollywood: At dinner one evening producer Billy Wilder's lovely wife Audrey (Wilder is responsible for *Some Like It Hot, Irma La Douce,* and a dozen other screen triumphs) announced blithely, "Darling, do you realize this is our anniversary?" Wilder poised a fork in midair and reproached her, "Please—not while I'm eating."

* * *

A marriage counselor was having trouble determining the cause of discord between a young husband and wife who insisted on talking at the same time. Finally establishing a semblance of order, he demanded of the wife, "What is the main block to your getting along together?" Grimly she ordered her husband, "You tell him, hon." "Ah," interrupted the counselor. "There's hope for your marriage when you still call him 'hon.'" "That," explained the wife coldly, "happens to be his name: Attila the Hon."

* * *

Asked one elderly lady of another at a Darien dinner party, "Doesn't it embarrass you to see your husband flirting so shamelessly with all the young unmarried daughters of your old friends?" "Oh, I just let him have his innocent pleasure," said the wife tolerantly. "He's like a puppy chasing automobiles. He wouldn't know what to do if he caught one. He just wants to bark at them a little."

*　*　*

"My wife," a sad-eyed husband told his doctor, "is getting to the stage where I think we'll have to move in with help of some kind. She bursts into tears at the drop of a hat. This morning she wept for an hour because she saw a dog with a broken leg."

"That's not so bad," nodded the doctor. "Many women are particularly sensitive about the suffering of animals. I think my own wife might cry at the sight of a dog with a broken leg."

"You didn't let me finish my story," said the husband. "This particular dog was in a box of animal crackers."

*　*　*

A whimsical Oklahoman who signs himself "Elisha J. Unlikely" submits the story of a cowboy who brought his bride to Chicago for a honeymoon. The bride had read a great deal about kidnapers before she arrived, and was afraid to be left alone in their hotel room. So when the cowboy left to look up some old pals, he locked her in the room, and took the key with him.

Hours later, after a delightful—and liquid—get-together with his friends, he suddenly remembered his bride. "Holy cow," he cried, jumping to his feet. "You gotta excuse me, boys. I done left Sally Lou locked in a room all night and I ain't neither fed nor watered her!"

*　*　*

To conclude this section on a gentler and more sentimental note, I quote this heartwarming ad from the classified section of a dignified metropolitan paper:

"I am responsible for all debts and obligations of my wife, Selma, both present and future, and am delighted to be the provider for a woman who has borne me two fine children, listened patiently to all my gripes, and with an overabundance of love and care made the past fifteen years of my life the happiest I have known. On this, our fifteenth wedding anniversary, I am proud to express my gratitude publicly."

6. *"It's Only a Game"*

BASEBALL

The official baseball records include the names of twelve
rank amateurs who participated in a single major league game.
The date was May 18, 1912, and the team they engaged in
combat was the Philadelphia Athletics.

This unusual turn of events was precipitated by the Georgia
Peach, Tyrus Raymond Cobb. On the afternoon of May 17,
1912, Tyrus took exception to the heckling of a fan in the
grandstand, climbed up to where he was seated, and socked
him in the jaw. For this act, Cobb was fined and suspended,

and the whole Detroit team, in sympathy with their illustrious center fielder, walked out on strike.

That's when the Athletics' management engaged the sand-lotters to substitute for the Detroit Tigers. Several thousand fans turned out to see what would happen when a big league ball team played a bunch of rank amateurs. They saw plenty. The Athletics made twenty-six hits and nosed out the amateurs, 24–2. The strike was settled that night.

*　*　*

One day when Ty Cobb was at the height of his career, a kid from his own home town in Georgia joined the squad and naturally came to Cobb for counsel. "I guess what's kept me tired so far is being a horse's aid," he opined. "Whaddya mean, a horse's aid?" asked Ty. "Wal," drawled the lad, "I git up every morning at four and fetch water and feed for the horses. Then I curry them and give 'em a morning workout. Then I clean out the stables all afternoon. After giving them supper I play phonograph records to keep them feeling happy-like and do other little chores till the owner lets me go home nights about eleven."

"Son," said Ty Cobb, "I've got news for you. A horse's *aid* you're not."

*　*　*

Al Lopez, stellar pilot of the Chicago White Sox, once caught for the Brooklyn Dodgers, and tells of a later year when the Brooklyn team brought up a young left-hander who had a world of stuff, but less control than is generally expected even from southpaws.

"I'll tell you how wild that young fellow was," enthuses Lopez. "One evening they sent him out to pitch batting practice at Ebbets Field, and he hit a man in the eye who was watching TV in a bar at Coney Island!"

*　*　*

The most famous double-play combination in baseball history must be the heroic Tinker, Evers, and Chance trio that brought pennants to the Chicago Cubs early in the century.

Nor will oldsters forget Giant-rooter F.P.A.'s ode to these stalwarts:

"These are the saddest of possible words:
Tinker to Evers to Chance.
Trio of Bear Cubs and fleeter than birds:
Tinker to Evers to Chance.
Thoughtlessly pricking our gonfalon bubble;
Making a Giant hit into a double;
Words that are weighted with nothing but trouble:
Tinker to Evers to Chance."

Incidentally, the name of the third baseman who completed that famous Cubs' infield was Harry Steinfeldt. See how many old fans remember *that*!

*　*　*

In the days when Babe Ruth was hanging up his home run records, General Pershing once visited Yankee Stadium, and press photographers persuaded him and the Babe to pose together for a few pictures. Babe was not given to much small talk, but he did feel that this occasion warranted a special effort on his part. So he draped his arm around General Pershing's shoulder and asked amiably, "Say, kid, you was in the war, wasn't you?"

*　*　*

One baseball record established by the New York Yankees' peerless outfielder, Joe DiMaggio, probably will stand for many years to come. He hit successfully in fifty-six consecutive games. His string was almost broken some games earlier when his own brother Dom, wearing the livery of the Boston Red Sox, robbed him of a sure triple with a wonderful catch against the center-field wall. DiMag got his needed hit on his next and last time at bat, but still was shaking his head over brother Dom's catch when he came back to the clubhouse. "This speaks well for the integrity of the game," he remarked, "but the kid sure didn't have to rub it in that way—especially when he's coming to my house for dinner tonight!"

*　*　*

Frank Frisch recalls one game with the old Boston Braves in which the great Dizzy Dean had struck out another of Joe DiMaggio's brothers, Vince, twice. In the ninth inning, Vince came to bat for the third time. After taking two called strikes, he popped a puny foul behind the plate. "Don't catch it," Dean screamed to the catcher. "Let it drop!"

Manager Frisch stormed out of the dugout, hollering, "What's the big idea?"

"I bet a guy ten bucks I'd fan DiMag three times today. This is my last chance." And then, while Frisch still fumed, Dizzy burned a third strike past DiMaggio at the plate and collected his ten-spot.

*　*　*

For one Fourth of July doubleheader, the owners of the St. Louis Cardinals baseball club (then known as the Gashouse Gang) hired a band. Dizzy Dean ran out to center field to confer with the leader, with the result that when the trio of umpires appeared for action, the band struck up "Three Blind Mice."

One of the umps pointed a finger at Dizzy and told him, "I ain't got no proof of who done this, but I got eight to one it wasn't nobody else but you!"

* * *

Bob Feller, famous pitcher of the thirties for the Cleveland Indians, was dragged to a five-hour-long opera one evening. "How did you like it?" he was asked later. "I'm not sure," admitted Feller. "I dozed through the first four innings."

* * *

Birdie Tebbetts tells of the spring day he asked a raw baseball rookie to name his best playing position. The rookie answered, "Kinda bent over, like this."

* * *

A second-string catcher on the Los Angeles Angels once set out in hot pursuit of a Pasadena millionaire's daughter. Weeks later his manager asked, "Howya doing, Buster, with that society babe?" "Not so good, Rig," admitted the catcher. "So far it's no hits, no runs—and no heiress."

* * *

Joe Garagiola, onetime big league catcher, has become an accomplished after-dinner speaker, though his name is frequently misspelled in the banquet programs. Governor Faubus had occasion to question Joe's name. "In the hills where I was born," averred Faubus, "we would take a name like that, get two girls' names out of it, and have enough left over for three boys."

Joe Garagiola says he played football, too, when he was a boy—until he nearly drowned in one game. Joe was playing on a field so uneven that it was covered with mud puddles. He was thrown for a loss on one play—right in a puddle, face down, and the entire opposing line fell on top of him. When they

untangled the mess, Joe was about to go under for the third
time. After that, he stuck to baseball.

*   *   *

There's been a lot of grumbling about the time it takes these
days for a game of big-league baseball to be played, what
with pitchers posing as statues for minutes at a time, adjusting
their caps, pants, belts, socks, and what have you, and managers calling conferences at every turn of a television camera.
The president of one of the leagues sent a secret memo to certain officials asking for suggestions as to how play might be
speeded up. The likeliest suggestion came from one cynic on
the *Journal-American:* "Play only eight innings instead of
nine."

*   *   *

Allie Reynolds, one of the all-time great pitchers for the New
York Yankees, hit only one home run in his long major league
career. "It was off Early Wynn in Washington," recalls Reynolds. "I didn't see it good, so I ran all the way. When I gal-
loped by second, I saw the third base coach holding up his
hands, so I thought he meant me to go back. I slid back into
second base! It was pretty embarrassing, especially since it
was the opening day of the season and the President of the
United States was in the stands!"

* * *

In Minneapolis, a sportswriter interviewed a hard-boiled young pitcher recently added to the roster of the Minnesota Twins. "You're a tough hombre, all right," conceded the scribe. "I bet you wouldn't give your own mother a decent pitch." "Why should I?" countered the pitcher angrily. "She batted .297 with Sacramento last season."

* * *

Willie McCovey, the slugging first baseman and outfielder of the San Francisco Giants, likes his nine hours of sleep every night. A newspaper man phoned him very early one morning and asked, "Did I awake you, Willie?" McCovey admitted drowsily, "Some."

* * *

At a recent wedding in San Diego, each of the five hundred guests was given a sachet of rice, handsomely ribboned, to shower the bride and groom as they exited. All but one of the guests untied the lace bag immediately. The one who didn't— a lad of eleven—obviously proposed to throw the rice in the original package. "What's the big idea?" demanded his father. "It's my first chance," explained the boy, "to test a pitch Sandy Koufax taught us at school Wednesday."

* * *

At a banquet honoring stars of the Los Angeles Dodgers' all-conquering baseball team, a pitcher noted for his smoking fast balls reminded the audience, "Behind every successful ballplayer stands a woman." Leo Durocher brought down the house by adding, "Yes, and she'd better be wearing a well-padded catcher's mitt."

* * *

Max Kase has a great collection of stories featuring the one and only Yogi Berra. One day the Yankee catcher (now a Met, heaven help him) was asked what he'd do if he found a million dollars. "If the fellow who lost it was poor, I'd return it," answered Yogi. Another time he showed up only fifteen minutes late for an appointment instead of his usual thirty. "See,"

he exulted to the friend who awaited him, "I'm earlier late!"
Probably the best Berra anecdote is apocryphal. It concerns
the day he saw a little girl falling out of a window of a house
across the street. From sheer force of habit, Yogi rushed over
like a gazelle and caught the youngster in his arms before she
hit the pavement. But then—still out of force of habit—he threw
her to second base!

BOXING

An interesting sidelight on the ethics of the prize ring turns
up in a reminiscence of Kid McCoy, a popular champion of
his day. McCoy was matched one night with a dangerous con-
tender who happened to be stone deaf. McCoy only became
aware of his opponent's affliction near the end of the third
round—but then he acted promptly and without hesitation.
He stepped back a pace and indicated in pantomime that the
bell had sounded, marking the end of the round. Actually, it
had not. "Thanks," muttered the deaf opponent, and dropped
his hands—whereupon Kid McCoy immediately knocked him
out.

*   *   *

Murray Robinson tells about a time when John L. Sullivan,
burly heavyweight champion, was downing a few beers in a
Bowery saloon. A skinny little runt who had had a few too
many staggered up to the champ and challenged him to a fight.
John L. picked him three feet off the ground by the back of
his coat, and grumbled, "Listen, you—if you hit me just once
—and I find *out* about it . . ."

*   *   *

James J. ("Gentleman Jim") Corbett, popular heavyweight
who won the championship from John L. Sullivan in 1892,
held the crown for four and a half years, when he was de-
throned by Bob Fitzimmons, then was cut to ribbons in an attempted comeback against Jim Jeffries.
Later Corbett became a sportswriter, and distinguished him-

self by consistently picking the wrong man in fight after fight. "I'll bet you never picked a winner in your life," jeered a fellow scribe one evening. "Oh, yes, I did," answered Corbett very seriously. "The time I fought Jeffries, I picked him to win after the first round!"

* * *

A Los Angeles middleweight boxer was held up the other night and robbed of ten dollars. Asked why he surrendered his wallet without a murmur, he explained, "Shucks, I don't fight no more for them small purses."

* * *

Bernard Gimbel, the dry goods tycoon, won his title as Number One Fight Fan fairly and squarely at the famous Dempsey-Tunney "long count" heavyweight embroglio in Chicago.

The victorious Tunney was protected after his victory by a phalanx of police, but somehow or other Bernie Gimbel wangled his way into the dressing room. "The next thing I knew," reports Tunney, "there was Bernie, fully clothed, including raincoat and hat, standing happily under the shower with me, talking a mile a minute about the fight."

* * *

Rocky Graziano, ex-middleweight champion, was asked in a TV interview recently, "Were you ever afraid of an opponent?" The great man pondered momentarily, then blurted, "Naw, I was too stupid!" Later Rocky insisted that he once sent Sugar Ray Robinson reeling to the mat. "He tripped over my body," explained Rocky.

* * *

A prizefighter, having heavy going in his first important fight, was floored in the second round by a punch right on the button. He looked from the mat at his trainer with glazed eyes. "Let the referee count," yelled the trainer. "Don't get up till eight." The fighter nodded and asked weakly, "What time is it now?"

* * *

Saddest prizefight story of the month comes from Red Smith, who overheard a battered, about-to-be-knocked-out preliminary fighter gasp to his manager between rounds one and two, "If I had that bum's right hook I'd moider him!"

* * *

In Philadelphia a strip-tease queen asked Cassius Clay what he did just before a big fight commenced. "I pray that everything will come off all right," declared Cassius. The strip-tease queen nodded sympathetically and giggled, "Me, too."

* * *

Out on his feet after eight rounds against an infinitely superior prizefighter, a glass-eyed gladiator was implored by his manager, "Don't give up now, Eddie boy! You got a no-hitter going!"

BRIDGE

In an amusing book called *The Mad World of Bridge*, Jack Olsen tells about a player who was determined to signal his partner that he violently disapproved of his opening lead of a heart. The usual way to indicate this disapproval is to put a very low heart on the trick—but this player's lowest heart was an eight—and he knew his partner would consider that card a direct invitation to continue in the same suit.

What to do, what to do? The resourceful player found a solution. He deliberately dropped his entire hand on the floor, and as he stooped to retrieve the scattered cards, he remarked clearly, "Don't wait for me. I'm playing a very low heart."

* * *

Both the Warrens and the Smithers were vulnerable in a hotly contested bridge game, when Mrs. Warren felt a hand grasping her leg.

She calmly put her cards face down on the table and announced, "If that's my husband, I bid four spades. If it's you, George Smithers, I'm going to punch you in the nose."

* * *

In Palm Beach, a socialite told bridge authority Charles Goren quite seriously, "My wife loves the game of bridge passionately. It gives her something to occupy her mind while she's talking!"

* * *

Mrs. Axelrod, reading the evening newspaper, called out to her husband in the TV room, "They found an old hen in Ardsley today with two hearts." "I know," called back Mr. Axelrod. "I played bridge with her Sunday night."

* * *

At the Hillcrest Country Club in Beverly Hills, the afternoon bridge games are taken very seriously. George Burns tells of one hand where he and his partner bid seven spades, vulnerable. One of their opponents had recently recovered from a heart attack. After some deliberation, he took out a nitroglycerin tablet, placed it under his tongue, looked at his cards again, and said with a deep sigh, "I double."

* * *

If you are playing bridge, what do you think the odds are against your picking up thirteen cards in the same suit? They are precisely 158,753,389,899 to 1! And in poker, the odds against your picking up a pat royal flush are 649,739 to 1!

*　*　*

Twenty ladies, engaged in an all-female duplicate bridge tournament, were making such a racket that just past midnight, a policeman called to warn them that a complaint had been called in. Later that night the still-seething hostess grumbled, "I wonder who was nasty enough to make that complaint." Confessed her husband complacently, "I did."

FISHING

A stranger stopped his car to watch the strange behavior of a fisherman on a riverbank. First he hooked a big pike, but threw it back. Then he landed a beautiful, large trout, but threw it back, too. Finally he reeled in a tiny perch, and with a grunt of satisfaction, deposited it in his bag.

The stranger couldn't resist calling out, "Why on earth did you throw those two big ones back and keep this tiny one?" The fisherman explained tersely, "Small frying pan."

*　*　*

A ten-year-old boy was instructed to take care of his kid sister while his parents went to town on business, so he allowed her to accompany him on a fishing expedition. "I'll never do that again," he told his ma that night. "I didn't catch a thing." Ma said, "I'm sure she'll be quiet next time if you just explain to her." "Oh, it wasn't the noise," explained the boy. "She ate the bait."

*　*　*

With nary one fish to show for his day with rod and reel, an amateur fisherman stopped at a market on the way home and thoughtfully bought a dozen trout. He then ordered the fish man to throw them to him one at a time. "When I tell my wife,"

he explained to the mystified fish man, "that I catch fish—
I catch them!"

* * *

An impatient angler had tried four varieties of bait without
a single bite. Finally, in disgust, he drew in his reel, and threw
a handful of coins into the stream. "Okay," he hollered, "go and
buy something you *do* like!"

* * *

An avid fisherman was dragged away from his beloved Minnesota lakes and taken on a tour of Europe by his determined
wife. Back home he announced that the summer had been
pretty much wasted, but that Venice at least had proved tol-
erable. "What attracted you most there?" he was asked. "The
Lido or St. Mark's?" "Neither," said the great traveler. "What
tickled me most was that I could sit in my hotel room and fish
right out of the window."

* * *

The late President Hoover in his book, *Fishing for Fun and
To Wash Your Soul,* declared that one of the surest ways to
make political forecasts is to determine how the candidates

feel about fishing. He gave as an example President Coolidge. "Coolidge," he said, "apparently had not fished before election. Being a fundamentalist in religion, economics, and fishing, he began his fish career for common trout with worms. Ten million fly fishermen at once evidenced disturbed minds. Then Mr. Coolidge took to a fly. He gave his Secret Service guards great excitement in dodging his backcast and rescuing flies from trees. There were many photographs. Soon after that he declared he did not choose to run again."

*   *   *

President Hoover had a copy of this "Fisherman's Prayer" framed and hung in his study at the Waldorf Towers:

God grant that I may fish
Until my dying day!
And when it comes to my last cast
I humbly pray,
When in God's landing net
I'm peacefully asleep,
That in His mercy I be judged
As good enough to keep.

FOOTBALL

From Coach Buck O'Neill of Hamilton College comes a delectable football story of a climactic encounter years ago between Hamilton and its arch-rival, Colgate, in which the Colgate eleven was making damaging and consistent gains through the center of the Hamilton line. O'Neill finally sent in a substitute, Miller, for the varsity center, Doyle—and things immediately took a decided turn for the better.

After the game, Coach O'Neill warmly praised Miller for his key role in Hamilton's last-minute victory. "Thank you for the kind words, Coach," replied Miller, "but I really don't deserve all the credit. You see, when I went in, Doyle never came out."

*   *   *

"I'm not saying that the football players at so-and-so University are semi-literates who get paid under the table," grumbled a man whose own team had just been shellacked by the squad under discussion. "I'm simply telling you that the first time that 240-pound fullback of theirs won his varsity letter, somebody had to read it to him."

* * *

After two big-name football coaches had been chivvied into resigning by alumni of a big Eastern university who considered anything but an all-winning season a disgrace, the late Herman Hickman agreed to take the job. "What are you going to do about those pesky alumni?" he was asked. "My intention," Hickman announced, "is to keep them sullen but not mutinous."

* * *

Held up in the middle of nowhere by a blizzard, Coach Hickman had to eat dinner in a run-down, fourth-rate roadside diner. So he only ate three orders of ham and eggs and four slabs of apple pie. As he brushed the crumbs from his ample paunch, he remarked contentedly, "Gentlemen, let's face it: There is no such thing as bad food!"

* * *

There's a very homely girl in Ann Arbor who always seeks seats directly behind the goal posts at football games. It's the only time, she explains, that she sees men running right at her.

* * *

"Our coach," boasted the second assistant manager of the varsity football team, "thinks of everything. Today he ordered waterproof pants for the entire squad."

"Waterproof pants!" echoed the assistant manager's date with surprise. "Why, the big babies!"

* * *

At Georgia Tech, they're still talking about a football game where the visiting team was clinging to a precarious lead, 14–13, with only a minute or two to go. The coach of the team in the lead sent in a new quarterback with instructions to run out the clock by use of simple running plays only. The new boy, however, had dreams of glory and when he spotted one of his backs apparently in the clear, he uncorked a forward pass in that general direction.

Out of nowhere the home team's speediest back flashed into the picture, intercepted the pass, and was off for paydirt —but to the amazement of the onlookers, the substitute quarterback who had made the pass overtook him and brought him down on the five-yard line. Seconds later, the final whistle blew.

Later that evening the Georgia Tech coach grumbled to the coach of the winners, "I'll never understand how that sub quarterback of yours ever overtook the fastest boy on our squad."

"It's simple," was the reply. "Your boy was running for a touchdown. Mine was running for his life."

*　*　*

Mrs. George Allen, wife of the famous pal of F.D.R., Truman, and Eisenhower, read in the paper about a modest Navy football coach who, following the first Navy victory over Army in years, quietly left the train in Baltimore on the way back to Annapolis so his team could get all the huzzahs when it arrived home.

Allen nodded and said, "That's exactly what I would have done under similar circumstances." "The heck it is," hooted the knowing Mrs. Allen. "You'd have put the *team* off at Baltimore!"

*　*　*

Duffy Dougherty, renowned college football coach, remembers a wire he received from thoughtful alumni on the eve of a game that would decide the Big Ten championship. It read, "We're 100 per cent behind you, Boy, win or draw."

Dougherty boasts of Michigan's most understanding wife. "When I get home," he relates, "she's put out my slippers, robe, and lots of hot water. She knows I hate to do dishes in cold water."

GOLF

Golf was a rugged pastime in the United States in those distant days before electric carts and portable bars took the spirit of adventure out of an eighteen-hole round.

Mark Twain, for instance, was once playing a twosome with no less a personage than Woodrow Wilson when the future President cut under a drive and sent a shower of turf in all directions. Striving to conceal his embarrassment, Mr. Wilson remarked heartily, "I hope you're enjoying our links here, Mark."

Twain spat the dirt out of his teeth, and answered diplomatically, "I'll say this for them, Woodrow. They're the best I ever tasted."

*　*　*

Two weekend golfers out Grand Rapids way had their morning ruined by a couple of slowpoke females playing in front of them. To cap the climax, they caught up with one of the females on the fourteenth fairway stretched out in the sun, arms behind her head, while her companion thrashed about in the deep rough. "Don't you think you might at least help your friend find her ball?" snarled one of the men.

"Oh, she's got her ball," said the female dawdler with the sweetest of smiles. "She's looking for her club."

*　*　*

There's an old girl at an Eastern club who's getting mighty hard of hearing as she nears her eightieth birthday. Her memory isn't so good either—especially when she's toting up her score. Nevertheless, she negotiates eighteen holes every blessed morning.

On the ninth green, recently, her caddie said, "I guess I can put you down for a ten on that hole."

"What's that you said?" she demanded. "Speak a little louder, please—and make that a seven!"

❀   ❀   ❀

It was after 9 P.M. when Matt Coggins arrived home from
the golf club, listing slightly to port, but he had an airtight
alibi. "The guy I was playing in the semi-finals of the Class C
Tournament," he told his wife, "dropped dead on the eleventh
hole. From then on it was hit the ball, drag my opponent, hit
the ball, drag my opponent, all the way back!"

❀   ❀   ❀

Bob Hope overheard two sunbaked old biddies at the nineteenth hole discourse as follows: "Your husband seems to be
scoring better now that he has a new stance." "That's not a new
stance. That's a new husband."

❀   ❀   ❀

Near the end of a tense golf match, one of the contestants,
very temperamental, was thrown off his game when his caddie
developed a severe attack of hiccoughs. On the seventeenth
hole, he sliced his drive clean out of bounds, and growled
fiercely at the caddie, "That was on account of you and your
blank blank hiccoughs." "But I didn't hiccough then, sir," protested the caddie. "That's just the point," screamed the player.
"I had ALLOWED for it!"

❀   ❀   ❀

Morey Amsterdam tells about the first time two pinochle
addicts attempted a round of golf. Mr. L. shot the first hole in
47, nosing out Mr. G. by two strokes. As they approached the
second tee, Mr. L. mused, "You know something, Mac, this golf
has interesting possibilities. What do you say we play for a
nickel a hundred?"

❀   ❀   ❀

"I picked up a golfing companion at the first tee," reported a
West Florida vacationist to his wife, "but he was so bad he even
lost his ball in the washer."

❀   ❀   ❀

Poem for the golfing season penned by St. Paul's well-loved Ben Ridder:

The minister took seven putts upon one green
And uttered not a word profane.
But where he spat, ere exiting the scene,
No blade of grass will ever grow again.

* * *

Slammin' Sammy Snead tells of one temperamental golfer who hit four balls in succession into a pond on a three-par water hole. Enraged, he threw his bag of clubs into the pond, too, and stamped off to the locker room where he set fire to his clothes and slashed his wrists. Anxious friends summoned an ambulance. As he was being carried out to it on a stretcher he spotted old Horace, a member of his golf foursome, watching the proceedings. "Hey, Horace," he croaked weakly, "what time do we tee off tomorrow?"

* * *

A golf foursome was playing on a course where the first three holes parallel an interstate highway. As the foursome trudged down the third fairway, a limousine drove along the road, and stopped abruptly. Out hopped a beautiful girl in full wedding array. "Horace! Horace!" she sobbed, throwing her arms around one of the players. "Why have you left me waiting at the church?" "Now, now, Natalie," he said sternly. "Remember! I said *if it rained!*"

* * *

An avid golf enthusiast, anxious to get out to the links as quickly as possible, joined a funeral procession, whizzed through a succession of red lights, and eventually turned off into a side street. A motorcycle cop was right behind him, however. "No soap, buddy," said the unfeeling voice of the law. "Back in line! I saw you join that funeral procession. Now stay in it."

The poor golfer ended up at the cemetery, where the cop made him remain for the entire service.

* * *

"Why don't you play golf with Lew any more?" asked a wife one evening. "Hmph," snorted her husband. "Would you play with a sneak who puts down the wrong score and moves his ball when you aren't looking?" "I certainly would not," asserted the wife. "Well," said the husband, turning back to his paper, "neither will Lew."

* * *

Nat Wartels, a two-handicap golfer, stopped in at a sporting goods store just off Times Square and bought a dozen golf balls. "Shall I wrap them up?" asked the clerk. "Don't bother," said Wartels. "I'll just drive them home."

* * *

In the locker room, golfer Arnold Palmer told about a twosome involving the town's leading priest and rabbi. The priest made a little silent prayer before each putt and began sinking them from all corners of the greens. Obviously shaken, the rabbi said, half-jokingly, "If you taught me to say that little prayer, do you think my putts would start dropping, too?" "Not a chance," the priest assured him. "Why not?" demanded the rabbi. "Because," said the priest, "you're a terrible putter."

* * *

A golf neophyte teed his ball for the fifth time, swung violently, and watched with jubilation as a small object whirled away at a 45-degree angle.

"I got that ball off at last," he chortled.

"Mister," sighed the caddie, "that's your wristwatch."

7. *God Bless America!*

COMMUTERS

A commuter, anxious to catch his train, hailed a farmer standing at the edge of the road, "Is it okay with you, pop, if I take a shortcut across your field? I got to catch the 8:45."

"Go ahead, young feller," replied the farmer, "but if my new bull sees you, you'll catch the 8:15."

* * *

Henry Albritson is a dapper, law-abiding citizen of Mount Kisco with a deceivingly bland manner. Aboard a wretched commuter local one morning, a burly stranger squeezed in next to Mr. Albritson in a "non-smoking" coach, lit a foul-smelling stogie, and asked condescendingly, "My smoking won't bother you, will it?"

"Not at all," Mr. Albritson assured him, "so long as my getting sick won't bother you."

* * *

A wealthy commuter in Westchester was showing a Japanese visitor his estate, and saved for the *pièce de résistance* a brand new Japanese garden he just had installed. The Japanese visitor was properly impressed. "It's marvelous," he exclaimed. "If we only had something like it in Japan!"

* * *

There's a man in the Chicago Weather Bureau named Charles Fairskies! Furthermore, Mr. Fairskies received this message recently from a suburbanite in Glencoe: "Dear Mr. Fairskies: I thought you'd like to know that I have just shoveled eleven inches of Partly Cloudy off my driveway."

* * *

A new resident in a New England town was invited to join the volunteer fire brigade. "I'll do it," said the newcomer reluctantly, "but I must warn you that I'm not as young as I used to be, and I don't expect I'll be much good climbing up a ladder." "Don't let that worry you," the chief assured him. "Nine time out of ten, by the time we get there, there's nothing to lean a ladder against."

* * *

One midsummer morning a commuter announced to his wife at breakfast, "It's too nice a day to go to the office."

"Good," said the wife, "but don't think you're going to play golf. There are a lot of things that need doing around the house."

"Golf was the farthest thing from my mind," protested the husband. "Now would you mind passing the putter?"

* * *

Item from the obituary column of a Westchester gazette: "Hammond Wilson of North White Plains was accidentally killed yesterday when a bullet ricocheted while he was endeavoring to shoot a rabbit in his vegetable patch. Surviving are his wife, four children, and one rabbit."

*   *   *

At a country auction, Mrs. Peggy Weidman won a rare old handblown whiskey bottle with a bid of twenty-two dollars. An old farmer had watched her bidding with mounting disbelief. Now, as her bottle was delivered to her, he leaned over to take a closer look at it. "Gosh a'mighty," he gasped to his wife. "It's *empty!*"

*   *   *

Mrs. Heimerdinger had a dim opinion of the way her neighbor, Mrs. Nussbaum, kept house. "I'll tell you what a mess her place is in," reported Mrs. Heimerdinger to bridge cronies with obvious relish. "While I was having a cup of coffee with her yesterday afternoon, her telephone rang—and she couldn't find it!"

* * *

A bright young Madison Avenue man looked in vain for a seat on the crowded 5:15 train, then pushed his way to the last car and called out, "This car has developed a flat wheel and will be detached from the train. Please move up to cars ahead."

With nasty remarks about the railroad, the disgusted occupants of the car cleared out and the bright young man, very satisfied with himself, sat down, opened his newspaper, and waited—and waited.

Finally a conductor appeared. "You were the clever gent who announced this car wasn't going?" he inquired. "Yep," nodded the clever one. "Well," said the conductor, "it isn't. You were so convincing they just uncoupled the car."

* * *

Two bald-headed husbands, in their early fifties, were exchanging confidences at their country club. "As usual," sighed one, "I came home pooped from the office last night—and as usual my wife wanted to go to the movies or the theatre. I reminded her that we were plagued with a jurisdictional strike, that our new fall line was giving us trouble, and that I was far too exhausted to go chasing around all evening."

The other husband nodded sympathetically, then asked, "And how was the show?"

DRIVERS, MALE AND OTHERWISE

A Pennsylvania legislator, with time hanging heavy on his hands in Harrisburg one evening, came upon a disintegrating, dog-eared pamphlet published just after the turn of the century that set him up for hours. It had been published by a no-doubt worthy outfit that called itself the Farmers' Anti-

Automobile Society, and recommended several rules that motorists on rural roads would do well to follow.

One rule suggested that a car owner, propelling his vehicle after dark, should stop every mile, send up a warning rocket, and then wait for ten minutes to make certain that the road ahead was clear before advancing.

"If a horse is unwilling to pass an automobile," the Society declared on another page, "the driver should take the machine apart as rapidly as possible and conceal the parts in the bushes."

(Just as I finished getting this anecdote down on paper, author Truman Capote came tootling up to our house in a Jaguar geared to do 150 miles an hour. What a sixty years these have been!)

* * *

A speeding car came to a screeching halt at a busy crossroad, barely avoiding a little old lady who, having a green light in her favor, was ambling quietly from one side of the avenue to the other. The old lady didn't seem either frightened or annoyed. She merely smiled at the driver, and pointed to a pair of baby shoes suspended from his rear-view mirror. "Young man," she demanded, "why don't you put your shoes back on?"

* * *

An arthritic mountaineer came into a small and totally unexpected inheritance and decided to buy a second-hand jalopy to ease the burden of his declining years. The cheapest he could find in all Missouri was $235, but the dealer reminded him, "You get five good tires thrown in free; they haven't gone more'n forty thousand miles." "Forget the tires," said the mountaineer. "I don't want any on my car. When I'm auto riding I want to know it."

* * *

A slick college senior, out with his steady in his roadster, headed for the side of the turnpike the minute they were beyond the city limits. "But, Jerry," she protested, "why stop here

where everybody will see us? There are so many nicer places
down the road a way." "Here we stay," said the swain firmly.
"I believe in love at first site."

*   *   *

An automobile manufacturer confided to some drinking
companions in Detroit that his engineers have built a car that
can go ninety miles an hour and come to a dead stop in exactly
ten feet.

"When are you going to put it on the market?" he was asked.

"We're waiting," explained the manufacturer carefully, "until we can figure out a way to keep the driver from going
through the windshield."

*   *   *

The day after a sedate schoolteacher bought a second-hand
sedan she drove it back to the dealer's yard.

"What's wrong?" asked the dealer anxiously.

"Nothing at all," said the teacher sweetly. "I just want to
return these things for the dear little old lady you told me
owned the car before you sold it to me. She left this plug of
tobacco in the glove compartment, and this half-empty bottle
of gin under the seat."

*   *   *

A mortified lady motorist was hauled before a village justice
of the peace by a motorcycle cop who announced, "Judging by
the way this here woman handles a car in traffic, I don't think
she can see very well."

The justice didn't look too surprised. "We'll just give her
the little old eye test," he said. "Lady, please read the third
line of that chart on the wall."

"Without hesitation, the lady spelled out, "Y-M-P-J-C."

"Perfect," approved the justice. "Now let's hear the line at
the very bottom."

"I would like to purchase," read the lady, "some tickets for
the Policeman's Pageant and Field Day."

"Better still," boomed the justice of the peace. "How many?"

Short Circuits

"What mileage you can get out of these new economy model cars," boasted a young man just back from his honeymoon trip. "My bride and I had to stop at more gas stations than our car did!"

Val Carmichael writes that his motoring problems have been miraculously reduced since he found a way to stop his wife from being a back-seat driver. He stuffed her into the trunk.

Jack Paar is heartily in favor of shorter taxicabs. "When they knock you down," he explains, "they don't stay on you so long."

An inquisitive little girl asked her mother, "What happens to an automobile when it gets too old and banged up to run?" Mother answered grimly, "Somebody sells it to your father."

Nothing improves your driving, points out Madelaine Hurlock, like being followed by a policeman.

In Kentucky, a harassed motorist kept looking in his rearview mirror, wondering why a light truck was tailing him so persistently. He finally alighted to discover that the truck had no driver, and had been hooked to his rear bumper since he had backed into a parking space a hundred miles away in Cincinnati.

"What I hate most about women drivers," explained Harvardite Mike Frith, "is how they turn out to be men after you've criticized their driving to your girl friend."

Joyce Mizzari defines "perambulator" as last year's fun on wheels.

A complete biography in six words: GIN, SPIN, DASH, CRASH, NURSE, HEARSE.

Art Carney took his car into a Westchester garage for a tune-up and was handed a bill for $120. "Hey," protested Carney, "who did this tune-up? Leonard Bernstein?"

Old Man Babcock was inching his dilapidated jalopy down Main Street when a traffic officer signaled him to halt. "Don't worry, pop," said the officer reassuringly. "I just want to see what it feels like to put my foot on a running board again."

And let us not overlook the story of the woman who told her husband, "Be an angel and let me drive." He did—and he is.

* * *

From upstate New York comes the tale of the motorist who was tootling merrily westward on the Thruway. When he passed a sign reading "Twenty Miles to Buffalo," he was smiling happily. He was still in the pink when he flashed by the sign reading "Ten Miles to Buffalo." Only minutes later, however, he was discovered sitting dazed and battered, holding his head, at the roadside, his shiny new automobile a sorry wreck. "What happened?" demanded the first state trooper to arrive upon the scene. "I didn't heed that last sign," mourned the wounded motorist. "I covered the ten miles—and the damn buffalo rammed right into me."

* * *

Mrs. Wimpfheimer was ambling unconcernedly in her new convertible in the left-hand lane of a parkway, when, without warning, she suddenly made a sharp right turn and collided with another car.

"Blank, blank, blank!" roared the other driver. "Why the blank, blank didn't you signal?"

"Don't be absurd," countered Mrs. Wimpfheimer loftily, "I ALWAYS turn here."

* * *

A workman who was extremely fond of garlic boarded a bus in a Southern city, and plumped himself down next to a very haughty, sour-faced lady. She immediately became aware of the garlic fragrance, and observed icily, "It's a wonder they don't run a special bus for persons who insist on eating garlic." The workman answered cheerily, "They do, lady. You're on the wrong bus."

* * *

A motorcycle cop stopped a driver who was hurtling up the West Side Drive of Manhattan at breakneck speed, and gave him a ticket. "I clocked you doing seventy-five miles an hour," said the cop grimly. The driver nodded cheerfully, then asked, "Couldn't you make it ninety an hour, officer? I'm trying to sell this car."

* * *

Traffic officer (to pedestrian just bowled over by a hit-and-run driver): "Did you get that driver's number?"

Pedestrian: "No, but I'd recognize my wife's laugh anywhere."

* * *

A traffic cop flagged a lady doing eighty-five on a crowded thruway and dodging from lane to lane. He examined her license and returned it with this quizzical observation:

"Your license seems to be valid, Madam. Now would you mind telling me how the heck you got it?"

* * *

A foreign roadster rounded a corner on two wheels, knocked down a policeman and four pedestrians, and finally wrapped itself around a telephone pole. A sweet young thing climbed out of the wreckage. "Yippee!" she cried. "That's what I call a kiss!"

* * *

A New York traffic cop's attention was drawn to a lady motorist who was calmly driving down the wrong side of an avenue. He stopped her and inquired testily, "Don't you know what that white line in the middle of the avenue is for?"

The lady considered carefully, then hazarded, "Bicycles?"

* * *

A motorist paused at a roadside snack bar and ordered coffee and doughnuts. A few moments after he had been served, he called over the pleasant-faced young woman in charge and said, "I can tell you something about yourself. You have a small son who plays in the kitchen with a toy automobile."

"You're absolutely right," gasped the young woman. "You must be a mind reader."

"No, no," insisted the motorist. "Just put me down as the fellow you served a toy tire for a chocolate doughnut."

* * *

A New Yorker drove all the way to California without incident, but once within the city limits of Los Angeles, found himself hopelessly confused in the complex of overpasses, underpasses, and clover leafs of the Freeway system. Finally he pulled up alongside a man who had a lady and four children in the car with him.

"Mister," implored the New Yorker, "can you help me out? I've been trying to get to the Civic Center for six hours and I wind up at this spot every time."

"You're asking the wrong man, brother," replied the man with the lady and the four children. "I ain't even got home from my honeymoon."

* * *

A San Diego matron, driving a spanking new Mustang, turned too sharply at an intersection, reports Neil Morgan, and neatly ran over the left foot of a cop directing traffic. A shrill plea from his whistle brought her to a stop. Helpfully, she flipped into reverse and backed toward the officer.

"I knew it!" he roared in anguish. "Now you got the other one!"

* * *

A co-ed reported to police that she had been struck by a ship in the middle of a state highway. She was driving innocently along, it seems, when a speedboat broke loose from its trailer.

* * *

Heard about the eager young bridegroom who came home and found his wife knitting tiny things—seat covers for their Volkswagen?

* * *

A taxi driver in Chicago got his comeuppance from a habitual lady back-seat driver. "Haven't you got more sense than to leave that window open?" she scolded. "It's blowing my husband's hair too much."

"How far can a little wind blow a man's hair?" scoffed the driver.

"The last little bit," she replied, "blew it about three miles."

* * *

Bob Campbell overheard a Brentwood beldame gurgle happily, "I had my first driving lesson today. I think I did very well, too—but, my goodness, that ignition key is tricky."

* * *

A Mrs. Miller, of Des Moines, explained how her car had swerved off the road in the dark:

"I was following the white line, and the white line turned out to be a skunk."

* * *

A La Jolla pedestrian couldn't duck fast enough, and was struck amidships by a big, mangy dog who came loping over the crest of a hill and catapulted him into a ditch. He barely had arisen and started to dust himself off when a girl in a miniature foreign sports car hove into view and knocked him down again.

"The dog didn't hurt me a bit," he reported later, "but that tin can tied to his tail darn near killed me."

* * *

Cornelia Otis Skinner had a nerve-wracking experience when she saw a little boy stroll into the path of a convertible driven by one of the young ladies in her company.

She screamed, snatched him up under her arm, and jumped with him to safety on the curbstone.

He turned out to be a midget of forty, smoking a pipe, and with a quaint and extensive vocabulary.

* * *

A Wall Street broker was interrupted in the pursuit of his duties by a phone call from his eight-year-old son.

"Mama ran over my bicycle when she was backing her car out of the garage this morning," wailed the boy.

The unsympathetic father replied, "How many times have I warned you not to leave your bicycle in the middle of the front lawn?"

* * *

Albuquerque, New Mexico, is generally regarded as a respectable, law-abiding community, but the other day when a police officer asked Rosemary Collins to show her driver's license after a traffic violation the culprit only laughed at him. Nor was there a thing he could do about it. Rosemary had climbed into a car, and put it out of gear. The car then rolled downhill into another car—a police lieutenant's in the bargain. Rosemary was two years old.

FARMERS

A stingy old lady on an upstate farm hired a new hand, and followed him all the first day to make sure he didn't waste a moment. When dinner time came round, he noted with disgust that the entire bill of fare consisted of a couple of very thin slices of meat loaf, bread, tea, and a very small spot of honey in the center of the table on a big platter.

"I see, Ma'am," observed the new hand coldly, "that you keep a bee."

* * *

Squire Klopfer was constantly annoyed by motorists who scooted past his front porch at an average speed of eighty miles an hour. The wily squire put a stop to that nonsense with a large sign that has slowed drivers down to a very slow crawl. The sign proclaims, "Please proceed with care. Nudist camp crossing just ahead."

* * *

Two gabby matrons in a New England town were gossiping endlessly on a party-line telephone when they were suddenly interrupted by the unmistakable sound of a receiver being slammed down on the hook. "Well, how do you like that?" snorted one of the talkers indignantly. "Somebody's hung up on us!"

*   *   *

Harry Golden tells about the Carolina farmer who sold a Yankee an old mule. "What's the mule's name?" asked the Yankee.

"I don't know his name," admitted the farmer, "but I call him Bill."

*   *   *

Little Oswald toddled out to a field his Pa was plowing to report, "There's a strange man at the house. I dunno what he wants."

"Son," the father told him, "if it's the landlord, he wants his rent. If it's the banker, he's come to foreclose the mortgage. And if he's a traveling salesman, you run home fast as your legs will carry you—and sit in your maw's lap till I get there!"

*   *   *

Two sour-visaged farmers liked to complain about conditions together. "Never did see hay grow so short as mine this summer," sighed one. "You think yours is short," scoffed the other. "I had to lather mine to mow it."

*   *   *

The noted minister, Dr. Harry Emerson Fosdick, summering in Maine, recalled a romantic interlude that occurred there a few years back. The local blacksmith, only five feet one for all his muscles of steel, fell in love with a girl who towered fully a foot above him. Diffident for months, he proposed marriage to her one night in a sudden burst of courage, and was promptly accepted. He climbed on top of his anvil and kissed the girl rapturously. Hours later, walking home through a pasture, he asked if he might kiss her again. "No," she decided. "Let's not overdo our sparking."

"Shucks," said the disappointed blacksmith. "If I can't kiss you no more, I might as well stop lugging this anvil."

* * *

A farmer took a train for his very first visit to New York. He alighted at Grand Central and was led through an underground passage to the Roosevelt Hotel. He had dinner in the Grill, and then relaxed in the newsreel theatre in the Terminal. The next day he bought gifts for the family in Grand Central shops and took a train back to the sticks.

"Well, Paw," asked his wife, "how did you like New York?"

"It was wonderful," enthused Paw, "but why didn't somebody tell me it had a roof over it?"

* * *

In Wappingers Falls, a farmer was trying to sell a broken-down old horse to a city fellow. After walking him slowly around a field, he remarked, "Got a handsome coat, hasn't he?"

The city fellow listened to the old horse breathe for a moment, then replied, "I like his coat all right—but not his pants."

* * *

You've heard a lot about farmers' beautiful daughters, but Squire Kislik was one farmer who had himself a beautiful wife. When she went home to visit her parents, all the joy departed from his life, and when she finally wired she'd be home on the 5:50, he hitched up his bay stallion, and set out to fetch her at the station in a fever of anticipation.

The stallion had been cooped up in his stall for days and was rarin' to go. He wheeled into the turnpike at fifty an hour, and began picking up from there. Farmer Kislik turned white with fear, and when they just missed ramming into Deacon Lapolla's Stanley Steamer, he finally hollered to the stallion:

"You gol durn fool! Who do you think got that telegram? You or me?"

* * *

The Guggenheim herd in Sands Point includes one cow who's mighty hoity-toity. "Go ahead," she was heard mooing to the dairyman one evening. "Milk me! See if I give a dram!"

*　*　*

The proprietor of a small village drugstore was called out one sleepy summer morning, leaving the establishment temporarily under the sole management of a very old, and very uneducated porter. "Just answer the phone if it rings, Jim," instructed the proprietor.

The phone rang. "Hello," said the porter.

"Do you have streptomycin and aureomycin?" asked a voice at the other end. The porter scratched his head, then said, "Ma'am, when I said 'Hello' I told you everything I know!"

*　*　*

A farmer's wife went stark raving mad one morning. As she was being led away by attendants from the nearest asylum her husband scratched his head in perplexity and muttered, "I'm danged if I kin figger what's gotten into the old girl. She ain't bin out of this kitchen in thutty-two years!"

*　*　*

George Heister writes about the rancher who couldn't keep his hands off his beautiful young wife. Finally had to fire every one of them.

*　*　*

In Kansas, they seem to relish the story of a small-town wife who accompanied her husband to Topeka for a cattlemen's convention. She wore a homemade blouse of which she was inordinately proud, for on it she had embroidered every cattle brand she knew.

A veteran cattleman watched her with something akin to awe as she approached the registration desk. Then he cackled loudly to a friend, "Get a load of that critter, Tom! She's sure changed hands a lot, hasn't she?"

*　*　*

Why do rich society ladies have so many more neuroses and mental disturbances than farmers' wives? The following story, contributed by Jim Donaldson, may contain the key:

Mrs. Smith had raised nine children on a Michigan farm, fed them and the farmhands, done all her housework, and helped with outdoor chores. She'd never been ill a day in her life. A doctor implored her to reveal her secret.

"I constantly see young women," the doctor said, "who have one or two children, and whose homes are full of gadgets to lighten work, but who suffer from nervous exhaustion or psychosomatic aches and pains. How is it that you managed to go through all these years and never have a nervous breakdown?"

"You know, Doctor," said the hardworking woman, wistfully, "I've always wanted to have a nervous breakdown. But every time I was about to get around to it, it was time to fix somebody a meal."

GARDENS ARE TO NAP IN

It's just twelve years since I bought a house in the country and I confess that when we moved in I couldn't tell an oak tree from a willow. Now, of course, I can—just! A rose was a rose was a rose to Gertrude Stein, but roses aren't always roses to me. I call them as I see them. And sometimes I see them as geraniums.

I never have known anything about gardening and probably I never will—nor am I ashamed of the fact. I am just an underprivileged city boy in that respect. Lawns, trees, flowers, hedges—they're all beautiful and I love them—so long as there's somebody else around to take care of them. For me, gardens are to nap in.

In our household, the "somebody else" is a rare Scottish gentleman who is just about perfect in his job. Before he came with us an Army colonel with whom he had been associated for a decade called me on the phone. "I want to tell you three

things about Mac," said he. "First: he's the greatest gardener I ever met. Second: he's the kind of manager we dream of finding in the Army. You can go off on a two-year trip publishing and lecturing to your heart's content and when you get home you'll find everything just the way you left it—or better. Third —and most important of all—if Mac wants to do things one way in the garden and you want to do them in another—SAVE YOUR BREATH."

It's all worked out in dreamy fashion. Not only do I never want to do things in the garden in another way than Mac's; I don't *know* any other way. So we agree perfectly. My only contribution came when I discovered that rabbits and squirrels were eating five out of every six ears of corn we were growing and that those we did manage to smuggle to the dinner table were averaging us about two dollars apiece. "I've thought of a new method of getting corn," I told Mac—who registered polite disbelief. "It's called the A&P system," I continued. Mac approved at once. He definitely does not like rabbits and squirrels. In the space we formerly grew corn we now play badminton. It's a big saving.

A noted columnist in his day who *did* cultivate a garden was Franklin P. Adams (remember his caustic wit on that classic radio program, "Information Please"?). F.P.A. concentrated on raising peonies—probably just so that he could pun, "If you take care of the peonies, the dahlias will take care of themselves."

Another flower grower in the metropolitan area always bought her seeds at a great big department store south of Forty-second Street. One day she came charging into that store's complaint department seething with rage. It seems that a few months previous she had buried her husband and purchased several packages of carnation seeds with which to decorate his grave. Then she flew off to Paris to pull herself together.

The day after her return, she visited her husband's grave. It was decorated all right—but not with carnations. It was one full bed of ripe rhubarb.

"I don't know what she was screaming so about," protested the manager of the department store's complaint department later. "We were perfectly willing to refund the price of the seeds."

The most avid—and horrifyingly articulate amateur gardener I know boards my train one station down the line every summer weekday morning. According to him, he has such a green thumb they asked him to lead the St. Patrick's Day parade this year. When he isn't snipping away at his plants, he is supervising the pruning and spraying of his trees. His favorite time for spraying seems to be when his wife is serving drinks to guests in the garden. I can testify personally that tree-spray-on-the-rocks will never replace the martini.

To distract my friend one day I told him about the unfortunate tree surgeon who fell out of his patient, but he didn't think this was funny, having fallen out of a tree himself only an hour before. He soon rallied, however, threw a copy of Rachel Carson's *Silent Spring* angrily aside, and proposed, "Let us spray."

The most fashionable gardener I know is having a problem this year with her front lawn. "The trouble with grass," she complains, "is that it comes in only one color."

There are three standard, made-to-order garden jokes that sprout every spring as regularly as the trees and flowers.

Number One is about the gardener who did nothing but

hoe, hoe, hoe—and if you think that's funny, you've never worked in a garden yourself.

Number Two cites the suburbanite whose garden was such a success one year that his neighbor's chickens won first prize at the local poultry show.

And Number Three reports the cautionary message that a cynical seedsman has imprinted on the back of every packet he sells: "Don't throw away this packet when it's empty and you have finished planting your garden. Probably it will be just the right size for storing your crop."

A story *I* like to tell concerns a lonely little widow in Los Angeles who had one pleasure left in life: every morning a gentleman left a rose for her. "It's from his garden," she explained to a visitor one day. "Here he comes now." Sure enough, the gentleman handed her a beauty. "I grew this one just for you," he said with a gallant bow.

The visitor left with the donor of the rose, who then explained sheepishly, "I've never been in a garden in my life. I buy her a rose in the florist shop across the street every morning. It gives her such a happy look for a few moments."

And now I'm off to a garden myself. Madison Square Garden.

HILLBILLIES

Bob Burns loved telling stories about an uncle and aunt who picked on each other continuously for forty years. Uncle was an old gadabout; Aunt was a homebody. Uncle had one particularly hectic week: on Monday night he went to a lodge meeting; Tuesday night to a Salvation Army rally; Wednesday night to a church meeting; Thursday night to a YMCA lecture. On Friday night, his wife saw him reach for his celluloid collar and demanded tartly, "Where you headed this evening, playboy?"

*   *   *

A mountain lad was very late for school one morning, but his excuse was deemed adequate. "Maw woke up Paw at three in the morning," he explained, "because she heard a noise in the hen house. Paw grabbed his shotgun and ran outside. He pointed it at the hen house and waited for something to happen. Something happened, all right. Our old hound dog came up behind Paw with his cold nose, and we've been cleaning chickens ever since."

* * *

The villagers in a remote Arkansas community got their best laugh in ten years when a damyankee erected a tool shed and hired a night watchman to guard the tools and supplies therein. "As though," they jeered, "any sane man in these hills would steal anything to work with!"

* * *

A revenue agent, hot on the trail of a West Virginia whiskey still, suddenly heard a shot, and something grazed his left sleeve. Undaunted, the agent continued forward, whereupon a second shot whistled through his coattails. When a third bullet, neatly puncturing his slouch hat, still failed to halt him, a voice from the woods sounded.

"One more step, mister," it warned grimly, "and I begin takin' aim!"

* * *

An itinerant preacher in the Blue Ridge Mountains shook an old reprobate and thundered, "Are you ready for the Judgment Day?" "Mebbe yes, mebbe no," said the old rep cagily. "When's it coming?" "It might come this very day," warned the preacher. "Then again, it might come tomorrow."

By this time the old reprobate was registering genuine concern. "Don't tell my old woman," he begged. "She'd want to go both days."

* * *

After the biggest hillbilly wedding the Blue Ridge Mountains region had celebrated since the Hatfield-McCoy feud, one stalwart admitted to the bride's father, "I didn't like the way that bridegroom dragged himself to the altar. He acted like he had lead in his pants." The bride's father answered grimly, "He did!"

* * *

A fable from the North Carolina back country: The revenue agents found a number of trails leading into the deep forest. Reinforcements were brought up, and several agents were put on each trail. At a given signal, they all crept forward. Miles into the woods they discovered that all trails converged on one little cabin, where a bearded man sat working. Was he making moonshine whiskey? Not at all. He was building a better mousetrap.

* * *

Help was mighty tough to come by in an out-of-the-way Missouri town, and "Pop" Miller, who ran the biggest—in fact, the only—motel thereabouts was reluctant to part with his night clerk, despite the fact that said clerk was a hopeless kleptomaniac.

"Pop" Miller finally solved his problem. Over the desk in the lobby he hung this sign: "Leave your valuables with our night clerk. He'll get them anyway."

* * *

A Kentucky backwoods lad took unto himself a wife and off they went to Louisville for their honeymoon. When they got back home, a friend told the bridegroom, "We hear you treated your bride awfully good."

"Well, sir," admitted the bridegroom, "the first day I was pretty tough with her, but after that I couldn't look her in the face for a week. By then, I could see a little out of one eye."

DRINKERS

Two darling old ladies were having lunch in the dining room of a residential hotel. "I've forgotten the name of it," one of them told the waitress, "but we both want one of those appetizers my nephew bought me here last week. In a little glass you get a green olive, covered by a perfectly delightful clear white sauce."

* * *

A young bride in distress called her father and wailed, "I'm afraid I've married a drinking man. All last night Oscar kept mumbling in his sleep, 'No, Sidney, no. I don't care if it's free; not one more drink for me.'"

Interrupted the father wistfully, "Did Oscar happen to mention any address?"

* * *

The bride-of-a-month tittered nervously as she passed the cocktails at the first formal dinner party she hosted. "I do hope these martinis will hit the spot," she quavered. "We ran out of olives, so I had to pour a spoonful of olive oil into each glass."

* * *

Mr. Sneedle, wont to imbibe at least four martinis with every lunch, was not too spry when he wobbled back to his office. His secretary found a way of protecting him, however. She told callers sweetly, "Can Mr. Sneedle call you back later? He's still out from lunch."

* * *

Two inebriated gents were weaving their way down a rail-road track. "Golly," complained one, "this is a long flight of steps." "I don't mind the steps so much," countered the other. "It's the low railings that get me."

* * *

The town drunk tried to get to bed without disturbing his wife, but heard her clomping downstairs the moment he shut the door. He made a dive for the library, reached for a book, and was sitting under the lamp when his wife collared him. "Hello, darling," he mumbled a bit indistinctly. "I thought I'd catch up a bit on my reading tonight."

"You did, did you?" she replied grimly. "Well, you just shut that valise and come up to bed."

* * *

An imaginative bartender in Tel Aviv has invented a new cocktail he calls a Little David. Imbibe two and you goliath down.

* * *

An attendant in the Manhattan D.A.'s office recalls a wild night during Prohibition days when twenty-five of the town's top bootleggers were rounded up in a surprise raid. As they were being arraigned, the judge asked each one his occupation. The first twenty-four promptly replied, "Real estate broker." The twenty-fifth stanchly declared, "Your Honor, I'm a bootlegger."

Surprised, the judge permitted himself a laugh and inquired, "How's business?" The answer was, "It would be better if there weren't so darn many real estate brokers around."

* * *

W. C. Fields, never known as a teetotaler, was suffering from a really stupendous hangover one morning at the Paramount lot. "Let me fix you a Bromo Seltzer," suggested his director. "Oh, no, not that," groaned Fields. "I couldn't stand the racket."

* * *

A big fire in a Midwestern brewery caused a temporary beer shortage in those parts, and every bar and grill had to go on a quota. The proprietor of one roadside retreat called to plead for an additional shipment "toot sweet." "It's an emergency," he declared. "But you've had your quota for the week," the brewery superintendent pointed out. "I know *I* have," answered the caller, "but what about my customers?"

* * *

Mike Connoly started off the new year by reporting, "I slept like a log last night. I must have. I woke up in the fireplace."

* * *

Maybe you're not on the mailing list that has been receiving this touching *Ode to a Martini Drinker*:
Starkle, starkle, little twink
Who the deuce you are I think.
I'm not under what they call
The affluence of incohol.

I'm not as drunk as thinkle peep
I'm just a little slort of sheep.
Tee martoonis make a guy
Feel so dizzy, don't know why.
So pass the mixer and kill my fup,
I've all day sober to Sunday up.

* * *

Swifty Morgan, a statistician of great renown, looked up from the financial page and announced, "It says here that freight car loadings are going down, but that the sale of Scotch whiskey has gone up. This means only one thing: More people are getting loaded than freight cars!"

* * *

Two extremely intoxicated celebrants at a college reunion sought still another bottle to imbibe—and found one in the garage of the motel where they were registered. One took a long swig and gulped, "This is powerful stuff," and passed it to the other, saying, "Maybe you'll know what it is." The other sampled the liquid, and gasped, "Holy mackerel! You've been drinking *gasoline.*" "I know that, stupid," grumbled the first, "but what kind—regular or high-test?"

* * *

Gene Sherman was proceeding peacefully down Sunset Strip in Beverly Hills when he saw a gray-haired old lady of seventy-five or eighty peering intently into a doorway. As Sherman hesitated, she tapped his arm and quavered, "Is this place a restaurant or a saloon?" "It's a saloon, ma'am," Sherman warned her, "and one with a very unsavory reputation, too." "Oh, thank you, young man," said the old lady—and went in.

* * *

Once upon a time there was a terrible, terrible week when Jackie Gleason didn't touch a single drop of liquor. Gleason's friend Toots Shor took this as a personal affront, but Gleason blamed it all on his doctor. "He's put me off the stuff for life," he explained sadly. "Foofel and poofel," scoffed Shor. "I'll send you to *my* doctor. He'll let you drink all you want."

The next day Geason was still on the wagon. "Didn't you go to see my doctor?" demanded Toots. "I went," nodded Gleason, "but I couldn't get in. The office was too crowded."

* * *

A finicky wine connoisseur took unto himself a bride. "She was Wellesley '53," he explained to a fellow imbiber. "You'll recall that's a very fine year for women."

* * *

A minister dropped into a strange barber shop for a quick shave and had the misfortune to choose a chair presided over by a barber who was suffering from an acute hangover. His breath nearly asphyxiated the poor minister, and then, to cap the climax, he took a huge nick out of the minister's chin. "You see," said the minister reproachfully, "what comes from drinking intoxicating liquor?" "Yep," agreed the barber cheerfully. "It sure makes the skin tender."

* * *

From San Francisco comes the story of three Chinese gentlemen who stepped up to a local bar. The first one ordered a Mai Tai sour, the second a Hoong Wong on the rocks. The third, however, declared, "Nothing for me, thank you. I'm pulling the rickshaw."

*　　*　　*

A great big grizzly bear wandered down from the woods at Lake Louise, Canada, one afternoon and shambled into a saloon. There a well-oiled patron exuberantly put his arms around the bear and proclaimed, "Look at us, men!" The bear was having no part of this, however. He picked up the patron and very accurately threw him through the entranceway into the street.

The drunken one picked himself up at length, and mumbled disconsolately, "Isn't that just like a woman? Give her a fur coat and she thinks she owns the world!"

INDIANS

We've all learned in our youth about the supposedly simpleminded Indians who sold Manhattan Island for twenty-four dollars and a lot of glass beads. Waste no sympathy on said aborigines, counsels Don Russell in his *Book of the American West.* "Those Indians," he asserts, "were somewhat in the same position as the confidence man who sold the Brooklyn Bridge for ten dollars. They didn't own Manhattan Island at all. They chanced to be there for a weekend's fishing!" So it was Peter Minuit and his fellow Dutchmen after all who were the ones taken in by that famous transaction!

*　　*　　*

An old—very old—scout swears he once heard a forceful squaw tell Sitting Bull, "Well, don't just sit there—do something!"

*　　*　　*

Big Chief Pokum's favorite squaw promised to make him a new bead necklace but when the time came for the annual conclave of the tribe, it wasn't finished. Chief Pokum expressed his disappointment in no uncertain terms, but his mate reminded him, "School teacher always tell me I be heap slow beader."

* * *

Two Indians were having their first look at water skiing. Asked one, "Why boat go so fast?" Answered the other, "Lunatic on string chase 'em."

* * *

From Phoenix comes the story of a wise old Indian chief who led his son to a tall hilltop and pointed to the densely populated valley below. "One day soon," prophesied the chief, "all this land will belong to the Indians again. White men all go to the moon."

TEXANS

Before she hit the jackpot as a novelist, a now-famous Texas lady applied for the job of school teacher in a sparsely settled county adjoining the one where she had been reared. The school board president was relaxing on his front porch. "I know your family, Miss," said the president. "Is it true that one of your cousins killed a man and your father bribed enough witnesses to save him from the chair?" "Yes, sir," admitted the applicant. "I'm not denying it."

"Is it also true," he continued, "that another of your cousins killed her husband and is now serving a term in the penitentiary?" "No, sir," blurted our heroine. "She's out! They sent her up for five years, but she got out in three for good behavior. But," she added, "with all those facts, I don't suppose you'll want me to teach in your system."

"Lady," he assured her, rising to his feet, "you're the very one we *do* want. You can't hold your head above nobody!"

* * *

A Texas billionaire indulged himself with a new whim this season. Back from a New York trip that included a visit to its teeming East Side tenement district, he constructed back of his twenty-eight-room ranch house a replica of a slum area block, complete with pushcarts, manholes, bagel and pizza parlors, fire hydrants, and assorted debris. "This is the latest thing up in Manhattan," he boasted to his friends. "They call it a stickball court."

* * *

The famous Lon Tinkle tells about a West Texas cattle raiser who was asked what he did between the time he alighted from his air-conditioned automobile and got into his air-conditioned ranch house. Replied the Texan, "I run like hell."

Dr. Tinkle also claims he ran into an effeminate stevedore in Galveston who refuses to unload anything but hairpins.

* * *

Colonel James Cokesbury Albright, the pride of Dallas, says that when it comes to gallantry, Texans cannot be beat. He cites as an example a rough old gaffer from the oil fields who was just preparing to dig into a succulent piece of roast pig at a barbecue when someone careened into him from behind and knocked his plate to the ground. In a rage he bellowed, "You hawg! You want all the space there is?" and then he perceived the offender was the dignified wife of his host. Without a second thought he amended his statement, "Lady hawg, that is, Ma'am."

* * *

While making a personal appearance in Tulsa, Art Linkletter was persuaded by a wildcatter to invest five thousand dollars in drilling a new oil well. Some weeks later he received this telegram: "Struck ketchup at 6000 feet. Drilled into hamburger stand abandoned during dust storm in early thirties. Estimate

we need five thousand more to locate mustard. (Signed) Your
Partner."

* * *

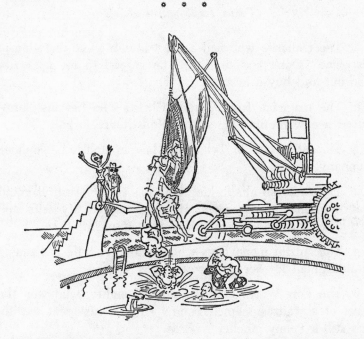

A millionaire's daughter came home to Dallas to find that
her father had a small surprise for her: a brand-new home
with forty bedrooms, three tennis courts, a nine-hole golf
course, and an Olympic swimming pool. Cavorting in the pool
when she came by was an assortment of handsome, bronzed
young athletes. The daughter clapped her hands delightedly,
and cried, "Oh, Daddy! And you've stocked it just for me!"

* * *

A Tulsa family man, delirious at the imminent arrival of his
first baby, set a new record between his bungalow and Tulsa
General Hospital. He made the five-mile trip through heavy
traffic in eight minutes flat.

Arrived at the hospital, he discovered, however, that, in his
excitement, he had made one slight mistake. He had forgotten
to bring along his expectant wife.

Texas Trillionaires . . .

1. The Dallasite who had a heart attack while dictating in his office. "Don't just sit there," he gasped to his secretary. "Go out and buy a hospital."

2. The magician from Corpus Christi who has just introduced a new routine. He saws a Rolls-Royce in half.

3. The oil tycoon in Tyler who has an unlisted telephone company.

4. The Amarillo alfalfa king who has three beautiful grand pianos in his rumpus room. His explanation: My wife and two kids all decided to take lessons at the same time.

5. The Austin moneybags who bought his wife a cleaning establishment for her anniversary—Las Vegas.

6. The Fort Worth financier, turned eighty, who won the heart of a waitress named Penny. Despite his great wealth, he's still a Penny pincher.

7. The Galveston magnate who pulled in a fish he thought was too small to take back to the club. So he persuaded two attendants to help him throw it back in the Gulf.

8. The sturdy son of a Bonham benefactor who came down to breakfast one morning and declared, "What a day! I feel like a million dollars." His mother, deeply concerned, cried, "Darling! What makes you so depressed?"

9. The El Paso rancher who's so rich he doesn't even know he's got six kids going through college.

10. The San Antonio hostess whose new mansion is so fantastic it has staggered even jaded Dallasites. "How many bathrooms did you say your new residence has?" inquired publisher Ted Dealey. The hostess answered modestly, "I can seat fourteen."

* * *

An expansive Waco character arrived at a Montana dude ranch with a great big motor launch tied down to his trailer. "Sorry," said the amused ranch foreman, "there's not a drop of water within a hundred miles." "I know," nodded the character. "The lake is arriving tomorrow."

* * *

A man from Texas, visiting in Alaska, was the butt of considerable humor about the fact that Texas was now only the second largest state in the Union. "True, true," conceded the Texan, "but wouldn't you half-frozen galoots up here like to have some of our herds of cattle? Everywhere you look in Texas, you see the finest, healthiest, most expensive cattle ever bred."

"Okay," joshed an Alaskan. "You've got a few head of mangy cattle. But you've got nothing like our majestic, towering, snowclad mountains up there."

"Not now," shot back the Texan, "but we did have, son. We had 'em before our cattle trampled 'em down!"

* * *

President Lyndon Johnson recalls a time when his fellow Texan, the late House Speaker Sam Rayburn, visited President Truman just after the latter had been sworn in. Said Mr. Sam, "You're now in the most powerful office on earth, Harry, and people are going to keep unpleasant things from you if they can. Pretty soon they'll have you believing you're the smartest man in the world. And you and I know, Harry, that *you're not!*"

8. The Great Society

RAGS TO RICHES

Rags . . .

John D. Rockefeller, never considered exactly a spend-thrift, was accosted outside his office by a smooth-talking panhandler who announced, "Mr. Rockefeller, I hoofed it thirty miles down here just to meet you, and everybody I met assured me you were the most generous man in New York."

Mr. Rockefeller thought this over for a minute, then asked quietly, "Are you going back by the same route?" "Probably," said the panhandler. "Aha," nodded J.D., "in that case you can do me a great favor. Deny the rumor."

* * *

Into a supermarket strode an emaciated man, obviously suffering from severe malnutrition, accompanied by five bedraggled, woeful little children. Even the hardhearted manager was touched. "Here," he volunteered. "Take this cart. Load it up with stuff for you and the kids. And tell the cashier I said there's to be no charge. It's on the house."

The father loaded the cart, then sought out the manager again. "Looks like you're all set," approved the manager. "Feel a little bit better now?"

"I do not," snarled the father. "*How about my green trading stamps?*"

* * *

His progress impeded by a derelict with the familiar whine, "Kinyu spare a quarter for a poor man to get a cup of coffee?" a busy magnate handed over a dollar saying, "Here, get yourself four cups," and hastened on his way. Next day the derelict was waiting on the same corner. "Say," he snarled, "aren't you the wise guy that slipped me a dollar for four cups of coffee? You big bum—I couldn't sleep a wink all night!"

* * *

Myron Cohen tells about a chronic borrower who begged an old friend to lend him a hundred dollars. "I'll pay it back the minute I return from Chicago," he promised. "Exactly what day will you return?" probed the wary friend. Shrugged the borrower, "Who's going?"

* * *

Characters: an old tramp and a young bride. Scene: the young bride's backyard. YOUNG BRIDE: I'll give you a big slice of the very first cake I ever baked if you'll chop some firewood for me. OLD TRAMP (after one bite of the cake): Tell you what I'll do, lady. I'll eat the firewood and chop the cake.

* * *

Art Buchwald tells of two old friends who met for the first time in years. One obviously had prospered; the other looked

terrible. Proposed the prosperous one: "Al, you've got to come
to work for me. I've got a good job for you. Now cheer up—and
here's fifty dollars on account. Get some food for your family
and have a jolly weekend."

Al turned up for work Monday morning looking worse than
ever. "I haven't eaten for five days," he confessed.

"What happened to the fifty bucks I gave you?" demanded
his friend.

"Well," said Al, "when I showed it to my wife and kids they
all smiled the first time in two years. And so, since we all looked
happy for a change, we went to a photographer's and had our
picture taken!"

* * *

Marvyn Carton, the sailing expert, was returning home from
his yacht club when a bedraggled individual stopped him to
beg for a quarter. His explanation, "I need it for the parking
meter!"

* * *

John Straley tells of a hobo who was sitting on a curbstone
in a fashionable neighborhood, munching contentedly on a
homemade sandwich. Along came a supercilious lady with an
equally supercilious poodle. Both sniffed disdainfully—but the

poodle picked up interest when he spotted the sandwich. "Shall I throw the doggie a little, Ma'am?" asked the hobo.

When the lady gave her condescending consent, the hobo seized the poodle by the collar and sent it sailing over a nearby hedge. "Thank you, Ma'am," he said. "If the doggie comes back, I'll be happy to throw him a little more."

* * *

Mrs. Dillenberg, on the veranda of the Comfort Arms, remarked, "I gave a bum ten dollars today." Her companion inquired, "What did your husband have to say about that?" Mrs. Dillenberg admitted, "He said thank you."

To Riches . . .

A millionaire, recalling the days when he was just beginning to claw his way up the ladder, mused, "Once I was living in California, while my parents were still in Michigan. I had just saved enough money to buy myself a bicycle when I heard my mother was sick. I jumped on my bike and pedaled all the way back to Michigan, only to be told that California air was the one thing that could save my mother's life.

"Gentlemen, I was equal to the occasion. I carted the bicycle over to my mother's bed, let the California air out of the tires —and she lived to the ripe old age of ninety-six."

* * *

A social climber in St. Paul has lost interest in his family tree. He paid a researcher two hundred dollars to dig up information about his ancestors. Now he's had to give the researcher a hundred dollars more to keep him quiet.

* * *

Miss Something-or-Other from away down South appeared at a cotillion in a new gown which, her beau informed her, looked just right on her. "Sho' nuff?" she purred. Blushing, he replied, "Sho' does."

* * *

Tony Randall tells of the post-debutante who called up her boy friend to advise him, "We'll have to postpone our marriage for a little while. I've just eloped with another man."

* * *

An oculist had prescribed expensive new glasses for a rich patient, and, meeting him soon after at Carnegie Hall, asked if the change had proved helpful.

"The new specs are just fine," beamed the patient. "My wife likes the frame, they fit well behind the ears, and for distance, they can't be beat. There's just one tiny flaw I might mention, however. I still walk off the wrong end of ferryboats."

* * *

A cautious suburban socialite makes it a point to tell all weekend guests when they check in, "If we get to drinking Sunday afternoon and start insisting that you stay over until Tuesday, *please* remember that we don't mean it!"

* * *

Along with the Cabots and the Lodges, the Adams family has dominated Boston Back Bay society for generations, and Charles Francis Adams was one of the most dignified and unapproachable of them all. A disturbing factor was another Charles Francis Adams, who owned the Boston Bruins hockey team, a race track, and other sporting interests. The socialite grew increasingly wrathful as he kept getting phone calls intended for the sports promoter. One night he was called to the phone at 3 A.M. and came clomping back to bed in a fine rage. "What's the trouble?" asked his wife. "Nothing to speak of," answered Mr. Adams curtly. "The Bruins' goaltender has been thrown into jail."

* * *

Cleveland Amory knows one very proper—and well-heeled —Bostonian who never saw asparagus growing until she was past fifty. The sight obviously unnerved her. "Why," she gasped, "I always thought that the cook braided the ends!"

* * *

"You Bostonians are always so loyal," taunted a Midwestern matron, "yet I notice that neither your father, your brother, your sister, or you yourself married a Bostonian." "Of course not," answered Amory smoothly, "we feel we have to spread the culture."

* * *

Two venerable members of a fashionable club were examining a new wall plaque in the card room. "The faults of our brothers," it read, "we write upon the sand. Their virtues we inscribe on tablets of love and memory."

Just then a loud crash was heard from the lobby below. "What's that?" exclaimed one member.

"Probably," said the other, "a truck delivering another load of sand."

* * *

One of the greatest New Year's Eve parties ever given in New York was hosted by the late editor of *Vanity Fair*, Frank

Crowninshield. Printed invitations read, "Admit Bearer and One Wife."

* * *

A couple prominent in the Social Register attended a masquerade party at a Long Island country club. After dinner, the wife developed a headache and elected to go home. Her husband so obviously was having a high old time, however, that she gave him a special dispensation to stay until the festivities were concluded.

At home, she recovered so rapidly that she decided to go back to the party, but sneakily put on another costume—her notion being that she might discover how her husband was comporting himself.

Back at the masquerade, she saw him sitting alone behind some potted palms. She disguised her voice and asked him if he'd like to dance. One thing led to another, and what with a full moon shining overhead, the two soon found themselves romancing in the back seat of a parked car. Finally she dis-

entangled herself, and returned home to await her erring
spouse.

When he finally came home he complained that his feet
were sore from dancing. "You mean you never left the dance
floor?" she asked sharply. "Only toward the very end of the
evening," recalled hubby. "Our old club bartender complained
that he never got in on the fun, so I loaned him my costume
and took his place behind the bar."

* * *

Joe Mankiewicz tells of another fancy dress ball that was
given in Rome when he was there for a couple of weeks producing *Cleopatra* with Elizabeth Taylor, Richard Burton, and
Rex Harrison. A chap well known in international society decided to attend the party as a wolf, but decided he was too
tired at the last moment. "I know how you've been looking
forward to this gala," he told the lovely young thing he had
been squiring all season, "so why don't *you* go as the wolf?"

She liked the notion well enough to discard the costume she
had originally intended wearing, and set forth as a reasonable,
if well-filled facsimile of Walt Disney's Big Bad Wolf. When
she came home, however, her costume was in tatters. "What
happened?" asked her anxious protector. "I don't know exactly," admitted the young lovely. "Who the heck were Romu-
lus and Remus?"

* * *

"Are you quite sure," asked a customs official loudly of a
lady on the dock, "that you have nothing to declare?" "Absolutely sure," insisted the lady. "Am I to understand, then,"
continued the official much more loudly, "that the fur tail
hanging from under your dress is your own?"

Maid to Order . . .

1. Before an important dinner in UN circles, a new maid
was cautioned by the hostess, "Remember to serve from the

left of each guest, and to clear the dishes away from the right. Is that clear?" "Yessum," nodded the maid. "You superstitious or something?"

2. Another new maid was asked by a Bar Harbor blueblood, "Do you know anything of my wife's whereabouts?" "Yes, sir," was the respectful reply. "I put them in the wash."

3. A proud Washington hostess instructed a maid taken on as an extra for a big diplomatic cocktail party, "Dress modestly —and don't wear any jewelry." The maid nodded, "Thanks for the warning, Ma'am."

4. A resident in a swanky midtown apartment-hotel noted that appreciable inroads were being made into his supply of bourbon by persons unknown. Very carefully, he made a small pencil mark on the label of the bottle on his side table opposite the current level of the liquid.

Returning home that night, he found this note from the chambermaid: "Please don't put any more pencil marks on this bottle, because I don't want to have to put water in such wonderful whiskey."

* * *

Mr. Sinsheimer was showing off his new eighteen-room duplex apartment to his less fortunate boyhood friends who still lived on the crowded Lower East Side. In the midst of the tour, an elegant butler appeared and announced, "Refreshments are being served in the Louis XIV dining room." "Thank you," nodded Mr. Sinsheimer. "Where is it?"

* * *

A prominent sportsman who practiced farming as a hobby fed a lot of torn-up racing forms to his chickens. The next morning he found them laying odds.

* * *

Trelawney was outraged to discover that his favorite club had passed a law allowing members to bring their wives into the sacred premises one evening a month. "Darn females barg-

ing in everywhere," he grumbled. "Besides, the rule is unfair
to bachelors like myself. Is it all right if I bring a girl friend?"

The chairman of the house committee pondered deeply,
then answered tentatively, "I hardly think anyone would object—provided, of course, that she's the wife of a member!"

* * *

The dignified London Tatler describes an anguished moment
at a great dinner given by socialite Mrs. Ronnie Greville for
the Foreign Secretary, Sir Austen Chamberlain, and his wife.

Mrs. Greville's butler, unfortunately, had been partaking
very liberally of the cocktails and wines intended for the
guests. Reluctant to make a scene, Mrs. G. handed him a note
which said, "Leave the room at once. You are drunk."

The butler nodded gravely, and promptly handed the note,
on a salver, to Lady Chamberlain.

* * *

Out in New Mexico they tell of a rancher who suddenly
struck it rich and decided it was time his son learned some
manners. The boy, tutored by a refugee from Harvard, got
along famously with his new course in etiquette until the
rancher decided to throw a big party in honor of his boy.

Decorators came all the way from Dallas to fix up the ranch

house and all the guests took their dinner coats out of the moth-balls. Everything went well until one guest made an insulting remark about the young heir, who jumped up in a rage and went for his adversary.

That's when the rancher pulled back his boy by the seat of his pants. "Doggone, boy," he exclaimed, "how often do I have to tell you? Put down that knife and go after him with your fork!"

*   *   *

Sylvia Kaye tells of a Palm Springs matron who has her desert mansion redecorated every winter. The precise shade that each room is to be painted is an obsession with her. Last fall she covered ping-pong paddles with the exact colors she wanted and left them for the painters to match.

When the job was finished, the painters had done such a faithful job that the gratified matron gave them a substantial bonus. "Best painters I've ever found," she enthused. They departed without telling her that they had made numerous mistakes, but had carefully covered them up by repainting the ping-pong paddles to match the walls.

*   *   *

P. G. Wodehouse, extolling the virtues of the once perfect, but now practically extinct English butlers, tells about one who presided over a mansion in Ireland. One day a gang of Sinn Feiners descended upon the place, and battered down the front door with axes. Inside the butler awaited them to tell them austerely, "His Lordship is not at home." They wrecked the house from cellar to attic, and finally set fire to it. On leaving, they found the butler still standing statuesquely in the hall. Flames were everywhere, and ceilings were crashing down, but the butler stopped the mob to ask, "Who shall I say called, gentlemen?"

*   *   *

A gouty old plutocrat sat cutting coupons in his club and grumbling about current political goings-on. "Blast those

Democrats," he rasped. "Do you think the Republicans are really any better?" asked a fellow member. "Not at all," admitted the plutocrat. "Blast them, too!" "Then what *are* you in favor of?" persisted the fellow member. The plutocrat's eyes gleamed. "The *feudal* system, sir," he cried, and tottered off to dinner.

* * *

That eminent man-about-town, Jack Baragwaneth, told about a day when one of the fabulous Du Pont clan came from Wilmington to New York for three important engagements. He kept the first two all right, but then, for the life of him, couldn't remember whom he was to meet on the third. No one to indulge in long-distance calls, he telegraphed home base, "Unfortunately have forgotten name my four o'clock appointment. Please advise." Back came this reply: "Name of your four o'clock appointment is J. P. Morgan. Your name Du Pont."

THE GAMING TABLES

A young writer who hit the jackpot this year with a surprise best-seller, and a subsequent six-figure sale of the property to Hollywood, allowed at a cocktail party as how he was contemplating a trip to Nevada. "I've invented a system for beating the roulette wheel," he announced, "that I believe is infallible."

Director Anatol Litvak, no stranger to the gaming tables himself, cooled off the young writer's enthusiasm somewhat by reminding him, "Nevada welcomes all gamblers with open arms when they blow into the state. But for gamblers *with a system,* my boy—they send an airplane!"

* * *

A customer beckoned the bartender in a Grand Bahamas gaming room. "Can you change a fifty-dollar bill?" he inquired. "My wife's playing the slot machines." "Sure thing," nodded the bartender. "How do you want it?"

"Humph," mused the customer, "shall we say two bucks in quarters—and the rest in drinks?"

* * *

A big chicken farmer from Oregon went to Puerto Rico one weekend and won ten thouasnd dollars in a hotel casino. "Turn the chickens loose," he ordered his wife by long distance, "and join me for a trip around the world."

Six months later the two of them were back in the U.S.A. and broke. "Well," sighed the farmer, "it's home to Oregon for us, I guess." "To recoup our losses?" suggested the wife. "No," said the farmer, "to re-coop our chickens."

* * *

The town's most notorious deadbeat boasted at the weekly poker game, "I give the little woman a check regularly every Saturday night so she can put it aside for a rainy day." "That's nice," commented one of his many creditors sardonically. "She can sew them all together and make a rubber raincoat."

* * *

Dean Martin tells of a gambler in the wide-open Capone era in Chicago who ran a slightly crooked roulette wheel. In fact, the house couldn't lose even if the players had every number covered. "If that happened," explains Dean, "the pill would jump off the wheel, hop out the door, and roll down Michigan Avenue."

* * *

One time the gambler was warned that the heat was on, and urged to take it on the lam. "I'll go on a huntin' trip," said the gambler. "Good idea," approved his mouthpiece. "Where'll you go?" "Milwaukee," said the gambler. "*Milwaukee?*" echoed the mouthpiece. "What the heck you gonna hunt in Milwaukee?" "Oh," said the gambler, "cats, dogs—whatever they got there!"

It Could Only Happen at Las Vegas . . .

This story comes from Bob Smith, television's famous Mr. Howdy Doody, who told it to me one morning in a TV studio:

A Brooklyn baker worked so hard and turned out such superior bread and cakes that at the age of fifty-five he was able to sell out his business for seventy thousand dollars. With seventy crisp, new thousand-dollar bills stashed away in his pocket, he and his wife boarded a plane for California, set on living the rest of their lives in peaceful retirement.

Over the Nevada desert, the plane developed minor engine trouble, and the passengers were told, "There is no danger whatever, but we're playing it safe and putting down at Las Vegas. We'll be grounded for approximately three hours; you may dine at any hotel you choose as guests of the airline. May we caution you, however, that if you choose to gamble, you're strictly on your own."

"Gamble," scoffed the baker to his wife. "Anybody who plays against those odds ought to have his head examined!" But the lure of the gambling tables was too much and he decided to risk a thousand-dollar bill on the roll of the dice.

Alas! The thousand dollars soon melted away, and the baker, now intent only upon recouping his losses, lost his head completely. He also lost his entire seventy thousand dollars.

The poor man headed unsteadily for the public washroom, but he didn't even have the ten cents that would gain him admission to that sanctuary. A fellow passenger from the plane understood his plight and pressed a dime into his hand.

"You're very kind," said the baker. "I've never borrowed a penny from anybody in my life, but I will take this coin with the understanding that I reimburse you at the first opportunity." He thereupon insisted upon writing down the man's name and home address.

Somebody, however, had left the door to the washroom ajar and when the baker came back to the lobby he still had the borrowed dime in his pocket. On an impulse, he put it into a slot machine and pulled the lever. He hit the jackpot! There followed one of the most amazing runs of luck ever seen at Las Vegas. The baker went back to the tables, doubled and redoubled his bets, and by the time he and his wife boarded the plane for Los Angeles, he had over a hundred thousand dollars in his pocket!

In California, the baker and his wife soon discovered that a life of idleness was not for them. They started another bakery, and because they knew their business so thoroughly, prospered from the start. In a few years, their assets were up in the millions.

One day the baker told his well-satisfied sales staff about his unnerving experience in Las Vegas. "This whole business— everything I've built up here in California," he said, "I owe, as you can see, to one man. I will leave no stone unturned to find out who he is."

"But I don't understand," interrupted the sales manager. "You told us yourself that the man who loaned you that dime gave you his name and address."

"He's not the one I'm looking for," explained the baker. "The man I want to find is the one who left that washroom door ajar!"

THE LECTURE CIRCUIT

"The human brain," opines William Nichols, "is a wonderful thing. It starts clicking the instant you are born and never stops until you are called upon to speak unexpectedly at a public gathering."

* * *

A Denver elocution teacher told Stan Peckham to practice speaking with pebbles in his mouth. "I was doing fine," recalls Peckham, "until one day I got the hiccups. I broke two mirrors and the picture window."

* * *

Judge Miles McDonald tells of the self-made millionaire, a pompous egomaniac, who hired a ghost-writer to turn out speeches and articles for him. He not only underpaid said ghost-writer, but subjected him to a continuous shower of criticism and abuse. The ghost-writer finally had his revenge. He provided his employer with a long speech to read at a very important conclave. The employer read the first ten pages of the speech in booming, confident tones, but when he turned to page eleven—in the middle of a sentence—he found only these words, printed in red: "FROM HERE ON, YOU OLD GOAT, YOU'RE ON YOUR OWN!"

* * *

Harry Hershfield, scheduled to be guest of honor at one of the innumerable banquets he attends, stood in front of a mirror in the washroom, straightening his black tie and adjusting his dinner coat. Pinching his cheeks to bring out the color, he asked the attendant, "How many great men do you reckon there are in New York City today?" The attendant answered solemnly, "One less than you think."

* * *

Harry Truman still splutters angrily when he recalls the evening he was guest speaker at a banquet in Des Moines. The coffee had been passed and the master of ceremonies turned to the former President to ask genially, "Shall we let them enjoy themselves a few moments longer, Harry—or should we have your speech now?"

*   *   *

A noted philosopher was delivering a speech in a California auditorium when a severe earthquake suddenly shook the building to its foundations. As big chunks of plaster began falling from the ceiling, the chairman made a dive for the shelter in the basement, pausing only to remark to the philosopher, "It is increasingly evident, Professor, that our premises will not support your conclusions."

*   *   *

Edmund Whitman, former V.P. of the United Fruit Company, confided to newshawk John Fuller that he won't consider his life complete until he's asked to deliver a June Commencement Day address at a respectable college. He's got his whole speech prepared already. It will go like this: "Gentlemen of the graduating class: I have only two thoughts to leave with you as you march forth from these cloistered halls: (1) There is no such thing as a free lunch. (2) You will never go broke taking a profit. I thank you."

*   *   *

The late President Henry Noble MacCracken of Vassar College once delivered a lecture in an Albany high school that neither he nor the audience ever forgot. There were to be accompanying lantern slides on "Campus Life," but by mistake, the pictures put into the slide box depicted scenes on a big dairy farm near Vassar.

Prexy MacCracken opened his talk by saying, "I'd like you to look at a picture of Matthew Vassar, who founded our college in 1861." Onto the screen came a picture of a great Holstein bull. A roar went up. The embarrassed MacCracken clicked the signal, and began again, "And here are some of our beautiful Vassar students." Out came a herd of cows, climbing over each other in their haste to get into green pastures.

By this time the audience was so hysterical that the poor college president had to call off the speech. The students went tottering off to green pastures of their own.

*　*　*

On a lecture tour, silver-tongued Norman Cousins found himself aboard a crowded Pittsburgh bus, when a young lady boarded same, laden with two large bundles and a howling baby. She took a quick look around, then deposited the baby squarely upon Mr. Cousins' lap.

Surprised, Mr. Cousins inquired, "Why, may I ask, did you pick me?"

"You have a kind face," replied the young woman without hesitation, "and besides—you're the only person wearing a raincoat."

*　*　*

A lecturer was instructing a ladies' club gathering on "What's Wrong with the Movies Today."

"The one I saw last night," he concluded, "is the worst yet. It includes murder, rape, arson, cannibalism, and perversion. If anything will justify censorship, this vile picture will do it. Now then, ladies, have you any questions?"

"Yes," cried three ladies in the audience simultaneously. "Where's it playing?"

*　*　*

Governor George Romney tells about the guest of honor at a banquet who discovered at the last moment that his upper plate had cracked. "You'll have to cancel my speech," he told the toastmaster. "Nonsense," said the latter. "Here's a spare upper I have in my pocket."

The guest of honor inserted the plate in his mouth, and essayed a few words with disastrous results. "No good," he announced, pulling out the plate. "It doesn't fit."

Like a magician taking rabbits out of a hat, the toastmaster produced a second plate, which didn't fit either, and then a third plate, which was exactly right.

The guest of honor made a fine speech, received an ovation, then turned gratefully to the toastmaster. "It was a lucky break for me," he said, "that you happen to be a dentist."

"Dentist nothing," said the toastmaster. "I'm an undertaker."

*　*　*

Rushing to redeem his hat and coat after a lecturer had overstayed his allotted time on the podium by a full forty minutes, a sore-bottomed but silver-tongued auditor consoled other disgruntled patrons with this reminder:

> It's never so bleak
> But it couldn't be bleaker:
> There might have been
> A second speaker!

And then he added these lines by R. Cheney:

> Charm and wit and levity
> May help you at the start;
> But at the end, it's brevity
> That wins the public's heart.

*　*　*

George Jessel, making one of his innumerable after-dinner orations, noticed with chagrin that his audience was growing rather restless. "Take it easy," he assured the wrigglers. "Like Lady Godiva on the last lap of her historic ride, I am drawing near my close."

*　*　*

And then there was the lecturer who announced that he had made a speech that would not be forgotten for a long, long time. "My audience," he added, "was composed entirely of elephants."

MEN OF LETTERS

Not every letter in the morning's mail is a bill, an advertisement, or a summons to some boring banquet at fifty dollars a head. It only seems that way! Comb the haystack carefully and once in a blue moon you'll discover a needle like the following (mailed to a hundred friends by an obviously overworked Wall Street broker):

"Dear Bennett: Perhaps you have heard of me and my nationwide campaign in the cause of temperance. Each year I make a tour of the South lecturing on the evils of drink.

"On these tours I have been accompanied by my friend and cashier, Mr. Oswald Shucat. Oswald is a pathetic case, a man of good family and excellent background whose life was ruined by excessive indulgence in whiskey and gin.

"Poor Oswald would appear with me at my lectures, sitting on the platform, drooling and besotted, staring popeyed at the audience while I would point him out as a horrible example of what drink would do.

"Now poor Oswald has died. A mutual friend has given me your name and I wonder if you would care to accompany me on the fall tour this year in his place? Yours in hope, Aloysius Drybone."

*   *   *

Letters Magazine printed this revealing exchange of notes between a patient's wife and the doctor who had been treating him.

1. "Dear Doctor: My husband was for years the perfect mate and father. Since consulting you, however, he has become a hopeless gadabout, critical of my housekeeping and our children, an ogre about bills, vain, arrogant and unfaithful. It is my belief that you have been giving him hormone shots which have entirely changed his personality. Mrs. A. Jones."

2. "Dear Mrs. Jones: In answer to your letter, I have not been giving your husband shots of any kind. I have simply had him fitted with contact lenses. Dr. Shallbe Nameless."

*   *   *

How does a man tell his wife that he has accepted an important new job in another city—necessitating his leaving his family temporarily behind?

Here, in essence, is how one Virginia gentleman broke the news to his wife:

"You may believe me, my dear, that far from seeking this new appointment, I used every endeavor in my power—but in vain—to avoid it. Not only was I reluctant to part with you and the family, but I was conscious that the new trust might be too great for my capacity. How well I know that I would find more real happiness in one month with you than I shall in my new post, though my stay be seven times seven years!"

It was via this letter that Mrs. George Washington learned

that her husband had been appointed Commander-in-Chief
of the American Army.

* * *

John Fuller, of *Saturday Review*, quotes this communiqué
from an author in Maine to her publisher, who had neglected
to report on a manuscript she had submitted to him several
weeks before:

"GENTLEMEN:

I have sent you a manuscript
which you have failed
to consider, and I think you are
a big jerk, and I mean
the biggest. I also think
when it comes to stupidity
you deserve all there is
in the book. You're not known
for your astuteness and judgment
but I *do* know your total idiocy,
which is beyond man's reason.
I cannot express what I think.
If prizes are to be awarded for

imbecility, you surely deserve
the very biggest, and the greatest
prize; and there is no doubt
you richly deserve this top award.
P.S. If you decide to accept my novel, please read only every
other line."

* * *

Ingenious and persevering fellows, these post office authori-
ties! One of them, according to Bill Feather, came upon a letter
addressed to:
Wood.
Mr.
Mass.
and promptly and correctly delivered it to:
Mr. Underwood
Andover,
Mass.

* * *

Dave Sherwood, of St. Cloud, Minnesota, sent me a copy of
this letter, which a local merchant received (with a check enclosed):
"Sir: I understand you desire to have me pay my account
in full, but the present condition of my bank balance makes
that impossible. My shattered financial status is due to federal
laws, state laws, county laws, corporation laws, liquor laws,
mother-in-laws, sister-in-laws, and outlaws.
"Through these 'laws,' I am compelled to pay a business tax,
amusement tax, school tax, gas tax, water tax, sales tax, and
income tax. My brains are taxed most of all. I am required to
carry fourteen different forms of insurance and my wife discovers one more charity a day to which I must contribute.
"My business is so governed that I'm no longer sure who
owns it. I am inspected, suspected, disrespected, rejected, examined, re-examined, summoned, fined and confined until I

provide a constant source of revenue for everybody but myself and my legitimate creditors.

"Fortunately, the wolf that comes to my door daily just had pups in my kitchen. I sold them—and here's ten per cent of what I owe you. I'm afraid you won't be so lucky next month. Faithfully, etc."

*　*　*

Teacher Berenice Hoffman, of New York, had an eight-year-old student named Susan who could read faster and more intelligently than any other kid in the class, but she was a chronic dawdler and couldn't seem to get to school on time in the morning. To punish her, her mother decreed that Susan could not borrow another single book from the school library.

Reader Susan chafed under this restriction for a week, then happily presented this note to teacher Hoffman: "Susan has been on time to school now five mornings straight, so you can let her have all the books she wants. Love, My Mother."

*　*　*

A school teacher in the Southland received a form letter from a loan company that began, "Because you are a teacher you can borrow $100 to $1000 by mail." His reply began, "Maybe I can borrow this money because I am a teacher, but I couldn't pay it back for the same reason."

*　*　*

Aristides Perkins, Harvard '22, hired a new salesman who could talk a mile a minute. Two weeks later the salesman sent in his first order—a whopping one—with this note attached: "Dear Boss: I seen this outfit which they ain't never bought a dime's worth from us, but the owner's daughter kinda took a shine to me and I sold them twenty thousand dollars worth. Next stop: Sinsinate." The next letter arrived two days later: "Dear Boss: Sinsinaty is my erster. Here's an order for ninety thousand, C.O.D."

Letter number three went out from Aristides Perkins to all

his other salesmen. It enclosed carbons of the new man's two
notes and orders and this comment from Mr. P.: "We bin
spendin' too much time here it seems tryin' to spell insted of
tryin' to sell. Lets watch them sales. Read our new mans letters,
and then I want you should go out and do like he done. Sin-
serley, Aristides Perkins."

* * *

The Missoula Lumber Company has achieved noteworthy
results with this rather offbeat collection letter to delinquent
accounts: "It has been said that a man who squeezes a dollar
never squeezes his wife. In looking over your account, it has
occurred to us that your wife is not getting the attention she
deserves."

* * *

A cute, freckled little girl in Iowa was given a sizable speech
to memorize for the school's graduation program. Two days
before the big event, however, the elocution teacher received
this note from the little girl's mother:
"I'm sorry to say Audrey will not be able to recite Friday
morning. Our goat ate her speech."

RESTAURANTS AND HOTELS

Graybeards who cry in their champagne for the good old
days are particularly depressed by the passing of a building
on the corner of Fifth Avenue and Forty-fourth Street, New
York, that once housed the establishment of society's favorite
restaurateur, Louis Sherry.

Here, at the turn of the century, the most dazzling debs of
the year made their bows in society and their fathers hosted
"stag" dinners topped off by "Jack Horner" pies—huge concoctions, decorated in whipped cream that, when cut open, revealed a covey of nymphs in their birthday suits.

Capitalist C. K. G. Billings, self-styled "American Horse
King," staged a banquet at Sherry's on March 28, 1903, that,

to quote historian Grace Mayer, "reached uncharted heights
in planning for the discomfort of his guests."

Mr. Billings was bent on publicizing his newly opened two
hundred thousand dollar stable at 196th Street and Fort Washington Road, now Fort Tryon Park.

He converted the grand ballroom of Sherry's into a woodland paradise by means of ten thousand dollars' worth of full-
scale scenic props, artificial foliage, potted palms, and a
tanbark floor covering, borrowed, at Mr. Sherry's insistence,
from the Barnum & Bailey Circus.

Thirty-six mystified horses were conveyed up to this bosky
dell by freight elevators, and the guests, appropriately attired
in white ties and tails, gingerly climbed aboard when Mr. Billings chirruped, "Tally Ho!" Only one fell off. Miniature tables
had been attached to the pommels of the horses' saddles, and
apprehensive waiters dressed as grooms served course after
course to the miserable company.

The horses ate right along with their riders—out of oat-filled
troughs thoughtfully decorated with gold foil.

❋   ❋   ❋

Sherry's bitterest rival was Monsieur Delmonico, who was doing a land office business diagonally across Fifth Avenue. Both were gifted with the patronage of the prize playboy of all time, "Diamond Jim" Brady, who boasted an income of a million dollars a year, and spent it cheerfully on diamonds, pretty girls—and food.

Brady had thirty sets of diamond studs, and sometimes wore several sets at a time. "Them as has 'em, wears 'em," he explained. He was a Gargantuan eater, thinking nothing of putting away at a single sitting four dozen oysters, six lobsters, two steaks, and an entire tray of French pastry.

Small wonder that he tipped the scales at close to three hundred pounds. Sherry hailed him as "the twenty-five best customers I ever had."

*   *   *

To gauge the diminishing purchasing power of the dollar, it is necessary only to recall that less than fifty years ago such fashionable New York hotels as the Waldorf, Biltmore, and Plaza were serving free lunch to their bar patrons, and that thousands of well-heeled businessmen ate their noonday fill at the cost of two schooners of ten-cent beer!

The menus were varied, too. An old ad for the Knickerbocker Hotel offered free chicken salad, lobster Newburg, cold corned beef, Virginia ham, and even chafing dishes.

*   *   *

World War I put an end to that nonsense. True, the late cinema star, Norma Talmadge, spotted a restaurant in the thirties that still advertised a ten-course dinner for forty-five cents, but when she asked her husband of the moment, George Jessel, how they could afford it, he explained glibly, "The music is terrible."

*   *   *

This year prices have reached a point where a Detroiter, experimenting at a highly touted new restaurant, told the waiter, "I'm not very hungry, so I think I'll try your ten-dollar dinner."

"Very good," noted the waiter. "Will you have your coffee black or with cream?"

"I'll decide that," said the Detroiter, "when I've finished my dinner."

"Pardon me, sir," corrected the waiter. "Coffee *is* our ten-dollar dinner."

* * *

Earl Hall, of Mason City, ordered a ham sandwich at a fancy new restaurant and got a bill for three dollars and fifty cents. "I've got to wire my readers back home," chortled Hall. "According to this bill, every pig in Iowa is worth six thousand dollars!"

* * *

During the Saturday night rush at a popular Long Island inn, one of the parking attendants was summoned to help check hats and coats in the jammed-up cloak room. In his first quarter of an hour he dented nine overcoats.

* * *

Near O'Hare Airport in Chicago there's a motel with one of those African shrunken heads behind the bar. The sign that adorns it reads, "He asked for credit."

* * *

A real estate agent was showing a very blonde, very well-developed female through a luxurious penthouse atop a resort hotel. "Now in this wing," said the agent, "we have the master bedroom, bath, and den."

The blonde interrupted suspiciously, "And den what?"

* * *

Claude Terrail, proprietor of the luxurious La Tour d'Argent Restaurant in Paris (it overlooks the Seine and is a "must" for all American tourists) has his own explanation for the superstition about having thirteen at a table. "The reason is," he says, "that most people have sets of only twelve knives, forks, and dinner plates."

* * *

A customer had been trying in vain to get some service in a crowded midtown restaurant one lunchtime. Finally he beseeched the majordomo, "Can't you change my table, please? I'd appreciate something nearer a waiter."

* * *

A restaurant proprietor told his wife happily, "Well, I finally found out today what's been happening to all those oysters we've been missing in the kitchen. That fool new cook has been putting them in the oyster stew."

* * *

Mr. Weybright came home from the office one evening with a horrendous tale of the lunch he had eaten. "The restaurant looked inviting," he said, "so I tried it for a change. Sure enough, the soup, salad, and beef were delicious. But the pie was inedible and the coffee was slop. Do you know what I discovered? The place had changed hands right in the middle of my meal."

* * *

"The world's two greatest point-killers," declares Don Quinn, "as everyone must know, are waiters and telephones. Most of us have experienced that shattering moment, when, lunching with somebody we want to make sure realizes we have a great sense of humor, we've crept up to the punch line of our very best story, only to have the waiter barge upon the scene, demanding, 'Who gets the roast beef hash?'"

* * *

Overheard at an East Side restaurant:
"Hey, waiter, this sauerkraut isn't sour enough."
"Mister, that isn't sauerkraut. It's noodles."
"Oh, for noodles it's sour enough."

* * *

Overheard at Sardi's: "Be sure that red wine is imported because I can't tell the difference."

*　*　*

A family group, dining at Danny's Hideaway, reached the dessert course. The ten-year-old daughter summoned the always-on-the-job Danny, and asked, "What kind of pastry do you have?" Then, before he could answer, she added, "And, by the way, what *is* pastry?"

*　*　*

A man with a passion for yeast was just receiving an order of same in a health restaurant when a clumsy waiter bumped into him. The powdery yeast went all over his clothes. The title of this sad little tale is "Yeast Meets Vest."

*　*　*

A high-flying, expensively attired public relations counsel brought his equally haughty date to an expensive restaurant, and boasted loudly all through dinner—especially when the waiter was within hearing distance—of the big deals he was engineering and the important new clients he was acquiring. When he left, his waiter commented to the wine steward, "Did you hear that braggart? He lives in a rear flat of one of my apartment houses. Tomorrow, first thing, I'm going to double his rent!"

*　*　*

In search of a snack at his private refrigerator (this story comes from G. A. Houdershal, of York, Pennsylvania), the longtime tenant of a residential hotel could find nothing but a dog biscuit. He bit into it tentatively, liked it, and the next morning told his wife to put in a large supply.

Mr. Binswanger, local restaurateur who was the source of supply, observed, "You don't need so many biscuits for a dog as small as yours." "They're for my husband," she corrected him. "These biscuits are strictly for dogs," grumbled Mr. Binswanger. "They'll kill your husband."

Six months later the wife admitted that her husband indeed

was dead. "I told you those biscuits would kill him," Mr. Binswanger reminded her. "It wasn't the biscuits," said the wife. "He was killed chasing cars."

❅   ❅   ❅

Myron Cohen knows a waiter who suffered a severe cramp and was rushed to the hospital. As he lay doubled with pain on an emergency ward table he grabbed a doctor hurrying by and implored, "Help me, help me. I'm dying." "Sorry," snapped the doctor. "This isn't my table."

9. *It's a Good Life!*

CHRISTMAS STORIES

The Christmas issues of some of our big magazines have to go to press so early these days that the poor writers usually have to compose their tales of Yuletide cheer in the middle of an August heat wave.

* * *

On a sun-drenched beach at Atlantic City, in the closing hours of a Miss America Pageant, Mitch Miller, waxing nostalgic, suddenly sighed, "Oh, for those good old Christmases—when whiskey came in ordinary bottles!"

* * *

Florenz Ziegfeld always bought Christmas trinkets for his beautiful Follies girls early in the season—but paid for them, if at all, very late. One day he instructed his treasurer to hop over to Tiffany's to buy a diamond bracelet for his leading lady.

"But why Tiffany's?" asked the treasurer. "I know where we can pick up a bracelet wholesale for a thousand dollars less."

"What's the difference?" inquired Ziegfeld cheerfully. "I'm not going to pay for it anyhow."

*   *   *

An intrepid jurist named Manges paid a visit to Kris Kringle's workshop at the North Pole recently, and promptly named old Santa's helpers "Subordinate Clauses."

*   *   *

In a crowded department store last holiday season, a man dropped a shopping list his wife had given him, and spent several anxious moments retrieving it from under the feet of the jostling throng. Not until he was out on the sidewalk did he discover that the trampled-upon paper he had snatched up was not, alas, his shopping list, but a printed reminder the executive office evidently had passed out to every store employee. It read, in big, red, capital letters: "Remember: try to sell last year's merchandise first!"

*   *   *

A ten-year-old boy insisted that his father tell him exactly what he wanted as a Christmas gift. "If you don't tell me," the boy explained, "how will I know how much money I have to borrow from you?"

*   *   *

An ingenious toy store proprietor in a suburban shopping center decided last holiday season to present Santa Claus in a full-size replica of an Eskimo igloo. Furthermore, he provided a shiny red sleigh to transport delighted youngsters to the igloo. One eight-year-old girl didn't relish the idea at all, but was persuaded by her mother to climb into the sleigh nevertheless. Just before the sleigh rounded the last turn before the igloo, the little girl panicked, and hopped out of the sleigh, leaving her mother alone to complete the journey. Santa Claus regarded the embarrassed mother with a twinkle in his eye and commented, "Some people never give up, do they?"

* * *

A wife, to her intense dismay, came down with a virus attack on the very day the town's biggest department store opened its mammoth pre-Christmas sale. Tearfully she persuaded her very reluctant husband to go in her place, and purchase a few items she had marked in the store's newspaper ad.

"If you have trouble fighting your way to the counter," she reminded her husband at the last moment, *act like a lady!*"

* * *

Harassed by a surging mob on the last shopping day before Christmas, a clerk shook her head sadly and paused while writing down an impatient customer's address. "It's a madhouse, isn't it?" sighed the clerk.

"Not at all," replied the customer haughtily. "It's my private residence."

* * *

Ed Condon writes jubilantly that his wife has at last completed knitting a pair of socks for him originally intended for a 1964 Christmas present. "They're magnificent," adds Condon, "but just the least bit tight under the arms."

* * *

Returned home from the Christmas holidays, a blithe young bachelor found two notes awaiting him. One, from a prosperous girl friend, was in his mailbox. It read, "There was no answer when I rang, so I left your Christmas gift in the mail chute." The second note was in the mail chute. It read, "Thanks a million for the wonderful bottle of Scotch. (signed) Your Mail Man."

* * *

In old Vienna, when the Hapsburgs still reigned, recalls Vincent Starrett, the good burghers had so much food to consume at Christmastime, and so many waltzes to dance, that parties, starting on Christmas Eve, sometimes lasted seventy or eighty hours. Retiring late on December 28, an exhausted host could take comfort in the thought that a Viennese Christmas came only three days a year.

Parting guests, incidentally, were given a ripe apple and a knife. Everyone bisected his apple at once, and if he managed that without cutting through a single seed, it meant that a wonderful New Year lay ahead for him.

*　　*　　*

Diplomats and heads of state exchange costly holiday gifts, too. David Ben-Gurion, destined to be the head of an Israeli state not yet in existence, once visited a wealthy Eastern potentate who presented him with a magnificent full-blooded Arabian stallion. Ben-Gurion was unimpressed.

"I hate gifts that can eat," he said.

*　　*　　*

A Westchester prep school presented its annual Christmas Nativity play last year, and assigned the role of innkeeper to a promising new student. In early rehearsals, he delivered his line, "There is no room at the inn" perfectly, but in the dress rehearsal he was overcome with brotherly love and when he opened the door, called out, "Welcome, welcome!" "No, no," cried the director. "You're ruining everything. You must recite your line as it was given to you!"

The contrite young actor promised to do just that, but when the curtain rose for the evening's performance, the director had certain apprehensions. And how justified they proved to be! When the visitors knocked loudly on the door our young innkeeper pulled it open and declared, "There is no room at the inn—*but*, gentlemen, come in and have a drink, anyhow!"

* * *

Carl Goerch recalls a Christmas program in a school outside Raleigh, North Carolina, that had an unrehearsed finale. Two groups of parents, unbeknownst to each other, had persuaded a Mr. Willet (weight 212) and a Mr. Hopper (weight 236) to give the kiddies a happy surprise by bursting into a party dressed as Santa Claus. The Santas arrived simultaneously.

"What do you think you're doing here?" asked Mr. Willet menacingly.

"I'm Santa Claus," maintained a slightly unsteady Mr. Hopper.

"Like heck you are," cried Mr. Willet, "and besides, you're plastered."

Mr. Hopper picked up a loose guitar and broke it over Mr. Willet's noggin. The kids whooped with joy. Mr. Willet thereupon uncorked a Sunday punch that knocked Mr. Hopper flat. The kids were delirious. Fortunately, the principal had once been a football star. He threw out Mr. Willet and Mr. Hopper and for the rest of the evening played Santa Claus himself. May all your Christmases be equally eventful and joyous!

HAPPY ENDINGS

Here are a few little stories that will, I think, make the world seem a little bit brighter.

1. There lives an obstetrician in Dayton who has two fixed charges. He sends patients a bill for either one hundred or two

hundred dollars. "Do you look up your patients' financial rating before you decide on your charge?" he was asked one day by a friend.

"Not at all," answered the doctor. "I base my fee on the first question the father asks when I come out of the delivery room. If he asks, 'Is it a boy or a girl?' he gets a bill for two hundred dollars. But if he asks, 'Is my wife all right?' I only bill him for one hundred dollars."

2. In Montreal, the same sleek limousine stands in front of the same exclusive club every afternoon. Promptly at four a down-at-the-heels old derelict lurches by, nods to the chauffeur at the wheel, and announces loftily, "I won't be using the car this afternoon, Fergus. A walk home will do me good." "Very well, sir," says the chauffeur respectfully, tipping his cap.

One afternoon a reporter demanded of the chauffeur, "That can't be your boss—or is it?" "My boss?" echoed the chauffeur, "I don't even know who he is. But he always says the same thing. It obviously makes him feel good—so what have I got to lose?"

3. A bus was bumping along a back road in the South recently. In one seat, a wispy old man sat holding a bunch of fresh flowers. Across the aisle was a young girl whose eyes came back again and again to the old man's flowers.

The time came for the old man to get off. Impulsively he thrust the flowers into the girl's lap. "I can see you love them," he explained, "and I think my wife would like for you to have them. I'll tell her I gave them to you."

The girl accepted the flowers, then watched the old man get off the bus and walk through the gate of a small cemetery.

4. An old lama in India, given to long hours of stroking his chin and meditating in silence, one day turned up at the retreat with a big drum he had borrowed from a neighborhood boy. "I had no idea you could play the drum!" exclaimed a fellow monk. "I can't," chuckled the lama, "but now—neither can the boy!"

5. A young miner was badly injured in an explosion and hovered between life and death in a hospital ward. His anxious

mother begged so earnestly to see him that the doctor waived rules and conceded, "All right—but put on a nurse's uniform so the boy won't know it's you. Otherwise, the excitement might prove fatal."

The mother tiptoed into the ward and put her hand softly on the fevered brow of her delirious boy. He relaxed, smiled through his bandages, and whispered hoarsely, "Thank you, nurse; that feels as good as mother."

6. An ancient king decided to honor the most worthy of his subjects. Candidates appeared from all over his realm. One was lauded for his wealth, another for his knowledge of the law, a third for his powers of healing the sick. In the wake of this illustrious company, however, came a stooped, shabbily dressed old woman, from whose dim eyes shone the light of understanding and love.

"Who is this woman?" asked the King. "What has she done to earn her entry into company like this?"

"You have seen and heard all the others," said his minister. "This is the one who was their teacher when they were young."

The King descended from his throne and placed the wreath of honor on her brow.

7. Writes Stephen Still, from Melbourne, "I could tell from the bus driver's greeting when the blind lady climbed aboard that she must be a frequent passenger. She sat down directly behind him and they carried on an animated conversation as he drove.

"When we reached the woman's stop the driver got out and escorted her through heavy traffic to the other side of the street. When he returned to his seat I noticed the woman still standing where he had left her. 'She won't budge till she knows I got back safely,' he explained. He honked his horn three times, the woman waved, and off we drove. 'I feel good,' said the driver. I answered, 'So do I.'"

8. One of the greatest mayors New York ever had was Fiorello La Guardia—"The Little Flower." Every New Yorker remembers the day Fiorello read the funny papers over the radio—with all the appropriate excitement and inflections—

when a strike kept the Sunday journals off the stands. They
remember too his squeaky fulminations against the "crooks,"
and "tinhorns" in our town, and his weekly radio sign-off, "Patience and fortitude."

One time the ubiquitous mayor chose to preside in a Night
Court. It was bitter cold outside. A trembling man was brought
before him, charged with stealing a loaf of bread. His family,
he said, was starving. "I've got to punish you," declared La
Guardia. "The law makes no exceptions. I must fine you ten
dollars."

But The Little Flower was reaching into his own pocket as
he added, "Well, here's the ten dollars to pay your fine—which
I now remit." He tossed the ten-dollar bill into his famous
sombrero.

"Furthermore," he declared, "I'm going to fine everybody
in this courtroom fifty cents for living in a town where a man
has to steal bread in order to eat. Mr. Bailiff, collect the fines
and give them to this defendant!"

The hat was passed and an incredulous old man, with a light
of heaven in his eyes, left the courtroom with a stake of $47.50.

A-HUNTING THEY DID GO

Invited by millionaire tool manufacturer J. A. Wilkie to join
him on a safari vacation, author Don Weldon promptly flew to
Southern Rhodesia where the party was already in progress.
A jeep, a Portuguese chauffeur-interpreter, and two native
guides were waiting to take Weldon to the camp where his
host was hunting elephants. After a three-day trip into the
heart of darkest Africa, they reached a clearing where Wilkie
was "roughing it" in a mammoth aluminum trailer—specially
designed, stocked with delicacies, and shipped over for the
holiday—with forty native cooks, butlers, and miscellaneous
servants in starched white uniforms to attend his every whim.
Weldon's waggish greeting was, "Dr. Livingstone, I presume!"

* * *

Woodland idyll: A hunter lost his bearings and wandered about the forest in a daze. Suddenly he spied another man. Dropping his rifle, he threw his arms about the other's neck and chortled, "Boy, am I glad to see you. I've been lost in these woods for three days!"

"Restrain your enthusiasm," cautioned the other sourly. "I've been lost here a week."

* * *

Sign outside a deluxe Adirondack hunting lodge: "If you have a chance to bag a moose near the lodge, be sure you don't shoot the fellow milking it."

* * *

"My, my," reminisced a bogus old party at a sportsmen's dinner. "The tigers I shot in my day in the wilds of Africa!" "Very interesting," interrupted a disgusted listener, "but there do not happen to be any tigers in Africa." "Of course not," agreed the old party without batting an eyelash. "I shot them all."

VACATION TIME

In the Mountains . . .

"Spend your vacation in your own backyard," suggests Bill Vaughan, "and your friends will know the kind of man you are: sensitive, introspective, home-loving—and broke."

* * *

The late Fred Allen's suggestion for lazy vacationists: detachable blisters for folks who abhor sun-bathing; self-wetting bathing suits to make diving into a rough surf unnecessary; and shoes with built-in pebbles for people who prefer having a beer on a cool porch to hiking through the poison ivy in the woods.

* * *

A young minister was vacationing in the White Mountains when he learned that a lady guest of the hotel, recently arrived from Boston, was gravely ill. Anxious to cheer her up he paid a courtesy call, murmured a wish for her speedy convalescence, and concluded, "I should like to say a brief prayer for your recovery before I leave."

The sick lady rallied at once, and snapped, "That will be quite unnecessary, young man. I am being prayed for in Boston."

* * *

Stan Holworthy's pretty little wife had been picking on him all the way up to Lake Placid, so as they stepped into the crowded hotel elevator with all their baggage, he squared accounts. He threw his arm around her and inquired in a very loud voice, "What did you say your name was, honey?"

* * *

Jackie Gleason dropped in at a summer resort in the Catskills where business was so phenomenal that the management turned away a young unmarried doctor.

* * *

On the porch of Tannenbaum's Manor, a stout lady earnestly assured the occupant of the next rocker, "My husband holds an extremely responsible position. No matter what goes wrong, he's responsible."

* * *

Eddie Fisher was writing a letter in the library of a hotel in the Catskills when he sensed the presence of a kibitzer behind him trying to read what he was putting down. So, after signing his name to the letter, Eddie added in a postscript, "I can't say more in this epistle because a nosey stranger is snooping over my left shoulder."

Whereupon the kibitzer drew himself up and demanded haughtily, "Who's snooping?"

* * *

Mr. Campbell finally has discovered a foolproof system for keeping relatives from dropping in for weekends in his mountain hideaway. "I borrow money from the rich ones," explains Campbell happily, "and lend it to the poor ones. None of them come back."

* * *

After British humorist Ronald Searle returned home from his first comprehensive American tour, he reported, "I asked a mountaineer in West Virginia who was 103 years old how he passed his time. He told me that in winter he mostly sleeps, in spring he chases some likely female cousin around the rocks, in the summer he makes moonshine whiskey out of potato peelings and coffee grounds, and in the fall he drinks it."

* * *

Explaining why his first night at a mountain hotel had been a sleepless one, Mr. Wartels told the room clerk, "That honeymoon couple occupying the next suite were arguing until 5 A.M. about their wedding. They couldn't agree on where to have it."

* * *

A penniless Jewish lad immigrated to the U.S.A. in the steerage in 1905, and worked his way westward. Now, sixty years later, he was living in great luxury at Aspen in the Rockies.

"Only in America could this happen," he exulted at a testimonial dinner in his honor. "Sixty years ago I didn't have a penny to my name. Today I'm a senior partner in the great Denver House of Nussbaum and McCarthy. And this, my friends, is the most wonderful part of all: *I'm McCarthy!*"

At the Seashore . . .

Jack Kofoed swears he saw this happen in the dining room of a swank Palm Beach hotel. A clumsy waiter spilled a whole plate of soup on the white jacket of an outraged guest. The manager rushed up immediately and purred, "Give that coat to me, Sir. I'll have it sponged immediately and returned to you absolutely spotless before you've finished your meal."

Five minutes later, the waiter who had spilled the soup poked the guest indignantly on the shoulder, and demanded: "Don't you know you're not allowed in this dining room unless you're wearing a jacket?"

* * *

Mrs. Appleby had talked her husband into taking her to Florida for a winter vacation, and here they were after dinner in Miami Beach one evening, looking up at a full moon, hidden from other tourists by a big potted palm.

A young man and his girl sat down near them, and not realizing they were being observed, fell into each other's arms. Whispered Mrs. Appleby to her husband, "Oh, Luther, he doesn't know we're here, and he's going to propose. Shouldn't you whistle and warn him?"

"Why should I?" objected Mr. Appleby grimly. "Nobody whistled to warn me!"

* * *

Nick Morgan tells of a bather on a chilly, overcast morning who ordered hot coffee from a beachside snack bar.

"Cream or sugar?" asked the waitress.

"It doesn't matter," shivered the bather. "I'm going to pour it on my feet."

*　*　*

A young toddler at a crowded beach reported tearfully to a lifeguard that he was lost. "Why didn't you hang on to your mother's bathing suit?" asked the lifeguard. The toddler explained, "I couldn't reach it."

*　*　*

Walter Evans was spending his first hours at one of those fashionable seaside hotels that advertise off-season rates of six dollars a day—with a steak dinner included. When he asked the waitress for his steak, however, she announced, "The steak is all over today."

"All over what?" asked the puzzled Mr. Evans.

The waitress explained, "With."

*　*　*

An astonishing conversation, allegedly overheard at a Miami Beach luxury motel, involved two girls friends who met accidentally after a year of separation. "So what's new?" asked one. "A terrible thing," answered the other. "My doctor just told me I seem to be turning into a man." The first girl nodded absentmindedly and inquired mildly, "So what else is new?"

*　*　*

Two red-hot mamas were acquiring a suntan on the sands of Montego Bay. "See that girl in the bikini over there?" whispered one. "She's my daughter-in-law. In one year she turned my poor son into a pauper." "That's nice," said the other. "A boy or a girl?"

*　*　*

Jack Benny believes that the waiters at Miami Beach's swanky Fontainebleau Hotel are the classiest and most cultured he's ever encountered. "Of course," he adds, "most of them were guests of the hotel when they arrived a week earlier."

*   *   *

At an elegant hotel in the Bahamas a prosperous merchant was urging his wife to complete her toilette.

"Should I wear my Dior dress or the one from Mainbocher?" she asked. "Wear the Dior," he said.

"And my hat—should it be the one from Mister John or the Lily Daché?" "The Mister John," he said.

"And my fur coat—should it be the chinchilla or the sable?"

The husband's patience was exhausted. "Wear anything you please," he shouted, "but for Pete's sake, come on downstairs for breakfast!"

*   *   *

The purchaser of a spanking new pleasure boat was not averse to female companionship on his moonlight cruises. The way he'd lure a debutante aboard the boat was to assure her, "You'll be crazy about my new boat, and you must come out on it with me. Incidentally, I wonder if you know that I named it after you."

No girl could resist a pitch like that! It was only when she came to the marina and saw the boat bobbing at the landing that she realized she had been had. The letters on the stern read "AFTER YOU."

*   *   *

A wealthy New York garment manufacturer was persuaded to try his skill at skin diving. Equipped with all the latest paraphernalia, he was lowered to the bottom of the sea, and was poking gingerly about when he spotted his arch-competitor flailing about in nothing but a bathing suit.

"Morris," cried the garment manufacturer. "What are you doing here without a diving helmet?"

Morris replied sourly, "I'm DROWNING!"

*   *   *

A man who believes in logic is H. Allen Smith. "It is a known fact," says he, "that most major hurricanes along the Atlantic Coast occur in August and September. The solution is therefore simple. Do away with August and September."

❋   ❋   ❋

Then there were the two crystal ball gazers who were marooned in their seaside home by a hurricane and forty-foot waves crashing in from the sea. "You know," said one, "this storm reminds me of the one in 1988!"

hor... such a... relish served before or be... courses of a meal. [t. F: asiue ... (the main body of the) work]

cow¹ (kou), *n., pl.* cows, (Archaic) kine. 1. the female of a bovine animal, esp. of the genus *Bos*, that has produced a calf and is usually over three years of age. 2. the

"DEFINITIONS"

Upheld too long to damyankee joshing about the way the English language is spoken south of the Mason-Dixon line, Winston McCord of Baton Rouge, Louisiana, strikes back justifiably with a few definitions he compiled while visiting the Greater New York area:

Oily: The opposite of late.
Sore: Viewed: "I sore it in *Try and Stop Me.*"
Dare: "Not here, stupid—dare."
Verse: Barbara Cook's got a good one.

Use: A pronoun: "Where use going, Al?"

Ax: To query: "I wanna ax you something."

✦ ✦ ✦

Possibly Mr. McCord had been musing over definitions like these, published in his own home territory in *The Dixie Dictionary*—which sells for "50 cents: Yankee money."

Auto: "I auto go to work, but Ahm tared."

Barn: "I was barn in Kentucky."

Balks: "Pass me that match balks."

Did: He's did.

Gull: A young female human.

Rat Cheer: Lay it rat cheer (not there).

Yawl: Yawl come to see me soon.

(The pamphlet also warns strangers to always say, "Pass them grits," since there is no such thing as one grit.)

✦ ✦ ✦

From a long list of definitions being circulated surreptitiously in Washington's huge Pentagon Building:

A program: An assignment that cannot be completed by a single telephone call.

Consultant: Any average man more than fifty miles from home.

To activate: To make carbons and add more names to a memo.

To implement: To hire more people and wangle additional office space.

Reorientation: Getting used to working again.

Committee: The unwilling, recruited from the unfit to do the unnecessary.

✦ ✦ ✦

A little girl, fond of dismissing any problems with an airy "It's nothing," was asked finally just what she thought "nothing" meant. Her imaginative definition was, "Nothing is like a balloon with its skin off."

✦ ✦ ✦

Another budding Webster is Norman Collins. He defines a family swimming pool as "a small body of water completely surrounded by other people's children."

* * *

And here are some other definitions you'll find in no standard dictionary:

Acoustic: What you use when you shoot pool.

Adolescence: When a girl begins to powder and a boy begins to puff.

Alimony: The fee a woman charges for name-dropping.

Aloha: A Pullman berth.

Anatomy: Something everybody has—but it looks better on a girl.

Anecdote: A revealing account of an incident that never occurred in the life of some famous person.

August: The month you can't open the car window you couldn't close in February.

Bachelor: A man who has faults he doesn't know about yet.

Banjo: Let's not invite Joseph.

Basso profundo: A deep-thinking fish.

Bath mats: Little dry rugs that children like to stand beside (*John Ciardi*).

Bust truster: A man who is sure his girl doesn't wear falsies.

Caddy: A lad who stands behind a golfer and didn't see the ball either.

Carbuncle: An auto collision.

Career girl: One who'd rather bring home the bacon than fry it.

Coincide: What you do when it starts raining.

Conscience: A little gimmick inside you that makes you tell your wife before somebody else does.

Conservative: One who believes that nothing should be done for the first time.

Debate: It lures de fish.

Desk: A trash basket with drawers.

De trop: A forward pass.

Deuce: The unkindest cut of all.

Dogma: A canine female parent.

Egoist: One who is always me-deep in conversation.

Experience: The only thing most people get out of life.

Forger: A man who gives a check a bad name.

Gladiator: What the cannibal said after he ate the female explorer.

Guest towel: A small square of absorbent linen completely surrounded by useless embroidery.

Heredity: Something you subscribe to wholeheartedly when your son's report card shows all A's.

Hoosiery: Stockings made in Indiana.

Inflation: Something that cost $10 to buy a few years ago and now costs $20 to repair.

Intuition: The instinct whereby a woman can tell she's right whether she is or not.

Jaywalking: An exercise that brings on that rundown feeling.

Kindergarten teacher: One who should know how to make the little things count.

Knob: A thing to adore.

Minor operation: One performed on somebody else.

Money: Jack of all trades.

Monologue: A conversation between a real estate promoter and a prospect.

Officer: A cop whom you can talk out of giving you a ticket.

Operator: An employee who takes the padding out of his shoulders and puts it in his expense account.

Pedestrian: A chap who knows what the lady motorist is driving at.

Pessimist: A man who's always building dungeons in the air.

Pharmacist: Man in a white coat who stands behind a soda fountain and sells ball-point pens.

Platonic lover: One who holds the eggshells while somebody else eats the omelette.

Procrastinator: Man with a wait problem.

Reno: The city of otherly love.

Repartee: What a person thinks of after he becomes a departee (*Sid Skolsky*).

Slang: Language that takes off its coat, spits on its hands, and goes to work (*Carl Sandburg*).

Small fry: A one-dollar steak.

Sneezing: Much achoo about nothing.

Taxidermist: A man who knows his stuff.

Theory: A hunch with a college education.

Toothache: A pain that drives you to extraction.

Violin: A bad hotel.

Wallflower: A girl without a gent to her name.

Wife: A person who can look in a bureau drawer and find the husband's tie clasp that isn't there.

Will power: The ability to eat *one* salted peanut.

11. *Only on Sundays*

A young minister, just out of divinity school, was assigned a parish in a tiny Blue Ridge community in Virginia, where he promptly was called upon to perform a wedding ceremony for a mountain couple.

He did his part beautifully, and the bridegroom told him, "Parson, it's easy to see you're going to be a big hit in these parts. I'd like to start you off real good too, but I'm sorry to say I ain't got no money to give you. Tell you what I'm gonna do. I got an ole houn' dawg I was aimin' to sell for ten dollars—and I'm gonna let you have him for five!"

*   *   *

Taken to church for the first time, a four-year-old girl was mystified when the entire congregation kneeled. "What are they doing?" she asked her mother. "Ss-s-h," cautioned the mother. "They're praying." "What?" exclaimed the four-year-old. "With their clothes on?"

*   *   *

The services of one congregation in West Palm Beach always include a group reading of the Twenty-third Psalm. One Sunday a visitor with a shrill, penetrating voice got about ten words ahead of the rest at the beginning and maintained her lead doggedly to the very end.

At the end of the services, one resident member asked another, "Who was that irritating lady who was always by the still waters while the rest of us were lying down in green pastures?"

*   *   *

A clergyman once assured his congregation, "Every blade of grass is a sermon."

Two days later, as the clergyman was moving his lawn, a member of the congregation passed by and nodded approvingly, "That's the stuff, Reverend! Cut your sermon short!"

*   *   *

Baptist minister Carl Winters, of Oak Park, is one cleric who appreciates the value of humor. "I definitely try," he says, "when I preach, to make people laugh. And while their mouths are open, I put something in for them to chew on."

*   *   *

St. Peter gazed solemnly at twenty-seven wives, just arrived, and seated before him. "Now, girls," said St. Peter kindly, "I want every one of you who ever was untrue to your husband on earth to stand up—and remember, no fibbing. I have ways of checking up on you, you know."

Sheepishly, twenty-six of the wives rose to their feet, but the twenty-seventh steadfastly remained seated.

St. Peter nodded, and put in a phone call to the devil. "Satan," he said, "I'm sending down twenty-seven untrue wives to you—and I advise you to be particularly careful of one of them. She's stone deaf."

* * *

Jerome Beatty's nephew announced he was going out on the lawn to play ball with God.

"How do you play ball with God?" asked Beatty.

"It's easy," explained the nephew. "I just throw the ball up in the air and God throws it back down to me."

* * *

A minister in Evansville had fallen into the habit of placing his sermons on the pulpit about an hour before the church service. One young rascal discovered this habit, and one day, before the congregation convened, he neatly detached the last page from the manuscript.

The minister delivered his sermon in ringing tones, and read the last line of what was now the final page: "So, Adam said to Eve . . ." Searching in vain for the following page, the minister made a mental note to give his secretary what for, cleared his throat nervously, then concluded his sermon weakly, "So, Adam said to Eve—there seems to be a leaf missing!"

* * *

When Bishop Stephen Bayne, Jr., was appointed executive officer of the Anglican Communion, he was asked as he embarked for London how he regarded his new duties. "I am rather like a mosquito in a nudist camp," admitted the bishop with a wry smile. "I know what I ought to do, but I don't know where to begin."

* * *

A venerable bishop got tired of receiving pleas for aid from the pastor of one of his most impoverished parishes, and wrote to the pastor, "These pleas must stop. I can do nothing more for you." For a full two months, not another word was heard from the chagrined pastor. Then, one day, the bishop got another letter from him. It read, "This is not an appeal. It is a report. I have no pants."

* * *

After extraordinary displays of patience, the parents of a three-year-old tomboy had taught her to say grace before meals. Then one day they heard her carefully reciting the prayer while she was taking her bath.

"This isn't the time to say grace," called in her mother. "You do that just before you eat."

"I know," called back the youngster cheerily. "I just swallowed the soap."

* * *

To stress his conviction that the people of today are too commercial and material in their outlook, a British bishop cited a question asked of a London stockbroker by his precocious offspring. "Father, why is it that so many churches have plus signs on them?"

* * *

Brian James tells of a well-heeled tourist who dropped into a tiny village church in Essex County, England, for the Christmas service. Before it began, he buttonholed the rector and said expansively, "I mean to give you a handsome contribution. I only hope you'll put on a good show today." The rector answered quietly, "It won't be a bad one. It's been running now for almost two thousand years!"

* * *

Cartoon in a religious weekly depicts an usher passing a collection plate at a church wedding. The caption reads, "I admit, sir, it's a bit extraordinary—but the bride's father insisted on it."

* * *

Rear Admiral George Dufek, one of the first Americans to actually reach the South Pole, was surveying the ice-capped landscape there at lunchtime one day with Father Linehan, geophysicist from Boston College. In his hamper, the admiral found ham and roast beef sandwiches. "None for me," said Father Linehan regretfully. "It's Friday, you know."

Admiral Dufek is not the man to be stopped by a thing like that. "If you'll step about fifteen paces to the left," he suggested, "it will still be Thursday." Father Linehan did just that and enjoyed the sandwiches immensely.

* * *

Two clergymen were talking animatedly at the corner of Madison and Fiftieth when a third man of the cloth appeared. The first two looked pleasantly surprised. One stuck out his hand and exclaimed heartily, "Well, speak of the devil . . . !"

* * *

Dr. Lee Fairchild recalls the story of the village priest who told his congregation, "Next Sunday I propose to give a sermon about liars. I suggest that before then you all read Chapter Seventeen of St. Mark's."

Came the following Sunday, and the priest began, "Will all those who obliged me by reading Chapter Seventeen of St. Mark's please raise their hands." Every right hand in the congregation shot up.

Observed the priest, "There happen to be only sixteen chapters in St. Mark's. I will now deliver my sermon on liars."

❊   ❊   ❊

A beatnik wandered into church, and on the way out, told the Reverend, "You were swinging, Daddy-o. You were way out."

"What was that again?" inquired the Reverend, knitting his brow.

"I mean," amplified the cat, "I dug your jive. I read you so good I put ten big fish in your collection plate."

"Ah," beamed the Reverend, grasping the beatnik's hand. "Cool, man. Cool!"

❊   ❊   ❊

The Reverend Andrew Poole tells about a fellow clergyman who was invited to a child's fashionable birthday party. Arriving tardily, he heard sounds of jollity in the rumpus room, and told the maid, "Don't announce me. I'm going to surprise them." He thereupon dropped to his hands and knees and crawled into the rumpus room, barking like a dog.

Looking up, he found six adults staring at him incredulously.

He had come to the wrong house.

❊   ❊   ❊

Have you heard about the new sport developed by Fathers Clancy and Hallorhan behind their Pawtucket parish house? It's played with rackets and a shuttlecock. They call it goodminton.

❊   ❊   ❊

Things weren't going too well in the first-year Sunday school class. Nobody seemed able to recall the identity of St. Matthew. Nor did they do any better with St. Mark. Finally the teacher said hopefully, "Surely somebody will remember who Peter was?"

A small boy in the last row came to the rescue. "Teacher," he piped, "wasn't he a wabbit?"

* * *

Copy of a prayer discovered by a correspondent in a room at a Long Island inn:

"Lord, Thou knowest better than I know myself that I am growing older.

"Keep me from getting too talkative, and thinking I must say something on every subject and on every occasion.

"Release me from craving to straighten out everybody's affairs.

"Teach me the glorious lesson that occasionally it is possible that I may be mistaken.

"Make me thoughtful, but not moody; helpful, but not bossy. Thou knowest, Lord, that what I want most is a few friends at the end."

✿ ✿ ✿

E. H. Taylor tells this tale at the expense of Bishop Bompas, the first Anglican missionary to venture into the Yukon.

The good bishop discovered a tribe of Indians who had never recorded a baptism, a confirmation, or a marriage service. The bishop soon rectified this situation, baptizing and confirming everybody in sight, and winding up by uniting every beaming couple in holy wedlock.

Later the tribal chief told Bishop Bompas that his tribe hadn't had so much fun in a month of Sundays. "And what part of the ceremonies," asked the bishop, "did you enjoy most?" "The marriage service," replied the chief, happily. "We all got new wives!"

✿ ✿ ✿

An unscheduled transcontinental airliner was definitely in trouble: one engine out, and the others backfiring, but the passenger in seat 9-A took some comfort from the fact that the priest sitting alongside him seemed quite undisturbed. "Do you think we'll get down safely, Father?" asked the passenger. "I certainly hope so," said the priest. "But what can we do if these other motors conk out?" persisted the passenger. "I can't answer that," admitted the priest. "You see, I'm not up in administration; my department has always been sales!"

✿ ✿ ✿

They tell about a fifteen-year-old boy in an orphans' home who had an incurable stutter. It was agony for him to talk to strangers.

One Sunday the minister who came out regularly from town was detained, and the boy, to the surprise of the people in charge, volunteered to say the prayer in his stead. He did it perfectly, too, with the proper reverence and not a single stutter. Later, he explained, "I don't stutter when I talk to God. He loves me."

✿ ✿ ✿

An enthusiastic minister, who liked to wave his arms to emphasize salient points in his sermons, had trouble keeping his shirttails in his trousers, and got into the habit of stuffing them in surreptitiously whenever he had the opportunity. One Sunday, while preaching away, he fished around behind his back in the usual way, and found more material than usual to push out of sight. He persisted manfully, however. At the close of his sermon he discovered that he had about half of a United Nations flag stuffed into his pants.

* * *

The late and great Pope John one morning granted a private audience to a newly appointed bishop, who complained that the complexity and responsibilities of his new office prevented him from sleeping. "The very same thing happened to me in the first few weeks of my pontificate," Pope John reassured him, "but then one day my guardian angel appeared to me in a daydream and whispered, 'Giovanni, don't take yourself so seriously.' And ever since then I've been able to sleep!"

12. The Professions

ARTISTS

Along about the year 1500 or so, an irreverent Italian legend has it, a young girl in Milan beseeched a famous artist she knew to paint her portrait. "I'm far too busy," he is purported to have told her. "Why not ask that fellow Da Vinci across the courtyard, Mona? He needs the business!"

* * *

Le Gallidaut, a meek, undersized Parisian sculptor, had never fashioned anything longer than a woman's hand, so everybody was mildly surprised when he turned out nothing less than an elephant in marble.

"But Le Gallidaut," marveled his oldest friend, "how could you sculpt such a perfect likeness without a model?"

"There was nothing to it," explained Le Gallidaut airily. "I simply chipped off every piece that didn't look like an elephant."

* * *

Dan Melnick, rising young theatrical and TV producer, and his wife, Linda, who is a daughter of composer Dick Rodgers, are in the process of acquiring a first-rate collection of modern paintings, abstractions, and expensive pop art.

A few weeks ago, a lady arrived at the Melnick home to bind a new rug. She gazed intently at the paintings on the wall, clucked appreciatively, and announced: "Nice pictures you've got here. Who's the artist in the family?"

* * *

Speaking of abstractions, a little boy in Arizona was stopped cold by one at an exhibition of local talent. "What's *that*?" he asked his mother. She explained, "It's supposed to be a cowhand and his horse." The little boy cut right to the heart of the matter. He asked, "Well, why ain't it?"

*   *   *

A business tycoon who painted for diversion got short shrift when he asked a young lady of his acquaintance to pose for him in the nude. "I'm not a model, I'll have you know," she said haughtily. "That's all right," soothed the tycoon. "I'm not an artist."

*   *   *

A wealthy dowager, very *avant-garde*, had her portrait executed by a new painter whose technique consisted of splattering great blobs of paint on the canvas. "It's the best I've ever done," he announced when he delivered the finished portrait, "although I'm not entirely satisfied with how your nose turned out."

"Why don't you change it?" asked the dowager.

"Frankly," admitted the painter, "I can't find it."

*   *   *

At an art class in California a young model slipped out of her clothes, then covered her face with shame. "I'm so embarrassed," she confessed. "I forgot my teeth."

*   *   *

While a Greenwich Village sidewalk artist was munching a hot dog, some rascal painted a mustache on his portrait of Elizabeth Taylor.

"What are you going to do about it?" the artist was asked after he had surveyed the damage.

"Raise the price," said the artist.

*   *   *

The owner of a picture gallery on Fifty-seventh Street tells of a night when Pablo Picasso supposedly caught a burglar red-handed in his château in southern France. The burglar tore loose from Picasso's grasp, but the artist later assured the police he could draw a rough sketch of the intruder.

On the basis of the drawing, the police promptly arrested the minister of finance, a visiting lady columnist from New York, a Univac machine, and a replica of the Eiffel Tower.

* * *

A friend once brought Picasso three paintings to sign. Picasso refused, declaring that all three were palpable fakes. "But," protested the exasperated friend, "I saw you paint these pictures with my own eyes." Picasso's unabashed answer was, "I can paint fake Picassos just as well as anybody."

* * *

A fabulously wealthy Argentine playboy dropped in to a famous Paris art gallery with his wife one blustery December day and bought all the Picassos, Gauguins, Klees, Hans Hofmanns, and Jackson Pollocks in sight. "Well, that's done," he told his wife happily. "Now that the Christmas cards are out of the way, let's get started on the real presents we've got to buy."

* * *

Salvador Dali, the eccentric artist, can come right down to earth when occasion warrants. At the Stork Club recently, for example, he was heard earnestly assuring a beautiful young hat-check girl, "Never take a fur coat from an amorous customer, my dear. A fur coat is like a painting by me: you have to explain both to your mother."

* * *

A water color specialist found an old Indian squaw in New Mexico who struck him as a perfect model for a painting. Promised sufficient wampum, she agreed to pose, but after remaining absolutely still for a half hour, she began to squirm. "Be patient," urged the artist, "I'll soon be finished." Ten minutes later she started wriggling again. "I thought Indians were patient and stoical," grumbled the artist. "What makes you so nervous?"

"Well, for one thing," explained the Indian squaw, "I'm sitting on a swarm of bees."

DENTISTS

On Madison Avenue, a lady patient descended upon society dentist Ed Pullman's office for the fifth time to command him to grind down her false teeth again. "I tell you they don't fit," she insisted. "Okay," said Dr. Pullman reluctantly. "I'll do it one last time. But by every test, they should fit your mouth perfectly as they are."

"Who said anything about my mouth?" snapped the lady. "They don't fit in the glass."

* * *

If the American Dental Association is on the ball, it will give serious attention to John Fuller's suggested slogan for the tooth-pullers of our nation: "Nothing dentured, nothing gained."

* * *

Arlene Francis, backstage before a "What's My Line?" broadcast, was talking about a man who began his professional career as a dentist, later became an internationally renowned brain surgeon. "How did he ever make so radical a change?" wondered Dorothy Kilgallen.

Explained Arlene, "His drill slipped."

* * *

Dr. Villard closes his clinic each day at six, and pauses on the way home for a Daiquiri cocktail—or two—at a Madison Avenue bar. One afternoon he noticed that the barkeep was sprinkling the top of his cocktail with grated hickory nuts. "Is that a new fad?" asked Dr. Villard. "Not at all," the barkeep assured him. "That is simply a hickory Daiquiri, Doc."

* * *

They sneeze, insists Irene Keepin, thisaway:

A dentist: Ah chew.

A R.R. engineer: Ah choo-choo.

A travel agent: Where choo?

A banker: Cash shoo.

A dancer: Ah cha-cha choo.

* * *

A world-wise ten-year-old, asked to write a school paper on "Care of the Teeth," came up with these three basic rules:

1. See your dentist at regular intervals.
2. Brush your teeth after every meal.
3. Watch out for shovers at the drinking fountain.

DOCTORS

An elderly lady in Baltimore was a hopeless hypochondriac who called her doctor at all hours of the night to complain about imaginary aches and pains. The doctor finally had to tell her, "If you wake me up once more in the middle of the night with one of these cock-and-bull stories, Mrs. Hilliard,

I'm going to have to ask you to transfer your business to another doctor."

Two weeks later, however, the poor lady fell down a flight of stairs, breaking a leg, four ribs, and suffering a concussion into the bargain. The doctor examined her from head to foot, shook his head approvingly, and said, "Well, Mrs. Hilliard! At last you're beginning to get the real hang of it!"

◦ ◦ ◦

"The time has come," Dr. Nudnick told his patient, "to wheel you to the operating room. Don't fret about the outcome. I've lost my last eleven patients straight, and if there's anything at all in the law of averages, you'll pull through. Is there anything I can do for you before we start?"

"There certainly is," said the patient grimly. "You can help me on with my shirt and pants."

◦ ◦ ◦

"I don't get it," declared one pretty girl as she divested herself of her garments. "I tell the doctor my sinus is bothering me, and he asks me to strip." A nude redhead with a satchel on her lap replied, "My case is even more puzzling. I'm here to tune the piano."

* * *

A hypochrondriac was discussing his various ailments with a doctor he had encountered aboard a transatlantic liner. "Take the matter of kissing my wife," he proposed. "The first time I kiss her, I feel very warm and perspire. But the second time, I am chilled and shiver with the cold. How do you explain that?"

"Before you answer, Doctor," interrupted the hypochrondriac's wife, "you should know that the first time he kisses me it's July and the second time it's January."

* * *

Dr. Morris Fishbein tells about a nurse who was given three demerits. She was absent without gauze.

* * *

A trustee of Lenox Hill Hospital has dug up a copy of the 1888 rule book for the School of Nursing at that superb institution. One of the startling statements in the 1888 compendium made it clear that "any nurse who smoked or had her hair done at a beauty shop gave the director of nurses good reason to suspect her worth, intentions, and integrity."

Among other duties that nurses in 1888 were expected to perform were mopping floors, cleaning chimneys, trimming wicks, and fetching coal. Hours were from 7 A.M. to 8 P.M., except on Sunday, when they were off between noon and 2 P.M.!

As an incentive, nurses who performed faultlessly for a period of five years were given an increase of five cents a day—providing there were no outstanding hospital debts at the time!

* * *

Overheard at a mountain resort: "I'll tell you how good my son, the doctor, has become after one year of practice: in three weeks he cured that rich Mrs. Teitelbaum of fourteen hundred dollars!"

* * *

In a pleasant little town in northern Westchester, there's an elderly doctor whose battered jalopy is the subject for considerable merriment to the young fry who hang out in front of the new supermarket.

The good doctor remains unperturbed by their jibes. "Yes, boys, this car is getting mighty old," he told them amiably one morning. "It's also fully paid for. If you'll check with your parents, you'll discover most of you ain't!"

*   *   *

A middle-aged matron in Scarsdale startled the clerk in a dairy when she ordered twenty-four quarts of milk. "Oh, I'm not going to drink them," she explained. "The doctor told me to take a milk bath, and I figure it will take twenty-four quarts to fill the tub." "Pasteurized?" asked the clerk. "No," said the matron. "Just up to my neck."

*   *   *

A new patient appeared in a doctor's office to explain, "Doctor, I'm disturbed. A week ago I came home to find my wife in the arms of another man, who talked me into going out for a cup of coffee. The next four nights, exactly the same thing happened." "My good fellow," said the doctor, "it isn't a doctor you need; it's a lawyer." "No, no," insisted the patient. "It's a doctor's advice I want. I've got to know if I'm drinking too much coffee."

*   *   *

Dr. George Stevenson, of the National Association for Mental Health, offers these suggestions for calming tensed-up nerves:

1. Don't bottle up anger. Find some way of venting it, such as sawing wood or taking a long hike.

2. Find a sympathetic ear. Putting vague fears into words helps ease them.

3. Listen to the other fellow's troubles. Everybody has plenty of them. They'll put your own in better perspective.

4. Practice "giving in" on some points. Always insisting on having your own way takes a high toll.

5. Turn your back on your problems for a while. A trip, a show, or above all, an amusing book can give your jangled nerves a valuable respite.

* * *

The whole neighborhood shook from the explosion in the rear of the town's oldest pharmacy. The pharmacist himself staggered out, his glasses broken, streaks of black besmirching his white uniform. "Lady," he implored a customer who was wiping debris from the soda counter off herself, "would you please ask your doctor to copy off that prescription again—and this time I hope he'll PRINT it!"

* * *

Have you caught up with the story of the Las Vegas transient who awoke with bad pains in his stomach one night and put in a hurry call for the house physician? That gentleman gave him a quick examination, folded up his stethoscope, and said, "I'll give you four to one you have acute appendicitis."

* * *

A sweltering midsummer afternoon had famous gynecologist "Sunshine" Rodgers in a swivet. Noticing his foul humor, a sympathetic patient asked, "These hot August mornings getting you down, Doctor?"

"Not these hot August mornings at all," scowled the good doctor. "It's those cold nights last November!"

* * *

In Ohio there lives a medical student who spent his summer vacation building up his sadly depleted cash reserve. He worked as a butcher in the daytime and was a hospital orderly at night. Both jobs, of course, involved wearing similar white uniforms. One evening he was instructed to wheel a patient on a stretcher into surgery. The patient, a stout, very frightened lady, looked up at the student and let out an unearthly scream. "My God!" she wailed, "it's my BUTCHER!"

* * *

"You certainly seemed fascinated by that medical magazine in my waiting room," observed a doctor as he prepared to examine a patient. "Indeed I was," agreed the patient. "The issue you have out there announces the discovery of ether."

* * *

A man with a very sore throat indeed went to the home of a doctor and rang the bell. The door was opened by the doctor's wife. In an almost inaudible croak, the man inquired, "Is the doctor in?" In a conspiratorial whisper, equally low, the doctor's wife answered, "No. Come on in."

* * *

Nancy Parks reports the meanest doctor in Flatbush. He keeps his stethoscope in the deep freeze.

* * *

A husband wandered nervously about a doctor's waiting room while his wife underwent a complete checkup inside. After some time the doctor stuck his head out of the door, summoned the husband, and said, "To be blunt, I don't like the looks of your wife."

"Neither do I," responded the husband, "but she's great with the children."

* * *

The laziest man in Westchester County fell off a couch and had to be taken to the doctor's in an ambulance. A doctor examined him and reported, "I'm afraid I've got some bad news for you, sir. You will never be able to work again."

"Thank you, doctor," said the lazy one. "Now what's the bad news?"

* * *

A Cleveland doctor, reports Jerome Beatty, recently treated a young girl for an angry, infected insect bite on her right lower leg. She phoned the following day to say that the pain and itching were gone, but the calf was purple. The Cleveland doctor promptly told her, "I never saw a purple calf. . . ."

* * *

A couple of newspapermen were having a cold soft drink at the corner drug store one afternoon when a pretty girl, neatly dressed, came in and asked the pharmacist to read a letter for her. It was obviously a rather intimate letter, too, because the girl blushed while she listened, and gave the pharmacist a hug and a kiss before she rushed happily out of the store.

"Don't think she's an illiterate," the pharmacist hastened to explain to the newspapermen. "Matter of fact, she's a senior at Radcliffe. But her boy friend is a doctor—and only a pharmacist like me can make head or tails of his handwriting."

* * *

"I note," murmured a young doctor to a very pretty nurse, "that 317 isn't chasing you any more. How did you bring it off?" "It was simple—once I thought it through," laughed the nurse. "I took the tires off his wheelchair."

*　*　*

In a chic Park Avenue office, a doctor gave a socialite a checkup, then asked, "Have you been living a normal life?" "Indeed I have," the socialite told him warmly. "Well," said the doctor, "I'm afraid you'll have to cut it out."

*　*　*

Margery Bartlett tells about a stranger in town who was lured by a doctor friend to a dance at a deaf and dumb institute. "How the dickens do I ask a deaf and dumb girl to dance?" he asked the doctor. "Just smile and bow to her," explained the experienced doctor. It worked. The stranger picked out the prettiest girl on the floor, smiled and bowed to her, and away they went. After a full hour he was still dancing with her, happy as a clam at high tide, when a tall, dark man suddenly approached the girl and said, "Darling, when are you going to have a dance with me? After all, I'm your fiancé." "I don't know, dear," sighed the girl, "I can't seem to get rid of this poor deaf and dumb fellow."

*　*　*

Joe E. Lewis tells about a surgeon who had imbibed a few too many before he showed up in the operating room. Presently he told the nurse, "It's okay to wheel the patient out." "But, Doctor," she protested, "we haven't wheeled him in yet." "Indeed," declared the surgeon icily. "Then what do you think I've been doing the past ten minutes?" "I *know* what you've been doing," said the nurse. "You have amputated a leg of the operating table."

*　*　*

Miss Edna Ferber sent flowers to a sick friend in the hospital recently, enclosing a card that made the recipient feel better on the instant. It read, "If loving thoughts are a comfort, my dear, you are lying on cream puffs."

* * *

"Wouldn't you know it?" sighed Dr. Busby. "The worst blizzard in years and at 3 A.M. the patient who lives farthest from the Thruway gets sick and I have to go see him."

Through the snowdrifts Dr. Busby fought his way to the side of the stricken man. After examining him, he shook his head gravely, and ordered, "Get your lawyer, your family, and your friends over here on the double!"

When he got back home, Dr. Busby told his wife the instructions he had given. "Poor fellow," she sighed, "is he really that sick?" "Not at all," grinned Dr. Busby. "He'll be perfectly well in twenty-four hours. But I was darned if I was going to be the only sucker out on a night like this!"

* * *

Victor Borge urges caution in the use of those new rejuvenation pills. "Take the case of a cousin of mine in Copenhagen. He took some pills guaranteed to make him fifteen years younger and they all but killed him. You see, he was only twelve at the time."

* * *

The young doctor's very first patient was a beautiful maiden with entrancing curves. "Steady, boy," the doctor admonished himself, but the stethoscope kept slipping from his fingers.

"What's the trouble?" whispered the girl softly. "You seem rather nervous."

"Not at all," the doctor assured her, then added, "Once more now, if you please. Deep breathely."

* * *

Old Dr. Boosey, general practitioner in Gooseleg Falls for nigh on fifty years, was dozing peacefully on the veranda of the Mansion House when a young man hailed him loudly, pumped his hand, and declared, "I want to thank you for your invaluable treatment."

"Never saw you in my life before," harumphed Doc Boosey. "You can't be a patient of mine."

"Me? Certainly not," agreed the young man cheerfully. "My uncle was your patient. And I'm his sole heir."

* * *

A young mother, being examined by her doctor, made no effort to control her son, who, despite the remonstrances of the doctor's secretary, was raising cain in the waiting room. Finally, a crash of bottles disclosed the fact that he had reached the doctor's cabinet of supplies. "I hope," simpered the mother, "that Billy's mischievous ways are not distracting you." "Not a bit," replied the doctor grimly. "Besides, he'll be quiet in a minute when he gets to the next shelf. That's where I keep the poisons."

* * *

Doctor's explanation to a three-hundred-pound patient: "These pills I'm prescribing for you are not to be swallowed. You just spill them on the floor twice a day and pick them up one at a time."

* * *

The inmates at a well-run loony bin chipped in and bought the new doctor a great big red balloon. "It's to show how much better we like you than the doctor who preceded you," explained the spokesman of the inmates. "Somehow you seem more like one of us."

* * *

A man who often confused himself with Young Lochinvar cherished a number of interesting ideas about the lovely young nurse who took care of him for some days at a local hospital. "Honey," he confided to her one morning, "I've fallen so deeply in love with you that I don't want to get well." "Don't worry," she assured him. "You won't. Your doctor, who happens to be engaged to me, saw you kissing me last night."

* * *

Two doctor cartoons have given me a special laugh recently. One, in the *Journal of the American Medical Association,* shows a newly graduated surgeon sawing the arm off a patient. "What kind of an operation do you think you're performing?" asks a nurse. "Operation!" gasps the surgeon. "I thought this was an autopsy." Another, mailed in by a thoughtful reader, depicts an obviously delighted medic standing over a patient on the operating table and telling the other doctors: "Gentlemen, this is Mr. Hellman, author of the best-selling *All Doctors Are Quacks. . . .*"

* * *

The classic doctor story is about the fine old country doctor who had neither time nor inclination to dun patients for payment. He died in his second-story office one morning, and one of his few worldly possessions was the wooden sign that had stood on his lawn for fifty years or more.

His loyal patients would have liked nothing better than to buy him an imposing tombstone, but they were just as poor as he was. After his funeral therefore, they uprooted the wooden sign and lovingly planted it on his grave. It read, "Dr. Farnum, upstairs."

BOTH SIDES OF THE LAW

The time was the cocktail hour, the scene the club car of a transcontinental train, and the cast of characters composed entirely of well-heeled legalites bound for their annual convention in San Francisco.

Every lawyer had a case to tell about, of course, but now Mr. Richards of New York had the floor—and indeed had had it for a full half hour. He wound up in a blaze of oratory. "Masterful as you will agree my defense was," he asserted, "the jury, inflamed by newspaper headlines, brought in a verdict of guilty and my client got twenty years in the clink."

Lawyer Brown of Louisville was the first to congratulate lawyer Richards of New York. "Not only was that a magnificently told story," he boomed, "but I can safely say it's the first case lost aboard this train in over eight hundred miles."

* * *

The rising young comedy team of Allen and Rossi have come up with an ingenious plan to relieve New York City's appalling traffic problems. They propose nothing less than making *every* crosstown street in Manhattan one way in the *same* direction —going west. "What good would that accomplish?" they were asked. "What good?" echoed Allen and Rossi. "Put the plan into operation on Monday—and by Wednesday the whole problem will be New Jersey's!"

* * *

A distinguished judge had a wife who was just a bit too fond of the grape. At a party one afternoon at the mayor's mansion, he reproved her, "My dear, that's the seventh time you've gone up to the bar and asked for another whiskey sour. Doesn't it embarrass you?"

"Why should it?" she answered happily. "I just explain I'm getting them for you."

* * *

Myron Cohen tells about a fellow who was having a running battle with his landlord. "I'll tell you how I keep *my* landlord in line," volunteered Myron. "You just do the same."

Three weeks later Cohen got this note from his friend: "I took your advice, and I expect no more trouble from that dirty landlord. Sincerely, Joe Schwartz. Sing Sing Cell Number 208."

* * *

Roommates at Vassar both had boy friends at Columbia Law School, which worked out very nicely for weekend parties. Suddenly, however, the ardent love letters of both law students ceased, and the girls had to content themselves with dry, non-committal little notes. "What's the matter with you two goons?" the girls demanded one Saturday afternoon. "Don't you love us any more?" "We do, we do," insisted one of the law students, "but, you see, we're studying breach of promise cases this month."

* * *

Donlin was on his way home through a dark alley when three thugs attacked him. Donlin fought like a wildcat, but finally was overcome and robbed of all the change in his pocket —thirty cents, to be exact. "You're a fighting feller," grunted one of the thugs with something like admiration in his voice, "but why would you be wanting to put up such a battle for a measly thirty cents?" "Sure," confided Donlin, "I thought yez wanted the ten dollars I've got hidden in me shoe!"

* * *

A Yale professor was toddling nervously along a dark back street of New Haven when a tough-looking character suddenly accosted him. "Would you be gracious enough," suggested the sinister character, "to lend material assistance to a forlorn, unfortunate fellow who is out of employment? All I've got in the world is just this here loaded pistol."

*   *   *

A clumsy shoplifter was nabbed pocketing a wristwatch in a jewelry shop. "Give me a chance," he pleaded. "I'll pay for the watch." When a bill was made out for him he turned pale. "This is more than I planned to spend," he quavered. "Can't you show me something less expensive?"

*   *   *

Stickup men become more sophisticated daily. Take the gunman who suddenly popped up at the paymaster's window of a mammoth assembly plant and barked, "Never mind the payroll, bud. Just hand over the welfare fund, the pension fund, the group insurance premiums, and the withholding taxes."

*   *   *

Two prisoners on the rock pile suddenly started slugging each other. A warden pulled them apart and asked the aggressor, "Why did you attack this man?" The prisoner's surly explanation: "He called me a dirty number!"

*   *   *

Defendant Nails Epstein, convicted for his ninth robbery, pleaded for mercy, whining, "I just finished a term of ten years, Your Honor." His Honor decreed promptly, "You are hereby sentenced to twenty more. One good term deserves another."

*   *   *

In a small town in Maine, the sheriff doubles as the vet. In the middle of one cold night he received an emergency call. "Do you want me as sheriff or vet?" he inquired. "Both," came the agitated reply. "We can't get our dog's mouth open—and there's a burglar's rear in it."

*   *   *

A short biography, submitted by Serena Babbitt: 1. High chair. 2. High school. 3. High stool. 4. High finance. 5. High hat. 6. "Hi, Warden."

* * *

In a busy suburban bank, a mean-looking hombre silently slid a note to the paying teller which read, "Put every dollar in your cage into a bag and don't open your mouth or I'll shoot." The teller obediently slid back the bag of money with a note of his own, which read, "Straighten your necktie, sloppy. Your picture is being taken."

* * *

"Hello! Is this Police Headquarters?" came an anguished voice over the telephone. "This is the Old Maids' Home. Send a riot squad quick! A burglar has broken in!"

"Okay, okay," soothed the lieutenant at the desk. "Who's this speaking?"

"It's the burglar," answered the terrified voice.

* * *

A chronic bad check passer suffered his greatest indignity recently. He received a call from his Red Cross blood bank. It seems his blood bounced.

* * *

Clancy, traffic cop at a busy Main Street corner for twenty years, celebrated his birthday just a bit too riotously and had to call the station house to say he was so ill he couldn't report for duty. The chief urged him with unexpected understanding just to go back to bed and sleep it off. "The chief is getting soft in his old age," reflected Clancy contentedly. Of course, he couldn't know that at that very moment the chief was telling his sergeant with a chuckle, "Poor Clancy's got one beaut of a hangover. Wait 'til he realizes this is his day off!"

* * *

A pretty stenographer brought a paternity suit against her very uncomfortable boss. The judge listened to the mass of most incriminating testimony, and when the time came to announce a verdict, pulled a cigar out of his pocket and handed it to the defendant. "Congratulations," said the judge. "You have just become a father."

*　*　*

Judge Jacob Brande tells of a young lawyer who had just passed his bar exams and was representing his first client in a city court. He put his brand-new overcoat and brand-new hat on a bench in the courtroom, and, obviously nervous, stepped forward before the judge to do or die.

The judge was a wise and kindly man. He peered at the fledgling lawyer over his glasses and remarked dryly, "Young man, I gather that this is your very first appearance in this court." "It is, sir," quavered the young lawyer. "I thought so," nodded the judge. "Now before we get started, get ahold of your coat and hat and put them where you can keep your eyes on them!"

*　*　*

"What do you do for a living?" asked the judge.

"I'm night orderly at the hospital," lied the prisoner.

"Thirty days for pan-handling," said the judge.

*　*　*

A mugger invaded a delicatessen shop, pointed a gun at the proprietor, and demanded, "Give me all your money." The proprietor quavered, "To take out?"

*　*　*

Patrolman Michael Conlin was banished to a beat in the darkest and dreariest part of town. His sin? He inadvertently arrested a man climbing into a taxi in a convict suit, only to discover that said man was an irascible judge on his way to a fancy dress party.

Patrolman Conlin has learned his lesson. "That's the last time," he swears, "I'll ever book a judge by his cover."

*　*　*

Alan King asked a veteran city judge, "How do you usually decide a case?" The judge answered, "First, I read the facts of the case. Then I listen to the plaintiff. Then I render my verdict." "Don't you listen to the defendant, too?" demanded the astonished Mr. King. "Never," insisted the judge. "That would get me all mixed up."

* * *

The police finally caught a bank robber red-handed in a corruption-ridden city. This not-so-clever robber was attempting to hold up the bank with a sawed-off shotgun. Unfortunately for him, he had sawed off the wrong end.

* * *

A police teletype was registering "wanted" notices and an operator at the station house read the reports into the radio microphone. This one brought conversation to a halt: "Lefty Loomis. Height: 5:9. Eyes: brown and blue. Hair: blond and dark brown. Nose: flat and bulbous. Mustache: yes and no. Marks: jagged scar on one chin." "This Loomis clown," muttered Sergeant Epstein, "sounds like he's got two heads." "That's right," nodded the operator, "he has." "Hmm," pondered Sergeant Epstein. "Not much to go on except the scar."

* * *

"Nails" Flanagan's wife turned up for the first time in months to see him on visitors' day at a federal penitentiary. "Nails," she said earnestly, "you been in this jail now for two full years and the children are starting to ask questions." "Yeah?" mumbled Nails suspiciously. "What kind of stuff do they want to know?" "Mainly," said Mrs. Flanagan, "where you stashed the 'loot."

* * *

When Ronnie Anville won his fourth straight breach of promise suit, he told reporters jubilantly, "These cases never bother me. No dame has been able to pin anything on me since I was ten months old!"

* * *

"I've got a skunk in my cellar," wailed a housewife over the phone to the police. The officer receiving the call assured her, "Nothing to get excited about. Just make a trail of breadcrumbs from the basement to the yard and wait for the skunk to follow it outside."

An hour later, the housewife was back on the phone, more frantic than ever. "I did what you told me," she announced. "Now I've got *two* skunks in my cellar."

* * *

The defendant in a big fraud case showed signs of panic on the witness stand. His high-priced lawyer, seeking to restore his confidence, told him in a stage whisper, "Take it easy, man. All you've got to do is tell the jury, in my words, exactly what happened!"

* * *

A crook high on the list of "most wanted" by the police of twenty states sneaked up the stairs of an ornate suburban mansion and headed for a cache of diamonds and pearls, when from the bedroom a shrill voice was heard:

"What do you mean, I spend too much money on clothes? That chinchilla you're always yapping about is four years old. I haven't had a new evening dress in months. Your partner's

wife spends more on herself in one week than I do in two years.
. . . Blah, blah, blah. . . ."

The crook tiptoed out of the house and rejoined his accomplice on the lawn. "It's no use," he sighed. "I can't go through with it. It's too much like robbing my own home."

* * *

The victim of a bus mishap had just collected fifty thousand dollars in damages in court, but his jubilation ended abruptly when his lawyer announced that he intended to keep 70 per cent of the sum for himself. "You're a damnable extortionist," blustered the accident victim. "Don't forget I'm the man who was involved in the accident." "Agreed," nodded the lawyer, "but it was my legal know-how and power of persuasion that won the case for you. Any imbecile can get knocked down by a bus!"

* * *

A Milwaukee judge, inspecting the state prison at Waupun, needed a shave, so took a chair in the prison barbershop. The barber lathered his face, then suddenly recognized him as he was stropping the razor. "Say, you're Judge So-and-So," he growled. "You sent me up here for twenty years!"

The judge, who never lost his presence of mind, jumped up from his chair and exclaimed, "By Jove! What a coincidence! I'm up here to get a pardon for you!"

* * *

The Detroit Athletic Club *News* printed a cartoon recently that had lawyer members chuckling. It showed a legalite about to read a will to a roomful of beady-eyed relatives. The legalite opened the session by confiding, "Before I read this will, I'd like to announce my engagement to Miss Hudson in the second row."

* * *

A recent Supreme Court ruling prompted this story from Herb Stein in California: A group of schoolchildren were kneel-

ing on the floor just before class was to begin. The teacher
walked in, and deeply concerned, asked, "What are you children doing kneeling on the floor?" Replied one of the youngsters, "We're playing marbles." "Oh, that's just dandy," said the
teacher, relieved. "I was afraid you were praying!"

MUSICIANS

M. Tippit was at one of those parties where the host made
a reluctant offspring play the violin for helpless guests. The
offspring, visibly seething, snarled, "Folks, I hereby dedicate
the piece I've selected to my former music teacher—who chick-
ened out."

*   *   *

At the conclusion of one of his most triumphant concerts before a packed house in Carnegie Hall, pianist Sergei Rachmaninoff was asked by a critic, "What sublime thoughts were
passing through your head as you sat down at the piano to
begin your concert?" Rachmaninoff answered frankly, "I was
counting the house."

*   *   *

Sir Thomas Beecham, internationally famous orchestra conductor, adamantly refused to hire female musicians. "If they're
pretty," he explained testily, "they distract my male musicians.
If they're not pretty, they distract me."

*   *   *

During composer-conductor Igor Stravinsky's first tour of
the United States, his command of the English language was
sketchy, to say the least.

One day in Milwaukee, the first violinist made the same
ghastly mistake three times at a rehearsal. Stravinsky never
ceased addressing the miscreant in the most polite terms.

Later a friend complimented him on his control. "How you

could speak so politely," he marveled, "when you obviously were seething in rage inside beats me."

"Ah," explained Stravinsky in his native tongue, "that is because I have learned only polite phrases in English. You should have heard what I was calling him under my breath in Russian!"

* * *

That eminent composer and band leader, Duke Ellington, who understandably is not displeased when disciples refer to him as "The American Bach," often quotes that same Bach in his casual conversation. The Duke once was heard to remark, speaking about piano playing, "As Bach says, if you ain't got a left hand, you ain't worth a hoot in hell."

* * *

Jascha Heifetz once spent a summer vacation in Lake Placid, in the Adirondacks. The lady in the cottage next door practiced piano regularly for an hour each morning, Heifetz or no Heifetz. What's more, she played terribly.

One day a stranger appeared at her door and said, "I'm the piano tuner." "I didn't order any piano tuner," expostulated the lady. "You didn't," agreed the piano tuner, "but Mr. Heifetz did."

* * *

Mrs. Glogauer, fat, rich, and fortyish, was about to give her first recital after years of arduous vocal lessons. The audience was large, if unenthusiastic, consisting of Mr. Glogauer's employees, who had been ordered to attend—or else.

"Oh," wailed the jittery Mrs. Glogauer, "if I only could learn what to do with my hands while I'm singing."

"Why not," suggested Mr. Glogauer wearily, "just hold them over your mouth?"

* * *

A famous opera star rests up between acts at the Met by performing Yoga exercises. "There's one person who gets a bigger kick out of this than I," he told a fellow artist, "and that's

my little boy. I heard him explaining to a friend this morning,
'It's great when Daddy stands on his head. I grab all the
money that falls out of his pockets and my dog licks his face.'"

* * *

Victor Borge once confessed to Irving Berlin, "Every time
I stop telling jokes to an audience, and sit down at the piano
to play a little Mozart, I hear a voice whispering in my ear:
'Don't play it!' the voice says, 'For heaven's sake, don't play
it!'"

"Do you recognize the voice?" asked Berlin.

"I certainly do," Borge assured him. "It's Mozart."

* * *

John Rosenfeld tells about the lady musician who was fired
in disgrace from a nationally famous orchestra. "We had a concert date in Dallas," she explained tearfully, "and I forgot my
harp."

* * *

Theme song of the Association of Nearsighted Citizens: "I've
Lost My Glasses—So I Wonder Who's Kissing Me Now."

* * *

A college student explained how he picked up a few dollars
each week working as an extra in the opera. "All I do," he

laughed, "is carry a spear—and keep my mouth shut." "But after a hard day of classes, all that extra work!" gushed an elderly lady. "How do you keep awake?" "That's the least of my worries, lady," said the student. "The fellow behind me carries a spear, too!"

* * *

According to expert Sigmund Spaeth, a tabulation of the three songs most often sung by Americans would include neither "The Star-Spangled Banner," nor "Home Sweet Home," nor "Dixie." Number One, in fact—and by a wide margin—is "Happy Birthday to You." Number Two is "For He's a Jolly Good Fellow." And Number Three is "Auld Lang Syne."

* * *

"Often a song that fails completely is given a brand-new title by its composer and publisher and then promptly scores a smash hit," notes Louis Sobol. "Make Me a Star," for instance, renamed "Blue Moon," quickly made the Hit Parade. Other temporary flops that followed a similar pattern were: "Turkish Tom Tom" changed to "Dardanella," "Smile and Show Your Dimple" renamed "Easter Parade," "If I Were on the Stage" changed to "Kiss Me Again," and "I Have No Words," republished as "Something to Remember You By."

* * *

Along about 1930, a young man named Irving Caesar wrote the lyrics for a song he hoped would make him famous. It was called "Louisville," and wasn't very good. The point of this story, however, is that Caesar persuaded a composer named J. Fred Cootes to set the words of "Louisville" to music—and Cootes' melody was very good indeed.

In fact, Cootes remembered the melody some four years later when another lyricist named Gillespie popped up with lyrics that impressed everybody in Caesar's office. The words of the new song and the melody written for "Louisville" fitted together like ham and eggs, or Scotch and soda—and the result was published just in time for the holiday season of 1934. It has sold over a million records and copies of sheet music every

year since, and promises to go on for many years more. The
song: "Santa Claus Is Coming to Town."

* * *

The audience was still applauding the first number rendered
by the Wappingdale Falls Marching and Chowder Club band
when the trombonist leaned over and asked the flute player,
"What number do we do next?" "The Washington Post March,"
answered the flute player. "Holy cow," gasped the trombonist.
"That's what I just finished playing!"

* * *

Morris Fishbein tells of a man who bought his wife a piano
for Christmas, but by Valentine's Day had persuaded her to
switch to a clarinet. "How come?" asked a friend. "Well," was
the explanation, "when she's playing the clarinet, she can't
sing."

* * *

After Carl Sandburg had played his guitar for a TV show
recently, the director apologized for all the sneezing and
coughing that had been done by the audience. "They didn't
do it on purpose," said Sandburg indulgently. "They're like
the little boy who sneezed in church, and was reprimanded
by his mother. The boy explained, 'I didn't sneeze the sneeze,
mama; the sneeze sneezed me.'"

* * *

A draftee from Kansas was sent to Honolulu and was en-
raptured by the supple hula dancers he encountered there. He
wrote to his father, "I've got to tell you, Dad, that those girls
sure know to shake hay while the son pines!"

* * *

In his amusing autobiography, *What Time's the Next Swan?*
Walter Slezak tells how his father, the famous opera star Leo
Slezak, was put on a strict diet when his weight became alarming. For a week he howled that he was being starved, then
suddenly began accepting his meager fare with amazing seren-
ity. His dog betrayed him by taking a stand at Slezak's desk,

holding a rigid point, and barking like mad. Mrs. Slezak investigated and found inside the desk a two-foot-long Hungarian salami.

For showing up his master, the dog was renamed Judas Iscariot.

* * *

Famous novelist William Styron has a four-year-old daughter who fancies herself as a connoisseur of fine music. She was listening intently to Leonard Bernstein leading his orchestra on TV one morning when her father inquired, "Do you know what they're playing?" The daughter answered haughtily, "I'm not sure, but I suspect it's one of those symphonies by Boat-Haven."

* * *

Karl Haas, Director of Fine Arts at Station WJR, Detroit, has a rare sense of humor. Asked to prepare a program to entertain sick students at Wayne University, he labeled the concert, "Music for Ill Literates." A morning TV program of rock 'n' roll selections he listed as "Music to Steal Hubcaps By."

* * *

Teachers as well as parents have their problems with teenagers. Harold Dunn, for instance, who teaches music in Jefferson City, Missouri, submits these five excerpts from classroom essays:

Joseph Haydn was born in 1732, and soon became the father of classical music. Later, at the age of twenty-eight, he got married. Haydn had a lot of will power. He died in 1809 and is still dead.

Bach was the most famous composer in the world and so was Handel. Handel was half German, half English, and half Alsatian. He was rather large.

Chopin had many fast friends. Among the fastest was Miss Sand.

Paganini was a famous fiddler. He fiddled with many of the greatest singers in Europe.

Requiems are usually played for sad occasions like funerals

and marriages. Fugues are also popular. The most popular fugue was the one between the Hatfields and the McCoys.

* * *

Jack Benny recalls a day in his youth when he was practicing on his violin in old Waukegan, Illinois. A dog stood outside the window howling his head off. Benny's father stuck his head inside the door and implored, "For Pete's sake, Jack, play something that dog doesn't know!"

* * *

How long will the Beatle craze last? The Beatles themselves know how quickly idols of the teen-agers can topple, but they are not too concerned. "When it's over and done with," reflected Ringo Beatle unemotionally, "I imagine we'll have nothing to do but sit on the deck of our yacht—and sulk."

* * *

At Carnegie Hall, in New York, a famous pianist took a final bow, then retired moodily to his dressing room, barring old friends and autograph hunters. He had given a slipshod performance and knew it. "Cheer up," counseled his manager. "We all have our off days. You had one coming to you."

The pianist finally was consoled, and he and his manager went to a nearby Russian tea room for refreshments. There one of the pianist's bitterest rivals appeared suddenly and cried, "Dear boy! You were magnificent tonight! You outdid yourself."

The pianist paled visibly and whispered to his manager, "Damnation! Was I *that* awful?"

* * *

Art Buchwald tells of the day an ambitious and aggressive mother conned the great pianist, Artur Rubinstein, into listening to her ten-year-old son murder a nocturne by Chopin. At the conclusion of the massacre, Rubinstein announced, "Madam, that is undoubtedly the worst piano playing I ever heard." Whereupon the mother nodded happily and told her son, "You see, stupid? Now will you give up those expensive piano lessons and try out for the Little League baseball team?"

PSYCHOANALYSTS

At the conclusion of a first—and most painful—session with a brand new patient, a psychoanalyst cleared his throat and murmured, "Now about weekly bills and where they're to be sent. . . ." "Ah," interrupted the patient. "I see you are concerned about my credit rating. Don't you worry about a thing, Doctor. You're going to get every penny I ever owe you or my name isn't Napoleon Bonaparte!"

* * *

Another glassy-eyed character who was convinced he was Napoleon burst into an analyst's study, thrust his hand inside his vest, and announced, "It isn't myself I've come to see you about, Doctor. It's my wife Josephine. She thinks she's Mrs. Margolies!"

* * *

"You've got to straighten out my husband," said a wife to a Park Avenue psychiatrist. "He thinks he's a jet plane." "Bring him here Thursday at two," suggested the psychiatrist. "That time is impossible," said the wife. "He's got to appear in court that afternoon—for flying low over Flatbush."

* * *

A new patient, signing up for treatment, confided to a psychiatrist, "I'd better tell you before we begin that I suffer from marked suicidal tendencies." "Very interesting," nodded the psychiatrist. "Under the circumstances, I'm sure you won't mind paying me in advance."

* * *

Heard about the sheep who simply couldn't get to sleep at night? In despair, he sought a psychiatrist, and told him, "You simply have to find a way for me to fall asleep nights—and please, Doctor, NO WISECRACKS."

* * *

A new patient from a publishing house informed his analyst, "I have just finished writing a play called *The Taming of the Shrew*." "My dear fellow," sympathized the analyst, "*The Taming of the Shrew* was written by William Shakespeare." "That's a coincidence," mused the patient. "They told me the same thing when I wrote *Hamlet*."

* * *

Paul Pearlman relays a story about a weirdie who wandered into a psychiatrist's office and stuffed tobacco into his left ear. "Obviously you need me," said the doctor. "I sure do," agreed the man. "Got a match?"

* * *

A proud but disturbed gentleman who had convinced himself he was General Robert E. Lee was brought by relatives to a famous New Orleans brain specialist. After a year, however, the specialist had to admit he could provide no cure. He gave up the case and submitted his bill. "General Lee" paid it promptly—in Confederate money!

* * *

Molly Berg has a neighbor whose husband became convinced he was a cannibal. The distressed wife finally persuaded him to visit a psychiatrist. Molly met him on the way home. "Nu?" she inquired, "What's the fancy psychiatrist like?" "Delicious," beamed the husband.

* * *

Then there's the worried lady who called her doctor to report, "My husband has suddenly gone off his rocker. He seems to think he's George Washington."

"When can I see him?" asked the doctor.

"Just take a look out of your window," said the lady. "He's out in your backyard chopping down your cherry tree."

* * *

"Now," said a head doctor to his new patient, "we're going to find out just what makes you tick."

"That won't be enough," mourned the patient. "I also want to know what makes me chime every quarter of an hour."

* * *

A desperate man sought an analyst. "I've developed a phobia," he reported, "that is ruining my business. Crowds make me violently ill." "What's your business?" asked the analyst. The patient answered, "I'm a pickpocket."

* * *

"My poor husband," moaned a woman to the town's leading psychoanalyst. "He's convinced he's a parking meter." The analyst regarded the silent, woebegone fellow holding the wife's hand, and asked, "Why doesn't he say something for himself? Can't he talk?" The wife said, "How can he—with all those dimes and nickels in his mouth?"

13. *The Printed Word*

AUTHORS

What must be one of the most cynical remarks ever made—as well as a frightening insight into the mental attitude of a world-famous author—was a comment of Somerset Maugham. Said Maugham acidulously, "It is not enough that a writer succeed: his friends must also fail!"

* * *

Other authors on authors:

"I don't understand how two men can write a book together. To me that's like three people getting together to have a baby."
—Evelyn Waugh.

"No man but a blockhead ever wrote except for money."
—Samuel Johnson.

"An author is a fool who, not content with having bored those who have lived with him, insists on boring future generations."
—Montesquieu.

"The good writing of any age has always been the product of someone's neurosis. We'd have a mighty dull literature if all the writers who came along were a bunch of happy chuckleheads."—William Styron.

* * *

The author of two fantastic best sellers remarked at a literary cocktail party, "I went over to the Cannes Festival on the *United States* and came back on the *Queen Elizabeth*." From the rear came the audible whisper, "Boat-dropper!"

* * *

The wife of one of America's most distinguished authors sued him for divorce recently, claiming that she could no longer stand his clomping around the house day after day. "I married him," she explained, "for better or for worse—*not* for lunch."

* * *

It is not unusual for an author to disdain his publishers, but William Makepeace Thackeray was more vociferous on the subject than most—possibly because his masterpiece, *Vanity Fair*, had been turned down by eighteen publishers before one was found willing to take a chance on it. Thackeray found himself, with a friend, in the drawing room of a publisher's home, awaiting the publisher, one morning. The carpet in the room was of a gaudy design of red and white. When the publisher appeared, Thackeray announced, "We have been admiring your carpet, sir. It is most appropriate! You wade in the blood and brains of authors!"

* * *

In a fascinating book called *The Fine Art of Literary Mayhem*, Myrick Land describes a variety of bitter feuds and vendettas in which world-famous authors climbed down from their ivory towers and exchanged insults that left everybody concerned gasping for breath.

The great historian, Thomas Carlyle, for instance, characterized the poet Algernon Swinburne as "sitting in a sewer and adding to it," and dismissed none other than Ralph Waldo Emerson as a "hoary-headed and toothless baboon." Henry James, rallying to Emerson's defense, deprecated Carlyle as "that same old sausage, fizzing and sputtering in his own grease." Most vitriolic of all was George Bernard Shaw, ready always to take on all comers. He once infuriated Henry Arthur Jones, reigning London playwright of his day, with such a string of insults that Jones counterattacked Shaw in a public letter beginning, "The Nag Sedition was your mother and Perversity begot you; Mischief was your midwife, and Misrule your nurse!"

* * *

Who says great writers and thinkers are undependable? Viscount Hailsham recalls the morning philosopher Immanuel Kant suddenly remembered he had proposed marriage to a lovely neighbor—and been accepted. He hastily donned his best clothes and rushed over to his prospective bride's home—where he found to his intense disappointment she had left town—some twenty years before.

* * *

From the moment Sherlock Holmes became a byword in England, his creator, Arthur Conan Doyle, was pestered by people of all kinds demanding solutions of problems that perplexed them. A lady who sat next to Doyle at a large dinner, for instance, annoyed him greatly. "Mr. Doyle," she asked so loudly that all other conversation at the table ceased, "there has disappeared from the inside of my country home within a single week one broom, one box of golf balls, a left riding boot, a dictionary, and six tin plates. What would Sherlock Holmes do in a spot like that?" "Very simple," snapped Conan Doyle.

"Sherlock Holmes would tell you that you keep a goat in your home."

* * *

Edith Wharton, author of such great books as *Ethan Frome* and *The Age of Innocence*, was no heroine to her hoity-toity relatives, who considered writing books no fit occupation for a young lady of quality. One uncle up in Newport, in fact, admitted that he rated Miss Wharton slightly more erratic than another unfortunate relative who "spent his last years sitting on a marble shelf in the happy illusion that he was a bust of Napoleon."

* * *

In the days when everybody was reading *Little Women*, Bronson Alcott, high-living and work-disdaining father of authoress Louisa May, regularly dropped into the offices of her publisher in Boston, Little, Brown and Company, in search of cash. "Just charge it against Louisa's royalties," he would suggest grandly. Finally, his daughter had to call a halt; thereafter he was given cash only when he could produce a written authorization from her.

Today, framed at Little, Brown is one of Miss Alcott's notes, reading "Please give my pa $50." Pa had thoughtfully crossed out the "$50" and made it read "$100." Nobody knows whether or not he got away with it.

* * *

Mark Twain was something of a practical joker. A seedy old acquaintance met him at the Hartford railroad station one morning and begged, "Help me once more. Treat me to a ticket to New York." "I'm pretty low on funds myself right now," answered Twain, "but I'll tell you what I'll do. You stow away under my seat and I'll hide you with my legs."

The acquaintance agreed. When the train pulled in, he scrambled under Twain's seat. When the conductor came around, Twain presented two tickets. "The second one," he explained loudly, "is for my friend cramped up under my seat here. He's a bit on the eccentric side—and this is the way he likes to ride."

* * *

When the great Irish poet and dramatist, William Butler Yeats, won the Nobel Prize in 1923, a group of his admirers in Dublin insisted upon giving a banquet in his honor. Yeats, a very shy, introspective man, writhed with embarrassment as speaker after speaker sang his praises. He sank lower and lower in his chair on the dais, but was suddenly revived when the chairman presented him with a check for twenty-five hundred pounds—over ten thousand dollars in those days—the gift of several wealthy gentlemen present. Yeats rose to his feet, stared at the check for a moment, then startled his audience by remarking, "Twenty-five hundred pounds, eh? I must say that's damn little for all the lies I've had to listen to this evening!"

* * *

Hesketh Pearson recalls an evening he spent with the George Bernard Shaws. While G.B.S. told one story after another, Mrs. Shaw sat silently doing needlepoint. "What are you working on so diligently?" whispered Pearson to Mrs. Shaw. "What difference does it make?" she whispered back. "It's just that I've heard these stories of his five hundred times, and if I didn't do something with my hands, I'D CHOKE HIM!"

* * *

Minneapolis sage "Mox" Lindquist met an old friend who had taken up story writing as a career. "Have you sold anything yet?" asked Mox. "Yes," nodded his friend. "My dress suit, some furniture, and my watch."

* * *

A distinguished author who summers in Provincetown received a note there from a schoolgirl which read, "I have chosen you as my favorite author. Please write me immediately in not less than three hundred words and tell me why."

* * *

Writers are famous procrastinators, and seize on any kind of excuse to put off getting down to work.

Novelist Graham Greene found a brand new way of procrastinating. A friend visited him at his English country estate and reported, "Every day Graham would disappear mysteriously for hours from the house. When I finally asked what he was up to, he explained that he could not write another word until a certain combination of numbers—987—appeared to him by accident. He was spending hours by the roadside waiting for those numbers to pass on a license plate.

"Well, it's a poor country road, and there are not many motor cars. So Graham didn't write a single word for the entire week."

* * *

A distinguished novelist was complaining at the Overseas Press Club one evening that his wife had been driving him batty for ten years and more. "Why don't you give her the air?" asked a sympathizer. "I can't," mourned the novelist. "She's the only typist I know who can read my damn handwriting."

*   *   *

With censorship battles raging throughout the land, it might be interesting to read what two famous writers had to say on the subject.

Noted George Bernard Shaw: "All censorships exist to prevent anyone from challenging current conceptions and existing institutions. All progress is initiated by challenging current conceptions, and executed by supplanting existing institutions. Consequently, the first condition of progress is the removal of censorships."

And Eugene O'Neill noted: "Censorship of anything, at any time, in any place, on whatever pretense, has always been and always will be the last cowardly resort of the boob and the bigot."

*   *   *

One of Noel Coward's Jamaica acquaintances was bemoaning the fact that the ranks of his old friends were being depleted at an alarmingly accelerated rate. "Two funerals this week alone," he sighed. Coward assured him grimly, "Personally, I'm delighted now if they last through lunch!"

*   *   *

Bill Saroyan, of *Daring Young Man on the Flying Trapeze*
fame, returned one day in triumph after he had made a fortune, to the San Francisco grocery store where he had clerked
briefly in his youth. Everybody crowded around to hear the
famous man give his views on life and love. Later the proprietor of the grocery story was asked, "What was the most important thing Saroyan said?" The proprietor answered testily, "He
didn't say *anything* important. All he did was eat up my
fruit."

*   *   *

Honor Tracy, witty and brilliant Irish author of *The Straight
and Narrow Path*, was not too pleased with the looks of the
English edition of her succeeding effort. She sent the London
publisher a copy of the ever-so-much handsomer American
edition of the book with a note reading, "As the cock said to
the hens when he showed them an ostrich egg, 'I am not
disparaging; I am not criticizing. I merely bring to your attention what is being done elsewhere.'"

*   *   *

Frank Sullivan, beloved sage of Saratoga, consented to an
interview recently, what with the local racetrack closed for the
season and a birthday coming up. "What do you think of
American women?" began the interviewer. "They should be
torn down," said Mr. S. briskly, then added, "Oh, pardon me,
that's my answer to what do you think of the newfangled New
York skyscrapers. As for American women, I'm not sure there
are any nowadays. Everybody wears pants and how is a fellow
with astigmatism and myopia going to tell which are women
and which are men?"

Mr. Sullivan also commented on the state of American
belles-lettres. "It's in a state of flux," he opined. "This chap
Katherine Anne Porter seems a good bet, and so does this
other chap, Walt Whitman. As for the Russians," he concluded,
in no uncertain terms, "they'll never amount to anything until
they get rid of the Czar."

* * *

Shortly before his death, William Faulkner, one of America's greatest authors, told me that editor Albert Erskine was the finest literary craftsman whom he ever had met. "When he approves a manuscript of mine," said Faulkner, "I know it's ready for the printer."

"Coming from you," I said, "that is a great, great compliment. Have you told that to Erskine? I know how delighted he would be."

"No, I haven't," admitted Faulkner with a slow smile. "In my book, when a race horse is running good, Bennett, you don't stop him to feed him a piece of sugar!"

* * *

Faulkner enjoyed the reputation for being a prodigious imbiber of bourbon whiskey, but his brother John reveals that many of his most celebrated binges were just playacting. He would get word to his family in Oxford, Mississippi, that somebody must come and fetch him. The "somebody" almost always was his mother, a gallant, indomitable wisp of a woman who knew her son Bill merely wanted to be fussed over.

Once she tricked Faulkner by serving him iced tea with just a dash of whiskey to lull him. When he stammered that he was sozzled, and couldn't get out of bed, she told him calmly he had been drinking tea for ten hours straight. The sheepish Mr. Faulkner rose silently and trudged off to work.

* * *

A young novelist began his speech at a Book and Author luncheon by quoting from a letter he had recently received: "You are the finest young writer in America today. You combine the skills of O'Hara, Faulkner, Hemingway, and Michener. Furthermore, you are the handsomest man I've ever encountered."

The audience was obviously taken aback by the young novelist's conceit—until he added, "Incidentally, the letter is signed 'Mother.'"

* * *

Jean Kerr, wife of drama critic Walter Kerr, notes that when a collection of her old magazine articles was published in book form under the title of *Please Don't Eat the Daisies*—and promptly zoomed to the top of the best-seller lists—her mother wrote to her saying, "Darling, isn't it marvelous the way those old pieces of yours finally came to the surface like a dead body!"

* * *

Poet John Ciardi cherishes this note received from a young admirer, whose name he thoughtfully refuses to disclose: "Dear Mr. Ciardi: I think your new book of poems for children is very funny. I read it in church. I thought it was much better than the sermon. P.S. Please don't tell my daddy about the sermon because he's the minister."

* * *

Have you heard about the astronaut who buttonholed a famous novelist at a cocktail party and told him, "I read your new book while I was in orbit last week. *Couldn't put it down!*"

A PLEA FOR THE UNKNOWN WRITER

Like the Broadway theatre, the book business today is suffering from a rash of "me-too-ism" that has the country in its grip. Every visitor to New York wants to see the same few smash-hit shows and spurns the broker who tries to sell him tickets for a play that his neighbor has not boasted of seeing when *he* visited the Big City. By the same token, people are buying books today not because they have a particular message, but because their neighbors are reading them or at least displaying them on their library tables—or because they are Number One, Two, or Three on national best seller lists.

This insistence of the American public to read and see what everybody else is reading and seeing has proved a bonanza, of course, for the few fortunate authors of the smash hits and best sellers, but what about the authors—just as deserving and

often more so—whose plays and books have not hit that magic circle? More important still, what about the authors who are totally unknown and have just seen their very first novels appear in print? If nobody will give these newcomers a hearing, how are they ever going to get started on the road to success?

I cannot emphasize the difficulty a publisher encounters today in getting a hearing for a new writer. There are exceptions to the rule, of course; maybe once or twice a year an unknown hits the jackpot, but for every *To Kill a Mockingbird, Goodbye, Columbus,* and *Catch 22,* there are at least a hundred extremely good first novels that not only sell fewer than two thousand copies, but that are never given as much as a one-paragraph review in leading literary journals and book sections. Booksellers do not even want to stock a couple of copies of these first novels, despite the fact that they have full return privilege from the publisher. How often have I heard them say, "First, you create a demand for the book and then I'll order copies. Meanwhile, I don't want to clutter up the shop with books nobody has ever heard of."

It's disheartening to tot up the number of the shining literary American greats of the past generation who have disappeared from the scene in recent years. Just think of the stars who have died in that brief span: Theodore Dreiser, Thomas Wolfe,

Sinclair Lewis, Willa Cather, Edna St. Vincent Millay, and within the past three years Ernest Hemingway, James Thurber, and William Faulkner. In the theatre, we have lost Eugene O'Neill, Robert Sherwood, Moss Hart, and George S. Kaufman. This is but a partial list. How are we going to develop replacements for these great stars if we don't encourage our promising newcomers?

This, then, is an urgent plea to every reader of this brief piece: the next time you go to a bookstore in search of something to give a sick friend or to take for yourself on a vacation, let a clerk whom you trust persuade you to buy a book by somebody who has never had anything published before. Then, if you like what you have read, beat the drum for your discovery. Tell people about it. Help, possibly, to launch another Hemingway or Faulkner on the road to fame!

BOOKS

Richard Armour, wise to the ways of the literary hucksters, notes:

> The publisher riffles the lukewarm review
> To find him a bookselling blurb
> Consisting of adjectives three or two
> To one paltry noun or verb
> Though many the words of another stripe,
> A flattering few he frisks.
> What he wants, he prints in a bold, black type,
> What he doesn't, he asterisks.

* * *

Two venerable gentlemen met on the veranda of a New England inn one summer's day in the eighties. One of them spiced his conversation with so many elaborate quotations that the other grew curious and interrupted with, "What did you say your name was, my good sir?" "Bartlett," was the answer. "John Bartlett."

* * *

An Eskimo sat in his igloo, reading a Shirley Temple Fairy Tale collection to his little boy. "Little Jack Horner sat in a corner," began the father, when the son interrupted him to inquire, "Daddy, what's a corner?"

* * *

Sidney Harris, acidulous Chicago critic, won the undying enmity of a fat, prolific lady novelist with a one-sentence review of her newest potboiler. "Miss Black's new book," noted Harris, "is underwhelming."

* * *

The day after the late Lloyd Morris's *Postscript to Yesterday* was published, the noted critic, Orville Prescott, gave it a glowing review, and Morris's agent rushed over to read it to him. "Prescott says the book obviously was written by a great gentleman of leisure." At that moment, Morris, having parted company with an incompetent servant the day before, was on his hands and knees scrubbing the kitchen floor.

* * *

An ambitious book salesman was endeavoring to sell a Los Angeles retailer a hundred copies of a handsome new gift edition of Elizabeth Barrett Browning's *Sonnets from the Portuguese*. The retailer snorted, "What do I want an item like that for? There aren't a hundred Portuguese in this whole neighborhood!"

* * *

In Bermuda, a formidable lady spent an hour poring over the stock of a book shop near the Salt Kettle House. After rejecting numerous suggestions, she finally decided, "Oh well, I'll take this Ian Fleming paperback." The clerk gave her a startled look, and then said gently, "But, madam, this is the book you brought in with you."

* * *

The type in some of the mammoth new paperbacks gets smaller and smaller and one anguished reader has struck back at his tormentors.

"I propose," he writes, "that these typographical monstrosities henceforth carry this legend on the last page:

'A NOTE ON THE TYPE IN WHICH THIS BOOK WAS SET.

The type in which this book was set is known, quite unfavorably, as one-half point Myopia, and was designed in 1622 by that noted sadist, Feodor Astigmatism. It bids fair to become one of the most heartily disliked faces this side of Fidel Castro. It is perfect for engraving the complete text of *The Brothers Karamazov* on the head of a pin.'"

❋ ❋ ❋

Authors of books intended to make readers laugh spend more time on dedications than do their more serious confreres. Here's the dedication Carl Winston came up with for his titillating *How to Turn a Million into a Shoestring*: "I should be remiss, indeed, if I failed to acknowledge my indebtedness to the People's Bank of Bridgeport, the Connecticut Light and Power Co., the New England Telephone Co., Sears Roebuck, Casey Fuel, the West Redding Market, the Internal Revenue Department, and another creditor whose name is Morris H. Legion. The total is $17,886.05. Hi, Fellows!"

❋ ❋ ❋

A few other inspired book dedications:

Inez McEwen dedicated her *So This Is Ranching* to "My infant grandson, the only gent on whom I've been able to pin anything."

Mark Hellinger dedicated one of his volumes to the bargain basement of a department store, for designing "underwear that doesn't bind while seated at a typewriter."

Vice President Tom Marshall dedicated his memoirs to "President Woodrow Wilson, from his only Vice."

Franklin P. Adams inscribed one volume of verse to his

"Loving wife, but for whose constant interruptions, this book would have been finished six months earlier."

* * *

Officials in New York's Public Library receive a lot of strange requests in the course of their work, but this one from a recent arrival from Tokyo just about takes the cake:

"Sir or Lady: To look for of see to make me a dictionary of thirty thousand words in double from Japanese to English. If no in your book warehouse, I have great need for he now, so interest another warehouse deposit please and see with price how to cost. If no is nowhere twenty five thousandth you give and to you send money in check of bench. Inrespectfully yours . . ."

* * *

A salesman stepped gingerly into a publisher's office and asked the receptionist, "Is His Nibs in a good mood this morning?" "I never saw him in a good mood," admitted the receptionist. "I've only been here three years."

* * *

"If you had occasion," asks Vincent Starrett, "to send a letter to the following characters of history and legend, what addresses would you write on the envelopes? 1. Sherlock Holmes; 2. Solomon Levi; 3. Dr. Manette; 4. Alice's Right Foot, Esq.? Here are the answers: 1. 221-B Baker Street, London; 2. 149 Salem Street, New Haven; 3. 105 North Tower, Bastille, Paris; 4. Hearthrug, near the Fender, with Alice's Love."

* * *

Critic J. Donald Adams, in an idle hour, jotted down the names of ten world-famous books whose authors are virtually unknown today. How many of them do you think you can recall?

Here are the books: 1. *The Swiss Family Robinson;* 2. *Quo Vadis?;* 3. *Black Beauty;* 4. *Baron Munchausen;* 5. *Lorna Doone;* 6. *The Four Horsemen of the Apocalypse;* 7. *East*

Lynne; 8. *Elsie Dinsmore;* 9. *The Covered Wagon;* 10. *Ben Hur.*

The authors: 1. Johann David Wyss; 2. Henryk Sienkiewicz; 3. Anna Sewell; 4. Rudolf Erich Raspe; 5. Richard D. Blackmore; 6. Vicente Blasco Ibáñez; 7. Mrs. Henry Wood; 8. Martha Finley; 9. Emerson Hough; 10. Lew Wallace.

* * *

George Hecht of the Doubleday book shops thought he had heard about everything until a rather brassy young lady sashayed into the Fifty-second Street branch and announced, "I'm looking for a good mystery story to read this evening while waiting to jump out of a birthday cake."

* * *

A distinguished English scholar named George Ordish is working on a history of the Incas, and he went all the way to the Vatican Library in Rome for a look at a book he heard would provide special illumination on the subject. Unfortunately for Mr. Ordish, the head librarian in the Vatican reported that the volume wanted was missing. "Yes, it's too bad," sighed the librarian. "Our records show that the book you wanted to examine has been missing since 1635!"

* * *

One hears a great deal of talk these days about so-called "pornographic" literature, but who is to be the judge of what books really deserve banning on that score?

D. H. Lawrence, observes critic John Hutchens, considered Charlotte Brontë's *Jane Eyre* pornographic, though it is now recommended to high school students. On the other hand, Lawrence cried "Unfair" when his own *Lady Chatterley's Lover* was banned. When Thackeray edited the *Cornhill Magazine,* he rejected a manuscript by Elizabeth Barrett Browning. Why? It contained the word "harlot"! Pornography's all-time best seller, *Fanny Hill,* hasn't one word your maiden Aunt Emma could blush at. On the other hand, Chaucer's *Canterbury Tales* has dozens of them.

In other words, as George S. Kaufman once remarked in a review of ancient Asian wars, "One man's Mede is another man's Persian."

* * *

Early in 1936, the late Wendell Willkie, then President of the Commonwealth and Southern Corporation, attended a convention in Atlanta, Georgia. One of the delegates told him, "Remember meeting my wife the last time you were here? Well, she's written a novel, and a publisher has accepted it. If it sells enough to earn five thousand dollars, we are going to buy a new house." "Good for her," enthused Mr. Willkie. "Although I never have done anything like this before, I'm going to write a letter over my signature to every stockholder urging him to buy a copy of your wife's book."

He was true to his word, and for years thereafter laughingly demanded some of the credit for getting the book off to a rousing start. The name of the book was *Gone with the Wind*.

*   *   *

Norman Kline is one literary light who believes firmly that the title of a book can mean the difference between a rousing best seller and a dismal failure. What might have been the fate, he asks, of seven all-time favorites, had they been named: 1. *Moby Richard;* 2. *This Side of Paramus;* 3. *Farewell to Feet;* 4. *Happiness Is a Hot Dog;* 5. *Gulliver's Trips;* 6. *Treasure Peninsula;* and 7. *Canoe of Fools?*

*   *   *

A notorious gangster decided to give his mother a leatherbound Bible for a birthday gift, but felt a bit conspicuous in the shop where he bought it. He handed the Bible to the clerk rather surreptitiously and asked, "Will you please put this in a plain wrapper?"

*   *   *

Dorothy Parker ended one of her scathing book reviews with a characteristic flourish. "I suppose," she conceded, "that this is another of those young writers who is worth watching. Not reading; just watching."

*   *   *

In Oshkosh, a cagey bookseller put two copies of *Rabbit Raising for Profit* on his shelf one evening, found six there the next morning.

* * *

When the late Carolyn Wells earned enough money to buy some long-wanted books for her library, she pasted this plate in every volume: "They borrow books; they will not buy; they have no ethics or religions. I wish some kind Burbankian guy would cross my books with homing pigeons."

* * *

Jack Fuller discovered a rare two-volume edition of the Essays of Montaigne that evidently never had been opened, since the pages were still unsliced. "Oh, yes," nodded the bookseller, "this is the uncuttest kind of all."

* * *

Mrs. Healy was the kind of reader who couldn't resist sneaking a look at the ending of a book before she was halfway through it. One day she began reading the dictionary, and true to form, turned to the last page before she got down to the last of the words beginning "*ad.*" "Hah," she exclaimed triumphantly. "Just as I thought. The *zebra* did it!"

MAGAZINES

A would-be fiction writer in Wyoming submitted a story some time ago to the editor of a big magazine. The editor read the story with some interest, then wrote the man who had submitted it, "I thought the story you sent us was excellent. I always have thought so. Unfortunately, I promised Bret Harte that I would only publish 'The Luck of Roaring Camp' under his own name." The editor figured that would shut up the plagiarist once and for all—but he was wrong. Back from him came another letter to the editor, reading, "You were a darn fool ever to have made him such a promise!"

* * *

A brilliant young editor on a big national magazine received steady promotions and salary increases for years, and seemed headed inevitably for the post of editor-in-chief. Then, unaccountably, he fell out of favor with the capricious owner and was banished to a minor post abroad. In his indignant wire of resignation to the owner, he demanded, "Why did you keep me on tiptoe so long if you weren't going to kiss me?"

* * *

This letter is framed and hung on the wall behind the desk of Herbert Mayes, brilliant Pooh-Bah of *McCall's:* "SIR: My wife was about to divorce me until she read your touching article about the evils of a broken home. Now she says she is going to stick to me through thick and thin. Please cancel my subscription."

* * *

Harold Ross, founder of *The New Yorker* Magazine, received a letter one morning from a famous short story writer. Engraved on the letterhead were not only the author's name and address but laudatory quotes from summaries of the writer's work.

Ross stewed about this for a week, then had some letterheads of his own printed just so he could answer the famous short story writer in similar style. Ross had *his* name and address engraved on each sheet, plus these two quoted tributes to himself: 1. "A splendid fellow"—John Wilkes Booth; 2. "Among those present was Harold Ross"—Account of a murder trial in the New York *Journal.*

* * *

One of the probably apocryphal stories concerning a running feud between Editor Ross and his star but temperamental contributor, Alexander Woollcott, concerns the time Woollcott turned in a "Shouts and Murmurs" column for *The New Yorker* a little too dripping with schmaltz and purple prose. Ross sent it back to Mr. W. with this note crayoned across the margin: "What you need, Woollcott, is a good, stiff ride on the subway in the rush hour."

＊ ＊ ＊

Cruelest blow dealt a doughty magazine editor came from a mere wisp of a girl—a very pretty one, too—who submitted a short story in longhand. "Your story's first-rate and I mean to buy it," the editor told her cheerily, "but we had the devil's own time deciphering your handwriting. Why didn't you type the story?" "Type it?" jeered the girl. "Do you think I'd waste my time writing stories if I knew how to type?"

＊ ＊ ＊

The editor of a brand-new digest magazine wired a famous author in Switzerland offering him five thousand dollars for a "definitive article on the significance of the idealistic split between the Soviet and Red China." The writer accepted the assignment. "Fine! Fine! Go to it," enthused the editor, "but please remember to confine your article to fifteen words."

＊ ＊ ＊

A woman submitted a torrid love story to a popular magazine and awaited word in vain from the editor for several weeks. Finally she wired, "Please report on my story immediately as I have other irons in the fire." An answering wire—collect—read, "We have considered your story and advise you to put it with the other irons."

NEWSPAPERS

In the middle 1830's, Richard O'Connor points out, there were fifteen daily newspapers circulating on the streets of New York—as opposed to six in 1965. But those papers of the 1830's had little to offer their readers in the way of news or features. A murder was dismissed in a few lines if it was mentioned at all. Court actions, misbehavior by socialites or celebrities, and business misfortunes were absolutely taboo. One man changed all this. James Gordon Bennett, whose irreverent

New York *Herald* was introduced on May 6, 1835, soon set a new pattern that was the direct forerunner of the kind of newspaper we're accustomed to reading today.

Before they had to emulate Bennett to escape bankruptcy, however, his competitors labeled him "an obscene vagabond," "a leprous slanderer," "a profligate wretch," "a pestilential scoundrel," and "a vile nuisance." They capitulated when the *Herald's* circulation soared to fifty-one thousand—against thirty-six thousand for his three principal rivals combined!

❊ ❊ ❊

In his youth, James Gordon Bennett was a reckless gadabout. His wild driving of a four-horse tally-ho once caused a crash in which one of his loveliest companions, Miss Jennie Jerome, was injured. Fortunately, she recovered—and went on to marry Lord Randolph Churchill. One of her sons was Winston Churchill.

Bennett was as vain as he was capricious. He demanded personal credit for every triumph earned by his staff; when any employee was accorded public recognition on his own, Bennett sacked him. One day Bennett demanded by cable that a list be given him of all the men on the *Herald* staff the managing editor considered indispensable. A list of his fourteen best men was promptly supplied. Bennett immediately fired every one of them! He told his secretary, "I will have no indispensable men in my employ."

Stupidity of this sort left Bennett and his *Herald* an easy victim when newspaper giants like Hearst and Pulitzer appeared upon the New York scene.

❊ ❊ ❊

This clipping from what he claims is a leading New Hampshire newspaper has been turned up by an eager young Harvard upperclassman: "Jared Hemp, one of the oldest residents of Pewter County, N.H., celebrated his ninety-seventh birthday at his home yesterday. When interviewed, Mr. Hemp was winding his watch. 'Yes, I still wind my own watch,' he said with a twinkle in his eye. 'I attribute my virile old age to my constant use since I was a boy of licorice lozenges and to my never wearing a collar. This gave me adequate saliva and health-improving neck-play.' Mr. Hemp entered the business of making lasts at the age of eleven and has lasted ever since. He has fourteen children, all of whom are in jail."

* * *

Damon Runyon landed his first newspaper job in Denver, Colorado. He waited in the anteroom of the city editor while an office boy announced his presence. The office boy reappeared and said, "The boss wants you to send in a card."

Runyon had no card—nor did he ever have one after he became famous—but he did have a pack of playing cards in his back pocket. He carefully extracted the ace of spades and told the office boy, "Give him this!" The city editor not only hired him, but treated him to lunch.

* * *

Lester Markel, for many years the brilliant but crusty editor of the Sunday Magazine section of a big newspaper, often made contributors rewrite an article several times before he blessed it with his O.K. He admitted at a staff conference, "We once asked England's great economist, Barbara Ward, to rewrite a piece five times." "Right," chimed in Markel's assistant, "and you printed all five versions."

✿ ✿ ✿

One of the reasons Bob Considine has more friends than almost anybody else in the newspaper business: he was overheard explaining to a first-time visitor at his apartment: "Millie and I have four children, two of whom we adopted. I forget which two."

A Few Classified Ads Culled from Small-Town Dailies and Weeklies . . .

1. "Will the mother whose little boy laid his half-sucked lollipop on a mahogany end table please come in again? She can have the end table for exactly one dollar, with the lollipop still intact."

2. "Attractive kitten seeks position purring in a nice little girl's lap. Will also do light mouse work."

3. "For sale: diamonds: $3; microscopes: $2.75."

4. "Will the party who picked up the black cocker spaniel puppy Friday on the boardwalk either return him or come back and get the heartbroken four-year-old boy he belongs to?"

5. "Send for a box of our homemade soap. It doesn't lather. It doesn't float. It contains no secret ingredients. It is designed solely to keep you company in the tub."

6. "Wanted: smart young lady to act as deceptionist." . . .

7. "For sale: 38-foot cruiser. A beauty equipped with two bailing pumps. May be seen by appointment. Bring diving helmet."

8. "Will the lady who saved $90 on electric washer I advertised in last week's *Gazette* please get in touch with me? It was the drier my wife wanted to sell."

9. "For sale: modern house with 4 bedrooms, 3 baths and rumpus room in cellar. Extra attraction: the family next door is building a swimming pool."

10. This plaintive classified ad was inserted in a Missouri gazette by the minister of a Presbyterian church: "Wanted! Men, women and children to sit in slightly used pews on Sunday morning."

* * *

A gentleman's umbrella was pilfered at a town meeting in the Midwest. After spending twice the price of the umbrella in ads for its recovery, he still had not gotten it back. His ad was worded:

"Lost from town meeting last Friday: a black silk umbrella. The gentleman who took it will be handsomely rewarded by leaving it at number seven, National Bank Building."

A high-powered copywriter sniffed, "No wonder your advertisement produced no results," and rewrote it as follows:

"If the man who was *seen* taking an umbrella from the vestibule at Friday's town meeting does not wish to get into trouble and have an indelible stain cast upon his Christian character, which he values so highly, he will return it *at once* to number seven, National Bank Building. *He is well known.*"

Next day the man who had lost the umbrella found twelve of them propped up in his anteroom.

* * *

The late Arthur James Pegler was a newspaper reporter in the grand tradition, a rootin' tootin' daredevil of a man, who risked his own life a hundred times to bring home a good story.

Once, Pegler was held up by a blizzard in Iowa. Seeking refuge in a farmhouse, he discovered that the owner had just passed away; the widow asked him to sit up with her husband's body while she went off to make the funeral arrangements. Pegler dropped off to sleep. When he awoke, the "corpse" was observing him critically. "You're dead!" gasped

Pegler. "Heck, no," was the reply. "It's just my fits. The old woman has tried to bury me three times before this!"

Pegler always said this was the one moment in all his wild life as a reporter that he was terrified. He also tried to persuade his son Francis not to follow in his footsteps. "Be anything but a newspaperman," he counseled son Francis, who later changed his name to Westbrook, and did not take his father's advice.

* * *

Jack Fuller has come up with a new game called "Reporters and Newspapers." Examples: Brown from the *Sun;* Cutt from the *Blade;* Justice from the *Tribune;* Left at the *Post;* Noyes of the *Bugle;* Plato of the *Republic;* and Lowering of the *Standard.* The one I like best is Alice of the *Mirror* (the London *Mirror,* that is). I'm sure readers of *Laugh Day* can come up with more of the same!

* * *

John McPhaul tells of a morning when a Washington businessman dropped in at a Chicago newspaper office endeavoring to collect a $150 debt owed to him for many a long day by one of the featured columnists on the paper. He failed in his mission, but for his pains he did get this attention in the columnist's next outpouring: "Mr. So-and-So, the well-known Washington banker, is in Chicago for a few days looking after some of his permanent investments."

* * *

A sadder but wiser newspaperman in Buffalo is looking for a new job. He lost his old one when the chief auditor spotted this item on a big expense account tab he tried to get away with: "Dinner with the sports editor of the Congressional Record: $46."

* * *

At a Westchester country club, a member told the owner of a big metropolitan newspaper, "Say, I owe you a vote of thanks. Your paper proved just the thing to stop my two kids from raising the devil this morning." Obviously pleased, the newspaper owner inquired, "What particular article did the trick?" "No article at all," explained the father. "I just rolled up your paper and whacked them with it."

*　*　*

No approver of all the newspaper mergers that have studded the history of American journalism in recent years was the late James Thurber. "One day," predicted Thurber dourly, "we're going to end up with just one newspaper for the entire country —and *the whole front page will have to be devoted to the name.*"

14. *Punsters on Parade*

If it's true, as many pun-dits aver, that the more ludicrous the buildup, the more shattering is the pun, Don Addis, of Hollywood, richly deserves first place in this staggering compundium for his story of the lad who was counting on his Uncle Al to take him to the circus.

Came the big day, however, and his mother told him that Uncle Al had flown to Australia to see the Davis Cup tennis matches. "I didn't know Uncle Al liked that game so much, Mom," mourned the lad. "Oh, but he does," she assured him. "Many's the time I've heard Alfred laud tennis, son!"

* * *

Last New Year's Eve, recalls William Travis, of Birmingham, a neighbor of his, named Early, gave a costume party, and to insure its success mailed invitations far in advance. Two eager guests, dressed as an old man and a dazzling young girl, to represent May and December, showed up for the party on Halloween. "You've pulled the boner of the year," scoffed the host. "Not at all," corrected the masqueraders. "We're two months, Early."

*　　*　　*

Playing golf at the Century Club, the curvaceous Mrs. Manges hit a niblick shot fully thirty yards beyond the second green. "What did I do wrong?" she asked her husband, a prominent attorney. "You didn't dig deep enough," he explained. "You only took af-fadavit." (The penalty for this sort of thing at most clubs is two strokes and distance.)

*　　*　　*

In an obviously enchanted forest near the home of Mrs. Mary O'Brian, in San Bernardino, lived two families of amiable, hard-working gnus, who often enjoyed picnicking together. Each family boasted one young mischief-maker, however, though each mother was convinced her own little gnu was the innocent dupe of his evil friend.

"You should punish that rascally brat of yours," shrilled one mother finally. "A sound spanking might do him some good."

"Spank *my* son, indeed," huffed the other. "Why don't you go paddle your own gnu?"

*　　*　　*

Nominated for the worst of the year: the story of the three Indian squaws who were admitted to the maternity ward at the same time. Chief Wampum, head obstetrician, assigned one to a buffalo hide, the second to an elk hide, and the third to a hippopotamus hide (now where did he get hold of *that* one?). At any rate, the squaws on the elk and buffalo hides each produced a six-pound son. But the squaw on the hippopotamus hide mothered healthy, six-pound twins. All of which proves, of course, that the sons of the squaw of the hippopotamus equal the sons of the squaws of the other two hides.

* * *

John Hutchens reports that a man intent upon reading up on locusts (there's a new plague of them due, we're told) was annoyed by the cost of books covering the subject, and declared forcefully, "What this country needs is a good five-cent cicada."

* * *

Miss Beatrice Lillie managed to remember she was a punster, too, even when a waiter spilled a whole cup of coffee on her costly new evening gown. "Go," Miss Lillie told the crestfallen waiter, "and never darken my Dior again."

* * *

A man, later identified as Tunis Conquy, was walking down a Southern road one day when, caught in an unexpected downpour, he sought shelter in a farmhouse. The friendly folks there invited him to join them for dinner. Said the hostess, "The meat on the plate on the left comes from a North Carolina piggie; the ham on the other plate comes from a little piggie from South Carolina. Which do you prefer?"

Whereupon Mr. Conquy replied (what a way to repay fine old Southern hospitality!), "Either one, Ma'am. Any pork in a storm."

Punsters by the Score . . .

1. The fire chief who responded to a call from a lingerie shop, but found no sign of a blaze when he got there. His official report read, "falsie alarm."

2. The poet who insists that a pond on his farm is the smallest body of water in the U.S.A. He's named it Lake Inferior.

3. The crow who perched himself on a telephone wire. He wanted to make a long distance caw.

4. The snake charmer who wooed and won a lady undertaker. One of their most cherished wedding gifts was a set of towels, marked—how else?—"hiss" and "hearse."

5. The effeminate Indian who checked in at the Waldorf. He registered as "homo the brave."

6. The Eskimo who stabbed himself with an icicle. He died of cold cuts.

7. The San Antonio restaurateur whose pie list suggests "remember the alamode."

8. The exasperated bus rider who suggests the Chicago Transit Authority adopt the slogan "no bus oblige."

9. The talkative musician who can't hold on to a job. Every time he opens his mouth he puts his flute in it.

10. The advice-to-the-lovelorn editor who insists "if at first you don't succeed, try a little ardor."

11. The commuter whose Volkswagen broke down once too often. So he consigned it to the Old Volks Home.

12. The bookseller who was dawdling over a second cup of coffee one Sunday A.M., reading *The Canterbury Tales*. His

wife demanded, "What have you got there?" He answered, "Just my cup and Chaucer."

13. The Broadway publicity man who bought a new electric typewriter and crawled under the desk with the extension cord to plug it in. A client caught him in the act. "You press agents," he chortled. "Always looking for a plug."

14. The baseball star who made his debut as a singer at one of the Playboy clubs. "Tonight," he quavered, "I'm like a girl who flirts with the butcher. I'm playing for big steaks."

15. The poker shark who once had an extraordinary run of big hands—and was smart enough to quit before his luck changed. "Not another hand, gentlemen," he announced firmly, as he cashed in his chips. "I intend to fold my tens and silently steal away."

16. The impetuous young man who deliberately threw three pairs of trousers into the furnace one Sunday, then told his wife, "No longer can you accuse me of being a stick-in-the-mud, unwilling to take a chance. I have just burned my breeches behind me."

17. The two hundred-pound lady who always insists she's on a diet, though none has ever spotted her observing it. Her husband calls her "the wishful shrinker."

18. The police captain, regarded as something of an egg-head by subordinates, who was shown two sets of fingerprints of a suspected robber. "These can't belong to the same man," objected the captain. "They're whorls apart."

19. The Pennsylvania farmer with relatives in East Germany who heard that a food package he had sent them had never arrived. Putting a brave face on things, he assured them, "Cheer up! The wurst is yet to come."

20. The promoter of a big flower show in Pennsylvania, who, told that a postponement was necessary because the ex-

hibits could not be installed on time, explained to his backers, "We simply were caught with our plants down."

       *   *   *

"Cheerful people," declares Dr. Wilbur Abercrombie, "resist intestinal diseases better than gloomy ones."

What the doctor obviously means is that the surly bird catches the worm.

       *   *   *

"Don't let the word 'paronomasia' throw you," advises good old Dr. John Fuller. "All that it means is an old-fashioned pun."

Dr. Fuller therupon gives a few examples, such as the missionary who was seized by cannibals, tied to a post, and jabbed with daggers so that the savages could drink his blood. After a week he told the chief, "Look: I'm tired of being stuck for the drinks."

Fuller also identifies Hawaii as "the place where men make passes at girls who wear grasses" and claims that what Sir Lancelot *really* asked Lady Guinevere was, "Who was that last knight I saw you out with, Lady?"

Then there was the great composer Bach, who, whenever he worked away from home, developed a prodigious appetite. So every time he went any place he packed a valise with six sandwiches, three apples, some cheese, and a selection of cookies. This became known as a Bach's lunch.

Well, at least we now know what a paronomasiac is!

* * *

A youngster found a salamander in his backyard and put it into a tank with his pet alligator. The alligator promptly swallowed the salamander. "Something awful's happened," wailed the youngster to his mother. "Sally's in our alli!"

* * *

A local district attorney was informed that the cheesemakers of Wisconsin had produced 1.9 million pounds of Limburger in 1958. Said the D.A.: "That's quite a phew."

* * *

Erudite critic Walter Kerr likes to pun as much as the next fellow. He found on the breakfast table one morning a misaddressed invitation to a dinner that had been held four nights previous. "Well," he commented, tossing the outdated invitation over to his wife, Jean, "There's one fete accompli!"

* * *

Mrs. Lanning Humphrey, of Waban, Massachusetts, tells of a wealthy gentleman who took time out from a world yacht cruise to give his crew a Christmas party in port. He went ashore to round up evergreens, victuals, musicians, gifts, and local notables. When he returned to the dock he found all the greens installed—but on the wrong ship. "Ahoy!" he shouted. "You're treeing up the wrong barque."

* * *

An artistic Indian erected a new wigwam and decorated it with costly manufactured baubles, purchased via a mail order catalogue. His neighbors, miffed because the new wigwam was getting too much attention, disparaged his efforts. Sneered they, "Cheap Sioux veneer!"

* * *

Frank Sinatra once engaged a chef freshly imported from Bombay, but after serving the same menu six nights running, he was discharged. Explained Sinatra, "This was one poor guy who got fired for favoring curry."

* * *

Unquenchable punsters have now turned to new color desig-
nations for interior decorators to conjure with. What do you
think, for instance, of Conquered Grape, Foreseeable Fuchsia,
or Enry Iggins Just You White? Then there's Zane Gray, Bi-
partisan Slate, and World Cerise. See what we mean?

* * *

A nearsighted debutante turned up for a soiree very much
under the weather. "I can't see," she mourned. "I couldn't put
in my contact lenses because my poodle bit me in the eye this
afternoon." "What did he do that for?" asked the hostess.
"Heaven knows," admitted the debutante. "Probably he felt like
having an eyeball before dinner!"

* * *

There was an unscheduled dustup in a Bagdad harem one
day long ago. The sultan barged in unexpectedly—and his sixty-
two wives let out a terrified sheik.

* * *

There has come to light an episode in the early life of William Penn that I believe has escaped the attention of many young Philadelphians.

It appears that Mr. Penn had a couple of aunts named Natalie and Ellie who were past mistresses in the art of whipping up a mince pie or an apple strudel. When greedy Quakertown bakers formed a combine and tripled the price of their pastries overnight, Aunt Natalie and Aunt Ellie decided to teach the greedy fellows a lesson. They put *their* delectable pastries on the market at absolute cost—and then proceeded to reduce the price five cents every day.

In no time flat, of course, the good citizens of Quakertown were discussing only one topic: the pie rates of Penn's aunts!

❋ ❋ ❋

The late Heywood Broun liked to tell about the zoo that imported the biggest yak ever seen in America. Every morning at breakfast time the animal, who was very fond of pancakes with maple syrup, would yawn prodigiously, and get up. Of course you know what song Broun declared this brought to mind? "Mighty Yak Arose."

❋ ❋ ❋

They say that what Christopher Columbus really told Queen Isabella when he got home from his American tour was: "Well, I bet I'm the first man who ever got nineteen hundred miles on a galleon." . . . Have you noticed how ship news photographers favor clothes-up shots? . . . And Charlie Poore discloses that a highly rated rock 'n' roller was run out of Newport recently. They guitarred and feathered him.

❋ ❋ ❋

There is an eccentric artist in the south of France who cultivates carp in the natural pool in his garden. When the carp attain full growth, he catches them, skins them, and makes gentlemen's wallets out of the skins. He is, in fact, the only man on the face of this earth who is noted for his carp to carp walleting.

15. *Right up the Riddle*

The late and unlamented craze for elephant riddles left countless parents, teachers—and elephants—reeling. Lest we forget, I've assembled here ten of what I think were the best of them.

1.

Q. Why do elephants need trunks?
A. Because they have no glove compartments.

2.

Q. What do you call elephants who ride on jets?
A. Passengers.

3.

Q. How do you get six elephants in a Volkswagen?
A. Put three in the front seat and three in the back.

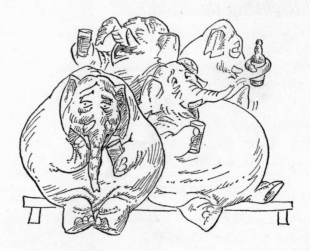

4.

Q. Why do elephants drink?
A. To forget!

5.

Q. What do you do when an elephant sneezes?
A. Get out of the way.

6.

Q. How do you get an elephant out of the theatre?
A. You can't. It's in his blood.

7.

Q. How can you tell when there's an elephant in the refrigerator?
A. The door won't close.

8.

Q. What weighs four thousand pounds and sings?
A. Harry Elefonte.

9.

Q. What do they call a girl who eats elephants?
A. Big Mouth.

10.

Q. What happens when you cross an elephant with a jar of peanut butter?
A. You get either a jar of peanut butter with a wonderful memory or an elephant that sticks to the roof of your mouth.

*　*　*

Since my riddle anthology ("Riddle-De-Dee": Random House) was published a few years ago, a veritable flood of new ones has come along. The following may be valuable for the student of 2100 who wants to know how the lighter-hearted set was passing its time in 1965:

Q. What's yellow and writes?
A. A ball-point banana.

Q. What's red and goes putt-putt-putt?
A. An outboard apple.

Q. What wallows in mud and carries colored eggs?
A. An Easter piggie.

Q. What do ducks do when they fly upside down?
A. They quack up.

Q. What color is a burp?
A. Burple.

Q. What's the difference between a schoolteacher and a railroad train?
A. The teacher says, "Take that gum out of your mouth"; the train says, "Choo, choo."

Q. Are carrots really beneficial for the eyes?
A. Well, have you ever seen a rabbit wearing glasses?

Q. What does a two-hundred-pound mouse say?
A. "Here, kitty, kitty."

Q. What is green and red and rents for $175 a month?
A. A two-room watermelon on East 62nd Street.

Q. What has a gray skin, four legs, and a trunk?
A. A mouse on vacation.

Q. What has eight legs, wears feathers, and says, "Ba-a-a, ba-a-a, ba-a-a"?
A. An Iroquois Indian quartet singing "The Whiffenpoof Song."

Q. Why did little Mary say, "There's a grape sitting in the bathtub" when it really was a giraffe?
A. Little Mary is color-blind.

Q. What is the most arrogant insect in the world?
A. A cocky roach.

Q. How can a leopard change his spots?
A. By going from one spot to another.

Q. What can a cat do to get fat?
A. Go to a butcher shop and meow for it.

Q. What kind of a waiter never accepts a tip?
A. A dumb waiter.

Q. What's the difference between a radio and a clothesline?
A. A radio draws waves. . . .

Q. What happens when you get stung by a bee and bitten by a mosquito simultaneously?
A. You sting along with itch.

Q. What did Mason say to Dixon?
A. "I suppose we've got to draw the line somewhere."

Q. What's yellow, soft, and goes round and round?
A. A long-playing omelette.

Q. What's black and white and hides in a cave?
A. A zebra who owes money.

Q. What's white outside, green inside, and hops?

A. A frog sandwich.

Q. What sentence of twenty-nine letters contains every one in the alphabet?

A. "Quick-wafting zephyrs vex bold Jim."

Q. How can a person go down Pike's Peak without first going up?

A. By being born at the top.

Q. What weighs six ounces, sits in a tree, and is very dangerous?

A. A sparrow with a machine gun.

Q. What would we have if every automobile in the country were painted red?

A. A red car nation.

Q. Why did the cookie crumble?

A. Because his mother was a wafer too long.

Q. How do you make a rhinoceros float?

A. With two scoops of ice cream, a rhinoceros, a dab of whipped cream, and a maraschino cherry.

16. *Still out on a Limerick*

There was a young maid from Kuwait
Who was rated as tops on a dait.
Though she started out slow
'Twas the lads who cried "Whoa!"
At a point we're not free to relait.

I thought that I had rounded up enough good (and print-able) limericks to last for a lifetime in *Out on a Limerick* (Harper's, $2.95)—but how new ones do keep rolling in! For instance:

1.

Most limericks discreetly called laundered
Are ones where the washer has wandered
Far off from his tub
And neglected to scrub
The lines over which he has pondered.

2.

The latest report from the Dean
Concerning the teaching machine
Is that Oedipus Rex
Could have learned about sex
Alone, without bothering the queen!

3.

Crooned a whimsical King of Siam
To his drinking pal, Omar Khayyam,
"Whoo and toot-toot,
They say you're astute,
But right now you're drunker than I am!"

4.

An imaginary line is the waist:
It never stays long where it's placed,
But rises or slips
From shoulder to hips,
According to popular taste.

5.

The kings of Peru were the Incas
Recognized everywhere as great drincas.
They worshiped the sun
And had barrels of fun
But their subjects considered them stincas.
                                        —*Reed Warsham*

6.

A young man down in old Allegheny
Proposed to a typist named Janey.
Groaned his friends, "You can't win:
She's as ugly as sin."
He explained, "But the day was so rainy!"

7.

A Briton who shot at his king
Was doomed on the gallows to swing.
When the rope was made fast
He cried out, "At last!
I'm getting the hang of the thing!"
                                        —*David Ross*

8.

There was a young pastor in Kew
Who kept a brown cow in a pew.
There he taught it each week
A new letter in Greek,
But it never got farther than *mu*.

9.

There once was a co-ed, quite dapper,
In psychology classes a napper,
But her Freudian dreams
Were so classic, it seems,
That now she's a Phi Beta Kappa.

10.

There was a young lady named Lynn
Who thought that to love was a sin.
But when she was tight
She considered it right—
So everyone filled her with gin.

           —*Rosemary Johnson*

11.

A gallant young blade from Duquesne
Went home with a girl in the ruesne
Said she with a sigh
"I wonder when Igh
Shall see such a rain-beau aguesne."

12.

There was a young maid from Kuwait
Who was rated as tops on a dait.
Though she started out slow
'Twas the lads who cried "Whoa!"
At a point we're not free to relait.

13.

An opera conductor named Paton
Conducted a score with his hat on.
By wiggling his ear
His toes and his rear
He contrived to dispense with a baton.
                    —*Joseph Rosenthal*

14.

A spendthrifty fellow named Si,
Who charged everything he could buy,
Said, when hailed into court,
With his bank account short,
"The Government does: Why can't I?"

15.

A cute little feminine specter
Got scared when another spook necked her.
She gave such a start
That her bones fell apart,
And it took quite a while to collect her.
                    —*Don Augur*

16.

A sweet little miss near Fort Bliss
Told her G.I. 'twas sinful to kiss
When that resourceful young rat
Asked, "You mean, dear, like *that?*"
She said, "Yes, and like *this* and like *this.*"
—*Staff Sergeant George McKeshnie*

17.

There was a young lawyer named Pique
Who was blessed with a prominent bique.
But one mortified client
Grew extremely defiant
And gave that proboscis a twique.

18.

A stylish young gent in St. Pierre
Had a girl friend and oft went to Sierre.
She was Gladys by name
And one eve when he came
Her mother said, "Gladys St. Hierre."
—*Roy Baldridge*

19.

Two starry-eyed, reckless young beaux
Were held up and robbed of their cleaux.
While the weather is hot
They won't miss them a lot—
But what will they do when it sneaux?

20.

History is being made at such a breakneck pace these days that even Harvard's erudite David McCord seems a bit befuddled. Muses McCord:

> There once was a man in the moon,
> But he got there a little too soon.
> Some others came later
> And fell down a crater.
> When was it—next August? Last June?

THE ARMY

General Matt Ridgway was reminiscing at the Pittsburgh Field Club about his days as a cadet at West Point. "I recall the first sergeant in my life," he said with a happy gleam in his eye. "He lined us up and roared, 'Men, I want three volunteers for K.P. duty and that means you and you and you.' I was one of the yous."

*   *   *

At an infantry officers' training camp, one tough, officious captain was the pet hate of every candidate. Yet at graduation ceremonies, every newly hatched second lieutenant contributed happily for a present to the detested captain.

It was a framed picture of Lassie, neatly inscribed, "With love, from Mother."

* * *

A one-star general was assigned to training draftees in the hottest, sandiest corner of West Texas. He staggered back from a ten-mile hike at the head of his troops one evening and fell moaning on his bed. "These boots," he announced, "are about to kill me. I swear they're three sizes too small." "Let me get you a new pair," suggested his orderly.

"Not on your life," cried the general. "We have no clear water, women, golf, or movies. Taking off these blank blank boots is the only pleasure I've got left!"

* * *

Now it can be revealed that canny news correspondents at the various fronts in World War II hit upon a new way of hornswoggling their home offices with inflated expense accounts. Aware that Army censors clipped entire paragraphs out of many letters sent back to the U.S.A., the correspondents would list formidable expenses on their tabs, then carefully cut out the explanations, leaving only the net amounts.

The home treasurers, truly impressed with all the top-secret stuff the censors apparently had cut out, invariably paid the bills without raising an eyebrow.

* * *

John Toland reminds us of the day a rewrite man in Rome was doing a piece on General Mark Clark and cabled his home office, "How old Mark Clark?" A joker at the home end cabled back, "Old Mark Clark just fine. How you?"

* * *

A pompous broker was reminiscing interminably about his glorious exploits in World War II. "I hadn't had my wings in the Air Force for a month," he asserted, "when I blew up four ammunition dumps and shot down nine fighter planes." "Ah, yes," sighed the lady next to him wearily. "I presume that's when they decided to send you overseas."

* * *

When General Patton was in an expansive humor, he liked to tell a story about a valuable officer under Napoleon who developed a brain tumor and had to submit to an emergency operation. The surgeon, maintained Patton, unscrewed the officer's cranium, took out the brain, and laid it on the table.

Just then a messenger arrived with the glad tidings that the officer had been promoted from colonel to general. With a whoop of joy he bounced up from the operating table, slapped on his cranium, and headed for the nearest exit. "Wait a minute," cried the surgeon. "You've forgotten to put back your brain."

"I won't need it now," called back the patient. "I'm a general!"

*　*　*

Shortly after D-Day in World War II, an aviator was dispatched over the Rhineland to drop propaganda leaflets. He didn't check back in at headquarters for three weeks. "Where you been?" demanded his squadron leader crossly. "How could you take three weeks just to dump a load of leaflets over enemy territory?"

"Dump them?" repeated the pilot in a hollow voice. "I thought you wanted me to slip one under every door!"

*　*　*

A V.P. at an aircraft factory, enlarging upon the virtue of initiative to the four o'clock shift, told of the day in World War II when General MacArthur summoned one of his Army engineers and asked, "How long will it take to throw a bridge across this stream?" "Three days," was the answer. "Okay," snapped MacArthur. "Have your draftsmen make blueprints immediately." Three days later the general asked if the bridge was under way. "It's finished," smiled the engineer. "You can send your troop across it this minute if you don't wait for those damn blueprints. They aren't started yet."

*　*　*

At a gay reunion of World War II veterans, the conversation got around to cartoons that had made the nation laugh a bit during the grim days before the tide turned in America's favor at Guadalcanal. It was surprising how clearly some of those cartoons—and the exact wording of the captions—were remembered, almost as clearly, in fact, as the famous pinup of Lana Turner looking back over her shoulder in a white swimsuit.

Favorites: Two goats chewing up top-secret reports at the Pentagon, with one grunting happily, "Best darn propaganda I ever ate!"; a general's hatchet-faced wife collaring him at the door of his home to snarl, "You're not going to go inspecting barracks until you tidy up the mess in your own room!"; the G.I. having a tooth yanked at the dispensary, gasping, "Ouch—Sir!"; and an admiral jumping up from his chair with a shriek of anguish while his aide whispers to a J.G., "I think the admiral's found that Japanese carrier that was missing from his chart."

*   *   *

A crusty professor of comparative literature registered distinct annoyance when a student just out of military service was late for class for the third morning running. "Tell me," rasped the professor, "exactly what did they say in the Army when you sauntered in late like this?"

"Well," mused the unperturbed student, "first they saluted. Then they inquired, 'How do you feel this morning, sir?'"

* * *

In Korea, an ace correspondent, pressed into emergency service at a field hospital, observed a young nun calmly assist in the amputation of a cruelly mangled Chinese soldier's leg. The correspondent, ashen-faced and trembling himself, told the nun, "I wouldn't do that for a million dollars." The nun nodded and said, "Neither would I."

* * *

The lieutenant at a small outpost had a new recruit assigned to keep quarters bright and clean. He was quiet, competent—and always called the lieutenant "Major." A sergeant drew him aside one morning and said, "Soldier, haven't you been in this man's Army long enough to know that one gold bar denotes a looie, not a major?" "If it's all the same to you, sergeant," implored the recruit, "you won those stripes your way; let me earn mine my way."

* * *

Reservists being recalled for active service are griping about shortages in equipment and uniforms. They recall a jest current during World War I: a recruit mourning, "I reported at Yaphank Monday morning, and by Tuesday I had a uniform, hat, shoes, and puttees that fit me like a glove. I don't understand it. Can I be deformed?"

* * *

The raw recruits were lined up for their first review and the colonel stopped before one very sad sack. "Your face is unshaven," snapped the colonel. "Your boots are unpolished. Your tunic is unbuttoned. Who told you you're a soldier?"

Weakly the sad sack replied, "My draft board."

*　*　*

The tough M.D. at a Texas Army post, death on any poor G.I. who reported for sick call, was on his way to a show in town when the motor in his car stalled. Very meekly, he called out to a group of privates lounging in front of barracks, "Hey, fellows! I can't seem to get my car going. Would you know what to do for it?"

"Sure thing Doc," one of the group answered happily. "Paint it with iodine, and mark it 'Duty'!"

*　*　*

Private Goodkind was whistling happily as he cleaned out the cages of the carrier pigeons. "Well!" observed a passing lieutenant, "that's the first time I ever saw a private happy performing a job like that."

"Yes, sir," beamed the private. "This job doesn't bother me a bit. Before I was transferred here I was in the cavalry."

*　*　*

Booked to emcee a vaudeville show at a veterans' hospital, lavish George Jessel sent an orchid ahead of time to each and every nurse. The nurses wore them, too. Georgie had overlooked one detail, however. All the nurses were male.

*　*　*

Outside an Army area that houses parachute troops and test pilots for supersonic planes, there's a sign that reads: "Danger! You are now entering a state thruway. Good luck!"

*　*　*

Captain V. R. Fernandes recalls the day a two-hundred-man Army group arrived to begin training as parachutists in an airborne outfit. A tough major welcomed the already apprehensive newcomers with a crisp, "So you're gonna be parachutists, hey? Fine! Your jump training will be conducted in three stages. The first week, we'll separate the men from the boys. The second week we'll separate the boys from the idiots. And the third week we'll let all you idiots jump!"

* * *

In the jungles of Viet Nam, a high-ranking officer was staring moodily into the pitch black night. "You haven't slept in forty-eight hours, sir," an anxious aide reminded him. "You need rest desperately." "My work is never done," answered the officer grimly. "My autobiography is due next Tuesday and I'm only up to Chapter Twelve."

* * *

A Pentagon official had occasion to call one of our astronauts recently. The astronaut's young son answered the phone. "Where's your dad?" asked the big brass. "He's orbiting nine or ten times around the globe," answered the lad. "He ought to be home in an hour." "Let me talk to your mother, then," requested the b.b. "Oh, she's out shopping at the bargain center," said the boy. "She won't be home till tonight."

* * *

Because the spectacular goings-on in the world of guided missiles and space ships is utterly mystifying to me, I had not realized until I visited Cape Kennedy in person that since 1953 Pan Am is the prime contractor for operations there, with RCA the principal sub-contractor. As one Cocoa Beach newshawk explained to me, the whole Atlantic Missile Range operates on three levels: 1. Pan Am talks with N.A.S.A. (The National Aeronautics and Space Administration) in terms of billions of dollars. 2. Pan Am then talks with RCA negotiators in terms of millions of dollars. 3. Pan Am VIP's then go to their homes and demand of their wives, "What do you mean, tomatoes have gone up to thirty-five cents a pound?"

* * *

N.A.S.A. is planning to put a hundred head of cattle into orbit at one time. A. C. Spectorsky points out that this will be the herd shot round the world.

THE NAVY

Sailor Wilhelm shambled into a Navy recruiting office on Tremont Street and diffidently tapped the officer in charge on the arm. "Say, Bud," he pleaded earnestly, "gimme that old sales talk again, will you? I'm getting mighty discouraged!"

* * *

A U. S. Navy supply ship put in for a spell at a Pacific island famed for its voluptuous and scantily clad maidens. One sailor spent a memorable day on shore posing groups of the cooperative beauties, and photographing them with his miniature camera. An ensign watched him silently for some time, then inquired, "Where do you think you're going to get all those films developed?"

The sailor replied, "Films? Who's got films?"

* * *

How to get ahead in the Navy: The Secretary of the Navy was inspecting a recently launched carrier. The entire crew stood at attention. "I suppose," said the Secretary jokingly to the carrier's captain, "you know the name of every man on the ship." "I think I do," was the captain's unexpected reply.

"Aha," smiled the Secretary. "What's the name of the third man from the left there in the rear rank?"

"William Jones," said the captain.

The Secretary addressed the seaman himself.

"What's your name, lad?" he asked.

"William Jones, sir," replied Seaman Jonathan Abernathy.

* * *

"One of my most challenging wartime experiences," recalled a not-too-reliable sea captain, "came in the icy North Atlantic. I was torpedoed and lived for nine days on one can of sardines." "Remarkable," nodded the man next to him at the bar. "How did you keep from falling off?"

* * *

Two attractive girls sauntered down Broadway, with a lone sailor dogging their every footstep. Finally one of the girls wheeled around and announced angrily, "You there, Mr. Fresh! Either quit following us this way, or get another sailor!"

* * *

A young British naval lieutenant, reports John Fischer, commanded his first ship—a frigate—during practice maneuvers. He succeeded in bumping into the admiral's vessel at the very outset of the operation.

The admiral signaled, "What do you propose to do now?"

The lieutenant's answering signal—rapidly to become a British naval legend—was, "Buy a small farm, sir."

* * *

On a U.S. cruiser the officer of the deck asked the starboard lookout, "What would you do if a sailor was washed overboard?" "I'd yell 'Man overboard,'" answered the lookout snappily.

"Good," said the officer. "Now what would you do if an *officer* fell overboard?"

The lookout asked, "Which one, sir?"

* * *

There's a winsome lass stationed near the outer gate of a Navy base who's been kissed by so many sailors her lips go in and out with the tide.

* * *

At a Navy officers' dance, a young lieutenant's eyes were attracted to a brooch worn by a hostess assigned to him. It depicted a cluster of Naval signaling flags, and the girl explained, "This brooch was a present from my bridegroom. The flags mean, 'I love you.'" The lieutenant held his peace, although he knew full well there was no such word as "love" in the naval signal manual. He could hardly wait to get back to the barracks and dig out his own copy of the manual.

What the flags actually signaled, he discovered, was, "Permission granted to lay alongside."

* * *

In a time when all mail from military personnel was heavily censored, the father of a valiant young sailor received three letters, spaced some weeks apart, from his son. Letter One began, "I cannot tell you where I am, but yesterday I shot a polar bear." Letter Two began, "I cannot tell you where I am, but yesterday I danced for over eight hours with a hula girl." Letter Three began, "I still cannot tell you where I am, but yesterday the doctor told me I should have danced with the polar bear and shot the hula girl."

THE MARINES

A hardened Marine veteran, his discharge in sight, signed up for a correspondence course in electrical engineering and was puzzled by one question on the application blank. "How long has your present employer been in business?" it said. The Marine finally answered, "Since 1776."

* * *

Cocky Marine sergeant Timothy McShane, no blushing violet, found a member of his platoon engrossed in—of all things—a hardbound book. "Reading, huh?" marveled Mc-Shane. "What's the name of the book, son?" The private answered, "It's called *What Twelve Million Women Want.*" "Hey," cried the good sergeant. "Lemme see that book a minute. I want to know if they got my name spelled right!"

* * *

Newly arrived in boot camp, a volunteer Marine from Long Island received this letter from his mater: "Dear Sebastian: Now that you are on your way to being a hero in the Marine Corps I trust that you will arise on time every morning so that the other young gentlemen in your set will not have to sit at the table and wait for you to come downstairs before they can begin eating their breakfast."

* * *

A nationally famous general in the Marine Corps recently was met at Kennedy Airport by his very fat wife. While they stood waiting for his baggage, a trim, red-headed airline hostess swayed by, and the general beamed. "Hope we fly together soon again, Miss Fenichel," he said. "How do you know her name?" demanded the wife. "It was posted up front," explained the general, "right under the names of the pilot and the co-pilot."

"I see," nodded the wife. "Now tell me the names of the pilot and the co-pilot."

18. *Time Marches on*

BABIES

A young lady at Cook County Hospital in Chicago had given birth that morning to a healthy, strapping baby girl. Some hours later a nurse found her propped up in bed poring through the pages of a telephone directory. She explained that she was looking for a name for the baby.

Said the nurse, "We have a little book here that lists a thousand first names for boys and girls. Let me get it for you." "That's not what I'm looking for," protested the young mother, clinging to the phone directory. "I need a *last* name."

✸   ✸   ✸

Great-great-grandmother Johnson studied the newborn babe with obvious satisfaction. "If my memory doesn't fail me," she cackled, "it's a boy!"

* * *

In Paris, a lady on the eve of producing a baby was in a grumpy mood indeed. "What you need," prescribed her husband, "is a bit of diversion. Tonight we're going to the Folies Bergère." "I should say not," countered the wife. "Think of the prenatal influence. Our child might be born stark naked!"

* * *

A noted punster was told by the doctor that his wife had just given birth to quadruplets. Dazed but game to the core, the punster exclaimed, "Four crying out loud!"

* * *

Papa Herlihy marched his five-year-old son up to the maternity ward to give him his first look at his baby brother, born six hours earlier. Said baby brother was howling piteously. The five-year-old studied him carefully, then nodded his head and commented, "No *wonder* Mom hid him under her coat so long!"

* * *

Bessie Moore tells of the Little Rock father who told his seven-year-old son, "Floyd, I have a surprise for you. The stork flew in last night and left a little brother for you. Why don't you write your sister the good news?" The boy wrote as follows: "Dear Sis: You owe me two bucks. It's a boy."

* * *

The newest thing in baby care has been introduced by the wily Parisians. Aboard the ocean liner *France,* in the children's nursery, where the desk of the nurse in charge adjoins the infants' sleeping quarters, a numbered bell tinkles every time a baby's diaper needs changing. Moisture in the linen activates a signal.

* * *

Elbert Sisson's wife was bathing the baby when he heard his four-year-old daughter Clare demanding the scissors. "Not now," answered Mrs. Sisson. "I'm bathing the baby." "I hate babies," announced Clare. "Now you stop saying that," commanded Mrs. Sisson. "Remember *you* were a baby yourself not too long ago."

"I know," admitted Clare, "but I didn't want the scissors then."

* * *

"The quickest way to make a tossed salad," suggests Clementine Paddleford, "is to feed vegetables to an eighteen-month-old child."

* * *

Delphine Koshland overheard two pert nursemaids in converse in Central Park, as they wheeled their daintily attired charges down the Mall. "Why can't you come with me to Radio City tomorrow?" pouted one. "For the simple reason," answered the other, "that I'm afraid to leave this poor baby alone with its mother."

* * *

I am indebted to Rev. Charles Nober, of Syracuse University, for this wonderful definition of a baby: an alimentary canal with a big noise at one end and no sense of responsibility at the other.

BOYS AND GIRLS TOGETHER

Precocious children continue to make cute and quotable remarks at an ever-accelerating pace and, what's more, there always seem to be a couple of parents, neighbors, and columnists within earshot, pens in hand, ready to record the remarks for posterity.

Years ago the late Robert Benchley tentatively suggested that the least the precocious children could do in return was to set down some of the cute remarks made by their *parents*. One Alfred Deedee, aged three, of Deedee, D.D., according to Benchley, actually acted upon this suggestion, but then the movement died aborning. This was Alfred's memorable contribution:

"My father asked my mother if she thought he was made of money. 'I'm not sure what it is you're made of,' she replied, 'but I'm pretty sure it isn't money.' This amused my father so that he hauled off and whammed her into the china closet, much to the surprise of the cups and saucers."

Boys . . .

A Milwaukee four-year-old brought a wriggling worm home with him from play-school and deposited it on the dining room table. "What," demanded his horrified mother, "are you doing with that worm?" "I met him on the lawn," explained the boy, "and I thought I'd show him our house."

* * *

Sam Levenson tells about the day his mother collared him just as he was about to drop an empty milk bottle on the noggin of his public school principal from a window in his seventh-story apartment. "Have you lost your mind?" cried his mother, giving him a whack over the ear. "The grocer gives us five cents apiece for empty milk bottles like that."

* * *

A little boy deposited two overdue books on the desk of a public library, and handed his past-due letter, plus the eighteen-cent fine called for, to the clerk. Then he asked, "Please, can I have the letter back? It's the first one I ever got!"

* * *

A young mother looked into the nursery and found her six-year-old son laboriously putting a bandage on his thumb. "What happened?" cried the mother. "I hit it with a hammer," said the boy.

"You poor darling," sympathized ma. "I wonder why I didn't hear you cry." "What was the use of crying?" explained the boy. "I thought you were out."

* * *

An English lad was walking across a village common when he saw a rabbit. "Look, Mum, there goes a rabbit," he exclaimed. "Nonsense, boy," scoffed his mother. "It must have been your imagination." The lad pondered a bit, then demanded, "Mum, has imagination always got a white behind?"

* * *

Nanette Fabray was describing the son of an acquaintance who had "freckles as big as nickels." "Big deal," scoffed her companion. "Lots of kids have freckles as big as nickels." Miss Fabray raised her eyebrows. "With *buffaloes* on them?" she asked.

* * *

"Cyril," said a teacher one bright morning, "do you feel that there is one thing you can do better than anybody else in the world?" "There is," said Cyril firmly after the briefest hesitation. "Read my own handwriting."

* * *

"Now, John," a mother coaxed her seven-year-old son, "you've been horsing around way past your bedtime. It's time to go to sleep." "I just can't, Mom," argued John. "My mouth is still full of words."

* * *

"For ten dollars," proposed Papa Giogrido to his son, "I'll teach you to talk like an Indian." The skeptical son asked, "How?" "See," beamed Papa, "you're learning already!"

* * *

Papa Erskine reacted as expected when his eight-year-old son Cuthbert brought home a report card containing four D's. "Cuthbert," said Papa, "I'll give you an incentive to improve your work in school. Come home with a better set of grades next month and I'll give you a crisp new dollar bill."

The next morning Cuthbert was waiting at the teacher's desk when she came in. "Teacher," he proposed cheerily, "how would you like to make yourself a quick fifty cents?"

* * *

John Drury tells of a south Georgian boy who was taken to Chicago one January and saw snow for the first time. He stared in wonder from his hotel room window at the snow-blanketed street below and cried to his mother, "Look, Ma! Grits all over!"

*   *   *

A sturdy lad asked his father, "Do you know if Mary's lamb followed her to school every day?" "That she did," said Father. "And how," pursued the lad, "did it all end?" "They finally separated," said Father. "The lamb graduated."

*   *   *

A mother and her two adolescent sons were trying to decide what to give Pop for his birthday. "I know," cried the younger son finally. "Let's let him drive the car this weekend!"

*   *   *

A number of five-year-old Timothy's playmates gathered beneath his window and shrilly importuned him to come out and play. Timothy finally appeared at the window and replied, "Can't you see I can't come down now? I'm taking my nap."

*   *   *

One minute little Warren had a big, fat, candied apple in his hand, the next minute it had vanished. "A man took it," he wailed to his father. "Imagine a man mean enough to steal an apple from a kid this size," exploded the father. "What did the man look like, Son?"

Little Warren pointed promptly to a tall, dignified gentleman who was strolling some paces ahead—with a big red candied apple dangling from the seat of his pants!

*   *   *

Young Danny, fooling about in his father's den, succeeded in swallowing a shotgun shell. His frantic mother rushed him to the doctor. "Let's keep our heads about all this," counseled that wise gentleman. "I won't be able to operate until Friday. Meanwhile, keep the boy from jumping around too much—and don't point him at anybody!"

*   *   *

Jim Backus lives near a rich movie tycoon whose overindulged twelve-year-old son ran away from home the other day. The outraged father called over to Backus, "How do you like that? A twelve-year-old brat running away from his mother and father!" "Take it easy," counseled Backus. "Your son is like many other youngsters, rebelling against authority. All twelve-year-old kids at one time or another run away from home."

"What?" roared the movie tycoon. "In a Thunderbird?"

* * *

Max Shulman describes the remarkable progress made by the son of a neighbor in Westport. "He began," recalls Shulman, "as an unwanted child, but today, at the age of seventeen, he's wanted in twenty-two states."

* * *

An Illinois lady heard an unholy racket in her backyard, and upon investigation, found her young son Michael clinging desperately to the back of a very shaggy sheep dog who was trying with equal desperation to escape. Michael, hanging on to the dog for dear life, begged his mother breathlessly, "Help me hold on to him, Mommy. Can we keep him? He followed me all the way home!"

* * *

The teenage son slumped dejectedly in his chair, and his mother anxiously whispered to his father, "What's biting him now?" "It's nothing worth whispering about," said the father resignedly. "He wants to go to the drugstore down at the corner—but the car won't start."

* * *

Young Mauruss kept a firm clutch on his first report card from school. "Maybe," he told his dad, "I should explain you the system first. A means wonderful, B means excellent, C stands for all right, and D is what I got."

* * *

Little Cyril came home from Town School with a black eye and a bloody nose. "Tsk, tsk," sighed his mother, "you've been fighting again." "Yes," admitted Cyril, "with Pete." "Didn't I tell you," the mother reminded him, "to count to fifty before you became involved in another fight?" "I did," insisted Cyril, "but Peter's mother told him to count to twenty-five."

* * *

A geography teacher had just been explaining to her charges the differences between the frigid, temperate, and torrid zones. At the conclusion of her talk she asked young Andrew what sort of zone he lived in.

Andrew answered, "Brooklyn, 18."

* * *

A Seattle five-year-old smelled a pancake breakfast being readied in the kitchen. "Mom," he called out happily, "my stomach is smacking its lips!"

* * *

Harlan Miller reports that the fourteen-year-old son of one of his colleagues has purchased a little black book for addresses and telephone numbers. On the outside, the lad, no blushing violet he, has confidently written "Volume One."

* * *

A fond grandmother, visiting her family, was freshening up for dinner when her four-year-old grandson brought his puppy in to see her. "I'm busy, dear," she said absently. "Wait for me downstairs." The grandson asked her tearfully, "Grandma, aren't you even going to speak to your granddog?"

* * *

Bob McGovern, of the famous McGovern fighting clan, initiated his four-year-old son into the manly art of self-defense. The very next afternoon the lad ran into the house in a fever of delight. "I did it, Dad! I did it," he exulted. "I hit her!"

* * *

It was his father's birthday, and seven-year-old Timothy Carson insisted on shining his shoes as a gift. Reluctantly Father Carson, already late for the office, took off his shoes and handed them to his son. They were returned in due course— glistening black.

"Great work, Tim," enthused the father—then whispered to his wife, "Well, there goes my only pair of brown oxfords!"

* * *

The playroom of a pampered lad in a lakeshore duplex is filled with cloth animals: lions, tigers, and what-not. One day the lad's mother decided the menagerie needed cleaning, and consigned the animals to the electric washing machine in the laundry. While she was superintending the operation, her phone rang. The boy answered. "Mother is home," he conceded, "but she can't come to the phone right now. She's stuffing an elephant into the washing machine."

There was a pause at the other end of the line and then a man murmured weakly, "I see. I guess I have the wrong number"—and hung up.

And Girls . . .

A five-year-old girl in Wellesley Hills, reports Ernie Heyn, was looking forward with wild excitement to her first day in school. When the great day dawned, she bounced out of bed at seven, and was outside waiting for the bus at eight. She was still enthusiastic when she got home that afternoon.

The next morning, however, when her mother woke her at seven-thirty, the little girl wasn't quite so happy. "What?" she protested angrily. "*Again?*"

* * *

An inexperienced nursemaid, taking a baby for a ride in the park, encountered a friend of the family, who peered inside the carriage and observed, "I see the poor little thing has her father's nose."

"Good heavens," gasped the nursemaid. "I thought that was a nipple."

* * *

An enchanting but temperamental little girl of eight received a phone call from a schoolmate the other evening. "Please call me back in ten minutes," she requested. "I'm in the middle of a tantrum."

* * *

Cuddly Tillie Expresso had the prize excuse of the week for being late to school: "I guess I overwashed."

* * *

Hank Meyer took his precocious three-year-old daughter with him into a voting booth. After he had pulled down a number of levers, he asked her, "See how it's done?" "Yes, Daddy, I see," she replied, her eyes shining. "Now where's the gum?"

*　*　*

Danny Kaye was a houseguest of the talented Mills family in Britain when Hayley Mills, then five (how the time flies!) came running downstairs at midnight in a near-panic. "I've got to see mother at once," she told her father. "My heart has stopped!"

*　*　*

Mother to perverse girl who won't eat her spinach. "Try a mouthful of it, darling. Pretend it's mud."

*　*　*

A rising suburbanite started to put on his dinner jacket the other evening, preparing to escort his wife to a country club dance. His young daughter, however, registered disapproval. "Please don't wear that suit, dad," she begged. "It always gives you such a terrible headache the next morning."

*　*　*

Sister Annette writes about the time she took some third-graders in her parish to visit the zoo, then asked them to write a paragraph about the animals that interested them most. Wrote one moppet: "The animal that interested me most was the Warning Stand Back. Every time we looked at it he spit at us."

*　*　*

"Look at that funny man across the street," suggested a little girl to her mother. "What's funny about him?" asked the mother indulgently. "He's sitting on the sidewalk," reported the little girl, "talking to a banana peel."

*　*　*

A Park Avenue matron took her six-year-old daughter up to see a very large stable in the Bedford Hills sector of West-chester. The youngster's attention was captured immediately by a newborn colt. "Look, Mommy," she caroled. "A foreign horse!"

*   *   *

A wide-eyed little girl from the slums was given her first two-week vacation in the country by a big newspaper. Things went tolerably well the first day until it was time for her to retire for the night. Her hostess took her to a lovely guest room with a wide, spotless, cool bed and said, "My dear, this is all yours." To her surprise, the little girl burst into tears. "I want to sleep in a regular bed," she sobbed—"one with five or six people in it!"

*   *   *

A whimsical teacher asked her class, "Would you say that 'trousers' is singular or plural?" Observant nymphet Virginia answered promptly, "Both: singular at the top and plural at the bottom."

*   *   *

John Fischer, erudite editor of *Harper's Magazine*, spotted a beloved child perched precariously on the peaked roof of a barn and asked her what she was doing there. "Her answer," says Fischer, "covered the situation like a horse blanket." She called down, "I'm trying not to fall off."

*   *   *

A ten-year-old girl, described by her doting mother as "tem-peramental," raised particular tantrums every time she was told it was time to go to bed. "I hate bed," she exclaimed one night. "If I took bed in school it would be my worst subject."

*   *   *

There's an eight-year-old girl up north of Boston whose pas-sionate love of pastries and hamburgers has kept her waistline indecently oversize—and expanding continuously. Her mother keeps admonishing her, "Fat girls find it hard to get husbands! Pull in that stomach of yours!"

The other day the poor girl came home from school bathed in tears. "During Salute to the Flag this morning," she sobbed, "I pulled in my stomach like you always tell me to—and my skirt fell off!"

* * *

A tense moment in a fifth-grade Austin, Texas classroom came when a teacher asked, "Who said, 'God's in His heaven, all's right with the world'?" One little girl answered, "Mrs. God."

* * *

A very small girl in Atlantic City, whose sunburn had reached the peeling-off stage, was overheard grumbling, "Only four years old, and I'm wearing out already!"

* * *

On a TV program in Detroit, a seven-year-old city-bred girl boasted that on her first visit to a farm she had gotten around to milking a genuine cow. "Did you enjoy the experience?" asked the master of ceremonies. "Oh, yes," enthused the little girl, "but I didn't get much milk out of it."

* * *

Late for school the third time in one week, ingenious young Malvinia came up with a brand-new alibi. "This time it really wasn't my fault," she told her teacher solemnly. "I was walking behind a slow dog."

* * *

The four-year-old daughter of an advertising executive in Connecticut asked her father how she might catch a bird. "Sprinkle salt on his tail," he advised soberly. That evening she came home with four birds.

* * *

A conscientious father had promised his wife that he would chastise their ten-year-old daughter for repeated digressions, and this time he laid it on good. The surprised little girl took the tongue-lashing in utter silence, then stamped off to the library and pulled a volume of the Encyclopedia off the shelf.

She sat engrossed in this volume so long that the father couldn't resist stealing up behind her to see what she was reading.

The little darling was studying up on poisons.

* * *

Erasmus Hall High School boasts an intriguingly built sophomore who's constantly mimicking Miss Bardot. Classmates have affectionately dubbed her the "Brooklyn Brigitte."

* * *

Jean Kerr tells about a seven-year-old little girl who got into a fight at a friend's birthday party and was sent home in disgrace. And when she arrived home, she found that her cat had been run over on the highway. Completely undone by all this, she burst into tears and wailed, "This is the worst day I've ever been to!"

* * *

On the wall of a building near his residence, Mike Nichols noticed a chalk inscription one morning that read "I LOVE GRILS." The next morning a line had been drawn through this declaration and a new line printed below that read "I LOVE GIRLS." The third day that line had been crossed out, too, and a third line substituted—in letters twice as large. It read, "WHAT ABOUT US GRILS?"

Together . . .

Seven-year-old Peter came home from the little girl next door to report disconsolately to his mother, "Agnes just broke our engagement. She returned my frog."

* * *

Mrs. Gumbiner came back from her canasta party and asked the baby sitter, "Did you bathe the children as I instructed you to?" "Yes, Ma'am," said the baby sitter, "and they behaved like lambs about it—all except the biggest boy. He fought like blazes before I could get him undressed and into the tub."

"What do you mean, biggest boy?" inquired Mrs. Gumbiner. "We have only one son. Which biggest boy?" "The one with a bald spot and eyeglasses," said the baby sitter. "Good heavens," gasped Mrs. Gumbiner, "that's my husband!"

* * *

A distinguished author in Connecticut has an enchanting four-year-old daughter who wants desperately to be older than she is. One afternoon recently she came tripping into her mother's study to announce blithely, "I am now *five* years old." "My dear," corrected the mother, "you know perfectly well you are only four." "No, no," contradicted the daughter, "I'm five. I just met another year coming down the driveway!"

* * *

Young Jonathan returned from school in disgrace, with a note from the teacher explaining that he had put mud in a little girl's mouth. "What made you do a crazy thing like that?" demanded Jonathan's mother. "Well, for one thing," he explained, "her mouth was open."

* * *

A poignant tableau revealed in Yellowstone National Park one day this summer: a father with four unruly kids in tow gazing pensively at a sign reading, "Deposit your litter here." The father sighed, and confided to a bystander, "Don't think I'm not tempted!"

* * *

Fourth-graders in a class for gifted children were asked by their teacher to complete a sentence beginning "Let's be as quiet as . . ."

Here are some of the answers, as reported by William Feather: "A leaf turning colors . . . a feather falling from a bird . . . time passing . . . the first star coming out . . . a gentle rainfall . . . when you pray . . . a butterfly flying . . . a soft breeze."

* * *

A self-satisfied mother, when her offspring went off for his first day in school, sent along this note: "The opinions expressed by this child are not necessarily those of his mother's side of the family."

* * *

A tough teacher asked her third-grade class to write a sentence beginning with the word "than." All but one of the kids was stymied. (Wouldn't *you* be?) The resourceful one's sentence read " 'Than' is a word with four letters."

     ❊   ❊   ❊

At the conclusion of five-year-old Bartlett's first month in kindergarten, his father asked, "Well, have you grown to like the little boys who scared you so at first?" "Yes, I have," admitted Bartlett. "And the girls?" Bartlett assumed an expression of deep disgust. "Oh, come now," chided Bartlett's father, "you at least like Susan, don't you?"

Bartlett's face was a study in shocked disappointment. "*Susan*," he echoed. "Is *she* a girl?"

     ❊   ❊   ❊

H. Allen Smith quotes this paper written for a history class by a fourth-grade genius in Mount Kisco:

"One day when Alfred the Great was wandering around the English countryside, he stopped at the house of a certain lady who was supposed to be baking cakes, but the lease said about that the better."

     ❊   ❊   ❊

Armand Deutsch gleefully came upon this essay on geese by an eight-year-old nature lover: "Geese is a low, heavy-set bird which is mostly meat and feathers. His head sits on one end and he sits on the other. Some geese, when they grow up, has curls on their tails and is called ganders. Ganders don't have to sit and hatch, but just eat and loaf and go in swimming. If I was a geese, I'd rather be a gander."

     ❊   ❊   ❊

And this is an essay about ants by a Kentucky eight-year-old: "My subjeck is ants. Ants is two kinds: insects and lady uncles. Sometimes they live in holes, and sometimes they live with their married sisters, and they always are in the sandwiches at pikniks. That is all I know about ants."

     ❊   ❊   ❊

From "Doc" Mack in Atlanta comes the story of two Cub Scouts whose younger sister fell into a lake. The two Cubs rushed home with tears streaming down their countenances. "We tried to give her articial respiration," sobbed one to their mother, "but she kept getting up and walking away."

* * *

A tired-looking mother entered a supermarket with her four boisterous youngsters and begged, "Haven't you got some brand of cereal that will sap their energy?"

* * *

From an essay by a ten-year-old scholar in New Orleans: "I hate Fidel Castro for two reasons: (1). He brought communism to Cuba and (2). He invented Castro Oil."

* * *

Another time, Art Linkletter entertained a little girl named Ellen, and a boy of the same age she obviously adored named Stevie. "When I grow up," confided Ellen (all of five) "I'm going to marry Stevie." "That's great," enthused Linkletter. "Do you feel the same way about Ellen, Stevie?" "Nah," scowled Stevie. "Never as long as I live." "Why not?" persisted Mr. L. "Because," explained Stevie with some dignity, "every time I turn around at school, she paints my nose."

* * *

Art Linkletter, waiting for one of his TV shows to start, suggested to the kids who were his guests that day that they draw pictures of what they wanted to be when they grew up. One lad depicted himself as a plane pilot. Another drew himself in the engine cab of a streamliner. But one little girl just handed Art a blank piece of paper. "I want to be married," she explained earnestly, "but I don't know how to *draw* it."

* * *

Herb Stein reminds us that the old-fashioned wall telephone had its advantages. For one thing, the kids couldn't reach it.

* * *

Steve Allen, who has learned by experience, contends that the best way to make your children heed your advice is to find out exactly what they want and then tell them to do it.

* * *

Nine-year-old Peter came home from dancing school to announce that every girl in the class was a clumsy cow. "All they can do," he explained with disgust, "is dance backwards."

* * *

A young lady carted a bundle of wash to a laundromat the other day and registered disbelief when the attendant informed her that it weighed nineteen pounds. "Ridiculous," she snorted—and together they sorted out the dirty wash. That's when she discovered the baby in it, cooing contentedly.

* * *

A solemn youngster with a fantastically high I.Q. keeps asking his socialite mother questions she can't answer—but to keep him quiet, she must give some sort of reply, so she makes things up as she goes along. "Invention," she sighs, "is the necessity of Mother!"

* * *

"A kid is the last container of a genuine sense of humor," maintains Dr. Seuss, author of the all-conquering *The Cat in the Hat*. He continues, "This sense of humor disappears as the kid gets older, and learns to laugh only according to the way the boss, society, politics, or race want him to. Then he becomes an adult. And an adult is an obsolete child."

* * *

Katheryn Launtz, of Washta, Iowa, assures us, "A man may have a battered hat and his trousers may be shiny, but if his children have their noses flattened against the window pane a half hour before he is due home for supper, you can trust him with anything you have."

* * *

The sheriff's office in a Texas city deserves some sort of Oscar for distributing a wonderfully wise and ironic list of rules titled "How to Raise a Juvenile Delinquent in Your Own Family." You may already have seen quotes from it in your newspaper, but I think it's worth reprinting. Here are a few highlights:

Begin with infancy to give the child everything he wants. This will insure his believing that the world owes him a living.

When he picks up obscene words, laugh heartily at him. Soon he'll acquire a vocabulary that will blow off the top of your head.

Pick up everything he leaves lying around. This will teach him he can always throw off responsibility on others.

Take his part against neighbors, teachers, policemen. They are all prejudiced against your child. He is never wrong.

Finally, prepare yourself for a life of grief, brother. You're going to have it.

CAMPERS

Many of the letters-to-parents-from-summer-campers that pop up in the columns and midsummer "news" items obviously are the brainchildren of professional gag-writers and TV scripters. Some of them, however, must be genuine, and if they're funny, what's the difference?

Here are some of the best of the recent crop:

1. "Dear Dad: We've been taking some pretty long hikes this week. Please send my other sneaker. Walter."

2. "Dear Mom: I left home in such a hurry I think I forgot to hang up the phone. Gwen."

3. "Dear Folks: What is an epidemic? Kerry."

4. "Dear Mommy: Please bring some food when you come to visit me. All we get here is breakfast, lunch, and supper. John."

5. "Dear Mom: Three of the girls in my tent have the dire rear. Chris."

6. "Hear ye, Parents: There are 190 boys in this camp. I wish there were 189. Your loving son, Ronald."

7. "Dear Folks: Yesterday our counselor told us all about where babies come from. You lied to me. Love, Margaret."

8. "Hi, fans! Your worries are over. I'm really growing very ladylike. All we talk about here is boys and sex. Please send me my water pistol and catcher's mitt. Love, Jill."

9. "Dear Parents: Oh boy, is this place wonderful! When I get back to the city, can I go to night camp? Willie."

10. "Dear Ma: Who said it was never hot in Maine? Please mail me some ice cream. P.S. You know what? I think this is a girls' camp. Pat."

* * *

When F. Scott Fitzgerald's daughter Frances was eleven years old, the famous novelist (author of *The Great Gatsby* and *This Side of Paradise*) sent her this capsule of advice while she was in summer camp:

"Darling Scotty: It's okay to worry about these four things: courage, cleanliness, efficiency, and horsemanship. But don't you *ever* worry your pretty little head about popular opinion, dolls, the past, the future, growing up, parents, boys, disappointments—or failure unless it comes through your own fault."

COLLEGE DAYS

A lady who ran a boarding house for students in a New England college town checked in a gangly new student who paid a month's rent in advance. A week later the lady received a note from the new student's mother. "Thank you for taking in my poor, lonesome boy," it read, "and I'll appreciate your keeping an eye on him, seeing that he gets enough sleep and eats enough wholesome food. This is the first time really he's ever been away from home—except, of course, for two years in the Navy."

* * *

A fraternity house in Michigan went in for a thorough spring cleaning, which involved sending all the window curtains to the laundry. This brought an angry note from the sorority across the road. "Gentlemen," it read, "we must insist that you put back the curtains in your upstairs windows immediately. We are not interested in a course in anatomy."

Back went this note from the fraternity brothers: "Dear Girls: This course is not compulsory."

* * *

Ray Washburne found a student sound asleep in his Williamstown bookshop the other day. Explained the student, "I was just drowsing around."

* * *

In some fashion that I do not understand, a Purdue sophomore swallowed a ping-pong ball and was rushed to the infirmary to have it removed. He bore up bravely while the surgeon made an incision, but began to squirm when this was followed by two more jabs. When the surgeon wielded his instrument for a fourth time, the student cried, "What's the big idea of cutting me in so many places?" "Relax, man," suggested the surgeon. "That's the way the ball bounces."

* * *

They're talking about the rich man's only son who had to leave the college of his choice because of bad eyesight. He mistook the Dean of Women for a co-ed.

* * *

Overheard at a college prom: "She reminds me of Bardot." "Brigitte?" "No, Guy Lom."

* * *

A sophomore at a Southern university, asked to write an essay about Shakespeare's *Hamlet,* was gratified to receive an "A" for his effort, but then was summoned to his professor's inner sanctum.

"My boy," began the professor, "you probably are not aware of the fact that I am a fraternity brother of yours—and spent my undergraduate days in the very house you live in now. What's more, we used to keep a pile of old student essays on hand just as you do today. You have had the bad luck to copy word for word a paper on *Hamlet* that I happened to write myself.

"Now, I suppose you're wondering why I gave you an 'A.' Well, when I turned in that paper, the fool who was giving the course at the time marked it "C-minus." I've always believed it rated an 'A.' "

* * *

The manager of a motel, reports Bob Sylvester, was asked if he could handle adequately a party of eighty teen-agers. "We have the room," he answered honestly, "but I'm afraid we haven't enough outlets for their electric guitars."

* * *

There sat a classroom full of bright-eyed Vassar sophomores, the new fashions clearly revealing the cute dimples in their knees. The puritanical visiting lecturer from Boston eyed the girls apprehensively, and murmured, "What, oh what, will the styles be up to next?"

* * *

Some time ago the superintendent of the Boston Public Library system was visiting a branch where an elderly gentleman had just borrowed a dozen lurid detective stories. "Don't you think," suggested the superintendent to one of the librarians, "that you could improve that man's literary tastes by suggesting that he read an occasional book a bit more meaningful and profound than a mystery?"

"I thought so myself," replied the librarian, "until I found out who he is. That's the president of Harvard University!"

* * *

"A fool," sighed Professor Wolfe, "can ask more questions than a wise man can answer." One of his students murmured in barely audible tones, "No wonder so many of us flunked your last exam!"

* * *

A Bowdoin sophomore called to his buddy across the hall, "Hey, Daly, your laundry's back." "Some service," approved Daly. "I only sent it in this morning." "That's right," agreed the sophomore. "The laundry refused to take it."

* * *

Supposedly it was a Princeton hopeful who started on a shoestring—then worked his way up until he got slapped in the face.

*   *   *

A student at Oregon State, challenged to include both the words "analyze" and "anatomy" in a single short verse, promptly came up with:

> My analyze over the ocean,
> My analyze over the sea.
> Oh, who will ride over that ocean
> And bring back my anatomy?

*   *   *

Once upon a time there was a rich man's son who was so slow on the uptake it took him seven years to go through high school—yet he longed to go to college. The father reluctantly agreed to stake him *if* he could answer a few simple questions. The first question propounded by Pop was "What's what?" "I don't know," admitted the son—and was promptly put to work in a menial job at Pop's plant.

Came the time for the son's first vacation, and off he went to the big city to see the sights. In a bar, a very beautiful girl indeed suggested that he buy her a drink or two, and several hours later, to his surprise and delight, he found himself in the girl's apartment. She left him momentarily, then returned in a lovely informal gown. The boy pointed to her hips and inquired, "What's that?"

"What's what?" asked the beautiful girl.

"Holy mackerel," gasped the boy. *"If I'd known that two years ago—today I'd be in college!"*

*   *   *

There's a freshman up at Dartmouth this year who bids fair to make his mark as a social commentator. His first paper for a philosophy section contained this summary: "Socrates was a famous Greek who went around giving people excellent advice. They poisoned him."

*   *   *

Co-ed to her studying companion: "What more could any girl want on a cold evening than a warm robe, a glass of milk, a good book to study, and—oh, thank heaven! The phone is ringing!"

* * *

Crew coach Darrow looked over a bowlegged freshman and inquired, "So you're aiming to come out for the crew, eh? Ever rowed before?" The freshman confessed, "Only a horse, sir."

* * *

A co-ed at Baylor University paraded around the campus with two silver bars conspicuously pinned to her sweater. "I take it," commented an observant English professor, "that you have an army captain for a boy friend."

"No, sir," said the co-ed cheerfully. "Two lieutenants."

* * *

In the hallway outside a university library in Tennessee there's a row of hooks with a sign reading "For Faculty Members Only." A campus wit added in pencil below, "May also be used for hats and coats."

* * *

"They tell me Stanford is a great college," grumbled the father of a student at that noted institution, "but my son's handwriting seems to get worse and worse up there. Here's a letter that just arrived from him this morning, for instance. I can't even make out how much he wants me to send him!"

* * *

A Syracuse junior, back from an expensive weekend at Vassar, composed this melancholy couplet:

> Pretty dishes
> Are avaricious.

* * *

Not unlike many other college athletic departments, the University of New Mexico's was worried by the disappearance of sundry supplies, notably sweat shirts with the University's name emblazoned thereon. Dean Sherman Smith may have been responsible for the stratagem that effectively dissuaded would-be athletes in search of these status symbols. The manufacturer was instructed to mark all new shirts, "U. of N.M. Athletic Department: THIRD STRING."

* * *

The Dean of the Columbia Graduate School of Journalism, Ed Barrett, tells of a rich trustee who called a college president and said, "Send somebody over to address our home-builders' convention next week, Sam. But please don't send anybody lower than a dean." The prexy answered dryly, "There *is* nobody lower than a dean!"

* * *

The morning after a big class reunion at a university some fifty miles from New York, an old grad called a friend to ask if he had gotten home all right. "No," complained the friend, "I missed my train and had to doze on a bench in the station for six hours." "You're lucky," nodded the old grad. "I got home."

* * *

The late and famous editor, Ellery Sedgwick, offered this challenging advice to a graduating class at Amherst: "It is my constant endeavor to persuade young men just starting their business careers that, instead of joining some company organized, successful, and regimented, they should sign up with a leaky ship, scrape down her decks, caulk her seams, refit her sails; for it is on the slipperiest decks that adventure beckons, and a speedier chance provided for rising in the world."

UNDERGRADUATE HUMOR

Every September, "welcome-back-to-the-campus" numbers of countless college comic magazines are pressed into the hot little hands of not-always-receptive undergraduates. Meanwhile the collegiate editors will be chortling loudly, and slapping each other on the back over puns and wheezes they have conjured for the text pages. Any resemblance to puns and wheezes of previous decades will be commented upon only by spoilsport fathers with fiendishly good memories.

It is just possible that some of the following stories will bob up in the months to come. They always have!

1. A pert Vassar junior, emerging from a conference with her renowned old professor of drama and literature, remarked ruefully to a roommate, "That old boy may be eighty, but he's still in there pinching!"

2. A Bradley senior is in the doghouse with his lady love's parents. "I promised to get her home before twelve last night," he admits, "but she had fifteen—and passed out."

3. *Fair co-ed:* Now before we start on this picnic you may as well realize that I neither smoke, drink, nor neck.
Experienced Princetonian: You're quite mistaken.
F.C.: You mean that I do do those things?
E.P.: No, I mean about starting on this picnic.

4. "Tomorrow is Marshall and Mary's wedding—so we bridesmaids are staying in this evening to give Mary a shower."

"Not a bad idea! I guess we ushers will stay home too and wash off old Marshall a bit."

5. "Were you ever troubled with athlete's foot?"

"Once—the time a Michigan State fullback caught me out with his girl."

6. Professor Binswanger defines "teen-age" as the time in life when girls begin to powder and boys begin to puff.

7. U.C.L.A.-ristocrat Rudy Toyt, known as "Hoity" Toyt by envious classmates, says that in his exclusive suburb, there are so many foreign cars, it's two years since anybody's been hit above the knees.

8. *Sophomore:* You like girls, I gather.

Junior: I like girls anybody gathers.

9. A romantic young bride, just graduated from Smith, persuaded her groom to stop the car on their honeymoon to lunch at an inn on the edge of a steep, lovely valley.

When they drove off later, she enthused, "What a wonderful gorge that was, darling!"

"Agreed," nodded the bridegroom, "but I could have done with one more piece of that apple pie."

10. *He:* I hear you neck.

She: Pardon me. I'll be more quiet the next time.

11. They tell of a lad who took so long to get through Harvard that he had ivy growing up his left leg. He met his fate

when he fell out of a speeding airliner. His last words were, "Gad! I guess that wasn't the washroom after all!"

12. An exhilarated U. of Texas promtrotter was driving the wrong way on a freeway. A cop overtook him and hollered, "Hey, you crazy or something? Can't you see those arrows?"

"Are you kidding?" replied the promtrotter gravely. "I can't even see the Indians!"

13. *Professor:* I will use my hat to represent the planet Mars. Any questions?

    Student: Yes. Is Mars inhabited?

14. *Groom:* Nothing but toast for dinner this evening?

    Bride: Yes, Michael. The bread toasted when the steak caught fire and fell into the chocolate pudding and I had to use the tomato soup to put out the blaze.

15. *From Texas:*
    Uncle's health is much improved
    Since he had bad things removed.
    Purified of lewd desire
    He sings soprano in the choir.

16. *From Indiana:*
    The thunder god went for a ride
    Upon his favorite filly.
    "I'm Thor," he cried.
    The horse replied,
    "You forgot the thaddle, thilly."

17. *From Ithaca:*
    She wore her stockings inside out
    Straight through the summer heat.
    She said it cooled her off to turn
    The hose upon her feet.

18. "Hey, little boy, can you direct me to the best movie in town?" "Yeah. For fifty cents." "Isn't that pretty high?" "Not for a movie director."

19. *Sailor*: "Are you nautical?"
Pretty young thing: "No, I'm niceical."

20. "I owe all I have to one woman."
"Your mother?"
"No, my landlady."

21. Aboard a Mediterranean cruise ship:
"What's that white stuff on yonder hill, Steward?"
"That is snow, Miss."
"I thought so—but that creep on the bridge keeps telling me it's Greece."

22. Mary Newlywed had just cooked her first dinner. "It was great," enthused the bridegroom, "but didn't you think the lamb was just a teentsy-weentsy bit tough?" "Come now," chided Mrs. Newlywed. "Let's not talk chop."

23. *Football coach*: Miss Barber, what are you doing with that varsity letter on your sweater? Don't you know you're not supposed to wear that unless you've made the team?
Miss Barber: Well?

25. She was only a chimney sweep's daughter but she soots me fine; a printer's daughter, but I like her type; a hash slinger's daughter, and can she dish it out; a moonshiner's daughter, but I love her still; a lawyer's daughter, so she goes from bar to bar; a real estate agent's daughter, but, oh, what a development!

26. Observation by an indignant faculty adviser: "When I was a kid there was no such thing as juvenile delinquency. We were all hardened criminals."

27. A motorist gave a lift to a beatnik, and after several moments of desultory conversation, asked him, "Is there something bearing down on us from behind?" The beatnik looked, and told him, "Nothing but a dog." So the driver slowed up a bit and there was a terrific crash. While waiting for the ambulance, the driver grumbled, "I thought you told me nothing

was coming but a dog." "Yeah, man," nodded the beatnik. "A Greyhound."

28. "Does a sweater do anything for your wife?"
"Naw. Just makes her itch."

29. "Have you ever been pinched for going too fast?"
"No—but I've been slapped."

30. Ad in a New Haven daily: "Encyclopædia Britannica complete set, for sale cheap, never used. *My wife knows everything.*"

31. "What do you think of the new captain of the crew?"
"He's a gentleman and a sculler."

32. *He:* Do you neck?
She: That's my business.
He: I see. A professional.

33. *Sophomore co-ed:* Are you wearing that skirt to make you look shorter?
Junior co-ed: No—to make the boys look longer.

34. *Visitor:* Where can I get hold of your sister?
Little boy: I wouldn't know. She's ticklish all over.

35. *He:* If you refuse me I'll get a rope and hang myself right in front of your door.
She: No, no! You know how my father detests your hanging around here.

36. *Redlands:* My uncle knew a month before his death the exact date he was going to die.
U.C.L.A.: Did he learn it from a fortune teller?
Redlands: No. The judge told him.

37. *Customer:* Waiter! I just found this hair in my turtle soup.
Waiter: Well, well! So the turtle and the hair finally got together!

38. *Father:* What do you mean, you have to have a new car? Look at all these jalopies parked here on the campus!

Ohio State '67: Pa, you just don't understand. Those are the cars that belong to the faculty.

39. Have you heard about the unfortunate co-ed at the University of Kansas whose nickname is Turnpike? Not a curve in sight!

40. *Student:* How much is a haircut?
Barber: One-fifty.
Student: How much is a shave?
Barber: Sixty cents.
Student: Okay. Shave off my hair.

41. *New bride:* What's worrying you, Joe? Remember your worries now are *our* worries.

Bridegroom: Wonderful, darling. We just had a letter from Syracuse from a girl who's suing us for breach of promise.

42. Letter from a freshman co-ed to her friend back home: "I now weigh 108 pounds stripped, but I'm not sure that the scales in front of the campus co-op store are accurate."

43. *Sue:* When I get down in the dumps, I buy a new dress.
Prue: Oh, I was wondering where you got them.

44. Three men were busy repairing telephone wires. As a Wisconsin co-ed drove along in her convertible, she saw all three climbing poles. "Look at those nuts!" she told her seatmate. "You'd think I'd never driven a car before!"

45. *Movie patron at Chinese movie:* "Usher, I smell punk."
Usher: "That's O.K. Just stay where you are and I won't seat anybody near you."

46. The students of Iowa State have taken to writing ballads in their spare time. Here's one of the soul-searing results:

A bunch of the germs were hitting it up
In a bronchial saloon.
Two bugs on the edge of the larynx
Were jazzing a hay-feverish tune.
While back of the teeth in a solo game
Sat dangerous Dan Kerchoo,
And watching his pulse
Was his queen of the wultz,
The lady that's known as Flu.

47. "Here's an autograph of Mark Twain."
"All I see is an X."
"Well, that's his Mark."
"Where's the Twain?"
"Down at the station."

48. A nearsighted lady pointed to a round object at a Cambridge supermarket and inquired, "Is that the head cheese you're advertising?"
"No, Madam," replied the Harvard clerk politely. "That's his assistant."

49. A group of sidewalk superintendents were watching a new building go up in Austin, Texas, when a luscious co-ed, clad in a tight blue serge dress, ambled by.
For a moment silence reigned while all eyes turned from

one type of construction to the other. Then a learned U. of T. senior piped up, "It'll never work, men. Too many moving parts!"

50. A young man approached a cigar counter behind which stood a cute young thing and inquired, "Do you keep stationery?" Answered the c.y.t. thoughtfully, "Yes, up to a certain point. Then I just go all to pieces."

You have been listening, ladies and gentlemen, to the Voice of the Future.

SUNSET YEARS

Old Mr. Hardrocks sat rocking in his chair at the window of the Union League Club, favoring his young friend O'Connor with an occasional remark. "My wife," he finally grumbled, preparing to decamp, "won't believe I spend my afternoons here. *She* thinks I'm out chasing women. Gad, I wish she was right!"

*　*　*

"The middle years?" David Savage describes them as "that quiet, peaceful, serene period between completing the children's college education and starting in to help with the first grandchildren." "The middle years," he adds as a clincher, "usually last from three to five months."

*　*　*

The manager of a Connecticut brokerage office relates how he stepped outside during a blizzard last January to see an elderly gentleman poking with his cane into a piled-up snowbank at the curb. Assuming that the old fellow was blind, the manager suggested, "Can I help you across the street?" "Now why should I want to cross the street?" countered the oldster irritably. "I'm looking for my sports car."

*　*　*

Vincent Peel tells of a gray-haired lady waiting for a Madison Avenue bus. She was overweight and obviously crippled with rheumatism. Her arms were loaded with packages.

As she prepared to climb aboard the bus, a man behind her volunteered a helping hand. The old lady declined with a sad smile. "I'd best manage alone," she explained. "If I get help today—I'll want it tomorrow."

* * *

On his seventieth birthday, Henry Wadsworth Longfellow wrote this letter to a friend: "You do not know yet what it is to be 70 years old. I will tell you, so that you may not be taken by surprise when your turn comes. It is like climbing the Alps. You reach a snow-crowned summit, and see behind you the deep valley stretching miles and miles away, and before you other summits higher and whiter which you may have strength to climb or may not. Then you sit down and meditate, and wonder which it will be. That is the whole story, amplify it as you may. All that one can say is, that life is opportunity."

* * *

Dr. Robert McMillon, of Winston-Salem, North Carolina, has compiled "A Coronary Decalogue" which contains the following excellent nuggets of advice:

1. Thou shalt not try to be a champion athlete after 50.

2. Thou shalt consider losing thy temper a luxury to be indulged in sparingly.

3. Thou shalt avoid worry. (The government probably will take care of thee.)

4. Thou shalt take regular vacations.

5. Thou shalt keep thy alcoholic intake below the point where it may delude thee into thinking thou art a better man than thou ever were.

6. After a certain age, thou shalt not take unto thyself a young and frisky wife, nor even a reasonable facsimile thereof.

* * *

Old Colonel Beauregard was a devil with the ladies, still charming the daylights out of them at seventy-seven. In fact, on his seventy-seventh birthday he adopted the practice of cutting a notch on his cane to mark each new conquest. That's what killed him on his seventy-eighth birthday. He made the mistake of leaning on his cane.

* * *

A rhyming calendar from a Victorian English miscellany:
    JAN et, aged, fell ill one day
    FEB rile troubles came her way.
    MAR tyr-like she lay in bed;
    APR oned nurses softly sped.
    MAY be, said a lord judicial
    JUN ket would be beneficial.
    JUL eps, too, though freely tried
    AUG ured ill for Janet died.
    SEP ulchre was sadly made
    OCT aves pealed and prayers were said.
    NOV ices with many a tear
    DEC orated Janet's bier.

* * *

Shortly before his own death, author Ben Hecht wrote a book about departed cronies he remembered best: famous individualists like H. L. Mencken, Charles MacArthur, and Gene Fowler. "There's one thing," wrote Hecht, "that keeps surprising you about stormy old friends after they die: their *silence*. For a while an echo stays in your ear. You hear a laugh, a revealing phrase or two, a certain quality of enunciation. Then—nothing. Another death takes place: VOICES."

* * *

The Chinese Reds are trying to stop circulation of a story about a country woman who was found high in a remote mountain wilderness, sobbing beside a freshly dug grave.

"My grandfather was killed on this spot by a man-eating

tiger," she wailed. "My father met with the same fate. And now my only son has been killed here, too."

"Why not move to Shanghai, where there are no tigers?" urged a young Chinese Communist. "No, no," protested the sobbing woman. "I'd rather take my chances with the tigers!"

* * *

And from Hong Kong, frighteningly close to Red China's border, comes a poignant tale about a boy named Po-yu. Po-yu misbehaved and cried bitterly when his mother chastised him with a stick. "You never used to cry when I thrashed you," observed his mother. "Why do you cry now?"

Po-yu answered, "When I did wrong and you thrashed me it always used to hurt. But now my mother's strength has ebbed to the point where it hurts no longer. And that is why I cry."

* * *

Sick joke from Chicago: a one-legged man died at the ripe old age of ninety-two. His nephew was in court in connection with the will when a well-wisher told him, "I was sorry to hear that you had lost the rest of your uncle!"

* * *

A young visitor, anxious to please the late Bernard Baruch, told him on his ninetieth birthday, "My, sir, you're looking well!" Angrily, Mr. Baruch replied, "The fellow who announced that there are seven ages of man was wrong. There are three, my boy. The first is Youth. The second is Middle Age. And the third is, 'My, sir, you're looking well!'"

19. *Trade Winds*

ADVERTISING

The pretensions and exaggerations of a handful of exhibitionists in the advertising field have put a whole and long-established profession on the defensive. There *are* frenzied account executives who bandy expressions like "Let's toss it around and see if it makes a salad" or "Let's smear it on the cat and see if she licks it off," but most of the advertising folk you'll encounter on Madison Avenue are as sober and conservative as—well, book publishers.

Furthermore, not every advertising man is afflicted with an ulcer, either. A panel recently queried fourteen hundred ad executives on the state of their health for the express purpose

of scotching this canard. Only 4 per cent admitted that they
suffered from ulcers!

* * *

Making tall claims is no new manifestation of the advertising
fraternity. An unearthed clay tablet of Babylon bears an inscription of cattle and feed for sale at "unheard-of low prices."
At least one Egyptian papyrus is an advertisement for a health
resort. Circus-like wall posters were discovered in the ruins of
Pompeii.

* * *

Consider this coffee come-on from the "Publick Adviser,"
published in London over three hundred years ago:
"In Bartholomew Lane, the drink called Coffee, which is a
very Wholesome and Physical drink, having many excellent
virtues, closes the orifice of the Stomach, fortifies the heat
within, helpeth Digestion, quickeneth the Spirits, maketh the
heart lightsome, is good against Eyesores, Coughs, Colds,
Rhumes, Dropsy, Gout, Scurvy, King's Evil and many others,
is to be sold both in the morning and at three in the afternoon."
What that copywriter could have done with *instant* coffee!

* * *

You will hear nothing on television today more jarring than
this magazine ad of the 1880's:
　　Though love grows cold
　　Do not despair:
　　There's Ypsilanti
　　Underwear!
A patent medicine outfit of that day got away with this in
the most conservative newspapers:
　　Lucinda Cordial! Barren wives
　　It turns to mothers fair
　　And the fond name of father gives
　　To husbands in despair.

* * *

The status of the account executive has definitely improved since the day, in the 1890's, when adman pioneer Frank Presby opened his agency in downtown New York. The morning he entered the building as a tenant for the first time he spotted this sign over the entrance: "Peddlers, book agents, and advertising men are not allowed in these premises."

* * *

Frantic copywriters, wallowing in a maze of secret formulas, astounding discoveries, giant economy sizes, and non-irritating filters, spend their days and nights seeking new keys to the public's pocketbooks.

One ingenious soul came up recently with the notion of printing ads backwards on the reverse sides of postage stamps, so that when you licked one, you would involuntarily carry the slogan around on your tongue for the rest of the day.

Unfeeling post office authorities gave him and his idea the heave-ho.

* * *

It's easy—if you know how—to spot a vice president in an advertising agency, states John Straley. "If he stays out to lunch for four hours," says John, "and nobody misses him—he's a vice president."

*   *   *

On a transcontinental plane trip, somebody asked chewing gum tycoon Philip K. Wrigley why he continued to advertise so extensively when his business already was a fantastic success. "For the same reason," replied Wrigley, "that the pilot of this plane keeps the engines running when we're already twenty-nine thousand feet up in the air."

*   *   *

David Ogilvy, one of the big men in advertising today, tells of a time when Max Hart, the men's clothing tycoon, summoned his advertising manager to complain that he was using too much copy in his new campaign. The ad manager disagreed violently. "Furthermore," he proposed, "I'll bet you ten dollars I can write a whole newspaper page of solid type and you'll read every word of it." Hart took the bet. "I won't have to write a line to prove my point," the ad manager than declared. "I'll only tell you the headline: *'This page is all about Max Hart.'*"

*   *   *

A well-known gourmet in the advertising world carries his own tiny, gold-trimmed pepper mill around with him. When luncheon is served at the restaurant he chances to be patronizing, he whips out the pepper mill and grinds elegantly. A sneering rival hails him as "the fastest pepper mill in the East."

*   *   *

A polltaker up Boston way has perfected an action-guaranteed approach. He smiles sweetly and announces, "Good morning, you unbelievably ugly old ape: we're conducting a survey to see how touchy people are."

*   *   *

One unattended, itty bitty advertising magnate in the Twin Cities, according to Jerry Beatty, coined the following six unintentional malapropisms in the course of one five-day, thirty-six-hour week:

1. Chafing at the dish.
2. Dropped it like a ten-foot pole.
3. Get on your bicycle and run like crazy.
4. He's just an ignorant ramus.
5. Let's not downgrade this up.
6. There's a dirge of good music on the radio.

* * *

There's a big ad agency on Madison Avenue whose quick-tempered boss fires about five employees a day. Anybody who lasts a full year is secretly awarded a medal by astounded colleagues. One of the v.p.'s of the agency was recalling the day he first worked there. "I didn't mind too much," he sighed, "that my name was printed on the door with chalk—but I did think the wet sponge hanging on the doorknob was rather disturbing."

* * *

Two high-powered advertising geniuses were talking about a third member of the fraternity, whose sudden death had been something of a shock. "What do you think the poor fellow had?" asked one in a properly mournful tone. "Nothing to speak of," sighed the other. "Just a small publishing account and a deodorant client. Nothing really worth going after."

* * *

Charles Brower, of Batten, Barton, etc., warns eager young account executives that if they had courted their wives the way they court prospects, their patter would have sounded something like this: "I can see you are a smart girl: the kind that can't be fooled on value. So you'll notice that I am wearing a three-hundred-dollar suit. That suit, girlie, is only an outward indication of the super-hydraulic, synchromesh, patented double-action heart that beats beneath it. Now listen carefully to something I tell only a chosen few. I am in limited sup-

ply. There are a lot of women after me. So for one day only,
I'm offering to marry you. But you'll have to hurry—hurry—
hurry—before I'm all gone."

*　*　*

A big talent agency was trimming its sales staff and fired
two of its most high-powered agents. While they were bemoaning their fate, a cockroach walked across the floor. One
of the agents stepped on it.

"I hope you realize," said the other bitterly, "that you have
just destroyed our corporate image."

BUSINESS AS USUAL

"When I find myself depressed over present conditions,"
said Roger W. Babson, "I can, within one hour, banish worry
and turn myself into a shouting optimist. . . . Here is how I
do it. I enter my history library, close my eyes, and reach for
a book, not knowing whether I am picking up Prescott's *Con-*

quest of Mexico or Suetonius's *Lives of the Twelve Caesars.* I then open my eyes and read for an hour; and the more I read, the more sharply I realize that the world has always been in the throes of agony, that civilization has always been tottering on the brink. The pages of history fairly shriek with tragic tales of war, famine, poverty, pestilence, and man's inhumanity to man. After reading history for an hour, I realize that bad as conditions are now, they are infinitely better than they used to be. This enables me to see and face my present troubles in their proper perspective as well as to realize that the world as a whole is constantly growing better."

* * *

In *Why Did They Name It?* Hannah Campbell tells how some of America's best-selling products got their names. Maxwell House Coffee, for instance, is named for a hotel in Nashville, Tennessee, where the coffee was so excellent, Teddy Roosevelt declared impulsively, "It's good to the last drop." Mr. Heinz was selling many more than 57 varieties when he registered his trademark in 1896. He just liked the number 57. Camel Cigarettes came along in 1913 when Turkish tobaccos were in vogue. The original camel was a venerable dromedary named "Old Joe" who lumbered through Winston-Salem with a circus just when R. J. Reynolds' were seeking a name for their new brand. Not sure they were right, they put "Old Joe" on their package. The rest is history. And Kodak? It means nothing at all. In Rochester, Boss Man George Eastman's favorite letter happened to be "K," so he invented a name that began and ended therewith.

* * *

"One thing you must say for people today," admits Frank Morris. "They're willing to do a day's work. But they want a week's pay first."

* * *

Cleaning up his cluttered desk for the first time in months, a successful but careless businessman found wedged into a crack at the bottom of one of the drawers a redemption check for a pair of shoes he had left for repair way back in 1933—thirty years ago. The shop, he knew, still existed, just around the corner, with the same sign on the outside: "Joe Antonio: Shoes Repaired While You Wait." Joe was an artisan of the old school—a man who took intense pride in his work.

More or less as a joke, the businessman presented the check at Joe's, saying, "I know it's thirty years since I left these shoes here, but it occurred to me you just might be able to find them." "Wait here. I go see," said the unsmiling Mr. Antonio. He handed back the check a moment later, explaining casually, "They'll be ready Tuesday."

* * *

The president of a big corporation let his eyes roam over the faces of his board of directors—which consisted of his own son, three sons-in-law, and his good-for-nothing nephew.

"Well, gentlemen," he said, "I suggest you give me all your ideas as quickly as possible—before my two tranquilizer pills wear off."

* * *

An antique shop up Bedford way featured an extensive collection of old snuffboxes. "They were handed down to me," explained the proprietor, "by my dear departed grandmother." "Oh," nodded a customer, "your grandmother took snuff." "Not at all," said the proprietor. "She took snuffboxes."

* * *

The vice president of an electronics firm had to excuse himself in the middle of an important meeting recently. "I hate to leave," he explained to his sympathetic fellow directors, "but my mother-in-law is arriving on the five o'clock broom."

* * *

"America," proclaims Tom Stevens, "is still the land of opportunity where a man can start out digging ditches and wind up as a top executive behind a desk—if he doesn't mind the financial sacrifice." (George Killian defines an executive as a man who leaves his air-conditioned office to drive in his air-conditioned car to an air-conditioned club to take a steam bath.)

* * *

Douglas Watt overheard a distressing conversation at a midtown snack bar. "You're nothing but a bum," upbraided a seedy-looking father. "Yeah?" answered his son. "Who brings home the unemployment checks?"

* * *

A publicist who lived high on the hog was frowning over a huge dinner check placed before him by the maître d' of a famous restaurant. His girl friend kidded him about his worried look. "Don't misunderstand," he assured her. "It's not the size of the check. I'm just trying to figure which client to charge it to."

* * *

Asked why he had lost his job, a worker in a mill explained angrily, "You know what a foreman is like these days: a faker who stands around and watches other men slave? Well, my foreman got jealous of me. Visitors to the plant all thought I was the foreman!"

* * *

On the second floor of a huge cigarette factory the secret formula for the company's most popular brand was concocted —a mixture of tobacco, tar, charcoal, and heaven knows what else. Then the finished product was funneled into a huge steel conveyor to the ground floor where the actual cigarettes were produced and packaged.

One day the top scientist produced a brand new secret ingredient to be added to the mixture, then pointed to the steel conveyor. "Okay, men," he ordered, "put *that* in your smoke and pipe it!"

* * *

A prosperous purveyor of rare orchids on Park Avenue is intoxicated about four working hours out of every five. He now is known as "the petrified florist"!

* * *

A venerable graybeard hobbled in to a credit manager's office to announce, "I'm here to pay the final installment on a baby carriage." "Thank you," said the credit manager, "and how's the baby today?" "Oh, I'm doing as well as could be expected," answered the graybeard.

* * *

A new industrial plant was opened in Chicago, and local stockholders were invited to see a mammoth metal-bending machine. "The first thing to remember about this machine," they were cautioned by the foreman, "is not to get your fingers caught in it."

* * *

Remember when Valentine cards were all sweetness and light, dripping with gooey sentiment? Well, here are a few *current* Valentines, spotted in those immaculate gift card racks that now take up so much space in alleged book shops:

1. A little lady with an obviously disgusted bird on her head. Coos the lady: "A little birdie told me all about you, my Valentine—cheep, cheep, cheep."

2. A not-too-bright-looking young man, with a bouquet of flowers, intoning, "Valentine, I'd like to lay the whole world at your feet—but you're so clumsy, you'd probably trip over it."

3. "Candy is dandy—but remember, My Valentine, that necking won't spoil your teeth!"

4. "Be loved! Be adored! Luckily you won't need sex appeal, charm, talent, or good looks—just three dollars for a small dog."

How could *any* girl in her right mind reject romantic appeals like these?

* * *

The president of a big importing house hired a new secretary the other day and put her to work at once taking down long letters to agents in Hong Kong, Buenos Aires, Rome, Stockholm, and Hawaii. A short time later the girl poked her head in his door and reported cheerfully, "Mission accomplished." "That's quick work," beamed the importer. "Where did you learn to type letters so fast?"

"I didn't," admitted the girl. "I just phoned those agents instead. That's much faster than writing."

* * *

"I'll tell you how ugly my new secretary is," mourned a debonair broker to his luncheon companion. "When I chase her around the desk, I *walk!*"

* * *

A secretary had just been told that she was fired, as of Friday evening, so she spitefully added a few parenthetical comments of her own to one of her boss's standard "alibi" letters. The result:

Replying to your urgent letter about non-delivery of your order of eleven weeks ago, unforeseen circumstances (I was away playing golf) prevented my answering sooner. Your order was marked for personal attention by our sales manager (he lost it) and he is heartsick at having failed you. (He's still looking for it.)

Please forgive us: this will never happen again (till next time). Your friendship means too much to us. (This is no kid-

ding, either. You're one of the few customers we have left.)
Faithfully (like my wife always said before running away with
the head shipping clerk). . . .

*   *   *

Alan King tells about the secretary who handed her boss a
letter written on heavily perfumed note paper. "This letter
was marked 'Strictly Personal,'" she told him, "but it isn't
very."

*   *   *

Eager to make good in his new job, Eustace Filligrew arrived at the office at eight-thirty sharp, only to find the curvy,
blonde secretary sitting on the boss' lap.

The next morning he showed up at eight-fifteen. The boss
and the secretary were locked in a tight embrace. As Eustace
tiptoed out of the office, the boss looked up at the clock and
hollered, "Filligrew, if you get in here tomorrow at eight—
you're fired!"

*   *   *

Ben Cassell lists the four faux pas that lost the beautiful receptionist in his office her job:

1. "Insurance? I'm sure the boss is interested in a new policy. Go right into his private office."

2. "I forgot to tell you yesterday. President Johnson called
from Washington while you were out to lunch and wanted you
to call him right back on a very important matter. I guess it
just slipped my mind."

3. "You may be the boss's son—but you can't make passes at
me like that."

4. "I'm sorry, but you can't go in right now, Mrs. Marshall.
Your husband is dictating to that new red-headed secretary he
hired personally last Monday."

*   *   *

A prominent midtown dress manufacturer lavishly entertained an out-of-town buyer last week. The very next day he
got an order for three hundred more girls.

*   *   *

"There's no limit to the amount of work a man can do," insisted Robert Benchley, "provided, of course, that it isn't the work he's *supposed* to be doing at that moment."

* * *

Memo pinned on the bulletin board of a paper-box factory:
"To Our Employees:
"The Management of this organization, after due and careful consideration of certain regrettable practices which have recently been brought to its attention, is desirous of again reminding you of the fact—which has, of course, been pointed out on several previous occasions but which nevertheless has apparently been overlooked or ignored by an all-too-preponderant proportion of our present personnel—that all members of this organization should make an earnest, sincere, continuous, and persistent effort to eschew and avoid all excessive wordiness, repetitive phraseology, unnecessarily complicated sentence structure, lengthy, involved, or obscure paragraphs, and other tautological and/or grammatical errors to indite or transcribe an internal communication of any nature whatsoever to one or more fellow employees,

The Management
"P.S. In other words—make it brief!"

*   *   *

A very self-confident young man had just submitted to a long series of aptitude tests, and awaited results with lofty unconcern. "I suppose," he told the returning examiner, "I have an aptitude for so many fields that you fellows are a bit confused about it all."

"You have an aptitude for exactly one field," the examiner told him tartly, "and that is any field in which your father holds an extremely influential position."

*   *   *

Adam Gimbel tells about a man who went to a clothing store to buy a suit, and was immediately asked his name, address, family history, favorite pastimes, political affiliation, and his wife's maiden name.

"Why all these questions?" he demanded. "I only want to buy a suit." "Ah, my friend," said the salesman silkily. "Before we sell you a suit here, we make sure that it fits your personality and position in life. We send to Australia for the proper blend of wool for you. From France we import just the right lining, from Scotland the buttons you should have. Then five tailors in our shop make it fit you to perfection, regardless of the fittings that may prove necessary."

"Shucks," said the customer. "I need this suit to be married in tomorrow morning."

"Stop worrying," said the salesman. "You'll have it."

*   *   *

Colonel Duffy is bemoaning the plight of the mattress tester who got fired for standing up on the job.

*   *   *

Mourned the proprietor of a men's clothing emporium, "In our five-story establishment, with sixty fancy clerks, we sold exactly one suit Tuesday. Wednesday we sold nothing at all. And Thursday was even worse than Wednesday." "How could it possibly be worse," demanded a stickler for accuracy. "Because," explained the proprietor, "on Thursday the loafer who bought the suit on Tuesday brought it back for credit."

*　*　*

Mr. Rinswanger, with eight hungry mouths home to feed, braced his employer for a substantial raise. "For six years," he wailed, "I haven't been able to buy even one suit of decent clothes for myself. Lord how the threads are unraveling in this worn-out coat I'm wearing."

"O.K.," conceded the boss wearily, "You can have a ten-dollar raise. But please, I beg you, don't show me your stringy coat any more. This organization can't afford any fringe benefits!"

*　*　*

In the dark recesses of a Third Avenue antique shop, Mrs. Hayward asked a clerk, "What is that quaint old figure in the corner worth?" "About two hundred grand," answered the clerk. "He's the proprietor."

*　*　*

A stout lady in Dayton's approached a lovely young salesgirl and inquired as to the whereabouts of the perfume counter. The salesgirl suggested politely, "Just walk this way, Ma'am." "Hmpfhh," commented the customer. "If I could walk that way, my dear, I wouldn't need perfume."

*　*　*

A top official at Chrysler confesses, "When we have a tough new problem at the plant and our experts can't figure an easy way to solve it, we put our laziest man on the job. He'll find the easy way in forty-eight hours flat. Then we adopt his method."

*　*　*

Overheard in an air-conditioned office: "Makes me feel a bit guilty, sitting here in comfort, while the wife and kiddies suffer under the broiling sun at the seashore!"

*　*　*

A professor from the Harvard Business School was telling his six-year-old son the story of Cinderella. The boy paid flattering attention—particularly when his father came to the part where the pumpkin turns into a golden coach. He interrupted only long enough to ask, "Hey, Pop, did Cinderella have to report that as straight income, or did they let her call it a capital gain?"

* * *

Dave Balch, passing a fish store on Vesey Street, spotted two tubs of live soft-shell crabs, side by side. One tub had a sign reading "$2.50 a dozen"; the other a sign reading "$1.50 a dozen." While Balch watched, a crab in the $1.50-a-dozen tub pulled himself up laboriously from among his fellows, attained the rim of the tub, and climbed into the $2.50-a-dozen receptacle.

"That's the sort of thing," opined Balch with great satisfaction, "that can happen only in the U.S.A.!"

* * *

Congressman John Lindsay of New York tells about a shop owner with 148 employees who proposed a profit-sharing and pension plan—provided every employee signified his approval in writing. One hundred forty-seven men signed at once, but one maverick refused, thereby nullifying the entire project. For two weeks the holdout persisted, then one day marched into the boss's office and declared meekly, "I've decided to sign." "Good," enthused the boss, "but what finally persuaded you to change your mind?"

Explained the holdout: "This morning the two huskiest members of the union grabbed me by the collar and told me, 'If you haven't signed up by ten-thirty this morning we'll break both your arms, break both your legs, and knock out all your teeth.' Well, Boss, nobody had ever bothered to explain the plan to me so clearly before."

INGENUITY

A young man in a drugstore phone booth left the door of the booth ajar, so the druggist couldn't help overhearing his conversation. "I want to talk to the boss," was his opening gambit. "Please connect me. This *is* the boss? Well, how would you like to hire a new, on-his-toes office boy? You already have one who is entirely satisfactory? No way to persuade you to make a change? O.K., I'm sorry. Thanks anyhow for listening to me. Goodbye."

After the young man hung up the druggist told him, "I couldn't help hearing what you said over the phone just now. I like your initiative and I'm sorry you didn't connect on that job. Better luck next time."

"Thanks," said the young man airily, "but everything is just dandy. That was my own boss I was talking to. I was just doing a little checking up on myself."

* * *

When F. W. Woolworth opened his first store, a merchant down the block resented the new competition and hung out a big sign reading, "I have been doing business in this spot for over fifty years." The next day Mr. Woolworth hung up a sign, too. *His* read: "Established a week ago; no old stock."

❖   ❖   ❖

A garage man who owns the first of four closely bunched gas stations on a federal highway leading to the Mojave Desert erected a big sign proclaiming, "This is your LAST chance to fill up before you hit the desert. The three other stations you think you see are mirages."

❖   ❖   ❖

A senior at the University of Minnesota awoke one midnight at the height of a violent storm to find the ceiling of his top-floor room leaking like mad. The resultant puddle next to his bed was rapidly assuming the proportions of Lake Superior.

Our hero was equal to the emergency. He calmly took the proper tool out of his kit and drilled a neat hole in the center of the puddle.

❖   ❖   ❖

A visitor to a Sunset Boulevard confectionery parlor noticed that one salesgirl had a line of customers waiting to be served by her while three other salesgirls stood idle. Later the busy salesgirl explained her popularity. "The other girls scoop up more than a quart of ice cream and then start scraping away. I always scoop up less than a quart and then add to it."

❖   ❖   ❖

An irate gent in a jewelry store demanded a refund on a watch he had purchased there a few days before. "This watch," he asserted, "loses fifteen minutes every hour." "Of course it does," nodded the proprietor. "Didn't you see the sign '25 per cent off' when you bought it?"

❖   ❖   ❖

A young girl who got a job in a bakery was telling her mother of her first day's experience there. "They put me to work taking stock of all the cakes that were left and I just couldn't spell meringue." "What did you do?" asked the sympathetic mother. The girl explained, "Well, there were only seven left, so I ate them."

* * *

There once was a capricious tycoon in downtown New York whose office was overrun with dogs. Never less than thirty assorted poodles, pugs, Pomeranians, and terriers had the run of the premises. Furthermore, every applicant for a job had to run the gamut of these canines before being granted an audience with the boss. The reaction of the dogs was carefully noted. If they liked him, the job was his; if they growled at him, he never had a prayer.

One wily applicant learned of the tycoon's idiosyncrasy in time. He carefully lined the cuffs of his trousers and the inner band of his hat with strips of raw liver. Of course the tycoon's dogs greeted his arrival with wild barks of approval—and he was made office manager on the spot!

* * *

A college graduate wangled his way into a tony publisher's office and asked cheerfully, "Need a good editor?" "I do not." "A proofreader, perhaps?" "Nope." "A sixth assistant secretary?" "No. Sorry, but we haven't any openings at all at the moment."

"Then," said the applicant, "you certainly need one of these." And from his briefcase he produced a neat metal sign reading, "No help wanted."

* * *

"Lackaday," sighed a Chinese businessman in Hong Kong, "I have lent a tricky competitor a thousand gold dollars and he has not given me a receipt. What can I do?"

"Write sternly," suggested his friend, "and demand payment of the two thousand gold pieces."

"Most careless listener," reproved the businessman. "I told you it was only one thousand gold dollars."

"I know," nodded the friend, "and your competitor will indignantly write and tell you so. Then you will have your receipt."

*   *   *

Two small brothers, aged eight and three, entered an ice cream parlor, with the three-year-old vehemently announcing, "I want vanilla! I want vanilla!"

The supply of vanilla had been exhausted, and bystanders wondered how the eight-year-old would cope with the situation. He did not hesitate. He ordered two strawberry cones and handed one to his younger brother.

"Here you are," he said cheerfully, *"pink vanilla!"*

INSURANCE

America's big insurance and casualty companies never have been in healthier financial shape, but life remains rugged for their underlings setting out to peddle policies for the first time.

To them are allotted the most unlikely prospects—in the most inaccessible territory—and woe betide the neophyte caught resting his dogs by an agency head. "A man who gets holes in his pants before his shoes," warned one, "is obviously making his contacts in the wrong place."

One foot-weary agent resorted to the telephone, and after 293 prospects had hung up on him, decided to shoot the works. He dialed the richest old coot in town. "I don't suppose," he hazarded timidly, "you're in the market for some additional life insurance."

"It happens that I am," was the astonishing reply. "Would you care to come out here and write a policy for a million dollars?"

"Excuse me, sir," stammered the agent, "I must have the wrong number."

Another agent, more optimistic by nature, came home jubilant from his latest brush with an ornery prospect. "No vague promises this time," he told his wife. "He says he will definitely buy a policy when hell freezes over."

The library of the Atlantic Insurance Company boasts the most complete set of marine disasters in the world. "I'll bet," joked a broker, "they even have a record of Noah's Ark." Inquiry proved that somebody at the Insurance Company had an excellent sense of humor, at least, because back came this dossier: "Built about 2448 B.C. Gopher wood, pitched within and without. Length: 320 cubits; width: 52 cubits; height: 35 cubits. Three decks. Equipped to carry animals. Owners: Noah and Sons. Last reported stranded on peak of Mount Ararat."

✿ ✿ ✿

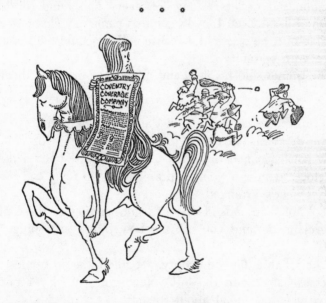

Insurance men will tell you that the most unpopular insurance salesman who ever lived was the killjoy agent who tried to sell a full coverage policy to Lady Godiva.

✿ ✿ ✿

Most people think "Lloyd's of London" is the most famous insurance company in the world. As a matter of fact, Lloyd's writes no insurance whatever. It is merely an association, whose members write policies strictly on their own.

Originally, Lloyd's was a London coffee shop, where marine

underwriters were wont to gather. In 1774, "Lloyd's Rooms" were moved to the Royal Exchange, and there a big bell was installed. For a hundred years, every important event has been announced via the tolling of this bell. It was salvaged from the frigate *Lutine*, sunk off the Netherlands coast in 1799 with a million pounds in gold bars and coins aboard.

Marine insurance is only one facet of the business done by Lloyd's today. Some years ago a professional flea trainer, for example, came to Lloyd's to insure his winsome performers. He was offered a policy, too, but the premium demanded was one hundred dollars a day for every five hundred dollars' worth of fleas! Even Lloyd's couldn't come any closer to a reasonable rate, he was told, because nobody could tell the age of a flea with certainty.

The trainer sold his fleas and opened a burlesque theatre.

*   *   *

An insurance salesman made the mistake of asking a prospect in the dress business how things were going with him. "I'll show you," moaned the dress man. He threw open a door to the stock room and pointed dramatically to rows and rows of dresses neatly arranged.

"Tens of thousands of dresses I got hanging on these racks," he exclaimed, "and you ask me how things are going. They ain't!"

"But what a fine inventory," soothed the insurance man. "Dresses hanging in the loft you've got, but clever partners you've got, too. What about them?"

"My partners?" sneered the dress man. *"They're hanging in the closets."*

*   *   *

The insurance adjustor was indignant. "How come," he demanded of the man who had sent for him, "that you didn't call the police the minute you discovered your car had been stolen?" "Well, for one thing," was the answer, "my wife was in it."

*　*　*

The formidable wife of a henpecked worm told an insurance salesman, "Let me be sure if I've got this right. You say that if my husband dies within even one year, I'll get the full fifty thousand dollars mentioned on Page One of this policy?" "Absolutely," the salesman assured her. "And within even a month?" "Yes, Ma'am." "And if he dies the day after I sign up?" "Then, Madam," said the salesman, snapping shut his briefcase, "I am confident you'll get the same fifty thousand—but they won't be dollars; they'll be volts."

*　*　*

An insurance broker in California sent his friends this announcement when his irrepressible sixty-seven-year-old mother graduated from college: "I announce with pleasure and relief that my mother finally nailed down her Bachelor of Arts degree this week. If you think it's tough putting your kids through college—just try your mother!"

*　*　*

A heavily bearded author invaded a book publisher's office recently, proposing an account of his six weeks on an uninhabited, treeless island without a bite to eat.

"How did you survive?" inquired the skeptical publisher.

"By luck," explained the author. "I had my insurance policy in my pocket. I found enough provisions to keep me going indefinitely."

SALESMANSHIP

An American shoe manufacturer read with interest about the upheavals in Africa, and correctly figured that along with their new freedom and opportunities, the African people would demand luxuries long denied to them.

The manufacturer hastily dispatched two salesmen Congoward to open new accounts. The bad salesman soon cabled back, "Returning next plane. Nobody can sell shoes here. Everybody goes barefoot."

The good salesman cabled, "Request permission open branch office here. Possibilities unlimited. Not a man or a woman in the territory knows what shoes are."

* * *

Another quick-thinking salesman is employed by a real estate broker on East Fiftieth Street in New York. The other day a lady on the telephone dialed him by mistake and inquired, "Do you sell maternity clothes in this shop?" "We do not," the real estate salesman told her regretfully, "but possibly I could interest you in a larger apartment?"

* * *

Lonesome George Gobel defines a salesman as "a fellow with a smile on his face, a shine on his shoes, and a lousy territory."

* * *

A conspicuous case of overselling is reported by Priscilla Platfoot, of Kansas City. A tiny runt of a man came into the emporium where she toils and asked for a job as store detective. "Nothing has escaped my eagle eyes in the past twenty years," he boasted breathlessly. "Why are you puffing?" interpolated the personnel manager. "You sound as though you climbed all seven flights of stairs to get here."

"I did," admitted the aspirant. "I couldn't find the elevators." (He didn't get the job!)

* * *

An overeager salesman got his comeuppance from a storekeeper in Maine. "You must remember that in this part of the country, young feller," said the storekeeper, "every want ain't a need."

* * *

A fur salesman was driving his wife along a mountain road when a small animal scurried across it in front of him. "What

was that?" he inquired. "A mink," said his wife. "Pfooie," sniffed
the furrier. "What a terrible fit."

IN THE SOUP

The nation's favorite beverage? Is it beer? Corn likker? Soda
pop? No, sir, it's soup!

According to a recent report, just about everybody in the
U.S.A. (approximately nine of every ten of us) has the soup
habit—and more and more of it is coming. Over ten billion
bowlfuls of soup were purchased by America's housewives in
1964.

*   *   *

No longer need mama slave long hours in the kitchen, or
worry which of her limited number of soup recipes she will
draw upon. Since the Campbells, not to mention the Heinzes,
Liptons, and others have been a-comin', she has only to heat
up some "mongol," "bird's nest," onion soup, bisque of lobster,
or bouillabaisse, and the family is served a treat comparable
with the fare at the most expensive restaurants. No matter
how fancy and infinite the varieties have become, however,
America's allegiance remains rooted to good old-fashioned
tomato soup, the sale of which tops all the others put together.

*   *   *

The succulent red tomato was unknown until it bobbed up
among the wild crags and rock-ribbed valleys of Peru. Thence
it spread to Mexico, where the Aztecs dubbed it *xitomatle*.
That was a little too much for marauding but appreciative
conquistadors, who reduced the name to its present form.

Soon these conquistadors, and their neighbors across the
Italian and French borders, were munching tomatoes at all
hours of the day and night. In Italy they became mixed up
with sauces and pizzas; in France, like so many other things
in that wonderful land, with sauces and sex. The French re-

named tomatoes *pommes d'amour,* and whispered that they possessed aphrodisiacal qualities.

The Puritans, after Cromwell's uprising, took no chances with this dangerous edible. They officially decreed that, aphrodisiac or not, tomatoes were *verboten,* and to be avoided as assiduously as toadstools and wolfsbane.

It remained for a publicity-minded benefactor named Robert Gibbon Johnson, of Salem, New Jersey, to put an end to this nonsense in the year 1820. He announced boldly that he would eat one dozen large tomatoes on the steps of the Salem courthouse.

A big crowd assembled, thoughtfully bringing two stomach specialists along with them, but Mr. Johnson calmly ate the twelve tomatoes, patted his midriff, and casually walked the five miles back to his farm. It was one of the stomach specialists who fainted.

*   *   *

From that day, tomatoes have ranked as our No. 1 home garden favorite, and indeed, what more satisfying sight can there be than a luscious tomato working in her garden? Tomatoes are ambrosial, whether in the guise of aspic, catsup, juice, chili sauce, salad, or cream of tomato soup!

* * *

But cream of tomato is not the only soup Americans have perfected to titillate the palates of gourmets the world over. The Pilgrims borrowed the idea of clam and fish chowder from the Indians. The Cajuns in Louisiana dreamed up creole gumbo. Philadelphians produced pepper pot, and Kentuckians the savory burgoo.

There are "mock turtle" and "mock kangaroo" soups, too, though if the animals named could read, they might be astonished to see what concoctions are merchandised with their names attached.

These are tasteful, but strictly non-turtle and non-kangaroo products devised by ingenious soup inventors and souper-douper selling organizations.

* * *

Plain soup, in fact, is far too healthful for the hoity-toity set. They now insist upon mixing it with gin, vodka, bourbon, and even rum, and labeling the results "bull shots," "bourbon beer," "monks' solace," and heaven knows what else.

In other words, they're now serving soup to nuts.

THE BULLS AND THE BEARS

Wall Street veterans are wont to talk about the crash of 1929 as though it happened just yesterday, but in 1929 all these commonplaces of 1965 were as yet unheard of (points out Joe Alex Morris in *What a Year*): jets, moon shots, the "sound barrier," Polaroid cameras, split-level houses, guided missiles, radar, bulldozers, electric typewriters, color TV, foam rubber, drive-in movie houses, bobby soxers, automatic transmissions for the family car, electric razors, the four-minute mile, and bubble gum—not to mention the United Nations—and the atom bomb!

* * *

Officials of the New York Stock Exchange treasure a request received by mail from a supplicant in Alabama who alleged that he was coming north to sell some hogs and would like "to get a couple of seats for the Stock Exchange which ain't behind no post or around in some corner where we can't see what's going on. Our Uncle Julius says you fellows put on the best show in New York."

Back in 1875, incidentally, a seat on the New York Stock Exchange was valued at $4750. In 1929, an all-time high was reached when a seat sold for $625,000. In the war year of 1942 the value plummeted to $17,000. Present value is in the $200,-000 range. There are 1366 seats on the Exchange today.

* * *

John Wheeler tells about a daring speculator named Charles Flint who operated in Wall Street at the turn of the century. Once he found himself in serious financial straits, and knowing J. P. Morgan, the elder, slightly, he approached him for a loan.

Mr. Morgan consented to take a stroll with him to the Battery. He talked polite nothings, however, the entire time. Finally, after about an hour, Flint blurted, "But, Mr. Morgan, how about that million dollars I want to borrow?"

Morgan held out his hand to say goodbye and answered, "Oh, you won't have any trouble getting it now that we have been seen together."

* * *

Hetty Green, famed "witch of Wall Street," was one of the richest women in the world when she died—also one of the stingiest and most detested. Arthur Lewis tells the whole story superbly in his book, *The Day They Shook the Plum Tree.*

Hetty Green dressed in rags, slept in cold-water flats, ate leftover scraps, and begged for free office space—so she could go on adding to the millions she already had stashed away. Worse still, she denied her son medical aid—so he was doomed to go through life a cripple.

The son, Colonel E. H. Green, when his mother died, proceeded to squander millions on patent medicines and such indulgences as an oceangoing yacht, which he ignored when he found that it made him seasick, and which gave him his first pleasure when it turned turtle and sank. He—and his only sister—derived as little real happiness from their great fortune as had their mother Hetty. Figure the moral for yourselves.

* * *

"A Wall Street security analyst," the late Herbert Bayard Swope liked to point out, "is as cautious as an Indian elephant. When one of these sagacious mastadons comes to a bridge, he tests it first with his trunk. If it holds firm, he next plants his front feet on it. If it still stands, he sits on it. After that, he sends another elephant over first!"

* * *

At the annual meeting of a company that was going from bad to worse, the president was interrupted in the middle of his address by his secretary who whispered hoarsely, "The treasurer wants to give his financial report. He's on long distance."

* * *

A partner of a Wall Street brokerage house summoned a pert, capable girl from the outer offices and offered her a big raise and advancement to a different job. "Thank you, sir," she replied demurely, "but if it's all the same to you, I think I'll keep my present pay and hang on to taking care of the stamp box and the petty cash."

* * *

John Straley tells of the stockbroker who was trying on a suit and told the tailor, "I think you might take these pants in about an inch." The tailor squelched him with, "In this business, mister, it's like in yours. You should never argue with the tape." Straley, meanwhile, is toying with the notion of opening a brokerage office in a dirigible moored above Broad and Wall Streets. That way he'll always be able to sell stock for his clients above the market.

* * *

A new customer asked for the head of a Wall Street brokerage house, and once admitted to the inner sanctum, explained succinctly, "I have a really tough investment problem." "We're here precisely for cases like yours," the broker assured him cheerily. "Just what is the nature of your problem?" The customer said, "I haven't any money."

* * *

Dick Bobbitt tells about a wealthy financier who became the virtual slave of a reigning musical comedy queen. After squiring her aggressively for months, he decided to propose matrimony, but cautiously hired a private eye to shadow her for a spell to make sure she wasn't two-timing him. A fortnight later, he received this report: "Miss So-and-So enjoys a spotless reputation, and until this year her behavior has been exemplary. In recent months, however, she has wandered sadly from the paths of virtue, and is now being seen constantly with a banker who is said to be the biggest crook in Wall Street."

* * *

A hard-driving young securities salesman phoned a prospect who chanced to be a certified accountant, and gave him a terrific pitch about a new business equipment stock which he claimed "was certain to double or even triple in less than a year." "I'm glad you think so well of this company," said the accountant warmly. "I happen to be its financial vice president." "Well, I'll be darned!" exclaimed the salesman. "Tell me confidentially, sir, *is the company any good?*"

* * *

Popular story among well-heeled suburbanites: A teacher, lecturing on Puritan fables and customs, asked her class, "What sort of people were punished in the stocks?" To which a bright lad in the front row responded, "The small, unsophisticated investors."

* * *

J. K. Galbraith, witty Professor of Economics at Harvard, explains in his book, *The Affluent Society:* "The nature of a vested interest has an engaging flexibility. In ordinary intercourse it is an improper advantage enjoyed by a political minority to which the speaker does not himself belong. When the speaker enjoys it, it ceases to be a vested interest and becomes a hard-won reward. When a vested interest is enjoyed not by a minority but by a majority, it is a human right."

* * *

A fat dowager aboard a crowded Fifth Avenue bus trod upon the foot of an irritable merchant who was trying to read the stock tables in the evening paper. "Madam," he said coldly, "I will ask you to kindly get off my foot." "Put your foot where it belongs," she replied sharply. "Madam," he murmured reverently, "don't tempt me!"

* * *

Arthur Goodman claims there's a new electronic machine in a big Wall Street brokerage office that is being used to good effect for extracurricular purposes by the staff during the coffee break. One girl inserted a note saying that from the way her boy friend had acted the night before, she figured she was engaged. "What should I do?" she asked the wonderful machine. It answered, "GET IT IN WRITING." Then a customer's man asked about an opportunity just given him to get in on a deal on the ground floor. Advised the machine, "WATCH OUT FOR THE BASEMENT."

* * *

Financial experts will like the story of the securities analyst who came home early one day and found his wife being embraced by a strange gentleman. "What's the meaning of this?" he bellowed. "Keep your shirt on," counseled his wife. "I've gone public."

20. A Turn for the Verse

What sentiment, what emotion a clever versifier can cram into four short lines! Following are a few quotable examples.

Ruminates Rod Terrill:

> The good old days, the good old days,
> We all so fondly speak of,
> Which, if they ever should come back,
> No one could stand a week of.

Character sketch by Frank Connors:

> He wrecked his car, he lost his job
> And yet throughout his life,
> He took his troubles like a man:
> He blamed them on his wife.

Disgusted with a stretch of wretched weather, an English poet (who wouldn't sign his name) dashed off this rhymed lament:

> Oh, what a blamed uncertain thing
> This pesky weather is:
> It blew and snew and then it thew
> And now by jing it friz!

Sayeth Paul Flowers, the Memphis sage:

> All right, go lie upon the beach,
> To bake beyond the water's reach;
> But if you're blistered when you quit,
> Remember that you basked for it.

By Sheldon White:

> I've written lots of letters
> Filled with libelous intent,
> And don't regret a single one—
> Except the few I sent.

Colonel Corncrib's ode to a bore:

> If you can remember so many bad jokes,
> With all of the details that mold them,
> Why can't you recall, with comparable skill,
> All the countless occasions you've told them?

By Herb Ellafson:

> 'Twas in a restaurant they met
> Brave Romeo and Juliet.
> He had no cash to pay his debt
> So Romeo'd what Juli'et.

Frank Boyden, famous headmaster of Deerfield Academy, has a little poem always on tap for lazy students:

> You can't go far just by wishing
> Nor by sitting around to wait:
> The good Lord provides the fishing—
> But you have to dig the bait.

Barbara Jones suggests a new version of an old Mother Goose rhyme:

> There was an old woman
> Who lived in a shoe
> She had so many children
> Her government relief check came to $4892.

Reports Day C. Yeager:

> I took up golf to soothe my nerves,
> But one thing causes mutters:
> If the foursome playing ahead of me
> Instead of putting, putters.

Rueful meditation from D. E. Twiggs:

> Doc said he'd have me on my feet
> The last time I was ill,
> And that he did . . . I sold my car
> So I could pay his bill.

Laments Walter Jacobs:

> A lady drove her little car
> In manner swift and deft,
> But every time she signaled right
> The little car turned left.

Terse verse from Francis Duffy:

> He let his head get swollen up,
> And sniffed at those who hired him.
> He thought himself a great big gun—
> And that is why they fired him.

Ogden Nash, of course, is one of the great masters of the art of the four-liner. These two are included in his sparkling collection, *From Everyone but Thee and Me:*

1.

The truth I do not stretch or shove
When I state the dog is full of love.
I've also proved, by actual test,
A wet dog is the lovingest.

2.

The clam, esteemed by gourmets highly,
Is said to live the life of Riley;
When you are lolling on a piazza
It's what you are happy as a.

The prolific Richard Armour is another of my favorites.
Consider:

1.

You cannot buy, you cannot lease
As durable and crisp a crease
As that your trousers soon acquire
When hung on hangers made of wire.

2.

How cunningly the ice holds back
And lingers underneath
And lets you raise and tilt the glass,
Then smacks you in the teeth!

The late Sam Hoffenstein once sent these lines to a lady
love who was beginning to bore him:

When you're away, I'm restless, lonely,
Wretched, bored, dejected; only
Here's the rub, my darling dear,
I feel the same when you are near.

A knowing light versifier once whipped up this gentle lament:

> When late I attempted your pity to move,
> What made you so deaf to my prayers?
> Perhaps it was right to dissemble your love
> But—why did you kick me downstairs?

Now who would you name as the author of those lines? Ogden Nash? Dorothy Parker? Richard Armour? Phyllis McGinley?

The poet's name was Isaac Bickerstaffe, born in 1735, and dead and gone almost a century and a half ago.

Rhyme marches on!

21. *Wide, Wide World*

THERE'LL ALWAYS BE AN ENGLAND

Hear ye, hear ye, those who chafe under the restrictions of the income tax, to this protest from a recognized authority: "The income tax, we have been told repeatedly, was a temporary measure, and would soon be reduced, if not relinquished altogether. These sanguine expectations have now been proved in vain, and indeed, the income tax is pressing on us more heavily, in peace time, than it did during the war. The very minister, in fact, who told us it would cease, now proposes its augmentation. What practical man now expects to see its end? Who is credulous enough to hope for a year in which he will be granted a reduction?"

The paper in which these words appeared was the London

Economist. The minister referred to was William Gladstone. The date was February 23, 1861!

*   *   *

Peter Fryer, in his book, *Mrs. Grundy: Studies in English Prudery,* tells how one Victorian journal lashed out at the waltz as "an expression of those base, primitive instincts which it is the aim of civilization to suppress. It is an engine of Hell to do the Devil's work!" Another London newspaper, in an article by a pig-raiser on pork and bacon, substituted "sow bacon" for "sowbelly." A third chastely referred to a dancer's navel as her "waist dimple."

Fryer notes that the undergarments issued to the Women's Auxiliary Air Force in World War II were so ludicrously "modest" and hideous that the girls dejectedly dubbed them "passion killers."

*   *   *

The stately and ultradignified Queen Victoria was riding in the royal coach through the streets of London when a loyal subject suddenly burst past the cordon of police and hollered, "Keep up the good work, Vic, old girl!" The miscreant was hustled off, and the Queen was heard to grumble, "That should never have been allowed to happen—but it was gratifying, quite gratifying!"

*   *   *

England's great Prime Minister, Benjamin Disraeli, once discovered a deaf Member of Parliament listening to a dreary debate with the aid of an ear trumpet. Snorted Disraeli, "What a wanton waste of the mercies of God's providence!"

*   *   *

In a debate in England's House of Lords, a tiresome member had been speaking for an hour. When he drew himself up to his full height (5 feet 2) and declaimed, "And now the time has come to ask myself . . ." a voice from the opposite side of the hall interrupted him with, "Well, you're going to get a damn silly answer!"

* * *

A British lady, married to a dashing cavalier ten years younger than herself, was summoned to America and forced to leave her roving-eyed husband alone for the first time since their marriage. Just before she left, she introduced the new butler to her husband.

"This is Rumbold," she said. "Not only will he look after you while I'm away but he'll do the cooking as well."

Some nights later the cavalier invited an old university chum to dinner. The food was ghastly. "What's gone wrong around here, old chap?" inquired the chum testily. "You never used to be satisfied with food like this."

"I know, I know," sighed the husband. "But what kind of cooking can you expect from Scotland Yard?"

* * *

An American in London slipped and fell on Fleet Street one day and was sufficiently bruised to believe a visit to a doctor would be the better part of valor. He accordingly stopped a bearded passerby and asked for the address of the nearest physician.

"Turn up Hind Court and look for Gough Square," advised the passerby. "There's a doctor living on the left hand side, I believe. You'll see the name on a plate outside."

The tourist followed instructions faithfully. He had no trouble finding the house. And there was the plate as promised. It read: HOME OF DR. SAMUEL JOHNSON, BORN, 1709. DIED, 1784.

* * *

Robert Littell, in his book *It Takes All Kinds*, tells of frisky Oxford undergraduates who practice for future Alpine and Himalayan mountain-climbing feats by inching their way up the walls and monuments of the various edifices on the Oxford campus. The fact that this sport is strictly forbidden adds an extra attraction to the activity.

One corpulent don who had been a famous mountain climber in his younger days recently gave a group of these Oxonian

scalawags a surprise. Spotting them carefully ascending the
outside of the most hallowed building in Oxford, he hurried
around to the other side and, puffing heavily, managed to
reach the summit first. When the temporarily triumphant un-
dergrads got there themselves, the next voice they heard was
the don's. "Gentlemen," he asked calmly, "may I have your
names, please?"

* * *

Palm Beach gentry recall with pleasure a crusty, formidable
English earl who made his first visit to our shores shortly after
the end of World War II.

Austerity was the watchword in Britain that year, and the
earl, although one of the wealthiest peers of the realm, with
four castles and a hundred servants, felt a bit guilty about
evading London's wintry blasts. "I've got it," he suddenly told
his wife, Celia. "We'll go without my personal valet, Masters."

Masters had not been ten feet from the earl's side since
nursery days, and the news that he now proposed to spend an
entire winter without his valet caused a sensation in every club
on Pall Mall.

The earl got through the first two days aboard the *Queen
Elizabeth* beautifully, faltering only when he had to put on his
dinner coat and black tie. A crisis was avoided when the captain of the ship came down from the bridge and helped him
personally. But on the third morning, His Lordship looked a
fright when he came on deck. There were tufts of hair in odd
places on his face, and blood flowed from jagged cuts beneath
his chin. "Bertie," gasped his wife Celia. "What have they done
to you?"

"It's my beastly razor," explained His Lordship. Lady Celia
rushed with him to their suite and found the razor clotted with
rust, hair, and gore. "Silly boy," she chided. "You forgot to
change the blade."

The earl regarded her in a state of stupefaction. "The *what?*"
he inquired.

* * *

The earl referred to in the previous anecdote prided himself on his hunting prowess. "In my day," he informed a beautiful dinner companion at a Palm Beach affair, "I have shot every known variety of wild game but a bongo."

"No bongo," sympathized the beautiful dinner companion (who had never even heard of such a beast). "Why not?"

"It was my stupid beaters," explained His Lordship petulantly. "They couldn't coax one up to the verandah!"

* * *

The first Rolls-Royce automobile was built in an English shed in 1905, and since that day the radiator design has never changed. The No. 2 model, in fact, remained in continuous production for nineteen years.

When Sir Frederick Henry Royce died in 1933, the designers decided on a radical step. The previously red "RR" monogram was changed to *black!* Conservative Britons expressed their disapproval in no uncertain terms.

As for the design of the emblem itself, it has changed only once—and that was when Queen Elizabeth ordered a special ornament from the royal silversmith depicting St. George and the Dragon. Directly after it was finished, the mold was destroyed.

* * *

A leading book publisher, famous for his taste in books, wines, and vari-colored shirts, purchased a Rolls-Royce recently with the profits earned from two new books of poetry.

A week after the Rolls had been delivered, the publisher called the Rolls dealer to complain that wheezing noises were emanating from the front end.

"There is only one possible explanation," said the Rolls man huffily. "Your chauffeur has asthma."

* * *

Max Bygraves, British comedian, confesses in his autobiography, "When I was a small lad my dad gave me a penny every morning as he patted me on the head. By the time I was fourteen, I had several pounds—and a flat head."

* * *

Every session of Britain's House of Commons is called to order by the Speaker, who marches into the halls with the flowing train of his black gown held up by a page, looking for all the world like a character in Gilbert and Sullivan. On the way to the House, he strides through the visitors' hall, a herald preceding him to call out, "Hats Off, Strangers!" Tourists who have gathered from all parts of the world to watch the colorful and traditional ceremony obediently doff their headgear as the procession goes by.

One day a great personal friend of the Speaker, named Neal McLean, was in the gathering in the visitors' hall. The Speaker spotted him as he walked through and impulsively cried out, "Neal! Neal!" Every tourist present promptly dropped to his knees!

* * *

Joe McCarthy met an Englishman who had just returned from the Far North and was full of tales of the troubles he had encountered driving a dogsled team over the frozen wasteland. "I kept urging them on with 'Tally-ho,' 'Tally-ho,'" he mourned, "but the confounded dogs wouldn't budge. They just panted a bit and laughed in my face."

"You should have said 'Mush,'" advised McCarthy.

"All right," conceded the Englishman. "The dogs just panted and laughed in my mush."

*　*　*

Martin Gabel, who loves England and the English people, brings back this story of a weekend he spent at a fine old estate in Surrey, complete with stables, prize cattle, peacocks, and extensive gardens. For his first breakfast there, the butler inquired, "Tea, coffee, or milk, sir?" Gabel chose tea. "Very good, sir," said the butler. "And will you take Ceylon, China, or Assam?" "Ceylon," elected Gabel. "And do you use milk, cream, or lemon?" continued the butler. "Milk," said Gabel with finality —but the butler's quiz was not yet concluded. "Very good, sir," said the butler again. "Jersey, Guernsey, or Holstein?"

*　*　*

A distinguished English actor had condescended to play a part in a Hollywood movie—at about six times the salary he commanded at home—but this didn't stop him from criticizing everything and everybody within range. One evening he was invited to dine with the publisher of one of the biggest and best West Coast newspapers. As coffee was being served, the publisher excused himself, explaining, "Every evening we have a staff meeting to discuss policy, and check on the editorials and front-page stories that are going to run in the next day's paper." "Good heavens," exclaimed the English actor. "You don't mean to tell me that you get out that paper of yours *deliberately?*"

*　*　*

It is very difficult to police some of the giant housing projects that now abound in cities around the world. One low-cost development outside of London had so many robberies that the tenants formed their own protective committee, and erected this sign: "Notice to Thieves: You are too late. Early bird miscreants have already purloined from these premises all radio and TV sets in working order, cameras, furs, and jewelry. THERE IS NOTHING OF VALUE LEFT TO TAKE."

Three days later somebody stole the sign.

* * *

Bids were solicited for a long-projected tunnel between France and England. Several firms submitted approximately the same estimates: in the neighborhood of twenty million pounds. One little outfit, however—Goldfarb and Company— declared it could do the job for fifty thousand pounds net. Highly amused, the head commissioner sent for Mr. Goldfarb and said, "Your estimate stopped us cold, I admit. How do you figure you can do this enormous job for fifty thousand pounds?" "Nothing to it," shrugged Mr. Goldfarb. "My brother will take a shovel and begin digging from the French side. I'll take a shovel and begin digging from the English side. When we meet—there you are."

"Do you realize," demurred the commissioner, "that the most minute error in calculation will mean that you'll miss each other completely under the middle of the English Channel?" "So what?" said Mr. Goldfarb, unperturbed. "If that happens, you'll simply have two tunnels!"

* * *

Sir Winston Churchill, to quote Bob Considine, was more than Britain's "Man of the Century." He was "one with the ages, a titan without boundary, borne to his timeless niche on the wings of a funeral unmatched in a land famed for plumed pomp and circumstance."

Sir Winston's old friend, Somerset Maugham, summed up the unbelievable mark on history made by Churchill in ninety years of tumultuous life when he reflected, "Not one of us would be here today had it not been for him." Churchill himself was perhaps prouder of his eloquence, wit, and genius as a journalist and historian than he was of his achievements in

diplomacy. "Winston," protested one of his parliamentary opponents, "spent the best part of his life preparing impromptu speeches." His valet noted that the preparations often were made in the bathtub. He thought he heard Sir Winston calling him one morning from that sanctuary, but was reminded sharply, "I wasn't talking to you. I was addressing the House of Commons."

One day Churchill remarked ruefully, "There's nothing very good to say about history after 1900. If I were dictator of the world, I probably should kill all the scientists. I should make it a criminal offense for anyone to go around bothering molecules. And the little atom would be left in peace forever." But Lady Churchill demurred, "Why then, Winston, are you always telling the British scientists to get on with their work?" "Because," he explained patiently, "in the first place, I am *not* the dictator of the world. In the second place, I am most unlikely to be elected one on such a platform. So—we just have to keep our end up."

"And," concludes Emmet Hughes, "he did—his life through. He could cock a skeptic's eye at the whole age that hailed him as a hero. And no small man can see so far."

LA BELLE FRANCE

Art Buchwald tells a story that underlines the skullduggery of fake art dealers in Paris, with rich but unwary Americans their chief victims. One such American fell for the old gag of the masterpiece so valuable that the government wouldn't allow its shipment out of the country. "It's a Titian," whispered the dealer, "a Titian every museum director would give his eyeteeth to possess. There's only one way I can sneak it to America for you. Let my assistant Garachi paint over the Titian. Then, when you get home, have the Garachi wiped off, and *voilà,* you have your priceless Titian."

The delighted American wrote out his check for two hundred thousand dollars, went on to the Riviera, and issued the necessary instructions about the painting to his secretary in New York.

Three weeks later he received this cable from New York: "Have received Garachi and cleaned it. Found Titian. Cleaned Titian. Found Garachi. How far should I go?"

*   *   *

"*Mal de mer,*" explained Maurice Chevalier to a young lady about to embark upon her first sea trip to the land of De Gaulle, "is merely a Frenchman's way of saying 'You can't take it with you.'"

*   *   *

An American tourist, arrived at Paris's Orly Airport for his first visit abroad, stopped at the restaurant near the customs counter for a bite of breakfast. What an opportunity to try out the French he had studied so laboriously from a set of phonograph records! He hailed a waiter and nervously ordered "*Oeufs! Oeufs!*" (Eggs! Eggs!) The waiter regarded him in disbelief, so again the American cried "*Oeufs! Oeufs!*"

This time the waiter permitted himself the suspicion of a

smile and, in perfect English, said to the tourist, "If you'll stop barking at me, sir, I'll be happy to take your order."

* * *

Red Smith was extolling the virtues of a Paris suburb called Noisy-le-Roi when a not-too-couth associate interrupted him by echoing, "Noisy Leroy?" and adding, "Throw the bum out!"

* * *

A French playwright visited our shores this season with his new and beautiful wife in tow. Unbelievably jealous, he had her shadowed constantly by private detectives until American friends told him, "We don't do things that way over here. Your behavior is an insult to all womanhood. Call off those gum-shoes immediately." Reluctantly the French playwright followed their directive. The very next day his bride slapped him across the face, crying, "You do not love me any more!"

* * *

Charles Pintchman claims that cinema star Henry Fonda had a difficult time in a Paris restaurant recently resisting a waiter who insisted that he drink a full glass of absinthe before tackling his dinner. "Why are you so determined on this point?" Mr. Fonda demanded. "Because," said the waiter, "you are my favorite screen personality, and I want you to stay healthy. And I happen to know that absinthe makes the heart grow, Fonda."

* * *

Herb Caen tells of the American exporter who was at the airport, bound for Paris, when he remembered he had failed to equip himself with some negotiable French currency. He phoned his brand-new secretary, "Get me fifty dollars' worth of francs and hightail it out here." She arrived breathlessly twenty minutes later—with two hundred hot dogs.

THE CARING FOR THE GREEN

If you're ever lucky enough to visit Dublin by air, I hope you'll get the same greeting there that awaited my wife, my two boys, and myself: a covey of bright-eyed journalists who made up clever remarks for me in the next day's journals, and a beaker of Irish coffee—which contains more Irish whiskey than coffee, and is a concoction fit for the gods.

The ride into the city of Dublin from the airport is an exhilarating one, too. "Look at the signs on the shops," I exclaimed happily. "Clancy, Gilhooley, Gallagher, O'Toole . . . !" My wife, infinitely calmer and less emotional than I am, doused my childish delight with, "What were you expecting: Nussbaum and Manischewitz?"

Our driver pointed out a railroad crossing where a guard had left the gate half open the day before, causing a traffic tieup clear down to O'Connell Street. A policeman finally cornered the guard and demanded, "What's the idea of leaving this gate half open?" The guard explained, "I'm half expecting a train from Galway."

Our driver also waxed enthusiastic about the literary revival in Ireland. "Those of us who don't read books," he boasted, "are writing them. And those who do neither are writing letters to the newspapers demanding that any book that really says something be suppressed immediately!"

Arriving at Dublin's famous Shelbourne Hotel, our driver pointed out a man in the lobby who once was silly enough to confess to an editor, "My name is Patrick Dolan, but I'm not Irish." "When you get to heaven," advised the editor, "just tell 'em your name—and never say another word!"

And how the Irish love to tell stories about themselves! Before I had been in Dublin four days I had chuckled over scores of them. Following are some I liked best (and had time to jot down).

* * *

The archbishop had preached a rousing sermon on the beauties of married life. Two buxom ladies from Bray left the church feeling uplifted and contented. "'Twas a fine sermon His Reverence gave us this morning," observed one. "That it was," agreed the other, "and I wish I knew as little about the matter as he does."

* * *

Honor Tracy tells of a phone call that woke up a minister in the middle of the night. "Hi, Finnegan," there asked a blurred voice he recognized as a parishioner. "Please send around three quarts of Scotch immediately." "This is not Finnegan," said the minister severely. "This is your rector." "Well, for Pete's sake," came the voice in astonishment. "What the heck are you doing in Finnegan's joint?"

* * *

A pugnacious son of Erin, exactly five feet tall and three sheets to the wind, staggered into a bar and loudly declared, "I'm the wild bull of Killarney and I can lick any bum in this joint." The bartender leaned casually across the bar, hit him lightly in the stomach, and sent him sprawling to the floor. It took the Killarneyite a few seconds to regain his composure, and then he told the bartender reproachfully, "Never hit a wild bull in the stomach, man. It's the silliest thing you can do!"

* * *

Patrick Clancy was a fighting man from the word go, but unfortunately he was lost in a gale in Galway Bay last winter. A neighbor stopped by to offer the widow Clancy a bit of consolation.

"Poor Pat," sighed the neighbor, "no doubt he's hitting the harp with the angels by now."

"Not him," replied Mrs. Clancy. "If I know my Pat, it's more likely he's hitting the angels with the harp!"

* * *

To prove to you what a smart girl O'Shea picked for his bride, there's the day they went to be married but didn't have a cent to pay the clergyman. "Sorry," said the latter, "but strictly cash in advance is my motto."

"Might you," suggested O'Shea's girl, "be after givin' me leave to go git the money?" Permission granted, she sped off and soon returned with the cash. After the ceremony, she asked, "No matter what you do now, yer riverence, this marriage is official, isn't it?" "It certainly is," the clergyman assured her.

"Then bless yer heart," said O'Shea's girl. "Here's the ticket fer yer hat. I picked it up in the vestry and pawned it."

* * *

In the heart of Dublin, reports the *Irish Digest,* there dwells a soul so pious that he insists on wearing stained glass in his spectacles during Lent.

* * *

Irish wit Brendan Behan recalled that after his book *Borstal Boy* became an international best seller, a boyhood crony accosted him in a Dublin pub. "'Tis well you're looking these days, Brendan," he wheezed. "Could you be giving me the loan of five quid?" "Why should I," countered Behan coldly. "Ah, sure, Brendan," said the beggar with tears in his eyes, "don't I remember you when the rags were floggin' your back?"

"Sorry, Mick," nodded Behan, turning away. "You're out of luck. You don't remember it half as well as I do!"

* * *

The guard at the entrance to a flossy estate barred the way to Shaughnessy, an old drinking acquaintance, who unexpectedly appeared leading by a halter an enormous elephant. "Come now, Shaughnessy," protested the guard. "You know we don't allow no elephants in here."

Back came Shaughnessy the very next day, leading the same elephant. He had, however, pasted a slice of bread on the elephant's trunk and another slice of bread on its tail.

"Didn't I tell you yesterday," roared the guard, "that we don't allow no elephants in this place?"

"So what?" demanded Shaughnessy. "This ain't an elephant, me lad. This is a *sandwich!*"

* * *

A Hibernian laborer, warned not to smoke near explosives, lit his pipe, nevertheless, one day on the job and promptly was blown sky-high.

A foreman dashed to the spot and demanded, "Where's Cassidy?" "He left," explained a fellow toiler. "When?" demanded the foreman. "Boss," declared the toiler solemnly, "if Cassidy comes back as fast as he went, he should have been here yesterday."

* * *

Now that those confounded experts are down to identifying people by numbers instead of names, Elliot Sharp tells about a convivial soul at the Hemisphere Club who introduced two men, explaining, "Number 435-11-9974, it's high time you met your fellow member, Number 632-7-091." The men shook hands warmly, and one said, "Mr. 632-7-091, where do you hail from originally?" "Dublin, Ireland," responded the other proudly. "Funny," mused the first man. "Your name doesn't sound Irish."

❖   ❖   ❖

Two bricklayers, writes Jerry Shane, were working on a
building. A sidewalk superintendent paused to ask precisely
what they were building. The more stolid bricklayer replied,
"I don't know and I don't care. All I do is slap this crummy
mortar on these crummy bricks and pile them up in a crummy
line." But the second and more imaginative bricklayer enthused, "I'm helping to build a great cathedral with a beautiful
spire that will point straight up to heaven."

So the second man was fired because they were building a
garage.

ISRAEL

A story currently popular in Tel Aviv concerns the newly en-
listed spy in the Israeli Secret Service who is sent to America
on a top-secret mission concerned with finding more water
to irrigate the Negev Desert. "When you deplane at Kennedy
Airport," he is instructed, "proceed to 171 Riverton Street, ring
the bell of Rosenbluth's apartment, and say, 'The sky is blue
and the grass is green.' He'll tell you what to do from there on
in."

The agent proceeds without incident to 171 Riverton Street,
but is perplexed when he discovers that there are two Rosen-
bluths living there. He take a chance and rings the bell of the
Rosenbluth on the first floor. When it is opened, he quickly
whispers, "The sky is blue and the grass is green." The man inside tells him, "It isn't I you want, my friend. Rosenbluth, the
secret agent, is the one on the *fourth* floor!"

❖   ❖   ❖

Ephraim Kishon, who writes a popular daily column for a
Tel Aviv newspaper, describes Israel as "sprawled on the shore
of the Mediterranean in such a way that half an hour's drive
from any point in the country will take you either to the seashore or into captivity at the hands of the Arab Legion."

Once Kishon complained in court about being smacked by

a taxicab, but the magistrate quickly put him in his place. "See how Israel has progressed," boasted His Honor. "When the pioneers first came here, some of them had to wait eighteen or twenty years before there *were* any taxicabs to knock them down!"

* * *

An Israeli diplomat tells about a duck that was preparing to paddle across the Suez Canal one day when a scorpion appeared with a bag of grain and said, "All this is yours if you will let me ride across on your back." "My mother always warned me to beware of the treachery of scorpions," demurred the duck. "How do I know you won't sting me in midstream?" "Silly duck," scoffed the scorpion, "in that case wouldn't we both drown?" So the duck said, "Hop aboard," but sure enough, halfway across the Canal the scorpion stung it. As they both went under for the third time the duck gasped, "What made you do it?" The scorpion gasped back, "What else could you expect? This is the Middle East!"

* * *

Messrs. Lapidus and Moskowitz, two wealthy and highly respected merchants from New York, were making their first visit to Israel, and in the course of same, dropped into a Tel Aviv night club where a new comedian had scored a sensational success. His entire monologue was delivered in Hebrew. Lapidus listened to it in silence without cracking one smile, but Moskowitz roared with laughter at each sally.

When the comedian had quit the stage, Lapidus said, "You certainly enjoyed that fellow's routine. I never knew you understood Hebrew." "I don't understand one word of it," answered Moskowitz. "If that's true," countered Lapidus, frowning, "how come you laughed so much at what he was saying?"

"Aha!" beamed Moskowitz. "*I trusted him!*"

* * *

An American tourist in Tel Aviv stopped an Israeli young lady and complimented her on her fine-looking, buxom baby.

"What's his name?" he asked. "Nasser Goldfarb," she replied. "Nasser?" echoed the astonished tourist. "How could you name your son after the enemy of your people, Mrs. Goldfarb?" She corrected him, "Miss Goldfarb, please."

*　*　*

A bit of excitement was added to the daily routine at a fashionable Israeli seaside hotel recently. A beautifully proportioned debutante from the U.S.A. went up to the roof on the first day of her visit to Israel to acquire a suntan in the shortest possible time. She kept her bathing suit on for a while, but then, discovering there was not another soul in sight, slipped it off and stretched out, face downward, to absorb the sun's rays, with only a small towel stretched across her back.

Suddenly there was a commotion. A flustered little assistant manager of the hotel dashed into view and gasped apologetically, "Miss, we do not mind your sunning on the roof, but we must beg you to keep on your bathing suit."

A bit miffed, the debutante demanded, "What difference does it make? No one can see me up here, and besides, I've covered my back with a towel."

"I see that," conceded the assistant manager, "but unfortunately, Miss, you are lying on the dining room skylight."

*　*　*

Latest story from Tel Aviv concerns Israeli private Avrim who tried to wheedle a three-day pass from his captain. "Don't be silly," the captain told him. "To get a three-day pass in this man's Army, you've got to earn it with some spectacular exploit."

A few days later Avrim astounded everybody by capturing

a brand-new Arab tank. Of course, he was rewarded with a three-day pass. Less than a month later, he captured another Arab tank and snagged a second pass. When he bagged a *third* Arab tank he became a national hero, and was promoted to captain himself.

Some time later, Private Moshe, who happened to be Avrim's first cousin, suggested, "Hey, Captain Avrim, how about one of those three-day passes for your favorite cousin?" "Earn one like I did," snapped Captain Avrim. "I couldn't," mourned Moshe. "I haven't your courage, or initiative, or flair for the spectacular."

Captain Avrim locked the door of his office, pulled down the shade, then whispered to his cousin, "Listen, Moshe. It's not as hard as you think. Take one of our own tanks out of the compound some night and drive out into the desert. Pretty soon you'll meet up with some Arab tank driver who's also looking for a three-day pass. . . ."

PEACEFUL COEXISTENCE

Official Washington is likening Red Chinese tactics to those of Hitler when he was in the ascendancy. They call it the "old salami game." "They shave off a slice of salami at a time but never enough to fight over. Finally the victim is left with nothing but the string of the salami—and that's not enough to fight over either."

* * *

At the opening of a three-day conclave in Smolensk, avers Myron Cohen, Soviet Premier Kosygin thundered, "Today, under our wonderful Communist system, every citizen of the Soviet Union is entitled to an electric icebox and a color television set. Is there any comrade in this hall who hasn't got an electric icebox and a color television set?" "Me," declared a little man in the fourteenth row. "Ah ha," nodded Kosygin, "and what is your name?" "Plotzikov," was the answer. "See that Comrade Plotzikov gets what is coming to him," ordered Kosygin immediately.

Toward the close of the third day of the rally, another citizen demanded the floor. "I suppose," sneered Kosygin, "you want to know what's happened to Plotzikov's icebox and TV set?" "Not at all," countered the citizen. "I want to know what's happened to Plotzikov."

* * *

Movie producer Billy Wilder has two gimmicks up his sleeve that he hasn't yet been able to jimmy into a picture. Both involve operatives from behind the Iron Curtain.

In one, the Commies kidnap a great film star in West Berlin and brainwash her. They are completely frustrated, however, because they discover she has no brains to wash.

In the other, a top commissar takes it on the lam and seeks sanctuary in Paris. In revenge, the boys at the Kremlin liquidate his wife and six children. The commissar thereupon hotfoots it right back to Moscow. He's no traitor at all; he just wanted to get rid of his family.

* * *

Comrade Kazotsky dropped in at the polls on election day in Pinsk and was handed a sealed envelope to drop into the ballot box. An official jumped six feet when Kazotsky started to open it. "What's the big idea?" screamed the official. "I want to see who I'm voting for," explained Kazotsky. "You must be out of your mind," decided the official. "Don't you realize that this is a secret ballot?"

* * *

A bold wag in Moscow dared tell about a big bruiser who attended his first track meet and discovered that one of the featured events was the hammer throw. He climbed down from the stadium, doffed his coat, seized a hammer, and threw it farther than a hammer ever had been thrown before.

When the track officials rushed up to congratulate him, the big man said modestly, "You haven't seen anything yet. Let me show you how far I throw the sickle!"

* * *

Caskie Stinnett reports that a passel of French delegates to a Moscow trade fair, understandably alert to the possibilities of their hotel room being bugged, cut through a maze of multi-colored wires they discovered cleverly hidden under the carpet. The floor was thick, but not so thick that it deadened the sound of the chandelier crashing in the room beneath them.

* * *

"Do you know what those Red Chinese are up to now?" grumbled an indignant businessman. "They're making the world's most beautiful girl. They're using Elizabeth Taylor's eyes, Brigitte Bardot's mouth, Ginger Rogers' legs, and Verna Lisi's back." "Boy, oh boy," moaned a man at the next table, "what I could do with what they're throwing away!"

* * *

Russia's increasingly uncensored humor magazine, *Krokodil*, recently ran a cartoon showing William Tell preparing to shoot his arrow. But on his boy's head was a sign readers seemed to recognize. It read, "NO APPLES."

* * *

Peter Lind Hayes spotted the most poignant classified ad of the year on the inside page of an East Berlin newspaper. It reads—if you can believe Peter—"WILL EXCHANGE: One fourteen-room, fully air-conditioned East Berlin villa for a hole in the wall."

* * *

Two confused Polish Communists were trying to make some kind of sense out of the current chaotic international situation. "Thank the Lord," concluded one, "that between Poland and China there's still one nice buffer state—Russia!"

* * *

Two space ships—one from Russia, one from the U.S.A.— predicts Seymour Rankin, will land smack on the moon before 1967, whereupon we may expect this anguished message from lunar males: "Dogs and monkeys we okay for a starter, but from here out, for the sake of universal harmony, boys, send us a couple of dames!"

* * *

Wiley Buchanan recalls an old fable that Spanish statesman Salvador de Madaragia told every time he heard Soviet propagandists proposing world disarmament without full inspection. The fable concerned a disarmament conference attended by all the animals. Each animal enthusiastically endorsed the abolition of a weapon he didn't happen to possess. The elephant proposed the abolition of talons. The eagle was equally enthusiastic over the notion of abolishing tusks. The lion wanted horns outlawed; the tiger poisoned quills. And so it went until the bear demanded the floor. "Let's abolish EVERYTHING," declared the bear heartily—"that is, everything except the great universal embrace!"

* * *

A preoccupied society matron was giving a dinner-dance for two hundred guests at her Washington residence. One guest named Smith was introduced to her exactly six times. When she asked his name a seventh time, he lost his temper completely and shouted, "Smith, you witch." "Ah," she beamed, "from the Soviet legation, I presume!"

* * *

Sad story from Moscow: An impetuous student in early 1963 drew a ten-year sentence in jail for hollering, "Khrushchev is a bum." Granted an amnesty in late 1964, he decided to get back into favor with the powers that be, and ran into Red Square shouting "Hooray for Khrushchev." Now he's back in the clink for *twenty* years!

WELL PLAID

An American in Aberdeen called up the police station and reported, "In front of the MacTavish National Bank there are two Scotsmen who are violently insane." "What makes you think that?" asked the lieutenant. "They must be," explained the American. "One is throwing his money away on the street and the other is picking it up and handing it back to him."

* * *

The driver of a taxicab suddenly lost control of his vehicle, and it started careening wildly through the dense traffic near London's Trafalgar Square. The passenger, to make matters worse, hailed from Edinburgh. "Can't you stop this cab?" he cried to the driver. "No," admitted the driver, "it's out of control." "There's one thing then that you *can* do," rasped the Edinburgher. "Turn off the meter!"

* * *

MacPherson was driving his girl past a shopping center one hot summer night when they passed a popcorn stand. "Yummy," said the girl. "That popcorn sure smells good."

"Wait a minute," said MacPherson generously, "and I'll drive up closer so you can get a better whiff of it."

* * *

A spoiled young Edinburgh society lass had not been entertained one evening by a new beau in the style she hoped to become accustomed to. As she bade him goodnight, she added in acid tones, "Take care on the way home, Jock—I wouldn't like to hear that you'd been robbed of all that money you saved tonight."

*　*　*

Quizzing a prospective son-in-law, a retired Scotsman demanded, "Are you quite sure you can support a family? Think carefully, young man. There are seven of us."

*　*　*

A traveling Scotsman was given expense money to put over a big deal. His reckless and most unusual spending aroused the suspicions of the bartender on his block. "Don't worry," the Scotsman told him sharply, "I'll know when I get to my own money!"

*　*　*

Workers in the box office of the Majestic Theatre never will forget the night Callahan stood patiently in line for an hour to purchase seats for a melodrama called *The Great Miracle*. Directly ahead of him was a dour Scot, who eventually reached the ticket window.

"Our best orchestra seats," the treasurer told the Scot, "are six-sixty. In the balcony they run as low as two-twenty." "I'll take two of the six-sixty seats," decided the Scot, producing a twenty-dollar bill, "and you may keep the change for being so courteous."

Callahan abruptly stepped out of line and headed for the sidewalk. The man in the box office yelled, "Hey! Don't you want to see *The Great Miracle?*"

"Not me," answered Callahan. "I've *seen* it!"

*　*　*

The fire-spitting three-headed Loch Ness monster, Scottish hotelkeepers' pride and joy, made one of his spectacular appearances one July day and sent vacationers and tourists fleeing, panic-stricken. All but one indomitable American lady, that is. She put down her knitting and patted the three-headed monster gently on the back. "*My* dear boy," she beamed, "have I got a girl for you!"

TRAVEL IN THE JET AGE

By Air . . .

Airline pilots at Kennedy Airport are talking about the ravishing redhead who boarded a jet, stretched out at full length, and explained to passengers around her, "I've got a big day ahead of me in L.A. tomorrow. I have to get some sleep."

The jet roared off into the gloaming, and as the redhead turned and wriggled in her sleep, her skirt crept up and up.

Suddenly the young gentleman in the seat opposite jumped up and reached for the blanket in the overhead rack. Carefully, almost reverently, he draped it over the recumbent figure of the beautiful girl. She awoke with a start. "Beg pardon, Miss," he told her, "but I've got important work also in L.A. tomorrow, and *I've got to get some sleep, too!*"

* * *

For her hundredth birthday, an old lady in the Blue Ridge country was offered a ride to New York in a jet airliner. "You won't get me in one of those fool contraptions," she answered firmly. "I'm gonna sit right here and watch my color TV, like the good Lord intended I should!"

* * *

A lady who weighs something over three hundred pounds had an interesting experience while flying by jet from Denver to New York recently. Shortly after the takeoff a stewardess tapped her on the shoulder and invited her to move from the tourist section to a seat in the first-class compartment. "I'm flattered," said the lady, "but wonder why you've singled me

out for this V.I.P. treatment." "Madam," explained the stewardess candidly, "we have a weight problem."

＊　＊　＊

A jet was about to take off for Seattle from Kennedy Airport
when a man rushed up to the gate attendant and demanded,
"Will there be time for me to get on that jet and kiss my wife
goodbye?" The attendant answered gravely, "That depends,
sir, on how long you've been married."

＊　＊　＊

Aboard a jet, one passenger explained to his seatmate that
his home was in upstate New York. "How far are you from
Manhattan?" asked the seatmate. "I reckon about 250 miles,"
said the passenger. "Two hundred and fifty miles!" echoed the
seatmate. "In Los Angeles where I live, up*town* is farther
away than that!"

＊　＊　＊

As a London to Calcutta jet soared through the sky, a restless kid kept tugging at the steward's coat to inquire every
twenty minutes or so, "What are we flying over now?" After a
dozen attempts to give a reasonably accurate reply, the steward
finally gave the kid a flight schedule and told him, "If you look
at your watch, then study this schedule, you should be able to
figure out where we are by yourself."

This kept the young traveler quiet for some time, but suddenly he was back at the galley, demanding, "Where are we
now?" "I told you," said the steward testily, "to look at your
watch." "Somebody has stolen my watch," whined the boy.
"Stolen, eh?" said the steward. "Then we're over Albania."

＊　＊　＊

At the Honolulu airport, a tourist deplaned and Tony Randall overheard him asking a bystander, "How do you natives
pronounce it? Hawaii or Havaii?"

"Havaii," said the native.

"Thank you," said the tourist.

"You're velcome," said the native.

Stewardesses were being hired to staff a new transpacific airline and the question was asked, "What would you do if the plane had to be ditched, and you found yourself the only girl on a remote tropical isle, garrisoned by ten thousand soldiers and only one officer?"

An English applicant admitted, "I should probably faint."

An American applicant said, "I should expect the lone officer to keep his troops in order."

A French applicant said, "What is ze problem?"

By Sea . . .

Captain MacLean, handsome skipper of the luxury liner *Queen Elizabeth,* had a bit of a problem with a particularly ebullient Texan on a recent westward crossing. It seems the Texan had become so attached to the ship that he insisted upon buying it. Captain MacLean finally dissuaded him with, "I'm afraid it's impossible, sir. You see she's part of a set."

* * *

The *Queen Elizabeth* was about to pull up her gangplank and sail off one morning when a shiny Rolls-Royce glided up to the dock and discharged a heavily furred London matron, followed by fourteen suitcases. Breathlessly, she explained why she was so late: "I told that fool chauffeur to take me to the pier —and he took me to the Pierre!"

* * *

A rich Iowa farmer was such a hi-fi enthusiast that he insisted on taking some elaborate hi-fi equipment with him on a European tour. His favorite platter recorded a variety of railroad sounds—whistles, chuffs, and clangs. He had just played it full blast in his stateroom in midocean when a female voice in the next cabin was heard. "You idiot," screamed the lady in said cabin. "My first sea trip to Europe—and you have to pick out a stateroom next to a railroad yard!"

* * *

A young doctor applied for a job of ship's surgeon for a 'round-the-world cruise. "What would you do," he was asked, "if the captain fainted on the bridge?" "I'd bring him to," answered the applicant. "And if he was still wobbly?" "I'd bring him two more."

* * *

Once upon a time there was a steamship captain who had handled freighters for years and took it as a mortal insult when he was transferred to a spanking new deluxe passenger liner. In fact, he often declared forcefully that any landlubber passenger who dared to get seasick should be tossed overboard forthwith.

One day in a howling gale a deck steward made his way along a line of deck chairs warning the few passengers in sight that the skipper was in a foul mood and might put his idea into execution.

"Throw seasick passengers overboard?" croaked one unfortunate voyager already green around the gills. "Here's a ten-dollar bill for you. Make sure I don't miss my turn!"

To Europe . . .

Back from his first tour of Europe, a disillusioned college student reports that he couldn't get hamburgers in Hamburg, English muffins in England, London broil in London, French toast in France, or even eggs Florentine in Florence. The wines —and the girls—he admitted, however, were wonderful.

* * *

The police officer who headed the night shift in a station house on the outskirts of Paris answered the phone, and heard an agitated citizen quaver, "There's a duel to the death scheduled for 6 A.M. in the Bois tomorrow and it's up to you police to put a stop to it." "We know, we know," the officer assured him. "Your adversary has already called us."

* * *

In a very, very swank restaurant in Paris, just off the Champs-Elysées, an American tourist was ignored for an unconscionable time by his waiter. Finally he managed to capture the errant waiter's attention and blustered, "My wife and I have been waiting for you for fully half an hour. I want a bottle of your best champagne." "Certainly, monsieur," said the waiter soothingly. "What year?" The tourist cried, "Right NOW!"

* * *

Arlene Francis decided to study French cooking recently, and enrolled with a very famous, very expensive Parisian chef.

"Does he let you eat what you cook?" asked her friend, Joan Axelrod.

"Let us?" laughed Arlene. "He *makes* us."

* * *

Judge Manders returned from his first trip to the Continent bubbling with enthusiasm. "What a wonderful city Paris is," he reported. "If only I could have gone there twenty years ago!" "You mean when Paris was really Paris?" joshed a friend. "No," said the Judge. "I mean when Manders was really Manders."

*　*　*

Aboard a luxury liner bound from New York to Le Havre, one elderly first-class passenger was boasting to a chance acquaintance of comparable vintage of a wonderful new watering spot he had discovered in Austria. "I don't know what chemical qualities the water there contains," he declared, "but I do know it's guaranteed to take twenty years off of anybody's life." When the acquaintance registered acute skepticism, the elderly gentleman produced his clinching argument. "You'll believe me," he crowed, "when I tell you of my own experience there. I arrived with a beautiful female friend who was eighteen years old—and in three days she disappeared!"

*　*　*

George Mikes, a Hungarian by birth and an Englishman by adoption, has written an amusing survey called "How to Be an Alien in Britain, France, Italy, Germany, Switzerland, Israel, and Japan." "In Britain," he notes, "a criminal may improve and become a decent member of society. A foreigner cannot. Once a foreigner, always a foreigner. He may become British; he never can become English."

"In Italy," observes Mikes, "hotel bills are scrupulously honest. If here and there in some of the smaller places, they happen to add the date to the bill, it is an error, committed in perfectly good faith. The only case which puzzled me occurred in Naples. I wondered whether they were justified in adding 230 lire for heating to my bill in the midst of a July heat wave."

❋   ❋   ❋

A world traveler has brought back from Frankfurt a paperback English-German phrase book which offers neophytes bound for West Germany the Teutonic equivalents for such everyday English phrases as: 1. "Stand back, the train ran off the metals." 2. "Bring me the curling tongs for my mustache." 3. "Give me a dozen very high, detached collars." 4. "Do you prefer a valve or a crystal set?" Here is a book, obviously, that no tourist bound for Germany can afford to be without!

❋   ❋   ❋

Suggestion in a Vienna newspaper for crossing a busy street: "In Italy, traffic will stop promptly if you cross the street with a shapely blonde; in England, if you have a dog on a leash; in America, if you are accompanied by at least three children; in Germany, if you are wearing the uniform of a general."

❋   ❋   ❋

Author Aubrey Menen, whose mother was Irish and whose father was Indian, declares that the land in which he ardently desires to spend the rest of his days is Italy, and here is his reason why: "In the first half of my life, I learned to know three people well: the English, the Indians, and the Americans. They were diverse in their ways, but they had one thing in common: all three felt deep within them that they had fewer moral failings than the rest of mankind. They felt that they only had to set the world a moral example, and the world would follow them.

"I suppose the world might have, if they actually had set the example. But they never did. Now I've decided to live among the Italians, who have given up such illusions."

* * *

It's Louis Sobol's story about the American motorist in Rome who stopped a native and asked anxiously, "Do you have any black cats two feet long?" "A few, *signóre*," answered the native. "Any black cats four feet long?" "It is possible," conceded the native. "Well, have you any *six* feet long?" "But no, *signóre*, that is ridiculous," said the native. "It's like I told you, you dope," interrupted the motorist's wife from the back seat. "You've run over a priest!"

* * *

Mary Ann Mobley bought a pair of expensive imported Italian shoes in a Fifth Avenue bootery recently. She knows they're the genuine article, too. They keep pinching her.

* * *

Afdera Fonda tells about a fountain in a town in northern Italy where any wish you make, the legend has it, will ultimately be granted.

One day a tourist and his wife were gazing raptly at the fountain, making their wishes, when the wife suddenly lost her balance and fell in with a mighty splash.

"Golly," exclaimed the husband. "I never realized these things really work!"

* * *

Touring through the south of Italy, an American couple drove through one village square where a brass band of twelve musicians was blaring away, under the violent leadership of a perspiring, uniformed maestro, before a deserted house whose every door and window was tightly shuttered.

The driver stopped and asked an onlooker, "Who are they serenading?" "The mayor," was the answer. "Well, why isn't he at the window acknowledging the compliment?" persisted the driver.

"That's the mayor leading the band," explained the onlooker. "What do you expect him to do? Be in two places at the same time?"

＊　＊　＊

Two ladies from Montreal toured Italy by motor last summer and inevitably pulled up before the famous Leaning Tower of Pisa. While they were parking their car, a uniformed attendant appeared, handed them a pink ticket, and collected 100 lire therefor. When the ladies returned to their hotel, they asked the concierge, "Who gets the money collected for parking near the Tower?"

The concierge examined their pink ticket, smiled, and explained: "There's no parking charge in Pisa, ladies. What you did here was to insure your car against damage in the event that the Leaning Tower fell on it."

＊　＊　＊

Outside the Excelsior Hotel in Rome, an American tourist heard a fellow chanting, "Bananas! Bananas! Three for a shilling!" The tourist elbowed his way through the midday traffic and tapped the caller on the shoulder. "Son," he advised, "these Eye-tall-ians don't understand English—and furthermore, they trade in lira, not shillings."

A happy smile spread over the banana vendor's face. "You're just the fellow I've been waiting for," he beamed. "Which way is the railroad station?"

To Africa . . .

A Peace Corps worker from the Deep South, assigned to a turbulent new African state, reported to his superiors in Washington via transatlantic phone, "What we're trying urgently to plant here is peace and harmony." A month later a freighter arrived loaded down with split peas and hominy grits.

* * *

A tourist came back from Africa with a trunkful of shrunken heads he hoped to sell, but experienced some difficulty in locating a purchaser. Somebody suggested he try a big sporting goods store. He called up, and after a few moments was connected with a man with a very deep voice. "I want to talk to somebody about selling a collection of shrunken heads," explained the tourist. "You're speaking to the right party," the deep voice assured him. "I'm the head buyer."

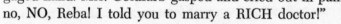

Miss Goldfarb, avid young do-gooder, joined the Peace Corps and was assigned a post in darkest Africa. Some months later, her mother answered the doorbell in her Chicago apartment. There stood her daughter, arm-in-arm with a huge man dressed in a lion skin, daubs of paint on his face, great gold earrings, an ebony splint in his nose, and a hideous mask in his disengaged hand. Mrs. Goldfarb gasped and cried out in pain, "No, no, NO, Reba! I told you to marry a RICH doctor!"

* * *

An African chieftain's daughter was offered as a bride to the son of a neighboring potentate in exchange for two cows and four sheep. It was agreed that the big swap was to be effected on the shore of the swift-flowing stream that separated the tribes. Pop and his daughter showed up at the appointed time on one side of the stream only to discover that the bridegroom and his livestock were waiting on the other side.

"Stupid fool," grunted the father of the bride. "He doesn't seem to know which side his bride is bartered on."

*　*　*

An intrepid explorer hired African natives to row him up a river where no white man ever had been seen. It traversed an impenetrable jungle and was laced with treacherous rapids.

For seven days the expedition doggedly progressed into the wilderness. Suddenly the explorer heard a beating of drums—ominous, insistent. Drums maintaining the same rhythm answered from farther up the river.

The explorer pulled out his pistol. "If these warriors attack," he promised, "I'll sell my life dearly."

"Keep your shirt on, mister," advised his boss guide. "Drums only say white sucker on way. Everybody raise prices."

*　*　*

Sick cannibal joke: Explorer in pot, about to be cooked. Chief asks victim if he has any last words to say. Explorer gasps, "Yes. I'm smoking more and enjoying it less."

*　*　*

It often happens, laments Olin Miller, that those who try to run the lives of others do more harm than good. Miller cites as an example the missionary who convinced a cannibal it was a sin for him to have five wives. So the cannibal ate four of them.

*　*　*

Changing world department: Well-informed cannibal chiefs are warning their subjects not to eat any more Americans. "Their fat," explained one fastidious fancier of human flesh, "is contaminated with chlorinated hydrocarbons, and is likely to produce ulcers, liver pains, and acute indigestion!"

Doesn't *anybody* love us any more?

To the Far East . . .

An American tourist gazed in awe at India's famous Taj Mahal. "And to think," he told his wife, "they were able to do it before anybody even had heard of such a thing as foreign aid!"

* * *

A fakir in Delhi cried out, "I've discovered two sacks of brand new nails." "Hurrah," cheered an even bigger fakir nearby. "Let's have a pillow fight."

* * *

Herb Stein tells about a tourist in Bangkok who was approached by a native and asked, "Hey, you like meet beautiful half-caste girl?" "No," said the tourist. "You like see nudist film?" "No." "You want to visit opium parlor?" "No." "What do you like then?" "Could you direct me to the public library?" "Hey, tourist! What's matter? You some kind of nut?"

* * *

Henry Morgan is credited with the story of a yachtsman whose boat foundered in the South Pacific. A giant wave finally swept him ashore on an uncharted island. Warily he crept into the underbrush, and suddenly spotted a wisp of smoke ascending from the foliage in front of him. Was this a nest of cannibals? He maneuvered within a few feet of the smoke-makers and it was then he heard a human voice. It was a woman's—and what she was exclaiming was, "You idiot! Why did you throw away your high trump on that trick? I ought to throw these cards right into your stupid mug!"

"Thank heaven, I'm safe," breathed the relieved yachts-man. "They're civilized!"

* * *

There's a very fat lady in Hong Kong who is threatening suit against the owner of a weighing machine there. She stepped on his scale one morning and reached for the card that was supposed to register her net tonnage. The card dropped out all right, but what it said was, "Come back in fifteen minutes—alone."

* * *

Danny Kaye, touring the world in behalf of the UN International Children's Emergency Fund, encountered one mean old curmudgeon who derided the whole idea. "The diseases, famines, and floods of the Far East," he insisted, "were always nature's way of counteracting overpopulation. Now you do-gooders are upsetting all the scales and what's the result? Seven hundred million Red Chinese! I don't mean to sound heartless, but . . ."

"Your logic is infallible," interrupted Kaye testily. "Why not put it to the test the next time your own child gets sick?"

* * *

Juliet Lowell reports receipt of the following note by a Japa-nese magistrate:

"Honorable Sir: I am writing school essay about American habits. Kindly enlighten me: how soon after marriage does great festival of divorce?"

* * *

To accommodate American tourists in Japan, the telephone company there, some years ago, slapped this notice in many public booths:

(A) Please ready with necessary yen coin, take off the transmitter, put in coin, and lastly send round the dial.

(B) When not connected, put on the transmitter if it was, and the coin will come on the return hole.

(C) For the suburbs communication, please notify it.

(P.S. Japan, infinitely more advanced today, and more conversant with American ways and speech, now has phone booths and equipment of the highest order—and the service is above reproach.)

* * *

A Japanese merchant has also made available for American visitors handy copies of local highway codes and regulations, thoughtfully translated by himself into English.

A typical paragraph: "On encountering pedestrians: when a passenger on the hoof hoves into sight, tootle the horn, trumpet to him melodiously at first. If he still obstacles your passage, tootle him with increasing vigor and express by work of mouth the warning: 'HI! HI.'"

* * *

A pompous history professor from the U.S. was invited to address a group of university students while he was visiting Tokyo. The Japanese dean acted as interpreter, writing the gist of the professor's remarks in Japanese symbols on the blackboard. Soon, however, the Japanese dean put down his chalk and stopped writing. Later the American professor asked him why. "Here in Japan," explained the dean with a respectful bow, "we only write when the speaker says something."

All-American . . .

A wily guide at Niagara Falls earns a big laugh—and extra tips—from every women's group he pilots by this sure-fire de-

WIDE, WIDE WORLD

vice: he herds them close to the brink of the cataract and declaims, "Now ladies, if I can possibly persuade you all to be
absolutely silent for two minutes at the same time, you will
hear the deafening roar of the cascading waters of Niagara!"

* * *

"I'll never forget the morning we first gazed on Niagara
Falls," confided Mrs. O'Connor. "My husband's face dropped
about a mile." "You mean," asked her friend incredulously,
"that Niagara didn't come up to your husband's expectations?"
"Not at all," Mrs. O'Connor assured her. "He fell over the rim."

* * *

A young mother was riding through Pennsylvania in a day
coach with her baby boy cradled in her arms when a man
across the aisle leaned over to say, "I must tell you that that
child of yours is just about the homeliest I've ever seen." The
outraged mother complained immediately to the conductor,
who did his best to soothe her. "We aim to please on this railroad," he concluded, "so I want you to ignore this man, and
move to a seat in the Pullman car ahead with our compliments.
. . . And, by the way, here's a banana for your monkey."

* * *

In Albuquerque they talk about a resident who drove all
day in 105-degree temperature with every window of his car
closed tight, then collapsed of prostration when he got home.
"Why didn't you open the windows?" wailed his wife. "What?"
he protested weakly, "and let everybody know we haven't got
an air-conditioned car?"

* * *

A tourist in New Mexico bought a beaded trinket from an
Indian for three dollars, upon the assurance that it represented
authentic tribal craftsmanship. "My squaw learn art from her
great-grandmother," said the Indian.

An hour later the tourist was back, hopping mad. "You faker,"
he cried to the Indian. "There's a fellow down at the railroad

station selling these same gadgets for a dollar. Shows you never can trust an Indian!"

"No," contradicted the unperturbed Indian. "Shows you never can trust white man. Feller who sold me these promised nobody else in town gettum."

✿   ✿   ✿

New Mexico historians point out with pride that it was an Indian chief from that state who first thought of installing electricity in the tribal washroom. Thus he became the first Indian ever to wire a head for a reservation.

✿   ✿   ✿

A certain distinguished gentleman from Arizona recently told an enthralled audience what happened when an apprehensive tenderfoot asked an old rancher, "What should I do if a rattlesnake bites me in the arm?" "Get a friend to open the punctures the rattler made and suck the poison out for you," advised the rancher. "And if I get bitten in the leg?" "Follow the identical procedure," nodded the rancher. "But suppose I'm unlucky enough to sit down on one of those darn rattlesnakes?"

"Ah, my boy," said the rancher solemnly, "that's the time you'll find out who your real friends are!"

✿   ✿   ✿

Epitaph in the cemetery at Tombstone, Arizona: "Here lies Jack Williams. He done his damndest."

✿   ✿   ✿

A Billings, Montana man told me of a vacation trip he took with his wife through Yellowstone National Park. En route, they met a quiet, amiable couple from New York, and made up a very compatible foursome. Back in Billings, my friend collected dozens of photographs posed by all in front of geysers, bears, waterfalls, and whatnot, and mailed them to the New York couple.

Two weeks later a slick lawyer appeared and announced, "Thank you for sending those pictures. Now I'll need you two

as witnesses. I'm representing your gentleman friend's wife in
a divorce suit."

"She didn't like the pictures I sent her?" faltered the Billings
camera shark.

"She thought they were extremely interesting," nodded the
lawyer. "You see, she wasn't the woman who was posing in
them."

*   *   *

Harry Golden tells about a West Coast lady named Sadie
whose twelve-year-old son snagged a job during his summer
vacation that paid twenty dollars a week. "And Mama," he
promised, "it all goes straight to you." When he handed her
his first pay envelope, the contents added up to only $19.90.
"Ah ha," said Sadie. "Taking out girls already!"

*   *   *

Notes Neil Morgan in his new book, *Westward Tilt*: Americans today are moving to California in greater numbers than
the annual entire immigration to the U.S. The five boroughs
of New York City would have to be emptied of every man,
woman, and child to match the population increase of the
past decade in our eleven Western states." He laments, however, that "people move to a place because it's different. But
the minute they get there, they start remaking it into a place
that isn't different at all."

*   *   *

A demon cartographer named Basil Konstantinos has determined that there is only one New York in the United States,
and that, of course, is the one that includes Manhattan, Brooklyn, and the Bronx. On the other hand, besides Boston, Massachusetts, there are Bostons in Arkansas, Georgia, Indiana,
Kentucky, Missouri, New York, Pennsylvania, Texas, and Virginia (nor should we overlook Bean City, Florida). There are
five Philadelphias besides the one in Pennsylvania, no less than
twenty-five Washingtons in addition to the nation's capital,

twenty-two Princetons, twenty-two Springfields, twenty-one Lincolns, and twenty-one Newports.

No wonder those hard-working lads in the Post Office Department occasionally get confused!

* * *

James Thurber told about two Alaskans who spent a summer vacation in the northernmost tip of Maine and had the time of their lives. As they were leaving, one of them told his hosts effusively, "Thank you! Thank you! Now I know what they mean by Southern hospitality!"

* * *

In the gold-rush days at the turn of the century in Alaska, recalls Boyce House, one of the most colorful figures in the territory was Wilson Mizner. To his dying day, Mizner boasted about the time it was so cold he broke three teeth on a frozen doughnut—also the night he pilfered the only typewriter in town and sold it to the butcher, who thought it was a cash register.

"Tragedy struck," reported Mizner, "on a colder day yet. The thermometer got stuck at sixty-nine below zero. The president of the bank stooped over to tie his shoelace and froze in that position. We had to bury the poor fellow in a drum!"

* * *

The peripatetic John Straley has been investigating the transit situation up in Nome, Alaska: "I wouldn't say in so many words that the transit system remains comparatively primitive in these parts—but yesterday was the first time I ever saw a crosstown bus that barked at me!"

*　*　*

The Eskimo had a reasonable explanation for leaving his 260-pound wife. He told a sympathetic judge in Sitka, "She wouldn't stop blubbering."

*　*　*

In Sitka they tell of a lucky Eskimo who won a trip to Seattle in a newspaper numbers contest. He came home with a long lead pipe that he set up in the center of his igloo, with one end protruding through the roof. When his wife asked the purpose of this installation, the Eskimo replied proudly, "New trick I picked up in Seattle. When you want more heat, you just bang on this pipe."

*　*　*

Anxious to be admitted to the most exclusive club in northern Alaska, a tenderfoot asked what he'd have to do to qualify. "Three things," he was told. "You've got to drink a quart of straight whiskey at one sitting, you've got to hug and kiss an Eskimo girl for three hours without being caught by her parents, and you've got to shoot a full-sized polar bear."

The tenderfoot promptly downed a quart of liquor, and reeled out into the stinging cold with a wild look in his eye. An hour later he was back, his clothing in tatters, and vivid scratches on his countenance. "O.K., O.K.," he reported. "Two out of three tasks accomplished. Now where's that Eskimo girl I'm supposed to shoot?"

*　*　*

A pair of bemused newlyweds were strolling on the white sands of Paradise Beach in the Bahamas. The groom looked out over the azure sea and declaimed, "Roll on, thou deep and dark blue ocean, roll on." His star-struck bride gazed out at the water for a moment, then gushed, "Oh, Sheldon, you wonderful man! It's doing it!"

*   *   *

Two cafe society phonies were discussing ways and means of promoting a loan for a Caribbean fortnight. "I'd call my broker," confessed one, "but his phone has been disconnected."

*   *   *

An American tourist fell in love with Montego Bay in Jamaica and decided to build a villa of his own there—offering overtime pay if it could be finished quickly. The contractor got it finished in record time—but the American found one thing missing when he moved in: there was no railing to the stairway. An army of native carpenters rushed out to the house immediately and built a railing in three hours flat. Two hours later the railing collapsed. The outraged owner called the contractor to raise more Cain. "Don't get so excited," soothed the contractor. "Remember: Nothing lasts forever."

*   *   *

Last word in optimism: the bullfighter, scheduled to face in the ring the fiercest bull in Mexico City, who put mustard on his sword!

*   *   *

Proud but easygoing Brazilians, says John Dos Passos, like to tell this story on themselves. When the Lord Jehovah had finished making Brazil he couldn't help boasting a little to one of his archangels. He had planted the greatest forests, laid out the biggest rivers, built the most magnificent mountains, bays, and beaches—then added untold treasures of gold, iron, and diamonds. "Is it fair, Lord," asked the archangel, "to give so many benefits to just one country?"

"You wait," chuckled the Lord Jehovah, "till you see the people I'm going to put there!"

22. *You Can Say That Again!*

QUOTATIONS

Some people collect stamps and others collect autographs. I collect quotes. I have a little black book that I carry around the country on lecture tours, and every time I read or hear a new or old quote that fascinates me, I make a note.

Here are some of my favorites:

Carl Sandburg: "A baby is God's opinion that the world should go on."

Arnold Glasgow: "A good leader takes a little more than his share of the blame; a little less than his share of the credit."

Ralph Peterson: "Experience is what enables you to make the same mistake again without getting caught."

George Burns: "Laughter feels good all over, but it only shows in one place."

Robert Balzer: "Life is what happens to you while you're making other plans."

William Allen White: "I am not afraid of tomorrow, for I have seen yesterday."

George Bernard Shaw: "Do not do unto others as you would that they should do unto you. Their tastes might not be the same."

Ralph Waldo Emerson: "The louder he talked of his honor, the faster we counted our spoons."

Harold Rome: "The trouble with being punctual is that nobody's there to appreciate it."

Frank Taylor: "A literary party is four authors and their wives who live in the same suburb and loathe each other."

George Santayana: "It is prudent to thank an author for his book before reading it, so as to avoid the necessity of lying about it afterwards."

From a book review by Dorothy Parker: "This is not a novel to be tossed aside lightly. It should be thrown with great force."

Wilson Mizner: "There is something about a closet that makes a skeleton terribly restless."

Franklin P. Adams: "Nothing is more responsible for the good old days than a bad memory."

Christopher Morley: "A man who insists on having his initials embroidered on his pajamas must be uncertain of himself. Surely you ought to know who you are by bedtime."

Somerset Maugham: "Only a mediocre person is always at his best."

Explorer Sir Vivian Fuchs: "If you actually look like your passport photo, you aren't well enough to travel."

George Ade: "A good listener is not only popular everywhere, but after a while he knows something."

Mark Twain: "Few of us can stand prosperity. Another man's, I mean."

Neil Morgan: "Behind every successful man is a surprised woman."

Will Rogers: "The best way to make a fire with two sticks is to make sure one of them is a match."

Abe Martin: "Never slap a man in the face—specially when he's chewing tobacco."

Tony Randall: "Those stretch pants so many young ladies are sporting these days come in three sizes: small, medium, and don't bend over."

Philip Wylie: "In the old days, men rode chargers. Now they marry them."

John Crosby: "A girl's biggest asset is a man's imagination."

Will Rogers: "A husband who is boss in his own house is probably a liar about other things, too."

O. O. McIntyre: "There are no illegitimate children. There are only illegitimate parents."

John Mason Brown: "Reasoning with a child is fine, if you can reach the child's reason without destroying your own."

Rod Cavanaugh: "My neighbor is mighty slow returning tools and commodities he borrows from me, but when it comes to bringing back my small children from his own little boys' birthday parties, golly, is he on time!"

Kim Hubbard: "Most parents don't worry about a daughter till she fails to show up for breakfast and then it's too late."

Doris Lilly: "To make a long story short, there's nothing like having the boss walk in."

Calvin Coolidge: "If you really want a job done, give it to a busy, important man. He'll have his secretary do it."

William Lyon Phelps: "The man who invented pills was a very bright fellow—but the man who put the sugar coating on them was a genius!"

Albert Lasker: "A salesman should never be ashamed of his calling. He should be ashamed of his *not* calling."

William Wrigley, Jr.: "When two men in a business always agree, one of them is unnecessary."

Tony Lema: "A hole in one, scored by pure accident can keep a complete duffer playing golf for the rest of his life."

Jack Benny: "Give me my golf clubs, the fresh air, and a beautiful girl for a partner, and you can keep my golf clubs and the fresh air."

Irving Lazar: "After eating a meal in a first-class restaurant nowadays, you need an after-dinner mint—such as the one in Denver."

Old Yankee pitching ace Lefty Gomez: "Remember this: a pitcher's success depends upon clean living—and a fast, friendly outfield."

Sinclair Lewis: "Don't fret about finding your station in life. Someone's sure to tell you where to get off."

Sigmund Spaeth: "Have you noticed how a concert audience will applaud a familiar encore after a few bars are played? They are applauding neither the performer nor the music. They are applauding themselves because they recognized it."

Sam Levenson: "My mother got up every morning at 5:00 A.M. no matter what time it was."

Chief Sitting Bull (as quoted by Dorothy Fields in *Annie Get Your Gun*): "I got three rules of life: no red meat; no get feet wet; no put money in show business."

David Burns: "In the old days, when a vaudeville comic allowed a pie to be thrown in his face, he wondered how many laughs he'd get. Now he wonders how many calories."

W. C. Fields (with a sensible amendment to an old proverb): "If at first you don't succeed, try, try, a couple of times more. Then quit. There's no sense making a fool of yourself."

Tony Randall: "Every time I find a girl who can cook like my mother—she looks like my father."

Arthur Godfrey: "Common sense gets a lot of credit that belongs to cold feet."

Groucho Marx (buying a frankfurter-on-the-roll): "Give me the bottom one: I'm always for the underdog."

Jackie Gleason: "The second day of a diet is always easier than the first. By the second day you're off it."

Dave Gardner: "Had it not been for Thomas A. Edison, people today would be watching television by candlelight."

Ringo Beatle: "Take a perfectly beautiful day, add six hours of rain and fog—and you have instant London."

Fable over the fireplace of a small hotel near Liverpool: "Fear knocked at the door. Faith went out to it and there was no one there."

Hindu observation: "Parting begins with the first meeting."

Lin Yutang: "When small men begin to cast big shadows, it means that the sun is about to set."

Persian proverb: "Give a horse to him who tells the truth. He'll need it to escape on."

Japanese proverb: "The cat is a saint when there are no mice about."

Vincent Hughes: "Politics is a profession where the paths of glory lead but to the gravy."

Mackenzie King: "The politician's promises of yesterday are the taxes of today."

Karl von Clausewitz: "A conqueror is always a lover of peace. He would like to make his entry into a coveted state unopposed."

Walt Whitman: "Bad officials are elected by good citizens who do not vote."

Adlai Stevenson: "There is nothing more horrifying than stupidity in action."

Ralph Erman: "These days the UN Building seems to be a site for sore allies."

Harry S. Truman: "The President of the United States hears a hundred voices telling him that he is the greatest man in the world. He must listen carefully to hear the one voice that tells him he's not."

Abel Green: "Eighty is a wonderful age—especially if you're ninety."

William Faulkner: "I decline to accept the end of man. I believe that man will not merely endure; he will prevail. He is immortal, not because he alone among creatures has an inexhaustible voice, but because he has a soul, a spirit capable of compassion and sacrifice and endurance."

23. Roundup

GRAB BAG

Does the number thirteen terrify you? If it does, points out Wes Lawrence, you are tempting fate every time you finger a U.S. one-dollar bill. The incomplete pyramid on its back has thirteen steps. Above the pyramid are the words "Annuit Cœptis" with thirteen letters. The American bald eagle holds in one talon an olive branch with thirteen leaves, in the other talon a bundle of thirteen arrows. These, of course, are reproductions of the two sides of the Great Seal of the United States, which had thirteen original states.

* * *

"In every organization," observes Dr. Charles Lapp, "there are three kinds of people: rowboat people, sailboat people, and steamboat people. Rowboat people need to be pushed or shoved along. Sailboat people move when a favorable wind is blowing. Steamboat people move continuously, through calm or storm. They are the ones who are masters of themselves, their surroundings, and their fate."

* * *

Jerome Beatty, Jr., has been investigating the new science of "thermodamnics," which concerns itself with the persistent cussedness of inanimate objects. It is hoped that thermodamnics eventually will reveal the secrets of why buttered bread always falls to the floor with the buttered side down, why squirting grapefruit juice always lands squarely on the spoonwielder's eye, why, when you're dressing in the greatest hurry, a shoelace always breaks, and why, when you're lighting your pipe with your last match, the wind invariably starts to blow.

* * *

Disillusioning bulletin from a highbrow quarterly: bulls are color-blind and don't "see red" at all. . . . Nero couldn't have fiddled while Rome burned because the violin was not invented until the Middle Ages. . . . And it couldn't have been an apple with which Eve tempted Adam, because apples don't grow in that part of the world. An apricot maybe? Or a fig?

* * *

We owe to John Fuller the incidental intelligence that (1) a Boston newspaper headlined a labor disturbance in Belgium "REVOLT IN BRUSSELS SPROUTS," (2) the call letters of a radio station in Arkansas, a region famous for its duck hunting, are KWAK, and (3) a scrupulously honest British writer has dedicated his first novel to "My friend Elspeth Grant, who wrote it for me."

* * *

Will Jones encountered a nudist with a beard down to his waist exiting from a nudist colony near Minneapolis. "Aren't those whiskers rather strange adornment for a nudist?" asked Jones. Explained the nudist, "*Somebody* has to go for coffee."

The man with the beard served another purpose at the camp, it developed. The leader admitted, "We were getting mighty tired of looking at the same faces all the time."

A police investigation at the camp some time later bogged down completely. The local D.A. alibied, "There wasn't a soul in the place I could pin anything on."

Gravestone Humor . . .

In New Mexico: "Here lies Les Moore, killed by four slugs from a .44. No Les, No Moore."

In Paris: Wife: I Am Waiting for You. A.D. 1920. *Husband:* Here I Am. A.D. 1952.

In Waukegan: Criminal Lawyer: The Defense Rests.

In Colorado: He Called Coyote Pete a Liar!

In Vermont:

> Under this grass and under these trees
> Lies the body of Jonathan Pease.
> But he's not here: only his pod;
> He has shelled out his soul, and gone to his God!

✿　✿　✿

Donald Ogden Stewart suggests this epitaph for the inevitable day when one becomes necessary: "Here lies Donald Ogden Stewart. IF NOT . . ." And Groucho Marx asks only this of posterity: "Bury me next to a straight man."

✿　✿　✿

Here's a pocket-size test by Jerry Beatty to see how well informed you may be:

1. What's the full Horace Greeley quote that begins, "Go West, young man"?

2. Was the Potomac the river Washington tossed the dollar across?

3. Did Hamlet say "Alas, poor Yorick: I knew him well"?

4. Was Frankenstein the name of Mary Shelley's monster?

(Answers.) 1. "Go West, young man and grow up with the country." 2. No, it was the Rappahannock. 3. No. His precise words were: "Alas, poor Yorick. I knew him, Horatio: a fellow of infinite jest, of most excellent fancy." 4. No. Frankenstein was the *inventor* of the monster who ultimately ruined his life.

✦ ✦ ✦

Variations on a theme:

One priest to another: "Read any Good Books lately?"
One bird to another: "Bred any good rooks lately?"
F.B.I. man to D.A.: "Booked any good Reds lately?"
One woman hater to another: "Fled any good looks lately?"
One jail warden to another: "Fed any good crooks lately?"

✦ ✦ ✦

A statistician, understandably breathless, reported recently that only one woman in 1150 now wears black lace panties. To which Olin Miller added this footnote, "What interesting jobs some people can latch on to these days!"

✦ ✦ ✦

Are you working too hard these days and worrying too much? You *might* bear in mind the soothing philosophy of the late Grantland Rice, who always advised his friends: "Take it easy —and don't forget to stop and smell the flowers on the way."

* * *

An ingenious hostess in Westport kept her guests reasonably contented during a sudden Sunday thunderstorm by demanding they attempt these four tasks:

1. Describe the taste of chocolate.

2. Assume that I am color-blind. Describe the color blue to me.

3. Keep your hands folded and describe how you tie your shoelaces.

4. Keep your hands folded and describe a spiral staircase.

* * *

Millionaire inventor Philip K. Saunders has written the story of his unusual life in *Dr. Panto Fogo,* a nickname he acquired one day when his trousers caught fire while he was taking a nap aboard a slow train in Brazil. A few of Mr. Saunders' passing comments bear repetition: (1) Laziness is the mother of nine inventions out of ten; (2) French food is not really good food. It is mediocre food cunningly cooked and disguised with sauces; (3) Africans never talk about sex because there are no sex taboos of any kind and therefore nothing about sex calls for any comment except the expressions of approval.

* * *

A new book called *The Girls' Book of Physical Fitness* conveys the information that just by lying awake but absolutely still you can use up seventy-five calories an hour! Raising your voice in song (whether in the shower or out) consumes 125 calories an hour and playing soft music on the piano burns up fifty. You can triple that hourly consumption at the ivories by shifting your repertoire to uninhibited rock 'n' roll. You can also get a good kick in the sit-spot from an irate neighbor while or immediately after this calorie-consuming activity is pursued.

* * *

Some towns you will agree just *ought* to be, have been invented by Kate Steichen and friends: Noah's, Ark., Near, Miss.,

Hoot, Mon., Either, Ore., Ballpoint, Penn., Fiveand, Tenn., Metre, Cal., Faux, Pa., Nohitsnorunsno, Ariz.

* * *

A learned gentleman named Les Goldman is convinced that people should choose professions that match their names. He has spent long hours, therefore, persuading one Walter Wall to lay carpets; Warren Peace to enter the diplomatic corps; Hugo Furst to become a paratrooper; Colette O'Day to assume the role of curfew officer; and Dinah Sklubb to go out and sell credit cards.

* * *

Once upon a time, legend has it, there were two tiny grains of sand in the Paleozoic ooze. One of the grains was possessed of curiosity, and the result is mankind. The other had no curiosity at all—and the result, today, is the oyster.

* * *

Editor Tom Dreier tells about a Missouri school superintendent who chose this method to present "a picture of the world his students could understand."

If, said the superintendent, the almost-three-billion persons in the world were compressed into a single town of 1000 people, the following contrasts could be seen:

60 persons would represent the U.S.A., 940 all the others.

60 Americans would receive one-half the income, 940 the other half.

303 would be white, 697 non-white.

The 60 Americans would have a life expectancy of over 70, the others of under 40.

The 60 Americans would consume 15 per cent of the town's food supply, and the lowest income group of the Americans would be better off than the average of the 940.

The 60 Americans would have 12 times as much electricity, 22 times as much coal, 21 times as much oil, 50 times as much steel, and 50 times as much equipment as all 940 remaining members of the town.

Still feeling sorry for yourselves?

FABLES

A great Turkish sultan lay dying one summer's day. His latest favorite, a beautiful lass of nineteen, sat weeping by his bedside.

Suddenly the stricken potentate rallied momentarily and ordered the girl to put on her finest raiment, and adorn herself with her costliest jewels.

"How could I do this when you are so ill?" asked the girl.

"Do as I say," commanded the sultan—then whispered to his chief advisers, "It occurred to me that when the Angel of Death comes for my soul, his eyes may light on this beautiful girl, and perchance he'll decide to take her instead of me!"

* * *

There is a fable about a very wise old man who was visited by a delegation of malcontents determined to tell him their troubles.

Suggested the wise man, "Write down your greatest trouble on a piece of paper." He then threw all the papers into a pot and said, "Now each of you draw a paper and by all the laws of probability you all will have brand-new troubles to fret over."

The malcontents followed his suggestion. Then they read the new troubles they had been saddled with. The result: Every single one of them clamored immediately to have his own trouble back!

* * *

Spoke an Arabic sage of a century gone by:

He who knows not, and knows not he knows not—he is a fool. Shun him.

He who knows not, and knows he knows not—he is simple. Teach him.

He who knows, and knows not he knows—he is asleep. Wake him.

But he who knows, and knows he knows—he is wise. Follow him.

* * *

A vain young creature in Wilkes-Barre, Pennsylvania, craved a pearl necklace. One dark night a genie appeared before her and said, "Make one wish. It will come true by morning."

The young creature murmured ecstatically, "Give me what I need for my neck." When she awoke she found next to her pillow a box containing six cakes of soap.

* * *

Once upon a time there was a snail, relates Simons Roof, who set out on a chill winter morning to climb the trunk of a bleak cherry tree. As he painfully inched his way upward, a beetle poked his head out of a hole and advised him, "You're wasting your time, friend. There aren't any cherries up there." But the snail didn't stop moving for a second. "There will be when I get there," he pointed out.

* * *

A young man saw some beautiful objects in a show window, carved from solid gold, and though the street was crowded with people, smashed the window and ran off with several of the costliest trinkets. Of course, he was immediately apprehended.

"How did you expect to get away with such an act in full view of hundreds of people?" asked the magistrate.

"Alas," murmured the culprit. "When I performed the act, I could see only the gold, and none of the people."

*   *   *

In Java they tell of a young blade who spied a beautiful maiden on the high road and followed her deliberately for a mile. Finally, she wheeled and demanded, "Why do you dog my footsteps?"

"Because," he declared fervently, "you are the loveliest thing I ever have seen and I have fallen madly in love with you at sight. Be mine!"

"But you have merely to look behind you," said the girl, "to see my young sister, who is ten times more beautiful than I am."

The gallant cavalier wheeled about and his gaze fell on as ugly a wench as ever drew breath in Java. "What mockery is this?" he demanded of the beautiful girl. "You lied to me!"

"So did you," she replied. "If you were so madly in love with me, why did you turn around?"

*   *   *

An extravagant king of Saxony once borrowed every cent that his court jester had put away for a rainy day. "Now," sighed the jester, "I understand the meaning of that old adage: 'A fool and his money are soon parted!'"

*   *   *

Olin Clark tells about the little boy who, despite all warnings and fables, continued crying "Fire." He turned out to be a wolf.

*   *   *

Chinese fable: A poor but honest laundryman maintained his modest establishment next door to a great big prosperous restaurant. Each day the laundryman would sit outside his shop, as near to the restaurant as he dared, and sniff the wonderful aromas from within.

One day the laundryman received a bill from his wealthy neighbor for "continuous smell of my food." He took his usual seat that afternoon with his tin money box in hand. After rattling it vigorously for a while, he cried to his creditor, "I hereby pay for the smell of your food with the *sound of my money!*"

* * *

Once upon a time there were two brothers—farmers both—named Elmer and Rockwell. Elmer was a hard worker who spent fourteen hours a day improving his land and healthy livestock. Rockwell was a bum, who let his fences fall down. His livestock roamed away and his barn burned down.

One day a man with a pocket full of gold came from Washington to buy land. He admired Elmer's beautiful farm, but he bought Rockwell's dilapidated layout because the government was seeking worthless land for a rocket-launching site.

Rockwell took the cash and bought a villa at Monte Carlo, where he dines with royalty, and has a high old time luxuriating in the sun. Elmer still slaves fourteen hours a day on his magnificent farm. He writes to Rockwell faithfully, but Rockwell is too lazy to answer. End of fable.

GHOSTS?

A brilliant and distinguished television producer I know (aren't they all?) has some rich, pedigreed relatives stashed away in a castle in the lake district of England, and this year he flew over by jet to get his first look at the ancestral seat.

It seemed a pretty gloomy place to him at first glance, and the tasteless dinner served to him by a toothless old hag depressed him further. Around the dining hall were faded portraits of what he presumed to be his ancestors—a forbidding lot—though one frame was conspicuously empty. "I must ask about that when I know these people better," he resolved, then, pleading a sick headache, he retreated to his bed-chamber.

There he found a pleasant surprise awaiting him. A young girl, rather oddly dressed but surpassingly beautiful, was bending over his suitcase.

"You don't have to unpack for me," he assured her. "I'm used to doing it myself."

By way of reply, the beautiful young girl did an unusual thing. First she favored him with a sweet, sorrowful smile, then she disappeared into thin air.

The producer rushed breathlessly back to the dining room and cried, "A beautiful girl has just vanished before my eyes."

"Damnation," grumbled his host, with no surprise whatever. "She's come back again, has she? That was your great-great-great-grandmother. She was murdered in that room by her husband—for good and sufficient reasons—in 1837."

The producer's glance wandered involuntarily to the frame that had been empty. There was the portrait of the girl from his room staring gravely at him!

*   *   *

Jerome Beatty tells about a friendly, publicity-loving ghost who whooshed into a photographer's studio and allowed as how he'd like to have a full-sized picture of himself. The obliging photographer set up his camera and lights, snapped the shutter once, and waved goodbye as the ghost dissolved into space. Alas! The photographer got no picture because the negative, it developed, was underexposed. To put it in a nutshell, the spirit was willing, but the flash was weak.

*   *   *

Four ghosts were engaged in a hotly contested bridge game when a fifth ghost opened the door to enter, loosing a gust of wind that blew all the cards off the table. "Confound it, Archie," grumbled one of the card-playing ghosts. "Don't you know what a keyhole is for?"

*   *   *

Ghosts seem to be especially prevalent in Scotland, but the doughty residents take them in stride. For example, an inn-keeper in the Trossachs acknowledged cheerfully at breakfast that the family's pet ghost had paid him a bedside visit on the stroke of midnight. "But he didn't stay very long," he added. "He vanished the moment I asked him for a small contribution to the community fund."

* * *

On a country highway, in the pale light of a waning moon, a forlorn pedestrian vainly thumbed a lift into town from the sparse number of automobiles that hurtled by. Finally, at the crest of a rise, one vehicle came to a halt, and the grateful pedestrian climbed in. The vehicle resumed its creaky advance.

A distant clock was just tolling midnight, when the pedestrian noticed that there was no driver at the wheel. Horrified, he jumped out. A shadowy graveyard loomed beyond him. He broke into a run.

Just then he noticed a figure climbing into the abandoned car. "Don't get in," he shouted. "There's something terribly wrong with that machine."

"You're telling me," was the reply. "I've been pushing the darn thing uphill for half a mile."

MARTIANS?

Those Martians are back in town again! The attention of two of them was attracted to a snazzy white motor scooter at a Third Avenue curb. "Isn't she a honey?" enthused one. "I think I'll take her back to Mars with us." "Careful, boy," warned the other. "She may be under age."

* * *

Two visitors from outer space ambled down Fourth Avenue, each one stretching his four legs and waving his six arms in the air. A tailor, standing in the doorway of his shop, saw them coming and cried out to his partner, "Quick, Mawruss, take down that 'Alterations Free' sign!"

* * *

A newly arrived spaceman arrived from Mars a week after his teammate, whom he found gazing intently at a mail-box and a fire alarm box. "The dumpy green fellow with the big mouth doesn't say a word," observed the teammate, "but I warn you not to fool around with the tall red character. He'll scream his head off!"

* * *

Bob Sylvester keeps bumping into Martians in out-of-the-way nooks and crannies. This time they were inspecting gas pumps at a roadside filling station. "What's the matter with those clunks?" worried one of the Martians. "All they do is stand around with their fingers in their ears."

* * *

One of those space travelers with a triangular head, square eyes, and ears made of piano wire landed on Delancey Street, and scared a pushcart peddler into fainting on the spot. The traveler thought the least he could do was tend the cart till the peddler recovered.

A youngster, passing by with his mother, gulped hard, and said, "Mom, isn't that the craziest-looking vegetable peddler you ever did see?"

The mother admitted grimly, "He may *look* crazy, but you'll notice he's getting sixty-one cents a pound for his potatoes!"

* * *

A Martian spaceman brought his contraption down in Las Vegas at the instant a slot machine player hit the jackpot. As the shower of silver dollars poured noisily out, the Martian patted the machine and remarked, "Buddy, you'd better do something for that cold."

* * *

At bustling Austin College in Sherman, Texas, I was solemnly informed by a fun-loving senior that Mars is inhabited by a strange-looking race called the Furries, and that the leader of said Furries is distinguished by a giant headpiece that looks like an enlarged hypodermic needle. Is it necessary to add that he is known as the Furry with the syringe on top?

SIGNS OF THE TIMES

Many signs along the nation's highways and byways prove conclusively that the imagination—and sense of humor—of enterprising operators continues to flourish. Even dignified Wall Street institutions are hanging out new-fangled signs these days to prove that the procession is not leaving them behind. One large bank has posted this warning at its entrance: "Careful, girls! Those attractive fellows in our windows are tellers!" A more conservative institution down the block suggests, "Kindly make your deposits quietly. You might wake one of the vice presidents."

* * *

A New Orleans dairy advertises, "Our cows are NOT contented. They're always striving to do better.". . . A Dallas restaurant, obviously patronized by oil magnates and booksellers, offers "All you can eat for $100." . . . In the window of a small Italian restaurant: "We offer you a pizza and quiet." . . . At a roadside beanery: "Try our enthusiastic stew. We put everything we had in it!". . . Up in Alaska: "Orange juice, 35 cents; Texas size, 20 cents.". . . Boasts a supermarket in

Paramus: "Here you will discover the finest liquors and the best fruits. It's where the beer and the cantaloupe play.". . . . Admonition of a health food shoppe: "Don't walk on the grass. It may be your supper.". . . . And above the door of a popular downtown eatery is this wonderfully provocative sign: "O'LEARY AND McGRATH. AUTHENTIC CHINESE COOKING."

What the Traffic Will Bear . . .

Warning on the main street of Beverly Hills: "Beware of children going to or from school—especially if they are driving cars."

On the back of a truck: "Watch my rear—not hers."

Outside of a garage: "Invite us to your next blowout."

In Houston, Texas: "Last Cadillac dealer for three blocks."

On the back of a honeymoon couple's car: "Amateur night."

In a Toledo auto repair shop window: "Save the next dents for us."

On a diaper service truck: "Rock a dry baby."

And on the outskirts of a northwestern college town this billboard has been erected by a concerned safety council:

> If heavy necking is your sport,
> Trade in your auto for a davenport!

* * *

Mike Connolly spotted this sign on a shuttered magic shop in Hollywood: "Vanished till next season." In the window of a Boston shop specializing in fireplace equipment: "Everything your little hearth desires." In a camera store in Paterson, New Jersey: "Visit our bargain basement on the second floor." On the sidewall of an otherwise prosaic sandblaster's headquarters: "Call us if you have any dirty stories." In a Niagara Falls gifte shoppe: "If you don't need it, we have it."

* * *

There's a warning sign posted seven feet high over the door to a famous basketball coach's office in Lexington, Kentucky. It reads, "If you don't have to stoop to enter here, keep out." . . . An ingenious distributor of fishermen's supplies in Colorado has a window full of new rods "guaranteed to get a pike's pique." . . . A Dayton tycoon has this reminder on his desk: "Things to do today: 1. Get organized. 2. Talk to wife. 3. Get reorganized." . . . And Bob O'Brien spotted this intriguing sign at New York's Hayden Planetarium: "This way to the Solar System and the ladies' and gentlemen's rest rooms."

* * *

On a church bulletin board: "This church is prayer-conditioned." . . . In an Arizona public garden: "Please do not write on the cactus." . . . A Boston necktie emporium beseeches, "Come in and tie one on." . . . A Rochester plumber suggests, "Do it yourself—then call us before it's too late." . . . A Shreveport realtor advises, "Get lots while you're young." . . . Outside a veterinarian's office: "Hospital zone: No barking." . . . In a fish store: "If our flounders were any fresher, they'd be insulting." . . . In a college book store: "Help fight TV: Buy a book!" . . . December sign in a toy department: "Five Santa Clauses. No waiting."

* * *

A scout reports that an automatic laundromat in Corona has two signs tacked alongside the door. The top sign proclaims, "Through this portal pass the finest folk in Corona." The lower sign adds, "Anyone caught putting slugs in the machine will be arrested forthwith."

*   *   *

Government operatives inform us that:

1. After a violent sandstorm had disrupted service in Saudi Arabia, this sign appeared in telephone booths: "Until further notice please limit calls to four wives."

2. In Moscow there's an imposing complex housing the "Commission on Electrification of all Russia." At the entrance there's a card suggesting, "Please knock. The electric bell is out of order."

3. A young porter at the Pentagon is obviously headed for bigger and better things. His wire basket is labeled, "For Top Confidential Trash."

4. A doctor recently was dispatched to an Army induction center to give antivirus injections. Above the entrance to his cubicle in the dispensary he tacked this notice: "To save time, draftees will please back in."

5. This summer the doughty head of a Cape Cod resort center's weather bureau posted this notice: "On account of the Fourth of July, there will be no weather today."

ELEVEN STORIES TALL

The late Irish author, James Stephens, who wrote *The Crock of Gold,* and insisted that he believed in elfs and leprechauns, often pointed out, "what a dull world this would be if every imaginative maker of legends was stigmatized as a liar!"

Trader Horn, for example, was a man after Stephens' heart. The Trader, or Zambesi Jack, as he liked to call himself, popped up in New York in the thirties with a bagful of preposterous reminiscences and an equally unbelievable capacity for liquor in any form.

Zambesi had a pet tiger, to hear him tell it, who insisted upon sleeping across the foot of his bed. One night he kicked the tiger in a moment of absent-mindedness. "Do you know that one kick broke my poor tiger's spirit?" he mourned. "Shows how careful you have to be of the other fellow's feelings."

* * *

One night the house of a neighbor of Lowell Thomas up in Pawling, New York, burned to the ground. With his own eyes, says Lowell solemnly, he saw the family dash to the lawn, followed by their faithful dog. Then the old dog dashed back into the flames to pull out a child they had overlooked. Then in he dashed again to rescue another missing child. It was a dashing affair.

Although everybody in the family was now positively accounted for, Fido fought his way back into the inferno a third time. He emerged just before the house collapsed, exhausted but triumphant. He was carrying in his mouth the insurance policy wrapped in a wet towel.

* * *

In Colorado, legend-loving Stan Peckham reports a Lothario, surprised by his girl's shotgun-toting pa, who made off so fast he overtook two jackrabbits and a gazelle.

He kicked the latter high into the air, muttering, "Get off the road and let somebody run who knows how."

* * *

In Princeton, Florida, according to W. E. Gaby, when pesky mosquitoes get so thick around him he scarcely can see, he just runs two or three times as fast as he can around a telephone pole and then jumps nimbly to one side, leaving the mosquitoes whirling around the pole till they die of dizziness.

* * *

As Mark Twain saw it, mankind can be divided into liars, damn liars, and statisticians. Probably it was in the role of statistician that he told of a night in Hannibal when Old Man Hankinson got locked in the washroom on the fourth floor of his house and hollered for help. There wasn't a ladder in town long enough to reach him.

"I admit I was the hero of the occasion," wrote Twain. "I snatched up a rope and flung the end of it up to Old Man Hankinson, yelling, 'Tie it around your waist!'

"He did as I told him—and I slowly pulled him down to safety."

* * *

Impressive indeed, I think, is this tall tale concocted by Sam Ridings, a grizzled cowboy of Chisholm Trail fame: A tenderfoot from the East, unaware of the abrupt changes of climate out West, once made for himself four harness tugs out of green buffalo hide. The first time he used them a sudden downpour filled his wagon so full of water he had to climb down and trudge beside his team. When he reached town, he turned around and discovered that his wagon was nowhere to be seen. The rawhide had stretched in the rain, and the wagon was a full mile behind on the tugs.

The tenderfoot started back to retrieve his wagon, but just then the sun reappeared and dried the rawhide, which contracted so quickly that the wagon ran right over its owner and killed him.

* * *

An unholy spell of weather hit Great Falls, Montana too, where the temperature got down to 38 below zero, and a man who left a friendly poker game because he was scared of his wife, froze to death at the first street corner.

"It wasn't so bad, really," explained one of the survivors of the poker game. "We hung a lantern on Old Charlie's ear and used him for a lamppost all winter."

* * *

Lightning shattered a tree under which Squire Erskine's hired hand had unwisely sought shelter. Squire Erskine found him there unharmed, however, but severely shaken when the downpour abated. "How close do you figure that lightning came to you?" asked the squire. "I dunno exactly," admitted the hired hand, "but my pipe wasn't lit before it struck!"

* * *

Clem Albright wins a medal for a prize whopper about hunting dogs. "My retriever stopped dead in his tracks one morning and pointed. I didn't see a sign of quail—just an old man napping in the shade. I woke the fellow and asked, 'Notice any quail around here?' 'Not a one,' answered the old man, 'but I've just been dreaming about a couple.'"

* * *

"Are the bears around here dangerous? Golly, yes," guide Ben Moody tells properly impressed tourists in the Banff, Alberta area. "One of them caught me drowsing in that open field yonder and chased me clear to that oak tree standing alone in the distance. My only chance was to leap up and catch the lowest limb which is a full twenty feet from the ground."

"Did you make it?" some tourist always asks.

"If you must have the truth," confides Moody, "I missed it clean going up—but I caught it on the way back down."

* * *

Vance Randolph tells about an Ozark mountaineer named Lissenbee who "was always blabbing things all over town. He didn't tell no lies; he just told the truth, and that's what made it so bad."

One day a talking turtle stopped him on the road and snapped, "Lissenbee, you talk too darn much." The startled Lissenbee made for the nearest tavern to holler, "I just seen a turtle what talks." Everybody in the tavern hooted in disbelief, but followed Lissenbee nonetheless to the place where the turtle still rested in the shade.

The pesky turtle, however, never said a word, and the crowd melted away in disgust. Lissenbee, brokenhearted, bowed his head in his hands, and muttered, "My reputation is ruined."

The turtle nodded, and said, "It's like I told you, Lissenbee. You talk too darn much."

WORDS TO SIGN OFF WITH

Minutes, the house organ of the Nationwide Insurance Company, has discovered a new language: "Realestatese," which embodies the art of making the description of a house bear as little resemblance as possible to the real appearance of same.

A few prime examples:

Newly decorated: The owner has repainted the front door.

Needs slight additional decorating: The buyer had better not make any weekend plans for the next three years.

Charming cul-de-sac: Deadend street behind a busy supermarket parking lot and a boys' schoolyard.

Magnificent view: The nearest bus stop is at least five miles away.

Prestige community: Two of the neighbors have maids.
Only two left: There were three originally.

✦   ✦   ✦

What about the incomprehensible gibberish often handed
out by government bigwigs and business tycoons? Is it unintentional or deliberate? Critic Granville Hicks thinks it usually is
deliberate.

"Evasion of clarity," writes Hicks, "is a trait of bureaucrats,
whether they are in government, business, or the professions.
Evasion of clarity is tantamount to the evasion of responsibility, and responsibility is what the average bureaucrat wants as
little as possible of. Evasion becomes a habit, and obscuring,
imprecise words often seem to issue automatically from the lips
of most bureaucrats, even when clarity could do no harm."

✦   ✦   ✦

In line with the above, George Brathwaits, up to here in
Pentagon longwindedness, thinks this is the way Washington
big brass might have delivered three reasonably famous dec-
larations:

1. It is my command that we relegate the torpedoes to per-
dition. Proceed at maximum celerity at 119 degrees NNE on
our erstwhile established course.

2. Let no homo sapien engage in the firing of his non-nuclear
weapon until the precise moment when the scleras of the
enemy are visible.

3. My expressed desire is to receive not more than one of the
following: (A) Complete freedom, entailing all its pleasures
and responsibilities, or (B) The loss of my life in a manner to
be determined at a later date.

✦   ✦   ✦

Collecting the quaint expressions of the Pennsylvania Dutch
is a favorite diversion of many Philadelphians. A few that pop
up on most lists are: 1. The sign on a door where the bell was
out of order: "Button don't bell. Bump." 2. The sound tip: "Bet-

ter it is to single live than to the wife the britches give." 3. The housewife's complaint: "The hurrier I go, the behinder I get."

* * *

Famous Critic Brooks Atkinson confesses that when he wants to add some very unusual words to his vocabulary, he consults the works of S. J. Perelman. It was from this prolific source, for instance, that he borrowed, "a firkin of butter and a hectare of gherkins" to describe the fare served at a picnic. Mr. P. shingled his country house, Atkinson discovered, with "second-hand wattles," and he "taps the dottle from his pipe" by "knocking it against the hob." He also frequently "muckles fibre towels" from airplanes that carry him hither and yon.

* * *

Words which are spelled the same way backwards as they are forwards are called palindromes. Examples are: ere, bib, did, bob, eke, ewe, eye, kayak, level, refer, radar, reviver, rotator, deified. Jason Lindsay lists four words which spell *another* word backwards: straw, diaper, deliver, dessert.

* * *

There are just two words in the English language that contain all the vowels (including the optional "y") in their regular order. They are "facetiously" and "abstemiously."

* * *

John Moore, in his new book *Your English Words,* lists some words even John Charles Daly hasn't used on TV. It's a hundred to one you never before encountered these specimens either: 1. quockerwodger; 2. skilligolete; 3. calibogus; 4. jobbernowl; and 5. rumblegumption. Their meanings? 1. A puppet; 2. A soup served sometimes to prisoners or sailors; 3. A mixture of spruce beer and rum; 4. A blockhead; 5. A Scottish word for common sense.

"Increase your word power" with these—if you *can!*

* * *

Come, James! We must clapperclaw that scomm before he wambles from a surfeit of quiddany.

A condensation of Dr. Johnson's famous dictionary has been published for the first time. A few of the unfamiliar words therein are clapperclaw, huzz, fleshmonger, scomm, doubry, quiddany, and wamble. Two to one you don't know the meaning of any of them. I certainly didn't!

* * *

At a conclave of half a dozen learned college professors, none could correctly define more than one of these four often-misused words: limpid, livid, stultify, and transpire. Try your own luck—before you go on to read that limpid means clear, transparent, free from obscurity; livid means dark grayish-blue, a bluish appearance due to a bruise; stultify means to make foolish or ridiculous; and transpire means to emit or give off waste matter, or to escape through the pores as moisture or odor. (The use of "transpire" to mean "pass" or "elapse" is distinctly frowned upon by practically all authorities on word usage but Bergen Evans.)

* * *

Henry Minott, of United Press International, after years of rigid copy editing, declares these to be the fifteen most commonly misspelled words: uncontrollable, changeable, gauge, naphtha, occurred, discernible, diphtheria, permissible, paraphernalia, likable, judgment, dietitian, embarrass, indispensable, harass.

✻ ✻ ✻

A student of semantics at Kansas State has summed up the career of a college football coach in eight words: Desired; Wired; Hired; Inspired; Admired; Tired; Mired; Fired.

✻ ✻ ✻

Cary Grant, a riddle addict of the first water, has found a new way to use the word "fundamental" in a sentence: "I went horseback riding yesterday, and now I have to eat fun da mental." And a precocious fifth-grade student in a Queens public school, asked to fit the word "influential" in a sentence, came up with "I dreamed I was in heaven, and influentials."

✻ ✻ ✻

The French philosopher Voltaire was told that a certain professor had a five-hundred-word answer for everything. "Heavens!" he exclaimed. "Is he as ignorant as all that?"

✻ ✻ ✻

Papa Smedkins, under the urgings of his wife, reluctantly postponed his golf game to give his young son a few customary words about the birds and the bees. At the end of his talk, both father and son were obviously impatient. "At least," concluded Papa Smedkins, "I guess you now understand why our cat is about to have kittens." "Thanks to you, pop," said Junior, "I do. She must have gotten stung by a bee."

✻ ✻ ✻

A very popular middle-aged farmer's wife in a Midwestern town was asked her secret for making and keeping friends. "There's no secret about it," she explained. "I'm just always careful to taste my words real good before I let 'em get past my teeth."

✻ ✻ ✻

Novelist Barnaby Conrad has compiled a volume of "Famous Last Words." Included is gourmet R. M. Milne's, "My exit is the result of too many entrees." Gambler Wilson Mizner's, "Well, Doc, I guess this is the main event!" And philosopher Hegel's, "Only one man understood me—and he didn't, really!"

Lord Duveen, art collector, died at Claridge's after a lengthy illness during which doctors repeatedly had told him he had only a few days left to live. His last words were, "Well, I fooled 'em for five years!"

*   *   *

A few other last words to remember are: The smart-alecky motorist's "Well, if he won't turn off his bright lights, I won't turn off mine!"; the chronic alcoholic's "I *thought* that last drink had a peculiar taste"; and the henpecked husband's "Hey, darling, hand me that stack of books to stand on so I can reach this curtain rod."

*   *   *

And here's a last word from the compiler of *Laugh Day*: There's no getting away from the world of today; you might as well get used to it. If you can adjust yourself to the pace, there's never been so exciting a time to be alive. More momentous things happen in a single year now than our grandparents experienced in a lifetime.

In fact, nobody's ever had it so good before. So laugh more! Make *every* day "Laugh Day"—and see how much happier you'll be!

Index by Categories

FRAMING HITCHCOCK

SELECTED ESSAYS FROM THE *HITCHCOCK ANNUAL*

SIDNEY GOTTLIEB
AND
CHRISTOPHER BROOKHOUSE

WAYNE STATE UNIVERSITY PRESS   DETROIT

Library of Congress Cataloging-in-Publication Data

Framing Hitchcock : selected essays from the Hitchcock
annual / [edited by] Sidney Gottlieb and Christopher
Brookhouse.
p. cm. — (Contemporary film and television series)
ISBN 0-8143-3061-4
1. Hitchcock, Alfred, 1899—Criticism and interpretation.
I. Gottlieb, Sidney.   II. Brookhouse, Christopher, 1938–
III. Hitchcock annual.   IV. Series.
PN1998.3.H58 F73 2002
79.43'0233'092—dc21
2002002978

CONTENTS

ACKNOWLEDGMENTS

I am especially grateful to Richard Allen for many conversations on Hitchcock, Hitchcock studies, and the specter of Hitchcock Inc., conversations that raised many issues that I at least tentatively explore in the introduction to this volume.

One of the truly happy accidents of my life came some ten years ago when Chris Brookhouse accepted my enthusiasm for Hitchcock as a credential and invited me to work with him on the *Hitchcock Annual*, work that has often been intense and time-consuming, but always pleasurable and rewarding. Were he not the co-editor of this volume, it would certainly be more formally dedicated to him, a dedication that I am quite sure would be signed not only by me but all the other contributors to the volume as well.

Sid Gottlieb

In 1990, when I found myself with the time and financial support to start the *Hitchcock Annual*, I wrote to Lesley Brill, Leonard Leff, Leland Poague, and Kristin Thompson, all of whom I knew only through their work, to ask if they would serve on the editorial board. Much to my surprise and delight, they agreed. The other original member was my former colleague Margaret O'Connor. Eventually Diane Carson brought her critical perspective to the group. In later issues, Loring Silet took up the burden of the book review section, for which I am extremely grateful.

Sid Gottlieb phoned me before the first issue appeared. He introduced himself and spoke of his keen interest in Hitchcock, as well as his experience editing and publishing a scholarly journal on George Herbert. Every issue of the *Annual* after the first one has been laid out and set and sent to the printer by Sid. Eventually Sid also took on more and more of the editorial work.

The *Hitchcock Annual* would not have prospered without the unselfish work of the above-named members of the editorial staff. I recall only once when anyone declined to read a submission, and to do so promptly. Not only were the readers' comments helpful to me, but also to the authors, whose work the readers inevitably improved by their suggestions. In a time when book and journal editing is often uncaring, our editorial board stood out for its thoughtfulness and dedication, and their efforts have helped shape each issue and, as a result, the present volume as well. As Sid and Richard Allen prepare to take the *Hitchcock Annual* into its second decade, *Framing Hitchcock* assembles a generous selection of representative essays illustrating the range and high quality of what we have accomplished in our first nine years.

Christopher Brookhouse

A NOTE ON THE TEXT

The essays in this volume are reprinted in substantially the same form as they originally appeared in when first published in the *Hitchcock Annual*, although in some places they have been lightly revised. Small errors have been silently corrected and citation methods have been regularized. Quoted dialogue is transcribed directly from the films, unless indicated otherwise.

FRAMING HITCHCOCK

INTRODUCTION

SIDNEY GOTTLIEB

More than a decade ago, the *Hitchcock Annual* began publication without any fanfare, manifesto, or statement of purpose, and without any felt need that such things were necessary. In a time of hype, theoretical sophistication, and self-consciousness, we simply, as it were, rolled up our sleeves and proceeded: independently (that is to say, without any sponsoring organization or academic affiliation), patiently, eclectically, and serendipitously. Through the years, the *Hitchcock Annual* has become established as a key source of historical information and critical commentary, written from a wide range of perspectives, on one of the central figures in the history of film, arguably one of the most important and in any event one of the most fascinating, widely recognized, influential, and admired artists, entertainers, and public figures of the twentieth century. Our one article of faith and guiding principle has been that Hitchcock merited, and film studies in general would benefit from, the kind of repeated, dedicated, and varied critical attention that a yearly publication focusing on him might provide.

The occasion of introducing a volume intended to represent and celebrate that principle also affords a good opportunity to examine it critically,
and to comment briefly and perhaps in some ways heretically on the current
state and growth of Hitchcock studies. Nonetheless, if a few reservations,
warnings, and suggestions create a momentarily sobering effect, they need
not undermine the prevailing spirit of celebration.

Not that many years ago, the study of Hitchcock was on the defensive.
However, Robin Wood's famous question, "Why should we take Hitchcock
seriously?" has been satisfactorily answered, both by Wood himself and by
several generations of critics and scholars.[1] There is at least a reasonably
secure consensus about the legitimacy of film as a major art form, film studies as a serious intellectual and pedagogical endeavor, and Hitchcock as far
more than a craftsman and popular entertainer. But the question that troubled Wood has also been reframed as well as resolved, and has given way to
other queries. While it would be a bit melodramatic to suggest that anyone
has proposed that there is a "danger" in Hitchcock studies, it is not overstating the case to note that varieties of the question, "Why should we take
Hitchcock *so* seriously?" abound. The rapid growth of Hitchcock studies,
alongside film studies in general, has been a proper expression of continuing
interest in a vital subject area, developed by an ever-increasing number of
scholars and critics, and aimed at and supported by a growing body of film
students and a general audience (and market) of film watchers. But there are
legitimate complaints about saturation and excess, and it is understandable
why some sigh out loud and wonder, "Do we really need another book—or
conference, or special session, or a journal—on Hitchcock?" Some libraries,
for example, on principle resist subscribing to single-figure journals, including the *Hitchcock Annual,* a policy that perhaps reflects not only budgetary
limitations but also serious reservations about what single-figure journals
signify, particularly about a state of criticism that threatens to become at
once too specialized and too unwieldy.

We are certainly at the point where we should more fully examine and
reevaluate the structure and consequences of the "Hitchcock apparatus,"
by which I mean neither the ensemble of cinematic techniques and practices nor the production and reception environments of Hitchcock the filmmaker, but the networks, vehicles, and pathways of Hitchcock criticism. The
fact that we so commonly speak of "Hitchcock studies" indicates that a very
worthwhile endeavor has been legitimated, but should also warn us that we
may be one short step from something potentially worrisome: "Hitchcock
Inc.," for lack of a better term, complete with a Hitchcock journal, research
center, websites, university courses, popular and academic books, confer-

ences, museum exhibitions, and extensive centennial events (which continue well beyond the centennial date), in addition to more biographies, televised specials, "making of" documentaries, and DVD commentaries on the way, as well as an endowed chair of Hitchcock studies at a distinguished university and serious talk of a Hitchcock Society. It may be unkind to describe these endeavors as mixed blessings, but one may envision their fruits as not only a substantial increase in valuable work on Hitchcock but also a constitution, franchises of various kinds, titles, dues, memorial statuary, secret passwords, and a ceremonial handshake.

More seriously, the "establishment" of Hitchcock studies may have some substantive effects that we should be wary of and that may limit our celebration of this generally worthy enterprise to, as E. M. Forster would say, two cheers rather than three. Let me summarize briefly four key areas of concern—none of which should surprise anyone conversant with the numerous contemporary analyses of the knowledge industries, channels of cultural capital, and history of how critical movements (whether defined by methodology, like New Criticism, deconstruction, or New Historicism, or by subject area, like Shakespeare studies) take physical as well as conceptual form. I acknowledge a great debt to these analyses that may not be fully evident as I adapt and apply them in a very abbreviated manner below. I am particularly indebted to Michael D. Bristol's *Big-Time Shakespeare,*[2] and my basic argument here is that one sign of the maturation—not just the growth—of Hitchcock studies would be a detailed and self-reflexive analysis of "Big-Time Hitchcock," some signs of which follow.

Valorization. As mentioned above, Hitchcock's status was, within recent memory, at risk. While I do not regret that Hitchcock's value is firmly established rather than constantly assailed, one may rightly be concerned by his current "taken-for-grantedness," to coin a phrase. Whether manifested in a specifically focused conference, journal, or book, the expanding number of courses on him, or other such aura-conferring activities, the enterprise of Hitchcock studies implicitly (if not explicitly) valorizes Hitchcock, often on uncertain and unstated grounds, even when he is not (although he frequently is) referred to as the Master or the Director. And almost by its very definition, Hitchcock studies betrays a lingering attachment to auteurism, a term that for many has been discredited and in the very least now requires careful enunciation and application.

Institutionalization. The dual danger signaled by this term is not only in turning Hitchcock into an institution (or, to mix metaphors, the proverbial 800-pound gorilla), but also in establishing certain bodies that direct or otherwise regulate work in the Hitchcock critical industry. (Such a "body,"

I should point out, need not be physical: it can take the form of a conceptual critical orthodoxy or dominant reference point for interpretive work.) Hitchcock, like other subjects of academic study, can be colonized and kidnaped, or, to use a somewhat less dramatic term, shaped—not always to his or our advantage—by the current Hitchcock apparatus.

Commodification. Because of his popularity and canonicity, both in and out of academia, Hitchcock-related artifacts have the potential to be valuable properties, and this exerts pressures on critical and even scholarly examinations of his life and work. Studies of films and filmmakers in general tend to aspire to the condition of the coffee table book or the prime position on the mass-market shelf. These are not disreputable aims, and synthesizing them with significant scholarship is by no means an impossible goal: for example, recent books by Dan Auiler, Bill Krohn, and Ken Mogg are important contributions to our knowledge of Hitchcock and fit nicely in the living room as well as the study.[3] Nevertheless it is well worth examining and monitoring the various ways that marketplace considerations make Hitchcock a desirable subject for commentary, make some approaches to his life and work more attractive than others, and can sometimes uniquely complicate, if not compromise, Hitchcock studies in general.

Proliferation. Taking stock of Shakespeare studies in the middle of the twentieth century, Jan Kott wrote that already at that time, "The bibliography of dissertations and studies devoted to *Hamlet* is twice the size of Warsaw's telephone directory."[4] Since then, the exponential growth has continued—and there is even an entire journal devoted to *Hamlet*. Depending on one's perspective, all this might add up to an abundance of riches or an annoyance, an inconvenience, and a quotable absurdity. Much is at stake. Information and communication theorists remind us that at a certain point a qualitative transformation occurs as an increase in messages, regardless of their content or quality, creates not knowledge but noise. The study of Hitchcock has not yet reached this pivotal moment where addition becomes subtraction, but scholars should be conscious of the fact that even our productivity and creativity (not to mention the purposeless and self-generating verbiage we sometimes spin out) can become not only unwieldy and overwhelming but also distracting and entropic.

While these are real sources of worry, there are, to be sure, countervailing forces and ways to address the above "certain tendencies" without abandoning or becoming cynical about the establishment and growth of Hitchcock studies. The following recommendations briefly address the four areas mentioned above.

1. Keep de-centering activities at the center of Hitchcock studies (an irony I fully intend). Residual concern for Hitchcock's distinctive genius will undoubtedly remain, but can be complemented by studies of the various contexts of his work (for example, the artistic and production systems and environments he worked in, his collaborators, his historical milieu, and so on) and a healthy awareness of his artistic limitations, weaknesses, and various missteps as well as his many achievements.

2. Keep the institutions of Hitchcock studies open and multiple. It is very helpful that there are many institutions—corporate, family, and amateur, as well as academic—at play in rather than presiding over Hitchcock studies. The resulting diversity should be applauded and maintained.

3. Let commodification serve access. Placing Hitchcock books on coffee tables and offering Hitchcock movies on cable television channels such as American Movie Classics (AMC) and Turner Classic Movies (TCM), in addition to making them available in DVD and video-cassette formats, does more than mere academic discourse in opening up a public sphere for Hitchcock studies, and the marketability of Hitchcock ventures may help materially support scholarly endeavors that are notoriously not self-sufficient.

4. Celebrate the growth and even occasional "noise" of Hitchcock studies. Proliferation need not lead to numbing excess, but perhaps can be mobilized to create a body of commentary that is rich and extensive but not overwhelming or impenetrable, and that presents Hitchcock (both the man and his films) as he might have wished—both familiar and strange, fresh and challenging, dense but not unintelligible.

We need to be wary of many aspects of "Big-Time" Hitchcock, but as Michael Bristol shrewdly points out, that phrase points in two different directions. In examining "Big-Time Shakespeare," he first addresses the long and enduring tradition of imperial and meretricious uses of Shakespeare's cultural and commercial power, a tradition that he insightfully describes and criticizes. But his primary focus is on a radically different and much more positive kind of "big-time" indebted to Mikhail Bakhtin's concept of an almost utopian "bolshoe vremja": a "great time" evoked by some art that links past and present, individual and group, low and high—an art that is "not for an age but for all time" because it is perennially "coming into being" (2–10), "richly dialogized and thus answerable to unforeseen social and cultural circumstances" (11). We should not push a Shakespeare-Hitchcock analogy too far, but we can safely apply the previous description to Hitchcock and acknowledge that he is truly "big-time" because his works, like Shakespeare's as described by Bristol, have "the uncommon capacity . . . to represent the complex pathos of Western modernity" (130). We indeed have world enough and time to take *this* Hitchcock so seriously.

The twenty-one essays and interviews gathered in this volume, drawn from the *Hitchcock Annual,* share a basic commitment to unraveling and re-articulating that above-named "uncommon capacity" of Hitchcock. These pieces reflect the diversity of current approaches to Hitchcock, and range widely across the various ways of "framing Hitchcock," as the book's title suggests: from archaeological investigations uncovering new information about his working methods and conditions to incisive analyses, informed by postmodern and feminist theories, of some of his central as well as some of his lesser-known works; from detailed investigations of recurrent visual and thematic motifs throughout the films to anecdotal commentaries on what is was like working with Hitchcock. While the essays are arranged in five sections under broad subject headings that indicate major areas of interest in the study of Hitchcock, they were not originally written with such headings in mind, and therefore more than occasionally expand beyond the boundaries designated by the title of the section they are placed within. But however provisional and limited, the structure we have chosen does establish clusters of essays on related topics and helps make useful links (and contrasts) among them more visible. Readers will undoubtedly make further links and note other interesting interactions among the essays on their own.

The first section, "Hitchcock: The Early Years," calls attention to what is perhaps the most important of the neglected areas of Hitchcock's work. "Neglected" is, of course, a relative term. There have indeed been substantial examinations of Hitchcock's silent films, including commentary in books by Maurice Yacowar, Tom Ryall, and, most recently, Charles Barr, in the context of broader discussions of Hitchcock's "British" films (that is, the films he made before moving to America in 1939) and in occasional articles or chapters, perhaps most notably William Rothman's detailed analysis of *The Lodger* in *Hitchcock—The Murderous Gaze,* which confirms that Hitchcock was indeed "Hitchcock" almost from the beginning, long before he made his most popular and esteemed films.[5] In general, however, critical studies skip over this period rather quickly, and there has not yet been a book or collection of essays devoted to it. With increasing access to these early films—video-cassettes and DVDs are now available for all the existing silent films except *The Pleasure Garden, Downhill,* and the version of *Blackmail* released without synchronized sound, and the BFI has recently issued restored versions of *The Lodger* and *The Ring* that make these films more watchable than they have been for many years—and much new information about Hitchcock's early life and career promised in Patrick McGilligan's biographical study,[6] I suspect that the next few years will witness a dramatic increase of critical interest in this "neglected" area, an early sign of which is evident in the three essays in the first section of this collection.

Two of these essays focus on Hitchcock and Germany, where he assisted on one film and directed two of his own, and which was also the source of many of the films and ideas about filmmaking that he was deeply influenced by. Even as I introduce detailed analyses that foreground this influence, though, I should add that it is important to keep in mind that Hitchcock's theories and practices were of course multi-determined, shaped by many forces and films and filmmakers from a variety of nations. For example, we need studies of "Hitchcock: The Russian Influence," emphasizing not only the films and writings of Sergei Eisenstein and Vsevolod Pudovkin, but also Hitchcock's felt kinship with the environment of Russian filmmaking of the 1920s, which was characterized by institutional control but also improvisation and self-determination under conditions of material scarcity and duress. It would also be well worth studying further "Hitchcock: The American Influence," examining the powerful influence of D. W. Griffith in particular, and in general trying to fathom exactly what Hitchcock meant when he spoke of himself repeatedly as "American-trained." And closer examination of the French influence on Hitchcock would usefully highlight the models for some of his early experiments with special effects and cinematic form. All these studies are necessary to complement an examination of the German influence and substantially expand our understanding of Hitchcock's early development. Perhaps these topics will be the subject of essays in future anthologies of Hitchcock criticism—or issues of the *Hitchcock Annual.*

In "Early Hitchcock: The German Influence," I survey the stylistic, thematic, and generic aspects of the German influence on Hitchcock, the relationship between Hitchcock and several key German directors (most obviously Fritz Lang and F. W. Murnau, but also E. A. Dupont), and the German background of some of the most characteristic elements of Hitchcock's "idea of cinema," expressed in his many writings and public statements as well as demonstrated in his film practice. The German influence is visible throughout his films in individual touches or moments, recurrent motifs, settings, and characters, and evident as well in some of his most deeply felt ideas about the "Autorenfilm" and commercially viable "Kunstfilm."

Joseph Garncarz's "German Hitchcock" focuses specifically on Hitchcock's work in Germany between 1924 and 1926 as screenwriter and set-designer for British director Malcolm Cutts's *The Blackguard* and director of his own first films, *The Pleasure Garden* and *The Mountain Eagle* (a "lost film" illustrated and described in great detail in a *Hitchcock Annual* essay by J. L. Kuhns that was unfortunately too long to include in the present volume).[7] Garncarz unearths and analyzes a wealth of contemporary German sources—including production records, reviews, articles, popularity polls of actors, actresses, and films, and other press material—to supplement and in some cases correct Hitchcock's own accounts of this period, and to paint an invaluable picture of the circumstances under which Hitchcock was given the resources and freedom as well as the cinematic models to help him fashion his characteristic style of visual narration and "success-oriented star image for himself."

Easy Virtue has come to be the most extensively analyzed of Hitchcock's silent films in the *Hitchcock Annual*.[8] Christopher Morris brings a shrewdly sophisticated theoretical perspective to bear on this fascinating film in "*Easy Virtue*'s Frames," where the figurative expression that Larita, the main female character, is "framed"—that is, manipulated by a social and legal system to appear guilty when she is in fact innocent—is the takeoff point for an examination of broader issues of representation that are, Morris suggests, inevitably prone to error. Although my brief summary here oversimplifies a complex argument, Morriss's premise is that since our awareness of the world operates by exclusion—concentrating on some things necessarily means we leave out others—the same process that makes knowledge and perception possible makes them inherently partial, fallible, and unstable. Highlighting its constant references to photography and its emphasis on how the camera "captures not so much life as the inevitability of the frame" and the futility of Larita or anyone escaping this predicament, Morris shows how *Easy Virtue* takes on new importance as an allegory of the cinema and a dramatization of aspects of the human condition that Hitchcock returned to repeatedly, perhaps most memorably in *Rear Window*: we are creatures of desire, always framed and circumscribed—visually, legally, morally, epistemologically, and, in a word, existentially.

The essays in the next section explore a variety of "Thematic Approaches to Hitchcock," each emphasizing either a particular theoretical methodology that offers substantial insight into important dimensions of Hitchcock's artistry, a cluster of coordinated and highly expressive images drawn from the films themselves, or a conceptual and structural category that shapes the films.

In "The Diabolic Imagination: Hitchcock, Bakhtin, and the Carnival-ization of Cinema," David Sterritt argues that while Hitchcock typically asserts a strong monologic control in his works, somewhat different from what we usually think of as a more open-ended and labile Bakhtinian dialogism and heteroglossia, he nevertheless displays a thoroughgoing "Bakhtinian preoccupation with the carnivalesque, the grotesque, the in-decorous, the socially 'improper' and culturally 'inverted' spectacle." Sterritt focuses primarily on *Rope,* with its Rabelaisian laughter and self-conscious sexual, moral, and philosophical perversity, *Psycho,* the "lower-bodily-stratum film par excellence of Hitchcock's career," and *Frenzy,* with its desta-bilizing doublings and boundary-erasing couplings of sex, food, and death, but he also suggests that these elements abound even in Hitchcock's "classic" works like *The 39 Steps* and *Notorious.* One of the many achievements of this essay is that it establishes comedy—at least as it is broadly interpreted and theorized by Bakhtin—as at the center of Hitchcock's art, temperament, and philosophical and moral vision, and defines his cinema as what I might call "vertuous": that is, one that characteristically, both playfully and seriously, inverts, converts, perverts, and subverts.

We see a different Hitchcock, although one who is similarly both playful and serious, in Frank M. Meola's "Hitchcock's Emersonian Edges." Without asserting any direct influence (it is far easier to imagine Hitchcock curl-ing up with a volume of, say, G. K. Chesterton than Emerson) or losing sight of crucial differences in attitude and philosophy (for example, Hitch-cock is in many ways suspicious of the eccentric, independent person that Emerson typically idealizes), Meola demonstrates the many ways in which Hitchcock "participates in America's ongoing Emersonian project." After his move here, the displaced and resolutely mannered Englishman never-theless proves to have American issues and themes at heart, nicely illustrated by Meola's analysis of Hitchcock's and Emerson's overlapping interests: in "vision" and "visionary possession," for example, central of course in *Rear Window* and *Vertigo*; in the danger of knowledge, particularly when it be-comes an instrument of power over others, as in *Psycho*; and in the Ameri-can contours of "threats to the soul," an elliptical phrase that becomes reso-nant and particular as Meola skillfully cross-references Emerson's "Nature," "Circles," and "Experience" and Hitchcock's *Strangers on a Train, Vertigo,* and *North by Northwest.*

My essay, "Hitchcock and the Art of the Kiss: A Preliminary Survey," fo-cuses on not only the frequency of kissing shots and sequences throughout Hitchcock's films but also the many ways in which his cinema is predicated on the kiss. Kisses are rarely incidental in the films, but rather appear as synecdochal representations of complex dramas: they tell the story and in some cases they are the story, embodying in miniature the dynamics of interactions and relationships as well as plotting the details and development of an individual's character, his or her desires and fears, successes and failures. The essay sketches a broad stylistics and thematics of the kiss, examining such moments as remarkable opportunities for Hitchcockian visual excess; offers a typology of kisses, giving examples of the variety of kisses Hitchcock portrays; and concludes with a close reading of one of his most famous kissing sequences, which takes place on the balcony in *Notorious,* to illustrate how intricately such scenes are embedded in the overall design of his carefully structured films.

Sarah Street similarly makes bold claims for the far-reaching significance of "Hitchcockian Haberdashery." Focusing on the recurrent image of a woman's handbag as "a central element of suspense and register of sexual tension" in such films as *Dial M for Murder, Rear Window, Vertigo, Psycho,* and *Marnie,* she demonstrates how what is often thought of as "a mere costume accessory" can, when deployed skillfully, function as a subtle mode of direct address to female spectators well-versed in the deep codes evoked by fashion, assert the "secrets" of "independent female identity" (the problematic core and flash-point of many Hitchcock films), and contribute substantially to the "female masquerade," a source of male anxiety and female power and versatility. Street credits not only Hitchcock but also the fashion and design advice from Edith Head and Grace Kelly in helping transform the handbag from a prop to an evocative "textual pointer," the decoding of which heightens our appreciation of the "enigmatic" and "complex presentation of the feminine" in Hitchcock's films from the mid-1950s to the mid-1960s.

Sabrina Barton nominates "Hitchcock's Hands" as one of the most critical components of his "cinematic body language" and uses examples from many of his most important films, including *Shadow of a Doubt, Notorious, The Birds,* and *Marnie,* to illustrate how "hands speak emphatically in Hitchcock's movies." According to Barton, hands evoke and enact powerful dramas, and besides functioning as key visual elements in spectacles that range from the subtle to the baroque, they often provide an index of a character's power or weakness, mental state, self-control, and competency, especially in times of stress. Barton is particularly concerned not only with how hands contribute to the complexity of Hitchcock's gendered representations of these latter qualities, but also with how such images "help shape audience's relationships with characters," affecting our sympathy with, interest in, value judgments about, and overall impression of the "humanness" of a character. She elaborates her argument by detailed textual analysis of (and frame captures from) key moments in Hitchcock's films, effectively pointed observations from cognitive and feminist film theory, and intriguing anecdotal comments drawn from real-life (rather than, as is so often the case, abstractly hypothesized) spectators from her class on "Hitchcock and Gender."

Thomas M. Leitch's essay could have been placed in the concluding section on Hitchcock's legacy, since one of the ways he defines "The Hitchcock Moment" is by comparing him with later so-called Hitchcockian filmmakers (a designation he disputes as sometimes too loosely awarded) who aspire to such moments and frequently fail: for example, Brian De Palma, whose overstated crescendos lack the "unobtrusive obtrusiveness" of Hitchcock's; Roman Polanski, whose unremittingly gloomy and oppressive nightmarish visions lack Hitchcock's multi-tonal wit; and David Lynch, whose films constructed of moments add up to less than the sum of their parts. But Leitch's essay also rightly fits in a section of essays that attempt to highlight particular defining elements of Hitchcock's artistry, and he persuasively argues that "Hitchcock's is preeminently a cinema of moments." Far from a catalog or simple appreciation of memorable shots or scenes—an approach that Hitchcock himself reinforced in his interviews by his habit of singling out particular moments for his own and then presumably the audience's notice and praise—Leitch's essay charts the intricate ways that such moments figure in the larger orchestration of Hitchcock's films, career, and critical reception. He relates Hitchcock's moments to a characteristic strategy of "disavowal" that enabled Hitchcock to both distance and involve his audiences, reminding them simultaneously that indeed a film can have extremely powerful effects but that ultimately "It's only a movie." The Hitchcock moment allowed him to reinvent himself constantly, to work within as well as against the Hollywood system, and somehow to become the kind of filmmaker who was if not all things to all people, then at least one who flourished, critically and commercially, in part because of his creative trickiness, flexibility, and versatility.

I wish that the following section on "Hitchcock and His Screenwriters" could have been longer, but we don't have more material to draw upon—at least from the *Hitchcock Annual*—that tells what it was like to work with Hitchcock on the scripts for his films. Hitchcock scholars should not lose sight of the great value of the recollections and observations of the many actors, actresses, technicians, and writers who worked directly with Hitchcock, and should continue to expand the oral history project of recording their comments while we still can. In any event, the two interviews here present an interesting picture of Hitchcock in the early 1960s, while he was making *The Birds* and *Marnie*.

Some of Evan Hunter's reminiscences about his contributions to these two films and problems with Hitchcock are fairly well known from previous interviews and his own short book *Me and Hitch,*[9] but Charles L. P. Silet elicits important comments about what drew Hitchcock to him initially (his "aesthetic respectability" as a novelist rather than his reputation as a mere screenwriter), the relationship between his television and film work for Hitchcock, and some of the details of their day-to-day working relationship and interaction. The more we investigate Hitchcock's working method, the more we learn about not only his remarkable attentiveness to details— "He was meticulous about the circumstances in the script," Hunter tells Silet—but also about his multi-faceted involvement in the writing process. The dramatic highpoint of this interview is Hunter's brief description of his by now famous blowup with Hitchcock over the "rape" scene in *Marnie,* resistance to which he says got him fired from the film. This incident, however, is placed in a broader context, just after less well-known but perhaps equally important details about Hitchcock's insistent reshaping of the script for *The Birds.*

In her interview with Richard Allen, Jay Presson Allen picks up the backstory of *Marnie* where Hunter leaves off and presents an interesting counterpoint to Hunter's account. Prodded by Richard Allen and questions and comments from the floor (the interview was conducted at a session held at the Hitchcock Centennial Conference), she asserts the value of the so-called "rape scene," which, in her opinion, far from ruining the film, adds to its psychological complexity. I use the qualifier "so-called" because Jay Presson Allen, with invaluable help from Robin Wood, alerts us to the many nuances of this pivotal moment in the film that may be elided if we simply call it a "rape scene." And much in contrast with Hunter's anecdotes about Hitchcock's occasionally intrusive and manipulative involvement in screenplays, she emphasizes not only the director's many contributions as she worked on the script—including a fascinating example of how cinematic inventiveness can resolve a writer's problems in moving characters from one place to another, in this case from wedding to honeymoon—but also his overall effectiveness as a teacher, particularly by giving her "a feeling of total freedom" to work and even "violate something that he had said he'd like with impunity." In addition, she comments candidly on Hitchcock's relationship with Alma (his wife and to this date largely uncredited and unappreciated collaborator) and Lew Wasserman (his former agent and later "boss"), the dynamics of Hitchcock's relationship with actresses, female production associates, and wives of other co-workers, and the reasons why she is both proud of and disappointed by *Marnie*. One particularly fascinating aspect of the interview is the interplay between Allen and the audience. Playing to a room filled with academics, she repeatedly insisted on her deeply held belief in the emotional, instinctive, and intuitive components of artistic creation and our proper response to art. But despite her many witty jabs at over-intellectualized critical and scholarly commentary that leaves her "stupefied" and "amazed," she was, if anything, energized and inspired by the questions, comments, and even intellectual interpretations offered not only by the interviewer on stage with her but by Peter Wollen, Slavoj Žižek, Robin Wood, Susan White, Walter Srebnick, and other members of the audience who made this a truly collaborative and dialogic occasion.

It may be a bit misleading to use the heading "Hitchcock: The Major Phase" for the next section unless I explain that this term is not meant to be restrictive. Critics have often been tempted to give shape to Hitchcock's career by periodizing it (for example, into early, middle, and late; English and American; the decade of spy films; the decade of war films; the Metro years; the "great" decade from *Rear Window* through *Marnie*) and charting various rhythms (such as rising and falling; success and failure; achievement and running for cover; innovation, consolidation, and repetition; apprenticeship, maturity, and senescence). This broad effort, in Thomas Leitch's phrase, to "find the director" is also to a certain extent an attempt to find the director's "major phase," his sustained peak.[10] But in many ways Hitchcock's "major phase" arguably stretches from *The Lodger* (1926) to *Family Plot* (1974), and it undoubtedly will not be long before a case has been made for nearly every Hitchcock film as a major one. I thus use the term loosely and perhaps a bit elliptically to introduce a section of essays that each focus on one key film and explicate particular aspects of its importance: that is, its creative achievement and continuing relevance to our ongoing attempt to reach a comprehensive understanding of Hitchcock. Four of the films discussed here are indeed commonly considered as high canonical works, beginning with one that Hitchcock often described as his favorite and moving through three acknowledged late masterpieces. But the section ends with a persuasive recuperation of his last film, which up until now no one has put forth as a favorite.

Throughout "Hitchcock the Feminist: Rereading *Shadow of a Doubt*, Thomas Hemmeter argues that Hitchcock can indeed be reclaimed for feminism and that this film is not, as some critics suggest, a misogynist fantasy that ultimately returns a transgressive young woman to a discredited and oppressive social order but rather a powerful critique of murderous and self-destructive patriarchy that may be resisted and at least tentatively escaped. *Shadow of a Doubt* certainly dramatizes patriarchy's far-reaching power of containment, so much so that a woman's options seem limited to either being crushed, if not murdered, or "triumphing" in ways that ironically reconfirm patriarchal values, a fate that Young Charlie skirts at the end, defeating Uncle Charlie only at the risk of becoming just like him in various ways. But patriarchy is also shown as a structure with pronounced "cracks and fissures," illustrating that the film ultimately "rejects patriarchal values" and charts a path by which they may be overcome. Hemmeter focuses particularly on how Young Charlie is able to escape the oppressive force of patriarchal binary constructs and misogynistic, pre-determined life-scripts by accepting a creatively fluid concept of identity, taking over the burden of "seeing" in the film and resourcefully becoming the woman who knows— not too much, overwhelmed by dangerous knowledge, but enough, and is liberated by useful and necessary knowledge. Hemmeter carefully avoids overstating Young Charlie's success at the end of the film, but by calling attention to her "marginal position" at the "provisional intersection of illusions," he nicely underscores that Hitchcock's highest achievement in the genre of suspense has less to do with mysterious plots than his haunting images of the existential condition of characters suspended in a "troubled state of grace."

Nearly everyone, of course, approaches *Rear Window* as a crucial example of Hitchcock's fascination with various forms of looking, but in "*Rear Window*, or the Reciprocated Glance" John A. Bertolini analyzes the pivotal moments in the film when looks intersect, with dramatic and deeply symbolic consequences. Most viewers can instantly recall the most striking and frightening of these moments—when Thorwald looks out his window directly back at Jefferies—but Bertolini also examines two other key reciprocated glances, tracing a fascinating nexus of gazes and a complex structural pattern that emerges during Hitchcock's cameo appearance. He stresses that Hitchcock's final word is that, despite the overall emphasis in the film on forbidden and dangerous looking, reciprocated glances may be comforting as well as fearful. Bertolini has an extremely fine eye for details in the film and how they are filiated into often subtle patterns, visual rhymes, links, and associations. Not the least of these details that he recognizes is the wonderfully therapeutic power of Lisa and Jefferies' reciprocated gaze just after he has fallen from the window, not to his death but literally back into the world from which his injury had temporarily removed him and perhaps into a new life that may be less solitary and alienated than his former one.

Leland Poague's densely layered "Engendering *Vertigo*" is as provocatively vertiginous as its subject. Only after we finish reading it do we become fully aware of how the punning title previews the complexity of his approach, suggesting not only that the essay engages with feminist criticism of Hitchcock and examines *Vertigo*'s play with gender, but also that this is part of a broader examination of the film as a "parable of birth giving and separation," related elements that become especially visible and comprehensible when we are aware of the intertextual "birthing" of the film in a generative sea of cinematic and critical texts. In assessing *Vertigo*'s "complex generic affiliations," Poague emphasizes the particular importance of the "comedy of remarriage" and the "melodrama of the unknown woman." These terms signal the centrality of Stanley Cavell in Poague's argument, and indeed much of the essay is a meditation on Cavell's philosophy of cinema and a plea for using it to break through what Poague takes to be the restrictions of contemporary criticism now dominated by a pantheon of Ferdinand de Saussure, Jacques Lacan, Louis Althusser, and Roland Barthes. Alongside much Cavellian philosophical speculation, adumbrating categories and schema, Poague also engages in another characteristic Cavellian maneuver of opposite as well as apposite juxtaposition and close textual analysis, and he squeezes out fascinating overtones and undertones, harmonies and dissonances, from startling collocations of *Vertigo* and, among many other examples, Frank Capra's films *It Happened One Night* and *It's a Wonderful Life*. Operating from the implicit premise that the film comes to life in part via Capra and Cavell, one of Poague's most intriguing revelations is the extent to which the true, and perhaps not altogether tragic, heroine of *Vertigo* is Scottie.

In "Avian Metaphor in *The Birds*," Richard Allen builds from previous psychologically oriented examinations of how this film associates tremendous chaotic and destructive energy with the feminine, and particularly the maternal, but stresses that to gain a comprehensive understanding of the "psychotherapeutic model of human relationships that underpins the narrative of *The Birds*" we need to supplement Freudian approaches with the somewhat "different picture of human motivation put forward in object-relations theory." The latter shifts attention from (without disregarding, Allen notes) sexual desire and the particular dynamics of the Oedipal environment to fears of abandonment and loss, broad concern about human connection, and a central focus on mother-daughter relationships and issues of female autonomy. From this perspective, the film remains extremely frightening as a picture of the consequences of our "emotional isolation and abandonment" and "inability to acknowledge" one another, but we also become aware of a potentially consoling "unresolved paradox" at the heart of the film and the human predicament: society is vulnerable to and must be protected from the ravaging power of hysteria, but this power is also linked with the feminine force that makes society possible in the first place. For Allen, the birds are thus not figures of an inscrutable and unrelenting apocalypse but an evocation of a kind of Shelleyan destroyer and preserver, illustrated by the appearance throughout the film of not only the more frequently noted demonic "death birds" but also the "love birds," signifying the powerful pull toward affection, bonding rather than biting. Melanie, Allen shrewdly points out, has qualities of both, but the latter—"her intuition, her contact with nature," therapeutic intervention into the life of Mitch and his family, and self-transforming acceptance of vulnerability—support at least a muted triumph at the end and confirm that "*The Birds* affords a space for the redemptive aspects of femininity."

Because of its position at the end of this section and its own freely chosen subject—*Family Plot,* Hitchcock's last completed film—a great deal of weight falls on David Sterritt's "Alfred Hitchcock: Registrar of Births and Deaths" as a valediction on Hitchcock's life and career, and it performs this function admirably. Like many of the other contributors here, Sterritt sees Hitchcock as not only the "Master of Suspense" but "the Master of Ambiguity as well," crafting works of "ambivalence," "indeterminacy," and "paradoxicality," qualities he "finds at the root of social and individual experience." And Sterritt also nicely summarizes the effort of many of the essays in this volume to describe Hitchcock as something more than an architect and analyst of pain and horror by stressing that even as he was nearing the end of his life and working under tremendous pain and pressure, he was "searching for loopholes in the human condition—hitherto unnoticed signs pointing toward renewal and regeneration rather than finality and closure." Hitchcock's films are frequently meditations on the Last Things in a broad sense, that is, confrontations with issues of ultimate concern, and Sterritt argues for the deep theological and metaphysical seriousness of Hitchcock's last film, which at the same time jokes so much about spirituality. Working from biographical material as well as contemporary theoretical constructs (especially Michel Chion's notion of the *acousmêtre,* the cinematic voice without a body, and Žižek's concept of the blot and attention to the uncanny and disturbing moments when the film looks out at its spectators), Sterritt reveals the many dimensions of *Family Plot* that "suggest that Hitchcock's investment in religious thinking has a value in Hitchcockian hermeneutics far beyond its usual limited role in explicating religiously inclined films— like *I Confess* and *The Wrong Man*"—and analyzing "his fascination with earthly guilt, sin, and redemption." There is an insistent subtext of transcendence throughout the film, as an emphasis on the body—especially the lower body, in keeping with Hitchcock's carnivalesque dimensions that Sterritt's earlier essay in the volume focuses on—gives way to a recognition of the non-material components of life and longing, visualized in a series of rebirths in the film and recurrent patterns of Christian imagery and supernatural contact. Particularly emblematic of all this, as Sterritt notes, is Hitchcock's more than usually symbolic cameo as a shadow cast on a well-deserved title, aptly describing the way he straddled two realms throughout his career as the "Registrar of Births and Deaths."

The final section in the volume focuses on "Hitchcock and His Legacy," exploring how Hitchcock's influence—a catch-all term meant to include the diversity of responses to his continuing presence, including various forms of imitation, transformation, and resistance—is registered not only in a wide range of films (including some rather unexpected ones) and directorial practices, but also in the continuing reconceptualization of genres he opened up and in the shifting codes, conventions, and conditions at work when we watch films.

In "A Hero for Our Times: *Foreign Correspondent, Hero,* and *Bonfire of the Vanities,*" starting from T. S. Eliot's provocative assertion that the present influences the past, Lesley Brill adopts a non-linear modernist and in some ways postmodern-inflected understanding of the dynamics of influence and intertextuality to analyze how "Frears's and De Palma's films at once allude to Hitchcock's and suggest a reinterpretation of it." The later two films seem particularly indebted to Hitchcockian themes, camera set-ups, and stylistic flourishes, as well as his attitude toward heroism and the demands of public life, a characteristic blend of "paradoxically realistic idealism" and "skepticism." But if *Foreign Correspondent* in some ways helps generate *Hero* and *Bonfire of the Vanities,* they in turn help reshape Hitchcock's film, or at least our understanding of it, turning it into a kind of proleptic homage to or intuition of our increasing fascination with, if not insistence upon, open endings and "multiple, unstable meanings."

Like Brill, James M. Vest works from the premises that "influence" need not connote an asymmetrical, "anxious" relationship and that an homage need not be primarily a signifier of self-denying deference. In "Echoes of Alfred Hitchcock's *Vertigo, The Birds,* and *Frenzy* in François Truffaut's *Story of Adèle H.,*" he traces the "discernible Hitchcockian imprint" in Truffaut's film, visible in recurrent high-angle shots; vertiginous camera movements; bird, dog, and bookstore motifs; and a pivotal cameo sequence inserting the director into the film.[11] But while he recognizes the depth and pressures of Truffaut's deep attachment to Hitchcock—and indeed notes that this is perhaps a critical subtext in a film about a young person's complex relationship with her world-famous and in many ways overpowering father—Vest emphasizes how Truffaut uses Hitchcockian elements ultimately to assert his independence and divergence, "saluting" Hitchcock "with ingenuity while establishing a distinctive, highly personal aesthetic vision."

Christopher Sharrett is attentive to Hitchcock's influence on particular directors, but he focuses more broadly on his major contribution to the collective enterprise of constructing and transforming a genre, in this case a genre that plays a pivotal role in contemporary attempts to represent, understand, and critique the "general psychopathology simmering underneath the superstructure" of "some principal assumptions of American middle-class life." In "The Myth of Apocalypse and the Horror Film: The Primacy of *Psycho* and *The Birds*," Sharrett explores not only the spectacular and dramatic but also the analytic power of these two films in figuring the unrecuperability of the world and its imminent end not as a metaphysical event but as a direct and explicable result of humanly constructed political, social, moral, and behavioral systems. Sharrett's essay is a necessary supplement and, in some ways, corrective to current work reexamining Hitchcock's "American" period and value as a cultural observer in his second home. Like Frank Meola in his essay in this volume and the essays in the recent collection *Hitchcock's America,* edited by Richard Millington and Jonathan Friedman, Sharrett argues that Hitchcock's later films constitute a far-reaching, even "systemic analysis of American life."[12] But he stresses far more than these other critics the deeply disturbed and disturbing "power of blackness"[13] in Hitchcock, and the extent to which *Psycho* and *The Birds* in particular mount an "assault on the empty belief systems of bourgeois society" and picture the devastating consequences of "the force of repression/oppression unleashed." Perhaps not unintentionally, a powerful irony underlines his demonstration of how contemporary horror films have learned the lesson of these two films in continuing their portrayal of the accelerating horrors of a society that has apparently *not* yet learned the lesson of these two films.

The final two essays in this section explore other aspects of *Psycho* as a pivotal component of Hitchcock's complex legacy. In " 'See It From the Beginning': Hitchcock's Reconstruction of Film History," Joan Hawkins examines how Hitchcock exerted control over an audience not only by the audacious internal textual design of *Psycho* but also by his instructions about how the film would be screened. While Hawkins praises Hitchcock's shrewd development and implementation of a marketing campaign that drew a great deal of attention to his film and also helped "discipline the audience" by making them wait in line and see the film only from the beginning, she analyzes this effort in the context of particular influences that Hitchcock was responding to and broader movements that he participated in. Upon close inspection, what we describe as innovations most often turn out to be "middles" as much as they are "beginnings," and Hawkins usefully points out that the positioning and exploitation of *Psycho* must be seen in terms of Hitchcock's debt to Henri-Georges Clouzot and the marketing of his "Hitchcockian" film *Diabolique,* released in 1955. Without at all undermining the stunning inventiveness of *Psycho*, Hawkins broadens our understanding of its tremendous impact by emphasizing how its textual formation as well as promotion and exhibition were grounded in "a cooperative effort between several cinéastes—from different cultures—working in the suspense/thriller/horror genre and art cinema mode."

The final essay, James Naremore's "Remaking *Psycho*," overlaps nicely with Hawkins' because part of it focuses on vivid recollections of his experience of watching the film when it first came out, in a carnivalistic atmosphere with the audience attending "for the sake of a roller-coaster ride of primal emotion." These enthusiastic comments, though, are set in the context of a far from enthusiastic review of Gus Van Sant's version of *Psycho,* a project that fails on all conceivable levels: as a horror movie, homage, intellectual exercise, or mass-marketed museum installation piece offering any significant meta-cinematic commentary. Ironically, the greatest achievement of Van Sant's *Psycho* is that it provides a foil to Hitchcock's, which comes to stand as a brilliant rarity in the age of mechanical reproduction, an "original." Naremore's primary intention is not to expand on the near-universal critical trashing of Van Sant's film but to comment on the logic and limitations of remakes in general, and return to Hitchcock's film with a renewed appreciation of such things as its counterpoint of austerity and artiness, the "boyish humor, pathos, and sinister grace" of Anthony Perkins' performance; the persistent rhymes and doublings that are part of a complex structural, tonal, and visual design; and the overall creepy wit and intelligence of this in some ways inimitable film.

NOTES

1. Robin Wood, *Hitchcock's Films Revisited* (New York: Columbia University Press, 1989), 55.

2. Michael D. Bristol, *Big-Time Shakespeare* (New York: Routledge, 1996). Further references to this book are cited by page number in the text of my essay.

3. Dan Auiler, *"Vertigo": The Making of a Hitchcock Classic* (New York: St. Martin's Press, 1998); Bill Krohn, *Hitchcock at Work* (New York: Phaidon, 2000); Ken Mogg, *The Alfred Hitchcock Story* (London: Titan Books, 1999).

4. Jan Kott, "Hamlet of the Mid-Century," in *Shakespeare Our Contemporary* (Garden City: Anchor, 1964), 57.

5. Maurice Yacowar, *Hitchcock's British Films* (Hamden, CT: Archon Books, 1977); Tom Ryall, *Alfred Hitchcock and the British Cinema* (Urbana: University of Illinois Press, 1986); Charles Barr, *English Hitchcock* (London: Cameron & Hollis, 1999); William Rothman, *Hitchcock—The Murderous Gaze* (Cambridge, MA: Harvard University Press, 1982), 6–55.

6. Patrick McGilligan. *The Dark and Light Side of Genius* Forthcoming in the fall of 2003.

7. J. L. Kuhns, "Hitchcock's *The Mountain Eagle*," *Hitchcock Annual* (1998–99): 31–108.

8. See Sidney Gottlieb, "Kissing and Telling in Hitchcock's *Easy Virtue*," *Hitchcock Annual* (1992): 1–38; Gottlieb, "Alfred Hitchcock's *Easy Virtue* (1927): A Descriptive Shot List," *Hitchcock Annual* (1993): 41–95; and J. L. Kuhns, "Comments on 'Alfred Hitchcock's *Easy Virtue* (1927): A Descriptive Shot List,'" *Hitchcock Annual* (1995–96): 126–33.

9. Evan Hunter, *Me and Hitch* (London: Faber and Faber, 1997).

10. Thomas Leitch, *Find the Director and Other Hitchcock Games* (Athens, GA: University of Georgia Press, 1991).

11. Vest has a particular interest in Hitchcock's cameos, which he has examined at length in two other essays, "The Controller Controlled: Hitchcock's Cameo in *Torn Curtain*," *Hitchcock Annual* (1998–99): 3–19, and "Alfred Hitchcock's Cameo in *Vertigo*," *Hitchcock Annual* (1999–2000): 84–92.

12. Jonathan Freedman and Richard Millington, eds., *Hitchcock's America* (New York: Oxford University Press, 1999).

13. I borrow this term from Harry Levin, *The Power of Blackness: Hawthorne, Poe, Melville* (New York: Vintage Books, 1958).

HITCHCOCK: THE EARLY YEARS

EARLY HITCHCOCK:
THE GERMAN INFLUENCE

SIDNEY GOTTLIEB

Hitchcock prided himself on being an Englishman and an English filmmaker, and in his early writings on film he emphasized the need for British directors to further explore British subjects (see, for example, "Films We Could Make," 165–67)[1]: especially the countryside and landscape of Great Britain as well as the city, and the middle and lower classes, largely neglected, he felt, by filmmakers (see "More Cabbages, Fewer Kings: A Believer in the Little Man," 176–78). Hitchcock was always shrewdly aware of some of the advantages of a "national" cinema, one that appealed to a "home" audience by a skillful manipulation of familiar stories and characters and that rested on the director's confident understanding of the audience's sense of humor and their enjoyment of fear and suspense. Nevertheless, during a time of a routinely international cinema, many of the early influences on Hitchcock were "foreign."[2] These influences are sometimes summarized by reference to particular filmmakers or films, an approach that perhaps works best in analyzing the French influence on Hitchcock, which may well have centered on a few experimental or avant-garde films, such as

Ballet mecanique and *Entr'acte*. But other "foreign" influences were much more far-reaching. For example, the American influence involves a particular debt to D. W. Griffith but also a more general notion of how to organize one's cinematic practices and work within a particular kind of studio system. (Hitchcock frequently remarked that his initiation to film was in a British-based but American-operated studio, and he often pointed out that in some ways he was an American filmmaker even before he moved to America.) The Russian influence may revolve around Eisenstein, Pudovkin, and Dovzhenko, but involves, more than a few particular works like *Potemkin*, a theory of montage, critical to Hitchcock throughout his career, and a sense of the political nature of filmmaking, an aspect of Hitchcock's films that deserves far more attention than it usually receives. Finally, the German influence, arguably the most significant, involves not only Hitchcock's debt to a few great filmmakers and a few important films but also an immersion in a broad-based production environment, culture, and aesthetic of cinema.[3]

Perhaps the best way to suggest the range and depth of the German influence on Hitchcock and the complexity of his response is to set up a few section headings. All are overlapping and interrelated, but each focuses on the topic from a different vantage point. First, we can examine the stylistic, thematic, and generic aspects of the German influence on Hitchcock. Second, we can look briefly at the relationship between Hitchcock and several key German directors. Third, we can examine how Hitchcock's "idea of cinema"—his vision of the ideal production system, the role of the director, the definition of film as art and entertainment, and so on—was deeply influenced by the German model.

STYLISTIC, THEMATIC, AND GENERIC ASPECTS OF THE GERMAN INFLUENCE ON HITCHCOCK

PURE CINEMA

Hitchcock frequently referred to the importance of his "German years" in his writings and interviews. He worked on several films as an assistant director with Graham Cutts and a British crew at the Ufa studio in Neubabelsberg, made his first two films, *The Pleasure Garden* and *The Mountain Eagle,* partly in the Emelka Studios in Munich, and reminisced about his German experiences in charming and perceptive detail throughout his life: see especially his early memoir, "Life Among the Stars" (27–58) and late interview, "Alfred Hitchcock: The German Years." But while in these pieces he related many interesting anecdotes about his often hilarious adventures and misadventures, he is his own best critic when he comments seriously on the most important lesson he learned from German filmmakers:

> The Germans in those times placed great emphasis on telling the story visually; if possible with no titles or at least very few. In *The Last Laugh* Murnau was able to do that, to dispense with titles altogether, except in an epilogue. . . . I've always believed that you can tell as much visually as you can with words. That's what I learned from the Germans. ("The German Years," 23–24)

Throughout his life, Hitchcock practiced what he called "pure cinema," emphasizing the visual dimension of film. Sound pictures, he frequently warned, had to steer clear of being "merely pictures of people talking" ("The German Years," 24), and it is interesting to see how Hitchcock's later films frequently contain long stretches without dialogue. In a letter to Hitchcock that was the first step toward setting up the interviews that would form the basis of the most important "Hitchbook" ever published, Truffaut pays Hitchcock perhaps the ultimate compliment from one filmmaker to another. Truffaut summarizes the main critical point of his remarks introducing the interviews:

> If, overnight, the cinema had to do without its soundtrack and become once again a silent art, then many directors would be forced into unemployment, but, among the survivors, there would be Alfred Hitchcock and everyone would realize at last that he is the greatest film director in the world.[4]

But Hitchcock knew that even silent pictures must avoid the easy temptation to be static and filled with explanatory and "talky" intertitles. Although whenever we speak of the German influence we tend to think first of exaggerated images, melodramatic actions, shadows, stairs, sudden eruptions of inexplicable violence, and so on, Hitchcock sets us straight by noting that, at least for him, German cinema was first and foremost a visual cinema.

EXPRESSIONISM

At the same time, though, we should not forget about nor underestimate the importance of shadows, stairs, mirrors, images of the double or "Doppelgänger," dark foreboding landscapes, sudden terrors, and all the other paraphernalia of many key German films of the 1920s that clearly had an effect on Hitchcock. Critics still debate whether the term "Expressionism" should properly be transferred from painting to film, but it nevertheless serves as a useful term to summarize many of the qualities of such films as Robert Wiene's *The Cabinet of Dr. Caligari,* Paul Leni's *Waxworks,* and Hitchcock's own *The Lodger* and *Blackmail.* Expressionism typically pictures the physical world as a dark, frightening, violent, and unstable place, often a projection of a disturbed person shown through striking set designs and lighting effects as well as subjective camera shots. Motion through this world is dramatic and dizzying, sometimes shown via a mobile camera, other times by a fixed camera focusing on a search, pursuit, or climactic chase. (Hitchcock refers to the "chase" as the "core of the movie" in an interview with that title, 125–32, and although he mentions primarily examples from Griffith, he was undoubtedly also influenced by dramatic chase sequences in early German films.)

In expressionist films, the self is typically tortured and fragmented, especially as powerful, even uncontrollable impulses battle with weaker forces of restraint, order, harmony, and gentle love, and often the self is doubled, paired with another character to illustrate a split but also the mysterious kinship between good and evil, light and darkness, normal and abnormal, love and hate, and so on. And there is frequently a sense of sympathy or identification with the monstrous: like Cesare in *Caligari,* the poor soul manipulated by forces beyond his control to murder, and like Jack the Ripper in Pabst's *Pandora's Box,* Hitchcock's shadowy lodger figure is sympathetic and attractive—only the first in a long line of Hitchcock characters who are charming as well as potentially or literally murderous. Throughout his career Hitchcock explored what might be called the guilt of innocence and the innocence of guilt, and this is a recurrent theme of the German films of the 1920s.

Cinematic Expressionism also calls to mind a particular ensemble of images and camera techniques that Hitchcock adopted. Shadows, nighttime settings, and so-called chiaroscuro lighting effects help establish a mood of unfathomable mystery; stairs often lead to places of horror; mirrors heighten the sense that characters are split and relentlessly and painfully self-conscious; and startling camera angles (sometimes unusually high, or low, or oblique) and quick changes in camera position have a destabilizing effect, signaling the inner and outer world of the main characters as precarious and volatile.

It is difficult to know exactly what attracted Hitchcock to the expressionist films of Weimar period Germany, but he drew on them throughout his career. While he was never a fan of the "horror" film, a genre that he felt merely exploited "sadism, perversion, bestiality, and deformity" ("Why 'Thrillers' Thrive," 111), he did believe that an imaginative immersion in the dangerous, the grotesque, and the fantastic could be not only "thrilling" but also therapeutic:

> Why do we go to the pictures? To see life reflected on the screen, certainly—but what kind of life?
>
> Obviously, the kind we don't experience ourselves—or the same life but with a difference; and the difference consists of emotional disturbances which, for convenience, we call "thrills."
>
> Our nature is such that we must have these "shake-ups," or we grow sluggish and jellified; but, on the other hand, our civilization has so screened and sheltered us that it isn't practicable to experience sufficient thrills at firsthand.
>
> So we have to experience them artificially, and the screen is the best medium for this. ("Why 'Thrillers' Thrive," 109)

Like the world of the Grimm brothers, which, as Donald Spoto notes, Hitchcock became enamored of during his days in Germany, the world of expressionist Weimar cinema had a lifelong effect on Hitchcock, and as early as *The Lodger* and as late as *Frenzy* he explored and analyzed and shuddered at and, if we believe his words, grimly enjoyed, with us, his recurrent evocations of that world.[5]

KAMMERSPIELFILME, STREET FILMS, THE "NEW OBJECTIVITY," AND FILMS OF THE CITY

While Expressionism gets most of the attention as the distinctive quality of German cinema of the 1920s and seems to be the movement most directly related to what we think of as Hitchcock's characteristic interests, we should note several other types of German films of this period that also influenced Hitchcock (surveyed briefly by Spoto, 73–74). The 1920s were a time of not only Expressionism but also documentary and social realism. *The Cabinet of Dr. Caligari* was, in its own rather bizarre way, a study of family and domestic relations, but there were other more understated and "realistic" examinations of these subjects, known as "Kammerspielfilme," filmed chamber plays emphasizing in often meticulous detail the life—and more often than not, the decay—of individuals living in claustrophobic environments. Before Hitchcock hit his stride, according to some, in the great thrillers of the mid-1930s, his work was characterized less by action, adventure, and suspense than by dramatic scrutiny of personal and social relations. Such films as *Easy Virtue, The Ring, The Manxman,* and *Murder!* obviously owe a lot to the British stage, but also show the influence of the German *Kammerspielfilme.* And this influence is a persistent one: Rohmer and Chabrol, for example, suggest that the combination of intimacy, the "deliberate mixture of the extremely concrete and the abstract," the use of many highly charged, even symbolic objects, and daring camera work in *Notorious* reminds them of certain *Kammerspielfilme,* especially of Murnau.[6]

The street film is, as Spoto notes, an offshoot of the *Kammerspielfilm,* focusing particularly on the attempt, invariably failed, to escape the boredom and limitations of domesticity. But the street or the road prove to be even more threatening than the home: that at least is the message of *Rich and Strange,* which Spoto sees as one early example of Hitchcock's "spiritual kinship" to this type of film (74). His most accomplished "street film," though, is undoubtedly *Blackmail,* which is a remarkable blend of elements from such films as Pabst's *The Joyless Street* and expressionist aspects from *Caligari* and Lang's *Metropolis.*

Finally, alongside Expressionism—and sometimes linked with it in intriguing ways—there was a resurgence of interest among German filmmakers in the late 1920s in forms of documentary cinema. The so-called "New Objectivity" aimed to capture the many details of life authentically, empirically, realistically. Although in one of his most well-known witticisms, Hitchcock spoke of his films as intended to give a slice of cake rather than a slice of life, throughout his career he attempted to do both, and perhaps we need to pay closer attention to the latter. There are, of course, a variety of cinematic influences on Hitchcock's "realism," including the British documentary movement in film, well in evidence in the 1920s even before its flourishing under Grierson and others in the late 1920s and 1930s,[7] and the documentary aspects of the Russian filmmakers more well known for their often flamboyant montage effects (especially Eisenstein, Pudovkin, and Vertov). But the German influence on Hitchcock in this respect was especially crucial. Hitchcock may not have seen such films as Erno Metzner's *Police Report: Hold-Up* (1928), recreating a crime in precise detail, but like Fritz Lang in *Spies, M,* and various films on the master criminal figure Doctor Mabuse, Hitchcock integrated documentary-like presentations of the mechanics of crime, detective, and legal work in many of his films: the best early examples are *Blackmail* and *Murder!,* but this documentary interest is critical even in later films such as *The Wrong Man, Vertigo,* and *Psycho.*

Hitchcock's interest in documentary also surfaces apart from his interest in crime, punishment, and detection. Some of his early films attempt to picture a social milieu in full realistic detail: *The Manxman* is his key work documenting provincial life; *The Ring* is not so much a tale of the boxing ring as an examination of a social circle, an image akin to Schnitzler's *La Ronde,* which Spoto suggests Hitchcock might have seen in Germany (77); and even a minor film like *The Farmer's Wife* owes its charm to Hitchcock's delight, however condescending, in following the country folk through their landscape of cows and chickens and often silly emotions and pretensions.

Hitchcock's additional interest in not so much the landscape but the cityscape perhaps owes a great deal to Walter Ruttmann's dazzling *Berlin, The Symphony of a Great City* (1927). Throughout his life Hitchcock told interviewers that one of the films he always wanted to make would be about twenty-four hours in the life of a city, told via a montage of documentary images. In discussing his unrealized projects with Peter Bogdanovich, for example, he described his planned but unmade film *Life of a City*:

> This is something I've wanted to do since 1928. The story of a big city from dawn to the following dawn. I wanted to do it in terms of what lies behind the face of a city—what makes it tick—in other words, backstage of a city. But the canvas is so enormous that it is practically impossible to get the right story. Two or three people had a go at it for me over the years but all failed. It must be done in terms of personalities and people and—with my technique— everything would have to be used dramatically.[8]

Hitchcock's model was clearly Ruttmann's *Berlin,* which told the life of a people by a rhythmic and stylized presentation of their comings and goings, their environment, their shapes and spaces, and so on. Although Hitchcock never made an entire film like this, he used these elements repeatedly— in the street scenes of *Blackmail* and *Secret Agent,* and the travelogue-type vignettes in *Rich and Strange,* for example—and always carried with him the lesson that documentary could be realistic as well as fascinating and fantastic.

HITCHCOCK AND INDIVIDUAL DIRECTORS

HITCHCOCK AND MURNAU

Modern viewers of Murnau's *Sunrise* (1927) invariably perk up their ears at one point in particular, when they hear the instantly recognizable music from Gounod's "Funeral March of a Marionette": instantly recognizable, that is, because it was recalled by Hitchcock and borrowed for his own purposes as the theme song for the very popular television series *Alfred Hitchcock Presents* (Spoto, 399). This is the most obvious but perhaps least important of Hitchcock's many debts to Murnau, whose films include the eerie and fantastic *Nosferatu, Phantom, Janus-Faced* (based on *Dr. Jekyll and Mr. Hyde*), and *Faust,* studies of the triumphs and tragedies of ordinary people in *The Last Laugh* and *Sunrise,* and his final tale of romance and native life, *Tabu.*

When he was in Germany with Graham Cutts making *The Blackguard* in 1924, Hitchcock met Murnau and watched him on the set during the production of *The Last Laugh.* This experience and this film in particular seem to have been pivotal for Hitchcock, and though it may be worth examining, say, the influence of *Nosferatu* on *The Lodger* (especially the use of shadows, disorienting camera angles, and the character of a mysterious vampire-like murderer) or of *Sunrise* on *The Manxman* (especially the use of a harsh landscape and the overall theme of romantically tortured lovers), much of Hitchcock's debt to or affinity with Murnau can use *The Last Laugh* as the key reference point.

As mentioned earlier, Hitchcock always emphasized the importance of Murnau as a visual story teller, working without heavy reliance on dialogue or intertitles. So much of this depended on his use of the camera and his expressive use of what we might call the architecture of space. When one thinks of *The Last Laugh,* what comes perhaps first to mind is the so-called "unchained camera," the unrestricted camera moving freely through space, sometimes to capture the bustling world around his main character, the head porter in a large and busy hotel, and other times to convey his increasing disorientation, drunkenness, and dizziness as the world bears down on him. Hitchcock was intrigued by many of the experimental and subjective camera shots that were common from the earliest days of cinema (e.g., *Grandma's Reading Glasses*), but Murnau helped move Hitchcock away from mere trickiness to a thorough integration of such techniques into a broader artistic construct. When the camera moves in Murnau, it moves with a purpose, not just because it could move, strapped onto the chest of the cameraman Karl Freund or pushed around in a wheelchair.

Hitchcock was particularly intrigued by Murnau's cinematic use of space and his meticulous set design. Hitchcock the technician—who was famous throughout his life for saying that his great interest and challenge was planning shots, not executing them—obviously recognized a kindred spirit in Murnau, whose creative illusionism confirmed for Hitchcock that cinema was an art of visual imagination wedded to concrete technical mastery.

Hitchcock recalled one set in particular from *The Last Laugh*, where Murnau used great ingenuity to create a scene of visual suggestiveness. Carefully foreshortened perspective allowed him to focus on a large clock in the foreground and still create the illusion of tremendous depth on a railroad set extending out into the background:

> The locomotive, a whole stream of coaches, and the glass roof of the railway station were all in perspective. The set had one drawback: as the perspective diminished there was no light in it. They solved that by putting a real train at the point in the distance where the lines met and had people coming out of the train." ("The German Years," 24)

As he notes in many of his writings and interviews, Hitchcock, like Murnau, was always fascinated by the architectonics of cinema. Rohmer and Chabrol link Hitchcock with Murnau (and Eisenstein) in praising him as "one of the greatest *inventors of form* in the history of cinema," but this is by no means to describe him as a "mere formalist" or to suggest that the link between Hitchcock and Murnau is purely formal. Far more important, for Rohmer and Chabrol form is the vehicle for emotion and the embodiment and expression of theme and attitude and philosophy. In Hitchcock and Murnau, we see both the "minute realism of details and the stylization of whole scenes," as in, for example, the prison interview in *Murder!*, so simple and powerful yet so carefully constructed in "the framing, the lighting, and even the decor."[9]

Thematically as well as formally and stylistically, *The Last Laugh* contains numerous Hitchcockian dimensions: the focus on a man overwhelmed by a cascade of not completely explicable—let alone justifiable—forces of society and fate; a sense of the precariousness of one's life, rising and falling suddenly, dramatically, unpredictably; the presence of an indifferent, if not hostile, world, captured memorably by picturing a neighborhood that can at a moment's notice turn menacing. *Nosferatu* captures the eerie and horrifying aspects of the Gothic world; *The Last Laugh* captures the eerie and horrifying aspects of the ordinary world. It is the latter that Hitchcock charted so powerfully throughout his career, and often in ways that evoked Murnau.

HITCHCOCK AND DUPONT

Of all the great German directors of the Weimar period, the least well-known and commented on now is E. A. Dupont, but during the 1920s he was highly respected, very popular, and influential, in England as well as Germany. For several years after his most important film, *Variety,* was released, it was referred to repeatedly in the British trade papers as not only one of the best of recent films but as a kind of benchmark standard toward which British films might aspire. Reviews of early Hitchcock films often compare them to *Variety,* released in England under the title *Vaudeville.* When the *Kinematograph Weekly* praised *The Lodger,* for example, the reviewer noted, "It is certainly one of the most remarkable British pictures made and is like *Vaudeville,* in that it will appeal to 'popular' and highbrow alike."[10] And when *Downhill* was released in 1927 reviewers often praised it by likening it to "one of the best films of 1926," *Vaudeville.*[11] Dupont worked in England for several years in the late 1920s, and while we don't know what relationship he might have had with Hitchcock, if any, we do know that they at least met: the March 1, 1928 issue of *Bioscope* contains a picture of Hitchcock standing alongside Ronald Colman and Dupont.[12]

Long after this meeting with Dupont, Hitchcock included *Variety* in his list of "My Ten Favorite Pictures,"[13] and the influence of *Variety* on his early works is easily recognizable, especially in *Murder!,* which is in several key ways unimaginable without Dupont's model. Like *The Last Laugh, Variety* was important for Hitchcock not only as a distinctive work in itself but also because it embodied so much of what was characteristic of the German films of the time. Dupont's cameraman was Karl Freund, so as we might expect the freely moving camera is much in evidence, capturing not only the energy and tension of the trapeze performers as they swing above the audience but also the anger and disorientation of the jealous husband as the world swirls around him even when his feet are on the ground. In *Murder!,* Hitchcock also swings his camera from a trapeze and this, coupled at a climactic moment with multiple superimposed images and a pulsing musical score, creates a powerful vertigo-effect that he would not equal again until many years later.

Variety is a masterpiece of trick shots, special effects (including several kaleidoscopic images of eyes representing and intensifying the shame of the cuckolded husband), striking camera positions (extreme close-ups as well as high-angle shots), and haunting chiaroscuro lighting effects, many of which Hitchcock adopted in *Murder!* and elsewhere. But perhaps equally interesting, as Lotte Eisner notes in her brief but remarkably perceptive analysis of *Variety* in *The Haunted Screen,* are the ways that Dupont mixes both Expressionism and an Impressionism that goes beyond "purely Expressionistic schematism" and "abstraction" to capture the "ebb and flow of light and movement."[14] Similarly, the Expressionism of *Murder!* is diffused, modified, intermittent, rather than static, geometrical, and pervasive. And Hitchcock also shares with Dupont a sense that the spectacle of the circus setting needs to be counterpointed with domestic, *Kammerspielfilm* elements: just as *Variety* shows some of the dull details of life out of the spotlight, *Murder!* occasionally—and with a characteristically aggressive and pointed Hitchcock sense of humor—places Sir John not only behind-the-scenes but fully in the mundane, down and dirty, babies and bathwater environment that is as much a part of "reality" as the theater and circus: the scene in which Sir John spends the night in a tenement and awakens to find himself covered with kids and cats is perhaps Hitchcock's visual equivalent of the shot in *Variety* showing a baby wetting its bed.

Although it does not adopt a narrative frame of the imprisoned murderer retrospectively telling his tale and adds an emphasis on the trial of an unjustly accused woman and the character of the investigator who comes to love her, *Murder!* shares many themes with *Variety*. The fairground or music hall setting not only allows for exotic and dramatic action but immediately announces that theatricality and passion will be the subjects. Both films are filled with "play acting," on stage and off, and Dupont and Hitchcock have a shrewd sense that the real histrionics of life—the impersonations, manipulations, lies, and melodramatic events—are just as likely to happen on either side of the curtain. They also share a fascination for the audience, the dynamics of audience response, and the question of audience "morality": audiences gather to witness a performance on the razor's edge of disaster, perhaps not altogether hoping that a catastrophe will be avoided. Eisner's description of *Variety* applies to *Murder!* and other Hitchcock films as well: shots of the audience "are felt to pulse with the collective madness which takes hold of an arena at the moment of truth. In its blind frenzy the crowd becomes a thousand-headed monster lusting for blood."[15] Needless to say, the audience in question is not only within the film but watching the film as well.

The primary passion, though, is that of the murderer. *Variety* is a detailed examination of a triangle relationship, and destructive jealousy seems to be an inevitable consequence of love. From the very beginning of his career, Hitchcock was very interested in triangle relationships: the triangle itself is a recurrent image in *The Lodger*; *The Ring*, despite its many circular images, is basically about a triangle; and three-shots of varying design, illustrating the fluctuating relationship between Alice, Frank, and Tracy, are a fundamental structural pattern in *Blackmail*. It may be stretching it to say that *Murder!* sets up a bizarre triangle, composed of Handel Fane, the woman he murders, and the "woman" he is or at least impersonates. But whether or not a triangle pattern is woven into *Murder!*, the film certainly dramatizes a man driven by uncontrollable passion. Like the murderer in *Variety* and so many other characters in German films of the 1920s, Fane is tormented, violent, and ultimately sympathetic, and Hitchcock learned a great deal about how to imagine, manipulate, and "shoot" such characters and their world from Dupont.

HITCHCOCK AND LANG

If there is one brief blurb that not only does Hitchcock justice but also points to the heart of so many of his cinematic interests and achievements, it is a British critic's observation in 1936, even in the midst of lamenting what he felt was the disappointing lack of intellectual substance in *Sabotage,* that "Hitchcock is our native Fritz Lang, and in many ways a true disciple of the master" (quoted in Spoto, 206). The relationship between these two directors, each of whom had an active filmmaking career of more than fifty years spanning the silent and sound eras and moving them from their native country to the American studio system, is far too complex to treat comprehensively in a short space, but even an outline of how they often overlap one another sheds a great deal of light on what, how, and why Hitchcock did what he did in many of his films. My focus here will be on Lang's early films, made before he left Germany in 1933, leaving for another time a discussion of the relevance to Hitchcock of later works showing the pursuit of an innocent "wrong man" or victimized and sympathetic guilty man (*Fury, You Only Live Once*), the maddening and disintegrating power of passion (*Vertigo,* while not of course at all a gangster story, still could be suitably titled *The Big Heat*), and the dangerous but ineradicable appeal of fascism on a political level, criminality on a social level, and sin and evil on a personal level.[16]

There is a remarkable variety in Lang's early films, and if he was sometimes the director of films with "high art" and "Gesamtkunstwerk" pretensions, synthesizing epic, myth, opera, and national heritage in spectacular productions like *The Niebelungs,* he was also the maker of action-adventure serials (*Spiders*), exotic fables of the past and future (*Destiny, Metropolis, Woman in the Moon*), crime stories (the Mabuse films), spy thrillers (*Spies*), and psychological dramas (*M*). Hitchcock drew from many of these, and perhaps not the least of what he drew was the sense that "high art" and "genre art" need not be incompatible. For Hitchcock, Lang was, along with Murnau and Dupont, an example of a respected and serious artist, a distinguished "auteur" even when working in the realm of popular entertainment, and throughout his works he expressed a worldview in a distinctive and compelling style.

The Lang "world" is remarkably akin to the Hitchcock "world." Hitchcock was particularly attracted to Lang's spy stories and thrillers, many of which could serve as textbook illustrations of Hitchcock's oft-repeated definitions of what I would call three of the cornerstones of his early films and theories on film: the emphasis on suspense rather than surprise, the enjoyment of fear, and the MacGuffin.

Very much like Lang, Hitchcock was less interested in quick moments of unexpected surprises than in creating protracted moments of tense expectation, worry, and audience involvement: the opening sequence of *The Testament of Dr. Mabuse* (1933), for example, with its pounding sound effects, mobile camera, and impending explosion is as "classic" an example of suspense as, say, the long sequence in *Sabotage* where poor little unknowing Stevie carries a bomb that everyone in the audience knows is ready to explode.

By the enjoyment of fear, as he explained in his essay of that title (in which he also discusses suspense, 116–21), Hitchcock refers not only to the simple paradox—if paradoxes can ever be simple!—that we get pleasure out of being frightened and deeply worried about the fate of characters we identify with, but also to the complex dynamic of involvement and detachment in the experience of film. Lang's films not only portray spectacles of audience manipulation and excitation (in scenes, for example, showing Dr. Mabuse's hypnotic power and control of his followers through media devices, and in various parts of *Metropolis* where crowds are swayed one way or another by speakers who tell them highly charged emotional tales), they *are* spectacles of manipulation and excitation, powerfully affecting his audiences. And yet there are interjections of detachment, sudden shifts from intimate close-ups to more distancing long or, more typically, high overhead shots, or other techniques that remind us that we are watching a film and that emotional involvement is only one pole of cinematic experience, paired with analytic detachment. We can enjoy the presentation of fear, Hitchcock points out, because we know that we are imaginatively but not literally in danger; and while watching his films and Lang's, we both share in the worrisome fate of the main protagonists and step back and study it.

Hitchcock's term the "MacGuffin" helped him to assert that his films were in fact not what they on the surface seemed to be about. As he explained to Truffaut:

You may be wondering where the term originated. It might be a Scottish name, taken from a story about two men in a train. One man says, "What's that package up there in the baggage rack?"

And the other answers, "Oh, that's a MacGuffin." The first one asks, "What's a MacGuffin?"

"Well," the other man says, "it's an apparatus for trapping lions in the Scottish Highlands."

The first man says, "But there are no lions in the Scottish Highlands," and the other one answers, "Well then, that's no MacGuffin!" So you see that a MacGuffin is actually nothing at all. [17]

The MacGuffin is simply the device that gets the action going, especially in a spy story or thriller: the secret or the missing papers, whatever it is that the characters in the film are searching for. The exact details, though, are inconsequential for the director, whose main concern is, as Truffaut commented, "not to *say* things" but "to *show* them." [18] Hitchcock refers to Kipling's spy stories as one model for the MacGuffin, but he might just as well have used Lang, who was not primarily interested in the specifics of the treaty bandied about in *Spies* or the particulars behind Dr. Mabuse's blackmail and extortions: his real effort was dramatizing the dynamics of power, tension, and suspense, and sketching a landscape of mystery that enveloped the protagonists and the audience alike. Similarly, the plans being smuggled out of the country in *The 39 Steps* and the "trivial and absurd . . . little tune of *The Lady Vanishes*," as Truffaut rightly describes it, [19] are no more than rocks thrown into the water that quickly sink to the bottom: Hitchcock's interest, like Lang's, is always in the ripples and reverberations.

Hitchcock and Lang share a fascination for crime on many levels. Lang is particularly interested in the larger than life master criminal who takes on mythical or even supernatural qualities, like Dr. Mabuse, who seems all-knowing, all-seeing, and all-controlling. Perhaps because he worked in a culture less infused with such master-myths and also perhaps because the specter of a real-life sinister archetype like Hitler was not as immediate in England as in Germany, Hitchcock is less concerned with the super-criminal (although we should note that there are evil geniuses throughout his works). But like Lang he has a strong sense of the all-pervasiveness of crime, not only because of the far-reaches of criminal networks and what one might call the institutionalization of crime, but also because of the basic presupposition that we are all rarely more than one step away from criminal behavior of our own. One of the distinctive characteristics of Hitchcock's films throughout his career is his ability to implicate and involve us with the guilty: we are fascinated by them, we sympathize with them, we analyze them, and often we recognize that we are them. *M* is Lang's classic work in this vein, and I suspect that it left a profound mark on Hitchcock, but even before seeing *M* Hitchcock made *The Lodger* and *Blackmail,* indicating that he, far more than merely Lang's disciple, made significant contributions of his own to this kind of film.

The above shift in terms from "crime" to "guilt" calls attention to the psychological dimensions of Lang's films, which he shared with Hitchcock. Their films characteristically portray the aberrant and bizarre, both the underworld of crime and the underworld of personality. As in so many of the German "Stimmung" films of the 1920s, the characters in Lang's films often seem motivated by powerful, uncontrollable, and ultimately inscrutable inner drives that erupt in a variety of lusts: for sex, power, and murder. The Seven Deadly Sins come to life in *Metropolis,* both allegorically as statues become animated and literally as the people of this futuristic but instantly recognizable contemporary city become embodiments of these and other vices. And even the "best" characters are split, part angel and part demon, to put it most simply. Freder is well-intentioned and compassionate, but subject to wild hallucinations and visions of decadent corruption that surrounds and infects him. Maria, the virginal and motherly dispenser of love and charity, is easily counterfeited and turned into her opposite, the "evil" Maria, who presides over lust and disorder just as credibly as the "good" Maria presides over the gentler forces of peace and harmony. Whether intentionally or not, Hitchcock's Alice in *Blackmail* echoes the split Maria of *Metropolis,* and without all the paraphernalia of robot technology is visually transformed from "good" to "bad" and enters into a hallucinatory world that is both eerie and familiar.

Lang and Hitchcock are not only concerned with individual psychology and the presentation of such figures as Jack the Ripper in *The Lodger* and the pathetic child murderer in *M*: they are also interested in mass psychology, the behavior of groups. Crowd scenes are prominent in Lang, perhaps partly the legacy of the theatrical spectacles of Irwin Piscator and Lang's penchant for what Kracauer calls "pompous ornamentation,"[20] but also undoubtedly because of his wish to dramatize the volatility of mobs: the masses in Lang's films are invariably ripe for exploitation, manipulation, and over-reaction. Hitchcock similarly includes recurrent scenes of mobs being misled (chasing after and abusing the "innocent" Lodger, for example, or cheering for the nonsensical rhetoric of Richard Hannay at the political meeting in *The 39 Steps*), erupting into spontaneous violence or panic (in the music hall sequences of *The 39 Steps,* for example), and generally failing to form useful and coherent communities, united in purposeful action (in *The Lady Vanishes*, for example). And for both Lang and Hitchcock, one of the most intriguing forms of the mob, explicitly and implicitly examined throughout their works, is the audience: essential to the art of cinema but basically unreliable, unpredictable, and infinitely problematic.

Lang and Hitchcock were makers of what Graham Greene later called "entertainments," but it is nevertheless legitimate to speak of the serious reaches of their art. There are important philosophical dimensions of Lang, for example, echoed by Hitchcock, especially the recurrent question of whether or not select individuals can place themselves beyond the applicability of moral law. Super-criminals like Mabuse, psychotics like Jack the Ripper and the murderer in *M*, and those in the service of the state and the "higher good" like Ashenden in *Secret Agent* and the conspirators in *The Man Who Knew Too Much*, each in their different ways and each with the backing of, say, Nietzsche, Dostoievsky, Hitler, or Lenin, pose powerful challenges to conventional morality. (My focus here is on early Hitchcock, but later Hitchcock as well continually gravitates towards characters who not only break but argue for the suspension of moral laws: *Shadow of a Doubt, Lifeboat,* and *Rope* are of course key works in this regard, but so too is *Vertigo,* perhaps Hitchcock's most stunning presentation of the claims of the "übermensch," aspiring to a "freedom"—a key but often overlooked term used in the film—that abolishes all restrictions, as well as those of the "untermensch," one driven by, in psychoanalytical terms, pure primary processes of desire that recognize no moral limitations.) Audiences paying to engage in the thrilling spectacles of Lang and Hitchcock nearly always find themselves drawn into moral and philosophical debates.

We find ourselves drawn into political debates as well, because both Lang and Hitchcock intend their works to be comments on contemporary events and institutions. Lang's world is one of overwhelming corruption and he repeatedly dramatizes not only the almost complete inefficacy of the representatives of the law but also the uncanny similarities between criminals on the one hand and police, lawyers, judges, and politicians on the other. In *M*, shots of the police investigators sitting around a table pass almost imperceptibly to shots of the criminals sitting around a table, and, ironically, all these characters share a common goal: the return to a state of "normalcy" during which, presumably, they can all get back to mutually beneficial business as usual. And in various other films nearly everyone is in the pocket of Mabuse, who is in some respects not an aberration but the embodiment of the ruling principles of government and business: greed, coercive power, and self-serving but ultimately self-consuming anarchic energy.

Much like Lang, Hitchcock also typically focuses on the ineptitude, venality, amorality, or corruption of the official custodians of law and order: Joe in *The Lodger* is only the first in a long series of Hitchcock's bumbling detectives; Frank in *Blackmail* is not so much bumbling as inevitably compromised, and he not only pursues but ultimately becomes a blackmailer; the police sent out at the end of *The Man Who Knew Too Much* don't so much combat as contribute to the anarchy; the real villain in *The 39 Steps* is a charming man of high social and political standing; and the government officials in *Secret Agent* blithely send out a good citizen on a mission of murder.

The breakdown of order and authority has metaphysical as well as political overtones for both Lang and Hitchcock. Each is critical of what humans make of the world, how they pervert and corrupt social relations, and so on, but each also has a vision of sadness, suffering, and disorder beyond human responsibility or repair. Late in life when asked by Truffaut to "single out a picture that made a special impression" in his early years, Hitchcock named Lang's *Der müde Tod,* and all the themes indicated by the title—literally the weary or sick death but usually translated as *Destiny*—echo throughout his films.[21] Lang and Hitchcock share a sense of life's inevitable chaos, characterized by fragmentation, decay, corruption, sudden eruptions of violence, and continual assaults on our notions of rationality and free will. The world is ultimately impenetrable and implacable, and we are constantly subjected to overwhelming and even determining pressures from outside and volatile and uncontrollable impulses from inside. Beneficent authority—whether human or divine—is almost always elsewhere in films by Lang and Hitchcock: if there is a God it is a God who watches us from a distance, leaving us to work out our own salvation—or, more likely, torture and confusion.

Lang's ability to give visual form to metaphysical ideas is part of his legacy to Hitchcock. For example, one of Lang's signature stylistic techniques is a sudden shift of perspective, from close to far and often from eye-level to high angle. Ironically, this is a God's eye point of view used to illustrate the distance, or detachment, or even absence of a helpful God, and it is a technique that Hitchcock adopted and used very effectively. In *Blackmail,* for example, Hitchcock cuts away from the violence in the artist's apartment to a high-angle shot out the window, showing a policeman passing by down below, oblivious to the trouble so close by. This is to a certain extent a wry critique of the police who are never there when you want them, but it is on a deeper level an assertion of how we are inevitably and inescapably left alone to meet our fate. And the abstract image of a spinning wheel used at the beginning and the end of *Blackmail,* like so many of the spirals and circles in *Metropolis* and the Mabuse films, not only reinforces the theme of the relentless power of fate but gives yet another reminder of how intimately related the distinctive Hitchcock touch is to the work of Lang.

HITCHCOCK, GERMANY, AND THE "IDEA OF CINEMA"

We tend to think of Hitchcock primarily as a practical artist rather than a theorist, but Truffaut usefully emphasizes that Hitchcock is not fundamentally "instinctive" but rather deeply self-conscious and meditative about his art. In short, Truffaut says, "he's really the guy who has given the most thought to cinema as both spectacle and style."[22] This "thought" emerges in Hitchcock's many interviews and essays, and takes more concrete shape in his films and in the production environment he constructed for himself as his career developed. While there were of course many influences on his film theory and practice, it is crucial to see how frequently German films and directors and his early experiences in Germany serve as his key reference points, models, and inspirations. The German influence on Hitchcock is visible not only in the many stylistic and thematic borrowings from and homages to such directors as Murnau, Dupont, and Lang throughout his works, but also in the development of what might be called his "idea of cinema": his definition of what cinema is, and what it can and should be; his understanding of the cultural and commercial aspects of films and film-making; and his vision of the ideal studio and the role of the director in film production.

As mentioned above, for Hitchcock Germany was the home of "pure cinema," telling stories and creating powerful meaning and effect primarily through visual means. Equally important, he looked to Germany as the home of "style," which he described as "perhaps the most significant and individually important thing about a director . . . evidenced by both his choice of subject and his manner of directing it" ("Film Production," 216). DeMille, Griffith, Ince, and Chaplin had style, Hitchcock acknowledged, but "On the whole, style was slower to manifest itself in U.S. pictures" (218). Not so in Germany:

> In the early 1920s the Germans gave great evidence of style. Whether or not it was something imposed by the studios, or individual to the directors, it is clearly in evidence in the work of Fritz Lang, F. W. Murnau, and many others. Some directors are more concerned with style and the treatment of the content than with securing new

themes. This is to say that, for the director, as often as not, what is important is the manner of telling his tale. The more original will revolt against the traditional and the cliché. They will want to show contrast, to present melodrama in a revolutionary way, to take melodrama out of the dark into the bright day, to show murder by a babbling brook, adding a touch of blood to its limpid waters. Thus the director can impose his ideas on nature and, taking what savors of the ordinary, can, in the way he handles it, render it extraordinary. So there emerges a kind of counterpoint and sudden upheaval in the ordinary things of life. (216–17)

Hitchcock appreciated the originality and adventurousness of the great German directors and their definition of a cinema as a free expressive art form. In discussing "Films We Could Make," Hitchcock speculated about making "really artistic films" (166) and used as an example "one German producer [who] even makes film studies of cubes and circles which change their shape as they move over the screen in rhythmic form like a Cubist painting in motion" (167). But in fact one of the great lessons of German cinema for Hitchcock was that film simply could not, at least for the present, be a purely "artistic medium" (167): it must exist within commercial confines, necessitating inevitable restrictions, limitations, and compromises for any dedicated artist. This sobering awareness of the real circumstances of film production, though, was not all bad news for Hitchcock: his lifelong sense that these limitations could be overcome, that compromises could be creative, that film could be a mass art, a profitable and accessible medium of popular entertainment as well as a serious, challenging, innovative, and complex art form, owed a great deal to the example of the German directors and producers of the 1920s.

Ufa was a studio and a corporation, and for a while at least it was run in such a way that the blend of art and commerce was an energizing dialectic rather than an unmanageable contradiction. In his fascinating and richly documented examination of *The Ufa Story*, Klaus Kreimeier notes that from the early 1920s until the end of 1932, "the presence of Erich Pommer, chief of Ufa's most important production team and an energetic opponent of vapid popular taste, guaranteed the production of films that were commercially successful and also drew critical acclaim at home and abroad." His "guiding principle that the 'commercial film' and the 'artistic film' had to form a synthesis had taken hold in the production teams and had become the standard for Ufa's regular actors, authors, directors, cameramen, and sound technicians."[23] In an essay published in 1922, Pommer expressed his confidence that shrewd and creative directors could serve two masters, synthesizing high and low, "crummy" setting and sophisticated style, art that lasts and product that sells:

> If by interesting lighting or focusing on the stairs or populating the scene with the right faces one can lend a touch of high style to a crummy bar patronized by thieves and whores, as, for instance, the old Dutch paintings do, then this crummy bar can emanate as much art as a Gothic cathedral can. It is immaterial what subject one chooses for making an artistic film. The only essential condition is that it be made by artists who know what the public wants but also know what they themselves want.[24]

These words are very close to Hitchcock's comments on style quoted above, and remind us that while he appreciated the fact that German film was a director's medium, he recognized that it was a producer's medium as well. Murnau, Dupont, and Lang were kindred spirits to him, but so too was Pommer, and Ufa provided him with a model of the extent to which an experienced production team, vast studio and technical resources, market knowledge and marketing ability, and support from above as well as below, as it were—from executives to staff, from critics to audiences—are essential to quality filmmaking. The more Hitchcock thought about filmmaking, the more he became aware of how much depended upon the producer, so much so that it wasn't long until he envisioned the ideal filmmaker as a director-producer, "one who must know all sides of the business and be a complete technician" ("Directors Are Dead," 183).

When he first arrived in Germany, he was immediately struck by the size of the film facilities: "The studio where I worked was tremendous, bigger than Universal is today. They had a complete railroad station built on the back lot. For a version of *Siegfried* they built the whole forest of the *Niebelungenlied*" ("The German Years," 23). Later in his career when he speculated on what he would do "If I Were Head of a Production Company," he noted first that "I want plenty of space" (172), large, permanent, and realistic sets, always available for use. "It pays handsomely," he says, "to have elbow-room" (173).

But as much as he was impressed by the spatial *largesse* available to the German filmmakers, he was equally impressed by their technical ingenuity and inventiveness, specifically their ability to create illusionistic effects, sometimes stunning and fantastic, sometimes more mundane. Hitchcock told the following story on numerous occasions:

If you're content to do a small portion of the set very accurately, it's much better than trying to do a whole street. This is a principle which I've stuck to ever since I was an art director. I was working on the Ufa lot in Germany in its heyday and there I picked up a great deal of insight into the techniques of set building and perspective of every kind. Once I had a scene to do against the doorway entrance into Milan Cathedral. It's one of the biggest Gothic piles in Europe. I only had to have a shot of a man going through the door into the black interior, so I had to decide how I was going to do it. I would never have been able to build the entrance of the Milan Cathedral; the doors are probably 100 feet high. What I did was solve the problem by building, in actual scale, the real thing— just one column on the left, but I made it about 8 or 9 feet high only. Its proportions were enormous, and I included half a dozen steps accurately measured, so that we got this big base of a Gothic column and the beginning of the door with a huge hinge on it and the eye did the rest for you. The lines went up out of the picture following the Gothic column and the lines of the set went out to the right. I went to the zoo there and asked for a few pigeons. So I had these few pigeons and they flew around and sat on the stone work, but the point was to do a little piece of the building accurately and well, rather than try to do a sort of cheaply built whole structure. ("Hitchcock Talks About Lights, Camera, Action," 309–10)

Hitchcock was also an early user of the German-developed Schüfftan process, allowing him to mix live action with photographically reproduced rather than actually constructed sets. Lang used this process to create parts of the futuristic city in *Metropolis;* Hitchcock used it in *Blackmail* for the climactic chase through one of the real landmarks of his own city, London's British Museum. Throughout his career, Hitchcock was always particularly intrigued by the technical challenges of filmmaking—"Well, of course, I'm a *technician* as well as a director," he noted in a late interview ("Hitchcock Talks About Lights, Camera, Action," 304)—and he shared with the Ufa directors a lifelong emphasis, in Kreimeier's words, not on mere "technical perfection" but on "the collaboration of technology and imagination."[25]

Cinematic ingenuity and inventiveness require more than technical resources, and mid-way through drafting his ideal working environment Hitchcock shifts his focus abruptly: "So much for physical space. Now for mental elbow-room. The director must have latitude" ("If I Were Head of a Production Company," 173). Hitchcock was impressed by the elbow-room and latitude allowed the German directors. Some years later he had his difficulties working with Pommer on *Jamaica Inn,* and described the production team of Pommer and Charles Laughton as "two extremely difficult men" (quoted in Spoto, 203). But in the 1920s Pommer was known and respected for supporting the freedom, independence, and adventurousness of his directors, a philosophy captured in what Kreimeier describes as his "famous challenge to the production team of *The Last Laugh*—'Please invent something new, even if it's crazy!'"[26]

"Mental elbow-room" involves not only directorial freedom within a studio but an even broader environment of respect and reinforcement. Germany in the 1920s was a country where film was taken seriously as an essential part of intellectual, artistic, and popular life, treated as culturally important, supported by the government, respected by the critics, and patronized by large audiences. This was the kind of cinematic establishment Hitchcock wanted to inhabit and that through the years he labored to find—and help create.

CONCLUSION

John Russell Taylor once summarized the depth of the German cinema's influence on Orson Welles (which Welles, incidentally, frequently denied) by remarking that "*Citizen Kane* may be the best American film ever made; but it just might be also the best German film ever made."[27] Perhaps this witticism can be adapted to describe Hitchcock as not only one of the great British directors and one of the great American directors, but also as one of the great German directors. However we come to phrase it, the German influence on Hitchcock is extensive and complex, and one we must fathom if we want to understand fully the origins and the exact contours of Hitchcock's remarkable achievements.

NOTES

1. Writings by Hitchcock referred to in my essay are from *Hitchcock on Hitchcock: Selected Writings and Interviews,* ed. Sidney Gottlieb (Berkeley: University of California Press, 1995), and are identified by title and page number in the text. The only exception is "Alfred Hitchcock: The German Years," an interview with Bob Thomas, published in *Action* (January–February, 1973): 23–25.

2. In the context of a brief but extremely illuminating discussion of Hitchcock's relationship to German Expressionism and Soviet montage, Robin Wood states, "I

find it significant—having in mind the whole Hitchcock oeuvre—that he should build the foundations of his style out of elements inherently 'artificial,' borrowed from cultures other than his own, and detached from the conditions that originally gave them their meaning" ("Retrospective [1977]," in *Hitchcock's Films Revisited* [New York: Columbia University Press, 1989], 208). I am well aware that for some critics the term "influence" is problematic and much-maligned, but in my essay I attempt to follow Wood's lead in his careful analysis of what he calls the subtle and complex "process of absorption into [Hitchcock's] style and method of these major influences," especially the German filmmakers and film industry of the 1920s and early 1930s. Theodore Price surveys much useful information about Hitchcock and German silent films of the Weimar period, but in some places his speculations and conclusions about possible influences are somewhat incautious and unconvincing; see Price, *Hitchcock and Homosexuality: His 50–Year Obsession with Jack the Ripper and the Superbitch Prostitute—A Psychoanalytic View* (Metuchen: Scarecrow Press, 1992), 288–354.

3. The German influence on Hitchcock and the presence of Germanic elements in his films is of course mediated in a variety of ways. Important articles on how the Continental influence was transmitted through the work of cinematographers, production designers, art directors, and other film technicians include Tim Bergfelder's "The Production Designer and the *Gesamtkunstwerk* in the British Film Industry of the 1930s," in *Dissolving Views: Key Writings on British Cinema,* ed. Andrew Higson (London: Cassell, 1996), 20–37, and three essays in *Gainsborough Pictures,* ed. Pam Cook (London: Cassell, 1995): Philip Kemp's "Not for Peckham: Michael Balcon and Gainsborough's International Trajectory in the 1920s," 13–30; Tim Bergfelder's "Surface and Distraction: Style and Genre at Gainsborough in the Late 1920s and 1930s," 31–46; and Duncan Petrie's "Innovation and Economy: The Contribution of the Gainsborough Cinematographer," 118–36. For a good introduction to the "Film Europe" movement of the 1920s and 1930s, an important context for Hitchcock's early films, see Andrew Higson, " 'A Film League of Nations': Gainsborough, Gaumont-British and 'Film Europe,' " in Cook, ed., *Gainsborough Pictures,* 60–79.

4. François Truffaut, *Correspondence, 1945–198,4* ed. Gilles Jacob and Claude de Givray, trans. Gilbert Adair (New York: Farrar, Straus and Giroux, 1990), 179.

5. Donald Spoto, *The Dark Side of Genius: The Life of Alfred Hitchcock* (New York: Ballantine Books, 1984), 77–78. Further references to this book are indicated in the text of my essay by page numbers only.

6. Eric Rohmer and Claude Chabrol, *Hitchcock: The First Forty-Four Films,* trans. Stanley Hochman (New York: Frederick Ungar Publishing Co., 1980), 86.

7. On Hitchcock and the British documentary filmmakers, see Tom Ryall, *Alfred Hitchcock and British Cinema* (Champaign: University of Illinois Press, 1986), especially chapter two, "British Film Culture in the Interwar Period," 7–31.

8. Peter Bogdanovich, *Who the Devil Made It* (New York: Knopf, 1997), 494.

9. Rohmer and Chabrol, *Hitchcock: The First Forty-Four Films,* 152, 28.

10. *Kinematograph Weekly,* February 3, 1927; from *The Lodger* scrapbook in the Hitchcock Collection, Academy of Motion Picture Arts and Sciences, Margaret Herrick Library.

11. *Downhill* scrapbook, Hitchcock Collection.

12. *Bioscope,* March 1, 1928; from *The Farmer's Wife* scrapbook, Hitchcock Collection.

13. March 15, 1939, newspaper unidentified; from the Hitchcock clippings file, New York Public Library.

14. Lotte Eisner, *The Haunted Screen: Expressionism in the German Cinema and the Influence of Max Reinhardt,* trans. Roger Greaves (Berkeley: University of California Press, 1973), 282, 284.

15. Eisner, *The Haunted Screen,* 283.

16. I also leave for another time a discussion of Hitchcock's possible influence on Lang and Lang's feelings about Hitchcock. Patrick McGilligan notes that "Lang himself detested the comparisons [between himself and Hitchcock], feeling that in the category of thrillers and suspense the critics tended to favor the upstart Englishman—who, after all, borrowed shamelessly from him" (*Fritz Lang: The Nature of the Beast* [New York: St. Martin's, 1997], 122). McGilligan refers to Hitchcock as "Lang's bête noir" (372n.), but also comments briefly on how deeply Lang was affected and perhaps influenced by *Rebecca* (353).

17. François Truffaut, *Hitchcock,* rev. ed. (New York: Simon and Schuster, 1984), 138.

18. Truffaut, *Hitchcock,* 139.

19. Truffaut, *Hitchcock,* 138.

20. Siegfried Kracauer, *From Caligari to Hitler: A Psychological History of the German Film* (Princeton: Princeton University Press, 1947), 149.

21. Truffaut, *Hitchcock,* 26.

22. Letter to Helen Scott, June 20, 1962, *Correspondence,* 184.

23. Klaus Kreimeier, *The Ufa Story: A History of Germany's Greatest Film Company, 1918–1945,* trans. Robert and Rita Kimber (New York: Hill and Wang, 1996), 196.

24. Erich Pommer, "Commercial and Artistic Film," quoted in Kreimeier, 97.

25. Kreimeier, *The Ufa Story,* 104.

26. Kreimeier, *The Ufa Story,* 104.

27. Quoted in David Cook, *History of Narrative Film,* second edition (New York: Norton, 1990), 348n.

GERMAN HITCHCOCK

Joseph Garncarz

This essay deals with Alfred Hitchcock's work in Germany between 1924 and 1926.[1] In 1924, Hitchcock worked as the screenwriter and set-designer of *The Blackguard* (*Die Prinzessin und der Geiger,* trans. "The Princess and the Violinist") for Ufa in Berlin, and in 1925/26 he directed his first two films, *The Pleasure Garden* (*Irrgarten der Leidenschaft,* trans. "The Labyrinth of Passion") and *The Mountain Eagle* (*Der Bergadler),* for Emelka in Munich. Ufa in Berlin was the largest German film company, and Emelka in Munich was its strongest competitor.[2] The first Hitchcock films premiered in Germany. *The Blackguard* premiered in Berlin on September 4, 1925.[3] *The Pleasure Garden* premiered on January 8, 1926 in Berlin,[4] and it was followed by *The Mountain Eagle* in the middle of May in Munich.[5]

Our knowledge of Hitchcock's German period is almost exclusively based on his own accounts.[6] These stories have also been used as the main sources by Hitchcock's biographers.[7] The problem with this approach is that it relies on these statements uncritically without asking what functions they serve. A close comparison reveals, for example, that the anecdotes about the production of *The Pleasure Garden* were modified over time to fit the image Hitchcock had constructed for himself. In the earliest account from 1936 there was no mention yet of his fear of the police during the smuggling of film stock over the border nor of his naïvete in sexual matters.[8] In accordance with his image as "The Master of Suspense," i.e., as a legendary director of thrillers, which had begun to take shape as early as the 1930s, he declared that the third film he directed, *The Lodger,* was "der erste spannende Film von Hitchcock" [the first suspenseful film by Hitchcock].[9] Because his German films did not belong to the thriller genre, he devalued them and even refused to talk about the films themselves. Instead, he only recounted some of the circumstances of their production, making life sound more thrilling than art, for example, by describing *The Pleasure Garden* as an "emotional drama that was being enacted on the other side of the camera."[10] Similarly, in order to further enhance his reputation for skillful visual narration, he stressed the importance of his experience at Ufa in 1924: "The Germans in those times placed great emphasis on telling the story visually; if possible with no titles. . . . That's what I learned from the Germans."[11] In a German television interview Hitchcock even maintained that this period represented the only external formative influence in his entire career.[12]

In this essay, therefore, I will try to reconstruct Hitchcock's career in Germany between 1924 and 1926 from contemporary German sources. Hitchcock's own statements will only be used if they can be corroborated by other information. Unfortunately, as far as I know, Emelka's documents on Hitchcock's work have not been preserved.[13] Except for censorship documents concerning *The Blackguard* and *The Pleasure Garden,* no unpublished source material seems to be extant.[14] However, a large amount of press material is still available: reports on contracts, articles on actors, descriptions of Hitchcock's work on the set, pieces of film criticism and, last but not least, an article on Hitchcock himself. On this basis a number of facts will be revealed that may serve to correct our view of Hitchcock's early work. Several aspects identified by researchers as being characteristic of Hitchcock's later work actually begin to emerge in the period between 1924 and 1926. In the work of those years we can already find an answer to the question of how Hitchcock integrated the style of European art films into commercial narrative cinema. We can also witness the birth of the "Hitchcock touch": its most important qualities are the emphasis on visual narrative and the dominance of individual attractive scenes over a concern for plot structure, and it serves as a double-strategy to address both film critics and the audience at large. We will also see how a specific image of Hitchcock begins to be formed in public discourse, and how it already includes some of the characteristics that were to gain central importance in his later career. A comparison between the contemporary material and Hitchcock's later self-presentation will enable us to understand some of the reasons for the strategies he chose in the construction of his image. When the conditions of production for the first two films directed by Hitchcock are reconstructed, we can see more clearly which options presented themselves to Hitchcock as a young director and how he made use of them. First, I will discuss which companies were involved in production, what the production conditions were like, which type of film was to be produced, and what kind of role Hitchcock was to play. Then I will consider whether Hitchcock lived up to expectations or whether he did things his way. I will also turn to the question of the critical and commercial success of Hitchcock's films in Germany.[15] Finally, I will examine the significance of Hitchcock's experience in Germany for his later career.

THE INTERNATIONAL PRODUCTION OF W & F FILM SERVICE LTD. AND EMELKA

Hitchcock had been working for the British production company Gainsborough since 1923 as a set-designer and an assistant director when he was sent to Munich in 1925, where he directed his first two films. The context relevant to his work is the cooperation between the German and the British film industries during the second half of the 1920s. The German film industry was extremely successful nationally, while the British film industry was only marginally developed. In Germany highly differentiated companies with large amounts of capital at their disposal, such as Ufa and Emelka, had already appeared by the end of the second decade of the twentieth century, whereas larger companies, such as Gaumont British Picture Corporation and British International Pictures, were not founded in Great Britain until 1927.[16] In 1926, 39.2 percent of the films submitted to censorship in Germany were of German origin, while the British film industry had a share of only 4.9 percent of the films released in its own country.[17] There was relatively little trade between the two countries, but even here the German film industry achieved a better balance. While only 0.4 percent of the films approved by censors in Germany were British, Germany held a market share of 5.8 percent in Britain, a figure even higher than the one the British film industry had achieved in its own country.[18]

Both the British and the German film industries were controlled by the film distributors. In 1924, the British distributor W & F Film Service Ltd. of London (hereafter referred to as W & F) signed a production agreement with the German film company Emelka, under which the first film to be realized was *Hidden Fires* (*Verborgene Gluten*).[19] Emelka was a production company that had its own theaters and its own distributor, Bayrische Film GmbH (i.e., it was vertically integrated like Ufa). W & F distributed and co-financed several films produced by Michael Balcon, who owned Gainsborough, where Hitchcock was employed (W & F became a part of Gaumont British in 1926; Gainsborough followed in 1928).[20] On March 26, 1925, before Hitchcock directed the second and third pictures under this bilateral agreement, it was "expanded to an extensive contract, the purpose of which is not only to co-produce films on the greatest scale and with stars of international acclaim, but also to organize the international distribution of the total production by both partners."[21] Emelka co-financed the films and produced them in its own studios.[22] W & F and Emelka were both able to save money through this bilateral agreement, and it also gave them the chance to release other films from their own production company in their partner's country. While Emelka had had an "absolutely secure financial base,"[23] W & F must have had financial problems, because the British negotiator, Franc Tilley, stated that the reason for the agreement with Emelka was "the previous failure of production in . . . Great Britain."[24] The British partner hoped to receive films that would prove to be more successful commercially due to the German production standards, which were far superior to the British standards.

The goal was to produce films for the European market that would be a guaranteed success with audiences. W & F set their hopes on a cooperation with Emelka, because both companies agreed about their policy that art films were a financial risk.[25] This conviction was entirely justified, considering Ufa's situation. Under the management of Erich Pommer (who had been an honorary member of the London Film Society since its foundation[26]), Ufa strongly emphasized art films, whereas Emelka produced films for the box office without artistic ambitions. This strategy was extremely profitable for Emelka. In 1926, three of the top ten films of the year were Emelka productions (*Ich habe mein Herz in Heidelberg verloren, Unsere Emden,* and *Die Försterchristl*), while only one was a Ufa production (*Ein Walzertraum* [*Waltz Dream*]) and another (the U.S. film *Ben Hur*) was distributed by Ufa.[27] Art films did enhance Ufa's prestige, but they were bad for business: due to an intention to further their directors' creativity shooting schedules and budgets were exceeded. Finally, Ufa even had to borrow money from the U.S. film industry (via an arrangement known as the Parufamet-agreement), and in 1927 it had to completely restructure its organization to avoid bankruptcy.[28]

A BRITISH PRODUCTION IN GERMANY

Even though *The Pleasure Garden* and *The Mountain Eagle* were produced in cooperation with Emelka in Germany, the British partner had the power of decision in all major points, according to the bilateral agreement. W & F could decide on the story and also employ their own personnel for all the important functions behind and in front of the camera. *The Pleasure Garden* is an adaptation of a contemporary British novel by Oliver Sandys (pseudonym for Marguerite Florence Barclay, later Evans); *The Mountain Eagle* is based on an original screenplay by Charles Lapworth (a colleague of Balcon's). Gaëtano di Ventimiglia, probably under contract at W & F, was employed as cinematographer.[29] And the Englishman Alfred Hitchcock, who had previously worked for Balcon as screenwriter and set-designer, was called upon to direct.

Almost all of the leads were cast with British or U.S. actors who were unknown to German audiences. The male leads were British (John Stuart and Miles Mander in *The Pleasure Garden*[30] and Malcolm Keen and John Hamilton in *The Mountain Eagle*[31]). Only a single major role was cast with a German actor: Bernhard Goetzke as Pettigrew (Petermann in the German version) in *The Mountain Eagle*. However, even though Goetzke had played in numerous well-known German films (e.g., Fritz Lang's *Der müde Tod* [*Destiny*, 1921], *Dr. Mabuse, der Spieler* [*Dr. Mabuse, the Gambler*, 1922], and *Die Nibelungen* [*Siegfried* and *Kriemhild's Revenge*, 1924]) before working for Hitchcock, he was not a star. Goetzke did not appear in any of the lists of the most popular actors that were regularly published in the German fan press. Rather, he was regarded as an excellent character actor,[32] and he was voted number two in the list of the best actors in 1926 (possibly even as a consequence of his performance in *The Mountain Eagle*).[33] A critic wrote, "At least they gave the role of the bizarre tyrant to the great character actor Goetzke."[34] Only the smaller parts were systematically cast with German actors (e.g., Ferdinand Martini as Mr. Sidney, Karl Falkenberg as the Prince, and Georg H. Schnell as the theater impresario in *The Pleasure Garden*); Emelka could use their own contract players in these cases.[35]

The female leads were cast with U.S. actresses: Virginia Valli (1898–68) and Carmelita Geraghty (1901–66) in *The Pleasure Garden*, and Nita Naldi

(1897–1961) in *The Mountain Eagle*. Contrary to a widely held opinion, the reason for this was not an intention to conquer the U.S. market. C. M. Woolf, the manager of W & F, used the U.S. film market as a source to expand his supply of films on the British market, but he did not consider it an export market for British films.[36] Similarly, the assumption that it was Balcon's intention to import top stars from the U.S. is incorrect. The stars of Hitchcock's films, Virginia Valli, Carmelita Geraghty, and Nita Naldi, were far from being top stars in the U.S.[37] Popularity polls and salaries are indicators of a star's market value. None of these actresses can be found on the lists of the U.S. audience's favorite stars of 1924.[38] In the same year, a U.S. star earned between $2000 and $3000 dollars per week, a top star even up to $10,000.[39] Nita Naldi, however, received only between $600 and $900 per week for *The Mountain Eagle*—obviously a much lower salary than the ones the U.S.'s favorite stars earned.[40] Her vamp image was simply out of date in 1926.

Incidentally, it is only a legend that Nita Naldi played the "native girl" in *The Pleasure Garden*.[41] There is no such reference in the contemporary German press. When images of the "native girl" are compared with some of Naldi's from her films (e.g., *Dr. Jekyll and Mr. Hyde* [1920]) or from portraits of her, it is obvious that they do not represent the same person, although there is a certain resemblance.[42] In 1937, Hitchcock refers to the "native girl" as "my little German girl."[43] The German trade press tells us that the German actress Elisabeth Pappritz played the part,[44] and photos of her were even reprinted in fan magazines.[45]

Nor could the strategy of employing U.S. actresses have been oriented towards the German market, because the chosen actresses had no market-value whatsoever in Germany. Virginia Valli, Nita Naldi, and Carmelita Geraghty were neither known to the German film critics, nor did they have any marketable name for the audience at large. Virginia Valli was described in one article as "the beautiful and well-known American," but this was probably nothing more than hype, because in another article it was remarked that with their casting of Valli Emelka had proved that they had "greater talent for discovering female beauties than most film-producers in Berlin."[46] About Nita Naldi the German press only wrote that she was American,[47] and that she was "known from the film *The Ten Commandments* [German premiere 1924]."[48] The German critics failed to notice, however, that she was cast against her vamp-image as the young teacher in *The Mountain Eagle*. None of the actresses managed to appear in any one of the popularity polls that were published in the German fan press for the years 1923 to 1926.[49]

Of over 15,000 votes in the year 1926, Valli, Naldi, and Geraghty could not have received more than five, because any person who received more was mentioned by name.[50]

Since the casting strategy of using U.S. stars for British films that were to be produced in Germany was thus neither commercially rational for the U.S. nor the German market, it can only be assumed that it was intended for the domestic, British market. Since I do not know of any British star popularity polls for the relevant period I cannot make a final judgement whether this strategy was justified, but only offer a hypothesis based on lists from a somewhat later period, which are the earliest British star popularity polls that I could find. A list from 1933 shows that U.S. stars were indeed popular with British audiences; but it should also be noted that there was a strong demand for British stars, especially when measured against the still relatively small supply of British films at the time.[51]

Furthermore, the bilateral agreement necessarily entailed some conflict of interest between the two partners, and the casting for *The Pleasure Garden* serves as an example. According to German press releases in June, 1925, "Maria Minzenti [and] the U.S. filmstar Margueritte de la Motte" were slated to play the leads in *The Pleasure Garden*.[52] De la Motte would probably have played the part later given to Valli and Minzenti the one given to Geraghty. Minzenti was under contract to Emelka, and she had worked in eight films for them in 1925 alone. This actress did have a market-value in Germany: in 1925, she reached number twenty in the list of Germany's most popular female stars.[53]

On July 2, 1925, Virginia Valli and Maria Minzenti were announced as the stars of *The Pleasure Garden*.[54] It was not until August 16 that Carmelita Geraghty was mentioned in the press. That day, it was reported that Hitchcock was directing the film's opening sequence in Geiselgasteig.[55] Hitchcock reports in 1936 that Alma Reville "had expected Miss Valli alone [referring to her arrival from the U.S. in Cherbourg]; but she had with her Carmelita Geraghty, one of Hollywood's current 'baby stars.' The two were travelling together and intended to stick together."[56] In 1925, Geraghty had indeed only just started out in her career. The nomination of Maria Minzenti in the German press together with Hitchcock's account leads us to assume that Carmelita Geraghty had not been considered for the role originally, but was cast when she arrived by coincidence with Virginia Valli in Europe. The reason for this change in casting was probably W & F's assessment that a U.S. "baby star" like Carmelita Geraghty would have a greater market-value in Great Britain than the German star Maria Minzenti.

THE START OF HITCHCOCK'S CAREER

Since co-production reduced the financial risk, it was easier to try creative newcomers. Thus, Hitchcock was given his first chance to direct. The special production conditions under the terms of the bilateral agreement allowed Hitchcock relative freedom to make the film. The reason for this was not so much the production's organization: the production was organized according to British, and not German practices. In the German film industry the director's freedom was traditionally much greater than in the British industry. German directors had an influence on the script and much freedom in its filmic realization, calculated the film's budget, and were responsible for its editing.[57] In Great Britain, by contrast, they played a less significant role: the director was not regarded as a second author, but as a technician who films a finished script by coordinating and supervising the necessary tasks on the set: "The director is inexorable. Equipped with his megaphone he takes the company through the action, explaining it in detail, to get it perfect before calling upon the camera-artist to turn the handle of his camera."[58] His creative control was very limited: "Very rarely has a director ever conceived the story he produces. A subject is thought of, and a scenario is written by a very gifted person, who may disappear after his script is completed. It is then passed to the director, who, with a group of highly skilled people—the art director (who has rightly become of great importance in the studio), the cameraman and, of course, the recorder—get together to plan the 'shooting,' but the director's dominating personality is not always there. He did not begin the picture by thinking of it, and writing the scenario, and he does not complete the production by cutting it."[59] The pre-industrial period of British film production of the 1920s still allowed the directors to edit their films, whereas the industrial period of the 1930s, from which the latter quotation dates, with its larger companies and more rigorous division of labor, deprived them of even this creative possibility.[60]

Therefore, Hitchcock's idea of becoming a star director was probably not conceived during his later British period, but rather stems from his experience as set-designer for Ufa in Berlin in 1924. Under Erich Pommer as head of production between 1923 and 1926, directors could benefit from a highly developed standard of production and exercise a degree of creative control that was unique in Europe.[61] As mentioned above, Hitchcock refers to his year at Ufa as the most formative experience of his life. Thus it is plausible to assume that not only the idea of visual narration can be attributed to German influence, but also Hitchcock's goal to become a star director who is the true creative force behind his films and whose reputation is the most important factor for their marketing.

During his first two directorial efforts, however, Hitchcock's creative freedom was constrained by British production practices: he had very little influence on the screenplay and the casting. He later complained about the script of *The Mountain Eagle,* and he did not approve of Nita Naldi's playing a village school teacher because of her vamp image.[62] It seems that he did, however, successfully insist on Bernhard Goetzke's being cast as the mayor. Goetzke related that Hitchcock had engaged him for *The Mountain Eagle:* "When I wanted to play the prosecutor [in *Dr. Mabuse*] Fritz Lang laughed at me, but he did let me play the part. And it was in this particular role that I was very successful, especially in England, where Hitchcock took notice of me and decided to contact me. We then met in Berlin. He was working on the sets for *The Blackguard.* And now he has called me to Munich and has given me a role that I really enjoy working on."[63] It is possible that Hitchcock was allowed to do his own editing for both his films, as this was still common practice in British filmmaking in the 1920s, but the German press casts some doubt on this: "[The film contains] dramaturgically dubious rifts and jumps, which are held together by texts, as if the director had not done the montage himself."[64] Be that as it may, working under the terms of the bilateral agreement did have one definite advantage for Hitchcock: he was responsible for a production that was not directly controlled by a producer on the set. Michael Balcon stayed in London, only sending telegrams now and then, and Hitchcock was free to make important decisions.[65] With the exception of script and cast, Hitchcock could do as he pleased artistically.

There is some evidence in the contemporary German press of the way Hitchcock exercised this freedom. He was described as a director who knew exactly what he wanted and who got things done his way: "Hitchcock's strong will guides the ensemble and overcomes all obstacles."[66] He was considered to be hard-working and untiring: "There are no breaks. Hitchcock toughly plods on from scene to scene."[67] He had to make himself understood to stay in control. Sometimes he would ask Fritz Sorg, the location manager, to translate:[68] "Again and again the spot-lights would flare up under Hitchcock's command, and his directions were translated into the jargon of Munich's film studios by an interpreter, often with lively questions on his part."[69] Sometimes he spoke German himself: "Even from a distance we can hear director Hitchcock's commands in broken German, which contains amusing grammatical mistakes."[70] Despite his difficulties with the German language, he spoke to journalists in German.[71]

HITCHCOCK'S ACHIEVEMENT
AS SEEN BY THE GERMAN PRESS

Hitchcock's achievement in his first film, *The Pleasure Garden,* was received merely indifferently: his style of directing was judged to be "neat and meticulous but somewhat stiff"[72] or "skillful and effective."[73] It was not until *The Mountain Eagle,* which Hitchcock himself later deprecated,[74] that Hitchcock's contribution met with much greater approval: "As far as the script provided an opportunity Hitschcock [*sic*] has delivered a piece of work of great quality."[75] His skill was thought to be equal to that of Emelka's directors, or even superior: "Hitchcock, an Englishman, directs. Although he has only directed two films in his life, both in Munich, his skill is already equal to that of Emelka's[76] own directors, or possibly even surpasses it."[77]

Opinions regarding the subject matter of Hitchcock's film differed. There were some statements to the effect that the content had a certain audience appeal, but most were less approving. The most important of the critics' arguments was that the films were "too English." One review of *The Mountain Eagle* reads:

> The aloofness and rarely moderated dryness of the script is entirely English. Suddenly a letter arrives: at that moment one is surprised to see that there actually is an outside-world beyond this village, because the terrible village Napoleon lives and rules here in such an improbably unhindered manner. Unfortunately the teacher, who has been transferred to the village school for disciplinary reasons, suffers all the more passively, and Amandus, who gives way to his father without a word, is passive as well. We are outraged at all this injustice, and even the final reconciliation cannot console us—all in all an English film with stolidness and cant.[78]

The style of Hitchcock's films was received much more favorably than their subject matter, but even in this respect the German press had some reservations. Hitchcock was praised for experimenting with artistic forms that were unpopular at W & F and Emelka. It is well-known that Hitchcock developed a special trademark: in the words of *Film Weekly,* "a reputation for eccentric technical tricks which the critics delighted to call 'Hitchcock touches.' "[79] As early as August 1925, during the filming of *The Pleasure Garden,* several film critics observed Hitchcock's use of unusual shots. One remarked, "Today we are watching the English director Alfred Hitchcock shooting a modern dance sequence with seven chorus girls and a pretty soloist in a theater and stage set." The following distinction between the layman and the expert is interesting, because it shows how Hitchcock caters to them both: "The layman is amused by the corn-yellow, poison-green and copper-red wigs of the slender-legged girls, the expert is more interested in the piquant shots (the camera is a strange English model, which is handled in a virtuoso manner by Gaëtano di Ventimiglia). Soon the lovely soloist Lucy Menne was framed in a close-up over the ramp."[80] The critic refers to a frontal, slightly low-angle shot meant to represent the voyeuristic perspective of the elderly men in the music-hall's audience.

The German film press, who always saw Hitchcock as an Englishman, especially valued his work because he had incorporated elements of the German style of filmmaking. In particular, the mise-en-scène (lighting, set-design) and the mastery of specific generic conventions showed an influence of the German tradition. Hitchcock's achievement was compared with that of Germany's creative staff and judged to be equal or even superior: "Its technique is the real strength of the film [*The Blackguard*], and it almost makes up for the flaws mentioned at the beginning [namely, that the film's content is "too English"]. The sets by N. Hitchcock[81] are of such picturesque beauty and architectural style that our foremost German masters could not have built them better. His English halls and the shop seen in the first scenes are splendid."[82] Hitchcock's sets, not only the famous stairway, but also the apartments, are done in the style of German Expressionism. They bring to mind Paul Leni's sets for the film *Das Wachsfigurenkabinett* (*Waxworks*, 1923), which was shown as the opening film during the founding ceremony of the London Film Society in 1925;[83] they are also similar to Robert Herlth's and Walter Röhrig's work for the film *Der Schatz* (1923, directed by G. W. Pabst).

Film critics praised Hitchcock's ability to use the style of German *Kammerspielfilme*. These films are a part of the German art film tradition. Ufa had participated in the production of the most noted ones, for example, *Sylvester, Hintertreppe* (*Backstairs*), *Scherben* (*Shattered*), and *Der letzte Mann* (*The Last Laugh*);[84] Emelka, which considered art to be a financial risk, did not produce any. *Kammerspielfilme* are naturalistic dramas about the lower middle-class or servants, and they usually have a tragic ending, for example, involving a protagonist's being murdered or committing suicide. These films usually show only interiors, they have only a few characters, who are socially typified (for example, "the train station agent" or "the porter"), and they are often technically innovative (for example, they use hardly any intertitles or show special camera effects such as the moving camera in *Scherben, Sylvester,* and *Der letzte Mann*).[85] The German critics placed *The Mountain Eagle* in this tradition: "A film, set in the highlands, of the *Kammerspiel* type. . . . The Englishman Hitchcock directed it. Even though he has only directed two films in his life, . . . he has . . . acquired the *Kammerspiel*-technique energetically, at least in its crude form. Perhaps he even shows it off a little too much."[86] The characteristics of the *Kammerspielfilm* can be described with the help of extant photos,[87] although no copy of the film seems to be preserved: a small group of characters, who are existentially dependent on one another, are involved in an intense conflict. The dominant shot-sizes used, from the medium close-up to tighter shots, accentuate the characters. Low-key-lighting, famous as a German lighting-style, further enhances the concentration on the actors. The theatrical acting style emphasizes the dramatic nature of the unfolding events.

However much the German film critics may have valued Hitchcock's films for their artistic merit, the German audience did not consider art to be a criterion of interest. For one thing, Hitchcock's films are not in the top fifty of the most successful films in Germany in 1926. Furthermore, it is on record that the co-produced films' financial performance did not live up to Emelka's expectations. As a result, "from the fall of 1925," Emelka initiated "a decidedly German period in Munich's film production," which was, as shown above, very successful.[88] The commercial failure in Germany of the films that Hitchcock directed for Emelka was probably due to the fact that the German audience simply preferred German films with German stars and subject matter.

VISUAL NARRATION

As I note at the beginning of my essay, Hitchcock himself, in retrospect, placed his work in the tradition of the German *Kammerspielfilm* by saying that he had emulated the German style of visual narration. However, this great respect for German films is an ideal that he did not quite attain in his work in Germany. The German critics agreed that Hitchcock's German films did not succeed in developing a language of images that was intelligible in itself, like the film *Der letzte Mann*, for example, but used intertitles instead of visual means of narration. To be able to understand what kinds of problems, especially concerning dramaturgy, the aspiration towards visual narration posed, and how Hitchcock's techniques in solving those problems developed over time, it is instructive to begin our analysis with the film *The Blackguard*, which Hitchcock did not direct, but for which he wrote the script, and also to take a closer look at its critical reception. A review of *The Blackguard* reads: "Maybe the film in itself would not be so incredibly ridiculous, if the intertitles, which are absolutely, positively hopeless, were better made and used less often."[89] Not only does the German press disapprove of the large number of intertitles, the use of the intertitles is also criticized as often being dramaturgically clumsy. The script, for which Hitchcock was responsible, "is disjointed and makes frequent use of bridging intertitles, which of course cannot fill in missing plot elements."[90] And also concerning *The Mountain Eagle* the argument is put forward that "in all those indirect intertitles [i.e., expository intertitles] suspense is anticipated. Through its over-use of explanatory words the film almost becomes an illustrated novel."[91]

Fortunately, a complete contemporary print including the original German intertitles of *The Blackguard* is still extant, so that we may examine the function of its intertitles more closely.[92] The film is 1,965 meters in length and contains 108 intertitles (excluding the credits). When the ratio between the number of intertitles and the number of shots is calculated, the result is 15.8.[93] Films such as Murnau's *Nosferatu* and Lang's *Der müde Tod,* which are famous for their visual narrative, surprisingly show a less favorable ratio (20.4 and 27.5, respectively). Thus, the statement that *The Blackguard* had too many intertitles is empirically incorrect when measured against contemporary conventions. Nor is the ratio between expository intertitles and dialogue intertitles in the least unusual (20:80).

Obviously, it was not so much the number of the intertitles but rather the way they were used that was responsible for the German critics' negative impression. In *The Blackguard,* expository intertitles are often used to solve dramaturgical problems—and not always convincingly. In several instances, characters simply disappear without explanation and later suddenly reappear. For example, Lewinski (played by Bernhard Goetzke), introduced to us as a violin teacher, disappears at the end of Act 1 and does not reappear until Act 5 as a leader of the Russian revolution; in between, he is mentioned only once in Act 3 (dialogue titles no. 14 and no. 15). This narrative gap is explained only through a single intertitle (no. 5 in Act 5): "The turmoil of the times had swept up the violinist Lewinsky." Another example can be found in Act 6; intertitle no. 6 reads "Miraculously, Michael had been able to save himself despite his severe injuries," again substituting for a visual dramatization of the event. The German film critic obviously had such examples in mind when he wrote that the film "is disjointed and makes frequent use of bridging intertitles, which of course cannot fill in missing plot elements."[94] In the first three acts our comprehension of the plot depends almost entirely upon the dialogue intertitles; it is not possible by visual means alone. For example, the intertitles no. 17 and no. 18 from Act 3 read: "Is that the jewelry from the store where I met you?" and "It was mine; I gave it away for the four violins!" This past event is related only in these intertitles; it is not shown.

When directing, Hitchcock depended on professional screenwriters to smooth over problems with the plot, as his own screenplay for *The Black-guard* demonstrates. As Charles Barr has argued, Hitchcock needed strong screenwriters, and he usually collaborated with a certain screenwriter for several films, a pattern he followed throughout his entire career (for the silent films, for example, this regular screenwriter was Eliot Stannard).[95]

From what we know of Hitchcock's way of working in connection with his later films, we may be tempted to assume that he only used these explanatory intertitles because he was not too concerned about the story and instead wanted to concentrate on opulent visual scenes. One of the most attractive sets of *The Blackguard* is the enormous stairway that appears twice in Michael's dreams. This set (for which, supposedly, the famous forest from Lang's *Die Nibelungen* had to be torn down[96]) can only be seen for a mere 90 seconds (based on a projection speed of 16 frames per second) in the film. The significance of this stairway is, again, only made clear through an intertitle, which is also shown twice: "You will become the world's greatest violinist, Michael, if you continue to love your art!" (Act 2, no. 2 and Act 4, no. 5). The visual potential created with such effort was thus hardly exploited.

Acknowledging Hitchcock's dramaturgical and stylistic difficulties in his early work, both as screenwriter and director, also sheds some new light on the first film Hitchcock directed in Great Britain, *The Lodger,* which he made directly after his return from Germany. It is well-known that Ivor Montagu, upon request of the distributor C. M. Woolf, reedited this film before its premiere, reducing the number of intertitles.[97] According to Montagu, the number of intertitles was cut from 350 or 500 to 80, i.e., by 60 or 80 percent. Apart from the fact that this number seems unbelievably large when compared with other films of the period, we may guess that, again, it was not so much the number of intertitles itself that was important, but rather their function; after all, in the case of *The Lodger,* changing the intertitles necessitated some reshooting as well.

Not only did the German film critics, who adhered to very specific standards developed in German art films, disapprove of Hitchcock's use of intertitles in his earliest films, but the British distributor also felt that improvements were necessary. Thus, Hitchcock was neither a born master of visual narration nor did Woolf pose an obstacle for Hitchcock, as is often claimed. Woolf did not hinder the fulfillment of Hitchcock's creative intentions by reediting *The Lodger*: he actually helped develop his style and enhanced his reputation. Hitchcock's characteristic dedication to narrating an entire story through images was the product of an interaction between different people of various functions in the film industry. Hitchcock strategically downplays these influences to present himself as the sole *auteur* of his films and to further the cult of his genius.

CONCLUSION

Until now, our knowledge of Hitchcock's work in Germany relied almost exclusively on the anecdotes that Hitchcock himself had told again and again from the 1930s onward. Since he used these anecdotes for the construction of a specific image, it is necessary to compare them with other contemporary sources, and this analysis leads us not only to modify of our view of Hitchcock's early work, it also has some consequences for our view of his later work. In summary, the beginning of Hitchcock's career as reconstructed from contemporary German sources can be interpreted as follows. Under the terms of an agreement between W & F and Emelka, international films, the realization of which was controlled by the British partner, were produced in Munich. Hitchcock, who enjoyed a high degree of freedom due to the special conditions of production, fulfilled his employer's ideas only partially and instead put his own into practice by experimenting with stylistic elements of German art cinema.

Hitchcock's films were unpopular with German audiences because they were "too English" in their mentality and casting. Most German film critics, however, highly valued Hitchcock's films, because they judged them as being artistically interesting and stylistically influenced by the German art film tradition. What all German film critics strongly disliked, by contrast, was the use of intertitles, which clearly opposed the aspirations of German art cinema.

When working for Ufa as set-designer in 1924, Hitchcock developed two cinematic ideals that he could not yet realize in his early work as a director in Germany, but which were to have immense importance in his later career from the 1930s on. The first was his style of visual narration. The second was his goal to become a director who would be the central creative force behind his films and whose reputation would be used as the most important marketing angle for his films. For this purpose Hitchcock created a clearly defined, success-oriented star image for himself, and it is only through an examination of contemporary sources other than his own accounts that the strategies behind the construction of this image are revealed.

Translation by Annemone Ligensa

NOTES

1. This essay is based on my contribution to the conference *Hitchcock: A Centennial Celebration,* New York, October 1999. I would like to thank the Deutsche Forschngsgemeinschaft for their financial support and also Hans-Peter Reichmann (Deutsches Filmmuseum: Frankfurt a. M.) and Werner Sudendorf (Stiftung Deutsche Kinemathek: Berlin) for their help in researching contemporary film journals. I am also grateful for the support and perceptive suggestions of Sidney Gottlieb, Annemone Ligensa, and Peter Krämer.

2. Tom Ryall's statement that Emelka was a part of Ufa is incorrect. See *Hitchcock and the British Cinema* (London: Croom Helm, 1986), 87.

3. Dr. M-l, "*Die Prinzessin und der Geiger,*" *Lichtbild-Bühne* 171 (September 5, 1925): 20.

4. Herbert Birett, *Database of All German Films Produced in the 1920s* (unpublished computer file).

5. Press screening on May 5, 1926, in Emelka's screening rooms; see Dr. W. K., "*Der Bergadler,*" *Der Film* 19 (September 5, 1926): 16. Concerning the premiere of *The Mountain Eagle,* see *Reichsfilmblatt* 20 (May 15, 1926): 11.

6. See especially Alfred Hitchcock, "My Screen Memories" (1936) and "Life Among the Stars" (1937), both in Sidney Gottlieb, ed., *Hitchcock on Hitchcock: Selected Writings and Interviews* (Berkeley: University of California Press, 1997), 7–26, 27–50, and François Truffaut, *Hitchcock,* rev. ed. (New York: Simon and Schuster, 1985), 25–42.

7. John Russell Taylor, *Hitch: The Life and Times of Alfred Hitchcock* (New York: Da Capo, 1996); Donald Spoto, *The Dark Side of Genius: The Life of Alfred Hitchcock* (New York: Ballantine, 1983).

8. "But my little German girl told me she'd got so bad a chill she couldn't go into the water. We couldn't wait for her to get well again . . . So I got the waitress at the hotel [i.e., probably the 400–year-old Hotel Villa d'Este at Cernobbio on the lake]. I convinced her she could like to be in the pictures. I told her all she had to do was wade out to sea and let Mander 'drown' her" (Gottlieb, *Hitchcock on Hitchcock,* 30). Hitchcock later (in Truffaut, *Hitchcock,* 34) changed the "chill" into the popular anecdote every biographer likes to quote: the actress could not go into the water

because she had her menstrual period (Spoto, *The Dark Side of Genius*, 88; Taylor, *Hitch*, 64).

9. Television interview with Hitchcock, "Hierzulande—Heutzutage—Almanach der Woche," March 10, 1966, WDR.

10. Hitchcock, "My Screen Memories," in Gottlieb, *Hitchcock on Hitchcock*, 10.

11. Interview with Bob Thomas, "Alfred Hitchcock: The German Years," *Action* (Hollywood) January-February (1973): 23–24.

12. Television interview with Hitchcock, "Hierzulande—Heutzutage—Almanach der Woche," March 10, 1966, WDR. Sidney Gottlieb, in "Early Hitchcock: The German Influence," *Hitchcock Annual* (1999–2000): 100–30 (reprinted in this volume), identifies stylistic, thematic, and generic influences of German films on Hitchcock.

13. I researched the following archives: Bundesarchiv in Berlin, Bayerisches Hauptstaatsarchiv in Munich, Stadtarchiv in Munich, and Cinémathèque Suisse in Lausanne.

14. Censorship card no. 10918 for *The Blackguard* in the Bundesarchiv Berlin; *The Pleasure Garden*, decision no. 777 by the Film-Oberprüfstelle in the Deutsches Filminstitut, Frankfurt a. M.

15. Unfortunately, I do not know of any source that could provide information on the commercial success of Hitchcock's German films in Great Britain.

16. Ryall, *Hitchcock and the British Cinema*, 46–47.

17. Kristin Thompson, *Exporting Entertainment: America in the World Film Market 1907–1934* (London: BFI, 1985), 125.

18. Thompson, *Exporting Entertainment*, 125.

19. "Emelka und England: Ein brauchbares Abkommen," *Süddeutsche Filmzeitung* 14/15 (1925): 8; see also Petra Putz, *Waterloo in Geiselgasteig: Die Geschichte des Münchner Filmkonzerns Emelka (1919–1933) im Antagonismus zwischen Bayern und dem Reich* (Trier: WVT, 1996), 71, and Rachel Low, "Die Anfänge: Gainsborough und Gaumont British," in Geoff Brown, ed., *Der Produzent: Michael Balcon und der englische Film* (Berlin: Spiess, 1981), 48.

20. Gainsborough was not mentioned by the German press. It was always said that Hitchcock worked for W & F: see, for example, J-n, "Große Pause in München," *Film-Kurier* [Supplement] 229 (September 29, 1925); Ryall, *Hitchcock and the British Cinema*, 46.

21. "Emelka und England: Ein brauchbares Abkommen," *Süddeutsche Filmzeitung* 14–15 (1925): 8.

22. Hitchcock said in 1937: "I was told that the picture was being half financed from London and by a German company." (Gottlieb, *Hitchcock on Hitchcock*, 28). Hitchcock himself said in 1936 that he had borrowed money in London and Munich when he was in financial difficulties (Gottlieb, *Hitchcock on Hitchcock*, 10). Hitch-

cock does not name the companies. Taylor speaks of a joint financing by Gainsborough and Emelka (*Hitch*, 62).

23. "Franc Tilley," *Film-Kurier* (May 27, 1925).

24. "Die Europäische Produktion der Emelka," *Der Film* 13 (1925): 31. Franc Tilley was an editor with *Kinematograph Weekly* until October, 1924. See "Franc Tilley," *Film-Kurier* (May 27, 1925).

25. See Putz, Waterloo in *Geiselgasteig*, and Robert E. Kapsis, *Hitchcock: The Making of a Reputation* (Chicago: University of Chicago Press, 1992), 18.

26. Heinrich Fraenkel, *Unsterblicher Film: Die große Chronik, von der Laterna Magica bis zum Tonfilm* (München: Kindler, 1956), 132.

27. Wherever possible, I have added the Anglo-American titles used most frequently; when no title could be found, this indicated that the film was probably not released in the U.S. nor in Great Britain. "Das Ergebnis der Abstimmung. 3500 Einzelurteile. Die führenden Kinos haben sich beteiligt," *Film-Kurier* 85 (September 4, 1927): cover. In detail: *Ich habe mein Herz in Heidelberg verloren* (no. 2, produced by Emelka/released by Bayerische Film GmbH), *Unsere Emden* (no. 6, produced by Emelka/released by Bayerische Film GmbH), *Die Försterchristl* (no. 7, produced by Zelnik, released by Südfilm), *Ein Walzertraum* (no. 10, produced and released by Ufa), *Ben Hur* (no. 4, produced by Loew Metro Goldwyn, released by Ufa). Incidentally, the number one film of the year 1926 was *An der schönen blauen Donau*. See Joseph Garncarz, "Hollywood in Germany: The Role of American Films in Germany, 1925–1990," in David W. Ellwood and Rob Kroes, eds., *Hollywood in Europe: Experiences of a Cultural Hegemony* (Amsterdam: VU University Press, 1994), 94–135.

28. See Rahel Lipschütz, *Der Ufa-Konzern: Geschichte, Aufbau und Bedeutung im Rahmen des deutschen Filmgewerbes* (Berlin: Energiadruck, 1932).

29. Dr. W. K., "*Der Garten der Lust*," *Der Film* 33 (August 16, 1925): 21; see also Hans Spielhofer, "Bei der Emelka in Geiselgasteig," *Süddeutsche Filmzeitung* 32 (August 7, 1925): 5–6, and "*Der Garten der Lust*," *Film-Kurier* (3rd Supplement) 191 (August 15, 1925). The title *Der Garten der Lust* (trans. "The Garden of Lust") was not approved by the censors and was replaced by the title *Irrgarten der Leidenschaft* (trans. "Labyrinth of Passion").

30. "*Der Garten der Lust*," *Der Film* 26 (June 28, 1925): 23.

31. "Einsendungen aus der Industrie," *Kinematograph* 1003 (May 9, 1926): 19.

32. See "Bernhard Goetzke," *Die Filmwoche* 9 (February 24, 1926): 210–11.

33. "Das Resultat unserer Umfrage," *Deutsche Filmwoche* (Berlin) 11 (March 18, 1927): 14.

34. Dr. W. K, "*Der Bergadler*," *Der Film* 19 (May 9, 1926): 16.

35. On Ferdinand Martini: "Ferdinand Martini has been a part of Emelka's staff in Munich for several years" (Walter Jerven, "Ferdinand Martini," *Film-Kurier*

[July 29, 1925]). Martini said of himself that he had been working for Emelka since 1921, "where he had been regularly employed." (See the article on Martini in Kurt Mühsam and Egon Jacobsohn, *Lexikon des Films* [Berlin: Verlag der Lichtbildbühne, 1926], 118). Martini played roles in eight films in 1925 and in five films in 1926 for Emelka. On Karl Falkenberg: "Then Emelka signed him and gave him an important role in almost every single one of their films." (J-n, "Karl Falkenberg," *Film-Kurier* [October 24, 1926]). Falkenberg, who played roles in two Emelka films in 1925 and also in 1926, gives Emelka as the address of his place of work (see the article on Falkenberg in Mühsam and Jacobsohn, 52).

36. Philip Kemp, "Not for Peckham: Michael Balcon and Gainsborough's International Trajectory in the 1920s," in Pam Cook, ed., *Gainsborough Pictures* (London: Cassell, 1997), 22.

37. Spoto classifies these actors as "top American stars" (*The Dark Side of Genius,* 82); Taylor calls Valli "one of the biggest stars at Universal" (*Hitch,* 65).

38. Richard Koszarski, *An Evening's Entertainment: The Age of the Silent Feature Picture, 1915–1928* (Berkeley: University of California Press, 1994), 262, bases his figures on polls in the journals *Photoplay* and *Film Daily.*

39. Koszarski, *An Evening's Entertainment,* 116.

40. Nita Naldi received £1500, according to Hitchcock's own report (Gottlieb, *Hitchcock on Hitchcock,* 33). When this amount is adjusted for inflation and divided by the number of weeks of filming, we have an estimate of Naldi's market value. Thus, with a total salary of $7290 (according to the figures in Statistisches Reichsamt, ed., *Statistisches Jahrbuch für das deutsche Reich* [Berlin: Verlag von Reimar Hobbing, 1928], 434), and with 8 to 12 weeks of filming (Putz has January to March 1926 [*Waterloo in Geiselgasteig,* 224], Taylor, October to December 1925 [*Hitch,* 68–69]; Taylor's figures seem to be more realistic, because in *Kinematograph* 983.4 (December 25, 1925): 3, there was an advertisement saying that "*The Bergadler . . .* is almost finished!"), Nita Naldi earned $600 to $900 per week.

41. Taylor does not mention Nita Naldi. Spoto, however, regards it as a fact (*The Dark Side of Genius,* 89). Before that, Naldi is mentioned in Peter Noble, *Index to the work of Alfred Hitchcock,* Special Supplement to *Sight and Sound* Index Series, No. 18 (May, 1949), 6; see also Charles Barr, *English Hitchcock* (Moffat: Cameron & Mollis, 1999), 215–16.

42. Hitchcock once said that the actress playing the "native girl" was doubled by a waitress from the hotel where the film team was staying for the scene in which she is ducked in the water by Mander (see note 8 above). In contrast to Taylor's description (*Hitch,* 65), however, she is not only visible from behind, but also quite clearly from the front. Is Hitchcock's story another one of his inventions?

43. Gottlieb, *Hitchcock on Hitchcock,* 30.

44. *Deutsche Filmwoche* 24 (October 9, 1925): 14.

45. *Deutsche Filmwoche*; see also "*Irrgarten der Leidenschaft*," *Illustrierter Film-Kurier* 7.341 (1925).

46. "*Irrgarten der Leidenschaft*," *Der Film* 30 (July 26, 1925): 15, and "*Irrgarten der Leidenschaft*," *Die Filmwoche* 4 (January 20, 1926): 92.

47. "Einsendungen aus der Industrie," *Kinematograph* 1003 (May 9, 1926): 19.

48. Hans Spielhofer, "*Der Bergadler*," *Reichsfilmblatt* 20 (May 15, 1926): 12.

49. "Wer ist der beliebteste Filmstar?," *Neue illustrierte Filmwoche* 23 (1924): 263; "Wer ist der beliebteste Filmstar?," *Deutsche Filmwoche* 19 (September 4, 1925): 8; "Wer ist der beliebteste Filmstar?," *Deutsche Filmwoche* 19 (May 7, 1926): 14; "Das Resultat unserer Umfrage," *Deutsche Filmwoche* 11 (March 18, 1927): 14; see also Joseph Garncarz, "Top Ten Stars, 1923–1926," in *The BFI Companion to German Cinema*, ed. Thomas Elsaesser and Michael Wedel (London: BFI, 1999), 228.

50. The U.S. audience's favorite female stars of 1924, Mary Pickford and Gloria Swanson, both appeared only once on Germany's lists: they were ranked as number 24 and number 39, respectively, in the same year. This means that Gloria Swanson, for example, received only about ten votes of 15,000. A total of 15,120 votes was collected; for the first fifteen ranks the number of votes is noted, for the next forty-two only the names but not the votes are given, and whoever reached a rank of only forty-two or lower had only received five votes or less.

51. David McGillivray, "Now You Know," *Films and Filming* 338 (November 1982): 42–43. The article lists the top male and female stars between 1933 and 1939; the original source is *Picturegoer*. In 1933, of 20 stars, 10 are from the U.S., 7 are British, and 3 from other European countries.

52. *Der Film* 26 (June 28, 1925): 23; *Film-Kurier* (June 22, 1925): cover.

53. *Deutsche Filmwoche* 19 (May 7, 1926).

54. Advertisement in *Film-Kurier* (July 2, 1925); Valli is also on the cast list in the following articles: *Der Film* 30 (July 26, 1925): 15, and *Film-Kurier* (June 30, 1925): cover.

55. Hitchcock had left for Italy on June 6 to begin location shooting (Spoto, *The Dark Side of Genius*, 86); see also *Süddeutsche Filmzeitung* 28 (July 10, 1925).

56. Gottlieb, *Hitchcock on Hitchcock*, 10; see also 8.

57. Kurt Mühsam, *Film und Kino* (Dessau: Dünnhaupt, 1927), 36–45; Urban Gad, *Der Film: seine Mittel und seine Ziele* (Berlin: Schuster & Löffler, 1921), 104; Kristin Thompson, "Early Alternatives to the Hollywood Mode of Production: Implications for Europe's Avant-Gardes," *Film History* 5 (1993): 386–404.

58. Frederick A. Talbot, *Moving Pictures: How They Are Made and Worked* (London: William Heinemann, rev. ed., 1923), 211–12.

59. Andrew Buchanan, *The Art of Film Production* (London: Isaac Pitman & Sons, 1936), 29–30.

60. Talbot, *Moving Pictures*, 218.

61. Thomas Elsaesser, "Kunst und Krise: Die Ufa in den 20er Jahren," in Hans-Michael Bock and Michael Töteberg, eds., *Das Ufa-Buch* (Frankfurt a. M.: Zweitausendeins, 1992), 96–105.

62. Gottlieb, *Hitchcock on Hitchcock*, 34.

63. J-n, *"Der Bergadler," Film-Kurier* (January 1, 1926).

64. Dr. W. K., *"Der Bergadler," Der Film* 19 (May 9, 1926): 16.

65. Taylor reports: "From London Balcon kept bombarding Hitch with telegrams . . . suggesting all kinds of Hollywood stars—mostly, like Agnes Ayres, rather *démodée* by this time. Eventually came the curt announcement that he was being sent Nita Naldi, best known for her vamp roles in DeMille's first *Ten Commandments* and opposite Valentino in *Blood and Sand*" (*Hitch*, 69).

66. "Münchener Porträts: Alfred Hitchcock," *Film-Kurier* (2nd Supplement) 274 (November 21, 1925).

67. *"Der Bergadler," Film-Kurier* (January 1, 1926).

68. Dr. W. K., *"Der Garten der Lust," Der Film* 33 (August 16, 1925): 21.

69. Hans Spielhofer, "Bei der Emelka in Geiselgasteig," *Süddeutsche Filmzeitung* 32 (August 7, 1925): 6.

70. *"Der Garten der Lust," Film-Kurier* (3rd Supplement) 191 (August 15, 1925).

71. "Münchener Porträts: Alfred Hitchcock," *Film-Kurier* (2nd Supplement) 274 (November 21, 1925).

72. *"Irrgarten der Leidenschaft," Kinematograph* 986 (January 10, 1926): 18.

73. Fritz Olimsky, *"Irrgarten der Leidenschaft,"* unidentified clipping from Stiftung Deutsche Kinemathek (SDK), January 17, 1926.

74. Truffaut, *Hitchcock*, 35–36.

75. *"Der Bergadler," Kinematograph* 1003 (May 9, 1926): 19.

76. It is not certain who is meant. Franz Seitz was head-director at Emelka.

77. *"Der Bergadler," Reichsfilmblatt* 20 (May 15, 1926): 12.

78. Dr. W. K., *"Der Bergadler," Der Film* 19 (May 9, 1926): 16.

79. Quoted in Alfred Gordon Bennett, *Cinemania: Aspects of Filmic Creation* (London: Jarrolds, 1937), 170.

80. Dr. W. K., *"Der Garten der Lust," Der Film* 33 (August 16, 1925): 21; see also Hans Spielhofer, "Bei der Emelka in Geiselgasteig," *Süddeutsche Filmzeitung* 32 (August 7, 1925): 5–6, and *"Der Garten der Lust," Film-Kurier* (3rd Supplement) 191 (August 15, 1925).

81. In connection with *The Blackguard*, the press has "N." (or sometimes "M.") instead of "A." Hitchcock. Since this mistake can be found in all the press items, it probably originated in the press material. The film's credits and the censorship card correctly use "Alfred Hitchcock."

82. Dr. M-l, *"Die Prinzessin und der Geiger," Lichtbild-Bühne* 171 (September 5, 1925): 20; see similarly *"Die Prinzessin und der Geiger," Film-Kurier*, and also

Fritz Olimsky, "*Die Prinzessin und der Geiger*," unidentified clippings from SDK, September, 1925.

83. Ryall, *Hitchcock and the British Cinema*, 87–88. Fraenkel comments, "Most of these films [which were regarded as having 'no commercial prospects' and were shown to the Society] were of German origin, and it was certainly no coincidence that Erich Pommer immediately became an honorary member of the Society with its foundation; that I myself, being at that time a young film journalist, received the same honor, was, however, due to the coincidence that I could point out German films of special interest to my British friends now and then" (132).

84. The *Kammerspielfilme* were shown for the first time in Ufa's large premiere cinemas in Berlin (Morzartsaal, U. T. am Kurfüstendamm, Ufa-Palast am Zoo), some with original musical compositions (by Klaus Pringsheim for *Sylvester*, Guiseppe Becce for *Der letzte Mann*). Following the film *Scherben*, the other *Kammerspielfilme* were all produced by Ufa (*Der letzte Mann* is a film by the Ufa production-company Union-Film), commissioned by Ufa (*Hintertreppe*, a film starring Henny Porten, is a film for Ufa's Gloria-Film GmbH), or at least released by Ufa (in the case of *Sylvester*).

85. See Joseph Garncarz, "Kammerspielfilm," in Ginette Vincendeau, ed., *Encyclopedia of European Cinema* (London: Cassell and BFI, 1995), 235.

86. Hans Spielhofer, "*Der Bergadler*," *Reichsfilmblatt* 20 (May 15, 1926): 12.

87. For reproductions of these photos, see J. L. Kuhns, "Hitchcock's *The Mountain Eagle*," *Hitchcock Annual* (1998–99): 31–108, and Dan Auiler, *Hitchcock's Notebooks* (New York: Avon Books, 1999), 6–11.

88. Hans Spielhofer, "Die Münchener Herbstproduktion," *Süddeutsche Filmzeitung* 36 (September 3, 1926): 3.

89. "*Die Prinzessin und der Geiger*," *Deutsche Filmwoche* 21 (September 18, 1925): 18.

90. Dr. M-l, "*Die Prinzessin und der Geiger*," *Lichtbild-Bühne* 171 (September 5, 1925): 20; see similarly "*Die Prinzessin und der Geiger*," *Reichsfilmblatt* 37 (1925): 43, and Fritz Olimsky, "*Die Prinzessin und der Geiger*," unidentified clipping from SDK, September, 1925.

91. "*Der Bergadler*," *Film-Kurier* (June 1, 1926); Dr. W. K., "*Der Bergadler*," *Der Film* 19 (May 9, 1926): 16.

92. National Film and Television Archive, London.

93. Herbert Birett, "Filmalter und Filmstil: Statistische Analyse von Stummfilmen," in Elfriede Ledig, ed., *Der Stummfilm: Konstruktion und Rekonstruktion* (München: Schaudig, Bauer, Ledig, 1988), 76–78. Birett calculates a measure Z, to measure the ratio between intertitles and shots: $Z = 100 \times Z'$, with $Z' = $ number of intertitles ÷ number of shots.

94. Dr. M-l, "*Die Prinzessin und der Geiger,*" *Lichtbild-Bühne* 171 (September 5, 1925): 20.

95. Barr, *English Hitchcock,* 22–77.

96. Spoto, *The Dark Side of Genius,* 74.

97. Ivor Montagu, "Working with Hitchcock," *Sight and Sound* (summer 1980): 190; Kapsis, *Hitchcock: The Making of a Reputation,* 18; Ryall, *Hitchcock and the British Cinema,* 89.

EASY VIRTUE'S FRAMES

CHRISTOPHER MORRIS

Given *Easy Virtue*'s unrelenting narrative of a woman's victimization—by a drunken husband, a lech-
erous artist, a patriarchal legal system, a weak second
husband and his manipulative mother, a crowd of
invasive male paparazzi—it may at first seem odd
that the film has attracted little notice from Hitchcock's feminist critics. On reflection, however, its
unequivocal revelation of a woman's oppression may
be problematic for critics, like Modleski, who advo-
cate reading Hitchcock's films "against the grain" in
order to discover in them a subversion of patriarchy.[1]
By contrast, the apparent feminism of *Easy Virtue*
seems so entirely "with the grain" as to momentarily unsettle the received construction of Hitchcock
the covert or overt misogynist.[2] Of course, reading
Hitchcock's films as feminist either against or with
the grain is already to engage in the grail quest of
hermeneutics that constrains critics, feminists and
others, to seek and define gender themes, whether
within particular films or threaded through them, a
project that has yet to achieve consensus.[3]

   Deconstructive criticism cannot, of course, move
closer to any such grail; however, it may propose a

way of understanding the critical quest as a correlative of the story's victim-ization of women.[4] That is, *Easy Virtue* narrates gender oppression as the imposition of the structures of male hegemony onto its protagonist, Larita, but it also allegorizes reading (and even seeing) as an analogous imposition of a frame onto arbitrary fields of signifiers. Such a double mistake, diegetic and critical, may be viewed as a cinematic instance of Derrida's metaphor of reading-as-tympan or the frame which privileges inside over outside as it marginalizes.[5] Reading, seeing, and distortion are equated in this allegory of seeing. But if such distortions are necessary to first comprehension, crit-ical pursuit of the film's gender theme may helplessly repeat its characters' mistaken frames.

II

That one of the interests of *Easy Virtue* is in an allegory of seeing, espe-cially framed seeing, may be evident from its credits, which appear over the image of a camera, and from key scenes of photographic representa-tion.[6] For example, the paparazzi aggressively take Larita's picture after her first trial. Later, at the Whittakers' estate, when Larita suspects her past may come to light, she desperately tries to smash a camera. And after the second trial, which ends the film, paparazzi harass her. Thus *Easy Virtue* is doubly framed—it is encircled with the activity of framing—or even triply framed if the credits are seen as framing the double frame.

With regard to Hitchcock's *oeuvre*, this subject has sometimes been dis-cussed in hermeneutic criticism in terms of "reflexivity," that is, of moral commentary on photography, film-making, the film audience, voyeurism, or the gaze.[7] Likewise, criticism of *Easy Virtue* has emphasized the idea of the camera as violator of identity—as a catalyst of Larita's downfall through its inexpungible record of her earlier "shame." The film's indictment of pho-tography has been linked to its broader attack on England's press, judiciary and class systems.[8]

On the other hand, reflexivity calls into question not only the social order but also the validity of visual representation itself. *Easy Virtue*, framed by the cameras of the credits and ending, explores the image of the frame as the medium for its critiques not only of the social system and the individual egos that seem to comprise it, but also of representation itself.

Framing is a metaphor for reading, a visual counterpart of the lin-guistic necessity for selection. For example, the film begins with a high-lighted newspaper column reporting legal proceedings, a technique that duplicates the eye's act of focusing. It selects-out the subject of divorce first from the rest of the news and then from other courtroom topics—probate and admiralty—and so associates framing with the processes of selection and reading. In other words, from the outset of the film, reading is made possible by what is excluded, marginalized, or not seen. The framing of the newspaper article is followed by two scenes of interpretation, linked by flashback, which extend this principle to the courtroom and artist's studio: both are sites where framing is depicted as necessary and taken for granted but misleading.

In the courtroom, the trial is depicted as a transparent fiction, an elab-orately costumed stage play performed before a credulous audience. The idea that legal proceedings misrepresent human subjectivity is suggested by the adversarial, alternating shots of Larita and her husband's attorney in sharp profile. The easy equations of these one-sided representations with innocence and guilt collapse when Larita's story unfolds and when the pros-ecutorial lawyer later becomes her confidante. Faces framed by wigs reveal expressive countenances to be only masks. The myopic judge and gossipy juror are dramatis personae, characters who jointly construct the verdict of "misconduct" against Larita.

The equation between the framed verdict and the representation of character—not unlike those made in hermeneutic criticism—is made by the gossipy juror's written responses to the testimony. The first ("Was the maid always present when Mrs. Filton disrobed?") betrays a kind of voyeuris-tic interest in the proceedings; the second ("The artist and the woman he pitied alone together. Pity is akin to love.") is redundant, given the love-note Claude writes to Larita. Because neither of the juror's responses supports a verdict of "misconduct" against Larita, viewer interpretation of character, including the juror's written "criticism," is allegorized as both necessary—some verdict must be reached—and mistaken.

The jury's verdict is made possible only by marginalizing instances of the more egregious behavior of both Aubrey Filton and Claude Robson. This verdict is thus "framed," arrived at only at the expense of what is excluded. As if to underscore its fictionality, the verdict is decided upon and announced in a courtroom presented as a series of frames: the accused inside a witness-stand, jury inside a box, judge behind bench, observers in orchestra and balcony sections.[9] The courtroom's interior ogives—these are echoed later in the artist's studio—further define the space of judgment as a series of artificial enclosures. When Larita leaves the courtroom only to be met in the doorway by a barrage of cameras, it becomes evident that the representations of photography only duplicate prior framings which have been allegorized as first conditions of reading and interpretation. So photography captures not so much life as the inevitability of the frame.

The film's juxtaposition of the law's outrageous fictions with artistic representation may be unsettling for the traditional humanistic confidence that art's relation to reality is somehow privileged; however, Claude Robson's painting of Larita is just as much a "frame" of identity as is the juror's verdict, the judge's sentence, the reporter's photograph—or (we may now begin to surmise) the film itself and its critics' views of it. None of these representations tells the truth; none can avoid a frame. Within the painter's literal, rectangular frame is an idealized or sublimated figure, a reduction and abstraction of the plot's triangular frame of desire in which Larita occupies the apex. The frames of art are evident, too, in the white statue, niched by an ogive and observable behind Larita as she sits for her portrait. The studio's numerous frames suggest the way artistic interpretations of character, including those of film, may be just as fictional as legal verdicts.

If painting, photography, and film—like the law—are helpless to render the world unframed, this debility may, by inference, be fated or inherent in life; if so, it may be impossible for film *not* to repeatedly allegorize this limitation. By no means restricted to newspaper, courtroom, and studio, frames in the world of *Easy Virtue* become ubiquitous, inescapable.

III

Escape (in the form of hiding her "scarred heart") is what we are told Larita longs for in the south of France, yet she first appears in a hotel lobby framed in white columns; like everyone else, she must enter her name within the ruled lines of the guest-register. Here human identity is equated with arbitrary signs within a frame. That Larita substitutes the surname Gray for Filton only makes the arbitrary nature of the framed name more apparent. It would appear that identity as the fictive construct of framing is not much affected by changes in venue. The room in which Larita finally kisses John Whittaker contains an alcove with a statue—as if she had not left the courtroom or artist's studio. The artifice of the wigs that framed jurists' faces is in France replaced by Larita's eye-concealing or broad-brimmed hats and by the tall silk hats worn by John and his driver. In these ways, the site of Larita's striving to recreate herself only makes more apparent the impossibility of transcending the artificial frames that construct selfhood.

The main link between the old and putatively new Laritas is established by her presence at the second court, another formally delimited space of ritualized conflict. The French tennis court—in history a famous nexus of sport and arbitrary law—is introduced by an impossible-to-ignore framing-shot, by means of which we view the players and bouncing ball first through a racquet. It is as if humans are subordinated to some network or mesh or fate larger than themselves. Of course, the seesaw motion of the tennis-game recalls the courtroom's images of alternating argument and counter-argument; the parallel likens the viewer, Larita, and the tennis-audience to the jury and to courtroom observers of the back-and-forth of framed human discourse struggling to issue in truthful representation.

Larita's exchange of one framed place for another provides no escape from the interpretation of identity or the triangulation of desire. John's pur-suit of her begins with the interrupted tennis-match and is strengthened by his jealousy of the attentions paid to Larita by the unseen "Duc de Val-lenville." Interestingly, this third term in the triangle presents itself as a mere signifier—a calling card with a signature. Of course, this framed assertion of identity repeats Larita's signature in the hotel guest-book. It is as if the embodied human triangle of London is replaced in France by the schemati-cally purer arrangement of man/woman/signifier. In any case, the depiction of John and Larita as always shadowed by various third terms comes up again in their carriage ride, when the presence of driver, horse, and fellow-travelers functions to expose the illusion of private selfhood or romantic union. Employing different methods, René Girard and Eve Kosofsky Sedg-wick conclude that literature represents gender relations as defined by trian-gulation; their common thesis has been invoked in the study of Hitchcock's films.[10]

In *Easy Virtue,* the triangle is one of many images that show love subor-dinated to a frame. The most dramatic example is the famous scene in which a telephone operator eavesdrops on John's proposal to Larita. This scene, praised as a virtuoso example of the way silent film "speaks" purely through visual images, dramatizes the way love is constructed in and through a frame, a pre-existing network—something akin to Derrida's notion of the postal, while at the same time the lovers mistakenly believe themselves to be the privileged origin and destination of the discourse.[11] (In fact, an inter-cepted love-message had appeared earlier in the film, when Aubrey Filton discovered Claude's letter to Larita; as a result, this scene's dramatization of the illusion of unframed, private discourse in love is already a redundancy.) The fact that the telephone operator's interception of the proposal inter-rupts her reading of a romance has the effect of equating the discourses of real and fictional characters.

The operator's vicarious identification with the lovers resembles that of a rapt reader or viewer of film. Indeed, when she shifts the site of her empathic reading, exchanging one framed discourse for another, the operator becomes the audience's surrogate, too. Her eavesdropping on the back-and-forth movement of the conversation aligns her with earlier spectators, in the English courtroom and at the French tennis court. The operator's "turning" also mirrors the viewer's move from the everyday world (which may after all be fictional) into the more enthralling movie theater. It is noteworthy that the operator literally turns, from left profile to full face, though this turn only leaves her again conspicuously framed, this time by Hitchcock's camera. Like the telephone operator, film audiences may imagine love and freedom on the condition of momentarily forgetting the frames that have constructed them.

IV

The switchboard scene is the center of the center of a symmetrical film framed by courtrooms, triangulated love, and pictorial representations of Larita: the return to England is marked by a famous metonymic dissolve which replaces a French poodle on a trunk at a way station with an English bulldog. The celebrated economy of narrative exposition here also condenses the film's allegory of the futility of Larita's, or anyone's, struggle to escape. The film's geographical circularity is only another frame. The lovers' carriage-ride across flat wastelands ends in the Whittakers' moated estate, rendered as a series of oppressive interior frames: the doorway, bedposts, and mirror of Larita's room; the interior ogives that recall the courtroom, artist's studio, and French hotel; the wooden carvings of saints looming over the dining room table; the double landings and balustrades which frame Mrs. Whittaker's first entrance and Larita's final defiance. Thus, the austere rigidity of the judicial frames is duplicated in the domestic world, which gradually "judges" Larita in a manner just as arbitrary as the court's. The dining table repeats the jury room, as the social repeats the legal verdict.

It is instructive that the catalyst for the Whittakers' condemnation of Larita is a pictorial representation: the magazine photograph that cites Claude Robson's painting. Once again, the implication is that the gross distortion of "framing" human identity is also inescapable, like fate: it will "come back" because it is never absent. When her ex-husband's attorney shows her the magazine, Larita realizes that the truth cannot be concealed; her subsequent camera-smashing makes it seem as futile to wish human identity unframed, unread, or uninterpreted as it is to attack the mechanical instrument of the framing. If framing is like reading or seeing, it is inherent in existence.

In this context, Larita's alterations of her party-dress and defiance of Mrs. Whittaker may signal an acquiescence in the inevitability of false constructions of human identity: since she cannot escape misrepresentation, Larita may as well play the "fallen" role assigned by her critics. Her final words to the courthouse photographers ("Shoot . . . there's nothing left to kill") establish an analogy between camera and weapon—one that Hitchcock would explore more explicitly in *Foreign Correspondent* and *Rear Window.* In *Easy Virtue,* the implication is that since photography is only another misinterpretation of a "subject" already shown to be constructed from the inescapable frames of prejudice, social convention, and art, it can do no further damage. Or, better: the necessity for framing dramatized in Larita's story brings to "nothing" our traditional, tenacious, human illusions of autonomous subjectivity, love, and meaning; once we understand that there is "nothing," in this sense, to shoot, the film ends.

Of course, Larita's defiance of the reporters does not deter them from "shooting." The implication for film criticism may be that hermeneutic interpretation—conceived as the attempt to establish the film's (or the director's, or even the viewer's) perspective on Larita's suffering, either with or against the grain of the film—cannot be stopped, despite the film's thoroughgoing exposure of its futility, for reading or seeing the film, in the first place, was the condition of arriving at its disillusioning end. For *Easy Virtue,* film criticism, too, is a fated or necessary error, the result of which will be, however, but another frame of "nothing."

NOTES

1. Following Edward Said, Tania Modleski, in *The Women Who Knew Too Much: Hitchcock and Feminist Theory* (New York: Methuen, 1988), describes her approach as a "frankly inventive" (13–15) way of giving voice to previously unheard women in Hitchcock; she does not mention *Easy Virtue.*

2. In *The Dark Side of Genius: The Life of Alfred Hitchcock* (New York: Ballantine Books, 1983), Donald Spoto describes Hitchcock as on occasion exhibiting a sadistic personality and abusing women; he believes Hitchcock's films sometimes reflect and rationalize these traits. In "Visual Pleasure and Narrative Cinema," in Constance Penley, ed., *Feminism and Film Theory* (New York: Routledge, 1988), Laura Mulvey argues that in Hitchcock's heroes, the "power to subject another person to

the will sadistically or to the gaze voyeuristically is turned on to the woman as the object of both" (66–67). In *Hitchcock on Hitchcock: Selected Writings and Interviews* (Berkeley: University of California Press, 1995), Sidney Gottlieb argues that Hitchcock rationalizes, rather than denies, the charge that he is a misogynist (70); he finds Hitchcock's writings about women "more than a little troubling" (71).

3. Among hermeneutic critics, there is no consensus as to the meaning of Hitchcock's films in general or of their gender relations in particular. In *The Hitchcock Romance: Love and Irony in Hitchcock's Films* (Princeton: Princeton University Press, 1988), Lesley Brill argues that Hitchcock endorses romantic love. Janet Bergstrom's emphasis on the power of viewer identification leads her to describe a Hitchcockian *oeuvre* far less recuperable for women's issues than that analyzed by Tania Modleski. See Janet Bergstrom, "Enunciation and Sexual Difference," in *Feminism and Film Theory*, 159–85.

4. For the distinction between hermeneutics and deconstruction, see Gary Shapiro and Alan Sica, eds., *Hermeneneutics: Questions and Prospects* (Amherst: University of Massachusetts Press, 1984), and John D. Caputo, *Radical Hermeneutics: Repetition, Deconstruction, and the Hermeneutic Project* (Bloomington: Indiana University Press, 1987). The best-known exponent of deconstructive film criticism in France is Marie-Claire Ropars-Wuilleumier; see her *Écraniques: Le film du texte* (Presses Universitaires de Lille, 1990). The most extensive investigation of the relevance of Derrida to film theory is Peter Brunette and David Wills's *Screen/Play: Derrida and Film Theory* (Princeton: Princeton University Press, 1988). An excellent deconstructive study of Hitchcock is part of Tom Cohen's *Anti-Mimesis from Plato to Hitchcock* (Cambridge: Cambridge University Press, 1994). My previous articles on this subject include "Feminism, Deconstruction, and the Pursuit of the Tenable in *Vertigo*," *Hitchcock Annual* (1996–1997): 3–25; "The Direction of *North by Northwest*," *Cinema Journal* 36 (1997): 43–56; and "The Allegory of Seeing in Hitchcock's Silent Films," *Film Criticism* 22 (1997–98): 27–50.

5. For Derrida's metaphor of the tympan, see "Tympan" in *Margins of Philosophy*, trans. by Alan Bass (Chicago: University of Chicago Press, 1982); the tympan as frame is discussed on xxvi-xxvii. In this introductory essay, Derrida announces his intention of examining the texts of philosophy from the point of view of their unjustly relegated margins (xxiii).

6. The credits of one of Hitchcock's earlier film, *The Lodger,* have also been likened to a representation of a camera's shutter. See Maurice Yacowar, *Hitchcock's British Films* (Hamden, CT: Archon Books, 1977), 33.

7. For commentary on Hitchcock's films that uses the idea of reflexivity in these ways, see, for example, Robert Stam, *Reflexivity in Film and Literature: From Don Quixote to Jean-Luc Godard* (New York: Columbia University Press, 1992), on *Rear*

Window, and Edward Recchia, "Through a Shower Curtain Darkly: Reflexivity as a Dramatic Component of *Psycho,*" *Literature/Film Quarterly* 19 (1991): 258–66, on *Psycho.*

8. Yacowar argues that the cameras suggest "voyeuristic intrusion" as part of Hitchcock's social satire leveled against both the upper class and the stigma of divorce (*Hitchcock's British Films,* 56, 57). In *Alfred Hitchcock* (Boston: Twayne Publishers, 1984), Gene D. Phillips sees in the photographers Hitchcock's satire of a "scandal-mongering press" (40).

9. William Rothman, in *Hitchcock—The Murderous Gaze* (Cambridge: Harvard University Press, 1982), first noted the relation between courtroom spaces and the film frame (353). For further discussion of this relation in *Easy Virtue,* see Sidney Gottlieb, "Kissing and Telling in Hitchcock's *Easy Virtue,*" *Hitchcock Annual* (1992): 3–38, especially 20 and 33.

10. In *Deceit, Desire and the Novel: Self and Other in Literary Structure,* trans. Yvonne Freccero (Baltimore: Johns Hopkins Univ. Press, 1972), René Girard argues that Western literature depicts romantic love—and the human subjectivity that seeks definition through it—as always mediated by some real or imaginary third term. In *Between Men: English Literature and Male Homosocial Desire* (New York: Columbia University Press, 1985), Eve Kosofsky Sedgwick elaborates upon a literary tradition according to which repressed bisexuality haunts male heterosexuality. Paula Cohen Marantz, in *Alfred Hitchcock: The Legacy of Victorianism* (Lexington: University Press of Kentucky, 1995), cites both writers in her discussion of triangulation in Hitchcock's films.

11. The technical virtuosity of the scene is praised by Yacowar (*Hitchcock's British Films,* 55) and Phillips (*Alfred Hitchcock,* 40). For Derrida's concept of the postal, see his *The Post-Card: From Socrates to Freud and Beyond,* trans. Alan Bass (Chicago: University of Chicago Press, 1987.)

THEMATIC APPROACHES TO HITCHCOCK

THE DIABOLIC IMAGINATION: HITCHCOCK, BAKHTIN, AND THE CARNIVALIZATION OF CINEMA

DAVID STERRITT

The purpose of looking at Alfred Hitchcock's films through the lens of Mikhail Bakhtin's theory is not to forge arbitrary links between a British-American film artist and a Russian-Soviet literary philosopher of very different backgrounds and tendencies. Rather it is to use Bakhtinian ideas as a means of connecting Hitchcock's *oeuvre,* or at least an important portion of it, with aesthetic traditions that have centuries of productive growth and development behind them. Central to this enterprise are two of Bakhtin's most important concepts. One is carnivalization, the deployment of a festive, parodic, often grotesque, ultimately subversive vision of the world. The other is dialogism, the theoretical acceptance and discursive use of relativized, destabilized meaning rooted in the continual interaction of different utterances. Monologism, opposed to dialogism, implies the rejection or avoidance of such relativization and destabilization.

As one might expect when dealing with a trickster like Hitchcock, such considerations lead almost immediately in an unexpected direction. One is normally tempted to think of dialogism and carnivalization as natural concomitants of each other. This is because dialogism tends to valorize heterogeneity, polyphony, and the potentially boisterous interaction of multiple voices, languages, and sensibilities; all such valorizations are compatible with the purposefully destabilized realm of carnival and its artistic manifestations. Monologism, by contrast, is associated with practices that level, close off, hierarchize, and generally work against diversity by favoring the presence of a single dominating consciousness, and by devaluing or obviating the presence of competing voices—thereby devaluing or obviating the carnivalistic urge as well.

A number of Hitchcock films demonstrate that carnivalism and dialogism need not function as a team, however, and that a profoundly monologic filmmaker can nurture a strong predilection for the grotesque, the indecorous, and the carnivalistic. It must be stressed that Hitchcock's carnivalism is not usually manifested through genuine merriment or festivity on the part of his characters. His is a morbid and dystopian carnivalism—more Halloween than Mardi Gras, in one critic's phrase—suffused with a darkness that reveals not only his own psychological proclivities but the relative weakness of English carnival traditions in general, with their burden of inhibited thought and behavior rooted in puritanism, Victorianism, and other such belief systems. Nor does Hitchcock appear to have a political agenda in mind; his propensities for undermining authority and celebrating impropriety seem motivated more by a sense of aesthetic mischief-making than by a purposefully antiauthoritarian spirit. Still, he excels as a carnivalizer, primarily in the attitude he shows toward classical cinema itself, which he subverts and denormalizes with surprising frequency.

After a look at Hitchcock's proclivity for monologic cinema—a proclivity that makes his carnivalism all the more startling—this essay will examine three Hitchcock films from three different decades for evidence of his carnivalizing impulses. Other films could have been chosen, including *The 39 Steps*, with its elements of vaudeville and the picaresque; *Shadow of a Doubt*, with its Uncle Charlie masquerade; *Strangers on a Train*, with its climactic amusement-park scene; *To Catch a Thief*, with its narrative puns on familiar genres; and so forth. The three selected here are not unique in their propensities, but show Hitchcock operating with particular vigor in his richest and strangest carnivalizing mode.

Bakhtin's emphasis on dialogism and carnivalism marks him as a champion of the diverse, the heterogeneous, the polymorphous, and—in his celebration of, for example, François Rabelais's extravagant gustatory and scatological fantasies—the perverse. Hitchcock, by contrast, is known as one of world cinema's most notoriously controlling personalities, attempting to govern every aspect of his films by means of meticulous preproduction planning, and treating his performers not as sources of free-flowing expressivity but as "cattle" whose inclinations toward spontaneity and inventiveness must be rigorously channeled and contained.

Yet the very tenacity of Hitchcock's control strategies may indicate the presence of precisely opposite tendencies within his artistic personality—tendencies toward the uncontrolled impulse, the unplanned urge, the anarchically unstructured thought and deed—which he felt impelled to suppress and counteract. These tendencies point toward a Bakhtinian preoccupation with the carnivalesque, the grotesque, the indecorous, the socially "improper" and culturally "inverted" spectacle. The presence of such tendencies is confirmed by Hitchcock's private life, where they evaded repression to a degree; he was an inveterate practical joker whose pranks sometimes transgressed all bounds of "good taste."

Hitchcock's insistence on control within his work nonetheless situates his *oeuvre* a great distance from Bakhtinian ideals of novelistic heteroglossia and dialogic visual/verbal complexity. It is characteristic of monistic (or idealist) ideology, Bakhtin suggests, to foster an environment wherein "the unity of consciousness, replacing the unity of existence, is inevitably transformed into the unity of a single consciousness."[1] In such an environment of "philosophical monologism," he adds slightly later, "the genuine interaction of consciousnesses is impossible, and thus genuine dialogue is impossible as well."[2] Hitchcock may readily be seen as a monologic artist in these terms. Following common cinematic practice, his films construct narratives in which many individuals, each with a unique consciousness, are depicted as existing alongside one another; yet these individuals/consciousnesses are inscribed through the monologic medium of Hitchcock's own all-controlling consciousness, which—in addition to shaping the diegesis itself, often with surprisingly self-reflexive overtness—frequently asserts its presence within the film through a hero or heroine who serves as surrogate for the filmmaker's unified and unifying perspective.

Even within the narrative worlds of such films as *Lifeboat* and *Rear Window,* which are clearly intended as microcosms of a large and diverse sociocultural "reality," the multiplicity of characters cannot be said to provide a truly dialogical quality, since the heteroglossia that might potentially characterize the coexistence of so many consciousnesses has been muted by their passage through Hitchcock's monologizing sensibility. This process takes different forms in different films. In some, including *Rear Window,* the protagonist serves as a dominating consciousness or "filter" through which all other consciousnesses are refracted and monologized on their way to the spectator's perception. In others, the "unified accent"[3] is imposed by evocation of a "special symbol"—in *Lifeboat* the assertive "voice" or "spirit" of American bourgeois values, in relation to which every character is implicitly viewed and assessed—that "joins and personifies"[4] what might in different circumstances be perceived as truly individual consciousnesses.

Hitchcock's consistency in monologizing his narratives displaces his work from the realms of heteroglossia and dialogism that Bakhtin's theory celebrates; yet his practice is consistent with his own worldview and cinematic vision. Hitchcock's narratives are predicated largely on physical, psychological, and moral conflicts between order and chaos, inscribed in a medium that itself partakes of a fundamental order-chaos ambiguity insofar as it constitutes, in Christian Metz's terms, a "language" without an embedded "language system" to provide a structurally consistent basis for articulative choices. Given the insecurity *vis-à-vis* order and chaos that pervades Hitchcock's *Weltanschauung*—reflected persistently in his work, wherein order often triumphs only uncertainly and belatedly over chaos— his monologizing tendency may be seen as a response to deeply rooted fears of heteroglossia and its potentially turbulent polyphony of different voices, languages, "contradictory opinions, points of view and value judgments."[5] Faced with the possibility of such turbulence, Hitchcock seeks a reassuring, albeit limiting, sense of structural certainty in a monologic "unity of viewpoint" that allows him to "weld into one both the most formal elements of style and the most abstract philosophical deductions."[6] Thus the unification of style, subject matter, and sensibility that often characterizes Hitchcock's work, and for which his work has frequently been praised, may be seen as a counterbalance to uncertainties and anxieties raised by the subjects of his narratives and images, often morbid or sinister in nature—and by the dialogic possibilities of cinema itself, which lead the filmmaker to impose monologic containment (and reductiveness) on what might otherwise emerge as polyphonic complexity (and open-endedness).

As suggested earlier, if it is true that monologue "closes down the represented world and represented persons,"[7] while contrastingly "there are no limits to the dialogic context,"[8] then monologism might be considered antipathetic to the expansive, uncontained, and relativistic nature of carnivalesque activity, while dialogism invites and encourages those qualities. Despite its monologic thrust, however, Hitchcock's work shows a vigorous urge toward the carnivalistic—most clearly in its relation to classical cinematic practice, which is a primary object of Hitchcock's impulse to invert, subvert, relativize, and parody.

Hitchcock's destabilizations may take ingenious forms. Consider a moment in *Notorious*, for example. Having stolen a key from Claude Rains, who now wants to kiss the hand holding it, Ingrid Bergman throws her arms around Rains's neck, lets the key fall behind his back, and uses her foot to push it under a chair. Robin Wood accurately notes that, were it filmed in an Otto Preminger-style single take from across the room, "this simple action would be ludicrously implausible: Bergman would first have to crane her neck over Rains's shoulder to see where the key had fallen (and, short as the actor was, this would involve some craning); she would then have to wrap one leg round his body to maneuver her foot into position, then move the foot several inches to conceal the key (which would not be very effectively concealed anyway)—and all this, of course, without Rains's noticing."[9] Wood, who cites this moment as an example of Hitchcockian spatial deception through editing, is correct in doubting that spectators caught up in the scene are likely to question its plausibility. Yet the filmmaker is here constructing a Bakhtinian grotesque body—a body with proportions, properties, and abilities of a nature not quite human, built through montage practices and existing only "in the cracks" of the film's ostensibly uninterrupted and "realistic" narrative flow. What is implausible in human terms—and would be equally so in certain cinematic terms, such as those of the single-take long shot—is entirely plausible in terms of Hitchcockian montage, which here constructs a grotesquerie so slyly naturalized as to pass unnoticed (that is, unnoticed as a grotesquerie) and be fully accepted by the spectator.

This violation of actual-world "realism" does not transgress norms of diegetic "realism," since the signified that it constructs in the spectatorial imagination does indeed seem plausible—at the moment of perception, if not during subsequent reflection—in real-world terms. That is, the spectator perceives the series of gestures and operations (protagonist dropping key, hiding key, deceiving antagonist) as a unified event that could indeed take place in noncinematic terms. Other violations of real-world possibility in Hitchcock may take more radical forms—in *Rope* for example, which leads the (characteristically) unreflective spectator to accept the sequential occurrence of a murder, a dinner party, the return of a guest, and the unraveling of the crime all within the space of some eighty minutes of action filmed in a "real time" technique. This is a most audacious chronotope indeed, to employ another Bakhtinian term.

Not all of Hitchcock's destabilizing and norm-breaching practices are undertaken in the service of narrative effectiveness and efficiency, moreover. Many can be seen as deliberate carnivalizing gestures aimed at reveling in grotesquerie, inverting social conventions, assembling "improper" combinations of image, activity, and word, fetishizing what Bakhtin calls "the material bodily lower stratum," and gleefully undermining decorum—not only that of characters within the films, but also (and crucially) that of Hollywood cinema itself.

Rope (1948) provides an excellent instance of such practice. Bakhtin observes that Rabelaisian laughter (a phenomenon steeped in the carnivalesque) serves as a mechanism for bringing out "the crude, unmediated connections between things that people otherwise seek to keep separate, in pharisaical error." To accomplish this linking function, Rabelais employs "the construction of series . . . of the most varied types, which are at times parallel to each other and at times intersect with each other." [10] The seven series in Rabelais's novel are those of "the human body in its anatomical and physiological aspects," clothing, food, drink and drunkenness, the sexual or copulatory, death, and defecation.

While there is no reason to posit a point-by-point relationship between Hitchcock and Rabelais, it is noteworthy that all seven of these series have a significant presence in *Rope*. The least important is the clothing series, although even here one may observe the irony of the socially "correct" clothing worn by the murderers as well as their guests—an irony that is underscored when suspicious Rupert finds a major clue to the murder in a hat left behind by the victim. [11] More important is the drinking-and-drunkenness series, since alcohol plays an important role in weakening the nerves of Philip, one of the murderers, and hence in alerting Rupert to the possibility of foul play. [12]

Still more important are the other five series, not only in themselves and in their parallel presences, but in the ways they intersect—often in an "improper," even provocative manner—during the film. The narrative begins with a close-up of a man dying (the anatomical/physiological human body series), and his corpse (the death series) will be a dominant, if unseen, presence throughout the film even though much of the narrative is ostensibly devoted to a commonplace social gathering. Dinner is served (the food series) from a trunk containing the corpse, and people eat while discussing the victim's activities and personality. The men who killed him and provided the dinner are apparently meant to be seen as homosexuals (the sex series) and their murderousness as a metonymic extension of gay perversity. [13] The defecation series makes its appearance most subtly, through anal implications that may be drawn from the murderers' homosexuality and through what may be the film's most-discussed and least-understood mechanism: the "hidden" splices that link the film's long takes on several occasions, most frequently by traveling into an extreme close-up of a male character's backside.[14] The presence of these Rabelaisian/Bakhtinian series and their various intersections in *Rope* indicate Hitchcock's interest in a certain kind of carnivalizing activity. We may say of Hitchcock, as Bakhtin said of Rabelais when discussing his use of absurd compound words and other bizarre verbal formulations, that "it must not be thought that [he] is preoccupied with form alone," but that he also aims "at destroying the established hierarchy of values, at bringing down the high and raising up the low, at destroying every nook and cranny of the habitual picture of the world," meanwhile seeking "to embody the world, to materialize it, to tie everything in to spatial and temporal series, to measure everything on the scale of the human body, to construct—on that space where the destroyed picture of the world had been—a new picture."[15]

Hitchcock's way of humbling the high and elevating the low relates not only to the Judeo-Christian tradition of imposing a form of ultimate justice on characters but also, and more interestingly, to a carnivalistic preoccupation with inverting the proprieties of mainstream cinema. He accomplishes this by "embodying" and "materializing" parts of life traditionally elided in Hollywood film (e.g., gay men and their backsides) and by employing series that, "gravitating toward the human being as 'body,' carry out . . . a disunification of what had been traditionally linked and a bringing together of what had been hierarchically disunified and distant, serving to bring about, therefore, the materialization of the world."[16] The linking of food and death reaches scandalous heights in *Rope*—there were calls in some American cities for the film to be banned[17]—as do less obvious linkages of various sorts: death and (homo)sexuality, for example, as Philip and Brandon kill their victim from behind and then discuss how they "felt" when he "went limp." Throughout these maneuvers one senses Hitchcock's mischievous insistence on concocting diegetic oxymorons, laughing at death, stressing the lower bodily stratum, and subverting the decorum of traditionally accepted movie content.

This does not exhaust the catalogue of carnivalizing practices in *Rope*. To cite another, the actions of Philip and Brandon constitute a deliberately risky "gamble" that might result in their exposure and destruction at any moment, recalling Bakhtin's suggestion that gambling is "by nature carnivalistic," that symbols of gambling have long been "part of the image system of carnival symbols," and that gambling provides "an atmosphere of sudden and quick changes of fate, of instantaneous rises and falls, that is, of crownings/decrownings" wherein "a person feels himself on *the threshold.*"[18] Philip and Brandon are on such a threshold during all of *Rope,* to be abruptly decrowned in the climax and denouement. To the extent that the spectator shares their suspense, moreover, the presence in gambling of a "special time," whereby "a minute is equal to years,"[19] may help explain the ability of *Rope* to sustain the highly nonrealistic chronotope mentioned above.

Bakhtinian theory may be deployed in discussing other aspects of *Rope* as well. The appropriation of Rupert's words (i.e., his quasi-Nietzschean theorizing) by Philip and Brandon points toward a whole realm of Bakhtinian concepts regarding language as a social phenomenon that "lies on the borderline between oneself and the other" and wherein the word is always "half someone else's."[20] The conspicuous double-voicedness of Philip's and Brandon's public remarks about their victim, of whose death they alone are aware, recalls—with bitter irony—Bakhtin's observation that the dead "are removed from the sphere of contact, one can and must speak of them in a different style. Language about the dead is stylistically quite distinct from language about the living."[21] Even in these areas, which are not directly carnivalesque, Hitchcock does some carnivalizing: Philip and Brandon do not just appropriate but brutally "<u>materialize</u>" the philosophical words that Rupert has "abstractly" made available to them, and the killers' smirking comments about their victim constitute some of the movie's most obvious jokes.

It is important to stress, however, that the laughter of such Hitchcockian jokes and ironies is rarely robust or cleansing. It acquires its Rabelaisian quality in that it "simultaneously denies and asserts,"[22] and what it asserts is profoundly ambivalent. Through such laughter and irony—the latter being "a form of reduced laughter,"[23] in Bakhtin's view—Hitchcock echoes the Rabelaisian practice of carnivalizing through linkage, in that "the very tone of this laughter shows that two opposite principles can be put together even in form."[24] *Rope* is an exercise in carnivalizing of the darkest sort, but carnivalizing nevertheless.

Psycho (1960) is the lower-bodily-stratum film par excellence of Hitchcock's career, and hence his most extravagant act of carnivalization via the subversion of Hollywood norms in particular and American-bourgeois norms in general.

Here we find Hitchcock indulging one of his favorite habits, that of situating violence and horror not in gothic gloom and shadow but in the most mundane setting imaginable, in this case a painfully ordinary motel on an underused Southwest highway. Thus does Hitchcock vent "the impulse to introduce the extraordinary into the very thick of the commonplace . . . and by an imperceptible process of conversion to push images and phenomena of everyday reality to the limits of the fantastic."[25] Like some social-adventure novels of the nineteenth century that Bakhtin cites, Hitchcock films may largely lack a "deep and free carnival sense of the world" in terms of gaiety and mirth.[26] Yet such a work as *Psycho* indeed manifests "an application of carnivalization to the portrayal of contemporary reality and contemporary everyday life; *everyday life* is drawn into the carnivalized action of the plot; the ordinary and constant is combined with the extraordinary and changeable."[27] Although it became notorious for its most extravagant elements, such as the extreme violence and kineticism of the shower-murder scene, Hitchcock carnivalistically labeled the film a comedy.[28] In its very outrageousness, *Psycho* recalls Bakhtin's suggestion that "Hyperbole is always festive (including abusive hyperbole)."[29] *Psycho* signals its carnivalesque preoccupations right away, announcing that the story will take place in Phoenix, a city named for a mythical bird that is (re)born from the ashes of its own death. One thinks immediately of the Bakhtinian grotesque body, in which "death brings nothing to an end."[30] The lower bodily stratum enters the picture as we enter the hotel room where Marion and Sam have had their tryst, and where the bathroom is dimly visible in the background as the camera makes its way toward the couple's bed; soon afterward, we will see the bathroom of Marion's own home as she prepares to flee with her stolen money. The defecation series is joined by the food series as we see Marion's uneaten lunch and hear numerous food references (plus one to licking postage stamps) in the dialogue.

Psycho is largely about anal activity, treated metaphorically, and its first symbol for excrement is money—specifically the forty-thousand dollars produced in the real-estate office by a childish (anal-sadistic) client who obnoxiously shows off what he has "made."[31] Again dialogue conjures up the lower bodily stratum—such words as "irregular" and "private" enter the conversation—and even the names point in this direction: *Lowery* speaks for itself, while *Cassidy* echoes Marion's remark that her behavior gives "excess [stomach] *acid*" to her boss. Such wordplay contributes yet another carnivalistic element to the film. The cash resembles excrement in that it is a normal object that becomes objectionable by being out of place, and

Lowery wants it removed to a proper receptacle, out of sight and mind. Marion retains it, however, removing it from Phoenix in her purse.[32] Among the imagined voices that resonate in her mind during her flight is that of Cassidy saying, "She sat there while I dumped it out," referring to his money in plainly excremental terms.

At the dealership where she replaces her car, Marion handles her illicitly carried material in a lavatory. During the same portion of the film we see (in close-up) the license plate of her original car: ANL-709, the letters virtually spelling out the film's most important symbolic key. This moment confirms the suggestions of lower-bodily preoccupation that have preceded it.[33]

Anality and sexuality continue their intersection as Norman proves unable to utter the word "bathroom" in Marion's presence, and as Mrs. Bates delivers an overheard harangue that refers to food, sexual appetite, and her son's "guts." Most striking of all the lower-bodily allusions during the motel portion of the film is Marion's disposal of ripped-up paper by flushing it down a toilet, which Hitchcock shows (complete with paper pieces floating in the bowl) in a full-screen close-up; she then removes her bathrobe as the toilet noisily finishes its flush. The toilet bowl is clearly echoed in subsequent close-ups of Marion's dead eye after the murder; the bathtub drain with water and blood being "flushed" away through its opening; the bathroom-sink drain as Norman cleans up after the crime; and (most hyperbolically) the swamp, itself a huge "toilet" overflowing with awful-looking stuff. Other lower-bodily references in the film's midsection include Norman's cry of "Mother . . . Blood! Blood!" which reminds us that much of *Psycho* can be read menstrually as well as excrementally; and the imposing presence of the phallic shower head during much of the murder scene.

Marion gives way to Norman as protagonist during the second portion of *Psycho,* and Marion's furtively retained money (now flushed down the swamp-toilet just as her scratch paper was flushed down the motel-toilet) relinquishes its role as the film's symbolically charged excremental material. What takes over in its place is something that *Norman* has furtively retained: his mother's corpse, which he has refused to dispose of in a socially approved way (out of sight and mind), just as Marion refused to deposit the bundle of cash. Arbogast, the detective, is the first character to draw near this forbidden object, showing his own anal-obsessive attentiveness when searching the motel office before meeting a fate similar to Marion's death. Unsettled by his unexpected visitors, Norman moves his treasure to the fruit cellar, bringing about a vivid intersection of the film's food series and death series via the fruit-cellar associations of ripening and decay. The camera dwells on his buttocks as he climbs the stairs to fetch his forbidden object. Remaining lower-bodily signifiers in this part of the film include a search of Marion's bathroom, the discovery of Mrs. Bates in the "bowels" of the house, and society's disposal of Norman by depositing him in a receptacle—the box-like room where his final soliloquy is delivered—that hyperbolizes the sort of repository (safety-deposit box, grave) in which the film's excrementally symbolic objects should "properly" have been placed earlier.

The excremental series in *Psycho* is worked out with great consistency, and constitutes what is probably the most flamboyant carnivalizing device in Hitchcock's *oeuvre*—in its obsessive fascination with the lower bodily stratum, and in the success with which it brings this fascination to the Hollywood screen, still under the domination of strong censorship forces at the time of the film's release. *Psycho* is a deliberate exercise in carnivalizing the Hollywood cinema. Its inclusion of a full-screen close-up of a toilet, an everyday object that had hitherto been rigorously excluded from mainstream American movies, is an overt example of this carnivalization. The close-up of the ANL-709 license plate (and our view of Marion's subsequent NFB license plate, squeezing an F—perhaps for Female—between Norman's initials) is another, putting to ingenious use the inherently polysemic nature of all initials, which inevitably (and dialogically) suggest a destabilizing plenitude of possibilities. Further examples include the death of the ostensible protagonist, Marion, around the midpoint of the film, in direct violation of "correct" scenario development; and more complex structural/symbolic elements such as the film's inclusion of three mutually referential searches wherein characters nose around (almost like animals) in quests related to lower-bodily-symbolic objects: (1) Marion's search for a place to hide her cash in the motel room; (2) the exploration of the corpse-containing house by Sam and Lila; and between these (3) Arbogast's search for the place where Marion was "flushed" out of the diegesis, which takes him to a number of motels in a classical-style montage that condenses various times and places into a concise chronotope that "echoes" the compactly located cabin and house where the other searches take place.

Psycho also contains elements as carnivalesque—and indecorous, by Hollywood standards—as transvestism (Norman masquerades in his mother's clothing), situational oxymorons (e.g., the sheriff's wife invites Sam and Lila to file a missing-person report over dinner), cinematic antigrammaticality (e.g., Marion's death occurs at a "wrong" place within the film's narrative structure), parody (e.g., Norman's imitation of a doting, restrictive mother), and a species of Bakhtinian relativity rooted in the fact that

Norman has thoroughly confused everyone in the film, including himself, over such seemingly simple matters as his own gender and various questions of who's alive, who's dead, and who's buried in the local cemetery.

Once again, it should be emphasized that *Psycho* is rarely carnivalistic in the sense of depicting festive behavior or building a mood of carnival freedom, gaiety, and so on, unless one accepts under this categorization such a morbid and perverse activity as Norman's voyeurism. Yet the film is deeply carnivalesque in its inversion of "correct" cinematic practice, beginning with Hitchcock's decision to treat such a violent narrative as a "comedy" in the first place. During preproduction, Hitchcock toyed with the idea of telling the entire story from a "fly's eye view," much as *The Birds* is told (in some respects) from a bird's-eye perspective.[34] Although this plan was carried out only in part, the opening crane shot indeed carries us into the hotel room with fly-like ease—a trope that puts the spectator in the position of a voyeuristic insect, and thus "uncrowns" the ticket-buying customers whom commercial films normally strive to seduce and flatter.

Psycho reveals still more carnivalesque features when examined in light of the comic tradition rooted in Menippean satire. Bakhtin identifies this ancient genre, dating back at least to the third century B.C., as "one of the main carriers and channels for the carnival sense of the world."[35] Although not every fundamental Menippean characteristic is present in the film, some of its tropes—e.g., the fly's-eye-view opening and the overhead shot of Norman carrying the corpse—recall Menippean "observation from some unusual point of view, from on high, for example." Also evident is "representation of the unusual, abnormal moral and psychic states of man—insanity of all sorts (the theme of the maniac), split personality, unrestrained daydreaming, unusual dreams, passions bordering on madness," not to mention "scandal scenes, eccentric behavior, inappropriate speeches and performances."[36] One quickly recognizes Norman's insanity, Marion's voice-over daydreaming, and other elements of *Psycho* in these phrases. The notion of "split personality" also recalls the film's frequent use of mirrors and frame-dividing objects to suggest "splits" in the diegetic world and in the consciousnesses that it contains. If we accept the hotel and motel as somewhat painful in their drab ordinariness, we may also find echoes of the "crude *slum naturalism*" that Menippea combines with such elements as "the free fantastic" and "the symbolic."[37] We may even find in *Psycho* a latter-day manifestation of the death-linked "threshold dialogue,"[38] to the extent that the Bates Motel—where Marion engages in soul-searching and life-questioning conversation shortly before her demise—is a "netherworld" in the depopulated void between Phoenix and Fairvale.

Of special relevance to *Psycho* is the evocative sense of grotesque-body fecundity that Bakhtin celebrates in relation to the carnivalesque—a sense of the old and decayed joyfully yielding up the new and uncontained, as when a laughing old woman dies in giving birth to her offspring. *Psycho* recuperates this image in strange and resonant ways. The relationship between Norman and Mrs. Bates is that of the offspring who refuses to allow the critical moment of birth-separation to pass, but seeks to retain or regain it forever. This takes place on a mental level (within Norman's consciousness) that seeks to substitute its own construction for the physical level of real in-the-world activity. "Just as the body is formed initially in the mother's womb (body)," Bakhtin suggests, "a person's consciousness awakens wrapped in another's consciousness."[39] In his desperation to recapture the "wrapping" of his mother's consciousness, Norman recreates her thoughts in his mental activity; recreates her appearance and movements in his physical activity; and recreates her words in both—intermittently during most of the narrative, but apparently on a permanent basis following his valedictory voice-over soliloquy. This is followed by the appearance over Norman's face of a death's-head image, presumably his mother's skull, in a moment that doesn't quite fit any Metzian definition of conventional superimposition or dissolve.[40] Norman smiles—reunited at last with the undifferentiated Other whose absent presence has been such a dominant part of his life—and the death's-head matches his grin, doubly carnivalizing the image. This is followed by the film's final shot, of Marion's car being hauled (rear first) from the swamp. One tail-light gazes at us in a dour echo of Marion's dead eye and all the film's anus-like empty circles; the car itself, with its load of corpse and cash, is connected by an umbilical cable to the camera's position and the spectator's gaze. The toilet-swamp of extinction becomes a resurrection-site of birth, in a final carnivalesque image of death-in-life and life-in-death.

"In living carnival images," Bakhtin suggests, "death itself is pregnant and gives birth, and the mother's womb giving birth becomes a grave. Precisely such images are produced by creative ambivalent carnival laughter, in which mockery and triumph, praise and abuse are inseparably fused."[41] All these elements are present at the end of *Psycho*—in the final merging of mother and Norman, death and reincarnation, toilet/grave and swamp/birthplace—aiming their collective ambivalence and Hitchcockian laughter at Hollywood cinema and all it represents. Resembling the phoenix invoked in the narrative's opening moments, moreover, the film ends by resisting its own termination—as if its eschewal of a conventional concluding scene were a nod to Bakhtin's dictum that "the carnival sense of the world . . . knows no period, and is, in fact, hostile to any sort of *conclusive conclusion*: all endings are merely new beginnings: carnival images are re-born again and again."[42]

Frenzy (1972) shows the persistence of carnivalizing impulses into the last phases of Hitchcock's career. Among its carnivalesque elements is one shared by *Rope* and *Psycho* as well as other Hitchcock films: the doubling of important characters. Not all *doppelgänger* stories are necessarily carni-valesque, of course, but the practice of doubling has ludic possibilities that Hitchcock exploits (often with his habitually dark inflection) many times in his work.

"All the images of carnival are dualistic; they unite within themselves both poles of change and crisis," observes Bakhtin, adding that "paired im-ages" such as twins and doubles—related to parody, which is itself linked to "the creation of a *decrowning double*" and the notion of an inside-out world—are very characteristic of carnival thinking.[43] *Frenzy* doubles its dark-haired hero with a blond-haired villain. The former is an innocent man whose bad temper and drinking, coupled with bad luck and circum-stantial evidence, get him convicted of rape and murder; the latter is a vi-cious psychopath whose likable demeanor, closeness with his mother, and other "respectable" qualities almost enable him to escape detection and continue his serial crimes. Their close relation connects the film to *Rope*, wherein Philip and Brandon double each other and both serve as inverted images of Rupert—evil instead of good, practice instead of theory, and so on—and to *Psycho*, wherein Sam and Lila are deliberately pallid doubles of Norman and Marion.

In each of these cases, Hitchcock uses doubling to explore characteris-tic "Hitchcockian" themes, particularly the ambiguity of good and evil and the transference of guilt and innocence. In the uncertainty, instability, and ambivalence that they evoke, such themes are clearly carnivalistic, especially when juxtaposed with the certainties of more formulaic specimens of Hol-lywood cinema. Hitchcock also constructs doublings not only of characters but of incidents, images, and so on. There are two murders in both *Psycho* and *Frenzy,* with the first murder depicted in far more detail—and providing a far more explicit grotesque-body image—than the second. *Frenzy* doubles the woman-in-potato-sack with a potato sack that passes before the camera during her murder. Norman's knife is doubled by Marion's wiper blades; the spinning hotel-room fan is doubled by a switched-off fan in the psychiatrist scene; each of these pairs doubles the other. And so forth.

Another strong example of carnivalization in *Frenzy* is its combination of the sexual series with the food series and the death series. We have already noted the carnivalistic practice of effecting "a disunification of what had been traditionally linked and a bringing together of what had been hier-archically disunified and distant."[44] This two-pronged operation contrasts strongly with the single-minded "project of separation"[45] from the female body that, according to Julia Kristeva, is engaged in by "patriarchal sym-bolic systems,"[46] and includes dietary prohibitions, the prohibition of incest on which these are based, and fear of "the maternal as unclean and im-proper coalescence, as undifferentiated power to be cut off."[47] The potency of undifferentiated maternal power within Hitchcock's psychic scheme, and the threat of malign coalescence posed by this power, has been amply demonstrated by Norman Bates's fate. The carnivalistic qualities of *Psy-cho*—grotesquerie, impropriety, relativity—arise in part from the fact that Norman does not *flee* but actually *courts* the domination of this power and its accompanying dangers, seeking to *bring together* that which is "prop-erly" (in life and "proper" cinema) disunified—this being, in the present instance, what Tania Modleski calls "female body and male law."[48]

A similar operation subtends *Frenzy*, wherein the "bringing together" is effected through a cannibalistic linkage of male voracity, food, and the female body. On one level, *Frenzy* may be said to carnivalize *Psycho* by inverting its devouring female, who "consumes" her son, via the trope of devouring males: the murderous psychopath who deals in foodstuffs and brackets a rape-murder with hungry bites from an apple,[49] and the police inspector who eats grotesque meals associated with the female body (e.g., an image-dialogue combination explicitly likens bread sticks to female fin-gers). On a broader level, *Frenzy* carnivalizes mainstream cinematic practice in general, by linking sexuality with cannibalism through its flamboyant combining of series that are normally separated. On a still broader level, it carnivalizes bourgeois social practice in a grand way, by evoking canni-balism and by making overt a more widespread phenomenon that is not acknowledged in "polite" company—what Claude Lévi-Strauss identifies as a "very profound analogy which people throughout the world seem to find between copulation and eating," activities that "are even called by the same term" in many languages.[50]

All these operations within the film are related to the carnival metaphor, which joins the cannibal metaphor in evoking "a kind of dissolving of the boundaries of self through the physical or spiritual commingling of self and other," to use Robert Stam's phrase.[51] As all the films discussed here demonstrate, Hitchcock's view of the possibilities of such "commingling" are richly ambivalent and heroically grotesque. And an even more riotous commingling takes place when other series enter the fray—the defecation series, for instance, already noted in *Rope* and *Psycho* and assertively present in *Frenzy* when (among other instances) the villain extricates a corpse from a sack of feces-like potatoes in what Modleski has carnivalistically called "a kind of macabre striptease."[52] Many other instances of carnivalism could be cited from these and other Hitchcock films. Although his art differs in profound ways from that of Dostoevsky, whose work impressed Bakhtin deeply, Hitchcock too constructs a world in which everything "lives on the very border of its opposite."[53] Writing about "the structural characteristics of the carnival image," Bakhtin asserts that "it strives to encompass and unite within itself both poles of becoming or both poles of an antithesis: birth-death, youth-old age, top-bottom, face-backside, praise-abuse, affirmation-repudiation, tragic-comic, and so forth, while the upper pole of a two-in-one image is reflected in the lower, after the manner of the figures on playing cards. It could be expressed this way: opposites come together, look at one another, are reflected in one another, know and understand one another."[54] Hitchcock accomplishes such acts of encompassing, uniting, reflecting, knowing, and understanding in a monologic manner; his consciousness, and the consciousnesses of his diegetic surrogates, tend to dominate others that might in different circumstances project individualized voices into a dialogic polyphony. Yet the carnivalistic qualities of these acts ring out clearly, complexly, and—on an aesthetic level, if not a political one—subversively. The conventions and commonplaces of standard Hollywood cinema are Hitchcock's prime targets, along with audiences who unquestioningly accept that cinema. Like the grotesque body that his films often graphically portray, his achievements in such works as *Rope*, *Psycho*, and *Frenzy* generate life, hope, and humor even as they depict the dead, the decadent, and the decayed.[55]

NOTES

1. Mikhail Bakhtin, *Problems of Dostoevsky's Poetics*, trans. Caryl Emerson (Minneapolis: University of Minnesota Press, 1984), 80–81.

2. Bakhtin, *Problems of Dostoevsky's Poetics*, 81.

3. Bakhtin, *Problems of Dostoevsky's Poetics*, 82.

4. M. M. Bakhtin, "Toward a Methodology for the Human Sciences," in *Speech Genres and Other Late Essays*, trans. Vern W. McGee (Austin: University of Texas Press, 1986), 163. Bakhtin uses the word "voice" when referring to such "symbols" in this essay, as in "the voice of life itself" and "the voice of the people." He uses the

word "spirit," as in "the spirit of a nation" and "the spirit of a people," when making essentially the same point in *Problems of Dostoevsky's Poetics*.

5. M. M. Bakhtin, "Discourse in the Novel," in *The Dialogic Imagination: Four Essays,* trans. Caryl Emerson and Michael Holquist (Austin: University of Texas Press, 1981), 281.

6. Bakhtin, *Problems of Dostoevsky's Poetics,* 83.

7. Bakhtin, *Problems of Dostoevsky's Poetics,* 293.

8. Bakhtin, "Toward a Methodology," 170.

9. Robin Wood, *Hitchcock's Films Revisited* (New York: Columbia University Press, 1989), 210–11.

10. Bakhtin, "Forms of Time and of the Chronotope in the Novel: Notes toward a Historical Poetics," in *The Dialogic Imagination,* 170.

11. The clothing series is more apparent in Hitchcock's film than in its source text, *Rope: A Play* by Patrick Hamilton, wherein the clue consists of a ticket that belonged to the dead man and is handled very differently from the hat in the film. Hitchcock's replacement of a ticket with a hat not only underscores the presence in his film of the clothing series—indeed a series since the hat joins a syntagma of proper middle-class clothing worn throughout the film—but establishes a subtly scatological "rhyme" between this object (given a pot-like appearance by its inverted position during the key close-up devoted to it) and the anal allusions that are rife within *Rope*.

12. Also in the realm of alcohol, Wood suggests that the team effort of Philip and Brandon in opening a champagne bottle near the beginning of the film provides a clue to their private sexual practice, i.e., masturbation.

13. Note that within Hollywood discourse, as within American culture in general, a small degree of homosexual inscription may be said to mark characters as sexual beings more emphatically than would a similarly minimal inscription of heterosexuality. Note also that while Hitchcock reduces the degree of gay signification found in Hamilton's play—eliminating some particularly suggestive dialogue, for instance, and a bit of male physical horseplay—he increases it near the end of the narrative, replacing Rupert's blowing of a police whistle (in the play) with the firing of a revolver, which suggests erection and ejaculation as Rupert extends his arm, penetrates the window's open space, and shoots. None of this is to suggest that Hitchcock's treatments of homosexuality are unproblematic, however. Wood calls appropriate attention to this issue by giving a chapter in *Hitchcock's Films Revisited* the punning title of "The Murderous Gays: Hitchcock's Homophobia." For all his carnivalization and even subversion of Hollywood cinematic norms, Hitchcock seems to have cared little about putting such practices at the service of larger social/cultural/political goals, such as raising the level of Hollywood discourse *vis-à-vis* homosexuality.

14. For a useful discussion of this trope, see D. A. Miller, "Anal *Rope*," *Representations* 32 (1990): 114–33.

15. Bakhtin, "Forms of Time and of the Chronotope in the Novel," 177.

16. Bakhtin, "Forms of Time and of the Chronotope in the Novel," 193.

17. Chicago and Seattle were the censorious cities. See Leonard J. Leff, *Hitchcock and Selznick: The Rich and Strange Collaboration of Alfred Hitchcock and David O. Selznick in Hollywood* (New York: Weidenfeld and Nicolson, 1987), 273.

18. Bakhtin, *Problems of Dostoevsky's Poetics,* 171 (emphasis in original). The crowning-and-decrowning of a mock king is one of Bakhtin's favorite symbols for the traditional carnival and its extension into other forms of activity.

19. Bakhtin, *Problems of Dostoevsky's Poetics,* 171.

20. Bakhtin, "Discourse in the Novel," 293.

21. Bakhtin, "Epic and Novel: Toward a Methodology for the Study of the Novel," in *The Dialogic Imagination,* 20.

22. Mikhail Bakhtin, *Rabelais and His World,* trans. Helene Iswolsky (Bloomington: Indiana University Press, 1984), 142. Bakhtin is quoting L. E. Pinsky.

23. Bakhtin, *Rabelais and His World,* 135.

24. Bakhtin, *Rabelais and His World,* 142. Bakhtin is still quoting Pinsky.

25. Bakhtin, *Problems of Dostoevsky's Poetics,* 103. Bakhtin is quoting Leonid Grossman, with whom he fundamentally agrees while pointing out that Grossman's analysis does not exhaust the matter.

26. Bakhtin, *Problems of Dostoevsky's Poetics,* 158.

27. Bakhtin, *Problems of Dostoevsky's Poetics,* 158 (emphasis in original).

28. Interview with David Sterritt, Boston, 1972.

29. Bakhtin, "From Notes Made in 1970–71," in *Speech Genres and Other Late Essays,* 154.

30. Bakhtin, *Rabelais and His World,* 322.

31. Money serves a similar purpose in Hitchcock's earlier *Shadow of a Doubt,* wherein Uncle Charlie's abnormality and lack of control are first indicated by cash immodestly spilling off his table and onto the floor. Later he criticizes his murder victims for having (almost literally) consumed their husbands' earnings, "drinking the money, eating the money." Again we see the intersection of a money series and a food/lower-bodily-stratum series. Note also in *Psycho* that Hitchcock makes his trademark cameo appearance just before we see Cassidy for the first time, and that the men look similar to each other, both being portly and wearing cowboy hats—an indication that Hitchcock is poking carnivalesque fun at himself through the Cassidy character. Hitchcock's practice of making walk-on appearances in his films is itself a strikingly carnivalesque gesture, of course, running through almost his entire *oeuvre.*

32. See the opening shot of Hitchcock's later *Marnie* for a vivid demonstration

of his interest in purses as symbolic objects charged with lower-bodily-stratum fascination.

33. The second half of the ANL-709 license plate presents an anus-like zero cushioned between buttock-like digits on either side. Along with its anal symbolism, the zero constitutes the first portion of a macabre visual rhyme that will be continued in the toilet close-up and completed at the film's climax when Mrs. Bates's empty eye sockets swing into view. Such eye sockets have a special fascination for Hitchcock during this period of his career, continuing in *The Birds,* his next movie. Although eyes are located physically on the upper bodily stratum, Freud has asserted the "substitutive relation between the eye and the male organ," as Margaret M. Horwitz has noted in connection with Hitchcock's work; see *"The Birds*: A Mother's Love,"* in *A Hitchcock Reader,* ed. Marshall Deutelbaum and Leland Poague (Ames: Iowa State University Press, 1986), 284 and also 287n. 10, where she cites Stephen Heath on this matter. The lower material bodily stratum and its carnivalizing functions live, however subtly, in all of these moments.

34. Stephen Rebello, *Alfred Hitchcock and the Making of "Psycho"* (New York: Dembner Books, 1990), 80: "According to a scribble found on a production sheet, Hitchcock was amused by a notion of screenwriter [Joseph] Stefano to sweep the viewer—almost as if he were to become a fly on the wall—into the hotel room window to spy on Sam and Marion, post-tryst." Other fly references were considered, including a helicopter buzzing fly-like in the sky during the initial crane shot, but most were discarded. Retained was the fly on Norman's hand (and in Norman's soliloquy) near the end of the film.

35. Bakhtin, *Problems of Dostoevsky's Poetics,* 113.

36. Bakhtin, *Problems of Dostoevsky's Poetic,s* 116–17.

37. Bakhtin, *Problems of Dostoevsky's Poetics,* 115.

38. Bakhtin, *Problems of Dostoevsky's Poetics,* 116.

39. Bakhtin, "From Notes Made in 1970–71," 138.

40. The death's-head image fades into view over a preexisting image, as if initiating a conventional dissolve, but then fades out with that image instead of remaining as an autonomous shot.

41. Bakhtin, *Problems of Dostoevsky's Poetics,* 164.

42. Bakhtin, *Problems of Dostoevsky's Poetics,* 165. Note, incidentally, that a 1983 sequel picked up threads that the original *Psycho* left open-endedly unraveled.

43. Bakhtin, *Problems of Dostoevsky's Poetics,* 126–27 (emphasis in original).

44. Bakhtin, "Forms of Time and of the Chronotope in the Novel," 193.

45. Julia Kristeva's phrase, quoted by Tania Modleski, *The Women Who Knew Too Much: Hitchcock and Feminist Theory* (New York: Methuen, 1988), 109.

46. Modleski, *The Women Who Knew Too Much,* 109.

47. Modleski, *The Women Who Knew Too Much,* 109. Modleski is quoting Kris-

teva again. She also cites Claude Lévi-Strauss on the link between the incest taboo and dietary prohibitions.

48. Modleski, *The Women Who Knew Too Much*, 109.

49. His chanted, "Lovely, lovely" during the rape has been compared with the standard British compliment for a well-prepared meal. The apple he eats also points—in this narrative set in Covent Garden—to a *Coena Cyprianiesque* parody of the Garden of Eden myth. Bakhtin has devoted considerable attention to the *Coena Cypriani,* an early-medieval parody that inaugurated a tradition of literature carnivalizing religious dogma and ritual.

50. Quoted by Modleski, *The Women Who Knew Too Much*, 105.

51. Robert Stam, *Subversive Pleasures: Bakhtin, Cultural Criticism, and Film* (Baltimore: Johns Hopkins University Press, 1989), 126.

52. Modleski, *The Women Who Knew Too Much*, 109.

53. Bakhtin, *Problems of Dostoevsky's Poetics*, 176.

54. Bakhtin, *Problems of Dostoevsky's Poetics*, 176.

55. Thanks to Bob Stam for his helpful suggestions on this essay.

HITCHCOCK'S
EMERSONIAN EDGES

FRANK M. MEOLA

In what ways can Alfred Hitchcock be thought of as an "American" filmmaker, concerned with "American" themes? Recently, some critics have begun to approach this question by moving beyond comparisons between the British and American periods. They attempt to analyze Hitchcock's American films as rich explorations of American society and culture, continuing a long tradition of "outside" observers of our national life.[1] In this essay, I want to consider the American Hitchcock from a specifically Emersonian point of view. In doing so, I am not asserting any overt influence of Emerson on Hitchcock, nor am I saying that Hitchcock is an Emersonian filmmaker in the sense that Frost or Stevens are said to be Emersonian poets. Rather, I want to discuss some of Hitchcock's signature films of the American period in terms of the way they consider enduring American cultural and, indeed, spiritual tendencies that were first and most powerfully articulated in the works of Ralph Waldo Emerson. Because Emerson worked through these crucial American concerns with such rigor, his work can help us see them in Hitchcock, who in turn forces us to examine ourselves as Americans by showing us—indeed, making us experience—our most deep-seated qualities (good and bad). An Emersonian perspective will help to continue the important project of seeing Hitchcock as at least in some important ways an American filmmaker (and, of course, one who questions the concept of "American" identity, and of identity itself).

We can point to several major Emersonian themes in Hitchcock: vision and its relationship to power; nature vs. artifice; the fluidity of identity with its exhilarations and its terrors; and the issues of authority, eccentricity, and "centricity." In general, Hitchcock's American films explore the possibility and difficulty of human relationships, place human constructs against larger annihilating forces, and obsessively return to the fear of isolation and solipsism within the disconnected self, thereby carrying forward themes that became pervasive in American literature and culture after Emerson. Of course, these are quintessentially "modern" and cross-cultural concerns, but I am hardly the first to point out that American literature has been in this sense "modern" almost since its beginnings. One reason that Hitchcock came to America was perhaps an instinctive attraction to the place where modernity had advanced (or degenerated) the farthest, and where the free, self-invented modern self was simply part of the cultural atmosphere.[2] Of course, his primary motivations were most likely career advancement and artistic opportunity, but these too can be seen as forms of self-development.

An Emersonian perspective on Hitchcock, then, helps us to see the ways in which he critiques certain American values. Emersonian readings, for example, provide new ways of thinking about such familiar labels for Hitchcock as "the master of suspense," since "suspension"—of identity, of belief, of forward movement—is a key Emersonian concern that speaks to deeply American urges and fears, ones that reach a particular crisis in the twentieth century, the "American" century and, of course, the century of film. I will therefore not only be pointing to correspondences between various Emersonian themes and motifs and similar ones in Hitchcock, but also trying to suggest how these similarities reveal American philosophical and cultural patterns in Hitchcock's work that, despite the abundance of critical commentary, remain under-explored. Only recently, indeed, as I've suggested, has the idea of Hitchcock as an American filmmaker really emerged as a specific focus, despite the fact that the American films include his greatest achievements and despite the growing awareness that works of art by and about "outsiders" and "the marginalized" are among the most powerful evocations of what it feels like to live an American life. Emerson is the progenitor of this art of American eccentricity, and Hitchcock, the displaced Englishman, is among its greatest twentieth-century practitioners.

Epistemologically too, the Emerson-Hitchcock parallel is fruitful, both for Hitchcock studies and for Emerson studies. One main corollary of asking, as Americans have always done, who we are is to ask how we know who we are, and where we are. Here as elsewhere, the work of Stanley Cavell is central, since Cavell has taught us to read Emerson as a philosopher of knowledge, backward in effect from such modern thinkers as Wittgenstein. More important for our purposes here, Cavell has established convincing connections between contemporary philosophy and American literary history, and has extended the latter to include American film. For Cavell, American movies, especially certain Hollywood films, engage fully in the central concerns of American literature, which reach back to Emerson and beyond. Cavell is, of course, particularly interested in pervasive Emersonian themes in American writing and film, and we might summarize those themes (especially as they emerge in Hitchcock) as what Cavell terms "our worldlessness or homelessness, the deadness to us of worlds we still see but, as it were, do not recollect (as if we cannot quite place the world)."[3] We can call this "alienation" or the state of mind of an immigrant, or a perpetual traveler.

Cavell, in other words, focuses on the Emersonian problem of reestablishing our knowledge of a physical world and finding a "home" in it, thereby moving beyond skepticism and nihilism. Also important here is Cavell's idea of the reestablishment of the domestic, or what he sometimes calls (particularly with reference to movies) remarriage. Film, which takes the visual world as its given, is an especially rich medium for the exploration of the self's alienation from and reconnection with the everyday world around us. And Hitchcock, particularly in his American films, evokes more powerfully than any other filmmaker a sense both of the world's absolute reality (sometimes hyper-reality) and of states of dislocation from that reality. This concern with the physical world is one reason that Hitchcock's American films repeatedly give us actual American locations, frequently landscapes, and also partly explains why those locations are often rendered in surreal, even blatantly artificial terms.

This approach to Hitchcock, therefore, can help us bring together two major aspects of his American work: his concern with American epistemological and psychological "homelessness," and his sustained critique of American culture. Hitchcock both celebrates the possibilities of America, including the Emersonian ideas of self-invention and reinvention, and analyzes the darker implications of those possibilities. Hitchcock displays an

Emersonian ambiguity about the individual self, the culture of commodities, the small town as a locus of renewal, and the relation of the marginalized to the normal, among other things. An Emersonian perspective can help us to see Hitchcock as an explorer of the American soul, the human soul in its American form.

One of the most striking ways in which Hitchcock can be said to have taken up Emersonian themes involves vision and the visionary, sight and insight, clear and impaired seeing, particularly with regard to nature. Perhaps because of his Catholic background, Hitchcock was drawn to questions of sin and redemption, and the fallen natural world, concerns that have been part of American culture since the Puritans. Like Emerson and writers whom he influenced (and who rebelled against his influence), such as Hawthorne, Melville, and Poe, Hitchcock tends to represent this fallen nature in terms of narrowness and restriction of vision, a failed transcendence. Like them, too, he is suspicious of visionary transcendence. I want to first briefly consider the idea of redeemed or clarified vision in Emerson, then discuss Hitchcock's engagement with this theme in some of his American films.

Emerson's most famous statements about vision and the visionary occur in his first book, *Nature*, which dates from a period of devastating personal losses in Emerson's life but also one of intense discovery, particularly of natural history and science. *Nature* attempts to redefine the Fall of Man in terms of our visionary relationship to the natural world, which is both utterly alien and potentially redemptive. The first sentences establish the vision-obsession of the work, and suggest a vision trapped in the past (a major Hitchcock motif): "Our age is retrospective. It builds the sepulchres of the fathers. It writes biographies, histories, and criticism. The foregoing generations beheld God and nature face to face; we, through their eyes."[4] The allusion here, of course, is to St. Paul, but the specific emphasis is on the contrast between looking back, which Emerson associates with deadness, and looking forward, which is to see more clearly, without obstruction (a state Hitchcock once described as his definition of happiness). Of course, this is a classically "American" idea: the renewal of vision and life, and the reinvention of self, in a New World through a virgin landscape.[5] Farther along in the opening of *Nature*, we find the famous "transparent eyeball" passage, in which Emerson declares that

> Standing on the bare ground—my head bathed by the blithe air,
> and uplifted into infinite space—all mean egotism vanishes. I be-

come a transparent eyeball. I am nothing. I see all. The currents of the Universal Being circulate through me; I am part or particle of God. (10)

Perhaps the strangest thing about this very strange passage is, as several critics have remarked, its use of the term "eyeball" rather than "eye," a usage that has the effect of rendering the lines both comic and somewhat grotesque. Instead of having the effect of nonmateriality and transcendence, the phrasing suggests a person transformed into an eyeball. In other words, language is inadequate to tell us what this transparency would be like, since language itself is not transparent. This is a problem of *media*, which for Emerson was a language problem and for Hitchcock a problem of film's illusory claim to represent an unmediated reality.

Yet Emerson believes in a strong connection between the power of seeing and the power of the soul, which he says "is a watcher more than a doer, and it is a doer, only that it may better watch" (36). The lack of "transparency," of clear vision, results in a peculiar sort of dizziness, indeed a sort of vertigo. As Emerson writes in *Nature,*

> the ruin or blank, that we see when we look at nature, is in our own eye. The axis of vision is not coincident with the axis of things, and so they appear not transparent but opake. (43)

Even more disorienting is the passage in the much later essay "Experience," where Emerson writes that "the discovery we have made, that we exist" is "the Fall of Man," which he links to uncertain vision:

> Ever afterwards, we suspect our instruments. We have learned that we do not see directly, but mediately, and that we have no means of correcting these colored and distorting lenses which we are, or of computing the amount of their errors. Perhaps these subject-lenses have a creative power; perhaps there are no objects. Once we lived in what we saw; now, the rapaciousness of this new power, which threatens to absorb all things, engages us.[6]

Emerson goes on to assert that "every evil and every good thing is a shadow which we cast." The essay "Circles" expresses this distortion in more physically vertiginous terms: "[W]e now and then detect in nature slight dislocations, which apprize us that this surface on which we now stand, is not fixed, but sliding."[7] Emerson pulls together many different vocabularies and issues here, in a way that Hitchcock would do using the hybrid medium of film: optics, point of view, solipsism, ambiguity of vision, and moral uncertainty—all are interrelated in this "modern" world-view.

This distortion of vision can have the effect of reducing the visionary to the voyeuristic, a theme that has engaged many American writers, as Richard Poirier argues in his classic study *A World Elsewhere*, which remains the best treatment of this theme. Poirier indeed titles one of his chapters "From Visionary to Voyeur," and he gives us a quotation from Henry James, Sr., a very American, very Emersonian passage that we can apply to several of Hitchcock's American films:

> The life of God in nature . . . is a life of perfect freedom or spontaneity. In that life, self-love freely subordinates itself to neighborly love, . . . [But] so long as . . . no man dreams of any other social destiny for the race than that which it has already realized, and which leaves one man out of all fellowship or equality with another—self-love is completely unprovided for, except in subtle and hypocritical forms, and is consequently driven to these disorderly assertions of itself by way of actually keeping alive. . . . The liar, the thief, the adulterer, the murderer, no doubt utterly perverts the divine life which is latent in every human form . . . but he nevertheless does all this [as] a mute, unconscious protest against an overwhelming social tyranny.[8]

In this kind of environment, the solitary observer becomes a sort of sociopath, as in the character of Coverdale in Hawthorne's *Blithedale Romance*, who spies on others while hiding himself, unaware of his own true desires and projecting them outward. In a democratic and nominally egalitarian social context, there is no authorized vision, and each person is thrown back into his or her subjective view, observing all others. Like Hawthorne, Hitchcock is very interested in the isolated self watching others, while at the same time he is acutely aware of its dangers. The outsider who attempts to incorporate the terrifying outer world into the seeing eye, to pull everything into an increasingly isolated self, can become a monster of eccentricity who asserts sometimes murderous power over others.

The pattern emerges, for example, in *Strangers on a Train,* where Bruno is perpetually outside looking in, a passive observer except when he acts violently in a twisted assertion of the self. Bruno spends a good portion of the film observing Guy, watching his movements, and many shots of Bruno emphasize his ardent gaze. We view the film's murder through a pair of eyeglasses knocked off the victim's face. Through these Emersonian "distorted lenses" we witness the result of one of society's extreme dislocations of vision, frustrated assertions of power, and of course we are seeing it through at least a double distortion, reflected in glass and projected on a screen. Hitchcock thus emphasizes the physicality, the materiality, of our eyes as we watch the screen, seeing dark things darkly, not face to face. Hitchcock disallows easy transcendence—of time, history, or the body. The film's climactic tennis-match scene is another example of obsessive watching, and of the ambiguity of seeing: Bruno sits among the crowd whose heads move back and forth along with the play of the ball, while only Bruno's gaze remains fixed—on Guy and/or on some entirely subjective reality, some psychotic inner world.[9]

In *Rear Window* and *Vertigo* we encounter characters (both played by James Stewart) who are less obviously deranged but nonetheless indulge in "visionary possession," to use Poirier's term for voracious seeing. Here we see Hitchcock's Emersonian concern with masculine power over the outer world, and over women, long associated in American frontier mythology with a landscape to be conquered and possessed.[10] Jefferies in *Rear Window*, confined to his small apartment by a broken leg representing both an emasculation and a spiritual crippling, substitutes for his world-wandering photography an obsessive interest in his immediate neighbors in their own cubby-hole apartments. Armed with his phallic lens, which of course gets bigger as the film goes on, he is blind to what goes on inside himself and begins to identify, and identify with, a wife-murderer—while trying to avoid marriage himself.[11] The film creates disturbing links among the desire to see, the desire to possess, and the desire to kill. Again, the voracity of these linked desires and their ambiguous relation to power over the outer world are tendencies Emerson insightfully analyzes. Moreover, Emerson foresaw that in the emergent American mass democracy, particularly in the urban context (where *Rear Window* locates itself), the visionary urge would be reduced to an obsessive curiosity about other people's lives, through gossip, cheap newspapers, and other forms of voyeurism and prurience. Movies and television intensified this process, and of course Hitchcock was deeply suspicious of these media, especially in their more vulgar and commercial manifestations. *Rear Window*'s central concern is this corrupted and corrupting desire to dominate others by observing and knowing them.[12] In recent years, this cultural tendency has gone even further, with the rise of blatantly voyeuristic—and utterly democratic—"reality" programs on television.

In *Vertigo*, Scottie's visions of the elusive Carlotta/Judy/Madeleine form the obsessive thread of the film, and here too an American everyman, inspired by visions of a lost masculine potency, attempts to dominate a woman—in this case by transforming her appearance before, in effect, killing her. (There are interesting parallels here to Edgar Allan Poe's tales of failed visionary transcendence resulting in murderous death, such as "Ligeia.") Here too we encounter the ambivalent American attitude toward the land and its history; Carlotta Valdes in some sense represents the buried pre-Anglo past of California (a Hispanic and Native American past) that "haunts" the present.[13] Scottie reenacts the Anglo-American desire to possess through women and land what Emerson terms "native force," a sort of primordial male grandeur, but this pursuit degenerates into the need to conquer. He is not content with the world nor with the quotidian (represented by the rejected Midge); for Scottie, the seen world is unfixed and sliding, in Emerson's terms, to a degree that finally drives him insane. He does not really "see" Midge, nor the real Judy, but sees only an ideal—an ideal, however, that is beyond this world and/or is death. He cannot learn to live within time, or in Emerson's words, "husband" the passing moments (and husband Midge, perhaps); this combination of seeing the ideal and the real is part of what Cavell terms "finding as founding," the quintessential Emersonian project. This "husbanding" of time is a form of redemption, akin to what Lesley Brill terms the "romance" aspect of Hitchcock's work, but the conditions of American life have made it extremely difficult; we are perhaps condemned to false visions of self-renewal that in fact pull us into traps of solipsistic darkness.[14]

All of which leads to *Psycho,* where the transcendent, God's-eye-view that opens the film quickly descends into a dark window, never in effect to emerge from that darkness and narrowness. Norman's eye peering through the wall becomes Marion's dead eye looking but not looking at us, a nontransparent eyeball, wholly of the body. The only hint at escape in the film comes at the end, when the car—that symbol of American mobility and independence—is pulled from the muck, but this is hardly a vision of freedom. Nor is the brief moment in *The Birds* when the camera views the human chaos from the air: there is a hint here of some larger view, and we of course share in it, but not for very long. We are immediately plunged back into the world of predator and prey, with only a residual sense that somewhere behind or above our view is a larger view, a greater power—perhaps benign, perhaps evil, perhaps beyond both.

Hitchcock, then, mainly dwells on the obstacles to vision, and the many ways in which what we might call (thinking again of that God's-eye-view) the "transcendental gaze" degenerates into—and indeed becomes indistinguishable from—egotism, power, the desire to "know" and to control other people, the need to escape all community and commitment, and related distortions of the visionary American self. And Hitchcock, again like Hawthorne and other great American narrative artists, refuses to exempt himself from examination. He acknowledges his own complicity, even as he forces his audience to acknowledge ours. Coverdale, in *The Blithedale Romance*, is a version of Hawthorne, and Bruno, Scottie, Jefferies, Norman Bates are all (as many have suggested) aspects of Hitchcock. This authorial complicity has been particularly well analyzed by William Rothman, whose notion of the Hitchcockian "murderous gaze" conjoins the concepts of vision and power in a way that illuminates Hitchcock's Emersonian awareness of the ambiguities of power. (This understanding of power is something we tend to associate with Nietzsche, whose ideas did interest Hitchcock, and who was without question influenced by Emerson.) In some sense, film's visionary desire, its attempt to transcend time and death, turns back on itself and reinforces our physical being in time. The power to transcend becomes the power to murder. As Rothman puts it in discussing *Psycho*:

> In its appropriation of Marion Crane's subjectivity, the camera reveals its appetite; but in Norman Bates, the camera discovers a singular subject fit to stand in perfectly for itself. The camera's relationship to Norman puts its relationship to Marion, and indeed all its subjects, in a new light. In Marion's ultimatum to Sam, in the theft of the money, in the journey to Fairvale cut short by the stop at the Bates Motel, in the dialogue with Norman in the parlor, in Marion's violent death, and in the aftermath of Marion's murder (in particular Norman's irreversible metamorphosis), Hitchcock formulates perhaps his profoundest reflection on the nature of the camera and the conditions of his own authorship.[15]

These "conditions" are also conditions of being human, including the ability to envision combined with the desire to spy, the need for freedom mingled with violent self-assertion, the impossibility of escape, and the inability to see things objectively or clearly, apparent clarity turning to opacity. In America, with its declared right to the pursuit of happiness and its promise of expansive freedom, these limiting conditions clamp down with a particularly fierce tenacity (another reason Hitchcock's American works are far more disturbing than his British ones).

At the same time, Hitchcock is supremely aware of the artificiality and the performative nature of most social arrangements, indeed of all "media," all things that mediate between people, as well as between human beings and the non-human. As Hitchcock moved from a "British" identity to a provisionally "American" one (the only kind of American identity perhaps), he also moved more deeply into the American obsession with issues of artificiality and naturalness. It is often assumed that American artists, following Emerson and Thoreau, always resolve this supposed dilemma in favor of nature. But that is not true. Even Emerson is aware of the impossibility of attaining what he terms "an original relation to the universe," some sort of prelapsarian state beyond society's presumed artificiality. Indeed, he understood that the artificial itself could be a manifestation of the forces it is meant to disguise or tame:

> We talk of deviations from natural life, as if artificial life were not also natural. The smoothest curled courtier in the boudoirs of a palace has an animal nature, rude and aboriginal as a white bear, omnipotent to its own ends.[16]

Hitchcock intuitively understood this Emersonian aspect of American artifice, and he repeatedly expressed the sense of nature's red-tooth-and-claw emerging from beneath surface civility. In fact, he displays a post-Romantic, American view of the proximity of the "primitive" to the "civilized": think, for example, of Bruno's discussion with bejewelled women of murder as a parlor game in *Strangers on a Train,* or the buffet served, in effect, on a coffin in *Rope.* But there is another side to this: the sense of entrapment in artifice, the inability to reconcile social codes, including language, with the more chaotic, disruptive forces of the natural world. Over and over in Hitchcock's films, we witness the awkwardness of civilized or citified characters when they are placed against backgrounds that dissolve social communication and identity.

I want now to discuss in some detail *North by Northwest,* which is a particularly rich consideration of American artifice and identity-confusion, before discussing more briefly other films concerned with these themes. We can begin with the famous moment when Cary Grant as Roger O. (for "nothing") Thornhill (aka ROT) stands alone in a gray business suit at the side of a lonely two-lane road, flat Midwestern fields stretching endlessly around him. Even before the true menace arrives, we feel a sense of threat, the threat of annihilation. The scene is silent, and Thornhill, the man of lying words, of superficial urban ironies, is little more than a vulnerable animal. Neither his suit nor his language will protect him from forces beyond the human.

Here, indeed, to quote again from Emerson's transparent eyeball passage, "all mean egotism vanishes," especially the egotism of human supremacy. Of course, after Roger O. Thornhill stands exposed to the awe-inspiring, ego-shattering vastness comes the film's most famous scene: the murderous plane, a mixture of killing machine and predatory bird. The forces that social convention, commodification, and mass urban life hide from us (and indirectly manifest) emerge with a vengeance in their purest form.

Another way to look at the Emersonian aspects of the crop-dusting sequence is suggested in a recent essay by Richard Millington, who astutely points out that *North by Northwest* locates Thornhill's "identity problem" as "distinctly the effect and expression of a particular set of cultural circumstances."[17] Millington's argument serves as a useful corrective to some of the more narrowly psychological and individualistic aspects of readings such as Cavell's and Rothman's. But there is finally no separation in Emerson's or in Hitchcock's works between the isolated individual and the culture of which he is a part. Indeed, one of the glories (and dangers) of the emerging mass democracy for Emerson is that social identities need perpetually to be reinvented, an issue *North by Northwest* treats with both tense drama and comic absurdity. The idea of a "representative man" (in Emerson's famous phrase) implies both great authority and utter anonymity—Thornhill (the iconic Cary Grant) is threatened with annihilation and also inflated to hero status. The figures on Mt. Rushmore are shot so as to appear both larger-than-life and ludicrously artificial, cold, dead. Millington suggests that, for Thornhill, to reinhabit a more "authentic" self is to become a sort of body-in-motion, which allows the self truly to value others while escaping the roles, the frozen identities, imposed by ideology and power.

But Hitchcock is not only interested in threats from the powers-that-be, he is also keenly aware of more obscure, less obvious dangers. He intuits the American awareness—clear in writers from Brockden Brown to Emerson, Poe, and Hawthorne to Faulkner—of threats to the soul. Hitchcock certainly confronts a culture of false roles and identities, but he looks toward self-invention as a solution only if it puts us further in touch with what we might term life-affirming energies. This is perhaps the core of Hitchcock's connection to American literary and philosophical tradition. His work looks toward the "reinhabiting" of the body and of social forms not as dead things but as vital incarnations. He dwells on deadness to emphasize the value of its opposite. This is part of what Cavell means when he writes, in his essay on *North by Northwest,* that the Mt. Rushmore scenes represent an attempt "to animate, or reanimate, or humanize the world and so achieve a reciprocity with it" (*Themes Out of School,* 167). The American land brings out in Americans both a positive and negative power, humanizing and dehumanizing, vital and violent. Social forms must be reimagined in America, in order "to establish the world as a home" (169). We cannot rest in the complacency of, say, Santa Rosa in *Shadow of a Doubt* (to rest is to invite death in the American/ Emersonian world-view), but must cultivate what Cavell terms "capacities for adventure and for improvisation" (169). This is the "lesson" learned by Thornhill and Eve Kendall on their cross-country journey, which is also a trial, so that they will be able to live together "on the road," in the dynamic conditions of American life.

However, as I've suggested, this "remarriage" is only a possibility for Hitchcock, who dwells on the precariousness of social forms and the dangers of the forces beyond yet within them. This is the emphasis of the somber films before and after *North by Northwest*. Recall, for instance, Tippi Hedren as Melanie Daniels, posed in her formal city attire against stark, bare landscapes in *The Birds*. It is commonplace to note the intense and comic artificiality of these scenes, but more perceptive viewers have understood that this awkwardness is part of Hitchcock's ongoing commentary on the fragility of American social and community codes, the self-styling (a shallow version of Emersonian self-reliance) that masks an underlying absence.[18] This, too, is something Emerson diagnosed: the bizarre American alternation between craven conformism and egotistical assertions of power. In *The Birds,* Melanie's ego is smashed to pieces, as is Lydia's (imaged by her shattered teacup). The destructive avian power has, of course, been analyzed as a "return of the repressed," on the personal level, but the birds are more than that: they are a kind of repressed or alienated power (in Emerson's phrase "alienated majesty"), the other side of Bodega Bay's all-American complacency. To assume that you have already arrived at some idyllic perfection (as an individual or as a group), to rest within one circle in Emerson's terms, is to invite disaster.

Another evocation of the forces beyond human artifice occurs at the center of *Vertigo*: James Stewart's Scottie and Kim Novak's Madeleine/Judy/Carlotta in the sequoia grove. Here of course the vastness evoked is not so much spatial as temporal, but the effect is similar: this is a landscape, common in the American West, of the pre-human and implicitly the post-human, and certainly of the non-social. As Emerson writes in the "Nature" essay, "Nature is loved as the City of God, although, or rather because, there is no citizen" (104). Nature appears to hold frightening and majestic forces because our life in society does not "live up" to those forces; our social forms are inadequate to them. *Vertigo's* perhaps most uncanny and chilling moment comes when Madeleine/Judy disappears from view altogether behind one of the ancient trees and we, like Scottie, are momentarily unsure whether she will reappear. We don't know if she has vanished, nor indeed if she was real at all. Briefly only the tree, the non-human earth, is visible: this is a quintessentially "American" and extremely Emersonian moment in Hitchcock. As we watch, we have the weird sensation that we ourselves have disappeared, and a strong sense (shared with Scottie throughout the film) of the desirability of such a disappearance, even as we are terrified of it. This fascination with a nature devoid of human presence pervades American literature after Emerson, and recurs in many Hitchcock films. The artifice of social codes—in *Vertigo* strongly linked to names and clothing—dissolves momentarily into the unknowable, unnameable something that creates and destroys human forms.

We can also read the theme of the making and unmaking of identity in Hitchcock's American films through some more lines from Emerson's essays "Circles" and "Experience," as we move farther out along some of these Emersonian edges and margins in Hitchcock's work. In "Circles," Emerson calls the circle "the highest emblem in the cipher of the world" (179), a typically tricky phrase. He goes on to quote St. Augustine's famous description of God's nature as "a circle whose centre was everywhere, and its circumference nowhere." The idea of world-as-cipher suggests, of course, an emptiness underneath everything, as well as an ultimate unknowability. Both the letter "O" and the image of the circle in general appear frequently in Hitchcock's films, especially those of the 1950s and early 1960s. We can link these recurring ideas of circularity, with their subtextual suggestion of the figure zero, with the Emersonian idea of fluid identities and the fluctuations between centrality and marginality. Hitchcock's 1950s films especially bespeak a sense of anxiety about identity, place, role, self-knowledge, and self-annihilation. Hitchcock emphasizes the bleaker side of all these uncertainties; his evocation of circles tends toward a spiraling downward, a loss of ground, or an endless repetition.

"Circles" and "Experience" describe not only the feeling of dislocation and dizziness, but also an alternation between feelings of what we might call ego-fullness (characterized by energy, power, a sense of knowing reality) and something else we can term, after Julia Kristeva, abjection (characterized by powerlessness, inertia, depression, and a sense of unreality).[19] Emerson describes this shift in "Circles" as the "vast ebb of a vast flow." "I am God in nature," he writes, "I am a weed by the wall" (182). This alternation recurs in Whitman and many others later; Whitman ascribes it to the paradox of American democracy: "One's-self I sing, a simple separate person / Yet utter the word Democratic, the word En-Masse," he declares at the beginning of

Leaves of Grass.[20] Hitchcock picks up this American theme of abjection and self-inflation, feeling outcast and feeling centered, in his first truly great American work, *Shadow of a Doubt* (with its broken family circle) and develops it in other 1940s films, but it begins to play a major role in the 1950s, that famously conformist (and anti-conformist) decade. For example, in *Strangers on a Train,* the marginal Bruno represents the outer edge of the circle within which Guy lives his privileged and complacent heterosexual life. Guy is forced, in Emerson's words, to "make the verge of today the new center," and is compelled into a slippage of identity. The two are, like many Hitchcock characters, aspects of a single character; good and evil slide into one another as the circle shifts. (Two circle images in particular stand out in *Strangers on a Train*: the emblematic eyeglasses upon which Bruno fixates, and the out-of-control carousel that kills Bruno at the end of the film.) Morality in America's late-Christian culture is not a simple dichotomy; as Emerson writes, "our crimes may be lively stones out of which we shall construct the temple of the new God," and "no evil is pure, nor hell itself without its extreme satisfactions" ("Circles," 188). Guy rejects Bruno but also needs him. Bruno's marginality generates an ambiguous power, both energizing and destructive, good and evil.

Later films have many more circle images, overlapping with images of eyes and of stairways, other Emersonian and Hitchcockian emblems. In "Circles," Emerson writes of scaling "a mysterious ladder" toward a "new prospect" that represents "power" (181), and is also a wider circle. In "Experience," this powerful prospect becomes more doubtful, closer to the Hitchcock world-view. "Where do we find ourselves?" asks Emerson. "We wake and find ourselves on a stair: there are stairs below us, which we seem to have ascended; there are stairs above us, many a one, which go upward and out of sight" (27). This sense of existing in an in-between state, when one circle of understanding and commonality has been broken but another has not yet been formed, is where Hitchcock's films of the mid- to late-1950s and early 1960s tend to leave us. We are suspended, on edge(s), as Scottie is suspended in *Vertigo,* a work filled with images of circles and stairs (and circular stairs), and abysses which might reveal a new, transcendent knowledge but might also produce madness and death.

These ambiguities of knowledge and power reach an abject extreme in *Psycho,* which is a sustained meditation on the darker aspects of eccentricity, of life at the isolated edges of America. In *Psycho,* Hitchcock continues and intensifies a critique of the radically marginalized self begun in *Rope,* whose ambiguously gay protagonists act out a twisted form of self-assertion that results from their life at society's edges. Philip and Brandon's cerebral "liberation" from presumably bourgeois standards slides easily into a socio-pathic need for a trans-human "superiority," an Emersonian/Nietzschean "transcendence"-as-madness. Emerson himself approaches this insanity (and backs away from it) in "Experience," but he nonetheless diagnoses an American individualist disease that is still with us: the alienated madman, filled with anti-social rage, who thinks he is above any common under-standing. A marginality that remains marginal, instead of incorporating itself into some new center, turns rotten.

Psycho enacts the most extreme form of this condition; the expansive Arizona/California desert through which Marion attempts to escape into a new life shrinks to the dimensions of a car trunk buried in a swamp, and a creature (Norman and not-Norman) confined to a cell and the prison of its isolated mind. Here again we have artifice juxtaposed with nature, most bla-tantly in the Bates house, a Victorian structure overfilled with objects from a long-dead past, including of course a dead body. The house stands, as the familiar American phrase goes, "in the middle of nowhere," in no context, between communities, especially since, as Norman says, "they moved away the highway." It is a shell from which the life-force has departed, the move-ment Emerson describes in "Self-Reliance" as "the darting to an aim," that American pursuit of the new and different.[21] But what of the human con-sequences of this restlessness, this movement through vast space that both equalizes all people and alienates individuals from one another? The Bates house and its adjacent motel of perpetual vacancy, these Edward Hopper-like images, are one Hitchcock response to that question. Another might be the shattered group in the isolated family car at the end of *The Birds,* with the caged lovebirds and Lydia's small gesture of comfort toward Melanie the only signs of stability and connection. This car, like Marion Crane's, cannot speed unencumbered toward escape and freedom: it must proceed slowly, taking care. Perhaps a new sense of loving community will emerge from the shattered Bodega Bay and the dissolved ego of Melanie Daniels, but we cannot be sure. Hitchcock provides no clear answer.

It is in these disturbing late-1950s and early-1960s films that Hitchcock's "old-world" wisdom asserts itself against the American grain of unlimited individualism. Emerson never truly resolved the issues arising from such radical statements as "there is no crime to the intellect" ("Experience," 45).[22] The life of perpetual expansion and self-expansion that Emerson often cel-ebrated breeds monsters (we might recall here William Carlos Williams' fa-mous line, "the pure products of America go crazy"). A balance must be struck between self and community, the eccentric and the centric. However imperfect, the circle of fragile civility represented by the slowly advancing car at the end of *The Birds* must continue to be drawn, and widened, for outside it the endlessly free self encounters only chaos.

And, finally, it is Hitchcock's understanding of the dangers of reliance on the fragile, asocial self that makes his American work a complicated embodiment and critique of Emersonian themes. Increasingly in the twentieth century, "modern" life became "American" life, and the celebration of the self grew both more insistent and more disturbing. Hitchcock builds upon and modifies the idea of perpetual self-invention by dramatizing the modern American self as liberated, comic, absurd, mad, despairing, violent (and sometimes all of these together), while holding out the possibility of redemption through community and love. He thus participates in America's ongoing Emersonian project while raising serious doubts about that "self" upon which Emerson tends to base his hopes for social and spiritual renewal.

NOTES

1. I have in mind specifically the anthology *Hitchcock's America,* edited by Jonathan Freedman and Richard Millington (New York: Oxford University Press, 1999). While I admire many of the essays in the book, my emphasis here is less directly sociological and political. I am more concerned with general cultural tendencies, in the manner of Richard Poirier and Stanley Cavell. Finally, however, I think these different approaches are complementary. Another recent study focusing on Hitchcock as an analyst of American society is Robert J. Corber's *In the Name of National Security: Hitchcock, Homophobia, and the Political Construction of Gender in Postwar America* (Durham: Duke University Press, 1993).

2. Indeed, Hitchcock to a great extent reinvented himself in America, in the public persona of the suspense master "Alfred Hitchcock," who was also the reserved, patrician Englishman. See Freedman and Millington's introduction to *Hitchcock's America,* 6–7.

3. Stanley Cavell, *In Quest of the Ordinary: Lines of Skepticism and Romanticism* (Chicago: University of Chicago Press, 1988), 32. Also see Cavell's *Pursuits of Happiness: The Hollywood Comedy of Remarriage* (Cambridge: Harvard University Press, 1981) and the essay *"North by Northwest,"* in *Themes Out of School: Effects and Causes* (Chicago: University of Chicago Press, 1988), 152–72. Cavell is to some extent continuing a tradition of seeing American literature as centrally concerned with epistemological questions, especially those involving self and other, skepticism and belief.

4. Ralph Waldo Emerson, *Nature,* in *The Collected Works of Ralph Waldo Emerson,* ed. Robert E. Spiller and Alfred R. Ferguson (Cambridge: Harvard University Press, 1971), 1:7. Further citations from *Nature* refer to this edition.

5. The list of studies of this theme is extensive, going back at least as far as Henry Nash Smith's *Virgin Land: The American West as Symbol and Myth* (1950; rpt. New York: Vintage, 1961). One fairly recent (and revisionary) example is Myra Jehlen, *American Incarnation: The Individual, the Nation, and the Continent* (Cambridge: Harvard University Press, 1986).

6. Emerson, "Experience," in *The Collected Works of Ralph Waldo Emerson,* ed. Alfred R. Ferguson and Jean Ferguson Carr (Cambridge: Harvard University Press, 1987), 3:43. Further citations refer to this edition.

7. Emerson, "Circles," in *The Collected Works of Ralph Waldo Emerson,* ed. Alfred R. Ferguson and Jean Ferguson Carr (Cambridge: Harvard University Press, 1979), 2:186. Further citations refer to this edition.

8. Henry James, Sr., *Christianity and the Logic of Creation,* quoted in Richard Poirier, *A World Elsewhere: The Place of Style in American Literature* (1966; rpt. Madison: University of Wisconsin Press, 1985), 112.

9. Of course, as some recent readings have pointed out, Bruno is forced into this subjective vision, this isolated world, by a society that will not acknowledge his homosexual desires. In a sense, he can see but not be seen. One such reading is Robert J. Corber's essay "Hitchcock's Washington: Spectatorship, Ideology, and the 'Homosexual Menace' in *Strangers on a Train,*" in *Hitchcock's America,* 99–119. Corber argues that Bruno represents the aspect of Guy (his homosexuality) that official American culture seeks both to suppress and to demonize.

10. On this general subject, see, for example, Annette Kolodny, *The Lay of the Land: Metaphor as Experience and History in American Literature* (Chapel Hill: University of North Carolina Press, 1975), Richard Slotkin, *Regeneration Through Violence: The Mythology of the American Frontier, 1600–1860* (1973; rpt. New York: Harper Perennial, 1996), and Richard Drinnon, *Facing West: The Metaphysics of Indian-Hating and Empire-Building* (New York: NAL, 1980).

11. These themes are discussed in, for example, Donald Spoto, *The Art of Alfred Hitchcock* (New York: Doubleday: 1976), 237–49, and Robin Wood, *Hitchcock's Films Revisited* (New York: Columbia University Press, 1989), 100–07 and 376–79.

12. Michel Foucault analyzes the relationship between systems of observation and forces of social control, especially the prison, in *Discipline and Punish: The Birth of the Prison,* trans. Alan Sheridan (New York: Vintage, 1979). Especially relevant to a consideration of Hitchcock and Emerson is Foucault's discussion of "panopticism" and the Panopticon, Jeremy Bentham's circular structure for the observation of prisoners and patients. The expert or supervisor can sit in the center and directly observe those under his control; the Panopticon thus combines vision, knowledge,

and power by placing the observed in a circle around a central authority. This is a Hitchcockian fantasy and nightmare: to be constantly observed and known, to observe and know others relentlessly.

13. This connection was suggested to me by a paper presented at the Hitchcock Centenary Conference in New York, October 1999, "*Vertigo,* Empire, and the California Mission Revival," by Martin Kevorkian and Stanley Orr. Paula Marantz Cohen remarks of Scottie's relationship to history that "he is a man seeking a past in another to compensate for the lack of one in himself" ("Hitchcock's Revised American Vision: *The Wrong Man* and *Vertigo,*" in *Hitchcock's America,* 167). Cohen also astutely notes that Scottie is not simply indulging in "a patriarchal power fantasy" but is also trying to fill a " 'lack' in himself" and attempting to revise his own identity (168).

14. Brill writes, "Crucial to most romances—and therefore at the center of the failure of romance in *Vertigo* and *Psycho*—is the confronting and overcoming of a voracious, enervating past. The cyclic, regenerative time that energizes romantic narrative returns from fall and winter to spring and summer. In ironic fictions time is linear, an unprogressive succession of days stopping in the endless winter of death. Romance and irony thus clash in their understanding of time's regenerative or entropic powers. The heroes of Hitchcock's romantic and ironic films both set out—as St. Paul puts it—to 'redeem the time, for the days are evil.' World and time in romance are sufficient and cordial to such an enterprise; in ironic narrative, paths of glory lead but to the grave" (*The Hitchcock Romance: Love and Irony in Hitchcock's Films* [Princeton: Princeton University Press, 1988], 200–37). I don't think Hitchcock so much veers between "romance" and "irony" as he works in a mode of romantic irony, combining the two, in an Emersonian way. Cavell's more directly Emersonian understanding of "redeeming time" involves "the stepwise overcoming of skepticism, say of the immeasurable distance from the world, by the process of nearing as indirection, so an instruction in mortality, finitude; an establishing of founding without a founder, a ground on which the power of mastery is common, is mastery of the common, the everyday" (*This New Yet Unapproachable America: Lectures after Emerson after Wittgenstein* [Albuquerque, New Mexico: Living Batch Press, 1989], 116–17).

15. William Rothman, *Hitchcock—The Murderous Gaze* (Cambridge: Harvard University Press, 1982), 255.

16. Ralph Waldo Emerson, "Nature," in *The Collected Works of Ralph Waldo Emerson,* ed. Alfred R. Ferguson and Jean Ferguson Carr (Cambridge: Harvard University Press, 1987), 3:106. Further citations from the essay "Nature" refer to this edition.

17. Richard H. Millington, "Hitchcock and American Character: The Comedy of Self-Construction in *North by Northwest,*" in *Hitchcock's America,* 139.

18. Again, Robin Wood was among the first to discuss this deliberate artificiality; see *Hitchcock's Films Revisited,* 161–62.

19. Julia Kristeva discusses and illustrates the concept of "abjection" in *Powers of Horror: An Essay on Abjection,* trans. Leon S. Roudiez (New York: Columbia University Press, 1982). She writes, "The abject is the violence of mourning for an 'object' that has always already been lost. The abject shatters the wall of repression and its judgments. It takes the ego back to its source on the abominable limits from which, in order to be, the ego has broken away—it assigns it a source in the non-ego, drive, and death. Abjection is a resurrection that has gone through death (of the ego)" (15). This forcing of the ego through a "death" and to its "limits" is very close to what Emerson describes in "Circles" and "Experience," and describes well the sort of experience undergone by many Hitchcock characters, especially in the melancholy films of the 1950s and early 1960s. For a full Lacanian/Kristevan analysis of Hitchcock's films, see Robert Samuels, *Hitchcock's Bi-Textuality: Lacan, Feminisms, and Queer Theory* (Albany: State University of New York Press, 1998).

20. Walt Whitman, *Leaves of Grass,* in *Complete Poetry and Selected Prose,* ed. James E. Miller, Jr. (Boston: Houghton Mifflin, 1959), 5.

21. Ralph Waldo Emerson, "Self-Reliance," in *The Collected Works of Ralph Waldo Emerson,* ed. Alfred R. Ferguson and Jean Ferguson Carr (Cambridge: Harvard University Press, 1979), 2:40.

22. There is, however, an implicit sense of terrifying solipsism and social dislocation throughout "Experience," as in the passage on crime and intellect, where Emerson writes that "The act looks very differently on the inside, and on the outside; in its quality, and in its consequences. Murder in the murderer is no such ruinous thought as poets and romancers will have it; it does not unsettle him, or fright him from his ordinary notice of trifles: it is an act quite easy to be contemplated, but in its sequel, it turns out to be a horrible jangle and confounding of all relations. Especially the crimes that spring from love, seem right and fair from the actor's point of view, but, when acted, are found destructive of society" (45). This is a good description of many a cool, self-absorbed, indifferent Hitchcock murderer.

HITCHCOCK AND
THE ART OF THE KISS:
A PRELIMINARY SURVEY

Sidney Gottlieb

The kiss: kiss me; kiss me, stupid; kissing fool; kiss off; kiss up; sealed with a kiss; kiss and tell; kissy face; kiss my ass; kiss that baby goodbye; kiss me goodnight; kiss me, kill me; French kiss; soul kiss; judicial kiss; kiss of peace; kiss of life; kiss me deadly; kiss the girls and make them cry; *besame, besame mucho. . . .* We live in a culture, a psychological and psychosexual economy, and a landscape of kisses, and my aim in this essay is to examine Alfred Hitchcock as one of the great explorers, analysts, and artistic geographers of the kiss. His interest in this subject, shared by his audience, is perhaps both adult and infantile, as Adam Phillips suggests in his brief but remarkably suggestive essay "Plotting for Kisses":

> Adults tend to have strong, mostly private and embarrassed feelings about kissing. But this squeamishness—it would be silly or arch to be interested in kisses—conceals an intense, originally infantile curiosity about kissing and a repertoire of different kinds of kisses.[1]

Hitchcock has many easily recognizable signatures, distinctively characteristic motifs, themes, images, and techniques that critics have traced throughout his films: sudden overhead shots; reflexive use of cameras; theatricality; varieties of the gaze; images of suspension; dramatic actions played against monuments; triangular patterns; repeated appearances of the blond woman, the guilty woman, the horrifying mother; images of bondage; patterns of diagonal lines; the conflict of love and duty; the exchange of guilt; the innocence of guilt and the guilt of innocence; and so on. To this list, and perhaps near the head of this list, we should add a central and abiding "curiosity about kissing and a repertoire of different kinds of kisses."

Hitchcock's "pure cinema" is undoubtedly composed of many "impure" things: to borrow a phrase from Susan Sontag, we cannot understand Hitchcock's aesthetics of film without understanding his erotics of film. This requires a detailed study of his kissing sequences, which turns out to be a surprisingly ambitious task, far beyond the scope of one short essay. But in what follows I at least attempt to set up a critical framework for examining Hitchcock and the art of the kiss, moving from a few general observations on kissing and cinema to a discussion of Hitchcock's particular fascination with kisses and how kissing sequences tie in directly to some of his recurring thematic and stylistic interests, then to a brief typology of kisses and what to look for in these kisses, and finally to an analysis of one sequence in particular to illustrate how Hitchcock integrates his kisses into the overall structural, emotional, and thematic fabric of his work.

In some respects, the prominence of the kiss in cinema is predictable, even inevitable, especially if we note, with Raymond Bellour, that one of the underlying purposes of the conventional film is to manufacture the couple, to dramatize, with however many variations, the archetypal bourgeois and patriarchal romance, processes in which the kiss plays a significant role. The kiss is also traditionally the most explicit and yet still allowable—that is to say, publicly performable and viewable—signifier of sexual activity. Not surprisingly, then, from the very beginning film, a medium that institutionalizes voyeurism and thrives on curiosity, display, and spectacularizing the private, has drawn from the long-standing artistic iconography of the kiss, and also, of course, developed influential conventions of its own.[2] All this helps explain why the 1895 film of the Irwin-Rice kiss is so typical, evocative, and foundational (in a way that, for example, the film of the Fred Ott sneeze is not). Controversial as well. The Hays Office guidelines of 1927 specifically discouraged "excessive or lustful" kissing onscreen, and Will Hays was particularly worried about the "proportions" of the Irwin-Rice kiss, duration here represented as length:

In spite of its popular appeal, a great many people disapproved of osculation to the extent of forty feet and to this day no one has ever definitely determined how many feet long a kiss may be and still remain a proper salutation.[3]

Hitchcock, on the other hand, was not worried but inspired, and it is perhaps only a slight overstatement to suggest that for him the archetypal "cinema of attractions" was the attraction of body to body, lips to lips. Even without direct evidence, I am convinced that Hitchcock recalled and repeatedly transformed the Irwin-Rice kiss—with its theatricality, wit, protracted duration, and blend of kissing and conversation—in his own films, part of a broader effort of which there is direct evidence: his lifelong homage to the days of "primitive" and early experimental cinema, and repeated tugging on the moustache of Will Hays and other such censors.

But while Hitchcock falls well within a tradition of cinematic kisses in some respects, kissing shots and sequences in his films are constructed with extraordinary care and carry an unusual amount of dramatic and thematic significance. For Hitchcock more than any director I know of, kisses are central, substantive, complex, emotionally charged, and problematic, as well as intimately—I use the term carefully—related to nearly all his key themes and concerns. Let me first briefly sketch out an overview of several ways in which the most distinctive aspect of the "Hitchcock touch" is the Hitchcock kiss.

His kissing sequences are typically *moments of stylistic excess.* By stylistic excess I refer to instances when on one or more levels a shot or sequence diverges from norms and expectations (of "classical" cinema, of Hitchcock's cinema, or of the particular film in which a kissing shot or sequence is embedded). In many cases, stylistic excess, partly by calling attention to itself, marks a moment as "special," particularly meaningful and worthy of aesthetic appreciation, critical attention, and emotional involvement. Along with chases, assaults, and murders, kisses provide Hitchcock with the most frequent opportunities for such stylistic excess, and since many of these moments are so memorable, perhaps all I need do is allude to a few typical techniques.

Camera movement. In key kissing shots Hitchcock uses a swirling, circling camera, most memorably in *Vertigo,* where the camera movement induces and embodies, literally traces, one of the conventional vortex-like images associated with vertigo (the entire film is filled with evocations of what I would describe as embedded vertigo, patterns of turning and wandering). Hitchcock uses this pattern in other places as well: in *I Confess,* for example, where the passion evoked in the remembered kiss is nostalgic and charming, but forbidden, and in *Strangers on a Train*, where the "romance" of the kiss of Guy and Anne is undermined by a pervading sense of worry and, even more damaging, emotional frigidity.[4] In addition to circling camera movement, Hitchcock uses complex crane and dolly maneuvering and panning to choreograph such elaborate set-pieces as the balcony kiss in *Notorious* (which I will discuss in more detail later) and the train compartment kiss in *North by Northwest*. Here and in many in other films as well, Hitchcock turns the kiss into a drama and a dance.

Camera placement. For Hitchcock, kisses invite intimate, intense, and sometimes intrusive, even invasive close-shots, perhaps imitating the way that a kiss itself is a breaching of what is normally defined as safe personal space. The classic example of this is when Lisa first kisses Jefferies in *Rear Window*, and this close-up effect is radicalized some years later in the storm scene in *Marnie*, which builds toward extreme close shots of a kiss. Both of these scenes powerfully convey excitement, satisfaction, and menace, a typical Hitchcock compound. In staging his kisses, Hitchcock also plays with a variety of other camera positions to add not only visual interest but tension or some element of disturbance: shots from above, shifting camera angles in quick cuts, off-center framing, and so on.

Special effects. These range from what we might call the ordinary baroque (there is conventional as well as unconventional stylistic excess), such as the high romantic kiss by the seaside in *Vertigo*, and the send-up of the high romantic kiss in *To Catch a Thief*,[5] with its shimmering light, swelling orchestral music, and fireworks, to the invocation of the fantastic in the dreamy slow-motion kiss in *Rear Window*[6] and in the kiss (also filmed with an intimation of slow motion) that opens all doors in *Spellbound*.

While kisses are associated with stylistic excess in Hitchcock's films, they are also rich with thematic implications. For Hitchcock a kiss is frequently not just—as it is conventionally—isolated, initiating, or climactic, but *metonymic*, capable of revealing the essence of a character, figuring and enacting the dynamics of a relationship, and embodying the crucial themes and plots of the entire film. We are as we kiss, Hitchcock suggests, and it is through their kissing or being kissed that we come to know a great deal about the multiply beleaguered and encircled Alice White, the witty and improvisatory Richard Hannay, the manipulative Johnny Aysgarth, the assertive and independent Lisa Fremont, the immature Francie Stevens, the hysterical and abused Marnie Edgar, the murderous Bob Rusk, and so many other key Hitchcock characters. The simplicity of these epithets, by the way, does not do justice to the complexity of the characters or their kisses: Hitchcock's kisses are indexes of desire, power, dominance, submission, trust, stability, vulnerability, and much more. And the way someone kisses indicates not only his or her character and capacity—or incapacity—for a relationship but illustrates the status and particular qualities of that relationship.[7]

Hitchcock frequently characterizes the couple and charts any development by their kisses. Sometimes a single kiss tells us virtually all we need to know about a couple. The concluding kiss in *The Lodger*, for example, is a remarkable evocation of a marriage defined as a happy ending but marked by tension, asymmetry, the terror of desire, a shadowy and ominous male, a shadowed and disappearing female, visible reminders of past horrors (the golden curls murders), and a foreboding sense of a future that is no release from this traumatic past. The kiss at the end of *Rich and Strange* undermines any sense that the couple has learned from their travels and returns them to their old, and bad, habits. The kisses at the end of *Young and Innocent* successfully transfer a young woman from her father to her lover. More ominously, the kiss in *The Wrong Man* after Rose hits Manny with her brush does not heal but rather heightens our sense of the fracturing of each character as well as their relationship. And some of Hitchcock's prolonged kisses show relationships being forged or negotiated, the best examples of which are, again, the above-mentioned balcony scene in *Notorious* and train compartment scene in *North by Northwest*.

Hitchcock also works with linked series of kisses throughout a film that dramatize complex character formations and changing relationships. The most fully articulated example of this structure is in *Rebecca*. Dispersed throughout this film are various kissing sequences that, when taken together, show the maturation of a young woman and, indeed, of a couple through the transformation of their kisses. As an experiment, I re-edited the film, linking all these kisses, and the result was a remarkably coherent 7 1/2 minute-long movie-within-a-movie that lays bare a progress from patronizing, infantilizing, passively received kisses on the forehead to mutually initiated and erotic but, perhaps more importantly, sympathetic, supportive, and "knowing" kisses on the lips as well as symmetrical embraces. And *Rebecca* is by no means the only film in which Hitchcock uses series of kisses as not only the key to a relationship but also as what might be called the deep structure of a film: other examples include *Easy Virtue, The Manxman, Rich and Strange, Suspicion, Spellbound, Notorious, Rear Window, To Catch a Thief*, and *Marnie*.

Kissing shots, sequences, and series contain a high emotional and stylistic charge but also a tremendous amount of information. Kisses not only punctuate the story: they tell the story and in some cases they are the story. There is such a close connection between kissing and telling in Hitchcock that I am tempted to say that for him kissing *is* telling: an essential and privileged mode of revelation and narration. Part of the reason for this is not only the inherent spectacular and dramatic qualities of a kiss but also a natural connection between the kiss and so much of what else fascinates Hitchcock, including the following ensemble of what many critics have suggested are some of his recurrent concerns: sexuality, intimacy, merging, separation, dominance, aggression, violence, voyeurism, and, more broadly, the precarious relationship between private and public worlds. There is much to be said about the relationship between kisses and each of these elements, but partly because of limited space and partly because I suspect that much about these connections is obvious and self-explanatory, I will make just a few comments.

I have already briefly discussed the kiss as the allowable and representable signifier of sexuality, the synecdochic expression of the full range of sexual relations and problems. The kiss also gives concrete spatial form to the dynamics of intimacy and distance, merging and separation, self-assertion and annihilation. Merging is both a desire and a threat in the Hitchcock world. Kissing sequences sometimes convey an ecstasy of absorption, swooning, and pleasurable self-loss: the typical markers are closed eyes, the head tilted or reclining, conversation stopped as the mouth is otherwise engaged, circular motion, melodramatic non-diegetic orchestral music, and so on. But kissing sequences also convey fear of merging, of being overwhelmed, of losing the self. This is often shown in dramatic form via resistance to a kiss, physical rigidity, pushing away, turning one's face, opening or keeping one's eyes open, and talking. And the dire consequences of merging are conveyed by visual imagery of erasure and pressure: on many occasions one head eclipses or shadows another during a kiss and one body forces another into tense, angular positions.[8]

Even beyond the ambiguities of merging and self-assertion, for Hitchcock kissing is frequently associated with a continuum of dominance, aggression, violence, and murder. That is to say, the lips often work for the teeth. Kissing and killing: relevant here is Truffaut's observation that Hitchcock films murders like love scenes and love scenes like murders—an observation perhaps prompted by Hitchcock's own repeated references to Oscar Wilde's famous assertion that, as paraphrased by Hitchcock, "You destroy the thing you love."[9] The larger expression of the kiss is the embrace, and frequently the embrace is barely distinguishable from an assault: Bruno lovingly murders Miriam in *Strangers on a Train*; Uncle Charlie nearly embraces young Charlie to death at the end of *Shadow of a Doubt*; one of the most memorable visual moments in *Topaz* is the deadly, flowering embrace; and when Mark kisses Marnie, in one of Hitchcock's most complex and carefully modulated examinations of the dynamics of a kiss, it is partially a passionate assault, but also a compassionate act, initiating not only an attempted suicide but also a lengthy process of healing and recuperation. Perhaps we need to add to Truffaut's insight, though, that this reversibility of love-making and murderous unmaking is uneven:[10] benign kisses have sinister overtones, but sinister, murderous kisses and embraces never appear benign. Phillips speaks of the elegiac quality of kisses.[11] Hitchcock's kisses often have that quality, but usually alongside a more strident note of alarm.

The connection between kissing scenes and voyeurism is both obvious and extremely important. Hitchcock's comments on the balcony scene in *Notorious* emphasize how important it was to him that "the public, represented by the camera, was the third party to this embrace. The public was being given the great privilege of embracing Cary Grant and Ingrid Bergman together. It was a kind of temporary *ménage à trois*."[12]

Kissing, perhaps more than anything else, mobilizes the gaze in Hitchcock's films, invites, involves, and excites the audience, and often establishes what I have previously described as a perspectival chain but might now describe as *hypervoyeurism*: scenes of looking at looking, and even looking at looking at looking, a complex construction that perhaps culminates but by no means begins in *Rear Window*.[13]

Finally, there is a close connection between kissing and what Hitchcock often described as one of his lifelong themes, the conflict of love and duty. I would broaden this and suggest that at the heart of his work is an examination of the complex and conflicting demands of the private and public worlds. The kiss is a critical moment and multi-dimensional signifier in this drama: partly because it pulls both ways—perhaps more toward the private, personal, smaller world, but also gesturing to the "social" world, however circumscribed, beyond the self—and partly because it typically calls attention to a moment of crisis or decision-making regarding one's negotiations between the private and public world. The kiss may be an affirmation, a bold move, an attempted resolution, but it is always, at least in Hitchcock's world, an announcement of an ongoing problem, a complex dialectic that I will illustrate in my concluding discussion of *Notorious*.

I have sketched out, however briefly, a broad stylistics and thematics of the kiss. Let me add a brief typology of kisses, indicating what kinds of kisses we find throughout Hitchcock's films and some of what to look for to understand their dramatic and thematic significance. Hitchcock names the "surprise kiss" and the "suspense kiss" to Truffaut, but there are many others we can add to the list.[14]

Occasional kisses. We should take note of the "when" and "why" of a kiss. We find a wide range of occasions for kisses in Hitchcock's films, including many conventional and predictable moments: ceremonial (e.g., wedding, holiday), domestic, superficial, formal, friendly, familial. In addition, there are kisses of greeting or parting, kisses as a prelude to lovemaking or a conclusion of lovemaking, kisses that represent a consolidation of intimacy or an affirmation of trust, and so on. But beyond these, there are more highly charged kisses.

Guilty kisses. Such kisses occur between people who should, by conventional standards, not be kissing (as in *Rich and Strange* and *Dial M for Murder*). Some of these are *overseen kisses* within the film itself (as in *Easy Virtue, The Manxman,* and *Notorious*). All screen kisses are in the very least, of course, overseen by the audience, and I have already commented on Hitchcock's self-conscious play with the voyeuristic attraction of kissing.

Near kisses. These are demonstrated by two people getting ready to kiss, hovering on the horizon of a kiss, but never actually initiating it (as in *Easy Virtue* and *The 39 Steps*). This adds tension to a scene: stepping into sexuality is always a highly charged moment in Hitchcock's films. Near kisses can take a variety of forms, including *attempted kisses, pseudo-kisses* (actions that are akin to but not quite kisses), *refused kisses* (as in *Suspicion* and *The Paradine Case*), and *resisted kisses* (essential to the intense drama in *Blackmail, Marnie,* and *Frenzy,* and the comedy in *Family Plot*).

Interrupted kisses. Hitchcock knows well that whatever drama and tension are built in to a kiss may be intensified by interrupting the kiss, heightening our awareness that no matter how much we hope it might be otherwise, a kiss is often not so much the resolution as the representation of a problem. Not surprisingly, interrupted kisses occur repeatedly in *Suspicion,* and at a key moment in *Rear Window,* Jefferies is more interested in stopping rather than enduring, let alone enjoying or giving in to, Lisa's kiss. For Hitchcock, a kiss is as likely a sign of rupture as rapture.

Conversational kisses. Kisses are sometimes a stopping of the mouth (of conversation and of breath), a transference of one kind of orality to another, but other times are an opportunity for talking. I take this conflation of actions to be a kind of drollery on Hitchcock's part, but as usual there is often a tension behind the drollery: conversation during a kiss continues intimacy but also keeps it at a distance by asserting that there are indeed two voices, two independent selves that continue on even through love.[15] The best example of a conversational kiss is the balcony scene in *Notorious,* but other examples may be found in *The 39 Steps, Suspicion,* and *Strangers on a Train.*

Kisses of self-assertion. Joan Fontaine in *Suspicion* asserts her independence and demonstrates that she is not a "spinster" as her father believes, by kissing Cary Grant, and Grace Kelly in *To Catch a Thief* boldly and surprisingly kisses, again, Cary Grant goodnight. Both of these instances, while acts of self-assertion, are also somewhat ironic attempts to express maturity, independence, and sophistication that these women do not yet possess. Kisses of self-assertion also take ominous and sinister forms as they blend into *kisses of hostility, aggression,* and *assault.* These are, unfortunately, aspects of the oral and erotic economy of many of Hitchcock's characters, especially men at work in such films as *Blackmail, Marnie,* and *Frenzy.*

Theatrical kisses. These include kisses of self-display that are stylized, meant to be seen, and may mark a testing of or even a flight from intimacy. It may be difficult (or ultimately impossible) to distinguish between Hitchcock's theatricality—he is, after all, the stage manager of everything that happens in his films—and that of the characters in the films. But there are instances where our attention is drawn to the theatricality of the characters in a kissing scene. At the end of *Murder!* Sir John and Diana Baring are finally established as a couple and bonded by a kiss, but as the camera pulls back we see that this kiss is set on a stage, complete with curtain and audience. This puts their relationship, as it were, in brackets, an action undertaken, presumably by Hitchcock and Sir John. And kisses can be theatrical without literally taking place on a stage, as in the railroad station kiss at the end of *Spellbound.*

Finally, in analyzing kisses we need to watch for not only the occasion and the type but the *geography and spatial form of the kiss.* Where one kisses is often revealing: on the lips, the cheek, the neck, the forehead, the top of the head, the hands, and so on. In *Rebecca* and *Marnie,* for example, Hitchcock works with a carefully articulated hierarchy of kisses, and a progression of kisses often charts the emotional rise or fall of a relationship. And Hitchcock also carefully constructs *asymmetries of kisses,* spatial patterns and positionings that indicate the unequal power or status of the characters in the relationship. All the following dimensions, having to do with the appearance of faces and bodies in the film frame, play a role in the meaning and effect of a kiss: higher/lower; foreground/background; profile/front/back view; light/shadow; visible/obscured (by the other person); eyes open/eyes closed.

I could go on establishing an even more detailed typology of kisses (e.g., kisses that domesticate rather than express or excite eros, as at the end of *To Catch a Thief*; "witty" kisses; deflected kisses), citing additional examples from Hitchcock's films that not only show but also discuss kissing (especially *Suspicion, Spellbound,* and *Rear Window*). But I'd like to conclude with one brief close reading, applying and synthesizing as much as possible of what I've said so far to illustrate that kisses are not merely interesting but isolated moments in a Hitchcock film. The example I've chosen is one of Hitchcock's most celebrated and familiar kissing sequences, the first balcony scene from *Notorious.* Hitchcock commented extensively to Truffaut on some of the particulars of this sequence: on the at least temporarily inseparable couple, the formation of the *ménage à trois* by adding the spectator to the couple, and the real incident of "true love at work" that he witnessed and used to help shape the scene in *Notorious.*[16] I would like to complement attention to these specific details with Hitchcock's own reminder that we need to examine how the scene is embedded in a larger whole.

In his essay "Production Methods Compared," Hitchcock uses the embrace as a key example in his discussion of the need to avoid the "tendency today . . . to shoot scenes and sequences and not to shoot pictures. The embrace can be shot from the front, from either side, or from above. If we are really going to be arty about the thing, it can be filmed from behind."[17] But, he goes on to say, "The angle from which that embrace is to be shot ought to flow logically from the preceding shot, and it ought to be so designed that it will fit smoothly into whatever follows it, and so on." Proper planning and script preparation help insure that "we will never think about shooting the embrace, but merely about shooting a picture of which the embrace is a part." What is ultimately so remarkable about the first balcony scene in *Notorious* is not only the many details that make it a technical *tour de force*—"the longest kiss in screen history," Truffaut remarked, quoting the "publicity blurbs"[18]—but the way it fits into and helps form a larger, more complex and powerful dramatic and cinematic structure.[19]

The balcony scene stages one of the key themes of the film: the attempt to assert a private world of love, privileged, set apart from the public world of distrust, politics, corruption, manipulation, duty, moral responsibility, time, and history. For me, this scene is the cinematic equivalent of a Donne lyric, imagining, describing, and enacting an ecstasy, an awakening and cementing of bodies and souls, a canonization, a dismissal of the larger world and a luxuriating in the immensity of a small, "pretty room" ("The Canonization"). The long shot of Devlin on the balcony shows the public world of Rio in the far distance, but initially the pull of duty preoccupies him, as we can tell by his expression and body language. The cut to a mid-shot eclipses that world, and the pull in to a tight close-shot excludes it. The faces of the two lovers fill the frame and their walk from the balcony into the room, to the phone, and to the door—"of course, they had to be in action," Hitchcock says—adds dynamism to the scene, a force of fusion in a film that also plays with various types of fission. [20]

The long uninterrupted take, the constantly maintained two-shot, the breathless tone of voice, the dance of motion, the rhythm of kisses: all this establishes an intimacy of the present. The past, the outside, and the separate, independent constructions of their character—Devlin as suspicious, cold, and manipulative; Alicia as confused, promiscuous, and compromised—recede. But there are disturbing intimations as well: the phone call is, if not an interruption, then at least a reminder of pressing responsibilities; the lovers move from full light, through shadows on both their faces, to a final image of a shadow primarily on Alicia's face, and the motion of the scene is both centripetal and centrifugal (perhaps a prefiguring of the kind of double motion at the heart of *Vertigo*), pulling them together but moving to and out the door, so that the drama here is one of initiation, consummation, and valediction.

As remarkable as this scene is, the depth of Hitchcock's genius and the intricacy of his structures, in general and in his kissing sequences in particular, become even more apparent when we examine how he reprises what we have just seen moments later in the second balcony scene. Hitchcock reinforces our awareness of this conscious paralleling with a line of dialogue: Alicia says "Hasn't something happened like this before?" But the parallel is set up for contrast, and the second sequence offers a point by point, technique by technique reversal of the first one. The second scene is marked by the following: a switch in Alicia's and Devlin's position at the beginning, perhaps a subtle announcement of the pattern of reversals that characterizes the entire scene; a normal rather than hushed and intimate tone of voice, not soothing but clipped and interrogative; primarily a rock-steady instead of moving camera, emphasizing immobility, unbridgeable distance and separation, and eliminating the earlier centripetal pull; long instead of close shots; a refused and conspicuously absent kiss; constantly interrupting cuts, including what qualifies as a shock cut at a particularly accusatory moment, from a two-shot to a one-shot of a startled Alicia; and reliance on shot/reverse-shot patterns, with a subtle insistence on fragmenting not only the couple but the individuals as well, inserting a shadowy edge of one's face into the frame while the other is talking. We move quickly—these scenes are separated by only 1 minute and 45 seconds—from a hopeful coming together choreographed around a prolonged kiss to a harrowing separation, in part the consequence of turning to public responsibilities.

The design is completed, though, and brought to harmony by the climactic return to a kiss at the end of the film. In a sequence that closely echoes the first balcony scene (and erases the second one), Devlin enters Alicia's bedroom and not only saves her from the Nazis but helps bridge all the gaps and banish the tensions that had risen earlier. Hitchcock mobilizes all the techniques of the balcony scene, but this time forcefully rather than tentatively. The camera pulls in to a close two-shot, and this view of the lovers united is either held or reasserted throughout the sequence: even when Devlin momentarily leaves the frame to open the door, Alicia holds him in her gaze and he maintains contact and presence by speaking to her until he reenters the frame. They each kiss the other, repeatedly, an affirmation of strenuously achieved mutuality and trust, and their conversation affirms a new level of maturity, even wisdom. It is now Alicia who talks about public affairs, telling the details she has found out about the spy operation. Devlin says, "We'll take care of that later" and concentrates throughout on confessing his feelings and expressing, as he never had before, his love. Neither the public nor the private world is sacrificed or avoided, and a kiss is no longer taken as a sign of an irresponsible turn inward.

Hitchcock shoots the kisses in ways that enhance the dream-like, almost hallucinatory qualities of the scene: quick cuts showing a kiss from slightly different angles, a circling camera action around the lovers as they kiss, and occasional off-center framing create a sense of disorientation; and keeping the camera close in on them as they kiss and make their way to the door adds to the impression that they are not so much walking as gliding, magically transported by love. But Hitchcock takes great pains to show that this is more than a dream, more than a fleeting fantasy of resolution. The door to the bedroom opens to a real world, signaled by a very noticeable shift in visual style and lighting, and the couple continues on, triumphing over the Nazis, their own inadequacies and fears, the soul-stultifying demands of the public world, and the threat of isolation and death. They have created, in the root sense of the word, a marvelous relationship, a sanctified space, where all, I think, do there embrace.[21]

In grand climactic moments, as in *Notorious,* but also in many less obvious, even apparently mundane moments in Hitchcock's films, despite what the song says, a kiss is not just a kiss. Truffaut spoke of Hitchcock's desire to fill his films with "highlights that linger on in the viewer's memory." Nearly every Hitchcock kiss is such a "privileged moment."[22] He once defined the chase as "the core of the movie," the "final expression of the motion picture medium . . . almost indigenous to movie technique as a whole."[23] But it is perhaps equally defensible to speak of the kiss as the core of Hitchcock's movies, essential in the construction and critical in our experience and interpretation of his works from the beginning to the end of his career.

NOTES

1. Adam Phillips, "Plotting for Kisses," in *On Kissing, Tickling, and Being Bored: Psychoanalytic Essays on the Unexamined Life* (Cambridge: Harvard University Press, 1993), 95.

2. Phillips suggests that we now learn about the "giving and getting of kisses" primarily from films ("Plotting for Kisses," 95).

3. Will Hays, *See and Hear* (New York: Motion Pictures Producers and Distributors of America, 1929).

4. In the middle of a brief but penetrating discussion of kisses in Hitchcock films, Robin Wood comments on "the stiff embrace, quite lacking in real intimacy, between Farley Granger and Ruth Roman in *Strangers on a Train*." [*Hitchcock's Films Revisited* (New York: Columbia University Press, 1989), 77.] Donald Spoto also makes some interesting observations about this scene and other memorable kisses in Hitchcock's films in *The Dark Side of Genius: The Life of Alfred Hitchcock* (New York: Ballantine Books, 1983), 427–28.

5. Hitchcock more than occasionally introduces elements of humor, parody, and satire into his kissing sequences. For example, in *Easy Virtue,* he deflates "high romantic" shots of lovers kissing and nuzzling by immediately following them with images of horses acting in a similar fashion (discussed briefly in my essay "Kissing and Telling in *Easy Virtue,*" *Hitchcock Annual* [1992], 29–30). And in *Strangers on a Train,* when Guy walks past Bruno's intimidating dog on the stairs, the dog's slobbering kiss—more precisely, he licks Guy's hand, but for all intents and purposes it is a doggie kiss of affection shot in a comically romantic mode—is exaggerated, like Grace Kelly's kiss in *Rear Window* and Ingrid Bergman's in *Spellbound,* by slow motion. Hitchcock frequently retracted his alleged statement that actors are cattle, but he didn't seem to mind slyly insinuating that lovers are akin to horses and dogs.

6. For Hitchcock's comments on this kiss and a special-effects kissing shot he planned but did not use in *The Birds,* see François Truffaut, *Hitchcock,* revised edition (New York: Simon and Schuster, 1984), 222.

7. I stress the "relational" aspects of the kiss, whereas Phillips explores what he considers to be the fundamentally narcissistic project of kisses, the desire, often

deflected but never satisfied, to kiss one's own mouth; see "Plotting for Kisses," esp. 94, 99–100.

8. If it seems as though I am viewing Hitchcock through the lens of Ingmar Bergman, let me turn that around and say that I think Bergman learned many lessons from Hitchcock. *Persona,* for example, is if not unimaginable without the example of Hitchcock then at least deeply indebted to him: thematically perhaps most obviously to *Vertigo* and *Psycho,* but visually to many of the moments in his other films that I have been cataloging in this essay.

9. Truffaut, *Hitchcock,* 153, 345.

10. I allude to Elaine Scarry because of the close connection in Hitchcock between the body in love and "the body in pain." See *The Body in Pain: The Making and Unmaking of the World* (New York: Oxford University Press, 1985).

11. The concluding line of his essay is: "Truly infectious, kissing may be our most furtive, our most reticent sexual act, the mouth's elegy to itself" ("Plotting for Kisses," 100).

12. Truffaut, *Hitchcock,* 261–62. Hitchcock goes on to describe the real-life experience lying behind this "romantic moment":

> I was on a train going from Boulogne to Paris and we were moving slowly through the small town of Etaples. It was on a Sunday afternoon. As we were passing a large, red brick factory, I saw a young couple against the wall. The boy was urinating against the wall and the girl never let go of his arm. She'd look down at what he was doing, then look at the scenery around them, then back again at the boy. I felt this was true love at work. . . . It was the memory of that incident that gave me an exact idea of the effect I was after with the kissing scene in *Notorious.* (262)

13. Gottlieb, "Kissing and Telling in *Easy Virtue,*" 24–25.

14. Truffaut, *Hitchcock,* 222.

15. Hitchcock illustrated his ideas on "dialogue in counterpoint" in a love scene by telling Truffaut about one such scene he did make (in *Notorious*) and one more outrageous scene he never made:

> Something I wish I could work out is a love scene with two people on each side of the room. It's impossible, I suppose, because the only way to suggest love would be to have them exposing themselves to each other, with the man opening his fly and the girl lifting her skirt, and the dialogue in counterpoint. Something like: "What are we going to have for supper tonight?" But I suppose that would come under the heading of out-and-out exhibitionism. Anyway, we used that counterpoint dialogue in *Notorious,* where

they talk about a chicken dinner and who is going to wash the dishes, while they're kissing. (Truffaut, *Hitchcock*, 262)

16. Truffaut, *Hitchcock*, 261–62.

17. Alfred Hitchcock, "Production Methods Compared," originally published in *American Cinematographer*, 30, No. 5 (May 1949), rpt. in *Hitchcock on Hitchcock: Selected Writings and Interviews*, ed. Sidney Gottlieb (Berkeley: University of California Press, 1995), 207.

18. Truffaut, *Hitchcock*, 261.

19. Ironically, one of the most detailed treatments of *Notorious*, Stefan Sharff's shot-by-shot analysis in *Alfred Hitchcock's High Vernacular* (New York: Columbia University Press, 1991), 13–86, covers this scene perfunctorily, perhaps because his attention is drawn largely to patterns established by cuts. For Sharff, the "most striking aspect" of this scene composed basically of one uninterrupted take is "the immaculate execution of the camera movement through the complex blocking" (29).

20. Truffaut, *Hitchcock*, 261. The mysterious radioactive substance in the film is no mere MacGuffin, as Hitchcock insisted, but a springboard to a deep investigation of volatile human energy. Like many of his films, *Notorious* is to a large extent about the nuclear family or nuclear relationship, and dramatizes interpersonal atomic bonds and explosions.

21. The emphasis on the reconstruction, not simply the construction, of the couple, along with the triangular love relationship, witty dialogue and visuals, and presence of Cary Grant, suggest to me that *Notorious*, not *Mr. and Mrs. Smith*, is Hitchcock's finest example (and transformation) of the comedy of remarriage. The classic study of this genre is, of course, Stanley Cavell's *Pursuits of Happiness: The Hollywood Comedy of Remarriage* (Cambridge: Harvard University Press, 1981). Kisses of many varieties are, as we might expect, prominent in comedies of this kind. In *Pursuits of Happiness*, Cavell briefly discusses *North by Northwest* as "adjacent to the structure of the genre of remarriage (33), and returns to this topic at the beginning of his essay "*North by Northwest*," in *A Hitchcock Reader*, ed. Marshall Deutelbaum and Leland Poague (Ames: Iowa State University Press, 1986), 249–64.

22. Truffaut, *Hitchcock*, 15.

23. Alfred Hitchcock, "Core of the Movie—The Chase," originally published in the *New York Times Magazine*, October 29, 1950, rpt. in *Hitchcock on Hitchcock*, 125.

HITCHCOCKIAN HABERDASHERY

SARAH STREET

In *Dial M for Murder* (1954) Tony (Ray Milland) has a problem. He needs to steal a latch-key which his unfaithful wife, Margot (Grace Kelly), keeps in her handbag, so that the man he has blackmailed to murder her can enter their flat, hide behind the curtains, and kill her when she answers the telephone. Margot's red handbag is a source of suspense from the beginning of the scene when Tony eventually steals the key. Suspense is initiated when we see her put the key in the handbag and place it on the desk. In several subsequent shots the handbag is blatantly displayed in the center of the frame. We are already alert to its potential suspense value because we know that Tony discovered Margot's affair by stealing her handbag, which contained an incriminating love-letter. The bag is visually identified with Margot by being the same red as her strident dress: she is the "scarlet woman" until she becomes a victim of the murder plot, and thereafter her clothes are less vibrant. There follows a consistent, obtrusive visual attention to the handbag that the viewer cannot ignore.[1]

Use of the handbag as a central element of suspense and register of sexual tension is not unusual in Hitchcock, as the *Dial M for Murder* example goes on to illustrate. Tony persuades Margot to stay in for the evening and cut out press clippings for him. We see him rummage in her needlework basket (another form of bag) for a pair of scissors that she later uses in self-defense. It is significant that Tony repeatedly invades his wife's "feminine" property in this manner: he also finds a stocking in the basket, another typically playful Hitchcockian use of female clothing. He then pretends he needs taxi money in a desperate attempt to get the key from her handbag undetected. The theme of the sacrosanct feminine object is clearly evident when Tony struggles with her to steal the key. As he opens her bag without asking, she protests, "Hey, you leave my bag alone!" She is worried about his interest in her "private space" where we already know she keeps her love-letters, her only vestige of privacy in the claustrophobic flat that has an intensely masculine appearance, featuring photographs of Tony at college and his tennis trophies. He tries to stop her taking the bag from him by holding it behind his back, forcing her to embrace him in a desperate attempt to continue the struggle. We see a close-up of his hand groping for the key, deftly opening the small black purse that contains it, and its eventual removal. Throughout the awkward tussle the pair maintain a semblance of superficial humor and civility which pervades their dialogue throughout the film, a form of communication which has presumably enabled them to keep secrets from each other: her affair and his pretense of being a loving husband.

In this essay I want to compare how the handbag is used in other Hitchcock films, most notably *Rear Window, Vertigo, Psycho* and *Marnie*.[2] These films feature the handbag as a powerful object, an expression of women's assertiveness within patriarchy. The handbag, a traditional "feminine" accessory, frequently functions in Hitchcock as a powerful object, rather than as a mere costume accessory. Perhaps surprisingly, in view of the standard claim that women in Hitchcock films are passive victims, the handbag is a signifier of female assertiveness rather than frivolity or passivity. The way it is used consistently demonstrates that in Hitchcock films femininity can be a powerful force to be reckoned with, often consuming the male protagonists with both fascination and fear.[3] As we have seen in *Dial M for Murder,* Margot is clearly *not* in control of her bag but its status as a private female object has nevertheless been signaled. As her husband, Tony takes advantage of domestic familiarity to invade her property: married couples are not supposed to have secrets. Superficially, they both abide by this "rule," but at the same time they both lead double lives. It is important that her marital status results in a different use of the bag than by the single women protagonists in the other films I want to examine. Its vulnerable position in this scene represents Margot's vulnerable status as Tony's wife; she is in danger of being exposed as duplicitous. The audience has also been provided with a further element of suspense: knowledge about the murder plan as part of Tony's masculine "game" of revenge.[4] Hence the struggle over the bag is invested with multiple layers of tension, not least sexual tension. It serves as a useful plot device but is also the primary signifier of the visual articulation of the film's representation of a stultifying middle-class marriage, held up by a facade of decorum and politeness, codes which disguise unhappiness and promote duplicity.

The period between *Dial M for Murder* and *Marnie* (1964) is a fascinating one in terms of its restrictive codes of femininity, before women became more overtly independent in the late 1960s. It is no accident that Hitchcock's films used handbags in such a dominant fashion during this period when resistance was often a covert activity. To this end I have found theories of the female masquerade particularly useful to inform my readings, which focus on masquerade as a positive way of enabling women in patriarchal society to use their femininity in a powerful, resourceful and often subversive manner.[5] This strategy is clearly often at work in Hitchcock films, residing in an ambiguous representation of "femininity" that is most clearly expressed by textual and subtextual uses of women's costume and accessories.

Analysis of the narrative role of costume and accessories can also function as a concrete focus for speculation on the impact of this direct address to the female spectator who would have been well-versed in contemporary costuming codes, meanings, and conventions.[6] In the many tie-ins between consumer culture and screen fashions, female spectators were targeted by appealing to their desire to see lavish costumes that they could use as models for their own "look-alikes" in an attempt to emulate their favorite screen heroines in dress and behavior.[7] Speculatively, it is likely that at the same time as digesting the obvious consumer address, contemporary female audiences might also have absorbed the implications of an intriguing representation of femininity in Hitchcock. In this connection after my readings of the films I want, briefly, to consider the related question of how far Hitchcock was actually responsible for the look of his heroines and demonstrate that on occasion there was considerable feminine input from the female costume designer and actresses.

The strategy of the female masquerade is clearly evident in Lisa's (Grace Kelly) use of her costumes in *Rear Window* (1954). After giving Jeff (James Stewart) a lecture on "feminine intuition," ("a woman has a favorite handbag and it always hangs on her bedpost"), she picks up her own bag, playfully remarking: "I'll bet *yours* isn't this small."[8] To Jeff's amusement, out cascades a nightdress and silk slippers from the black bag that looks as if it is a masculine briefcase. This gesture underlines the whole theme in the film of femininity as a threat ("preview of coming nightmares"), and as a masquerade. Lisa's feminine clothing is constantly contrasted with Jeff's huge phallic lenses. In these visual terms, therefore, his masculinity is directly pitted against her femininity. Lisa is in full control of her femininity—so much so that Jeff can only relate to her as an "action woman" (cf. the film's ironic ending, with Lisa holding up the *Harper's Bazaar* as evidence of her real identity). She displays her femininity knowingly in an almost aggressive way, precisely because Jeff cannot respond physically (he has his leg in plaster) or emotionally (he ridicules trappings of femininity and is scared of marital commitment).[9] The bag is thus a key visual symbol of the film's delineation of gender relations.

Vertigo (1958) is also extremely amenable to readings that depend on masquerade theory and these, in turn, have implications for studying the use of costume and accessories. Performing Madeleine, Judy knowingly played a role, obtrusively positioning herself in the frame for Scottie's gaze, for example in the scene when Scottie is hiding from her, but watching her in the graveyard. In this reading a stable masculine position is undermined because the woman-as-spectacle highlights the conditions of her own construction, thus destabilizing the voyeuristic/fetishistic mechanisms of the masculine gaze that would hold her subordinate. Or as Mary Ann Doane argues, in performing the patriarchal construction of femininity, "the masquerade doubles representation."[10]

In view of this interpretation, it is interesting to notice that Scottie's reconstruction of Judy as "Madeleine" leaves out, or renders impotent, the essentially problematic aspect of female costuming: the handbag. Madeleine, the construction of Elster and Judy, seldom has a bag, or when she does she does not use it and it is often lying on its side. This contributes to her image as ethereal and "otherworldly"—her enigmatic "feminine" demeanor. As participant in the masquerade, Judy knows this only too well. Madeleine's bag is unobtrusive: a smart, black coordinating fashion item. But when Scottie first encounters Judy she has a large white bag that swings from her shoulder. She uses it too—when he goes to her room she proves her identity and independence by showing him her driver's license, which she keeps in her bag.[11] The process of "transformation" back to Madeleine, however, repeats the previous bag pattern: when Judy is almost the same as Madeleine (save for her hairstyle) she has the impotent black bag. But when she is completely transformed into Scottie's ideal woman, emerging in a euphoric haze of green from the bathroom, she has no bag and remains without one for the rest of the film.

No bag, no threat of secrets or independent female identity. This is crucial in terms of what we have seen before: the signifiers of Madeleine's femininity have been exhaustively presented in the quest for the right shoes, dress, hairstyle, and Judy is frequently paralleled with Madeleine in the visual construction of the film. When Scottie follows her to her hotel, Judy is presented as less alluring than she was as Madeleine: entering a frame, she does not command the diegetic space she did as Madeleine; the curls on her forehead shorten her face, rendering it less photogenic; and the window she opens is in a seedy high-rise with a neon sign, rather than an old colonial mansion. This is part of the lengthy dissipation of the woman's control of her image, the emphasis shifting to Scottie's recreation of Madeleine. The terrible irony is that Judy is aware of what is happening, having participated in the scenario of masquerade before, using "femininity" as a conscious strategy, a crucial part of Elster's murder plan. As Scottie puts it, "You played your part so well."

In *Psycho* (1960) the bag is a transgressive agent associated with stealing, escape, and independence. Before the theft has been committed, Marion (Janet Leigh) has a white bag (matching her underwear in the first scene), signifying her innocence. Once she has stolen the money, her bag and underwear change to black. The changeover process is quite laborious as she puts the envelope containing the money into the black bag rather than in her suitcase, where it would be completely hidden. It is interesting that she chooses the handbag as the place of refuge for the money, presumably because she assumes that even if she was suspected of the theft most people would not insist on rifling through her handbag (as indeed the police motorcyclist later respects the sanctity of her bag by not insisting on personally investigating its contents). In spite of this rather crude demarcation of "good girl vs. bad girl," our identification with Marion as heroine is not so clear-cut; it becomes stronger once she has committed the theft.

It is of prime significance that the money she has stolen belongs to a rich tax-evader who will use it as a wedding present for his daughter "who has never had a day's unhappiness." Marion's "transgression," therefore, is not just stealing, but stealing money which has a clear patriarchal function. The perils of such an action are visually expressed by Marion's extreme anxiety over the money that she has hidden in her handbag. While she is driving, her bag on the passenger seat is a constant source of anxiety, particularly when she is stopped by the police motorcyclist. When he asks to see her driver's license we get a privileged look at Marion's furtive handling of the money in her bag. The camera shifts from his point of view so that we can see what she is doing, her anxious expression, and his sinister stare, accentuated by his dark sunglasses.

Once Marion reaches the garage, she continues the previous pattern of concealing the money in the bag and, significantly, disappears into a specifically female place, the ladies' room, to remove the cash from her bag to pay for her new car. Once again, we get a privileged view of her "transgression" as she counts out the money. The bag is a signifier of her duplicity and secrecy, but it also performs a key role in ensuring our identification with her as heroine. Her very anxiety and evident guilt about the theft persuade us that she is already a victim: not a literal victim in the way the narrative goes on to unfold, but a victim of patriarchal pressures. As a familiar fashion item, the bag endears her to us as she clutches it like a friend: a woman alone, driving in a state of emotional turmoil, completely unaware of the horrors that await her at the Bates Motel.

The bag, bulging with stolen banknotes, also symbolizes her rebellion against a world where it appears that happiness—the future she would like for herself and Sam—can only be bought. When Marion arrives at the motel she continues to cling to her bag, even when Norman takes her into the cabin. Once he has gone she relocates the money by wrapping it in a newspaper and putting it on the bedside table. Ironically, she and her bag are less powerful once she has tried to divorce herself from the theft. Her encounter with Norman persuades her to return the money, meaning that the rich man's daughter will have her marital home and perhaps Marion will return to her unhappy existence in Phoenix. Earlier she told Caroline (Pat Hitchcock), "You can't buy off unhappiness with pills," but her attempt to buy it off with stealing has left her haunted by guilt and shocked at her capacity to rebel. It is a double irony that once she thinks she has made the right decision—to try to undo her "transgression"—Norman Bates denies her even the possibility of further re-evaluating her "private trap."

Marnie displays Hitchcock's most distinctive use of the handbag in its opening shot of a woman carrying a yellow handbag and a suitcase.[12] We see the bag before the woman, whose face is concealed until the third scene. We then cut to a scene in which we learn that a robbery has taken place and the suspect is described by the men primarily in terms of her appearance: Mark refers to her as "the brunette with the legs." We learn the extent of her "resourcefulness" in the following scene, which reveals that the yellow bag holds Marnie's change of identity cards and stolen money—key symbols of her transgression against patriarchy and her rejection of men.

Inside the hotel room the two cases on the bed are intriguingly at odds with one another: one is being carefully arranged and packed with coordinating fashion items, whereas the other holds the remnants of a discarded disguise. This process of change prefigures the subsequent shots of Marnie changing her hair color and both events follow soon after the handbag opening, directly linking the accessory with her masquerade. In terms of plot the bag is a crucial element in the establishment of Marnie's independence. As in my other examples, it is also a signifier of her survival instinct in a world where she must exploit her knowledge of how to masquerade in order to maintain that independence. She also appears to derive great pleasure from her obvious expertise at manipulating the masquerade for her own ends.

Janet Thumim has written: "The problem for a female reader for whom Marnie's articulation may have some experiential resonances is that, no matter how sympathetic she may be to Marnie's analysis, in the end it is Mark's meanings to which she must subscribe as a consequence of the inexorable logic of Hitchcock's narrative construction."[13] But the non-visual significance of the bag at the end of the film goes some way to qualify this pessimistic view. The rhyme that the children sing when we first see Marnie visiting her mother, and again at the end of the film ("Mother, mother, I am ill; / Send for the doctor over the hill; / Call for the doctor, call for the nurse, / Call for the lady with the alligator purse; / 'Mumps' said the doctor, 'measles' said the nurse, / 'Nothing' said the lady with the alligator purse"), appears at two crucial moments, signaling danger to Marnie. The first is when we learn of the strained mother-daughter relationship. Marnie steals to be independent and provide for her mother, but mother and daughter misunderstand each other: Marnie thinks her mother does not love her; her mother is cold towards Marnie and thinks she is a prostitute. The tension created by this situation emerges as a cause of Marnie's own "coldness," which appeals to Mark's curiosity as a challenge to his romantic advances.

The second time we hear the song is at the film's ambiguous ending. Mark has blackmailed Marnie into marrying him and has forced an explanation for Marnie's frigidity out of her mother. In the course of the traumatic "confession," Marnie finally learns that her mother always loved her, but by now she is married to Mark as an alternative to jail. Ironically, knowledge of her mother's love has entailed the payment of a high price: loss of independence on her own terms. Although the ending would appear on the surface to be closed, the line "call for the lady with the alligator purse" who thinks that "nothing" is wrong with Marnie might act as a warning to Marnie to use her resourcefulness once again to escape from her new trap, or at least urge her to be cautious about Mark's "diagnosis," which has been motivated in good measure by his tenacious desire to investigate/possess her. Since her situation has changed, Marnie must develop new survival tactics, and renegotiate her relationship with her mother *and* Mark if she is to succeed in her new life. The major area of renegotiation must be with Mark, with whom she must insist on her own "meanings" and pleasures. The rhyme therefore allows for a feminist reading of the film at the end: we have come full circle from the powerful handbag imagery of the film's opening.

In view of the above readings, which reveal a complex and sophisticated knowledge of female behavior at work in Hitchcock, it is interesting that regarding the very area of concern—the "look" of female costume and accessories—Hitchcock might not have exercised total control (although obviously responsibility for how the accessories were shot and edited rests with Hitchcock). Edith Head designed many of Hitchcock's costumes, and in some cases there was clearly a negotiation of difference in the director-designer relationship. It is commonly assumed that Hitchcock maintained absolute authority over costuming (see his remark to Kim Novak when she complained about Madeleine's costume in *Vertigo*: "You may wear what you like Miss Novak, as long as it's in the script!"[14]), but there is some evidence that qualifies this assertion. He was definite about the colors of Novak's costumes, but Head commented that "other than colors, Hitchcock gives you a lot of room for your own ideas."[15] The Press Book for *Marnie*, for example, informs exhibitors that "Hitchcock went to extraordinary lengths to surround Miss Hedren with every possible aid to her portrayal. All of her clothes stemmed from the inspired drawing boards of Edith Head."[16] And this "feminine input" was not confined to the designer.

After *Dial M for Murder*, Hitchcock allowed Kelly considerable say in what she wore. Head recalled that when she was costuming *To Catch a Thief*, she bought all the bags and shoes with Kelly in Paris. Hitchcock's use of Kelly, an actress with "regal" connotations who exemplified the tie-in between high fashion magazines like *Vogue* and *Harper's Bazaar* and popular cinema, is interesting in respect to costume and accessories. She even had a handbag named after her, the "Kelly" bag created by Hermes, and she epitomized the 1950s trend to "accessorize" clothing with matching shoes, bag, and gloves, celebrated by many women's fashion magazines of the period. Although Hitchcock was extremely fussy about the colors used for her costumes, many of the actual designs were debated between Head and the actress.[17] Head collaborated extremely well with Kelly, saying that she "never worked with anybody who had a more intelligent grasp of what we were doing . . . I don't think people realize that there is a very analytical brain behind that beautiful face. I have never made sketches until I have worked them out with her."[18] It would appear, therefore, that women contributed in significant ways to the heroines' screen images.

There are many fascinating questions surrounding female spectatorship and Hitchcock, some of which I hope this essay has raised. Did the handbag "joke" remain purely a joke—an element of authorial "enunciation"— or did female spectators recognize the elements of masquerade that I have identified as so integral to the behavior of the Hitchcockian heroine? It is difficult to assess how far they would have been capable of readings that concentrate on the transgressive manifestation of femininity, but recent research has shown, for example, that as far as the retail market was concerned women "consumed" fashion in relation to the actresses they saw on the screen in intriguing ways: the desire to copy or adapt screen fashions could develop into a desire to emulate a particular actress' behavior.[19]

Audiences might have also have been influenced by contemporary reviews and fan magazines. Hitchcock's heroines had varying experiences with the press: Grace Kelly was admired, whereas Tippi Hedren was subject to reviews that revealed a confusing response to her image.[20] In 1956 MGM was deluged with more fan mail, mostly from women, for Grace Kelly than for any other star under contract.[21] In 1954 she was the subject of cover stories in *Look, Time, The Saturday Evening Post, McCalls, Ladies' Home Journal, Redbook, Colliers,* and *Cosmopolitan.* Women's magazines offered detailed analyses of costume, particularly in terms of color-coding and dressing for particular occasions. Many women purchased "Kelly" bags as part of that coding process. These codes would, no doubt, have been recognized by female spectators when watching actresses in Hitchcock films whose outfits were so carefully constructed.

The films make implicit, ironic statements about where real power lies in Hitchcock's work. He frequently appears to be making a joke about female clothes and accessories, and he often uses them as props for his suspense plots. But there is often a "gap" between the narrative role of the bag and its visual treatment, producing possibilities for readings that concentrate on femininity. The films also reveal a profound male anxiety about the threat of woman and her destabilizing impact, underlining the crisis of masculinity identified by several critics as a major subtext in many Hitchcock films.[22] Hitchcockian heroines have to be resourceful, using their costumes and accessories as a means of survival in a male world. They often resort to masquerade; the choice supports psychoanalytic readings that rely on the female masquerade in popular cinema. Single women have great control of their bags and are able to use them more powerfully than married women.

During the years 1954–64 Hitchcock was preoccupied with the theme of the masquerading blonde, and her costume and accessories played a key role in that representation. It seems that use of her bag involved an invitation to the audience to have a privileged look at female sexuality. Particularly when the bag functions as an element of suspense, it suggests that the spectator has superior knowledge given by the director (e.g., our view of Tony stealing the key from Margot's bag; our secret "look" at Marion removing her driving license from her bag, out of the policeman's sight; the opening scene of *Marnie*). But in so doing, Hitchcock presents us with an essentially enigmatic representation of femininity. Film spectatorship is not, however, informed by a single source, and when concentrating on this fascinating "space"—perhaps unwittingly supplied by Hitchcock—the female spectator can survey the implications of masquerade in its complete cultural context, thus rendering the handbag an "accessible accessory"—a convenient textual pointer towards an appreciation of the complex presentation of "the feminine" in Hitchcock films.

NOTES

1. *Dial M for Murder* was filmed in 3–D, a process which would have accentuated *mise-en-scène*, making the red bag even more obtrusive than in the exhibited version.

2. It would be interesting in a longer study to compare these films with Hitchcock's earlier films, for example *Suspicion* (1941), which features the handbag in a Freudian manner when Joan Fontaine rejects Cary Grant's advances on the hillside by shutting her handbag firmly between them. I have not included analysis of *To Catch a Thief* (1955) because its main signifying accessory is jewelry. *The Birds* (1963) has many scenes during which we are invited to contemplate Melanie wearing fashionable, color coordinated costumes and bags, but the bag is not singled out as obviously as it is in the other films.

3. Tania Modleski has also highlighted how "the strong fascination and identification with femininity revealed in Hitchcock films subverts the claims to mastery and authority not only of the male characters but of the director himself. . . . This fascination opens a space for the female spectator." See *The Women Who Knew Too Much: Hitchcock and Feminist Theory* (London: Methuen, 1988), 3.

4. In relation to Tony, the bag is used to place a rather crude Hitchcockian question mark over his heterosexuality. We already know that Tony married for money and displays no convincing affection for Margot; their relationship is characterized by cold civility. By contrast Tony tells his old college friend that when he was watching him he found him "quite fascinating. At times I felt that you almost belonged to

me." In relation to this theme, the bag plays an important role at the end of the film: the police hide it in a briefcase when it is sent to the station, to save the policeman from "being arrested." Tony has no such qualms when he retrieves the bag later, and his scheme to murder his wife is confirmed. Hitchcock is using the bag here not only to conclude this element of the plot but also to underline a subtext that has already been suggested: speculation about Tony's sexuality.

5. John Fletcher similarly interprets masquerade as subversive within patriarchy, in that it "constitutes a transgressive doubleness, an inscription of alternative wishes." See "Versions of Masquerade," *Screen*, 29, no. 3 (summer 1988): 55.

6. The best recent book on this subject is edited by Jane Gaines and Charlotte Herzog, *Fabrications: Costume and the Female Body* (London: Routledge, 1990)

7. One of the articles reprinted in Gaines and Herzog, *Fabrications,* is Charles Eckert's "The Carole Lombard in Macy's Window," 100–21, the first critical study to deal with the links between Hollywood studios and consumer product industries in the 1930s. Robert Gustafson, "The Power of the Screen: The Influence of Edith Head's Film Designs on the Retail Fashion Market," in *Velvet Light Trap* (1982), 8–15, shows how the tie-ins were often indirect: certain features of film costumes reached the retail fashion market because they had been adapted without acknowledgment by designers. On the question of emulation of screen heroines in dress and behavior, see Jackie Stacey, *Star Gazing: Hollywood Cinema and Female Spectatorship* (London: Routledge, 1994), 176–223. Also useful is Maria Laplace's "Producing and Consuming the Women's Film: Discursive Struggle in *Now, Voyager,*" in Christine Gledhill, ed., *Home Is Where the Heart Is: Studies in Melodrama and the Woman's Film* (London: British Film Institute, 1987), 138–66.

8. It is interesting in this context to remember that in Freud's famous case of Dora, bags and "reticules" feature prominently. In Dora's dream her mother's jewel-case is kept on her bedpost! Freud generally interpreted bags and jewelery as sexual symbols. See Sigmund Freud, "Fragment of an Analysis of a Case of Hysteria," in *The Pelican Freud Library* (Harmondsworth: Penguin, 1973), vol. 8.

9. See Modleski's reading of *Rear Window* in *The Women Who Knew Too Much,* particularly her remarks on p. 78. I have written on *Rear Window* at greater length in " 'The Dresses Had Told Me': Fashion and Femininity in *Rear Window,* " in John Belton, ed., *Alfred Hitchcock's Rear Window* (New York: Cambridge University Press, 2000), 91–99.

10. Mary Ann Doane, *Femmes Fatales: Feminism, Film Theory, Psychoanalysis* (London: Routledge, 1991), 26.

11. This is similar to Marnie's use of social security cards.

12. Raymond Bellour analyses the opening sequence without reflecting on the symbolism of the bag in his article "Hitchcock, the Enunciator," *Camera Obscura,* no. 2 (fall 1977), 66–91.

13. Janet Thumim, *Celluloid Sisters: Women and Popular Cinema* (London: Macmillan, 1992), 181.

14. Kim Novak, " 'He Was the Sexiest Man Who Played Opposite Me in 30 Years,' " *TV Guide,* March 1987, 10.

15. Edith Head, quoted in Joel W. Finler, *Alfred Hitchcock in Hollywood* (New York: Continuum, 1992), 120.

16. See Press Book for *Marnie,* British Film Institute Library.

17. See Edith Head and Jane Kesner Ardmore, *The Dress Doctor* (Kingswood, Surrey: The World's Work, 1960), 159–60.

18. Edith Head, interviewed by Gwen Robyns for her book *Princess Grace* (London: W. H. Allen, 1982), 88.

19. See Stacey, *Star Gazing,* 176–223.

20. See Thumim, *Celluloid Sisters,* 125–26.

21. Reported in Steven Englund, *Princess Grace* (London: Sphere Books, 1988), 82. Grace Kelly's image was of the respectable, ideal mate. Emphasis was placed on her being "a lady" from a good background. See Thomas Harris, "The Building of Popular Images: Grace Kelly and Marilyn Monroe," in Christine Gledhill, ed., *Stardom: Industry of Desire* (London: Routledge, 1991), 40–44.

22. See particularly Robin Wood, *Hitchcock's Films Revisited* (New York: Columbia University Press, 1989) and Modleski.

As for the hands . . . it is scarcely possible to describe the variety of their motions, since they are almost as expressive as words. For other portions of the body merely help the speaker, whereas the hands may almost be said to speak.

—Quintilian, *Institutio Oratoria*

HITCHCOCK'S HANDS

SABRINA BARTON

Watch Hitchcock as he takes you on a tour of *Psycho*'s set in that movie's famous trailer. Even as he ambles about the Bates Motel and mansion, Hitchcock's dark-suited body seems almost stationary next to the "variety of motions" (as Quintilian puts it) performed by his very active hands. Throughout Hitchcock's witty commentary on *Psycho*, his hands beckon, direct, even at times flutter like birds: "they are almost as expressive as words." Hitchcock's hands comment upon the horror and humor of *Psycho* at the same time that they also speak about aspects of the director himself: his fondness, for example, for using comedic gestures to direct and control public scrutiny of his body and identity.

SPEAKING HANDS

Hitchcock's own demonstrative hands led me to examine the expressive importance of the movements and meanings associated with characters' hands in Hitchcock films. In what ways does the camera repeatedly find and frame those hands? How do hands behave within a given framing? And what, thereby, do Hitchcock's hands seem to *say* to us? Cinematic body language tends toward volubility. It didn't take long to recognize that, among other things, hands in Hitchcock have quite a bit to say about gender. This study begins, more or less, from a question: What happens when feminist film criticism looks at a Hitchcock film, its manner of filming, and instead of concentrating on the "gaze" concentrates on the "hands"?[1]

For example, remember how *Vertigo*'s narrative begins: a pair of hands suddenly erupt into a murkily-lit screen and grab hold of a ladder rung. Thus we are introduced to . . . no wait, that's *not* our hero, that's *not* James Stewart. A criminal is attached to those hands, followed by the police officer (firing a gun), with Stewart as the detective bringing up the rear. But then the detective ("Scottie") fails to clear the leap across rooftops. He slips, dangles, clings to the gutter with both hands for dear life. The police officer courageously reaches down ("Take my hand! Take my hand!") to no avail. Scottie's incapacitated hands cause the officer to fall to his death. The implication that Scottie is a weak, failed, even feminized, hero is confirmed by the following scene: he's wearing a corset.

Hands in Hitchcock films inscribe a pattern of implicit claims about "femininity" and "masculinity." Christian Metz explains how film functions as a visual rhetoric: "A work's manner is a perpetual commentary on what the work says. This commentary is not developed. On the contrary, it is wrapped in the image."[2] I am interested in unwrapping Hitchcock's hand images and analyzing their gendered commentary. I am equally interested in examining how such images and commentaries may elicit spectatorial favor or disfavor for certain characters in the films.

After several years of teaching a course called "Hitchcock and Gender," I have found that feminist film theory's orientation toward the unconscious dimensions of spectatorship can make it difficult to work in a productive way with students' conscious experiences of "liking" characters they perceive as strong. What does it mean that such characters often wield, when it counts, controlled and competent hands? Why might viewers cognitively and emotionally favor those hands, those characters, that prove instrumental in carrying the narrative toward its happy (or at least its explicitly preferable) resolution? And how do such hands—controlled and uncontrolled, competent and incompetent—become gendered through textual arrangements of plot, *mise-en-scène*, editing, and cinematography?

READING HANDS

Narrative openings, as they evolved in the classical Hollywood tradition, play a disproportionate role in defining the audience's way of looking at plot and character. When *Vertigo*'s first sequence offers us the nerve-wracking image of Scottie clinging desperately to the gutter of a roof, the audience is primed for the crisis of masculine identity that follows. In fact, David Bordwell describes as the "primacy effect" the impact such defining information has on how an audience understands plot and character. For Thierry Kuntzel, a film's opening holds a condensed matrix of the motifs and unconscious fantasies that will unfold at length in the scenes to come.[3] Both of these concepts—the primacy effect, the film's matrix—usefully characterize the opening Pet Shop scene of Hitchcock's *The Birds*.

The movie's first several seconds light-heartedly instruct us to link women and birds. Melanie Daniels (Tippi Hedren) hurries on slim legs, with quick bird-like steps, across a busy intersection; she is whistled at appreciatively by a boy on the sidewalk; she looks up and notices the San Francisco sky filling with seagulls. As many critics have observed, these images indicate that Melanie notices birds on the loose and that she herself is a bird on the loose.[4] Melanie then enters the pet shop to pick up a myna bird that she has ordered for her aunt. What follows poses the question, for the first of many times in this movie: what happens when birds and women become uncaged, uninhibited, aggressive?

As Melanie stands alone at the pet-shop counter writing down her address, Mitch Brenner (Rod Taylor) enters the store, and momentarily mistakes her for a salesperson. Melanie, amused by his error, tries to pull off the ruse. But Mitch's smirk telegraphs that it is he who, having recognized Melanie from court, now controls the game. When Mitch slyly induces Melanie to remove a bird from its cage, she loses control of the situation altogether. She cannot keep the bird in her hand. What follows is a remarkable stylistic choice: an elevated and high-angled camera frames the bird as it flies wildly about the ceiling, leaving only the bottom margin of the frame for Melanie's flailing hands (fig. 1). Her hands flutter as erratically and ineffectually as the escaped bird.

The framing of female hands is at once humorous—look, flying hands!—and violent. The camera angle produces a severing effect that, by synecdoche, defines female identity. Melanie is "wrapped" in hand-images that offer "commentary" on her femininity as something grasping yet uncontrolled, something bodily and driven by impulse rather than by thought and agency.

FIGURE 1

Most people find a bird flying randomly about indoors quite unsettling. Yet reaction shots reveal an unfazed Mitch as he watches with amusement and waits. When the bird finally alights in an ashtray, Mitch acts. In one motion, he turns, raises his hat, then lowers it over the bird. The camera follows his action, ending on a close-up of Mitch's hands: one grasping the hat, the other taking hold of the trapped bird (fig. 2). The two women smile and twitter with gratitude and relief ("oh, there"; "wonderful!") as Mitch (reversing Melanie's earlier mistake) carries the bird back to its cage, raises the barred door with competent hands, and firmly restores the bird to captivity.

The formal symmetry of the Pet Shop scene—bird escapes from cage/ bird restored to cage—is narrative and stylistic, but it also (less audibly perhaps) advances an ideological commentary insofar as these two positions are closely identified with a gendered opposition: uncontrolled, incompetent woman (bird escapes)/controlled, competent man (bird restored). The close-up of the captured bird can also be read as rhetorical, inviting the viewer to associate selected images (Mitch's hands and hat) with masculine-identified prowess and achievement.

Such close-ups vividly illustrate how narration—the manner in which the story is told—also proffers an ideological commentary on that story, wrapped in each image. Jacques Aumont credits D. W. Griffith with developing the close-up into a "hyper-articulated writing" whose meaning exceeds "the causal and naturalising chain" of narrative events."[5] In other words, because a given close-up requires its audience to look at a selected

FIGURE 2

detail of the *mise-en-scène,* it thereby hyper-articulates the images: it says far more to us than is strictly mandated by narrative and thematic continuity. An active, analytical response to the close-up might ask: What is at stake (ideologically, for example) in looking at *this* image, in *this* way, at *this* juncture of the film? While one cannot easily make a mainstream narrative film without showing characters' hands doing things, Hitchcock's close-ups of hands (like Fritz Lang's) emphatically frame these gestures in a pointedly rhetorical manner.[6]

The Pet Shop scene's implicit gendered commentary becomes explicit when Mitch instructs his little feathered captive: "Back into your gilded cage, Melanie Daniels." Such insinuations do not necessarily make Mitch a more popular character. Indeed, many of us may find Mitch's patriarchal arrogance obnoxious. Still, the narration indicates that he is needed to maintain law and order, and he will become ever more so as the film progresses.

Melanie does not learn this lesson quickly. Resilient in her sense of fun and adventure, Melanie immediately plots revenge for her pet-shop humiliation. Her hands prove adept as she speedily jots down Mitch's license plate number, tracks his location, and sets off in her convertible with a pair of caged lovebirds to Bodega Bay. Yet how competent is she really? We are provided with numerous images (near and distant) of Melanie steering her convertible along twisting coastal roads at high speeds. Skillful driving signifies a character with agency. (When the shopkeeper in Bodega Bay asks Melanie, "Did you ever handle an outboard boat?" she replies, "Oh, of course.") However, a series of frontal shots of Melanie driving call attention mainly to her facial expression, revealing a preening complacency peculiarly disjunct from the challenging roads and the deafening sound of squealing tires. Low-angle shots that jokingly "match" Melanie's legs with the love birds further undermine her credibility.

Scenes of characters driving cars in Hitchcock films usually speak to us about those characters' agency and control, or lack of agency and control. *Notorious* offers a particularly relevant cluster of examples. Very early on in the film (again: "primacy effect," "matrix"), an exceedingly drunk and stumbling Alicia Huberman (Ingrid Bergman) invites her mysterious party guest (Devlin/Cary Grant) out for a spin in her car, groggily insisting: "I'm going to drive, that's understood." As Alicia weaves wildly around the road at top speed, two quick close-ups inside the car reveal (only to us) the hero's hand by the steering wheel, poised in hair-trigger readiness to take hold of the situation. These hand-images "hyper-articulate" his powers; Devlin *belongs* behind the wheel. Next, after the car has been pulled over for speeding, Devlin's hand, holding his official I.D., elicits patriarchal confirmation from a police officer's hand in the form of a respectful salute. When a furious Alicia still refuses to relinquish the steering wheel, Devlin's hand delivers a sharp and effective karate chop to the hysterical woman's wrist, after which he knocks her unconscious in order to take her place behind the wheel.

But each character's relation to his or her hands will soon shift. Paralyzed by ambivalence, Devlin finds himself sitting on a park bench for much of the film. Alicia, meanwhile, agrees to work undercover to expose a Nazi plot. In a pivotal scene, she secures the forbidden wine-cellar key (we see a close-up of her fingers removing the key). Unfortunately, Alex Sebastian (Claude Rains) chooses this moment to pry open his new wife's fingers in order to kiss her palms. Halting in one gesture both the sexual violation and the discovery of her own duplicity, Alicia throws her arms around his neck. A close-up behind Alex's back features Alicia's luminously lit hand deftly transferring the key to safety (fig. 3). The dynamics of gender, hands, and power will shift again by the end of *Notorious*. Devlin rescues a near-death Alicia, his hands once again on the steering wheel as he drives her off to safety and romance.

A similar deterioration of female agency and attitude occurs in *The Birds*, beginning with Melanie's return trip across the bay. The numerous shots of Melanie's desiring looks during the delivery-by-boat sequence have been interpreted as triggering, psychoanalytically-speaking, a retaliatory reversal in the double form of Mitch's gaze and the gull attack.[7] I wish to emphasize, however, the significance of Melanie's *hands* as they manipulate

FIGURE 3

birdcages and binoculars, oars and engines. Melanie's hands are narratively and stylistically highlighted as the necessary instruments of her desire, cognition, and agency. Equally, then, they represent the loss of those qualities. When Melanie is hit by a gull as she nears the dock, one hand by reflex goes to her head while her steering hand simply "flies" up into air. The boat is adrift. The camera cuts to an extreme-close-up of her gloved finger, now painted with bright red blood (fig. 4). When Mitch helps her up to the dock, he murmurs gently, "That's the girl."

As in *Notorious*, the formation of the romantic couple in *The Birds* depends upon the heroine's drastic loss of power, a loss signaled by her helpless hands. Near the end of the film, Melanie goes upstairs to the attic, alone, to investigate a noise. Two close-ups center on her hand, as it hovers near and then clasps the doorknob. But just as when she presumptuously opened the cage in the pet shop and then couldn't control the consequences, so here, too, when Melanie opens the attic door she utterly loses control of the situation. Instead of a single bird, countless birds swoop. Melanie's hands, once again, flail incessantly and ineffectually. Attempts to fend off birds with her flashlight or to get the door back open prove futile. Over and over the editing displays Melanie's once manicured, now bleeding, fingers as they are bitten by birds.

Mitch comes to the rescue. As he tends to Melanie, now collapsed on the sofa in a near-psychotic state, she abruptly tries to ward off an imagined attack, her hands once again like birds, flying randomly. Directed straight at the camera, these movements are especially unsettling as they momentarily

FIGURE 4

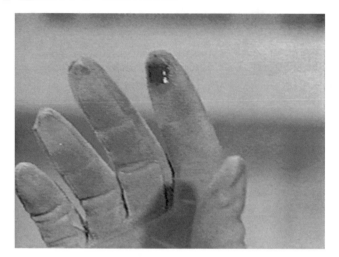

penetrate the organized space of the camera's own "fourth wall." When Mitch manages to pin Melanie's wings back across her chest, order is restored. Finally, Mitch fetches the car and guides a comatose Melanie into the contained space of the backseat (no more daredevil driving for her). Mitch belongs behind the wheel. He closes the car doors, gets behind the wheel, and begins to drive: everyone's fate lies in his hands.

I should note that, before this getaway, we are treated to shots of Mitch's hand getting savagely bitten by birds as he struggles to close a window-shutter during an attack. But, unlike Melanie, he keeps at it and manages to get the shutters closed, cleverly securing them with a lamp cord that he rips from the wall. With the attack still in full force, Mitch gathers the women, who have been writhing and huddling against the walls, and steers them onto the furniture. Mitch's gestures visually assert his mastery over the situation. He adeptly bandages his own hand, and resumes hammering planks and even furniture to doors and windows, securing the house as best he can. Mitch's showdown only shortly precedes Melanie's trip to the attic, thereby reinforcing the contrast between the two. His injuries, though painful, are on the surface: mere flesh wounds. Melanie's wounds extend into her core self, damaging her cognitive and emotional faculties (as the bandages wrapped about her head suggest). One might even argue that Mitch's protracted skirmish helps him finally to become the man—instead of the boy—of the house, while Melanie's fool's mission to the attic reduces her to a dependent girl.

TEACHING HANDS

These readings of *The Birds* and *Notorious* invite us to ask of Hitchcock's films: Whose hands open and close doors? Whose hands have the agency and ability to effect rescues? When I teach my "Hitchcock and Gender" course, some students become thoroughly disgusted with Melanie when she not only shuts the attic door behind her, but actually blocks it with her own body. Why, they want to know, can't the reasonably resourceful Melanie simply turn around, open the door, and escape from the attacking birds? That failure only makes sense when understood as gendered rhetoric: Melanie cannot open the door because this scene is *about* her incapacitation.

Usually at least one (female) student in my "Hitchcock and Gender" class is also disturbed by the sight of Melanie's chipped and scratched manicure, visible in close-up as she rests in Lydia's arms in the backseat of the car. Melanie's strong red nails have represented a sort of feminine armor, and the loss of that armor (mere varnish) elicits pity, but also revulsion. Melanie's damaged nails have become a visual trope for abject, bodily fragmentation.

All of these student responses raise a pedagogical dilemma: How can one teach productively those moments at which a film's rhetoric concerning gender differentiation derails a viewer's emotional investment in a woman character? Do we then simply condemn the movie for its negative image of a woman? Can we blame the tyranny of Hollywood genre conventions ("This is just what happens to women who go into attics alone in suspense-horror films")? But neither of these alternatives illuminates the mechanisms that underlie the gendered commentary.

Alternatively, by way of explication, one could draw on a post-structuralist psychoanalytic arsenal: "Listen up students: what matters here is how the film structures, for the spectator's unconscious, a sadomasochistic pleasure in the symbolic castration of the blonde object."[8] And yet, however well this rejoinder may articulate one underlying fantasy at work in *The Birds*, it fails to speak to the spectator's conscious engagement or disengagement with Melanie Daniels.

Feminist film scholarship needs, I believe, to become more attuned to when and why and in what ways viewers experience themselves as "liking" or "not liking" characters. After all, American feminist film critics of the early 1970s took for granted the importance for women in a patriarchal society of having popular cultural "role models" or "positive images" with which to connect. What can we learn by taking seriously those spectators who wish to admire and value and (consciously) identify with certain kinds of characters? As I argued above, filmic images such as shots of hands beckon us—and sometimes pull and push us—toward gendered perceptions of characters. What can we say about the cognitive and emotional consequences of those perceptions?

Here is an illustrative anecdote.[9] It was the week before Spring Break, and my "Hitchcock and Gender" students were discussing *Marnie* in the context of selected readings on the feminist psychoanalytic theory of masquerade. Sophisticated observations were made about Marnie's (Tippi Hedren) masqueraded—and hence elusive—subjectivity, which Mark Rutland (Sean Connery), for all his prowess, cannot entirely master. Well, well, I thought to myself, this class has certainly come a long way since the "I like/ I dislike that character" approach that dominated their responses at the start of the term. Then, with fifteen minutes left of class time, I decided, as a sort of informal review, to ask my students which of the Hitchcock films that we had thus far viewed most challenged or revealed the conventions of Hollywood gender representation.

That question triggered an instant return to the students' emotional connections with "strong" stars and characters: "I liked the two Ingrid Bergman movies the best"; "Yeah—she was really strong and memorable"; "It was a good strategy to start the course with *Rebecca*—there was no where to go but up from that washout wife"; "I agree, I couldn't identify with Joan Fontaine at all"; "But Charlie in *Shadow of a Doubt* was the best: she really stood up to her psycho uncle." Marnie's masqueraded identity fell by the wayside as soon as the students were allowed to voice their personal responses to the films' protagonists.

In retrospect, did I honestly expect my students to overlook that debilitating image, late in the movie, of Marnie's hand as it attempts and fails to steal money from the Rutland safe: her hand, once controlled and competent (if criminal), now neurotic and helpless? No longer taking orders, Marnie's hand quivers with a (disturbed) mind of its own, trapped within the rhythmic zoom-in, zoom-out close-up (symbolic, lest we miss the point, of her internal conflict over betraying Mark). This bit of camera rhetoric virtually shouts its commentary about Marnie's damaged identity, creating a caricature-effect that rarely fails to elicit hilarity from an undergraduate audience. How far our Marnie of the film's opening, defined by assured hands that cleverly arrange her next caper, has fallen.

Charlie Newton (Teresa Wright), the female protagonist of *Shadow of a Doubt,* follows a narrative trajectory dramatically different from that of either Melanie or Marnie: by the end of the movie, this woman has come to see more, know more, and do more. Charlie is the only member of her family who suspects her Uncle Charlie (Joseph Cotten) of being the infamous "Merry Widow" murderer; therefore, it is up to her to save her family and her town from a serial killer.

Charlie, I submit, is a positive image of a strong woman. I am not forgetting that what counts as "positive" or "strong" can mean many different things to different people and requires constant critical interrogation. (These days, Hollywood's answer to the strong woman character takes the form of muscular action heroines.) I suspect that, at bottom, one key axis that prompts us to admire and value and (consciously) identify with a character is the film's representation of that character's *selfhood* as fundamentally strong, constituting a unified and active agent whose efforts—in the context of the film—are coded as positive (as right or moral or desirable).

In *Shadow of a Doubt*, the female protagonist's agency is expressed through her controlled and effective hands. Charlie eventually does what so many heroines facing some form of jeopardy must do: she heads up the stairs alone to investigate a forbidden space. Women on staircases in 1940s gothics tend to appear either as visual objects or as non-credible investigators soon to be victimized.[10] However, when Charlie ascends and then descends the stairs (unlike Melanie heading for the attic), she is a subject with a plan: to search her uncle's bedroom, find the emerald ring he stole from one of his murdered widows, and use that ring as a weapon against her uncle.

With family and friends enjoying a reception for her uncle in the living-room below, Charlie descends the stairs, her well-lit hand displayed on the banister. Mid-toast, Uncle Charlie smiles as he catches sight of his niece. Then he freezes. The camera races in for an extreme-close-up of Charlie's hand: there, the incriminating ring gleams (fig. 5). The mere sight of Charlie's hand forces her uncle to reverse his planned announcement that he will be staying on in Santa Rosa. What makes Charlie so powerful here is her controlled agency in redirecting her uncle's course of action. Scarcely lifting a finger, she transforms his reception into a farewell party.

This is the Charlie championed during the "Hitchcock and Gender" discussion. Even though the students had, by that point in the term, acquired a critical understanding of filmic character as constructed from performative surfaces and psycho-cultural fantasies, that critical awareness somehow seemed to have lodged in a different part of their reception experience from their conscious enjoyment of Charlie as a strong woman. Whereas Melanie's and Marnie's ever more damaged and useless hands diminish the value attached to their characters, Charlie's increasingly capable

FIGURE 5

hands, employed to save her family and town, invite viewers to see her as strong and admirable.

What, then, can we do with this correlation: weak hands, weak woman; strong hands, strong woman?[11] Feminist critics may find it troubling that a viewer who values Charlie is, in fact, following the beckoning of the film's "commentary" on her character. The tendency of feminist film analysis has been to read against, not with, the grain of Hollywood films and their attendant ideologies of gender. But I am trying to envision a feminist film criticism that, alongside its skepticism, also acknowledges the powers exerted and pleasures elicited by positive images of strong characters. Such a goal prompts a question less self-evident than it may seem: What makes a movie's strong woman character—that is, one whose self is coded as (mostly) strong, active, and coherent—so successful in its bid for audience favor?

THINKING HANDS

I have found in cognitive psychology, as adapted through cognitivist film theory, some powerful explanations of what makes selves represented as strong so compelling for audiences. To date, feminist-psychoanalytic film studies, on the one hand, and cognitivist film studies, on the other, have been mostly indifferent, or even hostile, toward one another. That mutual indifference is unfortunate and unnecessary.

Cognitive science is an interdisciplinary field exploring the mental processes and procedures that enable humans, with such rapidity, to make sense of the massive influx of sensory data that we slog through every day. Human cognition, the field claims, relies on a variety of mental schemas (grids, patterns)—hybrids of hardwiring and acculturation—to transform that influx into meaning. Cognitive film theorist Murray Smith, in his study of how spectators form allegiances with movie characters, calls our attention to the "person schema." Person schema refers to the foundational cognitive grid used, transculturally, by human beings to divide and categorize sensory data as either *human* or *nonhuman*.[12] According to Smith, humanness is signaled, above all, by evidence of agency: that is, by a being's volitional relation to time and space (as opposed to responses driven only by need, reflex, and instinct). Humanness, in other words, is cued by such attributes as "thought, intention, self-awareness, self-impelled actions, and so on."[13] Such qualities perfectly describe the Charlie of the staircase/ring scene, where she earns privileged person-schema status. Note that Charlie's performance of the "strong woman" does not depend on physical strength; cognition and control alone signal her success. Hands must "think" before they act.

By this measure, Uncle Charlie loses person-schema status in *Shadow of a Doubt*. Paradoxically, the infamous "strong handed stranger" (as the local newspaper refers to the Merry-Widow murderer) is inherently weak: his hands and his mind are depicted as precisely *not* under control. Every time his niece moves closer to the truth, Uncle Charlie loses his grip. Not long after Uncle Charlie arrives at the Newton home, Charlie laughingly appropriates the newspaper page he's hidden away. A point-of-view shot from Charlie's perspective frames Uncle Charlie as he thunders up and wrenches her wrist to retrieve the evidence, jerking her forward. With Uncle Charlie holding her wrist, Charlie flinches and cries out, "Uncle Charlie, you're hurting me, your hand!"

Uncle Charlie's hands get the better of him on several occasions. One scene places us with Uncle Charlie by a window where he watches his niece waiting for Detective Graham outside. The framing drops to waist-level in order to emphasize how Uncle Charlie's hands suddenly twitch into a murderous choke-hold, causing his smoldering cigar to fall unnoticed to the floor. Images of involuntary hand movements comment on his mental instability.

The framing of hands and the movements of hands within that framing draw a distinction between the controlled agency of Charlie (coded as human) and the uncontrolled impulses of her uncle (coded as inhuman).

Torben Grodal argues that when a film character is represented as losing "humanness"—a loss cued first and foremost through her or his loss of agency—one effect is to impair spectator identification with that character:

> If [the character's] capacity for voluntary acts and thinking is blocked, this leads to a feeling of alienation, strangeness, and un-reality in the viewer, as experienced in watching horror films and science fiction, for example, when a person with whom we have a sympathetic relation suddenly becomes possessed by alien forces and behaves according to a "fixed pattern."[14]

Even if we have found Uncle Charlie intriguing and compelling (and he is the only character in the film who dresses with any flair), the more his intense behavior takes on the contours of a "fixed pattern," the harder it becomes (at least consciously) to identify with him.

Withdrawal from Uncle Charlie is reinforced by the film's narrational focus on and through Charlie's character. We are on her side, so to speak, as she learns to pull her hands and her self away from her uncle. When the uncle strong-arms his niece into the 'Til Two Club for a confrontation, she cries out: "Uncle Charlie, you're hurting me, again!" Then, sitting at a table inside the club, Uncle Charlie tries to take Charlie's hand as he quotes back her own earlier words: "We're more than uncle and niece." But Charlie quickly and successfully jerks her hand back off the table: "Don't touch me, Uncle Charlie." Although most feminist critics have read Charlie as losing a certain "phallic" force when she severs her transgressive identification with her uncle,[15] I would argue that, on the contrary, when she willfully detaches from him, Charlie becomes far better able to see, think, intend, and act. Don't forget the Charlie of *Shadow*'s opening, collapsed in bed, passive, and caught within a dangerously distorted perception of her uncle. When Charlie becomes an investigator, she moves up in the movie's person-schema hierarchy. "Massive viewer interest" claims Grodal "indicates that the phenomenon of 'humanness' has very strong cognitive and affective appeal." One dominant version of appealing humanness has been codified through Hollywood's rendering of the "acting, intending, and thinking subject."[16]

If the correlation of valued humanness with acting, intending, and thinking subjects seems familiar, perhaps that is because, like me, you hear the strong resonance this formulation has with Laura Mulvey's work. Left unexamined by Grodal, and touched on only tangentially by Smith, is the fact that Hollywood culture's privileged representatives of human agency also happen, far more often than not, to be male. Mulvey, like Smith and

Grodal, emphasizes the central significance of spectator identifications with character, but places her emphasis on sexual differentiation: "The split between narrative and spectacle supports the man's role as the active one of forwarding the story, making things happen."[17] This active male hero, as explained in psychoanalytic terms by Mulvey, elicits the (male) spectator's identifications with a phallic position, in part by reducing women to fetishized objects of the camera's and the hero's gaze.

Bringing in cognitive film theory can help to explain an additional layer of what I take to be the multi-layered spectator experience. When members of an audience find themselves "liking" a "positive" image of a woman, such feelings may be elicited (among other things) by that character's strong showing in the film narrative's (implicit) person-schema contest. Yet because the person schema has been acculturated under patriarchy, images of women tend habitually (by cognitive-classificatory habit) to be aligned with images of less-than-ideal or flawed human agency, which is why there is feminist value in laying claim to Charlie's personhood, to her efficacy as an active, intending, thinking character: "But Charlie in *Shadow of a Doubt* was the best; she really stood up to her psycho-uncle."

When Charlie comes down the stairs with that ring on her hand and confronts Uncle Charlie, she not only represents "virtue" riskily confronting "villainy" (to condense Noël Carroll's view of why audiences root for heroes in suspense thrillers);[18] she also represents, through stance and gesture, a particular version of thinking, intending and acting selfhood that has, as Grodal put it, "very strong cognitive and affective appeal."[19] *Shadow of a Doubt* is exceptional for what it allows its heroine—and her hands—to do.

There are, without question, powerful women with effective minds and capable hands throughout Hitchcock's works. Often, though (as we saw with Melanie Daniels and Alicia Huberman), their person-schema powers must in the course of the narrative give way to damage or punishment. Moreover, that punishment (as so much feminist film scholarship has explored) is overwhelmingly connected with, if not caused by, the culturally-defined "feminine" aspects of their selves, such as the sexualized surfaces of their bodies.

Still, I find that in Hitchcock films, more than most, a character's gender neither wholly encompasses nor neatly predicts what her or his relation to hands and agency will be. Although familiar cultural ideologies of gender identity are inevitably voiced, the "perpetual commentary" humming through Hitchcock films is complex, suggesting that configurations of hands, genders, and identities are far more subtle, variable, and shifting than one might think.

CHANGING HANDS

Hitchcock's male protagonists (usually problematic heroes at best) can have "hand problems" too. Earlier I invoked Scottie's hands in *Vertigo,* hands that fail, hands that are judged "weak" by a panel of men in the inquest scene. Popular audiences of the late fifties were dismayed and put off by Scottie and *Vertigo.*

Two years later, the same audience was captivated by Cary Grant's suave performance in *North by Northwest.* Initially, Roger O. Thornhill lacks commitment, competence, and control. His drinking and his divorces are coded as decidedly unheroic. However, by the conclusion of *North by Northwest,* Thornhill is scaling the walls of his antagonist's home like a veritable spider-man. A close-up shot displays for us the bloody scrape that Thornhill's hand incurs from this climbing feats, but (as with Mitch in *The Birds*) it's merely a flesh wound. In no time at all, Thornhill is clambering about Mount Rushmore. If the hero ends up dangling even more perilously than Scottie, by only one hand, that is because he has grabbed his falling blonde (Eve/Eva Marie Saint) with his other hand. Leonard (Martin Landau) steps over, delighted at the opportunity to trample and grind Thornhill's grip on the monument. But to no avail. Thornhill masterfully (indeed, magically) pulls Eve up from mountainside to train berth, in one grand gesture. His fingers' five tidy band-aids tell us (if we even notice them) how superficial the injuries are.[20]

Scottie's wounds, on the contrary, run deep, deep into his selfhood, and, therefore, into his manhood. No surprise that he is left, in *Vertigo*'s final shot, bitterly empty-handed. As Tania Modleski has persuasively argued, Scottie's feminized qualities are of a piece with Hitchcock's many "images of ambiguous sexuality," images "that threaten to destabilize the gender identity of protagonists and viewers alike."[21] What I have found is that in Hitchcock films hands that move involuntarily tend to signal a falling away (temporary or permanent) from the culturally-valued version of the person-schema. Furthermore, involuntary or simply excessive hand-movements tend to be coded as feminine and/or psychotic. Western culture's conflation of femininity not only with sexuality but also with weak cognition and control may well help to explain why so many male murderers in Hitchcock films are feminized or delicately wrapped in cinema's codified signs for male homosexuality.

Let's look at three examples of uncontrolled hands that signal queer-coded male killers. In *Rope,* as guests arrive at the dinner party given by co-killers Brandon (John Dall) and Philip (Farley Granger), the latter is mistaken for the two men's recently strangled victim, David (Dick Hogan). This confusion causes the already panicked (hence feminized) Philip to flinch and splinter his champagne glass; the camera methodically travels over to frame his bloodied fingers for us. Shortly afterward, hailed by Mrs. Atwater to get his palm read, Philip suddenly fixates on his own hands, now shaped into a choke-hold. In *Strangers on a Train,* the hands of increasingly out-of-control murderer Bruno Anthony (Robert Walker) repeatedly twitch into strangle-mode. Also, with regard to excessive hand movements, Bruno's hands (manicured-by-mother) flutter flirtatiously over and around the stiffly-withheld body of his object of desire, Guy (Farley Granger). And in *Psycho,* Norman's (Anthony Perkins) nervous hands constantly fidget and pop candy into his mouth, uncontrolled hands a bodily symptom of uncontrolled desires.

Hands that fidget from anger or impatience may connote masculine vigor. However, anxiously fidgeting hands tend to signal bodily and emotional hysteria, carrying connotations of femininity, even childlikeness. While this condition may not be entirely displeasing in the form of, say, Joan Fontaine in *Rebecca,* whose clumsiness and nail-biting provide Laurence Olivier with the pleasure of repeatedly reprimanding his new bride, in an adult male fidgeting (flinching, flailing, or fixated) hands cue something off-kilter or even unmanly about him.

After Charlie and Uncle Charlie are seated at the 'Til Two Club, and after Charlie refuses to let her uncle take her hand, he picks up a napkin, smooths it on the table, and begins to fold it. A cut to a close-up of Charlie's face reveals her startled expression, which in turn motivates a cut back to Uncle Charlie's hands as they unthinkingly twist—or rather, strangle—the napkin (fig. 6). A close-up of Uncle Charlie's face reveals that he suddenly notices her stare and, in response, he glances down a couple of times. Finally, the camera cuts back to his hands grasping the napkin and we hear (unrealistically heightened) the sound of twisting paper as Uncle Charlie slides his unsavory hands under the table and out of sight.

If gendered commentaries, wrapped in the image, prompt viewers (cognitively and emotionally) to perceive involuntary out-of-control hands as negative, then those of us interested in cultural identity politics may wish to look closely at which characters' hands, traditionally and currently, tend to fidget, flinch, or flail. The fact that Hitchcock's movies so often blur the boundaries of strong and weak, normal and abnormal, foregrounds but does not undo such classifications. While characters such as

FIGURE 6

the dandyish, incestuous Uncle Charlie may compel, fascinate, and elicit unconscious identification, he and Hitchcock's other boundary-blurring men are unlikely to be narratively rewarded, culturally valued, or claimed by admiring spectators as positive images and role models.

We have looked at how images of hands in Hitchcock films function—rhetorically, cognitively, emotionally, and culturally—to help shape audience's relationships with characters. Textual analysis remains an important tool for unwrapping the images that transmit a film's gender commentary. The goal here is neither to discount nor to celebrate the viewer's "I like/I don't like" responses to character, but rather to draw those responses into a new critical framework. The concept of the person-schema indicates that while at one level spectators are undoubtedly captivated by the transgressive potential of fluid subjectivities, they are also drawn to images of stable selves, to characters who think and act in ways that are socially valued and rewarded. For this reason, it is worth reclaiming the somewhat discredited hunt for positive images of those whose identities have been persistently devalued as less than human by cultural representations.[22]

As I teach my "Hitchcock and Gender" classes, I hope to do a better job of working with what my students perceive as positive and negative (strong and weak) characters. Perhaps a pedagogy and a criticism that pay close attention to the commentaries on identity so eloquently choreographed by Hitchcock's hands can help to expand our habitual sense of who and what counts as human, and which hands we want to hold on to.[23]

NOTES

1. In this essay, I generalize on the basis of a small sampling of Hitchcock's films in a rather risky way. I do so in order to develop a preliminary set of critical coordinates for thinking about Hitchcock's gendered hands. Most often, critics have commented upon Hitchcock's hands only in passing. For example, James McLaughlin's "All in the Family: Alfred Hitchcock's *Shadow of a Doubt*," in *A Hitchcock Reader,* ed. Marshall Deutelbaum and Leland Pogue (Ames: Iowa State University Press, 1983), 141–152, comments on Uncle Charlie's vampire-like grip and then, in an endnote, offers an eclectic sampling of Hitchcock's hand-images, which McLaughlin associates with vampirist, romance, or murder motifs (151n. 3). After the initial publication of my essay in the *Hitchcock Annual,* I discovered a short essay by Yuri Makino titled "Hands and Hitchcock," in *Focus 7* (spring 1987): 15–17. Drawing on Freud and German Expressionism, Makino argues that Hitchcock's characters' hands function as physical manifestations of "inner feelings that have been repressed," particularly feelings of guilt (15).

2. Christian Metz, "The Impersonal Enunciation, or the Site of Film: In the Margin of Recent Works on Enunciation in Cinema," trans. Beatrice Durand-Sendrail with Kristen Brookes, in *The Film Spectator: From Sign to Mind,* ed. Warren Buckland (Amsterdam: Amsterdam University Press, 1995), 156.

3. David Bordwell, *Narration in the Fiction Film* (Madison: University of Wisconsin Press, 1985), 38; Thierry Kuntzel "The Film-Work, 2," in *Camera Obscura 5* (spring 1980): 20.

4. Most recently, for example, see Richard Allen "Avian Metaphor in *The Birds,*" *Hitchcock Annual* (1997–98): 40–67 (reprinted in this volume). Criticism on *The Birds* has heavily favored psychoanalytic interpretations of the film. See, among others, Robert Samuels, *Hitchcock's Bi-Textuality: Lacan, Feminisms, and Queer Theory* (Albany: State University of New York Press, 1998); Slavoj Žižek, "The Hitchcockian Blot," in *Looking Awry: An Introduction to Jacques Lacan through Popular Culture* (Cambridge: MIT Press, 1991), 88–106; and Bill Nichols, "For *The Birds,*" in *Ideology and the Image* (Bloomington: Indiana University Press, 1981), 133–69.

5. Jacques Aumont, "Griffith: the Frame, the Figure," in *Early Cinema: Space, Frame, Narrative,* ed. Thomas Elsaesser, with Adam Barker (London: British Film Institute Publishing, 1990), 356. It is because of their specially marked significance that close-ups of hands dominate my essay's repertoire of examples. The visual rhetoric inscribed by Hitchcock's hands is very likely indebted to Griffith's own fascinating close-ups of gendered hands.

6. The significance of hand images in Lang's *M* is illuminated by Anton Kaes in *M* (London: British Film Institute, 2000). According to Tom Gunning, Lang spoke of using his own hand for a series of anonymous cameos: the director's hand would

stand in for an actor's during certain close-ups of hands. See Gunning, *The Films of Fritz Lang: Allegories of Vision and Modernity* (London: British Film Institute, 2000).

7. See Raymond Bellour's groundbreaking study, "*Les oiseaux*: Analyse d'une séquence," *Cahiers du Cinema* no. 216 (October 1969): 24–38.

8. I don't mean to parody this approach. Psychoanalysis has shed brilliant light on visual culture's compulsion to fetishize and attack the female body. In "Hitchcock's Hands," I begin to explore how the cognitive and psychoanalytic dimensions of spectatorship work with and against each other.

9. I included the following classroom anecdote in the endnotes of a previously published essay on related issues of gender, identity, and spectatorship, but did not analyze the discussion in the context of cognitive theory, as I will here. See Barton, "Your Self Storage: Female Investigation and Male Performativity in the Woman's Psychothriller," in *The New American Cinema*, ed. Jon Lewis (Durham, NC: Duke University Press, 1998), 187–216.

10. Mary Ann Doane, *The Desire to Desire* (Bloomington: Indiana University Press, 1987). The stairs, Doane argues, lead heroines to an "image of the worst" (136).

11. Distinguishing strong from weak hands can be tricky. In *Blackmail*, for example, the artist, Crewe (Cyril Ritchard), has masterful hands: he guides Alice's (Anny Ondra) hand in a sketch, plays the piano, adjusts her dress, and finally grabs and sexually assaults her. During the assault, Alice's arm suddenly protrudes from a curtained bedstead, flails, manages to get hold of a knife, then disappears behind the curtain again. Next, the rapist's dead arm drops through the curtain and hangs in the frame. However, Alice's active self-defense is not rewarded with further signs of strength or agency. Instead, she is haunted through the night by hallucinatory images of Crewe's stiff limb (superimposed on the arm of the beckoning traffic cop and on that of a man sprawled on the street). By the next morning, Alice cannot even keep the breakfast bread knife secured in her hand.

12. Murray Smith, *Engaging Characters: Fiction, Emotion, and the Cinema* (Oxford: Clarendon Press, 1995), esp. 20–31. Smith is indebted to David Bordwell's analysis of how even structuralist critics rely heavily on "person schema" inferences when dealing with filmic characters. See Bordwell, *Making Meaning: Inference and Rhetoric in the Interpretation of Cinema* (Cambridge: Harvard University Press, 1989).

13. Smith, *Engaging Characters*, 17.

14. Torben Grodal, *Moving Pictures: A New Theory of Film Genres, Feeling, and Cognition* (Oxford: Clarendon Press, 1997), 120–21.

15. See, for example, Diane Carson, "The Nightmare World of Hitchcock's Women," in *The Kingdom of Dreams*, ed. Douglas Fowler (Gainesville: University Presses of Florida, 1986), 11–20, and McLaughlin, "All in the Family: Alfred Hitchcock's *Shadow of a Doubt*." In an important divergence from this critical pattern,

Thomas Hemmeter offers a more affirmative feminist view of Charlie as left "in a marginal position between marriage and unmarriage." See "Hitchcock the Feminist: Rereading *Shadow of a Doubt*," *Hitchcock Annual* (1993): 24 (reprinted in this volume).

16. Grodal, *Moving Pictures*, 120.

17. Laura Mulvey, "Visual Pleasure and Narrative Cinema," *Screen* 16, no. 3 (1975): 6–18.

18. Noël Carroll, "The Paradox of Suspense," in *Suspense: Conceptualizations, Theoretical Analyses, and Empirical Explorations*, ed. Peter Vorderer, Hans J. Wulff, and Mike Friedrichsen (Mahwah, NJ: Lawrence Erlbaum Associates, 1996), 71–91.

19. Grodal, *Moving Pictures*, 120.

20. I would not have noticed them without the description in the screenplay: "He put his arms around her, and as they kiss lovingly, we see the hand that was stepped on. Each finger is neatly taped with a Band-Aid." Ernest Lehman, *North by Northwest* (London: Faber and Faber, 1999), 196.

21. Tania Modleski, *The Women Who Knew Too Much: Hitchcock and Feminist Theory* (New York: Methuen, 1988), 5.

22. Judith Butler has written extensively on representational systems in which certain bodies come to matter, while others are abjected, pushed outside the boundaries of the speakable and thinkable, much less the admirable. See especially *Bodies That Matter: On the Discursive Limits of "Sex"* (New York: Routledge, 1993).

23. Many, many thanks to Phillip Barrish for incisive comments on argument and revisions, Sidney Gottlieb for wise and gracious editing, Kelly Kessler and Brian Bremen for generous help with the images, James and Erica Haba for scrupulous read-throughs, and Robert Barton for putting Quintilian in my hands.

THE HITCHCOCK MOMENT

Thomas M. Leitch

Early and late, Alfred Hitchcock's is preeminently a cinema of moments. Who can forget the moment when Alice White, still dazed by her fatal stabbing of the artist who tried to rape her in *Blackmail*, is forced to sit through a conversation in which the word "knife" keeps leaping out at her? Or the moment in which the charwoman in *The 39 Steps* signals the discovery of a corpse in Richard Hannay's London flat by screaming, only to have the scream blend in with the whistle of the train carrying Hannay off to Scotland? Or the moment in *Young and Innocent* when the heroine despairingly announces that the villain she's seeking must be here *somewhere* and the camera obligingly cranes across two rooms to an agonizingly tight closeup of his twitching eyes? Or the moment in *Notorious* when Alex Sebastian tells his mother he's married to an American agent, and Mrs. Sebastian lights up a cigarette and instantly turns into Ma Barker? Or the moment in *Strangers on a Train* when Guy Haines, trying to get away from the psychopathic Bruno Anthony, plays a tennis match, and the camera shows Bruno's head the only one in a crowded grandstand that's not bobbing back and forth to watch the play? Or the moment in *Rear Window* when L. B. Jefferies, who's been spending the entire film snooping on Lars Thorwald, finally sees Thorwald peering back at him? Or the moment in *Psycho* when Norman Bates puts paid to Marion Crane's terror that somebody will catch her with the $40,000 she's stolen by casually tossing a newspaper with the money still hidden inside on top of her corpse and slamming the trunk door? Or the moment in *Frenzy* when Bob Rusk's mother sticks her head out an upstairs window to say hello to Richard Blaney, invoking in that one brief cameo an entire generation of lethal Hitchcock mothers?

For better or worse, the success of Hitchcock's films is intimately bound up with such moments. Reviewing *Secret Agent* in 1936, Graham Greene complained that Hitchcock's films consisted of "a series of small 'amusing' melodramatic situations. . . . Very perfunctorily he builds up to these tricky situations (paying no attention on the way to inconsistencies, loose ends, psychological absurdities) and then drops them; they mean nothing; they lead to nothing."[1] Hitchcock himself, describing his films to François Truffaut thirty years later, changed little but Greene's minatory tone in extolling the big moments in *The Lodger* and *North by Northwest.* And if many of Hitchcock's films, from *Secret Agent* to *Saboteur* to *Frenzy,* seem, as Greene suggests, to be in danger of collapsing into an anthology of overinflated, often self-plagiarized moments, the relative failure of such films as *Topaz* and *Family Plot* can be traced to their lack of memorable moments. To a surprising extent, Hitchcock's work stands or falls with the Hitchcock moment.

Whenever a reviewer anoints a new Master of Suspense—something that happens with alarming frequency—the piquancy of the Hitchcock moment is invoked. Yet the trademark moments that make Hitchcock's films so pleasurable are as distinctive as his famous cameos. Recent filmmakers working in the suspense genre have produced many big moments of their own, but these moments differ so strikingly from the moments most characteristic of Hitchcock's work that for the most part they may be used to define the Hitchcock moment in terms of what it is not.

The most obvious point to make about the Hitchcock moment is that despite its detachable status, its aptness for visual anthologies, it is not necessarily a big moment. With a few notable exceptions from *Psycho* and *The Birds,* the Hitchcock moment is not physically intense or kinetic. Instead of the speeding car chase so beloved of Hollywood filmmakers, for instance, Hitchcock gives us a circular chase, heading nowhere, on a merry-go-round in *Strangers on a Train,* or the pursuit of the good bus by the stolid, unwitting bad bus in *Torn Curtain,* or the absurd pursuit of Roger Thornhill by a crop-dusting plane in *North by Northwest,* or the world's slowest car chase in

Vertigo. When Hitchcock does present what looks like a straightforward car chase in *Foreign Correspondent*, the chase, punctuated by Huntley Haverstock's unexpected meeting with Carol Fisher and her decorous introduction of Scott ffolliott—"beginning, old boy, and they're both small f's"—ends with the disappearance of the killer's car in a field dotted with windmills, introducing a deceptively quiet, menacing sequence filled with more authentically Hitchcock moments: the moment when an alleged farmer surreptitiously rubs dirt on his hands, for example, or the moment when Haverstock sees the windmill's vanes change directions. Again, the chases in *To Catch a Thief*, a movie that might be described as nothing more than a series of chases with brief time-outs for drinks and sex, are repeatedly and comically undermined, from the opening police pursuit of the person who turns out not to be John Robie, to the film's central set-piece, in which the most urgent question is not whether the police will keep Robie and Francie Stevens in sight, but whether Francie will succeed in seducing Robie into admitting that he really is the Cat. Throughout *To Catch a Thief*, as in many of Hitchcock's other films, the pursuers do not really want to catch their quarry but rather to continue the chase forever—not exactly a recipe for the high-energy chases so beloved of contemporary action directors.

The unobtrusive obtrusiveness of these moments distinguishes them from the quasi-Hitchcockian moments in the films of Brian De Palma. The drug deals gone bad in *Scarface* and *Carlito's Way*, the 360–degree pans in *Obsession* and *The Untouchables*, the numberless shower scenes from *The Phantom of the Paradise* to *Blow Out*, all of them take off from Hitchcock—De Palma often seems to have spent his formative years locked in a projection booth with only prints of *Vertigo* and *Psycho* and a thousand-pound box of jujubes—but they are all based on the most inflated of Hitchcock's many memorable moments. The clearest sign of this inflation is the way De Palma literally stops time in his biggest moments by shooting in slow-motion, as in the climaxes of *Obsession* and *Carrie* and *Dressed to Kill* and *Body Double* and *The Untouchables* and *Raising Cain* and *Carlito's Way*. Each of these moments, like the split-screens De Palma favors in *Sisters* and the lyrical panning shots he affects throughout his career, abstracts a single instant from the narrative by inflating and aestheticizing it, as if the director could not bear to let it go. The narrative premise for prolonging these moments is that they hold off the much less pleasant moment of reckoning just ahead. In surrealistically prolonging the moment just before the bucket of blood falls on Carrie White's head or the razor slashes Liz Blake's throat, De Palma often shows a sadistically Hitchcockian sense of fun, but the most common emotional reaction is a delicious sense of anticipatory dread. De

Palma seems to be inviting us to wish we could freeze the last moment before the inevitable calamity. When Hitchcock wants to present the calm before the storm, he emphasizes the frustrating banality of the moment— the delays in *Sabotage* that keep Stevie from placing the bomb by 1:45, or the endless stationary long shot outside the Blaney Bureau that heralds the discovery of Brenda's body in *Frenzy*—and lets the narrative itself supply the tension. In general, though, Hitchcock never wants to freeze any particular moment; he's too eager to get to the moment right around the corner.

De Palma's big moments always pump up the suspense; Hitchcock's moments more often defuse it, typically by broadening the emotional range, or by introducing a discordantly comic note, or by undercutting the melodramatic conventions of the thriller. In this respect the Hitchcock moment is the opposite of the Roman Polanski moment. Films like *Repulsion* and *Rosemary's Baby* and *Chinatown* build their cumulative effect out of hundreds of visual and auditory details designed to produce a powerfully unitary tone. From the moment when the elevator carrying Rosemary and Guy Woodhouse to their new apartment refuses to stop exactly at the seventh floor to the moment when Rosemary's eyes widen in horror at her first glimpse of her baby, every moment in *Rosemary's Baby*—from the portentous long shots showing characters looming in distant doorways to the unbalanced framings that turn innocuous actions like phoning a new obstetrician into ominous set-pieces—is designed to foster a single, overwhelming sense of sunlit nightmare, all accentuated by the inescapable ticking of clocks and the distant strains of "Für Elise." Although the emotional tonality of Polanski's work varies from *Repulsion* to *The Tenant* to *Tess,* each individual film, like a single nightmare, is remarkably homogeneous in tone, with each moment, from J. J. Gittes's silent surveillance of the haunted Hollis Mulwray to the catastrophic note of the horn welling up from Evelyn Mulwray's car, intensifying the sense of claustrophobic oppressiveness. The ideal Polanski film would be a nightmare that never lets the audience wake up.[2]

The only Hitchcock film this description fits equally well is *Vertigo,* and since *Vertigo* seems to be De Palma's favorite Hitchcock film as well, perhaps we ought simply to conclude that it is Hitchcock's most typical film and the clearest bearer of his legacy. But there is another, anti-*Vertigo,* side to Hitchcock this conclusion would ignore: the comic sense of nightmare produced by the constant undercutting of melodrama by romance in *The Lady Vanishes* or irony in *Rope* or the ultra-civilized comedy of manners in *The Trouble with Harry* or the nasty in-jokes lurking in the dialogue of *Psycho.* The 1934 version of *The Man Who Knew Too Much* is an extended exercise in the art of pulling the rug out from under the audience so deftly and frequently that they come to expect, and enjoy, being double-crossed. This side of Hitchcock has no impact on Polanski, and not much more on De Palma—who inherits Hitchcock's sense of malicious fun without anything like his emotional range—but we do see it at work in David Lynch.

If the ultimate Hitchcock film really were reducible, as Graham Greene and Charles Thomas Samuels have suggested, to an unbroken skein of Hitchcock moments, then *Blue Velvet* would have some claim to be the ultimate Hitchcock film. It's filled with big moments, from the soft-focus pastels in its picture-postcard opening survey of Lumberton, U.S.A., to its closing shot of Dorothy Vallens finally reunited with her little boy; many of its big moments are little moments, like the image of insects chomping deafeningly away in the grass as Mr. Beaumont is having his stroke; and many of its most memorable moments are deeply, disruptively funny, from the tableau of the dog drinking from the hose clutched in Mr. Beaumont's unfeeling hand to the moment when the menacing car following Jeffrey and Sandy turns out to be driven, not by the murderous Frank Booth, but only by Sandy's jealous boyfriend, who, seeing Dorothy running naked across the yard toward Jeffrey, asks him, in a triumph of perversely misplaced innocence, "Is that your mother?" *Twin Peaks,* the television series Lynch co-wrote with Mark Frost, inflated such transcendentally wacky moments to a structural and thematic principle. Recall how much of *Twin Peaks* is invoked by a few repeated images—the dancing dwarf, the undulating crimson curtains, the spectral face of Laura Palmer—and a few tag lines: "fire walk with me," "the owls are not what they seem," "a damn good cup of joe." Lynch is the undisputed king of the dreamlike moment that is hauntingly resonant precisely because of its banality. Unlike Hitchcock, however, that is all he is king of. Whether or not Greene is right about *Secret Agent,* it is arguable that in *Blue Velvet* the moments are more memorable than the film, and indisputable that in *Twin Peaks* and *Wild at Heart* the moments, like Dr. Johnson's Shakespearean conceits, run away with the story—an eminently appropriate fate for a world that, as Lula tells Sailor, is "wild at heart and weird on top." If surrealistically intense moments were the guarantee of a coherent style, then *Twin Peaks: Fire Walk with Me* would be a masterpiece instead of a curio that did not succeed in attracting even a cult audience. Instead, it seems a test case of Pauline Kael's attack on auteurism: "The smell of a skunk is more distinguishable than the perfume of a rose; does that make it better?"[3]

Unlike Lynch's big moments, which are always threatening to run away with the story, Hitchcock's most characteristic moments are rooted in the story. Their potency depends on specifically narrative expectations, and they always have specifically narrative implications. Hence Hitchcock's well-known dictum—"Some films are slices of life. Mine are slices of cake"—should be taken to distinguish his slice-of-cake films not only from slices of life, but from fragmentary cake crumbs as well.[4] In this regard the Hitchcock moment survives most clearly in the films of Quentin Tarantino. Think of the moment in *Pulp Fiction* when Vincent and Lance are arguing over who's going to give the dying Mia Wallace a shot of adrenalin, or the moment when the Pop-Tart pops up from Butch's toaster, or the moment when Butch reaches for the samurai sword on the pawnshop's upper shelf, or the moment when Vincent, in the middle of asking Marvin whether he believes in miracles, accidentally blows off Marvin's head. Moments like these follow Lynch in marrying banality to a kind of lunatic transcendence, but without ever adopting Lynch's tendency to leave the narrative behind.

Even the most outrageously stylized moment Tarantino has yet given us—the moment in *Reservoir Dogs* when Freddy, the strung-out druggie not yet christened Mr. Orange, is almost unmasked by a suspicious police dog in a men's room—rebounds on its frame story, the undercover cop Freddy's single-minded attempt to persuade his buddies he's a user and a career criminal, with redoubled force. Like Hitchcock's cameos, Freddy's anecdote is a playfully self-conscious style break, a shamelessly pumped-up moment designed to bolster Freddy's mendacious cover story, that at once teasingly reminds us of the fictive nature of the story it punctuates and returns us to that story with renewed pleasure. And it illuminates the defining paradox of the Hitchcock moment: It is an interruption, typically an ironic defusing, of the narrative that broadens and intensifies the power of the narrative. As Michel Foucault concludes of René Magritte's painting, "Ceci n'est pas une pipe," multiplying modes of referentiality (in Magritte's case, verbal, iconic, and semiotic) in ways that heighten their contradictions ends by "restor[ing similitude] to itself—unfolding from itself and folding back upon itself. It is no longer the finger pointing out from the canvas in order to refer to something else. It inaugurates a *play of transferences* that run, proliferate, propagate, and correspond within the layout of the painting" (my emphasis).[5]

The director's ritual cameo plays a pivotal role in this "play of trans-ferences" by reminding the audience that they are watching a Hitchcock movie by playing their awareness of the filmmaking apparatus against their immersion in the film's diegetic world without breaking that world's spell. And it is no coincidence that Hitchcock is the filmmaker who has chosen to publicize himself by parading his image through films the director himself stands outside of. When Polanski appears as the Man with the Knife (his official billing) in *Chinatown* or stars as Trelkovsky in *The Tenant,* the creator seems to have been swallowed up by his creation. But Hitchcock never plays a character or takes a narrative role in his cameos; his sole function is to be recognized by audiences so that he can enrich their enjoyment of the film by confirming their awareness that, after all, it's only a movie.

This awareness enriches the audience's experience instead of simply undermining it because it does not break the spell of a fictive world in which we had been utterly immersed, but rather reminds us that we were never entirely immersed to begin with. Hitchcock's relentless stylization works to make us always, and pleasurably, aware of his films as films even as their narrative complications work to pull us into their world. The Hitchcock moment is designed simultaneously to be seen into, as a gateway to the world of the characters and their fears and desires and obsessions, and seen through, as a self-conscious artifice reminding us not to take those problems too seriously—or, more precisely, to take them seriously within the context of the Hitchcock world, the world of Hollywood film. The Hitchcock moment thus serves at once as a window leading into the narrative, through the identifications that bring us close to the characters, and a mirror reflecting our knowing awareness of the narrative's enabling conventions of style, economy, and wit.

This paradox will seem daunting only to movie audiences who actually believe that the story they're seeing played out on the screen is real. But the effect of the Hitchcock moment, like the set speeches in Marlowe and Racine or the coloratura arias in Italian opera or the ritualized gunfights in Hollywood westerns or dance numbers in Hollywood musicals, is to remind the audience of something they already know perfectly well: they have come to the theater specifically to enter—more accurately, to participate in— a fictive world that can be pleasurably pregnant with style and meaning precisely because it is fictive, and that their fundamental attitude toward this world is not credulity but disavowal. Every one of these moments offers the dizzyingly seductive promise of a instantaneous rhetorical transcendence— a sheer vertical swoop, a moment of Dionysiac ecstasy, as the stylistic needle leaps off the chart—coupled with the reassuring promise of a return to the womb-like Apollonian security of the horizontal narrative that frames our desires and expectations by limiting them to the rhetoric of the diegesis. And the Hitchcock moment, even more than the corresponding moments in the films of De Palma, Polanski, and Lynch, is the site of disavowal, the moment when we are most deeply immersed in the film's world at the same time we are seeing through it.

Setting the Hitchcock moment against the corresponding moments in De Palma and Polanski and Lynch is not the same thing as arguing that Hitchcock's films are better than the work of these other filmmakers, or even that the Hitchcock moment is more distinctive. Indeed, the opposite is the case. Hitchcock is the quintessential Hollywood filmmaker precisely because of the characteristic way his privileged moments focus the audience's disavowal. It is this focus on disavowal, however it has been identified, that has given Hitchcock, and not De Palma or Polanski or Lynch, a central place in narratives about Hollywood history.

More generally, claiming a special distinction and centrality for Hitchcock is not the same thing as claiming classic (or even relatively higher) status for his films. Hitchcock may be a classic, but to set him against other filmmakers who are not classics is a tricky business. When Barbara Leaming attempted in 1981 to define Polanski by contrast with Hitchcock, she emphasized Polanski's subversive immersion in violent spectacles, noting that his "disconcerting proximity to his material gives his films an aura of personal risk" and "conceals nothing"—as against Hitchcock's "sustained aesthetic distance," the "lucidity and formal brilliance" that made him "a classic director."[6] Leaming's distinction is eminently reasonable, but undermined by its lack of historical perspective. For in his unflinching assault on the audience's sensibilities, Leaming's Polanski resembles no one so much as William S. Pechter's Hitchcock, described in Pechter's 1963 essay "The Director Vanishes" as unleashing "a virtual war of aggression through the inventions of his films, subjecting his audience as his protagonists to the terrors of paralysis, agoraphobia, confinement, vertiginous heights, impotence, and above all, the unknown."[7]

Hence Leaming's assessment of Hitchcock as a classic serves a function more purely historical than evaluative. Historicizing her description reveals her to be judging Hitchcock from a perspective considerably less outraged than Pechter's, partly because Hitchcock's films have mellowed with the passing of years, partly because the Universal publicity machine has been working overtime, as Robert Kapsis has pointed out, to establish Hitchcock's credentials as a classic, partly because the films that took their inspiration (for example) from *Psycho* are so much more explicitly violent that they make their great progenitor seem positively sedate. Leaming has arrived at a moment in which she can still recall and revisit her initial shock at what Pechter had called Hitchcock's war of aggression, but finds the assault shaped and tempered, as Pechter did not, by Hitchcock's invention of "new cinematic possibilities."[8] In short, Leaming is inhabiting a Hitchcock moment of her own, a moment when the visceral experience that originally compelled her attention is balanced by her aesthetic admiration of Hitchcock's artifice.

This privileged moment in Hitchcock criticism—the director is elevated to classic status in order to make room for a younger filmmaker who can claim Hitchcock's former place—does not so much mirror as expand the privileged moments within the discourse of individual Hitchcock films. In *Find the Director*, I described Hitchcock's entire career as Master of Suspense as a series of disavowals of the enabling conventions of his earlier films, as each new series of thrillers began by breaking the rules of the old.[9] Just as the Hitchcock moment invites the audience to disavow their uncritical immersion in a particular film narrative, Hitchcock's key films (the 1934 *Man Who Knew Too Much, Rebecca, Rope, Rear Window, Vertigo, The Birds*) are structured as disavowals of his earlier work, which they use as the basis for an implied contract it is his pleasure to break. Going further, we might elaborate on Kapsis's argument that Hitchcock's entire public career, including his posthumous career, has been a series of media constructions and adjustments by defining each stage of that development as based on privileged moments of disavowal, the denial that Hitchcock was something the audience was already convinced he was.[10] Writing in the 1950s, the *Cahiers du Cinéma* critics contended that Hitchcock was not a mere entertainer but a creator whose stylistic and thematic preoccupations remained remarkably consistent from one project to the next; a decade later, the publicists at Universal, with the help of Andrew Sarris, tried to position Hitchcock as a serious artist who was also a popular entertainer; still later, Raymond Durgnat argued that Hitchcock was a minor aesthete rather than the major artist described by Sarris and Robin Wood. Leaming's attempt to define the peculiar status of Polanski's thrillers by disavowing Hitchcock's title to the same status indicates the ways in which the Hitchcock moment, once established in a given film, provokes a disavowal that takes an inevitably historical development, leading to a chain of disavowals from moment to moment, film to film, history to history.

In short, the disavowal that characterizes the Hitchcock moment—both the distinctively transcendental moments in individual films, the privileged moments marking turning points in Hitchcock's development, and the continuing retrospective evolution of his career—is inescapably an historical function. Because they link textual markers with historical analysis, the Hitchcock moment and the disavowal it provokes have the power to play a decisive role in resolving the deadlock of contemporary film studies between erotics, the modern psychoanalytic spin on aesthetics, and history.

Thirty years ago Susan Sontag contended that "instead of a hermeneutics we need an erotics of art."[11] And up to a point, that is exactly what poststructuralism has given us, most persistently in the work of Julia Kristeva, most systematically among the followers of Jacques Lacan, most influentially in Roland Barthes's *Pleasure of the Text,* which Richard Howard describes as "an *erotics of reading.*"[12] Barthes's distinction between the kind of readerly *plaisir* we get from following the directives a text prescribes for us and the kind of writerly *jouissance* we get from actively rewriting the text— ignoring its directives, reading against its strictures, using it to write our own irreproducible, irreducibly different text—has defined the new erotics of art largely through a turn away from the sort of *plaisir* long associated with the obvious manipulation of Hitchcock's funhouse narratives. The poststructuralist erotics of art is preeminently an erotics of the moment, a swoon away from the fascistic imperatives of narrative manipulation into a realm of— depending on the theorist's orientation—Barthesian *jouissance* or the Lacanian imaginary or the Kristevan semiotic or Derridean freeplay. By breaking the stranglehold of linguistic categories over the audience's freedom, poststructuralism frees us to write our own texts. In film theory, this tendency has had several results: its reorganization around the privileged moment— the mirrored portal between the imaginary and the symbolic—instead of the gross narrative so beloved of structuralists; its preference for psychoanalytic theories of desire rather than rhetorical theories of pleasure; and its sovereign disdain for the aesthetic of manipulation that the *Cahiers* critics first used to establish Hitchcock's reputation as an auteur. By rights, contemporary film theory should have declared Hitchcock off-limits long ago.

Of course nothing like this has happened. Auteurism, which championed the authority and potency of the individual director, may be a dead aesthetic, but Hitchcock himself, like Mrs. Bates, stubbornly refuses to stay buried. He is the one auteur whose work, properly characterized in auteurist terms as Hitchcock movies, continues to provoke a steady outpouring of scholarly books and articles, the one dead filmmaker about whom it would not be surprising to find pressed into service for still another conference, still another volume, still another measure of value for some aspiring filmmaker.

Why has Hitchcock, virtually alone of the directors enshrined among Sarris's pantheon of auteurs, survived the pogrom of auteurism? The answers depend to a surprising extent on the special potency of the Hitchcock moment. The simplest reason for Hitchcock's survival is of course the continuing appeal of his films as commercial entertainment for a mass audience. Even Hitchcock's oldest films are studded with moments that make them more compare favorably with other landmark films made during the same period—*The Lodger* versus *Mother, Blackmail* versus *The Jazz Singer,* the 1934 *Man Who Knew Too Much* versus *The Private Life of Henry VIII*—as entertainment for a contemporary audience. The most characteristic moments in some of Hitchcock's films—*Notorious, Strangers on a Train, To Catch a Thief, The Trouble with Harry, North by Northwest*—seem hardly to have dated at all. Even the films whose fashions or performance style or political topicality have dated their leading moments most dramatically—*Murder!, The Lady Vanishes, Lifeboat, Torn Curtain, Topaz*—maintain their currency as documents of their eras. Shorn of their status as the timeless masterpieces of an auteur, *Rear Window* and *Marnie* continue to be studied as fables of fifties domesticity or cold-war sexual repression. More generally, Hitchcock's films have not dated; they have simply been historicized in a process that turns the iconic status formerly assigned to their defining moments to new use. If *Foreign Correspondent* can no longer be uncritically inhabited as a clarion call to war, it can be studied as an unusually stylish example of propaganda. Though the proportions of belief and skepticism may have changed over half a century, audiences continue to see into the world of the film even as they see through it.

A second reason that Hitchcock's reputation continues to flourish despite the decline of auteurism is the way their most distinctive moments so perfectly capture the Hollywood style, in which, as Michael Wood has observed, "it is all too much—overplayed, overwritten—and it is all just right." The over-ripeness that keeps the Hitchcock moment from ever passing itself off as realistic is a hallmark of the Hollywood aesthetic of excessiveness that reminds us that we are at "*the movies,* an independent universe, self-created, self-perpetuating, a licensed zone of unreality, affectionately patronized by us all."[13] Although audiences that already know *Vertigo* or *Psycho* will have a profoundly different experience of those films from any audience that is coming to them for the first time, no audience ever outgrows its initial infatuation with Hitchcock's movies, or movies generally, simply by wising up to their corny shifts and conventions, because the ironic awareness of Hollywood's perfectly judged over-expressiveness is present from the very beginning as the disavowal that defines our relation to the movies. As in the experience of watching *Foreign Correspondent,* the terms of disavowal inevitably change, but the fact of disavowal, in Hitchcock's work as in Hollywood films generally, does not.

If the defining moments in Hitchcock's films have kept his work and his reputation before the general public longer and more consistently than those of any other auteur, another kind of disavowal has played a corresponding role in Hitchcock's survival among film students and historians:

his equivocal status, along with Howard Hawks, as the consummate studio independent—that is, the filmmaker who spent virtually his entire career within, though never entirely within, the studio system, first in England, then in the U.S. This view of Hitchcock has kept his reputation alive by tapping into the other mainstream in contemporary film studies: the critical study, fueled by the New Historicism, of archival material from the studios, in which, as Thomas Schatz has put it, "the West Coast management team" displaces the heroic individual director as the driving force behind film production. [14] This new wave of historical studies is interested in Hitchcock not because the distinctive moments of his films put the audience through a distinctive experience, still less because they express a distinctive sensibility, but because they reveal, in Schatz's muted echo of Sarris's earlier formulation of the director as hero, "that the producer and director could break free, if not from the system at large, at least from direct studio control." [15] Schatz's Hitchcock has been developed in more detail by Leonard Leff as an aspiring independent filmmaker working in a town whose "studios never defined 'independent' as 'not subject to control by others.' " [16] In Schatz's and Leff's hands, Hitchcock emerges as on the one hand an active collaborator in the system, maintaining his independence through a constant series of movements from studio to studio, and contract renegotiations within a given studio, and the kind of subversive collaborator capable of rising above the constraints of the studio system—and, on the other hand, himself a commodity to be packaged, marketed, and consumed in the ways recounted by Kapsis. Hence the historical dimension of the Hitchcock moment, which establishes the typicality of Hitchcock's films, explains the continued fascination of Hitchcock the auteur, whom for the sake of brevity I will call "Hitchcock," as well.

Contemporary historians of Hollywood, in other words, instead of scrapping the old auteurist image of Hitchcock as unfashionable, have taken it for granted as a starting point for their own historical revisions and demystifications. Like audiences of individual films, these historians see through "Hitchcock" as a means of seeing into Hitchcock. Schatz's and Leff's work in studio history finds in Hitchcock a valorizing challenge to emerging economically-based accounts of Hollywood production, an apparently independent spirit who turns out to be an endlessly resourceful collaborator. And in his tellingly subtitled *Hitchcock: The Making of a Reputation*, Kapsis, himself a sociologist rather than an aesthetician, manages to valorize auteurism by treating it archaeologically, as a dead aesthetic. In his volume-length pathology of Hitchcock's changing reputation, Kapsis does not so much bury the reputation of "Hitchcock" as historicize it, simultaneously repackaging "Hitchcock" for a new generation of film students prepared to be fascinated by auteurism as an historical movement that is as immutably past as the Vietnam war. If Kapsis is correct in pointing out that "acceptance of the auteur view of Hitchcock as a serious artist produced its own kind of halo effect," his own analysis, however it may tarnish the auteurist halo of "Hitchcock," leaves Hitchcock as firmly entrenched as ever in contemporary film studies precisely because he once had a halo to tarnish.[17] In focusing not on Hitchcock the greengrocer's son and British emigré but "Hitchcock" the auteur, Kapsis valorizes a new kind of Hitchcock moment precisely: the historical moment when the disavowed "Hitchcock" becomes the discursive figure constructed to account for a career and a certain way—actually several changing ways—of thinking about the movies as art and entertainment.

In their own way, poststructuralists, who ought to have no truck with Hitchcock the auteur, have found not only his films but "Hitchcock," the director as a paradigmatic figure, equally useful. *Vertigo* plays a crucial role in Laura Mulvey's seminal essay on the fetishizing male gaze and indeed in feminist theories of spectatorship generally.[18] Tania Modleski's book on Hitchcock seems to have been written as if in response to Robin Wood's question, "Can Hitchcock be saved for feminism?"[19] And the essays in Slavoj Žižek's exuberantly titled collection, *Everything You Always Wanted to Know About Lacan (But Were Afraid to Ask Hitchcock)*, take as their point of departure Hitchcock the auteur as the " 'postmodern' phenomenon par excellence" and then proceed to deconstruct him, or it, through a rigorous, frequently maddening, interrogation of the telltale moments that open the gaps among Hitchcock the realist, Hitchcock the modernist, and Hitchcock the postmodernist—or, as we might say, between Hitchcock the canny author of meaning and "Hitchcock" the commodity, the ultimate blue-ribbon brand-name for Hollywood's consumer market.[20]

This malleability of Hitchcock, his availability as a commodity to be deconstructed, is the final reason for the survival of Hitchcock studies. Just as studio historians have found Hitchcock's fingerprints all over the archival records (if not as the subject, then as the object, of meaning), poststructuralists have found in Hitchcock the most cordial, even conspiratorial, invitation to practice their own writerly craft.

Hitchcock has survived, and Hitchcock studies incongruously continue to flourish, because the permutations of the Hitchcock moment so multiply the uses to which "Hitchcock" can be put: to defend the energy of American popular culture, to organize audiences' evaluations of particular films, to establish film studies as a serious academic discipline, to serve as a touchstone for new critical or theoretical or historical analyses. Since disavowal is at the heart of each of these activities—from Truffaut's use of Hitchcock to bludgeon the Tradition of Quality to Žižek's selection of Hitchcock as the exemplary postmodern figure to be deconstructed, from Sarris' choice of Hitchcock as the quintessential Hollywood auteur to Kapsis' implication that history is itself no more than a series of variously directed disavowals— it is not surprising to find that both Hitchcock and "Hitchcock" have been so resilient.

But the survival of Hitchcock and Hitchcock studies comes at some cost. The result of all the scholarly ferment on Hitchcock is that instead of a single Hitchcock, we now have multiple Hitchcocks, and multiple concomitant Hitchcock moments (some textual, some intertextual, some retrospectively historical), which seem impossible to reconcile. Hitchcock studies, in a failure indicative of a crisis in film studies generally, has still not succeeded in theorizing the relation between the old Hitchcock—the sly auteur, the subject projected by the larger units of narrative, the ironic raconteur and funhouse barker who controls meaning by controlling the audience, the studio, the press, the system—and the paradigmatic postmodern figure "Hitchcock"—the touchstone for historical or psychoanalytic deconstruction, the object specifically constructed as an object of desire, the Hitchcock who emerges only in privileged moments from behind the curtain of narrative.[21] Nor is it surprising that we should have trouble with the even simpler problem of reconciling Hitchcock the Apollonian storyteller, the Hitchcock of Lesley Brill, with the Dionysiac reveler of the privileged moments Raymond Bellour has chosen to analyze, because the present state of film studies is similarly fractured between two powerful but disparate projects, both borne out of a flight from aesthetics: a dispassionate critical history of cinematic narrative, and an impassioned critical theory of the cinematic moment.

The first of these projects is figured by the paradigmatic subject of new Hollywood history, the West Coast studio management team that plays the critical role in Schatz's *Genius of the System*. This team is in the business of creating and marketing a single product: cinematic narrative, tailored to the measure of a collective fantasy they aim to market as well. In focusing on the economic apparatus by which that fantasy is created and manipulated as an on-screen projection of the audience's desire, Schatz, like Kapsis, works from the unitary commodity, the completed film, outward to the apparatus.

Poststructuralists working on the second of these projects, toward a theory of cinematic representation, begin at the same starting point, the film narrative, and then proceed in the opposite direction, working from larger, presumably consensual units of meaning to the privileged moments that deconstruct them. Even when historians and theorists share an agenda of demystification, as in the work of Modleski and Teresa de Lauretis, they are left with a gap between an ongoing project in cinema history that is essentially a history of narratives and an ongoing project in cinema theory that is essentially a theory of moments.[22]

In sum, contemporary film studies is torn between an erotics of desire, operating essentially through fetishized individual images, and an economic history of desire, operating essentially through a fetishized apparatus. Production companies, that is, keep turning out narratives that film theorists keep analyzing as anthologies of moments. The two sides of film studies are complementary, but they are impoverished both by their lack of a coherent theory of narrative—they merely debunk auteurist theories of narrative, whether expressivist or rhetorical, without substituting any theory of their own—and by their lack of a common conceptual vocabulary. There is no more telling evidence of this sorry situation than the current disarray of genre theory, which ought to be in the forefront of contemporary cinema studies, and no more promising ground for the meeting of film history and film theory than the Hitchcock moment, with its readerly promise of uncomplicated narrative *plaisir* and its writerly subversion of that promise through the invitation to *jouissance,* its simultaneous acceptance and critique of the norms of consumer culture, its standing both inside the system as the quintessential Hollywood commodity and outside the system as the moment that knows too much.[23]

If we had a theory of the Hitchcock moment, as the quintessential Hollywood product that both manipulates the consumer audience's desire and encourages the critical audience to speak its desire, we might well be on our way to achieving three landmark goals. We might replace the structuralist hermeneutics of cinema, not with an erotics of cinema, but with a historical economy of cinema that acknowledged, right from the start, that whoever is anointed today's nihilistic maverick—Hitchcock, Lynch, Tarantino—is likely to be accepted or dismissed as tomorrow's social moralist. We might locate disavowal properly at the heart of the cinema's appeal, recognizing the ways all audiences, from the most naive to the most sophisticated, use their awareness of the apparatus to inform and enrich their experience of the diegesis. And we might thereby acknowledge the ways in which the consumer audience and the critical audience, like Hitchcock the studio hireling and Hitchcock the subversive independent, might just, for all the differences in self-consciousness and pretension and writerly activity ascribed to them by both sides, be one and the same.

NOTES

1. Graham Greene, *Graham Greene on Film: Collected Film Criticism, 1935–1939* (New York: Simon and Schuster, 1972), 75.

2. Hence, *pace* Charles Thomas Samuels (see *Mastering the Film and Other Essays* [Knoxville: University of Tennessee Press, 1977], 72), it is not Hitchcock but Polanski, the poet of the unrelieved single effect, who is the true heir of Poe and Poe's aesthetic.

3. Pauline Kael, *I Lost It at the Movies* (Boston: Little, Brown, 1965), 297.

4. François Truffaut, *Hitchcock* (New York: Simon and Schuster, 1967), 71.

5. Michel Foucault, *This Is Not a Pipe*, trans. and ed. James Harkness (Berkeley: University of California Press, 1983), 49.

6. Barbara Leaming, *Polanski: A Biography: The Filmmaker as Voyeur* (1981; rpt. New York: Touchstone, 1983), 205, 31.

7. William S. Pechter, "The Director Vanishes," in *Twenty-Four Times a Second: Films and Filmmakers* (New York: Harper and Row, 1971), 177. See also Pechter's 1966 Postscript on *Torn Curtain*, whose central set-piece, the killing of Gromek, he describes as "graphic, prolonged, horrendous. . . . No detail of this act is euphemistically omitted. . . . It is dwelt on, but one would need to be mad to feel the experience of it could possibly be enjoyed" (194). The historical development from Pechter's Hitchcock, who delights in outraging his audience, to Leaming's Hitchcock, who is a model of classical equipoise to set against Polanski, the true provocateur, raises fundamental questions about the importance of disavowal in the evolution of the horror film, whose sensation-seeking target audience wants to be frightened but has already been jaded by so many previous examples in the genre that each new example must take all the others for granted and top them all.

8. Leaming, *Polanski: A Biography,* 205.

9. Thomas M. Leitch, *Find the Director and Other Hitchcock Games* (Athens: University of Georgia Press, 1991).

10. Robert E. Kapsis, *Hitchcock: The Making of a Reputation* (Chicago: University of Chicago Press, 1992).

11. Susan Sontag, *Against Interpretation and Other Essays* (New York: Farrar Straus Giroux, 1966), 14.

12. Roland Barthes, *The Pleasure of the Text*, trans. Richard Miller (New York: Hill and Wang, 1975), viii.

13. Michael Wood, *America at the Movies* (New York: Basic Books, 1975), 6, 8.

14. Thomas Schatz, *The Genius of the System: Hollywood Filmmaking in the Studio Era* (New York: Pantheon, 1988), 12.

15. Schatz, *The Genius of the System,* 294.

16. Leonard Leff, *Hitchcock and Selznick: The Rich and Strange Collaboration of*

Alfred Hitchcock and David O. Selznick (New York: Weidenfeld and Nicolson, 1987), 270.

17. Kapsis, *Hitchcock: The Making of a Reputation*, 243.

18. Laura Mulvey, "Visual Pleasure and Narrative Cinema," *Screen* 16, no. 3 (1975): 6–18.

19. Tania Modleski, *The Women Who Knew Too Much: Hitchcock and Feminist Theory* (New York: Methuen, 1988); Robin Wood, *Hitchcock's Films Revisited* (New York: Columbia University Press, 1989), 371.

20. Slavoj Žižek, ed., *Everything You Always Wanted to Know About Lacan (But Were Afraid to Ask Hitchcock)* (London: Verso, 1992), 2.

21. For a particularly telling use of privileged moments to deconstruct the larger meanings of Hitchcockian narrative, see Christopher Morris, "*Psycho*'s Allegory of Seeing," *Literature/Film Quarterly* 24, no. 1 (1996): 47–51.

22. This problem is by no means a recent development. As long ago as 1971, Brian Henderson pointed out in "Two Types of Film Theory" that neither Sergei Eisenstein nor André Bazin, architects of the two leading schools of film theory, had produced anything like a theory of the complete film; at best, Bazin had "a theory of the real" and Eisenstein a theory of the individual montage sequence. See *A Critique of Film Theory* (New York: Dutton, 1980), 27.

23. Since this essay first appeared, the publication of Rick Altman's *Film/Genre* (London: British Film Institute, 1999) and Steve Neale's *Genre and Hollywood* (London: Routledge, 2000) has opened new vistas for genre theory along just such lines.

HITCHCOCK AND HIS
SCREENWRITERS

WRITING FOR HITCH:
AN INTERVIEW
WITH EVAN HUNTER

Charles L. P. Silet

When Alfred Hitchcock began to prepare for the
filming of *The Birds* (1963), he chose a widely published and critically acclaimed New York novelist,
Evan Hunter, to write the script. Later he told Hunter
that he was in search of the artistic respectability
that had eluded him in the reception of his previous
films, and that choosing a famous novelist to write
this screenplay just might get him that elusive artistic
recognition that he sought.

Hitchcock had first become aware of Hunter's
scripting talents when he worked for him on *Alfred Hitchcock Presents,* his long-running television
show. Hunter had both supplied stories and written teleplays for the series. In addition, he had been
doing other script-writing in Hollywood and had recently completed adaptations of his best-selling novels *Strangers When We Meet* (1960) and *The Young
Savages* (1961). Hunter would bring to Hitchcock's
new film both experience as a scriptwriter and the
caché of prominence as a critically acclaimed author.

As Mr. Hunter recalls in the following interview,
perhaps the most important skill he possessed was

his ability to flesh out full-blown scripts from rather minimal material. Hitchcock planned to use Daphne du Maurier's famous short story "The Birds" as a basis for the movie, but he wanted only to retain the basic idea of birds attacking people and the title. He needed someone who could write a story from this sketchy outline. Hunter produced a fine script that contributed to the reassessment of Hitchcock's films that began around the time of the release of *The Birds*. And he was successful enough that Hitchcock also hired him to write the script for *Marnie* (1964), although as Mr. Hunter explains he was unable to finish work on that production.

The following interview provides a rare insight into Hitchcock's working methods and a privileged glimpse into the history of the shooting of one of his most famous films.

When did you first meet Hitchcock?

I met him after he had done "First Offense," which was a serious story of mine, on *Alfred Hitchcock Presents*. I didn't write the screenplay for that but it was based on my story. When I did write one, it was based on a story by Robert Turner. It was a difficult thing to do because the story was just an internal monologue, the kid thinking about the electrocution of his father at eleven o'clock. I transferred it to a bar where the kid's drunk and trying to get drunker and is obnoxious, and I put in all the bystanders in the bar to open it up. This may have been in Hitch's mind when he called upon me to do *The Birds*, because the Daphne du Maurier story, "The Birds," involves just two people in a cottage. They hardly say anything, there's no dialogue in the entire story. Hitch also told me later, and I learned later from other sources, that he was looking for some "artistic respectability" with *The Birds*. This was something that had always eluded him, and he deliberately chose to work with a successful New York novelist, rather than a Hollywood screenwriter, many of whom are much better screenwriters than I am. After I had finished the teleplay on the Turner story, they invited my wife and me over when he was shooting something and we met him there. He was always rather charmed by my former wife. I don't know why, but he was. Anyway, he was always very gracious to any woman who arrived on the set. I remember he was shooting a scene where a guy was under ice. They were shooting through these big cakes of ice covering the actor and Hitch walked away from it to talk to us while the actor was still under the ice.

Leaving this poor guy freezing.

Yeah, and they kept calling him, "Hitch, sir, Mr. Hitchcock, sir, could we possibly . . ." Very funny.

Can we talk a little bit about the experience of working on The Birds?

Hitch told me on the phone that he had called my agent and asked if I would want to do *The Birds*. I'd had some stuff done on his television show, so I vaguely knew him. But I wasn't familiar with Daphne du Maurier's story "The Birds," so I said, "Let me read it." I read it and it sounded interesting and I accepted the job. But when I spoke with him, he said, "Forget the story now that you've read it, because all we're using is the title and the notion of birds attacking people." He said, "That's it. So when you come out to the coast, come out with some ideas we can pursue and I'll have some and we'll talk further." In the first two days we shot down my ideas and his ideas and started from scratch.

And as you worked, you worked in tandem?

We spent a lot of time trying to figure out who the girl was going to be. That's Hollywood talk—"the girl," it ain't *my* talk, and "the boy"—and figured out how we were going to get the story going. I would come in every day having thought the night before and he would always say, "Tell me the story so far," and I would tell him and then he would start shooting holes in it. He was always thinking in terms of the shot he could get, and I was always thinking in terms of the logic of the actions of the characters. He wanted a scene where Melanie Daniels rents a boat and goes across the inlet and gets hit by a bird. That's the first bird attack. I would think, "Why is she going to all this trouble renting a boat when she could easily drive around?" But it was a good working relationship. He was meticulous about the circumstances in the script. There are holes you could drive Mack trucks through in some thrillers. He said, "In my films I'd like to think that if you'd reel it back you'd say, 'Oh, yeah, there it is.'" Nowadays of course we can do that through video replay.

You said that you worked with other directors and often times the script gets so changed its hardly recognizable. How much of The Birds *is really yours?*

Most of it is. The most noticeable deletion was not shooting the end of the script as I had written it. I had another ten pages of script that he did not shoot, or if he shot I never saw them. And the most noticeable addition was the scene where in an attempt to give the girl some depth at the birthday party for the children Rod Taylor takes her up on a hilltop and removes from one pocket of his jacket a martini shaker, and then from the other pocket two martini glasses, and pours martinis for them. On this hilltop they start talking about her empty life. It's a stupid scene and I don't know who wrote it. Rod Taylor said to me, the day they were shooting it and I was on the set, he said, "Evan, did you write this scene?" I read it and I said, "No," and he said, "We're shooting it this morning." I said, "Well, let me talk to Hitch about it." I went to Hitch and said, "This is a dumb scene. It's going to slow down the movie enormously, slow down the point where the birds attack the children at the birthday party, and it serves no purpose and I don't think it should be in the movie." And he looked me dead in the eye and he said, "Are you going to trust me or a two-bit actor?"

That was that?

Yes, it was.

What was in the ending that you wrote?

Mitch leaves with his family driving a convertible with a cloth top, and there was a reason for that. And the reason was that I wanted to make the final assault the birds attacking the car's top. Also in my version, as we leave the farmhouse we see the devastation that was wreaked on the town itself. We see overturned school buses and signs of people having defended their homes against the bird attacks. So it becomes not just an isolated attack on Mitch and his family but a town-wide attack with implications that it may have gone even beyond the town. Mitch and his family finally get to another roadblock and it's covered with birds, and Mitch gets out and moves some stuff and he gets back into the car. As they start driving through it, the birds all come up off the roadblock and start attacking the car as they're driving out of town. In that area in Northern California the coast roads have these horseshoe curves but the birds fly in a straight line after the car, and as they attack the canvas top, we see from inside the car looking up at all these beaks tearing at the canvas and finally the whole top goes back and the birds are hovering over the car. Just then the road straightens out and Mitch hits the gas pedal and the car moves off and the birds just keep falling back, falling back, falling back. In the car they all catch their breath and Mitch's sister says, "Mitch, do you think they'll be in San Francisco when we get there?" and he says, "I don't know honey," and that's the last line of the movie.

Why didn't Hitchcock shoot it that way?

I think he was very tired by then, and this would have required a lot of work with the scene in the car where four characters are in a tight space and the camera is in with them watching the beaks and then the scene of the birds hovering and the birds following and the helicopter shots, animation, everything. It was just too much to do.

What about the restaurant scene which you wrote in Connecticut and you shipped back to Hitchcock in Hollywood?

I love that scene. That was like a one act-play.

How did you do it?

Hitch called and he said, "I need something more." I don't know how we discovered where we would take them, the central characters, Melanie and Mitch, but once I knew it was a restaurant, the Tides, then I had the whole scene in place and it just wrote itself.

It's a scene which sort of explains, or provides a kind of logic, to explain the birds' behavior.

That's right. It's really a scene of great confusion because nobody knows what the hell is happening. We made, if you'll forgive the expression, an "artistic" decision early on that we were never going to explain the bird attacks, never. Otherwise the film would become science fiction and we didn't want to do that. I remember there was another scene he had cut out of the film. It was a good scene and I guess he replaced it with that dumb scene on the hill. It was a scene after the finches come down the chimney in the house. Melanie wakes up the next morning after the attack inside the house and she looks out the window and Mitch is in the backyard burning the birds. He's raking them up and burning them. Then we cut away in the movie to Jessica Tandy, Mitch's mother, going to the farmer's house. And what I had written there after Jessica leaves is that Melanie goes down and talks to Mitch about what happened the night before and they try to explain it. He makes a joke about it. Like maybe there's a little bird in the hills organizing all of these birds and urging them to revolt against humanity. The couple is laughing about it and she says, "Mitch, they came down that chimney in *fury*," and then he suddenly holds her close because she's frightened. And they kiss and this is what Mitch's mother sees when she's coming back from the farmhouse, she sees them in an embrace. In the movie this scene is gone, but she's all at once calling him "darling" and "honey." Something is missing.

It also helps to explain why the mother, who's been a little ambivalent about having her around anyway, becomes a bit more nervous.

More wary and guarded, sure. It was a good scene, and I'm pretty sure he shot that scene. I don't know why he decided not to use it. The ending he didn't shoot, but I'm pretty sure he shot that scene.

Has any of your Hollywood work had an effect on your fiction?

I don't think so, not really. Maybe in terms of having a camera move right in and keep a scene going. Only in art movies do you see the camera lingering on every object in the room, on a tic in somebody's eye. In most movies, the camera moves in on the scene and the actors play the scene without it lingering on everything in the room or the characters. When the camera lingers on something in a movie, it's pointing out the importance of that something. I read somewhere that you can always tell how important a writer feels about a scene by the amount of space he gives it. So perhaps that's a connection.

Was Hitchcock easy to work with?

Oh yeah, I loved working with him. He was like the father anyone wished he would have. He was intelligent, he was world-traveled. He knew everybody, he was famous, he was a star in his own right. I don't know how many people would recognize Steven Spielberg if he walked into a restaurant. Maybe in Hollywood, but I don't think they would in Iowa. But if Hitch walked in, they'd damn well know him. He was a big, big star. One of the few directors I think who has ever had such a high profile.

And he was generous with what you were doing?

Well, he was almost *possessive.* He'd call all the time. My former wife and I knew very few people in Hollywood, anyway, but we were starting to make friends. I remember once he called her and said, "Where are we going to dinner tonight?" And she said, "Gee, Hitch, we've made other plans." And he said, "Well then what am *I* supposed to do?" Once he took us to the track and handed us each $100 as we were walking in. He said, "This is for you, Evan, and this is for you, Anita." I said, "Hitch, we can't take that." He said, "Why not, you're my guests." Then I said, "Because if I lost it, it wouldn't mean anything and if I won any money I'd feel I should turn it over to you." He said, "In that case, give it back to me." But we had a lot of fun with him. He was an amusing man to be with.

Didn't you also work on Marnie?

Yeah, I wrote the first draft screenplay. I also got fired from that film because Hitch wanted to put a scene in it that was in the book we adapted that I did not want to write for the movie. I figured a different way around it. It was the scene on their honeymoon night when Mark Rutledge tries to make love to Marnie and she's all quivery and frightened and terrified of the fact and he rapes her. Sean Connery, who later played Mark, wasn't involved in it at the time. I didn't know who the lead was going to be. I just knew that Tippi was playing Marnie, and I said to Hitch we're going to lose all sympathy for the lead character because of the rape. Marnie's obviously not being coy, she's terrified, she's cowering in the corner, and any decent man would not rape her. She's his wife. I wrote the scene two ways, the way he wanted it and the way I thought it should be written with a little tenderness and gentleness and understanding—*no* rape!—and I put my version on white paper inside the body of the script and I put his version on yellow paper outside the body of the script. And I delivered it to him and I said, "I think this is the way we should go and I think you will agree when you've read both." I'd given them both my best shot. And I got fired the next day.

No particular explanation?

No. Peggy Robertson called and said, "Hitch is putting another writer on the film." I later did an interview with Jay Presson Allen, who wrote the final draft of *Marnie,* about her movies and everything else, up at the Writers Guild. And when I told her about my experience she said, "Evan, you bought your ticket back home right that minute, the minute you said you didn't want to do that scene. That scene was the only reason he wanted to make that picture." As a matter of fact, that scene became the whole purpose of *Frenzy* many years later, where he carried that idea to its extreme.

AN INTERVIEW WITH
JAY PRESSON ALLEN

Richard Allen

This is a lightly-edited transcription of an interview conducted at the Hitchcock Centennial Conference, hosted by the Department of Cinema Studies at New York University and held at the Director's Guild Theater, New York, on October 17, 1999. Questioners from the floor have been identified whenever possible.

RICHARD ALLEN: Jay Presson Allen is a writer and producer. Her plays include *Forty Carats, A Little Family Business,* and *True,* which she also directed. She wrote the screenplay for *Marnie* in 1964 as well as *The Prime of Miss Jean Brodie, Cabaret, Funny Lady,* and other scripts. Welcome Jay Presson Allen.

JAY PRESSON ALLEN: Thank you.

RA: So obviously, Jay, we're here to talk about *Marnie* and your collaboration with Hitchcock on that project. I wonder, first of all, whether you'd tell us how you got involved.

JPA: I had written *The Prime of Miss Jean Brodie,* and the producer's wife had become quite ill. And we postponed the play, eventually doing it first in London. Anyway, the play was sitting around in agents' offices, and Hitch got it and read it and called me and offered me the job. I don't think I was—I was not movie-oriented. In those days not everybody wanted to be a screenwriter. I don't believe I would have taken an offer—it was something I knew nothing about, cared nothing about—if it had been anyone but Hitch, but I thought that with him that it might be fun, and it was.

RA: I don't know how good your recollection of this is, but we've been talking a lot about the fact that Hitchcock in America often adapted or used English or British novels, and this one is an English novel. Can you tell us something about the process of adapting what is an English novel, partly about English class structure, to an American screen?

JPA: You make it into an American class structure. It's as simple as that. We just made the man FFV—"First Family of Virginia" kind of guy—and kept her as what she was.

RA: We spoke with Evan Hunter earlier in the conference. Are you aware that Evan wrote a full . . .

JPA: It's against our union laws for a producer not to inform a writer that previous writers have been on the screenplay and name them. Hitch didn't give a clue. I thought I was the first writer on. Not only did Evan do a version, but there was some guy before him.

RA: Joe Stefano told us that he also wrote a treatment of the film initially.

JPA: In any event, I was not told. Also, they're supposed to give you that previous work. I think, for the plain and simple reason that if two writers use the same structure—not dialogue, but structure—then whoever was there first gets credit no matter what. So obviously, if you get a job like I did and your structure is pretty much the same as the guys who came before you, to your astonishment, you will have a co-writer on there with you, which you didn't know anything about, which is what Hitch did to me. Although I didn't know . . .

RA: You weren't aware.

JPA: Oh no, not a clue. Not a clue. Never did.

RA: Evan Hunter told us how the reason he got fired from this job, he understood subsequently, was because the main reason that Hitchcock was interested in the book *Marnie* was on account of the "rape scene" in the novel.

JPA: I don't think that was the only reason Hitch was . . .

RA: Not the only reason.

JPA: No.

RA: One of the reasons.

JPA: A reason.

RA: Right. And Hunter felt uncomfortable with this scene in relation to his conception of the Mark Rutland character. He thought it out of character and that the audience would lose sympathy with that character if that scene remained. So he did two versions of the scene in his script, one with any kind of connotations of rape written out, and a second with the scene more or less as Winston Graham writes it in the novel. Did you have discussions about this scene with Hitchcock and did you think about the problems this scene would pose for your characterization of Mark when you wrote your draft of the screenplay?

JPA: No. Not at all. And I'm very fond of Evan, but I think he was psychologically a little naïve. There's a vast audience of women out there who fantasize the idea of rape, as has been proved over and over and over again.

RA: I'll leave that one for question time. One of the important changes that you made to the script was that there's two male characters in the original novel and these two male characters were retained in Evan Hunter's script. One was Mark Rutland, of course, and the other is a character called Terry Holbrook, and in the novel, and in Evan Hunter's script, the Terry Holbrook character is somebody who is unsympathetic. He's sexually aggressive towards Marnie. It makes us sympathize with Mark Rutland and identify with him and his attitudes towards Marnie. In your version of the script and in the final film, this character is eliminated. I wonder if this relates to the previous question about the rape scene. I wonder whether you eliminated this character in order to make the Mark Rutland character slightly less sympathetic and give us more sympathy towards the plight and predicament of the female protagonist Marnie. There's a second change too you made, which was to bring Mark Rutland right into the beginning of the film so he kind of overlooks her first robbery at Strutt's office and the realization of the theft. So he has this kind of controlling presence.

Yet I think my question is a leading one: Was this an intentional device on your part to make us slightly less sympathetic and more critical of the Mark Rutland character to prepare a way for an identification with Marnie?

JPA: No. We just thought)and I'm not at all sure this didn't come from Hitch, I just don't know)that Rutland should be the only real guy and that it needed another female character built up a bit. There was nothing about trying to make it easier for Rutland.

RA: Was your intention to make Rutland less sympathetic?

JPA: To me it had no meaning at all. I just didn't see what good the guy was going to do in the script.

RA: In the novel there's a scene—and this, again, was in Evan's script—there's a scene in the cinema where Marnie steals money from the cinema.

JPA: I would have liked that. If I had read that script, I would have kept that scene. I like scenes in movies.

RA: Yes. My question was . . . I presume that Hitchcock had read the novel or that Peggy Robertson had read the novel.

JPA: I'm sure Hitch read it.

RA: I wondered whether this scene was ever discussed, because it somehow didn't make its way into the film.

JPA: No.

RA: It was never discussed.

JPA: No.

RA: I have one more question. What do you think about all the analysis of Hitchcock's work that is embodied in this conference and has taken place over the past ten or fifteen years?

JPA: Of course, at least we're able to blame it on the French. I've been in this business, both theater and film, for well over fifty years and I don't remember ever meeting an intellectual—I meet a lot of very bright people, clearly, obviously—but artists tend not to intellectualize their work. It comes from the gut. It comes from instinct. It comes largely as a surprise to the artists themselves. Very little analysis goes into it. I think Hitch would have loved all this. I think he would have adored it, but I think it would have made him giggle.

RA: I'm going to open up questions to the floor.

PETER WOLLEN: I wonder if I can ask you a question about the ending of the film. In the novel the *denouement* is that we discover through Marnie, who turns up at her mother's house after the mother has died, that Marnie's mother has in fact strangled a child at birth. So that's different from the end of the film. I was wondering whether it was Hitchcock's idea or your idea to change that ending.

JPA: Tell me first what the ending of the movie is.

PW: The ending of the movie is that she goes back with Mark Rutland and discovers the trauma that has taken place in her childhood when one of her mother's clients is beaten to death. In the novel this doesn't happen. Marnie's mother has already died, and Marnie discovers from a newspaper cutting that there has been a scandal many years previously in which Marnie's mother has strangled a child to which she has given birth herself.

JPA: I'm sure that was Hitch's intent from the beginning. It's just neater the way it is and certainly more sympathetic for Marnie, I think.

RA: How much input did Hitchcock have in the formation of the script in terms of discussion about the infusions of color in the story?

JPA: We did discuss that at some length. I loved the idea, and he wanted to do it. So this was a little gift he was giving me. I don't think I would have ever done another movie if it hadn't been for Hitchcock. He was a marvelous teacher. My ignorance was glorious. I hadn't a clue. I'd had no training whatever, as I'd had in the theater, and the theater that long ago was very sequential. It didn't get really cut up and able to move it around the way it's done in film, the way it's done today, until Arthur Miller's *Beyond the Fall*. In any event, that was the first play I ever saw that moved like a movie. So all I knew was to bring somebody on stage, have them say their thing, have their little whatever, and get them off. So clearly a movie was very very far from any skill I might have had. But Hitch did something marvelous. He clearly influenced me in many, many, many ways. But, at the same time, he gave me a feeling of total freedom. My feeling was that I could write anything in the world I wanted to write and that I could violate something that he had said he'd like with impunity. This is a great teacher. Has everybody heard the thing about the flowers in *Marnie*, the wedding flowers?

RA: Tell us.

JPA: Well, I was writing the section where they get married. So I had them go into the church. I had them in the church, I had them coming out of the church, I had them in a limo, I had them going to the boat. And even I knew this wasn't going to work. So I called Hitch and said, "I've got a problem here." And when I told him what it was, he said—I'm so sorry I can't imitate him, but I can't—he said, "Why don't we, instead of that, why don't we start with the doors to the church opening and the guests coming out and the church bells chiming and before we see Marnie and Mark, we see flower blossoms that people are throwing. And we go close to a blossom and cut to a vase full of roses and the vase has a card on it that says 'Congratulations' and the water in the vase is sloshing, sloshing, sloshing." So you knew instantly they were married, they were on a boat. Certainly the best screenwriting lesson I've ever experienced or read about.

RA: Did you look at any other Hitchcock films before you wrote the script or had you seen any?

JPA: Oh, I think I'd seen everything. I wouldn't have gone otherwise. That's why I went.

RA: I have another question about adaptation. When the protagonist has her analysis in the novel, it's from a psychiatrist, not from Mark Rutland. In your script and in the film it's Mark who does the analysis. Was that Hitch's idea?

JPA: No, that was mine.

RA: Any other questions?

JPA: Incurious you are.

SLAVOJ ŽIŽEK: Just three short points. It interests me what you said about intellectuals because, as an utterly corrupted intellectual, writing un-readable analysis of Hitchcock, my problem with *Marnie* is that it is compared with *Spellbound* (these are the two films that most directly refer to psychoanalysis), which is a much too intellectual film. It doesn't work. Its flirting with psychoanalysis for me is a little bit too direct. Two concrete questions: first, you mentioned the rape scene.

JPA: The what?

SŽ: Rape. Rape. OK, sorry. You said it is not a problem. I unfortunately agree with you. But, nonetheless, why do you think people accept that scene? One reasoning would be that they see it as the state of Mark at that point when he still wants violently to dominate Marnie but that at the end, gaining a deeper understanding of Marnie, Mark redeems himself. It can be read in a much nastier way: that, in a way, on account of her frigidity, Marnie in a way deserves this or that. But it's not enough for me to just say that people accept rape. There must be some specific . . .

JPA: I didn't say that she deserved it.

SŽ: No, no, no. I only say that some people would not find that scene shocking, patriarchally oriented people who think, if a woman is frigid, that maybe a good rape will help her. I'm not saying that you meant this. I am just trying to find why people accept that Mark raped her and nonetheless he's redeemed at the end. Because otherwise, in a normal Hollywood film, if a leading guy does something like that, he is out, no?

JPA: Clark Gable raped Scarlett. I've never heard anybody complain about that. He scoops her up and takes her up and rapes her. It's just a movie. My own take on *Marnie* is that it's not a very good movie because I didn't know how to write it. I thought Tippi, who I like and who I like very much in *The Birds,* was miscast. She has a very brittle, edgy quality, and it would have been much easier on Hitch if he'd had a much more vulnerable woman. I don't know. I just think there are a lot of problems in the film.

RA: What do you think of Sean Connery?

JPA: Oh, well, Hitch called me one day and he said "There's a British actor who is making a James Bond movie and I've heard that he's marvelous. I can get some film on him. Do you want to look at it?" And I said, "Sure." And we sat there together and watched what we had of this cartoon of a British gentleman speaking with an extravagant Glaswegian accent. We instantly cast him as a Virginia gentleman. We just loved him.

QUESTION: John Waters has recently stated that *Marnie* is his favorite Hitchcock picture because how can you not love a story set in Baltimore? What kind of research did you do to write the Baltimore scenes?

JPA: I had forgotten that it was in Baltimore. My husband's family originally comes from Baltimore. They now live in Virginia hunt country. So I had a little help at home, but that's about all the research I did.

SUSAN WHITE: I wanted to point out that one of the differences between *Gone with the Wind* and *Marnie* is that Scarlett liked the rape and Marnie didn't, and in a way that's kind of interesting because it does further indict Mark. I'm wondering)we're all wondering)whether there was any discussion of Marnie's relationship to her horse, because it's so . . .

RA: Forio.

JPA: That's what I mean about intellectualism.

SW: Oh, come now. You've got all the Freud stuff going wild in that movie.

JPA: I realize that she says the same thing to the horse that she does to somebody else, but I have to tell you that was an instinctive thing. There was no analysis going on with that at all.

RA: It is in the novel too. Big time.

SW: What about the relationship to the mother? I assume that there wasn't really any explicit discussion about erotic undertones, or even with Lil. Although some people have written about Marnie's relationship with Lil as potentially lesbian.

JPA: So someone told me the other day. I have to tell you, when you do films or theater or television, if ever a serious critic deigns to review your work, you are always stupefied, amazed, and fascinated, and sometimes made absolutely hilarious by all the stuff you didn't know about what you'd written. You don't do that. Most people really don't do that.

SW: I just want to say that I adore *Marnie*. I think it's brilliant, and I just wanted to thank you.

JPA: Well, you're very kind.

RA: On the question of the mother, another change from the novel is in the character Lucy Nye. She's like the madwoman in the attic who reveals the secrets of the family house, and the secret as Peter mentioned is actually that she killed her baby in the novel. Instead, in your script, which I think is much better than the novel . . .

JPA: You're sitting right here by me. Let me say something about that. It's not a good novel, but really good novels don't always make good movies. Some of the best movies ever made have come from second- and third-rate books.

RA: In your adaptation, you develop the relation between Marnie and her mother much more fully, and I wonder whether that was a way, again, of trying to make the character Marnie more sympathetic, engaging to the audience.

JPA: I'm sure it was. I don't have any memory of deliberately doing that, but I'm sure it was. I mean, I like Marnie. I felt sorry for her.

QUESTION: One theme of conversation over the past few days, especially in speaking to screenwriters, has been the way in which the screenplay changes the source material and imposes or suggests new meanings. But your comment about Tippi Hedren and the way she played the role suggests something about the screenplay and the finished movie that suggests that between those two stages there might be room for creating new meanings . . .

JPA: Of course there is. That's what a director's job is.

QUESTION: Could you then comment about what you found surprising in the finished movie, things that might count as meanings or effects or responses that you had not yourself thought about?

JPA: No, I can't say that because I just don't have that kind of a brain. I don't analyze. I react absolutely emotionally.

QUESTION: But on an emotional level, when you saw the movie, were there any things that surprised you?

JPA: I was disappointed.

RA: What disappointed you about the film?

JPA: I thought it was filled with *longeurs.* I didn't think the Marnie character worked as well as it should have done. I think there were some very good scenes, some excellent scenes. And because I did write some good scenes, I think that's why Hitch liked me and wanted to work with me again. I don't know. It didn't hold together in some strange way.

RA: Tell us more about Hitch wanting to work with you again.

JPA: We became very, very good friends. In effect, I lived with Hitch and Alma for a good length of time I was in California. They were unbelievably generous and fun. They were fun to be with. Really fun, Alma just as much as Hitch. We said we wanted to work again. Obviously we'd have a good time. Hitch had two ideas: one, the Barrie thing, *Mary Rose,* and he said he had wanted to do *Mary Rose* for a long time and that

Lew Wasserman, who was head of the studio, didn't like it, but let's go ahead and have a shot at it. So I wrote a draft which Hitch liked, and Lew wouldn't do it. He just wouldn't make it.

RA: What were his objections to it?

JPA: I haven't a clue. I have no idea. I'm not even sure that Hitch did. It was a very strange relationship.

RA: Lew's and Hitch's?

JPA: Oh yes. Lew Wasserman, who was, certainly at one time, the most powerful man in Hollywood and still swings a very heavy stick, had been Hitch's agent.

RA: You know he gave us money for this conference?

JPA: Did he? Good. He should. That's exactly what he should do.

RA: That's what Pat Hitchcock said to me too.

JPA: In any event, he had been Hitch's agent, which means, in effect, that he worked for Hitch. Suddenly the outfit he was with took over a studio and they got divested of the agency business and he was suddenly Hitch's boss. This was not easy for Hitch. In fact, it was quite difficult for him.

RA: Was Lew Hitch's financial advisor?

JPA: I couldn't comment on that. What I was going to say is that the other thing Hitch had in mind for us to do was fun but insane. He wanted to take a John Buchan novel, and he was going to rent a yacht, and Alma and he and my husband and I and my dog were going to sail around the world, going from port to port, doing research for this John Buchan novel, and we were going to take two years doing it. It sounded great, but as Hitch was an old Turk of the deepest dye, he loved working with women, but he really didn't like their husbands. Lewis was so excited about the boat, and I said, "You fool! You'd be the first to go overboard. Before the dog!"

QUESTION: I like Marnie too. You said that you thought that Evan Hunter's script, or Evan Hunter in general, was psychologically simple-minded. I wondered how you went about writing Marnie's psychology, or if it was important at all to you or Hitch, writing the script?

JPA: I didn't say simple-minded! I said naive. And yes, the psychology was very important.

QUESTION: So what sort of prep work did you do? What sort of research if any?

JPA: I'm real good at that. I'm really good at the psychological stuff. Actually, that's my strongest point. I didn't do any research. I'd been reading all my life. I was in my forties, I knew a thing or two.

QUESTION: Was there a difference in writing *Jean Brodie,* say, and *Marnie?*

JPA: Of course. Everything is different. Nothing is alike.

QUESTION: Was there a different process involved?

JPA: No. It was always the same. Just go as fast as you can and get it over with.

WALTER SREBNICK: Just to follow up on the psychology question, clearly the script flirts with psychoanalysis consistently, but the one text that actually is mentioned in the scene in which Mark Rutland is playing therapist and word association games with Marnie, is *The Undiscovered Self,* which is Jung's text. Was that deliberate on your part to mention Jung as opposed to a text by Freud at that point?

JPA: No. It was just a useful line.

WS: Because it relates to the theme of the film.

JPA: It's an interesting question, but it just works in the scene. There was no analyzing of it.

RA: There's been a lot of discussion at this conference about the creative role of Alma Reville in Hitchcock's work, and Pat told us she is working on a biography of her mother.

JPA: She should be.

RA: Can you tell us a little about that from your perspective?

JPA: Alma was very, very, very smart, and she was grounded, really grounded in common sense. And she had been a highly regarded editor when she took up with Hitch and Hitch was nobody. Her skill at editing and at narrative was marvelous, and she contributed a lot to Hitch's career.

RA: Was she involved in *Marnie* in any way at all?

JPA: Well, we were always together. Hitch was jealous. He liked to get me alone because he liked to be the only one. I don't say that he didn't have some resentment at this stage of the game in Alma's input but he was mistaken.

RA: He had some resentment?

JPA: Not conscious. Not conscious at all because it was a very happy marriage. It was a very good marriage. Unconsciously he wanted to be "it"! Most artists do. Nothing wrong with that.

RA: Do you think he depended on Alma at all?

JPA: Oh yes. He depended on her for a lot of things. He depended on her for stability. Absolutely. She was marvelous, and she had a sensational sense of humor. She was what he needed.

RA: But it was a professional as well as personal collaboration.

JPA: Well, she never got credit on anything, but I know she had to do a lot of story stuff with Hitch because she had a marvelous sense of narrative.

QUESTION: I was hoping you could talk a little bit more about what it was like to be a woman screenwriter in the fifties and sixties and whether there were other women, besides Alma, who were mentors to you and supportive friends to you at that time.

JPA: No, there wasn't anybody else. I was very ignorant of the movie business although I had lived in California and had friends in the business. But my ignorance of it was really extraordinary. *Marnie* was the first thing I did, of course, and then *Cabaret* came after that. My presumption was that the woods were full of women writers. I didn't know there was virtually no one. And some journalist called me one day some years later and wanted to interview me as one of only two women who, up to that time, in talkies, had had two films made. And I said, "Oh, that's got to be a mistake. You better go to the union and check that out. That can't possibly be true." But it was. There just weren't any other women doing it.

   I must say that I was wonderfully treated by the men I worked for. I never had any real trouble with any of them. Most of them were extremely supportive. But this was pre-women's liberation and maybe I just didn't know how furious they were with me.

SLAVOJ ŽIŽEK: I am sorry to impose myself again, but just three very brief precise questions. First, at a certain point in the film, Mark gives to Marnie a kind of psychoanalytic explanation of her compulsion to steal, saying because you didn't get love, you must steal, and so on. This is what I mean by the film being too intellectual.

JPA: Maybe you're right.

SŽ: It doesn't have the right emotional resonance for me.

JPA: I clearly didn't know how to do this stuff. I could certainly do better today.

SŽ: Second point, which is an enigma for all of us, and I also congratulate you. I love *Marnie*. You remember two scenes which we experience as very artificial: one where Marnie is riding the horse, obviously roughly done background projection, the other the famous black ship at the end of the street. You probably know that some minority—I'm against them—claim this is just Hitchcock's senility, whatever. But you may be aware that there is a whole school of critics, theoreticians, who think that this gap, this artificial impression, was intended, crucial. As far as you aware, was it or not?

JPA: Hitch was very thrifty.

SŽ: Got it. Lil, that is to say the Diane Baker role: it's not so much lesbian but it's a certain figure that reappears in a whole series of Hitchcock's films, like Mrs. Danvers in *Rebecca,* you know this guardian of the house, usually a dark-haired woman, often shot on the first floor casting a threatening gaze down on the innocent arriving heroine. Were you aware of this precedence of the Lil role in previous Hitchcock films?

JPA: No. Not a clue.

ROBIN WOOD: A crucial motif in *Marnie*, I think, or perhaps *the* crucial motif, and I should say I've seen this film at least twenty times now, and I think it is an unqualified masterpiece . . .

JPA: Do you teach?

RW: Yes, I do. I plead guilty. But I've been told I am not an intellectual, that I'm an anti-intellectual. Anyway, what I wanted to comment on is the stroking or smoothing of hair. Near the beginning of the film, Marnie kneels at her mother's knee, wanting to have her hair brushed and the mother refuses. At the end of the film, Marnie does exactly the same thing. After her memory, she kneels at her mother's knee, and her mother Bernice reaches out her hand and can't bring herself to touch this terrible reminder of her past. Mark raises Marnie to her feet and strokes her hair, and Marnie accepts it, which I think is the crucial moment of the whole film, the moment the whole film moves towards. In the memory sequence, the sailor comforting Marnie also strokes her hair. And the sailor is connected to Forio, the horse, because of the "There, there now" when they die. Was it yours, was it Hitchcock's, was it unconscious?

JPA: No, that was mine. Some of it was unconscious. Not all of it.

QUESTION: You previously remarked that you felt that Tippi Hedren was ill-cast in the role of Marnie. Is there someone in particular who you envisioned in the role and, if so, why?

JPA: Clearly, even at the time, I think she was too old. But someone with an endless, bottomless vulnerability like Ingrid Bergman, although I don't think she was the right person.

RA: Hitch wanted Grace Kelly. What would you have thought of that?

JPA: I know he did. We discussed it at great length. I think it was the same problem that Tippi had. A little icy.

RA: Hitchcock liked icy.

JPA: Oh, he adored icy. He was mad for icy. He was having an old man's *crise de coeur* over icy.

ROBIN WOOD: Can I also, at risk of pushing this too much, go back to the so-called rape scene once more? I've always been bothered by the simple description of that as rape. I think it's more ambiguous, the way Hitchcock shoots it and perhaps the way you wrote it. What happens is Mark bursts into Marnie's room. He is obviously drunk and desperate.

He grabs her night-dress and tears it down so she's standing there in front of him naked and she looks appalled. He is ashamed. He seems to sober up immediately. He's very gentle with her. He takes off his dressing gown, his bathrobe, and puts it around her shoulders. She becomes completely passive. Now, the way I read it, Marnie knows she is being raped but Mark does not know he is raping her.

JPA: You're absolutely right.

RW: Oh, thank you.

JPA: My own feeling about the movie is that I was disappointed in it when I saw it and a couple of years later. Three years later, I was staying with my mother and father, and Mother was going to look at a television program of *Marnie* that night. She said, "Oh good, we can see it together." And I said, "I can't do it. I just don't want to." Anyway, I finally had to. It seemed much, much better but then I checked the time and realized how much had been cut. Very judiciously cut.

RA: When was the first time you saw the film?

JPA: At the studio.

QUESTION: After the script was written, was your input finished, or were you in on the filming?

JPA: I was there part of the time. I had a husband and a child. Hitch wanted me to stay the whole time, but I couldn't. He got very restless, not to say bored, during the filming of the show. He had done everything he was going to do before they got in front of the cameras, unless he had recalcitrant actors. All the creative work had already been done. He storyboarded a film like nobody I ever saw. I mean every single, solitary shot was up there.

QUESTION: But there was no doctoring afterwards?

JPA: All the creative work had been done, and then he was left with actors.

WALTER SREBNICK: There is a biographical theory aboard that annoys those of us who truly love this movie, which is that because of Hitchcock's, as you put it, old man's *crise de coeur*, the film was sabotaged by this. I wonder if you would agree with that or know anything about that or would reject that out of hand?

JPA: I would not reject it out of hand. I certainly don't know that it's true. Clearly, it could have been true. He was always kind of bored with everything he did after the challenging part was done. But I think when he realized he was not going to continue to be Pygmalion to Tippi a lot of the energy went out.

RA: There appear to me no more questions. I want to thank you very much for joining us this morning.

HITCHCOCK: THE MAJOR PHASE

An analysis of gender ideology in which women are always innocent, always passive victims of patriarchal power, is patently not satisfactory.
　　　　　　　　　　—Michele Barrett[1]

HITCHCOCK THE FEMINIST: REREADING *SHADOW OF A DOUBT*

Thomas Hemmeter

Because almost every film directed by Alfred Hitchcock depicts encounters between men and women reflecting the values of a patriarchal order, his films are not often claimed as feminist texts. Instead, many feminist critics conclude that, because his films mirror images and structures of a vicious and vengeful patriarchal system repeatedly subjecting women to male violence, the narratives close off any possibility of women escaping this oppression.[2] This critical perspective creates an allegory that projects onto a film text its own narrative assumptions: thus a film like *Shadow of a Doubt* is read as a patriarchal tale of a young woman's transgression, punishment, and return to the family structure.[3]

　I propose an alternative feminist reading of *Shadow of a Doubt* as a critique of the patriarchal ideology it represents, as a text that shows the cracks and fissures in the sexual roles born and existing in the institution of the family. From this perspective, the film becomes a feminist text. My critical approach is a textual feminism, open to the ambiguities and silences of the film text that reveal dislocations of the supposedly unified patriarchal voice; it is a critical approach that "seeks to expose, not to perpetuate, patriarchal practices."[4] Central to my reading is the notion that *Shadow of a Doubt* represents gender identities not as fixed, stable metaphysical essences (i.e., as patriarchal categories), but as subversive, divided constructs of a divided patriarchal order. Patrice Petro has said that "while the narrative development of *The Lady Vanishes* clearly works to fix and center traditionally patriarchal female and male positions, it also explores the negative side of this Oedipal paradigm"— women's power to resist, "to refuse, to withdraw from, and disturb the symbolic space."[5] *Shadow of a Doubt*, too, creates these negative, marginal spaces, spaces that this essay will explore.

In one of the best feminist studies of *Shadow of a Doubt*, Diane Carson concludes that Hitchcock is a misogynist because this film fixes women between two nightmare worlds: that of complacent submission to domestic tyranny and that of doomed rebellion against that tyranny.[6] This 1943 film paints a portrait of a typical American family in Santa Rosa, California: a stodgy father, fussing mother, college-age daughter impatient with her routine family life, and a boy and girl several years her junior. When their Uncle Charlie comes to visit the Newton family, the older girl, Young Charlie (Charlotte), first welcomes him as the person who will shake the family out of its lethargy and then discovers that he is a notorious murderer of widows, a discovery that leads her uncle to try to kill her. Eventually she turns to blackmail to force him to leave and must push her uncle to his death in order to save her own life.

Carson sees in Young Charlie's story a daughter punished for transgressing patriarchal laws that would keep women in the home. Carson also uncovers a second story, that of Charlie's mother Emma. Emma's repressed voice tells the story of a woman's life in protected domesticity: Emma feels trapped in her own family home, her identity eclipsed and her vitality sapped. This reading corrects the easy assumption that Emma is a happy housewife and that Charlie's Freudian mother fixation expresses a desire to "make an already happy Emma happy."[7] Carson's study makes clear that Emma's domestic life is unhappy, and the film presents no alternative for independent women like Charlie to escape from the oppressive nightmare of a patriarchal world. Because *Shadow of a Doubt* offers women a choice only of submission in marriage or in death, Carson claims that the film's misogynist hidden agenda is to convince the daughter to conform to the patriarchal order and to accept her mother's domestic nightmare in marriage.[8] This closed reading is shared by James McLaughlin, who like Carson sees Young Charlie's only choice as a return to her family—and indeed sees her in the film's final shot as coupled and ready to repeat her mother's grim family narrative.[9]

Though Carson's study makes us aware of the degree to which *Shadow of a Doubt* concerns itself with patriarchal values and the place of women in the family, I think its conclusion that Hitchcock therefore aims to keep women subject to men is incorrect. In resolving the film's structures into yet one more Hitchcockian double, that of a choice between two nightmares, Carson's analysis itself shares with patriarchal thought a dualistic approach to sexual difference: women are trapped in domestic nightmares; men create and enforce this entrapment. Like the feminist criticism of Kate Millett, Carson's and McLaughlin's analyses are guided by a "monolithic conception of sexual ideology" that refuses to recognize textual ambiguities, instead resolving everything into dichotomies of opposition.[10] Even essays attempting to argue that Hitchcock's films present feminist critiques can fall into this dualistic trap. Beginning with the title question "Alfred Hitchcock: Misogynist or Feminist?" a recent article can only conclude that Hitchcock offered an unconscious, unknowing critique.[11] As Toril Moi says in *Sexual/Textual Politics*, "The binary model of differences enclosed or captured between the two opposite poles of masculinity and femininity blinds us to that which escapes this rigid structuration."[12] A potential danger of feminist discourse, in other words, is to become as authoritarian as the text of the patriarchal film. From the perspective of Toril Moi's textual feminism, then, to stabilize Hitchcock's text as monolithically patriarchal is phallocentric criticism; to read the destabilizing forces in the text is feminist criticism.

It is easy to map various stereotyped, passive roles for women onto *Shadow of a Doubt*, each with its corresponding image of a male master. Young Charlie, her little sister, and her college-age friends are clearly, as Carson calls them, "handmaidens," girls awaiting their male lovers (their knights) to rescue them from their family boredom. Of course this romantic rescue leads inevitably to marriage and the unromantic return to the confining family the handmaiden sought to escape. The domestic roles for women, as mother and wife, represent unhappy entrapment and loss of identity for Emma Newton, who at one point says of her married life, "You sort of forget you're you." The only other roles for women in *Shadow of a Doubt* are created by death: a woman either becomes a widow when her husband dies (like the available Mrs. Green, Uncle Charlie's next potential victim) and/or becomes a victim of male violence if she, like Young Charlie, dares to assert a right to an independent life.

The unmarried handmaiden and the widow share a certain freedom from patriarchal oppression, but this freedom is only temporary since independent status exists only as a staging ground for the necessary choice of one of two victim roles, and the temporary freedom is gained at a terrible cost: violence and death. Widows, freed from oppressive male dominance in marriage, put themselves back into a dangerous maidenhood in seeking to be romanced as girls by men like Uncle Charlie, perhaps in hopes of returning to the supposedly safe status of marriage. Young Charlie saw her uncle very much as her family's knightly rescuer from its domestic routines, and in a sense she competes with Widow Green for his affections.

An exchange of rings between uncle and niece structures the film, with Charlie first rejecting the ring coyly, later accepting it, then returning it to her uncle when she learns that it had belonged to one of her uncle's victims, and finally stealing it back to blackmail her uncle into leaving. Though the dense symbolism of this multiple exchange may be interpreted in many ways, the ring exchanges overtly suggest that in some sense Young Charlie and her uncle end the film married, and she is therefore his widow after pushing him to his death. The reverse threatened, of course, and she might have lost her life, another victim of her uncle's violence, in a death symbolizing the total eclipse of self in marriage. The incestuous nature of Charlie's "marriage" to her uncle also suggests the smothering closeness of family relationships. Patriarchal forces clamp down hard upon women in this film.

A parallel set of roles may be mapped onto the other sex: Roger, Young Charlie's brother, is a spoiled baby of the family—as was Uncle Charlie— and may grow up into another demonic rescuer. While Uncle Charlie represents the knight available to rescue the handmaidens, whether young girls or widows, Joe Newton, Charlie's father, is the patriarchal husband who, having left behind the romance of the unmarried boy/knight, dreams of the freedom of the unattached male by reading murder mysteries. Though refusing the patriarchal role of husband and father, Uncle Charlie nonetheless dreams of the ordered family life of his youth, creating an illusion of Victorian harmony and peace in contrast to his disordered life outside the family as the killer and false knight/oppressor.

The men on either side of this dualistic structure dream of escaping to the life on the other side: inside the ordered family, the husband/father dreams of criminal disorder; outside the ordered family, the man dreams of peaceful order within an ideal family. In this patriarchal family order women do the same thing as the men, those on either side of this cramped structure dreaming of the comforts offered by the alternative: Emma dreams of some independence from her confining, no-name existence, while widows and girls like Young Charlie dream of a man to marry to take them out of family boredom. Women *and* men are victims of the patriarchal family ideology.

If one accepts Julia Kristeva's definition of femininity as a patriarchal construct, not a biological state, it follows that societal power can use men and women as both victims and enforcers of patriarchal conceptions of sexuality.[13] Originating in the dreams and illusions of the characters, patriarchal sex roles are not real essences in the fictional world of this film but socially created categories—ideological projections of dreaming people. Emma Newton, for example, is not simply a female victim of patriarchy but, through her dreams of escape, becomes an oppressor as well as a victim in this system. Her desire to escape her own oppressive family life, with its denial of meaningful identity, drives Emma to mother her brother (Uncle Charlie) much as he was mothered as a child. To enhance her dreamy remembrance of life as his sister, when she was an Oakley and not a Newton, Emma harbors her brother in her house and seeks to hold him there as long as possible to keep up the illusion that she is living a more glamorous life. Safe in the Newton home, Uncle Charlie makes two attempts to kill Emma's own daughter Charlie, once on the back steps and a second time in the garage. Emma's acceptance of the domestic dream of a family without oppression—the nostalgic family of her childhood—leads her to the dangerous delusion that she can dream away the realities of her family life.

Emma's family ideals clearly put her own family at risk. By nourishing idealistic delusions in both her brother and her daughter, she incubates forces that combine to threaten Young Charlie's life: Emma's dreaminess nurtures Young Charlie's dreams of escape from her home through the agency of her uncle, the savior. These dreams make Young Charlie vulnerable to romantic hopes and melodramatic despair and throw her into her uncle's homicidal path. Emma's dreams also nurture the patriarchal violence Uncle Charlie commits in hopes of recovering the old family life as it used to be. Sharing Emma's nostalgic image of the supposedly conflict-free Oakley family of earlier days, he takes out his frustrations at the failure of real life to meet his mental ideal by killing women who do not live up to the old standards. His sister Emma lives up to these standards; rich widows do not. Nor does his assertive niece Charlie, and he tries to kill her.

Uncle Charlie, whom Carson would identify as the enforcer of patriarchal values in Hitchcock's oppressive vision, instead represents the failure of the patriarchal ideology most clearly. Uncle Charlie short-circuits the ordinary progression of males into paternal authority within the family by refusing to cross the boundary from independent boyhood/knighthood into marriage—by refusing to live the life of the oppressed, resigned, ordinary husband and father like Joe Newton. He remains boyish, careless, the boy-knight turned satanic when he finds his ideals frustrated by the world. As he says to his niece, "Do you know the world is a foul sty? Do you know that if you rip the fronts off houses, you'd find swine? The world's a hell." This cynicism, coexisting in puritanical contradiction with an idealized vision of his past family life, impels him to condemn the lives of rich widows as unclean animals who live only to display their wealth in jewelry and furs. Thus one might initially conclude that Uncle Charlie embodies patriarchy's dual vision of women as angels of the house or treacherous destroyers.

Uncle Charlie's virulent misogyny, however, intersects with a curious femininity in his character, his dandyish manners and clothes contradicting his masculine cigar smoking. In one scene Young Charlie surprises him sitting in his room polishing his shoes, a domestic side he probably preferred she not see, given his violent response of ripping from her hands the article she teases him with. Once this feminine side of Uncle Charlie is recognized, it becomes possible to reinterpret images that suggest Hitchcock's misogyny. The oft-noted parallel opening visuals of Uncle Charlie lying on his bed followed by a similar shot of Young Charlie lying on her bed leads Carson to conclude that her position suggests a sexual availability: her uncle's position suggests a similar sexual availability, and is just as passively feminine.[14]

In positioning Uncle Charlie at the extreme of two sexual stereotypes, the super-masculine woman killer and the feminine dandy, the film reveals how the dualistic construct of man and woman unravels and overlaps. Uncle Charlie does not possess the stable, unchanging sexual identity that he might wish to lay claim to. He even shares many traits with the independent women he so despises: he wears fashionable and flashy clothes like his wealthy prey; he has, like his victims, a good deal of money and displays it flamboyantly (although he claims to despise it); and he has the same name as his niece, indicating that like other Hitchcock doubles he is much the same as his female counterpart.

The film further undermines the notion of Uncle Charlie as a stable, unchanging individual by demonstrating the degree to which he owes his existence to the imaginations of other characters. For the most part his identity is a construction of one woman, his niece Charlie. He exists as Young Charlie's rescuing knight early in the film, when she needs him to fill that role, while she plays his handmaiden. When later he violates her image of his proper role, she inverts the illusion and makes him the ravager of the family, a demon figure. Clearly, Uncle Charlie could play neither role without the enabling illusions of his Santa Rosa family and Young Charlie's belief in him as either savior or destroyer of her family. He is a creature of the patriarchal family and its illusions. Only such an ideology could permit the radical character transformations such as the ones Uncle Charlie undergoes, from savior to destroyer. In a clear rejection of the patriarchal view of sexual identity as essence, *Shadow of a Doubt* asserts that sexual identity is primarily a social creation, in this film a construct of other people's dreams.

Young Charlie's sexual identity is no more fixed than is her uncle's, for she not only assumes the roles of her uncle's handmaiden and, later, widow, she also assumes male roles, even that of the family patriarch in trying to protect her family. As her uncle says to her, "You're the head of your family, Charlie, anyone can see that." Finally she herself becomes another knight who must destroy her uncle in order that her mother and other family members be protected from the knowledge of his murderous deeds. After discovering the dark underside of her romantic dream, she, like Uncle Charlie, attempts to recreate the family she fled, burnishing it into a glowing image of an ideal state of innocence. That this perfect family which needs protection from her uncle never existed poses no obstacle, for she, again like Uncle Charlie, creates the lost ideal as a mental construct.

In killing her uncle at the end of the film, Young Charlie in effect exchanges identities with him, taking on his masculine role of preserver of patriarchy. Just as her uncle sought to kill her to preserve his and Emma's vision of the family, she kills her uncle in an effort to preserve this same vision. Because she can only work within the terms of patriarchy, Charlie's efforts to throw off the illusions of patriarchy lead her to reassert them. That is, in killing her uncle in the full knowledge that he threatens every value sacred to the family, she also preserves the false notions her family holds toward her uncle as the kind, bright-eyed best of the family. And since these same family-nurtured illusions helped turn Uncle Charlie into a widow-slaying monster, Young Charlie's efforts to protect her family from the reality of her uncle's murderous ways suggest that his actions will be repeated by another "Uncle Charlie." As her uncle did before her, Young Charlie finds herself in a conflicted position, sharing traits of both sexes, a patriarchal identity divided by conflicts born of the efforts of the ideology to protect itself.

I do not think, however, that *Shadow of a Doubt* merely turns Young Charlie into a version of her uncle. She does speak similar words, even threatening to kill him, and she does assert the masculine power to act as no other character does to confront her uncle, to threaten him, to frighten him, to learn his vision, to blackmail him, and finally to kill him. But it is important to recognize how Young Charlie's act of seeing dominates the film as the woman's perspective does in *The Birds,* another film in which Hitchcock supposedly reveals his misogyny. Uncle Charlie is her vision, her illusion of rescue from the family by a man and then her illusion of a hellish threat to the family. Though the visions are patriarchal, they are also hers—female— for in a patriarchal society women sometimes dream patriarchal dreams, using the terms available to them. Her uncle does not function merely as an agent of patriarchy to restrain her; she also reconstructs him as a satanic figure corresponding to her changing knowledge of the world. The film does not pit Uncle Charlie as the ravaging masculine against Young Charlie the embattled feminine, but pits the Uncle Charlie part of Young Charlie against another part of herself. Sexual identities are not stable essences, and Young Charlie is very much a divided subject, different from herself.

To read the film as a feminist film requires the recognition that in destroying her uncle, Charlie denies the validity of both her earlier-held patriarchal visions: man as knightly rescuer from family oppression and man as satanic destroyer of transgressing women. The film asserts that the patriarchal family is founded on these two illusions, held by men and women alike. From this perspective it would be difficult to conclude that a person as perceptive as Young Charlie would accept the woman's role—the oppressed wife or the victim—conferred by either of these two visions. The negatives of domestic conformity are presented all too clearly to conclude with Carson and McLaughlin that the agenda of the film is to convince Young Charlie to conform, to settle down into safe domesticity. While she is certainly aware of the violent potential of a man like her uncle, she understands as well that her own family nurtured his patriarchal violence and learns that her lover Jack Graham could not protect her any more than her father could from her uncle's violence. The film dramatizes the impossibility of a safe existence in any one category of dreams or in any one sexual role.

It is knowledge that separates Young Charlie from the other women in the film and that suggests the need for a new category beyond wife/mother or handmaiden/widow, a third term, something on the fringes of the other roles and made up of them though not the same. Knowing what she does at the end of the film, Young Charlie cannot settle into marriage, and yet she is no independent widow anxious for a dangerous fling of romance either. In writing about *Notorious,* Tania Modleski posits a " 'conflictual' narrative" which "functions not to integrate the individual into the social order, but to express women's experience of lived contradiction in patriarchy" and which places Hitchcock heroines in impossible positions.[15] Modleski goes on to argue that "women's modes of knowing in patriarchy" have to do with

"an awareness of contradiction" which Hitchcock's films, in their preoccupation and identification with women as victims, reinforce "in the female
spectator."[16] I believe that this knowledge exists not only in the female spectator but in a character like Young Charlie, whose tortured face bears the
weight of the contemporary spectator's knowledge within the diegesis of
the film.

While the film uses the terms of patriarchy, it rejects patriarchal values
by placing Young Charlie at the margins where the dualistic terms of patriarchy intersect: where ordinary family values intersect with extraordinary
values born of romance; where the qualities of the wife/mother mingle with
those of the unmarried woman; where the stereotyped traits of the feminine
come together with those of the masculine. At the end of the film, standing with Jack Graham outside the church where her uncle's eulogy is being
read, Charlie is fully aware of the two nightmares that threaten every man
and woman—oppressive marriage or solitary violence. The narrative makes
clear that she has not yet chosen either, willing neither a romantic death nor
the slow death of domesticity, but exists, unhappily, at the margins of these
two worlds in full knowledge of their threats. To close off the narrative in the
assumption that Charlie must return to the family in marriage to Graham
is to impose patriarchal values upon a text Hitchcock leaves open.

Though Young Charlie is temporarily free of patriarchy's nightmares,
her knowledge confers upon her the recognition that she will have to face
them again. Knowledge is paradoxical in Hitchcock's films because, while
liberating, the alternatives it presents are so grim. It confers on someone
like Charlie the power to act—to correct her own illusions and to protect
herself from the consequences of carrying her illusions out into the world—
but it also produces a kind of paralysis or stasis (e.g., as in *Rear Window*,
where the vision of L. B. Jefferies both promotes and prevents action at the
same time). Instead of revealing some brave new world of freedom for independent women disentangled from the lines of patriarchy, Charlie's knowledge returns the knower with new insight to the same old world. Better vision does not change anything other than the character who can see better.
Knowing the trap of her family and understanding her mother's smothered
existence; knowing that the family produces its deranged defenders whose
efforts to preserve family values would paradoxically destroy the family;
knowing that the family nurtures passive victims by encouraging romantic
dreams in women and willful ignorance and repression in parents: knowing all this, Young Charlie can only recognize that this is indeed her heritage. While the film narrative gives her nothing to do with this knowledge,

ending as it does with her recognition, it does not follow that the narrative pursues a logic of containment.[17] Instead it pursues a logic of analysis and critique.

Though it offers no alternative world to patriarchy, *Shadow of a Doubt* does make clear how patriarchal terms themselves work to tear apart patriarchy's unified vision of an ordered world. At the end of the film, Young Charlie finds herself at the gap where the discourse unravels. Supposedly the victim of her uncle for transgressing patriarchal laws, she succeeds in killing the enforcer, but in this very act finds herself substituting for her uncle as perverse protector of a system in which she does not believe. Uncle Charlie, the supposed protector of patriarchy, is its potential destroyer. If everyone shared his vision of families as pig sties, its obverse—the illusion of the family as ideal, which enables the oppression of women—would disappear. Without the romance of the family, romantic illusions of young women would no longer be nurtured; the ignorance of Emma Newton would no longer have to be protected; and a young woman like Charlie would be freed to pursue interests independent of the family.

Young Charlie, who manages to free herself from the illusion that her uncle is the apotheosis of good family values and romantic decency, finds herself echoing Marlow's lie to Kurtz's Intended in *Heart of Darkness,* hiding the truth about her uncle from her family members so that they can maintain their romantic illusions. To protect her family from knowing the worst, she sustains the family myth of a heroic Uncle Charlie and sustains as well this myth's power to promote the destructive illusions and disillusions of people like her uncle.

The end of the film sees Young Charlie waiting outside the church, near enough to hear her uncle being eulogized within as a pillar of the community but still on the outside, at the margins. Where first she lay inside her family's home, now she stands apart from her family, who listen inside the institution that complements the home. She knows the eulogy's notion of community to be a lie just as she disbelieves her uncle's vision of the human community as sty. Positioned between two inadequate roles for women (i.e., oppressed wife or victimized woman), she is no less positioned between these two inadequate discourses. Carson and McLaughlin read the final image of the film as a statement that Young Charlie has given in and has returned to her family, and since she is pictured in a two-shot holding hands with her boyfriend, this possibility exists. But there are counter-suggestions. The couple wait outside the church, not sanctioned by this legitimizing institution of patriarchy. Their grim pairing brings together the qualities of a funeral and a marriage.

As in the ending of many other Hitchcock films, the coupling is un-consummated, its tending-towards-but-not-completed quality suggesting a temporary stay against both the confusion of Uncle Charlie's world and the stultifying order of her family. *Shadow of a Doubt* leaves Young Charlie in a marginal position between marriage and unmarriage, a troubled state of grace but nevertheless a position other than the grim couplings constructed by the fixed duality of patriarchy in other Hitchcock films: the domestic nightmare of marriage or the violent nightmare of a murderous pair (think of *Vertigo* or *Psycho*). Young Charlie exists at this provisional intersection of illusions, a fragile third status beyond either of the confining poles conferred by patriarchy.

Though her position is a tentative one, Young Charlie might be read as a feminist construction attempting to deconstruct sexual categories and patriarchal stereotypes of women's roles. This perspective exposes the film's narrative as a rhetorical enterprise that analyzes the family roots of misogyny. *Shadow of a Doubt* shows the deadly transformations of patriarchal roles as men and women work to protect family values: Uncle Charlie, the stereotype of the male enforcer of patriarchal values who kills liberated widows, transforms himself into an unstable contradiction, the feminine dandy, while the feminine handmaiden, Young Charlie, is transformed into the masculine enforcer. These stereotypes appear overtly as constructs in service of a tangled ideology as the family sex roles tear apart at the seams. To conclude that the male filmmaker, Hitchcock, seeks authoritarian, patriarchal control of everything in his text derives more from the imposition of a critical methodology than from the text itself. Working from a feminist theory that can account for the "paradoxically productive aspects of patriarchal ideology," a critic can recognize in a film like *Shadow of a Doubt* that the oppressive order can backfire and allow some women to beat the odds.[18] Texts can say things forbidden by an apparently dominating ideology, and just as Carson found the quiet words of Emma Newton to be voicing her domestic hell, other critics may find other textual voices.

I think that Young Charlie's position at the intersection of conflicting patriarchal values expresses a feminist objection to the sexual roles created by this system. In leaving Young Charlie on the margins at the end of *Shadow of a Doubt*, Hitchcock subverts the patriarchal claims of family hegemony and creates a marginal feminist voice. To understand the female spectator's complex, contradictory response to Hitchcock films, Modleski argues for "an understanding of women's placement on the margins of patriarchal culture—at once inside and outside its codes and structures."[19] *Shadow of a Doubt* leaves us with this precise image of Charlotte Newton:

on the margins, the position of dissidence from which, Kristeva theorizes, oppressed women struggle against the central power of patriarchy.[20]

NOTES

1. Michele Barrett, *Virginia Woolf: Women and Writing* (London: Women's Press, 1979).

2. See, for example, James B. McLaughlin, "All in the Family: Alfred Hitchcock's *Shadow of a Doubt*," *Wide Angle* 4, no. 1 (1980): 12–19; Laura Mulvey, "Visual Pleasure and Narrative Cinema," *Screen* 16, no. 3 (1975): 6–18; and Linda Williams, "When the Woman Looks," in *Re-Vision: Essays in Feminist Film Criticism,* ed. Mary Ann Doane, Patricia Mellencamp, and Linda Williams. The American Film Institute Monograph Series, vol. 3 (Frederick, MD: University Publications of America, 1984), 83–99.

3. See, for example, McLaughlin, "All in the Family."

4. Toril Moi, *Sexual/Textual Politics: Feminist Literary Theory* (London: Methuen, 1985), xiv.

5. Patrice Petro, "Rematerializing the Vanishing 'Lady': Feminism, Hitchcock, and Interpretation," in *A Hitchcock Reader,* ed. Marshall Deutelbaum and Leland Poague (Ames: Iowa State University Press, 1986), 131.

6. Diane Carson, "The Nightmare World of Hitchcock's Women," in *The Kingdom of Dreams: Selected Papers from the Tenth Annual Florida State University Conference on Literature and Film* (Tallahassee: University Press of Florida, 1987), 11–20.

7. Paul Gordon, "Sometimes a Cigar Is Not Just a Cigar: A Freudian Analysis of Uncle Charles in Hitchcock's *Shadow of a Doubt*," *Literature/Film Quarterly,* 19, no. 4 (1991): 274.

8. Carson, "The Nightmare World of Hitchcock's Women," 19–20.

9. McLaughlin, "All in the Family," 18–19.

10. Moi, *Sexual/Textual Politics,* 30.

11. Sander H. Lee, "Alfred Hitchcock: Misogynist or Feminist?" *Post Script* 10, no. 3 (summer 1991): 47.

12. Moi, *Sexual/Textual Politics,* 154.

13. Moi, *Sexual/Textual Politics,* 166.

14. Carson, "The Nightmare World of Hitchcock's Women," 13.

15. Tania Modleski, *The Women Who Knew Too Much: Hitchcock and Feminist Theory* (New York: Methuen, 1988), 65.

16. Modleski, *The Women Who Knew Too Much,* 66.

17. See Barbara Klinger, "*Psycho*: The Institutionalization of Female Sexuality,"

in *A Hitchcock Reader,* 332–39, as well as McLaughlin, "All in the Family," and Carson, "The Nightmare World of Hitchcock's Women."

18. Moi, *Sexual/Textual Politics,* 64.

19. Modleski, *The Women Who Knew Too Much,* 116–17.

20. See especially Julia Kristeva, "A Partir de Polylogue," interview with Françoise van Rossum-Guyon, in *Revue des Sciences Humaines* 169 (December 1977): 495–501, and "Un nouveau Type d'Intellectuel: Le dissident," *Tel Quel* 74 (winter 1977): 3–8.

REAR WINDOW, OR THE RECIPROCATED GLANCE

JOHN A. BERTOLINI

Hitchcock's stories, which often have their roots in paranoid fantasies, resemble the delusions of psychotics: people are after me (the chase plot); people are persecuting me (the pursued is innocent); everyone's against me (the pursued cannot go to the police for help because they think him guilty of some crime); I'm in danger and no one will believe me (even the good people don't trust the pursued). *The Lady Vanishes* (1938) is paradigmatic in this regard in that it portrays the urgency characteristic of the paranoid in the protagonist's efforts to convince the world (and a particular man) that her apparent delusions are real. Insofar as *Rear Window's* (1954) basic plot concerns an individual's efforts to convince people that a murder has taken place, it conforms to the pattern of paranoid fantasy that underlies so many of Hitchcock's films. More specifically, one member of a couple usually has to persuade the other member to believe him or her, and then they together have to prove to the world that they are right. In doing so, by working together, they develop their romantic relationship until the end of the film when they can join together in love. For love to be created, Hitchcock suggests that the man or the woman has to enter into the private *Vertigo* mental world of the other; their fantasy lives must be shared.[1]

The mechanism of the film is on one level simple: everything L. B. Jefferies (James Stewart) sees out of his rear window has to do with his own emotional and professional worries.[2] After the credits, the camera moves to the window sill and watches a cat move swiftly up a flight of outdoors stairs leading to the courtyard of Jefferies' building (Hitchcock will later duplicate this shot when the camera watches Stella and Lisa enter the courtyard to dig up Thorwald's flower bed, as if the film were beginning over again or as if Lisa were completing the cat's tentative invasion of the world across the way from Jefferies' apartment), and then pans upwards to reveal the building across the way; it looks to the right, then to the left, then down to show the street beyond the building—these are the boundaries of Jefferies' view.[3] The shots establish the visual space of the film, roughly the shape of a proscenium stage (the three bamboo curtains being successively and evenly rolled up by an unseen agent during the credits also suggest a stage performance). Then the camera cuts back to the interior of Jefferies' apartment to show him asleep (dreaming); a close-up of his face shows him perspiring from the New York summer heat and humidity (a wall thermometer reads 94 degrees) and the camera shows us that he needs his morning shave.

The camera now cuts to various windows around the courtyard to look in on Jefferies' neighbors, and to tell us what he's dreaming about. First we see a songwriter shaving in front of a mirror on his mantelpiece (shortly we will see Jefferies shaving after he awakens); the songwriter hears a radio announcer ask, "Men, are you over forty? When you wake up in the morning, do you have that tired listless feeling?" The shaving suggests simple wish fulfillment: Jefferies dreams that he is already up and about, performing his morning ablutions, so that he can continue his pleasurable sleep. But the announcer's question is one that causes Jefferies anxiety: he is in love but reluctant to marry. And the songwriter's moving to shut off the radio is another wish-fulfillment, to repress the question. The songwriter is standing up and able to move about (as Jefferies cannot because of his broken leg). As the songwriter changes the dial on the radio, the camera cuts to show a couple sleeping on their fire escape awakened by an alarm clock. Jefferies' dreaming of someone else awakened by a clock allows him to sleep a little longer without guilt (the image also introduces the motif of time into the film). The transition from the songwriter to the couple is one of metonymic association: the radio dial being switched becomes the alarm clock being turned off; in both cases, time presses (Jefferies for his part feels the pressure of time because of his cast, which he refers to as his "cocoon").

The camera continues to pan left and watches (in long shot) a blonde young woman in her bathroom, from the back and from the shoulders up, arranging her hair, moving from her bathroom into her living room, fastening her halter top, the top coming unfastened; she bends, picks it up and refastens it; she dances a little to some music. The dancer has an obvious sexual appeal for Jefferies, but more importantly her dancing shows how intensely he desires freedom of movement. To one who is forced to be immobile, ordinary movement takes the dream form of agile, patterned movement. In other words, the dancer as a wish-fulfillment image condenses an analogy: a walking person is to a paralyzed person what a dancer is to a person who can merely walk. The camera next sees children dancing in the street as they follow and are cooled off by the spray from a street-cleaning truck. The wish-fulfillment nature of these images for Jefferies is obvious. The final image the camera sees before moving back into Jefferies' apartment is of a hand reaching outside a window to remove the cover of a bird cage, and this leads the dreamer back to reality. Jefferies, like the bird, is confined to his apartment because of a broken leg. Like the invisible hand that pulled up the bamboo curtains, the window is an active though apparently missing agent, for it functions like a looking glass; it projects as if onto a screen the fantasies, fears, and desires from Jefferies' psyche. That is why the camera is so mobile. It does not merely record what is there, it creates the images, it writes them. Its very potency in this regard emanates from the pressure of Jefferies' immobility.

Jefferies' immobility is not total; he is only relatively immobile by virtue of his confinement to his apartment in a wheel chair (his visiting nurse, Stella, will complain about his sleeping in the wheelchair instead of in his bed). Once inside his apartment, the camera pans around to establish two important points: that Jefferies is a photo-journalist, and that taking pictures of a car race has resulted in a broken leg and his confinement in a wheel chair. Then there is a fade out and fade in (he is awake now), and the camera moves to look out his window to see what he has been dreaming about: mobility (the dancer, as she moves around in her apartment, performs dance or calisthenic movements). Most important, for the film as a whole, the dancer is a figure of the artist, and for that reason signifies Jefferies' anxiety about being able to renew his artistic abilities as a photographer. Moreover, a photographer ordinarily has the power to immobilize a dancer in a picture. Here, it is as if the dancer by virtue of her power to move, and therefore to attract and hold his glance, has immobilized the photographer, in the way that moving pictures hold the glance of the audience.

In the exposition sequence of shots inside Jefferies' apartment, we see first a framed negative of a model's face, then the finished picture on the cover of a *Life*-like magazine. The blonde cover-model bears a resemblance to the dancer. Behind the tie between the photographer and the dancer lies the myth of the Medusa, the woman with snakes for hair (the dancer's lithe movements), whose threat to her male adversary, the power to give him an erection or turn him to stone (Jefferies' broken leg in a cast), can only be deflected by the use of a mirror-shield (Jefferies will save himself by blinding his would-be murderer with his flash gun—his professional reflecting shield).[4] By looking at the reflection of his psyche as projected across the courtyard in the costume jewelry salesman's murder of his wife, Jefferies avoids staring directly into the Medusa's eyes, and therefore enables himself to defeat the internal enemy. (The business of costume jewelry suggests Jefferies' fears that he could degenerate into a second-rate artist, a purveyor of shoddy goods.)

That Jefferies does not actually witness the murder and dismemberment, but only hears a scream in the dark and later dozes off while the salesman leaves the apartment with his mistress disguised as his wife, suggests how threatening a direct confrontation with his fantasy of ridding himself of Lisa would be. Jefferies' suspicion that the salesman has murdered his wife initially only flickers in his mind. Hitchcock makes it a literally subliminal suspicion when, in the sequence where Jefferies and Stella watch Thorwald directing the movers as they carry out the trunk possibly containing his wife's dead body, children's voices can be heard faintly, arising from the courtyard below Jefferies' apartment, shouting "Bang! Bang!"—as if they know a murder has been committed and are trying to make Jefferies fully conscious of it. Likewise, the wife's severed head, the idea of which Hitchcock keeps constantly in the audience's mind but the head never in direct view, functions as a Medusa's head in that it is too horrible for us to behold. Hitchcock himself hints at the way the myth of Medusa underlies the film when he explains to Truffaut what partly inspired him during the fashioning of the screenplay:

> The killing presented something of a problem, so I used two news stories from the British press. One was the Patrick Mahon case and the other was the case of Dr. Crippen. In the Mahon case the man killed a girl in a bungalow on the sea front of southern England. He cut up the body and threw it, piece by piece, out of a train window.

But he didn't know what to do with the head, and that's where I got the idea of having them look for the victim's head in *Rear Window*. What Patrick Mahon did was to put the head in the fireplace and light the fire. Then something happened that may sound phony but is absolutely true. Like in a stage play, just as he put the head in the fire, a thunderstorm came on, with lightning and thunder. Somehow, the heat of the fire made the eyes open wide, as if they were staring at Mahon.[5]

Hitchcock has various ways of alluding to the myth of Medusa by emphasizing the motif of the head, both in the dialogue and by way of camera movement and the framing of shots. For example, the way Hitchcock shoots Lisa's first entrance, a close-up of her face approaching the sleeping Jefferies, preceded by the shadow of her head gradually covering Jefferies' sleeping face, makes her approach seem menacing, as indeed, in his unconscious, it is. (The low angle shot of Lisa's approaching face will be duplicated when near the end of the film Thorwald lunges toward Jefferies to strangle him.) Later, Jefferies taunts Lisa with the question whether she's ever eaten fish heads and rice because, he warns her, if she marries him she might have to eat food made from things "you couldn't even look at when they were alive." Jefferies seems overly concerned with Lisa's hair (the night she comes to stay over he asks her somewhat petulantly, "What have you done to your hair?"). Lisa jokes that the only way she could get Jefferies' attention would be to move "into the apartment across the way" and do "the dance of the seven veils" (Salome's dance both traps the glance of the spectator and leads to decapitation/castration). Stella reproves Jefferies for peeping with the reminder: "In the old days they used to put your eyes out with a red hot poker." The punishment for looking at forbidden things (like the Medusa's head) is to be blinded, or castrated. But Jefferies' unconscious knows that for his own salvation—to be both an artist and a husband successfully—he has to survive his own anxieties. On the evening of the murder, Jefferies' anxieties about both drive him to quarrel nastily with Lisa. The residue of hostility from their quarrel, as it were, makes the salesman act to kill his wife. The mechanism of projection does work in that specific a way, but it also works in more general ways.[6]

Most of the individuals Jefferies watches are in some way artistic, but also frustrated somehow in the practice of their art (as the setting is Greenwich Village, Hitchcock can here be seen following his own principle of always using setting expressively).[7] The sculptress, for example, uses a hearing aid and in the trailer for the film the voice-over tells us that Jefferies calls her "Hearing Aid," but nowhere in the film itself does Jefferies so refer to her. Instead, we see her turning up her hearing aid so that she can hear a neighbor, the woman with the bird cage, say "Good morning"; like Jefferies, who cannot walk or see everything, the sculptress cannot hear everything. Her impairment seems to translate into her own art, for she tells the milkman that her sculpture is called "Hunger." Jefferies will later be frustrated in his attempts to eat the breakfast Stella has prepared for him because of his squeamishness over her speculations on how Thorwald cut up his wife's body. Furthermore, the sculptress doubles Jefferies as an image of immobility by her habit of reclining and dozing in a yard chair.

Like the sculptress and the dancer, the songwriter is a figure of the artist and, because of his recurring inability to finish the song he is working on and the resulting frustration, similarly suggests anxieties about waning artistic powers on Jefferies' part. But before we see the sculptress, the dancer, or the songwriter (the latter two have apartments on the same level with Jefferies' apartment, suggesting the level of awareness he has about the anxieties those two figures represent), we see on a level above and far to the right an image of a family, a father, a mother, and a child, the parents dressed for the day and sipping coffee on their balcony. The distance of the image measures Jefferies' anxiety about his ever marrying and having a happy family life.

The dialogue with the visiting nurse, Stella, sets up the sources of Jefferies' discontent. He is attracted to Lisa Fremont, his exact opposite in her love of fashion, of city night life, of stability, and because she's so different, he cannot reconcile his desire to pursue a career as a photo-journalist with his desire to marry Lisa. He continually protests that she would not be able to adapt herself to his adventurous life, but in keeping with the film's mechanism of projection, the truth is that he fears he cannot adapt himself to her needs. Hence, the appearance of the young newlyweds in the apartment across the way and to the left: the young wife's sexual demands on the husband—demands he finds increasingly difficult to satisfy—become a running joke in the film; more than a joke, because the configuration of the bride constantly calling to the groom, "Haarrrry," to return to bed, parodies the invalid Mrs. Thorwald's constant need for attention, showing that the two needs are connected in Jefferies' mind and are equally threatening.

All that he watches across the courtyard corresponds to an internal anxiety, wish, or ambivalence regarding the two questions central to his life: Can he return successfully to his career as an artist and can he succeed at love and marriage? His accident has immobilized him and thereby made him resemble the products of his own art, the photograph that immobilizes time and stops movement. And so he is forced into a contemplation of himself:

the artist as Narcissus is the paradigm for the whole film. Jefferies spies on his neighbors because they are a projection of his internal life; the shots of his neighbors' doings are reverse angle shots of his own psyche.

After he awakens the first thing he does is imitate the songwriter by shaving; then the phone rings (a version of the alarm clock going off for the couple on the fire escape) and he takes a phone call from his editor. While he talks on the phone, his reflection can be seen in the left panel of his rear window. Likewise when we first see Thorwald bickering with his wife, his reflection can also be seen in his window panel as he walks into their bedroom. These reflected images, coming so early in the film, not only link Jefferies to his projected murderous self, Thorwald, but also establish the motif of the mirror self. The audience in the theater vicariously experiences Jefferies' contemplation of his own psyche and survives. But Jefferies survives at the expense of another broken leg. His smile at the end of the film signifies the release from anxiety; his broken legs are now only broken legs.

Two moments of a reciprocated glance emblematize the central theme of the film: the first is Hitchcock's signature appearance which takes place fittingly in the apartment of the songwriter (the script does not indicate Hitchcock's appearance here, suggesting that Hitchcock devised it on his own). Hitchcock stands in front of the mantelpiece (where the songwriter earlier shaved in front of a mirror) with his back to us and to the songwriter, while the songwriter sits at the piano playing, with his back to Hitchcock. Presumably, the songwriter is auditioning his work for Hitchcock's approval. Hitchcock looks over his left shoulder at the songwriter, who in turn stops playing and looks over his right shoulder at Hitchcock. Hitchcock had been winding or setting or repairing a clock (and his activity figures his identity as the master of suspense, the controller of time).[8] After he stops, they exchange glances, looking at one another for a moment. Even more important, during the seven seconds Hitchcock can be seen on screen, his image is reflected in one of the window panels that is open, so that Hitchcock, the songwriter, and Hitchcock's reflection form a triangle, with Hitchcock himself forming the apex. Then the camera cuts to a shot of Jefferies, indicating that he is watching that exchange of glances between Hitchcock and the songwriter, and insofar as he is a spectator of the scene, he turns the triangle into a parallelogram by returning the glance from Hitchcock's reflection. By means of the reciprocated glance, Hitchcock not only fixes the theme of the artist contemplating his artistic self, but also tells us that his films are a looking inward. As befits the self-consciousness of the moment, the audience response is laughter at recognizing Hitchcock giving himself a role in his own fiction.

I would like here to digress in order to place Hitchcock's appearance in *Rear Window* in the context of his other signature appearances.[9] In *Young and Innocent*, Hitchcock's appearance as a press photographer is the first of his signature appearances that figures him as an artist. Previously, he had appeared as a bystander, passerby, or passenger, and after *Young and Innocent* (1937) he reverts to his usual roles, until *Spellbound* (1945), where he appears as a musician emerging from an elevator in the lobby of the Empire Hotel ostentatiously smoking a cigarette and carrying a small musical instrument case. This is the first of three appearances he makes as a musician in his films. In the two subsequent appearances, he carries each time a larger instrument case. In the *Spellbound* instance, Hitchcock indicates his awareness of his artistic self-consciousness by following his own appearance with the appearance of a parodic double of himself in the person of the masher (Wallace Ford), who smokes a big cigar and carries a package the size of a shoe box wrapped in plain paper and tied with string. The figure of the masher in every way grotesquely parallels Hitchcock's appearance.

In *The Paradine Case* (1947), Hitchcock appears at the outdoor archway of a train station (passing the protagonist played by Gregory Peck), carrying what looks like a cello case. Then, in *Strangers on a Train* (1951), he appears boarding a train with, as befits the *doppelgänger* nature of the film, a double bass in a soft case, an instrument that parodies his own shape. Moreover, as he boards the train, the protagonist (played by Farley Granger), is getting off, and must swing his suitcase to avoid a collision with Hitchcock's bass; their eyes momentarily make contact during this gracefully executed path-crossing. Hitchcock's appearance here as an artist figure who exchanges glances with the protagonist anticipates the same conjunction of role and action in *Rear Window,* and the over-the-shoulder glance is anticipated by his appearance in *Stage Fright* (1950), where he passes by Eve Gill (Jane Wyman) as she is walking down a street rehearsing out loud a role she is about to play. Hitchcock looks back at her askance—at least it seems so, because his regard is as ever impassive—and as he does so a double-decker bus goes by in the distance, and by a trick of perspective momentarily seems to join his head to Jane Wyman's with a double line.

Lastly, in the film immediately preceding *Rear Window, Dial M for Murder* (1954), Hitchcock appears in a photograph of a class reunion. Whether or not Hitchcock knew at the time he devised this ingenious appearance for himself that his next film would be about a photographer, his role as the subject of the camera's glance figures his own artistic self-consciousness. Indeed, Hitchcock's next several appearances are mostly figurations of his role as an artist. For example, in *The Trouble with Harry* (1956), he is seen through a window walking by an outdoor display of the protagonist Marlowe's paintings, while Marlowe (John Forsythe) is indoors advising the spinster (Mildred Natwick) on how to remake her appearance (clearly what Hitchcock liked to do for his actresses and what Scottie [James Stewart] does to Judy [Kim Novak] in *Vertigo*). Just before we see Hitchcock walk by, we hear Marlowe say "I was speaking figuratively of course," and then Hitchcock's familiar figure appears. In *The Man Who Knew Too Much* (1956), Hitchcock appears as the artist contemplating art, watching acrobats perform in the Marketplace of Marrakech, and right afterwards he shows us the "Teller of Tales" performing. In short, during the 1940s and 1950s, Hitchcock devises his signature appearances as figurations of his own artistic self-consciousness, and *Rear Window* is exemplary in this regard.

Just before Hitchcock makes his appearance, Jefferies has been watching Thorwald and his wife arguing, and while they are doing so Thorwald's reflection can be seen in their bedroom window panel. (Hitchcock and his reflection in turn replicate the images of Jefferies and Thorwald reflected in their respective window panes during their earliest appearances in the film.) Just after Hitchcock's appearance, Jefferies and Lisa have an exchange about the songwriter and his music, thus keeping in the audience's minds the scene of Hitchcock's self-conscious appearance. The exchange goes:

LISA: Where is that wonderful music coming from?
JEFF: Some songwriter over there in that studio apartment. Well . . .
     [*He looks admiringly at Lisa*] He lives alone. Probably had a very unhappy marriage.
LISA: Well, it's enchanting. It's almost as if it were being written especially for us.
JEFF: No wonder he's having so much trouble with it.

The second reciprocated glance in the film, when Thorwald realizes that Jefferies is the one who has been watching him, the one who knows he murdered his wife, reverses the effect of the first; it terrifies the audience. Let me locate this moment in context, for the context defines the moment's impact and import. Lisa and Stella have left Jefferies' apartment to enter the courtyard and look in the flower bed to see if Thorwald has buried his wife's head there, but they find nothing. Meanwhile, Jefferies watches them at work and simultaneously looks out to make sure that Thorwald does not return (Jefferies has tricked him into leaving his apartment by pretending over the phone to be a blackmailer who wants to meet him at a local bar). Lisa signals that since she has found nothing in the flower bed she is going to climb up the fire escape to get into Thorwald's apartment through his rear window. Jefferies does *not* want her to because of the danger, but part of him *does* want her to because she would thereby prove herself suited to his adventurous life. More important, by reluctantly permitting her to risk her life, Jefferies places Lisa in the situation of Thorwald's wife, so that he (Jefferies) can save her, and therefore cancel his wish to do away with her. During this entire episode, Lisa wears a flower print dress, thus reinforcing her connection with Mrs. Thorwald, who contemptuously discarded the flower her husband had placed on her breakfast tray, and whose head was temporarily buried in her husband's flower bed, which Lisa in turn digs up.

Stella returns to Jefferies' apartment and dissuades him from calling Lisa away from Thorwald's apartment. They both watch Lisa searching Thorwald's apartment for evidence that he murdered his wife. Jefferies watches through a telephoto lens, using a tool of his own art. However, Jefferies and Stella are distracted from their responsibility to watch out for Thorwald's return by "Miss Lonelyhearts," the woman in the first floor apartment under Thorwald's, because she has laid out sleeping pills in apparent preparation of suicide. Stella tells Jefferies to call the police. While he begins to do so, *we* see Thorwald returning before Jefferies and Stella notice him. Anyone who has watched the film with an audience will remember vividly the terror of this moment—Lisa unawares still searching in the apartment, Thorwald's hulk silently (because we cannot hear him) coming down the hall to his door, about to discover Lisa. Much of the pleasurable anxiety created in the audience by *Rear Window* (as indeed by much of Hitchcock) derives from a child's fear of being caught doing something it should not. Jefferies frantically calls the police, and watches as Thorwald discovers Lisa and then assaults her. Before Jefferies notices Thorwald returning, the camera has been watching across the courtyard in long shot from Jefferies' point of view. After Jefferies does notice Thorwald, the camera moves into medium shots, first of Thorwald, then of Jefferies. The change from long to medium shots decreases the psychological space between them, indicating the level of awareness on Jefferies' part of how much Thorwald now threatens him.

Thorwald menaces Lisa, forcing her back step by step from the living room into the bedroom, just as he had done to his wife after she discovered him talking on the phone to his mistress, and the visual replication makes clear Lisa's role in Jefferies' dream. As Thorwald and Lisa are struggling, Thorwald turns off the lights so that we and Jefferies are left to imagine how he is going to kill her. Jefferies' immobility and sense of powerlessness mimic the audience's feelings at this moment. We would like to save Lisa just as Jefferies would, but like him we are bound to our seats and can do nothing; Stewart's acting in this scene under Hitchcock's direction allows the audience into Jefferies' mind. His hands go to his neck as if trying to feel what he imagines Lisa is suffering at Thorwald's hands. He looks up at Stella and says with childlike pleading, "Stella, what'll we do?" The tension reaches its maximum and the police arrive. That Hitchcock intends Jefferies to be the audience surrogate at this point can be seen from an anecdote he tells Truffaut about the premiere of the film in which Hitchcock was sitting next to Joseph Cotten and his wife Patricia Medina, who, when Thorwald returned to the apartment, grabbed her husband and said, "Do something, do something!"[10]

The audience relaxes with relief and experiences a false sense of security: this will now become the pattern for the rest of the film—extreme tension, relief with a false sense of security created by some distraction, then a reinstating of the tension or apprehension augmented by the realization of some new and greater danger. As Jefferies watches Lisa negotiating with the police (he comments to Stella on how smart Lisa is to get herself arrested and so away from Thorwald), she holds her left hand behind her back and wiggles a finger with a wedding band on it, pointing at it with her other hand to show Jefferies she has found the evidence that Mrs. Thorwald has been murdered (since no woman would leave town without her wedding ring). The ironic symbolism of her gesture is perfect, since Jefferies' unconscious anxiety has been about his murderous impulses toward Lisa for her wanting to marry him, which he perceives as a threat to his artistic self. He punishes himself for having those impulses by watching Lisa almost get killed by Thorwald. Jefferies has been so tenacious in trying to prove Thorwald's guilt because Jefferies has been in pursuit of his own criminal self.

The whole image of the Thorwalds' marriage, in the fashion of dream-work, reverses his relationship with Lisa.[11] Just as Mrs. Thorwald is an invalid who resents her husband's mobility, taunts and ridicules him, so too is Jefferies immobile, and so too does he taunt and ridicule Lisa for her interest in fashion and the high life. The subtlety of the parallel can be seen from the incident between Thorwald and his wife when he brings her breakfast in bed with a flower on the tray and she casts the flower away. Similarly, Lisa brings Jefferies dinner from the 21 Club, a dinner that he criticizes because it's "perfect." Therefore, Lisa's pointing to the late Mrs. Thorwald's wedding ring on *her* finger, epitomizes in one single shot the whole complex relationship between herself and Jefferies.[12]

In an iris shot from Jefferies' point of view, we and Jefferies see Lisa wiggle her finger, but then the iris moves (and here I come to the reciprocated glance between Thorwald and Jefferies) from looking at the wiggling finger to looking at Thorwald looking at the wiggling finger. Thorwald realizes that she is signaling someone across the courtyard, and he looks directly into the camera—at us—at Jefferies. At this moment the audience's secret fear of being discovered when they thought they were hidden and protected is realized. Jefferies has spied on Thorwald all through the film and now Thorwald looks back, reciprocates the glance. The camera cuts to Jefferies who turns to Stella and says, "Turn off the light! he's seen us," and the camera quickly pulls back from him. For years I remembered that sequence as Jefferies wheeling himself back quickly to get out of the light. What I was actually remembering was the morning after the murder when Jefferies sees Thorwald stealthily looking out his window to see if anyone is watching him; there Jefferies did wheel himself back to get out of the light and into the shadow. To make us experience Jefferies' fear of Thorwald's glance, Hitchcock only has to pull the camera back to make us experience the movement as Jefferies, trying to hide from that glance.

Thorwald now does to Jefferies what Jefferies has done to him: he spies on him, telephones him, and finally invades his privacy by entering his apartment. Jefferies, like Perseus protecting himself from Medusa, uses a mirror-shield to protect himself.[13] As Thorwald approaches him, Jefferies repeatedly uses his flashgun to blind Thorwald momentarily. In this way he delays the attack on himself. As he does so, he shields his own eyes with his hands, protecting himself from the blinding flash and from the return glance of the murderer. Each time the flash goes off, the screen goes red, then gradually returns to normal.

Hitchcock's use of color here signifies more than a mimesis of Thorwald's point of view. In Hitchcock's black and white film, *Spellbound*, black lines on a white surface (which can be taken as a metaphor for film itself) evoke for the protagonist the memory of a death for which he was not responsible. At the end of that film, Dr. Murcheson, who had sought to transfer the responsibility for the murder he committed onto the protagonist, is told that he should not be held responsible for the murder, but he finally rejects that exculpation, turns a revolver on himself (the revolver pointed directly at the camera and hence the audience), and fires: at this point the screen goes red for an instant. In *Marnie*—which might be called Hitchcock's red film, as *Vertigo* is his green film—the color red evokes for the heroine the memory of a murder for which she was not responsible. And, lastly, Hitchcock gave as his reason for shooting *Psycho* in black and white rather than in color that he did not want to show Janet Leigh's red blood flowing down the shower drain. In each of these instances the principle of exculpation is at work. So too in *Rear Window,* when Jefferies makes Thorwald see red, he simultaneously fixes the guilt for the murder of Thorwald's wife on him and exculpates himself of the guilt for having desired unconsciously to do away with Lisa. And the means by which he does so is a tool of his art, the flash gun. He thus transfers a version of the punishment Stella warned him about ("They put out your eyes out with a red hot poker") onto Thorwald, temporarily blinding Thorwald with red by means of his mirror shield.

The ending of *Rear Window* involves a double punishment, for in punishing Thorwald, Jefferies also punishes himself. Thorwald does not succeed in his attempt to push Jefferies out of the window; rather, Jefferies loses his grip and falls by himself, breaking his other leg. I would call it, therefore, an unconsciously willed fall. Thus he expiates his murderous impulse toward Lisa. She cradles his head in her lap as he tells her how proud he was of her for braving the danger of entering Thorwald's apartment and getting the wedding ring.

Finally, though, *Rear Window* is about more than a single character's therapeutic experiences; it profoundly represents the anxieties attendant upon marriage, not the petty ones, but the serious ones, involving the question of loneliness versus marital strife. In the apartments across the courtyard, Jefferies confronts the fears he has about marrying and the fears he has about not marrying, most notably in Miss Lonelyhearts, whose suicide is prevented by the songwriter's successful completion of his song, "Lisa." The coupling of Miss Lonelyhearts and the songwriter at the end of the film, like the resolutions of the other stories—Miss Torso is really a faithful girl-friend waiting for her short unattractive soldier boyfriend to come home, the couple that sleeps on their fire escape gets a new puppy to replace the dog killed by Thorwald, the songwriter does finish his song—represents a wish-fulfillment dream for Jefferies, the resolution of the problems of marriage by art. These endings also represent Lisa's views: she was the one who insisted that Miss Torso was not in love with any of the "wolves" pursuing her, and Lisa believes all along that she and Jefferies can make a successful marriage. Her optimism is reflected in the happy endings for the neighbors' stories. She changes by entering into his fantasy life when she gets herself into Thorwald's apartment, and he changes by dreaming her optimism. Jefferies' obsession with his art of photography has all along prevented him from marrying Lisa, but the ending of the film shows him blissfully asleep dreaming happy endings to the stories he had imagined to represent his anxieties about the conflict between art and marriage, while the camera shows us Lisa putting down the book *Beyond the High Himalayas* in favor of *Harper's Bazaar* magazine. The conflict remains, and these are matters of life for both the man and the woman, but no longer matters of murder.

There is one story ending left to be interpreted: that of the newlyweds. Theirs is the last story the camera peeks in on. We hear the wife saying, "If I had known you quit your job, we wouldn't have gotten married," and the husband replies, "Aw, honey, quit nagging." This seems to be a repetition of the situation between Thorwald and his nagging wife, with the dire implication that the cycle of marital hatred is unavoidable, but it is not; rather it playfully recapitulates the nature of the gap between the romantic anticipations of marriage and its weekday actualities. It too can be understood as Jefferies' wish-fulfillment, for the husband quits his job, and his wife is displeased, as Jefferies would like Lisa to be displeased were he to quit his art.

The last shot in *Rear Window* is a continuous one, beginning with a pan across the courtyard from right to left, showing us the resolutions of the neighbors' stories, then pulling into Jefferies' apartment to show us his smiling, sleeping face, then moving down his body to his legs to show us that he now has two broken legs, and then, back up Lisa's reclining body to show us that she is wearing clothes suitable for a photo-journalist's wife. It would seem she has capitulated, and become the woman he wants her to be, but her taking up of *Bazaar* suggests that she can dress for the part without sacrificing her sense of herself.

Moreover, Lisa's outfit here, pedal pushers and a simple shirt, duplicates the outfit worn by the sculptress as she lies dozing in a lounge chair in the courtyard below, suggesting that in some sense Lisa herself has become an artist-figure, a match for Jefferies. Throughout the film, Hitchcock has made the various women across the way represent different aspects of Lisa's character by means of similar clothing—that is, Lisa's character as projected by Jefferies' psyche. When Lisa wears a chiffon dress with a black top and wrap and a white skirt, Hitchcock shows Miss Torso returning from a night on the town in a gown with a wrap, and then he intercuts shots of Lisa in her black chiffon dress with shots of Miss Torso in a black nightie. Thus Miss Torso's two outfits decompose Lisa's single outfit into fabric and color. Jefferies insistently makes comparisons between Lisa and Miss Torso precisely because he is afraid to marry a woman who treats love as a game. Miss Lonelyhearts always wears shades of green, until she is saved from suicide by the songwriter's completion of his song, and Lisa wears a green suit when she comes to stay overnight in Jefferies' apartment, because Miss Lonelyhearts embodies what both Jefferies and Lisa might become if love between them fails.

I have already discussed the significance of Lisa's flower print dress, but I would like to make one more point about it by way of conclusion. After Jefferies' fall out of his window into the courtyard below, which I see as both a willed self-punishment and a liberation from the prison of his own ego, he joins Lisa in the real world, having overcome the fears and unlawful desires which he projected onto the lives of the apartment dwellers across the way. As he lies on the ground, his head cradled in Lisa's lap, amid the print flowers of her dress, he exchanges glances with her, the final such reciprocation in the film. That image is powerful and satisfying because it shows his defeat of the Medusa's head, his fear of women. Mrs. Thorwald's head had been buried in the flower bed and we have imagined the discovery of that horrid sight several times. Here we are freed of those imaginings and in their place we see the unsevered head of Jefferies in Lisa's lap.

NOTES

1. Recently, Thomas M. Leitch has argued similarly: "In order for Jeff and Lisa to earn their happy ending, they both need to prove they can act as in accord with each other's wishes." See *Find the Director and Other Hitchcock Games* (Athens and London: University of Georgia Press, 1991), 172.

2. François Truffaut in his interviews with Hitchcock (*Hitchcock,* rev. ed., [New York: Simon and Schuster, 1984]) points out that the stories Stewart watches across the way "convey an image of the world" and "have a common denominator in that they involve some aspect of love" (216). Truffaut was anticipated by Jean Douchet, in "Hitch et son public," *Cahiers du Cinema* 113, November, 1960, rpt. in *Cahiers du Cinema 1960–1968,* ed. Jim Hillier, trans. David Wilson (Cambridge: Harvard University Press, 1986), 150–57, and followed by Robert Stam and Roberta Pearson, in "Hitchcock's *Rear Window*: Reflexivity and the Critique of Voyeurism," *Enclitic* 7, no. 1 (1983): 136–45. This latter article is a full-scale analysis of the film as an allegory of the cinematic experience, and is excellent, except for some small errors about the content of the film, e.g., the authors say that Hitchcock forsakes "his usual cameo appearance" (138), which is not so, and that Jefferies is the only person "allowed to look through the phallic telephoto lens" (143), while in actuality Stella looks through it to see the pills Miss Lonelyhearts is laying out. Robin Wood adds his own typically remarkable observations about how what Jefferies sees reflects his own unconscious fears and wishes. See *Hitchcock's Films Revisited* (New York: Columbia University Press, 1989), 100–07.

3. For a more extensive treatment of the use of space in *Rear Window,* see John Belton, "The Space of *Rear Window*" in *Hitchcock's Rereleased Films,* ed. Walter

Raubicheck and Walter Srebnick (Detroit: Wayne State University Press, 1991), 76–94.

4. Freud discusses the symbolic meaning of the Medusa's head: "The terror of Medusa is thus a terror of castration that is linked to the sight of something . . . it occurs when a boy . . . catches sight of the female genitals surrounded by hair . . . The sight of Medusa's head makes the spectator stiff with terror, turns him to stone." See "Medusa's Head" (1922), in *Sexuality and the Psychology of Love*, ed. Phillip Rieff (New York: Collier Books, 1963), 212–13.

5. Truffaut, *Hitchcock*, 222.

6. Patricia Ferrara rejects the idea of reading the film as either an allegory of movie watching or as a projection of Jefferies' psyche, and offers an alternative interpretation of the film as about the various ways in which people relate to one another through seeing. She argues her case coherently and powerfully in "Through Hitchcock's *Rear Window* Again," *The New Orleans Review* 12, no. 3 (1985): 21–30.

7. In the preface to his book of interviews with Hitchcock, Truffaut tells of an exchange he had with reporters:

> In the course of an interview during which I praised *Rear Window* to the skies, an American critic surprised me by commenting, "You love *Rear Window* because, as a stranger to New York, you know nothing about Greenwich Village." To this absurd statement, I replied, "*Rear Window* is not about Greenwich Village, it is a film about cinema, and I *do* know cinema." (11)

8. Hitchcock's control of cinematic time is most evident near the end of the film when Thorwald tries to push Jefferies out the window, and Hitchcock shows the neighbors coming to their windows or doors to see what is going on. The sequence is tremendously tense, and Hitchcock speeds up the film for the movements of the neighbors, which are intercut with shots of Jefferies struggling with Thorwald. Here Hitchcock creates psychological or subjective time: at such a moment of suspense, time races in the perception of the spectators, and so does the film. (Today's audiences, sophisticated in their perception of such effects, do notice Hitchcock's manipulation of speed, but I doubt that the audiences of 1953 did.) The sequence, like so many others in the film, has its earlier counterpart in the episode of the discovery of the murdered dog, where the neighbors successively come to their windows or doors to hear the woman who owned the dog denounce the neighbors for their indifference.

9. I here gratefully acknowledge Maurice Yacowar's superb treatment of this subject in his *Hitchcock's British Films* (Hamden, CT.: Archon Books, 1977), 270–78. Yacowar was, I believe, the first critic to refuse to take Hitchcock at his word when

he claimed that his appearances became a nuisance to be gotten out of the way as near the beginning of the film as possible.

10. Truffaut, *Hitchcock*, 73.

11. Hitchcock comments to Truffaut, "The symmetry is the same as in *Shadow of a Doubt*. On one side of the yard you have the Stewart-Kelly couple, with him immobilized in a cast, while she can move about freely. And on the other side there is a sick woman who's confined to her bed, while the husband comes and goes" (Truffaut, *Hitchcock*, 216).

12. Both Hitchcock and Truffaut comment on the symbolism of the ring (Truffaut, *Hitchcock*, 223).

13. Michael Powell also uses the myth of Perseus and Medusa in *Peeping Tom* (1960), where the murderer films his victims as he kills them with a stiletto extending from one of the legs of his camera's tripod. At the same time he has a mirror attached to his camera so that he can photograph the expression of fear on their faces as they watch their own deaths. His victims are all women, whom he fears only because they are women, and like Perseus he destroys their power over him by turning what he takes to be their murderous looks back upon themselves. Laura Mulvey frequently points out connections between *Peeping Tom* and Hitchcock's films in her running commentary on the Criterion DVD version of *Peeping Tom*.

ENGENDERING *VERTIGO*

Leland Poague

A motif haunting Hitchcock's *Vertigo*—musically, thematically, critically—is repetition.

As described by Kathryn Kalinak, the music Bernard Herrmann composed for *Vertigo*'s title sequence features "arpeggiated chords played in contrary motion in the bass and treble voices."[1] Though perfectly mirroring each other, the treble voice descending as the bass voice ascends, the effect is one of dissonance—given the particular chords themselves, the harmonic intervals between them, and the lack of clear distinction between melody and harmony lines.

A kindred symmetry of formal elements leading finally to dissonance and dissolution is enacted in *Vertigo*'s narrative line: in the way its action doubles back upon itself, constructing and deconstructing its own discourse on matters of similarity and difference, innocence and guilt, past and present, illusion and reality. Tania Modleski is hardly alone in hearing these repetitions as voicing the call of death, though she voices that call in the voice of another; she explains Scottie's embittered interrogation of Judy on their second ascent of the mission tower by reference to (feminism's) Freud and his theory of melancholia, where repetition, "as Freud has shown, is linked to unfreedom, to masochism, and to death."[2]

I gather these thoughts as prologue in part because *Vertigo* has so fascinated film critics over the years as to make any additional remarks on the film seem obsessive or obsessed—for being so obviously uncalled for, hence uncanny. Equally uncanny are the debts I have lately incurred to the work of Stanley Cavell, an uncanniness marked by the fact that Cavell's contributions to film study have been confirmed as much by repression as by elaboration. Though Modleski has lately accused Cavell of engaging "in conversations with himself," there have been precious few interlocutors for Cavell among the cadres of professional film scholars.[3]

There is good reason for film scholars to avoid Cavell. His vision of the task of criticism is capacious and intricate; it rivals at every turn the standard "SLAB Theory" (SLAB = Saussure-Lacan-Althusser-Barthes) by means of which a whole generation of film professors has undertaken to characterize the ideological force of the cinematic apparatus.[4] Though Cavell avows a specific loyalty to the transcendental romanticism of Emerson and Thoreau, it is his general claim that romanticism—as represented by such as Descartes and Kant and Rousseau and Nietzsche (in philosophy) and Shakespeare and Coleridge and Poe and Kleist (in literature)—fully anticipates the critique of culture undertaken more recently in the work of (in the names of) Marx and Freud, Lacan and Derrida. Certainly it is my more modest claim that Cavell's *The World Viewed* is the equal of Metz's *The Imaginary Signifier* when it comes to pondering the way cinema turns alienation into something like rapture; that Cavell's *Pursuits of Happiness* is fully the equal of Mary Ann Doane's *The Desire to Desire* when it comes to discussing how film genre is intricate with concepts of gender identity and social legitimacy.[5] Indeed, Cavell is unabashed in claiming that marriage is a trope of the social contract as the latter is elaborated in Milton and Locke and Lévi-Strauss while remaining fully mindful that marriage is equally a trope (and a tool) of patriarchal oppressiveness, as he elaborates via repeated discussions of Nora's revolt against Thorvald in Ibsen's *A Doll House*.[6] And there is nothing in the annals of academic film study to match Cavell's sustained reflections on the reaches and depths, the attunements and disappointments, of human language.[7]

Repetition, voice, alienation, identity: all are topics under study in Cavell's analyses of film genres. Crucial for our purposes are Cavell's "derivation" of "remarriage comedy" from its (mostly Shakespearean) sources in classical comedy and his subsequent derivation of "the melodrama of the unknown woman" from remarriage comedy, derivations that are describable (mythically) as a matter of conversation or interpretation or negation: "Let us think of the common inheritance of the members of a genre as a story, call it a myth. The members of a genre will be interpretations of it, or to use Thoreau's word for it, revisions of it, which will also make them interpretations of one another" (PH 31). "Interpretations," that is, where a feature in one instance takes the place of, "compensates" for, a related feature present in some other version of the story; "Negations," however, when the revision or substitution in question finally changes the story, makes it some other story.

Thus "remarriage comedy" derives from or interprets classical comedy, for example, by replacing the marriage ceremony that typically concludes the New Comedy story with a threat or fact of divorce between characters somewhat older and more maritally experienced than their New Comedy peers. "The central idea," writes Cavell in "The Thought of Movies," is roughly "that the validity or bond of marriage is assured, even legitimized, not by church or state or sexual compatibility" but "by something I call the willingness for remarriage, a way of continuing to affirm the happiness of one's initial leap. As if the chance of happiness exists only when it seconds itself. In classical comedy people made for one another find one another; in remarriage comedy people who *have* found one another find that they *are* made for each other."[8] In a number of instances this recovery of identity is expressed or troped by incest—as when, in *The Awful Truth*, Lucy Warriner proves her commitment to marriage by posing as her husband's sister, as if she and Jerry had "grown up together," "thus staking a final claim to have known him intimately forever" (PH 60).

Remarriage comedy also interprets classical comedy by shifting the folkloric "death and resurrection" feature of romance from the Old Comedy *senex* to the female member of the romantic comedy couple. Cavell often describes remarriage comedy as a "comedy of equality" (PH 82), equality understood as a matter of mutual acknowledgment or recognition; but he is careful to mark the asymmetry of social power under patriarchy, which leaves the female characters, if not exactly dead, then at least in a state of uncreation, "as if the women's lives heretofore have been nonexistent, as if they have haunted the world, as if their materialization will constitute a creation of the new woman and hence a creation, or a further step in the creation, of the human."[9] Because men, in their villainy, hold social power, the heroine's (luckily happy) task in remarriage comedy is to find (or refind) a man, call him a husband, who can provide acknowledgment in the form of education or, as Cavell puts it citing Milton, "conversation." In remarriage comedy, Cavell avers by reference to *It Happened One Night,* "talking together is fully and plainly being together, a mode of association, a form of life, and I would like to say that in these films the central pair are learning to speak the same language" (PH 88).

And what distinguishes remarriage comedy from the subsequently derived "melodrama of the unknown woman," especially in view of their shared concern for the re-creation or metamorphosis of the human female, is that in melodrama "this change must take place outside the process of a mode of conversation with a man (of course; since such a conversation would constitute marriage)." Bravely, in light of the latter comment, Cavell elaborates melodrama's negation of remarriage comedy by going on to speak from the vantage point, in the voice, of a melodramatic heroine addressing her comic sisters on the topic of their differences: "You may call yourselves lucky to have found a man with whom you can overcome the humiliation of marriage by marriage itself. For us, with our talents and tastes, there is no further or happy education to be found there; our integrity and metamorphosis happens elsewhere, in the abandoning of that *shared* wit and intelligence and exclusive appreciation."[10] Indeed, when women in these melodramas do talk to men the result is typically *not* a matter of conversation, of interchange between intellectual equals; rather, it results in what Cavell, speaking of Bette Davis in *Now, Voyager,* describes as a genre-defining "irony" that "serves to isolate the woman of this melodrama from everyone around her, or almost everyone. It is a question whether it also isolates her from us. Hence I speak of the genre, adapting its title from one of its members, as the study of the unknownness of the woman."[11]

There is a casualness to Cavell's (often narrative) descriptions of the genres and films he studies that belies the intricacy and specificity of the critical readings they subtend. The following remarks aspire to match the delicacy and density typical of Cavell's critical practice, however short of the mark they fall. In sections II and III *Vertigo*'s relationship to melodrama is pondered, by reference to William Rothman and Peter Brooks. In section IV, I elaborate the extent to which *Vertigo*'s parable of love lost and lost again evokes the tradition of remarriage comedy, if only as a measure of the hopeless aspirations that haunt Scottie and Judy throughout. Section V explores the intertextual relationship of *It's a Wonderful Life* and *Vertigo,* with special reference to George Bailey's status, elaborated with help from Shakespeare, Cavell, and Jessica Benjamin, as an "unknown woman." I will repeat myself.

II

Vertigo is not altogether unknown to Cavell's philosophy. Indeed, Cavell's most recent remarks on the film—in *Pursuits of Happiness* and in his essay on *North by Northwest*—measure it against his picture of remarriage comedy, as, for example, in evoking "the creation of the woman (or the human) by other means" than marriage (PH 222). That such creations lead generally to "catastrophe" in Hitchcock is a way of measuring the specific gravity of *North by Northwest,* where the burden of (human) sexuality is lighter, more bearable—and in large part because in *North by Northwest* "it is the man who undergoes death and revival (at least twice, both times at the hands of the woman) *and* whose physical identity," like that of the leading women in remarriage comedy, "is insisted upon by the camera," as if, in light of his previous sexual misdeeds, it is the man's task to educate himself so that he can "educate and hence rescue the woman."[12]

Cavell's other remarks on *Vertigo* are somewhat more difficult to summarize because they move into that region of Cavell's philosophy where questions of genre and epistemology intersect. In *The World Viewed* Cavell discusses the use of color in *Vertigo,* as in "More of *The World Viewed*" he discusses the famous 360–degree tracking shot of Judy and Scottie, as enacting the (ever unstable, thus deeply romantic) distinction between one world and another, "between meaning and loss of meaning, between possibility and impossibility" (WV 203). And in "What Becomes of Things on Film?" Cavell confirms the link between the literary and the philosophical by studying how, in *Vertigo* and *It's a Wonderful Life,* the particularly human "wish for a completer identity than one has so far attained" may "project a complete world *opposed* to the world one so far shares with others." "In both skepticism and romance, knowledge, call it consciousness as a whole, must go out in order that a better consciousness can come to light."[13]

In seeking to sketch a Cavellian picture of (some aspects of) *Vertigo,* I am not altogether alone; Marian Keane and Wendy Lesser have contributed importantly to our understandings on these accounts.[14] But the most immediate occasion for wishing to follow out my intuitions about *Vertigo* is provided by Rothman's finely wrought essay on the film in *The "I" of the Camera,* where he ponders and finally rejects the prospect of including *Vertigo* among those melodramas that Cavell has linked under the "unknown woman" rubric.[15]

I am less interested in refuting Rothman than in exploring the conceptual space between us. To the extent that Rothman's understanding of

Vertigo depends upon a particular view of melodrama and its relation to the camera, I know there are differences worth specifying. Moreover, I will eventually want to consider in some detail *Vertigo*'s heartbreakingly parodic relationship to the romance of remarriage comedy and to a picture of "intersubjectivity" or "identification" that I use in *Another Frank Capra* to substantiate the claim that *It's a Wonderful Life*'s George Bailey *is* an "unknown woman."[16]

Though he takes *Vertigo*'s Judy Barton to be an unknown woman "in precisely Cavell's sense—a woman who apprehends her condition more deeply than the men in her world, who possesses deeper vision, intelligence, and depth of feeling," Rothman describes a guilt at the heart of the film that effectively negates the unknown woman story by shifting our focus from the woman *within* the film to the "woman" *beyond* the film—Alfred Hitchcock (IC 171). If it is Elster's guilt and Judy's guilt that define *Vertigo* as "a Hitchcock thriller" and that "call forth" those guilty or murderous gestures by means of which Hitchcock contests Elster's "authorship," hence declares the "Elster" in his own authorship, then Hitchcock's camera "is an instrument of taxidermy, not transfiguration." It amounts to a vengeful identification with his characters and his audience in which "Hitchcock never gets beyond his own case, his own longing for acknowledgment" (IC 172).

Behind these views of Hitchcock and *Vertigo* are (I think) two interrelated claims, one derived from the picture of melodrama on view in Peter Brooks's *The Melodramatic Imagination* and the other derived from a picture of the possibilities of the camera derived from Cavell.[17] In opposing "taxidermy" and "transfiguration," for example, Rothman implies that the latter, if not the former, takes place "independently of human intentions." Rothman might mean that transfiguration happens automatically, photographically, since (in Cavell's words) "a great property of the medium is its violent transfiguration of creatures of flesh and blood, its recreation of them, let us say, in projecting and screening them" (NO 344). (Cf. Rothman: "The camera does violence to its subjects, fixes them, and breathes back only the illusion of life into these ghosts" [IC 172].) But to the extent that Rothman takes Hitchcock's "human intentions," his purposeful inflections of "transfiguration" in the direction of violence and horror, to set *Vertigo* beyond the realm of meaningful participation in Cavell's "unknown woman" genre, as Rothman's subsequent remarks on *Letter from an Unknown Woman* certainly imply, then there is reason for thinking that Cavell, at least, would disagree. In "What Photography Calls Thinking" Cavell notes the adjacency of horror films and remarriage comedy via "the camera's transfigurative power" as prologue to considering how Capra's *Mr. Deeds Goes to Town* participates in the genre of melodrama.[18] And in "Psychoanalysis and Cinema" Cavell takes the death-dealing barrage of images suffered by Stefan Brand in response to the unknown woman's letter as an Ophulsian picture "for the aesthetic working of film as such, an idea of some vision of horror at its basis" (PC 255).

The intentionality of the camera also plays a part in Rothman's related argument, in "Virtue and Villainy in the Face of the Camera," to the effect that "The role of the camera undermines the very basis of theatrical melodrama" because, in Hitchcock's films at least, "there are no villainous human beings responsible for creating what it is [a Hitchcock] film lays bare that is intolerable in the human condition."[19]

Rothman arrives at this (deeply apt and disturbing) conclusion by reference to cinema's inheritance of (break with) Victorian melodrama in Griffith and to Peter Brooks's description of French melodrama as depicting acts of "self-nomination" in which "Both heroines and villains announce their moral identity, present their name and the qualifications attached to it, in the form of revelation" (MI 39).[20] Rothman (understandably) interprets "moral identity" to imply moral absolutes, but he takes the camera's necessary collaboration in any such declaration as confirming beyond doubt the completely mixed and contingent character of the worlds and beings we view on film. "Evil, understood as an occult force that exists apart from human beings and their creations, has no reality in the face of the camera" (IC 78). Put otherwise, if the camera as a quasi-Hegelian "world spirit" or Kantian condition has a role in villainy's declaration, then a film-world where villainy matters can never be purely good; though the villain be purged, the camera remains and is tainted.

Though Rothman's terms for melodrama are derived from Brooks, and though his conclusions about the camera's moral implication in the actions it depicts are unassailable, his conclusion that film and melodrama are as if ontologically opposed is a view I cannot share, in large part because I read Brooks somewhat differently. That is, where Rothman takes "occult" as referring to an (absolute) ethical substratum "that exists apart from human beings," I read "occulted" as referring to the absence of moral certainty, an absence resulting from the "liquidation of the traditional Sacred" (MI 15), an absence made good by repeatedly "performing" and "imposing" the "signs of virtue" in a world where morality exists, as it were, unconsciously, as "the fragmentary and desacralized remnants of sacred myth" (MI 5). Virtue's tokens are "provisional," in that sense "performative" (MI 201, 85). "That they can be staged 'proves' that they exist" (MI 201). And where Rothman takes the theatrical as definitive of "The Melodramatic Imagination"—which means taking characters as existing singularly, apart from any narrating agency, so that the assertion of narrational presence displaces or replaces the character's presence, Hitchcock replacing Judy as *Vertigo*'s token of unknownness, say—I remember that Brooks's discussion of theater is prologue to a discussion of the novels of Balzac and James and that, even in its theatrical mode, melodrama as described by Brooks speaks a double "victory over repression." Melodrama, writes Brooks, "is motivated by a totally coherent ambition to stage a drama of articulation, a drama that has as its true stakes the recognition and triumph of the sign of virtue. There is a victory wrought both within the conflictual system of the play and within the medium of communication encompassing play and spectator, since the play strives toward making evident the very problematic that it takes as its subject" (MI 49).

III

In marking the difference that distinguishes my own path toward *Vertigo* from Rothman's, I am *not* disputing his central claim, that *Hitchcock* is the film's primary token of unknownness. Indeed, apart from grasping that fact there is no way of comprehending the power and poignancy of the film's last shot, no way of determining the degree to which *Vertigo* enacts a melodramatic "victory" of "recognition" over "repression." That something like repression *is* a central issue, however—though not much in doubt—can be helpfully elaborated by noting how *Vertigo* interprets certain clauses of the melodramatic story as it has been variously elaborated by Brooks and Cavell.

Reading Brooks's *The Melodramatic Imagination* with *Vertigo* in mind evokes the uncanny feel of the film itself; repeatedly, in Brooks, the settings and scenarios of *Vertigo* are (as if unconsciously) evoked and elaborated. Elster's class (and gender) relation to Judy is recalled when Brooks describes the "inherently feudal" social structure of melodrama wherein "Villains are remarkably often tyrants and oppressors, those that have power and use it to hurt" and in which "the victims, the innocent and virtuous, most often belong to the democratic universe" (MI 44). Scottie's wanderings are evoked in Brooks's description of the melodramatic "fascination with the city, either as the symbol of corruption lying in wait" or "as an unexplored world offering layers of mystery" (MI 88). In discussing melodrama's "space of claustration" Brooks alludes to monasteries and convents where "evil monks and nuns" work "at the behest of a guilty aristocrat" (MI 50). Elsewhere he cites the "enclosed garden" (MI 29) and the "tribunal scene" (MI 44) as *topoi* proper to melodrama. Among the many features of the film that Brooks helps to elaborate, however, one is crucial, especially given Cavell's emphasis on the fact of conversation and Brooks's own focus on melodrama's desire to "say all": the trope of "muteness," in which "Virtue, expulsed, eclipsed, apparently fallen, cannot effectively articulate the cause of the right" (MI 31).

Melodrama's "Aesthetic of Muteness" has several sources: material (in that the "patent theatres" in pre-revolutionary France held a monopoly on "the classical repertory" so that "secondary theatres" were restricted to mime and music and spectacular tableaux [MI 62]) and philosophical (to the extent that romantic theorists of the drama, like Diderot and Rousseau, saw gesture "as the first sign, the unmediated sign, dependent for its sig- nifying on presence" by contrast with "the existing sociolinguistic code," which proved inadequate "to convey a full freight of emotional meaning" [MI 66–67]). The (ironic) echoes of *Vertigo* are clear enough already: a se- ries of "falls"—of Scottie from roof to rain gutter, of the cop who tries to rescue him to the street below, of Scottie off a stepladder into the arms of Midge, of "Madeleine" into San Francisco Bay and later from the mission tower, of Judy from the tower in a reprise of Madeleine's "suicide"—have the effect of leaving Scottie, in some sense falling's chief victim, in a mute and hopeless trance. This is literally the case during the coroner's inquest and all the more so once Scottie's nightmare lands him in the psychiatric hos- pital. And, as is often noted, Scottie's more "normal" muteness is fully on view as he wanders—accompanied by spectacular (special effects) tableaux and Bernard Herrmann's deeply romantic and disturbing musical score— through the melodramatic landscape of Madeleine's own (mutely theatri- cal) entrancement. It matters more than a little that the film's last fall also renders Scottie speechless, as if forever.

But equally as relevant to the trope of muteness as those passages where characters are literally speechless or voiceless are the film's passages of con- versation, all but two of which (and those too, finally)—Scottie's first con- versation with Midge, Scottie's last conversation with Judy—take place un- der the sign of irony, an irony fully as villainous or vengeful as anything on view in *Gaslight* or *Now, Voyager*. The aspect of irony is, of course, doubled for knowledgeable viewers in all those conversations preceding Judy's reve- lation of her part in Elster's plot to kill his wife. Even on first viewing there is a sense of the uncanny in Elster's description of his wife's otherworldliness and in Pop Liebl's descriptions of "The beautiful Carlotta, the sad Carlotta" and in "Madeleine's" recountings of her "dream" to Scottie, the sense of another world adjacent to this one; on all subsequent viewings that "other world" becomes all the more demonic for being all the more clearly a version of the film world, a world of conversations scripted in advance, of language detached from purposes of attunement and communication. (Elster: "You and I know who killed Madeleine.")

This quality of conversational "deadness" fairly obviously haunts every conversation from the first scene between Elster and Scottie until the moment when Judy reveals herself to us, to the camera. But that revelation does Scottie no good—nor, perhaps, could it. And the conversations that follow, between "Judy" and Scottie, though no less haunted—if also, in some deep sense, far more honest—are nevertheless a far cry from the "meet and happy" conversation that typifies the couples in remarriage comedy. (Recall Judy's panic-stricken attempts to untrack Scottie's fashion fixations in the dress shop, for instance, or the agonized silences and stiltedness of the passage when Scottie asks Judy to change her hair color.) Here we might mark, for future reference, that the "aria of divorce" by means of which the melodramatic heroine in such films as *Gaslight* and *Stella Dallas* renders her presence (if only to the camera) by declaring her absence (to a husband, to a daughter) is here assigned to Scottie as he drags Judy to the top of the mission tower. And even here his words are achingly, uncontrollably, ironic, however free they are from the falsehoods perpetrated by Gavin Elster. "There's no bringing her back." Yet what else has he done just now but that?

In deriving "the melodrama of the unknown woman" from remarriage comedy Cavell notes that the woman's "metamorphosis" takes place "elsewhere" than the world of men. He often calls this elsewhere "the world of women" by noting the presence of mothers and (often female) children in these films—by contrast with remarriage comedy, where "The price of the woman's happiness" is "the absence of her mother (underscored by the attractive and signal presence, whenever he is present, of the woman's father) together with the strict absence of children for her, the denial of her as a mother" (PC 232).

More generally, the "world of women" trope refers to the crucial roles played by *other* women in these films—by Charlotte Vale's sister-in-law and niece in *Now, Voyager,* by Helen Morrison in *Stella Dallas,* by the "Sister-in-Charge" who forwards the unknown Lisa's letter to Stefan Brand in Ophuls' version of the story, by the near-deaf cook whose timely (theatrical) intervention helps restore Paula to sanity in *Gaslight.* Often the metamorphosis in question is less a matter of existence *per se* than identity, an identity often signed to the world as a matter of dress. Perhaps *Stella Dallas* is the classic instance here, where Stella uses the clothing code (among other class markers) to enforce a distance between herself and her daughter, which Cavell takes as asserting a kind of (deferred) kinship: "Stella's mutual recognition—almost—with the mother to whom she discovers she can entrust her daughter . . . nominates the woman at the same time as the mother Stella never had, from whom she receives . . . authorization to try the world on her own terms."[21]

Echoes of *Vertigo* are sounding here too. Certainly the fashion text of *Vertigo* is an open secret. So too, in a way, is the relation of Carlotta Valdes to her (lost) daughter. As Rothman points out, Judy's situation echoes not only Carlotta's (both are, as it were, throwaways; Carlotta and Judy both suffer exile at the behest of a pointedly nameless man) but also that of Carlotta's nameless daughter (both Judy and the daughter suffer a stepchild's fate). More than a few critics have been tempted to read Elster's "elaboration" of Madeleine's (female) ancestry as a further token of mother/daughter silence—to the extent that Madeleine, though given to wearing heirloom jewels, is, through her mother's reticence, completely ignorant of the family madness that resulted in Carlotta's suicide at age twenty-six. Here we might also note how Midge adopts the mother role with Scottie; he too is a lost child (Midge: "You're not lost—mother's here"). For that matter, so is the *real* Madeleine, somebody's daughter (more than literally) thrown out—whose San Francisco residency of roughly a year's duration makes it altogether likely that her family, like the family business, resides primarily, originally, in Baltimore, which puts a whole continent between her family and herself.

Vertigo's "world of women" hardly amounts to a feminist utopia. Indeed, the relation of Gavin Elster to his wife's family business gives reason (if reason is needed) for imagining that most of the women in the world of the film work for male bosses or businesses. That said, however, it is worth remarking how thoroughly "split" the social world of the film remains— Elster's obsessively masculine offices and his club and the coroner's hearing with its all male jury are set in sharp contrast to the feminine worlds on view at Midge's flat, the flower shop, the "Mission Dolores," the McKittrick Hotel, the dress shop, the beauty parlor. And it seems intriguingly the case that Scottie is far more comfortable in that "feminine" world, as his expert mimicry-depiction of neckline and sleeve length across the dress-form of his own torso makes (in my experience) laughably clear to most audiences. Within Stewart's famous "boyishness" is also a barely submerged "girlishness," which marks him as the "feminine man" of melodrama.[22] (So is this the place to note that in Hitchcock's next film it is Cary Grant who suffers the death-and-revival experience typically reserved for women in Cavell's construal of the remarriage genre?)

IV

What we might term the "standard" reading of *Vertigo* takes Scottie (and patriarchy with him) to task for indulging a regressive and therefore destructive relation to "The first love object," "the mother's breast." "The most obvious manifestation of this regression," writes Robin Wood, "is the phenomenon called 'romantic love,' with its demand for perfect union and its tendency to construct the loved person as an idealized fantasy figure, the necessary condition for 'perfect union' being the denial of otherness and autonomy."[23] In a similar vein, David Shumway (citing Juliet Mitchell and Denis de Rougemont) critiques Cavell's analysis of remarriage comedy for indulging an illusory (hence ideological, destructive) picture of marriage "as the goal—but not the end—of romance" as against the view that "Marriage must be the death of romance" because "romance seeks an idealized object, and when that object is attained, love ceases to be romantic."[24]

Against the implication that marriage is the death of romance, or that romance amounts to nothing other than death-dealing regressiveness, I find myself pondering the following passage, drawn from Cavell's *Pursuits of Happiness* discussion of *It Happened One Night*, specifically his interpretation of the censoring function played in the film by Peter's "Wall of Jericho" blanket, which Cavell links to Peter's problem "in putting together his perception and his imagination" of Ellie, a perceptual crux that amounts to Capra's way of framing "the problem of other minds": "The picture is that the existence of others is something of which we are unconscious, a piece of knowledge we repress, about which we draw a blank. This does violence to others, it separates their bodies from their souls, makes monsters of them; and presumably we do it because we feel that others are doing this violence to us. The release from this circle of vengeance is something I call acknowledgment" (PH 109). If words mean anything, these words signify Cavell's attentiveness to the violence of the human imagination, a violence exercised in and by repression, in this case the specific repression of Ellie's claim to be Peter's sexual and spiritual other, "somebody that's real, somebody that's alive," despite his insistence that "they don't come that way any more," an insistence that splits her in two, the "brat" from the woman.

Though there are other forms of violence on view in the remarriage comedies Cavell studies—Ellie's father slaps her across the face in the first scene of *It Happened One Night*, as Adam Bonner slaps Amanda across the rear in *Adam's Rib*—Cavell's primary interest, as befits a philosopher of ordinary language, is the violence of skeptical doubt understood as "a wish to transgress the naturalness of human speech" (PH 74), which amounts to "a wish for the connection between my claims of knowledge and the objects upon which the claims are to fall to occur without my intervention, apart from my agreements" (CR 351–52). Of course, "the mark of the natural in natural language is its capacity to repudiate itself," as if our "attunement with one another" were "arbitrary, or merely conventional" (IQO 48). But this repudiation, in Cavell's (oddly Lacanian) lingo, interprets "metaphysical finitude as intellectual lack" (IQO 51). In connection with *Othello*, Cavell calls this lack jealousy, and he interprets Othello's death-dealing entrancement with the (skeptic's) concept of "ocular proof" as a function of violence, possession, denial: "The violence in masculine knowing, explicitly associated with jealousy, seems to interpret the ambition of knowledge as that of exclusive possession, call it private property. Othello's problem . . . is that Desdemona's acceptance . . . of his ambition strikes him as being possessed, as if he is the woman."[25] In seeking a "possession that is not in opposition to another's claim or desire but one that establishes an absolute or inalienable bonding to himself," Othello's jealousy is thus directed at, amounts to a denial of, "the sheer existence of the other, its separateness from him" (DK 9). But this amounts in Othello's case to a denial of human finitude and contingency altogether, of himself *as* human, "For if she is flesh and blood then, since they are one, so is he" (DK 136).

Though but briefly sketched, the conceptual relevance of Othello's case in Shakespeare to Johnny-O's case in *Vertigo* is clear enough in outline; each seeks "ocular proof" in ways that hint at necrophilia and lead ultimately to the demise of a woman loved "not wisely but too well." I am also moved to adduce Othello's example, however, by Cavell's observation "that in beginning with a sexual scene denied our sight, [*Othello*] opens exactly as a normal comedy closes, as if turning comedy inside out" (DK 132–33). Both the skeptic and the romantic seek "a new intimacy in the self's relation to its world" (PH 15). Both are moved by, both risk, disappointment— disappointment in the intimacies of language, our necessary participation in and responsibility for the words we use and our uses of them, disappointment as well in the facts of sexual intimacy, in the fact *of* sexual intimacy, in the fact that marriage (two becoming one) foretells birth (one becoming two). It is exactly this combination of disappointments that Cavell's (concept of) "remarriage comedy" seeks to acknowledge or incorporate.

That is, remarriage comedy (contra Shumway) also "turns comedy inside out" by beginning with disappointment, with divorce, with an ending of romance. If male violence or its shadow "splits" the woman or the marriage, remarriage comedy heals the split by means of "conversation" and "repetition." "Marriage" in Cavell's usage "is always divorce, always entails rupture from something" (PH 103). All that legitimates marriage "is the mutual willingness for remarriage, for a sort of continuous reaffirmation" (PH 142). And the form that affirmation takes is conversation "of a sort that leads to acknowledgment; to the reconciliation of a genuine forgiveness" (PH 19). Cavell sometimes calls this marital realm "the domestic" so as to align it with the ordinariness of ordinary language. And behind that thought is Cavell's claim, deeply apposite in the present context, "that the ordinary has, and alone has, the power to move the ordinary, to leave the human habitat habitable, the same transfigured. The practice of the ordinary may be thought of as the overcoming of iteration or replication or imitation by repetition, of counting by recounting, of calling by recalling [or of marriage by remarriage]. It is the familiar invaded by another familiar. Hence ordinary language procedures, like the procedures of psychoanalysis, inherently partake of the uncanny."[26]

I detail these Cavellian themes partly to further undo the repression that film scholarship has visited upon his intellectual project. My more immediate purpose, however, is to establish a context for describing *Vertigo,* like *Othello,* as "a failed comedy of remarriage" in which "the reunion is hideously parodied and becomes possible only a moment too late" (PH 142). I am not, let me add, denying the claim that Scottie's idealization of "Madeleine" amounts to male violence in his failure to link perception and imagination, by letting one subsume or overtake the other—as when Scottie asserts possession of Madeleine by asserting that "no one [else] possesses" her. The latter phrase, indeed, is evidence of exactly that deadly strain of melodramatic irony that attends upon Elster's murder-plot and that negates the "meet and happy conversation" clause of remarriage comedy. But the echoes of remarriage in *Vertigo* are nevertheless pervasive and systematic. To the extent that we find the happiness pictured in remarriage comedy as honorable, as livable, to that extent we are bound to honor Judy and Scottie for having aspirations akin to our own. Put another way, though the repetitions at work in the world of *Vertigo* are deadly, especially to women, we could hardly care so deeply about the particular deaths in view if they did not also evoke (among other things, no doubt) our hopes for the kind of world pictured in films like *It Happened One Night* and *The Awful Truth,* where devotion to dailiness amounts to "The winning of a new beginning, a new creation, an innocence, by changes that effect or constitute the overcoming of revenge" (PH 261). How else can we account for the endless poignancy of Scottie's declaration that Judy is his "second chance"?

My specification of *Vertigo*'s participation in the genre of remarriage comedy can (and must) be brief—precisely *because* the links are so systematic. I will return to the "Capra" intertext of *Vertigo* in discussing the latter film's relationship (via Stewart) to *It's a Wonderful Life*. Let me mark in passing two moments of *Vertigo*, however, that link it to *It Happened One Night*: 1) the scene in Scottie's apartment, after "Madeleine's" fall into San Francisco Bay (I take the impromptu clothesline with Madeleine's "things" slung over it, stockings included, as a direct allusion to the first "Wall of Jericho" scene of *It Happened One Night*); and 2) Judy's declaration, as she and Scottie are preparing to dine at Ernie's, just before she puts on the necklace, that she is "hungry" (which takes up in short-hand form the equation of physical and spiritual appetites that Capra threads so carefully through his version of the story). And let me mark as well, now under the "Stewart" rubric, echoes in *Vertigo* of his role as Macauley Conner in *The Philadelphia Story*, where he is charged, among other things, with carrying a wet and water-shocked Katharine Hepburn from a body of water to a house (as Scottie fishes Madeleine from the bay and takes her home) and with delivering a speech in which he recognizes a woman's inner "magnificence," a matter of the way she speaks and stands and moves, which amounts finally to his astonished recognition that she is made of "flesh and blood" (as Scottie tells Judy, even before he sees the necklace, "It's you, too; there's something in you," as if Judy requires delivery, which also amounts to something like recognition, however delayed or deferred).

Perhaps the most concise demonstration I can offer of *Vertigo*'s intricate relation to remarriage comedy is the way it rewrites, as if reversing, the parable and problematic of Preston Sturges's *The Lady Eve*. That "falling" in both becomes a trope of the (comic, tragic) standing of human existence is beyond dispute. In each case, falling (in love) results in something like the "splitting" or "doubling" of a woman, a splitting that hinges on questions of sexual deception or transgression, and that resonates decidedly with the camera's transfiguring attentiveness to the precise physicality of an illustrious Hollywood actress. In each case the woman's deception, involving a story of illegitimate ancestry, is sponsored by a fatherly or avuncular figure with a British accent and a (melodramatic) taste for the theatrical. Somewhere in the middle of each film a central character (Jean, Scottie) wakes up panic stricken from a dream of sexual violation. And in each film the concept of remarriage is evoked in scenes that fantasize some prior state of knowledge or relationship: twice Hopsie/Charles tells Jean/Eve that it's as if he's known her forever ("You seemed to go way back") while Scottie assures "Madeleine" that her dream-vision of San Juan Bautista is real, a memory ("You've been there before"), the deadly reality of which is confirmed twice over. So the problem in both films involves finding some way back from the brink of distrust and recrimination, some (endless) path toward acknowledgment and forgiveness. In both, as it were, the path is downward— happily so, as Hopsie and Jean dash madly down the ship's staircase to Jean's cabin in *The Lady Eve*, tragically so as Judy exits screaming from the mission tower. Though I take the aptness of the comparison to be self-evident, I find confirmation in the fact that Hitchcock's next film is *North by Northwest* in which a lady named "Eve" also scrambles downward (across the face of Mt. Rushmore) before she is reborn into her marital berth.

North by Northwest concludes, as is often noted, by reference to both *Vertigo* and *Bringing Up Baby*: the former in Cary Grant's urging, amounting to a second marriage proposal, that Eva Marie Saint take his hand (which rehearses the cop's last line to Scottie before he tumbles to his death in *Vertigo*'s first scene), the latter in the shock cut from the face of Mt. Rushmore to Mr. and Mrs. Thornhill's Pullman cabin where Grant completes the task of rescue by pulling Eva Marie Saint into the top bunk of their marriage bed (as Cary Grant pulls Katharine Hepburn onto his museum scaffold as the brontosaurus collapses beneath her in *Baby*). *Vertigo* can be seen to interpret, by reversing, this down/up rhythm—in that Scottie pulls Judy up the tower stairs only to see her vanish over the edge of the world. Though I will return to the tower scene to consider why Judy falls, or what it is that prompts her reaction unto death, here I want to interpret the last conversation of Scottie and Judy in light of *Vertigo*'s complex generic affiliations.

I have already noted that Scottie is charged with delivering the "aria of divorce" normally assigned in melodrama to the unknown woman. Surely Scottie's angry and bewildered sense of victimization ("Why me?") is fully the equal of Paula's in *Gaslight* when she unravels, by mimicry, her husband's theatrical strategy for driving her mad (which includes, we might add, a false story about *her* "mad" mother). Scottie's tirade is only slightly less theatrical—in the sense that he is revealing artifice while simultaneously "staging" his "second chance"—but it is no less ironic, if only because Scottie's trauma is much less under control, is in that sense more hysterical. We might note that *he* is now the split character, carved forever into before and after, even as he tries to put Madeleine and Judy, past and present, together: "I loved you so, Maddie."[27] But his words don't take, are not taken up in their apparent spirit of triumph and dismissal. Judy faces him, embraces him, kisses him. He kisses back. About this, at least, he is wrong; it's not "too late." Not yet.

In this moment they remarry. What had seemed revenge has become forgiveness—though, as Thomas Leitch points out, Scottie's anger is far more directed at the deception practiced upon him by Gavin and Judy than by the murder most foul of the real Madeleine Elster.[28] (Here again Scottie follows the lead of Henry Fonda's Hopsie in *The Lady Eve*.) Does this make Scottie guilty too? Ironically enough, yes. He is both victim and accomplice—like Judy. But guilt and innocence are understood by melodrama and remarriage comedy alike as performatives, not essences; innocence is thus something one declares, enacts, as Judy declares her guilty innocence to Scottie, asserting her real identity by confessing her true desire: "I walked into danger and let you change me because I loved you and I wanted you." So Scottie is right in this, in his inchoate conviction that here and now is his second chance. (As always, for everyone.) In remarriage comedy, Cavell suggests, "innocence is not awarded once for all, but is always to be rewon" (PH 53). So innocence is recovered, reclaimed, acknowledged. But now it *is* too late.

V

During the graduation dance scene of *It's a Wonderful Life*, James Stewart's George Bailey, at her brother's behest, asks Mary Hatch/Donna Reed to dance. In so doing he interrupts the life-story monologue of a hapless high school Romeo. As George and Mary dance, the crestfallen suitor is joined by a cynical compatriot who poses the following question: "What's the matter, Othello, jealous?" Given Cavell's repeated emphasis on Othello's skeptical search for an ocular proof that will render his knowledge of others certain by turning them to stone, to private property, thus to assuage the horror of being something other than stone, say flesh and blood, it is easy to see the general relevance of the Shakespearean intertext to Capra's parable of a building and loan officer driven to hyperbolic distraction by the machinations of capital as personified by Henry F. Potter, "the richest and meanest man in the county." In trying to specify the relevancies of *Othello* to the graduation dance scene, however, complications arise—to the effect that, as neither is obviously Othello or Iago, both George and Mary are versions of Desdemona, Mary in her fanatical loyalty, George to the extent that he, as it were, grants Othello's wish that Desdemona had never been born, by wishing that wish for himself.

July 20, 2001The latter construal gains credence in light of Cavell's brief remarks on *Vertigo* and *It's a Wonderful Life* in "What Becomes of Things on Film?" In pondering his title question, Cavell is moved by the work of Bužuel and Bergman to consider the relationship between cinematic procedures "of unmarked juxtapositions of reality with some opposition to reality" (he calls this "the subjunctive") and the fact that films evincing these procedures seem to have found a natural subject in "the meaning, or limits, or conditions, of female identity, hence no doubt of human identity" (TOS 179). In both *It's a Wonderful Life* and *Vertigo*, the instability of the world—whether there is one world or two, one woman or two—is on display, and Cavell links this display to Jimmy Stewart's photogenetic "capacity to stake identity upon the power of wishing," implying "a willingness for suffering," a capacity that "would admit him to the company of the women" in melodrama "whose search for their identities" amounts to "the identifying or the inhabitation of a feminine region of the self" (TOS 180). (Kaja Silverman makes a similar point along more Lacanian lines in describing George as having a masochistic relation to the Symbolic regime of the film.)[29]

But then the *Othello* connection opens up a doubt about the direction of George's wishing. Is his desire never to have suffered birth a version of skeptical anger and rage, "self-consuming disappointment" seeking "world-consuming revenge" (DK 6)? Anger and rage, yes. But I have eventually come to see George's situation as Othello's turned "inside out." That is, where Othello's sense of himself as female follows from the fear that he is flesh and blood, an embodied human, George's sense of himself as female follows from just the opposite fear, that he lacks embodiment, that he has not yet been born. So his task in the film, endlessly expressed as a desire to get out, to leave, is the task of birth-giving; giving birth to himself.

Crucial to my elaboration of this picture of George Bailey is Jessica Benjamin's study (to quote her subtitle) of "Psychoanalysis, Feminism, and The Problem of Domination" in *The Bonds of Love*.[30] Key here is the way Cavell and Benjamin both describe the task of "differentiation" less as a once-and-for-all Oedipal/Symbolic accomplishment than as a matter of never-ending and creative *tensions* in the relations of self to other, though in Benjamin's view *establishing* that tension is the most difficult problem with which parents and children are tasked, especially in contemporary western societies. "The need of the self for the other is paradoxical," Benjamin writes in words that echo Cavell's speech-act theory analyses of "acknowledgment," "because the self is trying to establish himself as an absolute, an independent entity, yet he must recognize the other as like himself in order to *be* recognized by him" (BL 32); "at the very moment of realizing our own independence, we are dependent upon another to recognize it" (BL 33); "and this, in turn, means I must finally acknowledge the other as existing for *himself* and not just for me" (BL 36).

Central to Benjamin's picture of these matters is the "rapprochement" phase of psychological development in which the child's instinctive assertion of omnipotence is (ideally) matched by a caregiver's both asserting and *sharing* a recognition of human finitude or limits, the difference between wants and needs, say; narcissism or omnipotence on both sides of the parent/child dyad is given up in favor of the mutual attunement that *discovers*, as both revealing and creating, the "real world," the "intersubjective" world, a world of *shared* tensions and responsibilities (BL 41). Crucial to this phase is a process of "destruction," as defined by D. W. Winnicott, in which the child's natural aggression toward the parent takes the form of "a refusal, a negation, the mental experience of 'You do not exist for me,' whose favorable outcome is pleasure in the other's survival" (BL 38). (There is an obvious echo here of Cavell's whole "remarriage" paradigm, in which a marriage is "destroyed" so that it may subsequently and pleasurably "survive.")

When acknowledgment is refused, however, especially in infancy or early childhood, the whole world of reciprocal differences and acknowledgments goes with it; what's left is Hegel's Master/Slave version of the paradox in which the world is either dominated or submitted to, and from which there is no way out: "If I completely control the other, then the other ceases to exist, and if the other completely controls me, then I cease to exist" (BL 53). Thus "the drama of reversible violator and victim displaces the tension of interaction with the other. This drama now occurs within the omnipotence of mental life, the encapsulated sphere of the intrapsychic" (BL 71).

There is uncannily little to chose between this Hegelian picture of the psychology of human identity as mutual destructiveness and the standard picture of *Vertigo* as elaborated most cogently by Modleski and Deborah Linderman.[31] (Modleski: "The very effort to cure her, which is an effort to get her to mirror man and his desire, to see (his) reason, destroys woman's otherness" [WWK 93].) Thus the result of Scottie's failure to impose his identifications of the world upon Madeleine is a collapse of psychic reality altogether figured as his identification with her nothingness, her emptiness, by dreaming *her* dream, her nightmare: "Scottie actually *lives out Madeleine's hallucination,* that very hallucination of which he had tried so desperately to cure her, and he *dies Madeleine's death.* His attempt at cure having failed, he himself is plunged into the 'feminine' world of psychic disintegration, madness and death" (WWK 95). And if hope there is in Modleski's picture of Scottie's melancholy fall into madness, it is exactly in

Scottie's "regression" to a "narcissistic identification" with Madeleine/Judy, the pull and possibility of which is measured by his increasingly sadistic efforts to deny it.

A similar capacity for rage, as Rothman remarks, is displayed by George Bailey in the Capra movie, most emphatically in the sequence when he trashes his architectural models and terrorizes his family on Christmas Eve. But I have come to see that rage less as a token of regression *per se* than of a positive wish for embodiment *tout court*, an instance of "destruction" in Jessica Benjamin's sense that recapitulates an earlier failure of destruction to yield a world, a failure played out in George's relationship to his father. In essence, George's father never listens to him, never truly hears George's destructive characterizations of life in Bedford Falls; when we first see George he is shouting through a megaphone, and I take his subsequent loss of hearing as a displaced mark of his father's endless withdrawal from him, a mark earned by mimicking his father's brand of self-effacement in saving his younger brother from drowning. As a result, and especially when George's father suffers a stroke and thus withdraws for good on the eve of George's departure, George feels ghostly, unreal, uncreated—the Pottersville of the "unborn" sequence is the reality of his life everyday, a life he is not yet living, a life unrecognized ("Mary, it's George! Don't you know me!"). When Mary describes the old Granville place as "full of romance," George replies "I wouldn't live in it as a ghost." But he does and he is. I claim that George's sense of himself as a "wet nurse," as "nursemaid to a bunch of garlic eaters," as uncreated and unrecognized, makes him an unknown woman. So too, I now want to claim, is Scottie Ferguson in *Vertigo*.

Scottie's "feminine" status can be derived alike from *Vertigo*'s inheritance of melodrama or remarriage comedy. In the former case, Scottie is both "the feminine man" and the "unknown woman" whose silence is broken in delivering the "aria of divorce" that virtually defines the genre. Indeed, we have already observed Scottie's propensity for dwelling in a world of women, even and especially in his dreams. Modleski, moreover, has described Scottie as taking on Carlotta's role in the film's second half—as a "sad" mother desperately in search of a lost daughter whose whereabouts are known (in that there is no sense that the nameless father undertook to hide the daughter or her dwelling place; in the sense, as Rothman claims, that Scottie knows Judy is "Madeleine" from the moment he first sees her, framed, framing herself, in the characteristic right-profile pose that was her signature in the film's first half) yet maddeningly undiscoverable.

In the latter case, Scottie's literally doubled relationship to Judy, described by any number of critics as a kind of two-way mirror, each of the other *mise-en-abîme*, follows the remarriage model in leaving "ambiguous the question whether the man or the woman is the active or the passive partner, whether indeed active and passive are apt characterizations of the difference between male and female, or whether indeed we know satisfactorily how to think about the difference between male and female" (PH 82). Like the heroines of remarriage comedy, whom Cavell describes as non-existent, as haunting the world, Scottie lives a ghostly life, "wandering" in a curiously timeless labyrinth.

In pondering this ghostly element of Scottie's character, I am reminded of Jessica Benjamin's observation, after Winnicott, that intersubjective relations, by contrast with the intrapsychic representations of Freudian theory, are expressed spatially rather than symbolically (BL 126). Paradoxically, the "inner space" that enables one to "contain" or "to hold oneself, to bear one's feelings without losing or fragmenting oneself," especially when under attack in the rapprochement phase, tropes the "safe transitional space," the "open space" of childhood, which "allows us to feel that our impulses come from within and so are authentically our own" (BL 128). Where "identification with the holding mother" is lost, so too is "access to inner space," which amounts to a loss of sexual subjectivity (BL 163). The result, especially for the adult male, is that his "encounter with woman as an acutely desirable object may rob him of his own desire—he is thrown back into feeling that desire is the property of the object," which "robs him of the inner space to feel desire emerging from within—a kind of reverse violation" (BL 164)

The vertiginousness of this psychic scenario perfectly captures the sense in which Scottie both lacks desire and hysterically exudes it, is simultaneously empty or transparent, yet full. It underscores for me a quite literal reading of Scottie's otherwise mysterious decision to take up the case of Madeleine Elster against what seems his better judgment. Though he is no longer in the detective business, Scottie takes up the case upon learning: 1) that Madeleine is possessed, as if from within, by another being; and 2) that this possession is something of which she is unconscious, as if she were, in a sense, unknown to herself—as if her selfhood were a function of this unknownness. I take it that Scottie senses himself as unknown, as empty, as ghostly—a trope taken over quite literally from *It's a Wonderful Life* where Mary's mysterious disappearance from her bathrobe, only to reappear in a hydrangea bush, provides the "green world" prototype for *Vertigo*'s Muir Woods sequence, in which a fantastically evanescent Madeleine accuses Scottie of having taken, like George of Mary, no notice. But I also understand Scottie's identification with Madeleine as expressing his wish to be full, to be possessed from within, like a pregnant woman—a pregnancy cinematically depicted by the cocooning 360–degree tracking shot around the embrace of Scottie and Judy. That something like birth-giving is at stake in this identification is also depicted in Scottie's experience of "Madeleine's" dream, which can be taken as a micro-parable of human fatedness and finitude: "deflowering" (the disintegration of the nosegay corsage) is followed by the passage of a head through a mother's grave (pulsing and red, like a womb or a birth canal) which immediately yields entry into a world where arrival equals death. No wonder Scottie takes on a "motherly" stance toward Judy, dressing her up, showing her off, feeding her, and so on.

Another way of describing the "unknownness" of Scottie is simply to observe how little we know *of* him at first, especially when it comes to pondering *why* he feels so dead to the world, so unborn. We know absolutely nothing about *his* parents, presuming he had parents, beyond the following: 1) that Scottie is independently wealthy, from which we can infer that his parents were once well off, and might well be dead; and 2) that Scottie, though educated in the law, chose to become a cop rather than a lawyer, only to discover a pre-existing (and previously unknown) condition, only triggered by the death of his uniformed colleague in the film's first scene, which made even that profession, for some reason, unacceptable.

Hints of parent/child antagonism are in train here, of the normal sort in which a child will try to determine her own path in the face of apparently contrary parental desires—and are confirmed, in a curious fashion, by the apparently friendly but spatially and emotionally distanced relation on view between Midge (as "Mother") and Scottie. A more literal distance between parent and child is evident in the relationship of Judy and her mother. She *says* it was antipathy to her stepfather that occasioned her leaving home. Yet the scenario she acts out with Gavin Elster results in the death of a woman, not a man, as if her hostility were directed at the female parent. And yet there is a hint, for those with ears to hear, that Judy's hostility is of the positive form pictured in Benjamin's rapprochement scenario; that is, Judy *screams* at the last minute, as if she really wanted Madeleine to survive after all, despite the fact that Elster had broken his wife's neck before throwing her out of the tower.

I am inclined to read all this backwards, and as applying equally to both cases—to the effect that what binds Scottie and Judy together is a sense of mutual ghostliness, as if neither feels fully born because neither has really accepted the fact of birth, an acceptance foreclosed, like that of George Bailey in *It's a Wonderful Life*, by the death of a parent, Judy's father in her case, who knows which parent (or parents) in Scottie's, though perhaps the dead cop will do as a figure for Scottie's sense of abandonment (or so we might well conclude by the way the end of Scottie's birth-trauma nightmare visually rhymes with the image of the dead cop as viewed from Scottie's vantage in the film's first scene).

There is one other woman whose unknownness we must consider briefly before these remarks on *Vertigo* can be sent on their worldly way: the nun in the bell tower. Critics for whom it is axiomatic that Judy's death is chiefly attributable to Scottie's Hegelian brand of male villainy seldom give the good sister a second thought, beyond taking her as a *dea ex cinema* tasked with ringing down the curtain on Judy's sad story of female victimage. Though I fully agree with Rothman that Scottie's crimes against Judy, real as they are, would have been greater still had he not remained true to his love for Madeleine, who emphatically *is* Judy and *was* all along, I want to keep the feminist brief against Scottie in view as a reminder of the class and gender issues underscored when we considered *Vertigo*'s inheritance of melodrama, especially the clause pertaining to guilty aristocrats and their ecclesiastical co-conspirators.

In describing *Vertigo* as a parable of birth giving and separation—of wanting to be born and fearing that you haven't been—I might be understood as repressing the obvious fact that the film's most emphatic gesture of separation is the murder of Madeleine Elster by a man who worships "power" and "freedom." I take Judy's reaction to the nun's gothically staged appearance in the tower, in all of its mysteriousness and depth, as betokening her realization that, innocent or not, she can never be real in the world as it stands, a world where *all* women are, and will likely remain, uncreated, ghostly, possessed (as if from within) by male-authored fictions of deficient female inheritance or parenting, fictions made altogether too real by a world where women are silenced, their desires denied, their autonomy never sufficiently enough recognized to gladly suffer the rages of infancy in ways that will allow fantasy to yield (to) a genuinely human reality. Scottie and Judy come agonizingly close—to the extent that *she* creates a world for him by withstanding *his* rage. But the nun's appearance obviously raises a specter of ghostliness that Judy finds literally unbearable, however we eventually choose to identify the ghost—as the real Madeleine, as Carlotta Valdes, as Gavin Elster, as Alfred Hitchcock.

I hardly wish to imply that the nun who climbs the steps to the tower while Judy and Scottie speak their hearts to one another was specifically or consciously in league with Elster. But I *am* trying to account for certain facts: 1) that the only other instance in the film of a silhouetted figure unexpectedly appearing from the darkness was Judy, when, as Madeleine, she appeared at Scottie's apartment, framed in the doorway, to recount her "dream" of San Juan Bautista, a dream obviously scripted by Elster for Judy to act out; 2) that the nun, in Judy's hearing, is effectively silent—her "I heard voices" comes after Judy's anguished "Oh, no"—and that the specter of silent (or silenced) mothers looms large in the film's repertoire of wounded and wounding relationships; 3) that the nun, though representing "the world of women," also represents a denial of sexual difference or desire, as if the only way for women to exist is to deny their own (hetero)sexual existence. Indeed, a link between unrecognized or undecidable difference and death is forged in the logic that gets the nun to climb the tower in the first place—Madeleine's "suicide," I am presuming, has alerted the mission staff to the danger represented by the tower; and the sister (or "mother") hears "voices," which may or may not be taken to imply that she hears any difference between them. I imagine that the sight of the nun reminds Judy of her mirror-image relationship with Scottie, as if he were too much like her, too much her mother—not *different enough,* finally, to help render *her* real. Thus does Hitchcock trope the "incest taboo," a prohibition remarriage comedy encounters but successfully revises by interpreting marriage as (by) divorce. In the melodramatic world of *Vertigo,* there is, as Midge reminds us, "no losing it."

The call of strange voices brings the nun to the tower. To Scottie these same voices are uncannily familiar. He once heard a scream. Now he hears it again as Judy recoils from the nun and plunges to her death. In dragging Judy up the tower Scottie cites the scream, along with the necklace, as truth tokens—as if he had known from the instant he first heard it that the scream belonged to Judy, who stood above him, not to Madeleine, whose falling body flies silently past him as he cowers on the tower stairs: "Why did you scream? Since you'd tricked me so well up to then?"

Within the film-world, Scottie's tracking of the scream to its origin in space measures the relation of repression and desire—repression, to the extent that Scottie's knowledge seems to remain unconscious; desire, in the sense that Scottie is right to think that Judy *is* Madeleine, and has known it all along, a knowledge Judy knowingly appeals to in her apartment after their first date when she poses in silhouette profile (but her left, as opposed to her right, this time—showing her other side, say) and talks to Scottie, so that sound becomes the chief token of her identity. However brutal its enactment, however traumatic her rebirth, Scottie's re-creation of Judy-as-Madeleine thus amounts to a victory over repression, an acknowledgment of desire, his for her, hers for him. Here is where the film's indebtedness to remarriage comedy is most touchingly and clearly marked, and its inheritance of melodrama too.

Indeed, *Vertigo* shares with remarriage comedy a quality of "privacy"—typically figured in the couples' withdrawal to a place of perspective, beyond society—which finally allows us to distinguish cinematic from theatrical melodrama by distinguishing the depicted world of the film from the world of its depiction, the world of the film's narration. If it is melodrama's deepest ambition to "say all," we can say that little of substance is finally left unsaid in either *Vertigo* or *It's a Wonderful Life*. What more do we need to know? We are not in the least unsure, for example, of the political facts on the ground: that Potter drove Peter Bailey to a premature death and hence condemned George all the more certainly to uncreation, that Potter pocketed another $8000 of ill-gotten gain with nary a prospect of detection or imprisonment, that Elster murdered his wife for fun and profit and got off, as they say, Scott free (literally, as Scottie at film's end can hardly be imagined as a credible witness against Elster). But this knowledge lacks force in the world where it seems most applicable or most needed. Evil is not fully "nominated," especially in the world of *Vertigo*, so it cannot, finally, be purged, not *from* the world on view, not *by* the world on view. All is said, but only we can hear it.

Our world, Hitchcock's world, there is reason to hope, may be a different matter. In claiming that Hitchcock's gaze is murderous, Rothman underscores cinema's necessary participation in human finitude or fatedness; if cameras cannot literally kill, they inevitably mark their subjects as mortal beings. To the extent that we equate Scottie, Elster, and Hitchcock as male fantasists whose narcissistic enactments merely replicate a childish picture of womankind, making every woman, like Judy, a "copy," a "counterfeit," cut to the measure of male desire, then we must agree that all are villainous. Indeed, in Rothman's intuition that Hitchcock's studious dedication to unknownness, to the mysterious and the secretive, evinces "his desire to avenge himself on those who, beholding his creations, draw sustenance from them" without acknowledging his powers of creation and decreation, we hear uncanny echoes of Cavell's *Pursuits of Happiness* description of Peter Warne's villainy as reflexive, a matter of violence offered for violence suffered.[32] One way of taking *Vertigo* as a parable of human birth offered and refused is to say that the men in the film blame women alone for the fact of human nativity. This too is villainous.

But there is another way to understand the film and Hitchcock's participation in it. Partly this involves his legendary cameo appearance. In *Vertigo*, Hitchcock is visible walking down a sidewalk outside Elster's shipyard, a horn case in his hand, just before Scottie enters the frame en route to Elster's office. Hitchcock thus marks *himself* as mortal, as seeking no exemption, as humanly attuned.[33] Put another way, we are *all* "copies," *all* "counterfeits." Our existence does *not* depend upon complete independence or originality. As Benjamin and Cavell alike avow, a desire for absolute autonomy is a desire for death, marked in *Vertigo* by Elster's murder of his wife. Also deadly is identification with another so complete that all autonomy is lost. Carlotta's fate is a version of this, a fate replicated in Elster's fictional "Madeleine." It is thus also Judy's fate and finally Scottie's too. It is the fate of women in *Vertigo*'s world.

In our melodramatic desire to render judgments of the romantic or perfectionist fantasies that drive Hitchcock's characters to destruction, however, we must be careful not to condemn fantasy itself, fantasy *tout court.* As Cavell makes the point in *The World Viewed,* "It is a poor idea of fantasy which takes it to be a world apart from reality, a world clearly showing its unreality. Fantasy is precisely what reality can be confused with. It is through fantasy that our conviction of the worth of reality is established; to forgo our fantasies would be to forgo our touch with the world" (WV 85). Indeed, as Benjamin confirms, it is by experiencing the failure of destructive fantasies (not simply by abjuring fantasy altogether) that the world itself is discovered; Winnicott's "reality principle," contra Freud's, "is a positive source of pleasure, the pleasure of connecting," "the recognition of shared reality" (BL 40–41). It is thus from the interplay of similarity and difference, fantasy and reality, that *intersubjectivity* is born.

So here is my intersubjective fantasy of how Hitchcock manipulates the play of similarity and difference in *Vertigo.* He is like each of the major characters in some respect: an investigator like Scottie, a painter and illustrator like Midge, an industrialist like Elster, a lost daughter like Judy. But he also insists on a degree of independence from them all—via his emphatic use of moving camera, for instance, which acknowledges the presence of an audience for whom such gestures may be said to count. But such gestures also acknowledge his dependency, his own finitude and humanity, his presence in our world as well as in *his* world. This too betokens birthing, separation, letting go. Films must be, as they say, released.

I want to say that Hitchcock releases his authorship to Judy in the film's last shot in a way that renders undecidable whether she lives or dies, whether he lives or dies. The last thing we see Judy do is recoil from the nun; we presume she leaps from the tower. Similarly, the film's last shot recoils very emphatically from the nun and leaps backward into space. The nun, the very spirit of ill-timing, tolls the bell, which signals an accident, but which can also tell the hour. (But then all our hours are accidents of timing, of birthing.) The nun cannot see where Judy has gone. What Scottie sees we can only guess, though whether he sees *at all* is doubtful. For that matter, whether there is anything to *be seen* is an open question. The only evidence we have that Judy fell is her scream. Her last scream did accompany a fall, though not her own. I have no doubt that Judy, of course, is dead to Scottie, dead in his world. My fantasy is that she hovers in space, between his world and our world, like the hovering face of *Vertigo*'s credit sequence, a pulsing membrane, a film.[34]

NOTES

1. Kathryn Kalinak, *Settling the Score: Music and the Classical Hollywood Film* (Madison: University of Wisconsin Press, 1992), 5.

2. Tania Modleski, *The Women Who Knew Too Much: Hitchcock and Feminist Theory* (New York: Routledge, 1988), 98. Cited hereafter as WWK.

3. See Tania Modleski, *Feminism Without Women: Culture and Criticism in a "Postfeminist" Age* (New York: Routledge, 1991), 11. Film critics who *have* addressed Cavell include Dana Polan, "The Light Side of Genius: Hitchcock's *Mr. and Mrs. Smith* in the Screwball Tradition," in *Comedy/Cinema/Theory*, ed. Andrew Horton (Berkeley: University of California Press, 1991), 131–52, and Marty Roth, "Slap-Happiness: The Erotic Contract of *His Girl Friday*," *Screen* 30, nos. 1–2 (Winter-Spring 1989): 160–75. See also Naomi Scheman, "Missing Mothers/Desiring Daughters: Framing the Sight of Women," *Critical Inquiry* 15, no. 1 (Autumn 1988): 62–89.

4. David Bordwell, "Historical Poetics of Cinema," in *The Cinematic Text: Methods and Approaches*, ed. R. Barton Palmer (New York: AMS Press, 1989), 385.

5. Stanley Cavell, *The World Viewed: Reflections on the Ontology of Film*, enlarged ed. (Cambridge: Harvard University Press, 1979), cited hereafter as WV, and *Pursuits of Happiness: The Hollywood Comedy of Remarriage* (Cambridge: Harvard University Press, 1981), cited hereafter as PH; Christian Metz, *The Imaginary Signifier: Psychoanalysis and Cinema* (Bloomington: Indiana University Press 1982); Mary Ann Doane, *The Desire to Desire: The Woman's Film of the 1940s* (Bloomington: Indiana Univ Press, 1987).

6. On the use of marriage as a type of the social contract see especially Cavell's "Two Cheers for Romance," in *Passionate Attachments: Thinking About Love*, ed. Willard Gaylin and Ethel Person (New York: The Free Press, 1988), 85–100.

7. Nearly everything Cavell has written bears on the question of language theory. Citations for the present essay are drawn from *The Claim of Reason: Wittgenstein, Skepticism, Morality, and Tragedy* (New York: Oxford University Press, 1979),

cited as CR, and *In Quest of the Ordinary: Lines of Skepticism and Romanticism* (Chicago: University of Chicago Press, 1988), cited as IQO.

8. Stanley Cavell, "The Thought of Movies," in *Themes Out of School: Effects and Causes* (San Francisco: North Point, 1984; Chicago: University of Chicago Press, 1988), 13. Cited hereafter as TOS.

9. Stanley Cavell, "Psychoanalysis and Cinema: The Melodrama of the Unknown Woman," in *The Trial(s) of Psychoanalysis,* ed. Françoise Meltzer (Chicago: University of Chicago Press, 1988), 232. Cited hereafter as PC.

10. Stanley Cavell, "Naughty Orators: Negation of Voice in *Gaslight*," in *Languages of the Unsayable: The Play of Negativity in Literature and Literary Theory,* ed. Sanford Budick and Wolfgang Iser (New York: Columbia University Press, 1989), 343. Cited as hereafter as NO.

11. Stanley Cavell, "Ugly Duckling, Funny Butterfly: Bette Davis and *Now, Voyager,*" *Critical Inquiry* 16, no. 2 (Winter 1990): 217.

12. Cavell, "North by Northwest," TOS 171.

13. Cavell, "What Becomes of Things on Film?," TOS 181.

14. Marian E. Keane, "A Closer Look at Scopophilia: Mulvey, Hitchcock, and *Vertigo,*" in *A Hitchcock Reader,* ed. Marshall Deutelbaum and Leland Poague (Ames: Iowa State University Press, 1986), 231–48; Wendy Lesser, "Hitchcock's Couples," in *His Other Half: Men Looking at Women Through Art* (Cambridge: Harvard Univ Press, 1991), 121–44.

15. William Rothman, "*Vertigo:* The Unknown Woman in Hitchcock," in *The "I" of the Camera: Essays in Film Criticism, History, and Aesthetics* (Cambridge: Cambridge University Press, 1988), 152–73. Cited hereafter as IC.

16. Leland Poague, *Another Frank Capra* (Cambridge: Cambridge University Press, 1994).

17. Peter Brooks, *The Melodramatic Imagination: Balzac, Henry James, Melodrama, and the Mode of Excess* (New Haven: Yale University Press, 1976). Cited hereafter as MI.

18. Stanley Cavell, "What Photography Calls Thinking." *Raritan* 4, no. 4 (Spring 1985): 11.

19. Rothman, "Virtue and Villainy in the Face of the Camera," IC 77, 78.

20. Rothman and I cite different language from Brooks, though from the same passage of argument; I believe I have not distorted his view or use of Brooks in so doing.

21. Stanley Cavell, "Postscript (1989): To Whom It May Concern," *Critical Inquiry* 16, no. 2 (Winter 1990): 280. Cited hereafter as PS.

22. On "the feminine man" concept see Tania Modleski, "Time and Desire in the Woman's Film," *Cinema Journal* 23, no. 3 (Spring 1984): 19–30, and Cavell, PS.

23. Robin Wood, "Male Desire, Male Anxiety: The Essential Hitchcock," in *A Hitchcock Reader*, 228.

24. David R. Shumway, "Screwball Comedies: Constructing Romance, Mystifying Marriage," *Cinema Journal* 30, no. 4 (Summer 1991): 7, 11.

25. Stanley Cavell, *Disowning Knowledge In Six Plays of Shakespeare* (Cambridge: Cambridge University Press, 1987), 10. Cited hereafter as DK.

26. Stanley Cavell, *This New Yet Unapproachable America: Lectures after Emerson after Wittgenstein* (Albuquerque: Living Batch, 1989), 47.

27. On this point I am specifically indebted to Lesley Brill's *The Hitchcock Romance: Love and Irony in Hitchcock's Films* (Princeton: Princeton University Press, 1988), 219. Professor Brill's analysis echoes my own, in charting *Vertigo's* ironies against a background of romance, though his version of that background is drawn largely and productively from other Hitchcock films. I, obviously, rely on Cavell and Brooks.

28. Thomas M. Leitch, *Find the Director and Other Hitchcock Games* (Athens: University of Georgia Press, 1991), 203.

29. Kaja Silverman, "Male Subjectivity and the Celestial Suture: *It's a Wonderful Life*," *Framework* no. 14 (1981): 16–22. Two other deeply thoughtful articles on *It's a Wonderful Life* are: George Toles, " 'No Bigger than Zuzu's Petals': Dream-Messages, Epiphanies, and the Undoing of Conventions in *It's a Wonderful Life*," *North Dakota Quarterly* 52, no. 3 (Summer 1984): 43–66, and William Rothman, "Hollywood and the Rise of Suburbia," *East-West Film Journal* 3, no. 2 (June 1989): 96–105.

30. Jessica Benjamin, *The Bonds of Love: Psychoanalysis, Feminism, and the Problem of Domination* (New York: Pantheon, 1988). Cited hereafter as BL.

31. See Modleski, WWK, and Deborah Linderman, "The Mise-en-Abîme in Hitchcock's *Vertigo*," *Cinema Journal* 30, no. 4 (Summer 1991): 51–74.

32. William Rothman, *Hitchcock—The Murderous Gaze* (Cambridge: Harvard University Press, 1982), 340.

33. In the original version of this essay published in the *Hitchcock Annual*, I took the object in Hitchcock's hand to be a large flashlight, which allowed me to describe him as "enlightened." In "Engendering the Truth about *Vertigo*: Thoughts on an Article by Leland Poague in the 1994 *Hitchcock Annual*," *The MacGuffin*, no. 17 (November 1995): 14–26, Ken Mogg objects that I am factually wrong. In his editorial reply to my rejoinder (*The MacGuffin*, no. 24 [February 1998]), he describes my metaphoric extension of the error in the direction of Kant as "elaborate, pretentious interpretation" (p. 20). I gladly stand corrected on the factual matter. A horn case it is! But in light of Mogg's repeated insistence that I do not have sufficient evidence for claiming an intertextual connection between Hitchcock and remarriage comedy, especially Capra's *It Happened One Night*, I cannot resist noting how the horn case

evokes the biblical Joshua, whose trumpet players, on his order, famously toppled the Walls of Jericho. In popular culture, indeed, Joshua's order is itself a trumpet's call; in the words of the Negro spiritual, "his mouth was a gospel horn." Given that Peter Warne specifically denies he has a trumpet during the also famous "Wall of Jericho" scene in *It Happened One Night,* and that it is Ellie who finally breaches the wall, in the second auto-camp scene, I am moved to say that Hitchcock is here alluding to the Capra film (an allusion subsequently confirmed by the makeshift laundry line Scottie uses to dry Madeleine's clothes after her jump into the bay), hence identifying himself as much with Ellie as with Joshua, just as Scottie identifies himself both with Judy/Madeleine and with Elster.

34. Profound thanks for their timely comments and encouragement are due to Susan Poague, Richard Ness, Loring Silet, Neal Bowers, Nina Miller, Thomas Kent, Christopher Brookhouse, and Lesley Brill. I am grateful to Rebecca Burnett for editorial assistance on the latest revision of this essay. I responded to Ken Mogg's "Engendering the Truth about *Vertigo*" with "Engendering (More) *Vertigo,*" *The MacGuffin,* No. 24 (February 1998): 14–19, which replies to Mogg's criticism, explains the provenance of the original essay, and extends its argument to incorporate Pedro Almodóvar's *High Heels* as the last panel in a triptych of melodramas, as if the Almodóvar film were looking back at Hitchcock's across the space defined by Capra's *It's a Wonderful Life.* Many of the Cavell essays pertaining to melodrama cited above have been collected together as *Contesting Tears: The Hollywood Melodrama of the Unknown Woman* (Chicago: University of Chicago Press, 1996). Given my reading of William Rothman's reading of Cavell's "unknown woman" rubric, I should also point readers to William Rothman and Marian Keane's *Reading Cavell's* The World Viewed: *A Philosophical Perspective on Film* (Detroit: Wayne State University Press, 2000).

AVIAN METAPHOR
IN *THE BIRDS*

Richard Allen

Critics of *The Birds* have rightly sought to connect
the thread of domestic melodrama in the film with
the attacks of the birds that temporarily interrupt
that thread. But what is the nature of this connection? The orthodox interpretation of the film is an
Oedipal one. Thus Margaret Horwitz writes, "The
wild birds function as a kind of malevolent female
superego, an indirect revelation of Lydia's character.
She is a possessive mother, intent upon furthering a
symbiotic, Oedipal relationship with her son."[1] Horwitz's interpretation of the film is echoed by Slavoj
Žižek, who writes, "The terrifying figure of the birds
is . . . the incarnation of a fundamental disorder in
family relationships—the father is absent, the paternal function (the function of pacifying law, the
Name-of-the Father) is suspended and that vacuum
is filled by the 'irrational' maternal superego, arbitrary, wicked, blocking 'normal' sexual relationship (only possible under the sign of the paternal
metaphor)." The irrational maternal super-ego is the
liberator of pure chaos: the birds are a figuration of
the eruption of a "*lawless* impossible real" into the
domain of the law or the social order.[2]

There is much in the film to favor this interpretation. Melanie Daniel's entry into Bodega Bay on her quest to bring a pair of lovebirds to Mitch Brenner is the occasion for the birds to begin their attack, and she is the object of assault. Furthermore, her association with Mitch is viewed with hostility by Lydia who jealously guards his companionship in a manner that has clear Oedipal overtones. The film jokes about this when, upon her arrival at Bodega Bay, Melanie inquires as to where the Brenners live. "Mr. and Mrs. Brenner?" she asks. "No," is the reply, "just Lydia and the two kids." While Mitch is Lydia's son, he interacts with her as if he were her domestic partner and Lydia reacts to Melanie in the manner that she had reacted earlier to Annie Hayworth: both are her rivals for Mitch's affection. In a particularly telling scene in the Brenner kitchen, Mitch refers to Lydia as "darling" and "dear" as he dries the dishes, while Lydia taunts him with observations about Melanie's notoriety as a good-time girl prone to pranks like jumping nude into a fountain in Rome the previous summer. As Horwitz points out, in the very next scene that follows from a close-up of Lydia in the kitchen, Mitch repeats Lydia's observations about Melanie to her in a manner that suggests his sexual interest, but is accompanied by the increasingly ominous sounds of the birds gathering on the telephone wires against a lowering sky. Mitch casts an alarmed glance in their direction at the end of the sequence.[3]

This Oedipal interpretation is further supported by considering certain formal aspects of the work that link Lydia to the birds. Jessica Tandy's blank stare (fig. 1) cues the transition to scenes that feature birds gathering or attacking at several junctures within the narrative. The stare, together with her taut mouth, craning neck, and occasionally hysterical cries render her birdlike. So too does her hairstyle and costume. Her hair is black flecked with gray. She consistently wears a black-and-white-speckled wool coat (fig. 2), and later in the Brenner house she sports a black-and-white-speckled wool skirt. The relationship between black and white is central to the figuration of the birds and their relationship to the human. The opposition of black and white signifies morality via its association with light and darkness. It is an idea invoked by Daphne du Maurier in her short story from which the film was adapted, where the massing of the birds creates premature night and brings a black winter instead of a white one. While the tendency to think in black and white terms may indicate a faulty adherence to absolutes when what is at stake are finer shades of gray, the commingling of black and white may suggest the breakdown of category distinctions, an incipient chaos or monstrosity.[4] The black and white motif is announced in the credit sequence, as black birds that peck away at the credits flutter against a white background (fig. 3). It is echoed later when a flock of crows attacks the school children against the background of Annie's white-walled, black-roofed schoolhouse, which looms on the horizon like some gigantic gothic birdhouse (figs. 4, 5). It is repeated again when black bird and white bird, crow and seagull, combine in the final assault on the Brenner household and on Melanie, alone in the attic.

However, while such a formal analysis points to a connection between Lydia and the birds, it also reveals the inadequacy of imputing the agency of the birds to Lydia alone. The telling bird-like stare that often signals transitions to scenes featuring the birds is not just attached to Lydia but to Melanie (fig. 6), Annie (fig. 7), Mitch (fig. 8), and to a woman with two small children at the café who functions in the story as Lydia's double.[5] As the film draws to a close and the Brenner family is isolated and entrapped in their homestead under assault from the birds, Mitch, Melanie, and Lydia loom in the foreground of the image in low-angled close-ups that dramatize the angular, avian aspect of human physiognomy (figs. 9, 10, 11). The association between the birds and the human beings in general is reinforced through Hitchcock's deployment of the speckled black and white costume. Melanie dons a specked black and white wool suit in the opening scene of the film, a point to which I shall return (fig. 12). Mitch wears a black-and-white-flecked jacket in the aforementioned scene with Melanie outside the house, and throughout most of the remainder of the movie sports a gray and white flecked jacket, seagull colors (fig. 13). Finally, the woman in the café wears a black-and-white-flecked wool dress, as well as exhibiting the characteristic wide-eyed avian stare (fig. 14). The association that all the main characters bear to the birds in the film does not discount the centrality accorded to Lydia, but an adequate interpretation must consistently account for their role.

As Robin Wood was the first to point out in his unsurpassed interpretation of *The Birds*, the script takes great pains to explain why a Freudian interpretation of the film is inadequate.[6] Why does Lydia Brenner behave the way she does, Annie Hayworth rhetorically asks of Melanie Daniels: "Jealous woman, right? Clinging, possessive mother? Wrong! With all due respect to Oedipus, I don't think that was the case." Lydia, she continues, was "afraid of any woman who would give Mitch the one thing that Lydia can give him—love." Still, Melanie replies, doesn't that amount to a jealous, possessive woman? "No, I don't think so," Annie responds; she is not jealous in the sense that Melanie is implying: "You see, she's not afraid of losing Mitch. She's only afraid of being abandoned." To the extent that Lydia's relationship to Mitch is incipiently incestuous, it is a symptom of the fears she has of repeating the loss that she has already suffered in the death of her husband. Unable to mourn this loss and to relinquish her attachment, Lydia installs Mitch in her husband's place and jealously guards her relationship to him. Lydia cannot release Mitch, nor can Mitch leave, for we surmise that he believes that his presence in the house is indispensable to Lydia's well-being. "He'd just been through a lot with Lydia after his father died," says Annie. "He didn't want to risk going through it all again."

If Annie is to be taken seriously, the deeper significance of the birds' attack lies not in an Oedipal jealousy but in an uncontrolled rage that issues from feelings of isolation and abandonment. The principle agent of this rage is perhaps Lydia, but all the main characters either exhibit anger or have a reason to be angry on account of feelings of emotional isolation. As I have suggested, Lydia's plight is figured by the woman in the café, who, without a husband, struggles to protect her two children in the face of a cruel and hostile world like a mother hen protecting her young (fig. 14).[7] Annie has been abandoned by Mitch, and her subsequent lifestyle as devoted schoolmarm (to Cathy) and companion to Mitch has memorialized this abandonment, while Mitch himself continues to suffer the burden of his mother's sense of helplessness. Melanie knows all too well the pain of attachment and loss, the substitute gratifications it leads to, and the kind of anger it instills. Witness her conversation with Mitch on the hill before the birds attack the children's party:

MELANIE: You see—Rome—that entire summer I did nothing but—it was very easy to get lost there. So when I came back I thought it was time I began finding something again. [Melanie changes the conversation to a myna bird she bought for a straight-laced aunt who will be shocked by the four letter words it has picked up from her niece. Then the conversation continues]

MITCH: You need a mother's care, my child!

MELANIE: Not my mother's!

MITCH: Oh—I'm sorry.

MELANIE: What have you to be sorry about? My mother? Don't waste your time. She ditched us when I was eleven and went off with some hotel man in the East. You know what a mother's love is!

MITCH: Yes, I do.

MELANIE: You mean it's better to be ditched?

MITCH: No, I think it's better to be loved. Don't you ever see her?

MELANIE: I don't know where she is. . . . Well, maybe I ought to go join the *other* children.[8]

If the Freudian interpretation misconstrues the way in which the birds figure human agency, it is also overly narrow in its interpretation of who and what it is the birds are attacking. For while Melanie and her precursor, Annie, can be seen as the object of Lydia's Oedipal rage, this is scarcely true of Cathy and the other children who twice become the target of the birds. Although Melanie undoubtedly visits Bodega Bay in search of a mate—the lovebirds she brings are a gift for Mitch—the deeper significance of her quest lies in the fact that the visit to the Brenner house allows her to establish a relationship with a mother whose hostility she can at once experience and forgive, therefore enabling her to discover her own sense of self-worth. Lydia's problem is that she has a distorted relationship with her children that renders her incapable of the kind of love that allows her to let them go. In the psychotherapeutic narrative of the film, it is Melanie's task to conquer Lydia's fear of abandonment by offering the kind of unconditional love that will release Lydia from this fear and by the same token liberate Mitch to become her mate. If Melanie becomes the object of the birds attack because she is a rival for Mitch's affections, at a deeper level of narrative logic, she becomes the object of attack because she embodies a childlike emotional openness and directness that is so threatening to Lydia (and by extension to everyone who has experienced emotional isolation as a result of narcissistic wounds—humanity as whole). Thus Melanie is at once family therapist and martyr. Melanie bears an intuitive understanding of the kind that Hitchcock generally assigns women in accordance with cultural convention. She also experiences the suffering that accompanies this understanding. In both respects she is aligned with Annie, but Annie's understanding of human isolation is a result of her encounter with the Brenner household and it leaves her embittered. It is Melanie's prior experience of isolation and embitterment that offers her the possibility of personal renewal in the role of "family therapist."

Melanie is closely identified with Lydia's daughter Cathy, who is the same age as Melanie was when her mother died. As Melanie admits to Mitch, she is, emotionally speaking, a child like Cathy. Melanie's friendship with Cathy parallels her relationship to Mitch throughout the film and draws out the deeper meanings in the latter. While the lovebirds are a gift from Melanie to Mitch, they are equally a gift from Melanie to Cathy. Her identification with Cathy resonates in two distinct but related ways. She relates to Cathy as a mother to a child in a way that allows her to repair her own damaged relationship to her own mother. This is threatening to Lydia in a manner that demonstrates why Lydia's rage fails to be explained by Freud's theories. Lydia shows precisely the same resentment towards Melanie's relationship to Cathy as she demonstrates towards Melanie's incipient attachment to Mitch. She reserves a singularly glowering and prolonged bird-like stare for the moment when Cathy innocently bounds up to and embraces Melanie when she realizes that Melanie has, after all, decided to stay for her birthday party (figs. 15, 16). It is as if Lydia, in her bitterness, imputes the worst of ingratiating and self-serving motives to Melanie for her embrace of Cathy, when really she has done nothing wrong. It is just that Melanie responds to Cathy's warmth and spontaneity in precisely the way that Lydia is unable to do.

Melanie also identifies with Cathy as someone who needs recognition and acknowledgment from Lydia in order to secure a precarious identity. If the first manner in which she identifies with Cathy enables her to become the family therapist, it is this second affiliation that renders her so vulnerable. Her link to Cathy is first made explicit in what seems an otherwise strange and baffling moment in the hardware store where Melanie stops to ask directions to the Brenner household. The store is portentously decked out in Hitchcock's warning colors of yellow and red on white that are only intensified within the claustrophobic interior that anticipates the many images of entrapment in the film. Melanie asks what is the name of the Brenner girl and, unsure, the owner of the store turns for confirmation to Harry, who is out back. From a shot of Melanie looking, Hitchcock cuts to a point-of-view shot of the back of the store, a graphic configuration of the colors of danger (figs. 17, 18). Harry, off screen, responds with the wrong name. In this strangely jarring moment, what Melanie stares at, together with the spectator, is a visual array that seems to defiantly look back at her, suggesting that, in looking, she fails to grasp how what it is that occurs at this moment puts her own identity into question. The items cluttered within Melanie' visual field, filling every inch of space, provide a kind of visual correlative to the cluttered massing of the birds later in the film in whom the returned gaze is given a deadly embodiment that literally causes her breakdown.[9]

If there is a psychotherapeutic model of human relationships that underpins the narrative of The Birds, it is not that of Freudian psychoanalysis but a different picture of human motivation put forward in object-relations theory, then current and popularized by Harry Guntrip in his book *Personality Structure and Human Interaction*.[10] I cannot demonstrate here that Evan Hunter, the screenwriter of The Birds, read Guntrip's work, but his recently published journals on collaborating with Hitchcock suggest that he was regularly consulting with a psychologist over the script of Marnie that he was preparing at the same time.[11] But regardless of any proven influence of object relations psychology on Hunter's writing, his screenplays for both *The Birds* and *Marnie* articulate a picture of human motivation that is congruent with it. The stories of both films center upon searching for and sustaining contact with others rather than simply upon the satisfaction of desire. According to object-relations theorists, sexual desire is not the well-spring of human action but just one way that the search for attachment is articulated. The overvaluation of sexual desire that is demonstrated in, for example, Lydia's relationship to Mitch, manifests a distorted form of attachment that issues from a sense of isolation and loss. With its stress on emotional lack and loss of the mother as opposed to sexual desire and its prohibition by the father, object-relations theory is a psychotherapeutic model oriented towards mother-child and especially mother-daughter relationships, since, in traditional role playing, the problem of achieving autonomy from the mother is particularly resonant for little girls.

Critics overlook the significance of object-relations theory for *The Birds* because of the unquestioned authority still accorded by some to Freudian or Lacanian explanation, when what is at stake in the interpretation of a work is not the absolute truth of a given picture of human motivation but how that picture might inform the text being discussed. Also, arguably, there is a failure to take seriously the fact that Hitchcock is such an important film author because he is a successful collaborator, particularly with writers. The script of *The Birds* must be considered alongside Evan Hunter's other writings of the time, such as the script for *Marnie* and his novel, *Buddwing,* where human psychology is portrayed in a manner that has striking affinities with specific features of Guntrip's thought as well as object-relations theory more generally.[12]

I have tried to bring into relief a picture of human relationships that contrasts with the Freudian interpretation of this film, because I believe that it better illuminates the work. However, it would be foolish to dismiss the Freudian themes entirely for they are so obviously present. What, then, is their place? In an interesting departure from her emphasis upon the birds as an expression of Lydia's super-ego, Horwitz argues that the birds are associated, in a much more general way, with female hysteria and destructiveness. The birds, she writes, "are evocative of the mythological 'Harpies' which were depicted as flying creatures, part bird and part woman, armed with hooked beaks and claws. The birds also call to mind 'Furies' which were represented as female 'avenging spirits' who punished moral transgression."[13] This line of argument can be made to square with the Oedipal reading if the birds are seen as a kind of maternal super-ego writ large; this is, I think, the spirit in which Žižek interprets the film. The birds represent the perverse alternative to a patriarchal social order that temporarily failed to sustain itself through the male line.

While at first sight this interpretation remains inconsistent with the idea that there is a connection between Mitch and the birds, Mitch can be considered a man who has been "feminized," who is unconsciously or unwittingly carrying out the desires of his mother. However, the idea of the birds as a universal inscription of a female hysteria is equally consistent with the psychotherapeutic interpretation I have offered here, where the anger arises not so much from the breakdown of the patriarchal line but from a failure to be loved. Since it is women and not men, in Western culture, who bear the responsibility for loving, that is, for fostering emotional connection, women are also responsible for its breakdown. In one interpretation, the birds are expressive of the death-dealing power of an hysterical femininity that requires containment by the pacifying routines and hierarchy of the patriarchal family and social order. In the other, the power of an hysterical femininity to deal death is a consequence of the power of women to compel emotional response and mutual acknowledgment. Thus is generated the unresolved paradox or conundrum that defines *The Birds* and generates the Hitchcockian universe as whole. In *The Birds*, the social world of human interaction, embodied in the microcosm of the American family, is restored by containing feminine agency. Tippi Hedren is literally reduced to a catatonic child-like state. Yet it is feminine agency and the emotional connection it initiates that affords the possibility of the human, social world in the first place.

Thus far, I have focused on the way in which the birds embody the defensive rage that issues from a sense of emotional isolation and abandonment, and manifests an inability to acknowledge the other. But why birds? There are, I think, good reasons that Hitchcock uses birds to figure this rage. When we fail to acknowledge the other, in effect we no longer treat them as human: we act as if they do not have the emotional responses, and so on, that we have. Such a failure to acknowledge the emotional responses of others is constitutive of our own failure to respond emotionally. As Stanley Cavell has understood perhaps better than any other contemporary writer, dehumanization of the other is dehumanization of the self. In this respect the birds are carefully chosen for the role they play in the film, for they are an animal to whom it is hard to ascribe emotional responses, and therefore an animal that epitomizes the dehumanized and unresponsive other that the humans in the film threaten to become on account of their sense of emotional isolation. We ascribe emotions to human beings on the basis of their facial expressions and behavior. It is someone's tone of voice, flushed face, and exaggerated gestures that indicates she is angry. This is not to say that her anger consists in these expressions of anger, since one could be angry without exhibiting it; nonetheless, it is on the basis of this behavior that we understand what anger is.

The application of emotions to animals resides in our capacity to think of animal behavior in terms of human behavior. It is for this reason that we can far more readily respond to a pet Labrador than a cockroach. I do not mean that our ascription of emotion to animals is merely a fiction, nor that it is inherently sentimental (though it is prone to sentimentalization), just that its limits reside in the limits of our capacity to picture animal behavior in terms of human behavior. This is perhaps why Wittgenstein writes that if a lion could talk we could not understand it, for there is nothing that could count in the behavior of lions as something that we recognize as speech. Birds occupy a place of particular interest with respect to the grounds upon which we ascribe emotional predicates to animals, for in comparison to other animals of their size, they are unusually rigid: their feathers appear as a kind of armor, and they entirely lack facial expression. If their beady eyes suggest an inside, it is a hollow interior. This animal, whose emotions are utterly inscrutable, is also one that, at least to the nonspecialist, seems to exhibit a purposiveness without purpose, in its exuberant song, color, and flight. Thus birds seem to combine the absence of emotion with irrational drive and thereby epitomize blind nature in contradistinction to the human, and this makes them ideal figures for those forces that are destructive of human social life.

However, this is not the only role allotted to birds in the film, for we must not forget the love-birds that Melanie brings to the Brenner household, and to which her bird-like attributes are also connected. In the scene in the bird-shop that opens the film, Melanie meets Mitch, who has come to buy a bird, the English slang for a sexually attractive woman, and pretends to be selling them. Her angular posture, the fact that she is framed between bird cages, and her stare all render her bird-like (fig. 12). Mitch is the bird-catcher who shares some of the mannerisms of his quarry. Once Melanie sets out to Bodega Bay, she dons the pale green colors of the love-birds that she brings with her in courtship to Mitch, and this remains her costume for the rest of the film. She is associated with the love birds through their persistent chirping that we hear from off screen while we look at her, and she moves in sync with the love-birds as the car swerves around the bend with a bird-like screech of its brakes. As Lesley Brill established, the sense of artifice and the motif of bird-catching set out in the opening scenes have a decidedly romantic resonance that is made explicit in the love-birds themselves.[14] In the context of the film's preoccupation with the thematics of emotional isolation, Melanie's avian qualities are better understood here less as a sexual instinct—the reductive assumption of a Freudian interpretation—for she is not straightforwardly seductive in the film. They are better understood as manifestations of a "mating instinct," with its connotations of getting attached or getting close to someone. In this sense Melanie's avian qualities represent the very aspects of her character that seem to provoke those other birds, what we might call the death-birds, to attack her.

The qualities the love-birds represent appear at first sight to be antithetical to the qualities of the death-birds. Here, the affinity between the human being and nature appears beneficial to the human. Melanie's mating instinct challenges the emotional distance and sense of isolation that characterize the Brenner household and Lydia in particular. This isolation is inscribed in the location of the house at the edge of Bodega bay and it is emphasized by the way in which Melanie approaches the house across the bay by boat. It is underscored through the use of point-of-view editing that draws attention to relationships of proximity and distance in a manner that has been exhaustively analyzed by Raymond Bellour.[15] Yet, as a love-bird, Melanie is endowed with a decidedly cool and detached persona. Her blonde hair, pale green suit and off-white fur (feathers), painted nails (claws), and silver sports car all connote a coolly, almost glacially undemonstrative character, self-sufficient but emotionally distant. At first sight, she is scarcely the candidate for family therapist and substitute mother. She is the antithesis of the earthy school marm, Annie *Hay-worth*, whom we first encounter tending her gardens. Yet it is precisely Melanie's avian qualities that allow her to counter the figure of the death-bird, the figure of emotional isolation and aggression. For the very qualities of birds that inhibit us from applying emotional predicates to them are precisely the same qualities that provoke or test us to find in them the qualities of mind or emotion they appear to lack. In Hitchcock's avian female, we find a particularly telling figuration of Cavell's idea of the unknown woman, a woman who provokes us into acknowledging her humanity by dint of her self-containment and inscrutability, who provokes recognition through merely existing or being.[16]

Hitchcock's critics would no doubt point out that the image of femininity projected by Melanie Daniels is a decidedly patriarchal one. The equation of Melanie to a bird suggests that her emotions are inscrutable, her actions are irrational, and her purposive purposelessness is at the service of sexuality and reproduction. Yet, as usual in Hitchcock's treatment of gender, there is more than what meets the eye. For by exhibiting femininity as pure "nature," Hitchcock's use of Hedren in *The Birds* (and in *Marnie*) calls into question the naturalization of gender roles as "second nature." Hedren's avian postures represent an abstract, schematized, hyperbolic conception of femininity. Consider the way she purses her lips (as if she is about to give a peck on the cheek) as she plays a mating game with Mitch (fig. 19). Once established, this gesture is reproduced in her relentless smoking that molds her lips in the appropriate avian manner (fig. 20). Note the way in which she cocks her head (fig. 21) just prior to the first bird attack, which ruffles her feathers (fig. 22). Consider, too, the way in which she holds a dressing to the wound she receives on her forehead after the first bird attack in a manner that emphasizes the spindly quality of her arms and her too-feminine, all-too-clawlike finger nails (fig. 23). Once again this gesture is perpetuated through her smoking as she holds her elbow at an acute angle and displays her red claws.

These hyperbolic feminine gestures are of twofold significance. First, Hedren seems to be performing femininity rather than simply being feminine. This performativity of gender is characteristic both of other stars used by Hitchcock, for example the "masculinity" of Cary Grant, and the way Hitchcock uses stars. Hedren in this respect is peculiarly exemplary, for her star persona was one manufactured by Hitchcock himself, who literally put the quotation marks around "Tippi." Secondly, Hedren's performance of femininity is curiously detached from our capacity to ascribe to it a particular sexual object (specifically a heterosexual object). There is a temptation here, of course, to look at her performance in *The Birds* with the hindsight of watching her in *Marnie*, where her performance of femininity coincides with a hostility to men and connotes a desire not simply heterosexual.[17] However, even in *The Birds*, while she couples with Mitch, the triangle she forms with Lydia activates Annie's dormant mating instinct (she starts looking and sounding like Melanie) and eroticizes their encounter, most strikingly when Melanie returns to Annie's house to stay the night. Before Annie opens the door, Melanie preens herself (fig. 24), and Annie, as she opens the door, thrusts her breast forward in a provocative gesture of welcome (fig. 25). The house siding that forms a background to the shot serves to inscribe Hitchcock's characteristic compositional motif of parallel diagonal lines that like the color red characteristically indicates warning, threat, or disturbance in the fictional world.[18]

Melanie's expressions of emotion are so disguised in artifice, play, and the projection of an image, that one might indeed begin to wonder whether her expressions of desire are sincere. It is at this juncture that the line begins to blur between those qualities of Melanie's character that make her a catalyst who breaks down the boundaries of human isolation and those qualities of her character that seem to sustain it. Both the love-birds and death-birds are birds, and whether or not we see Melanie's bird-like behavior as evidence of artifice or authenticity depends very much on our attitude or point of view. Cavell has argued that the cinema provokes this skeptical standpoint by virtue of its realism.[19] I have argued elsewhere that the Bazinian conception of realism that underpins Cavell's argument is indefensible; however, I believe that his argument can be reconstructed from the standpoint of iconicity, rather than indexicality.[20] The realism of cinema lies not in the causal link between image and referent, but in the capacity of cinema to exactly replicate the coordinates of space and time.[21] By virtue of this capacity, cinema can exactly reproduce the repertoire of gestures and expressions that comprise human behavior. A defining characteristic of Hitchcock's cinema is the way that he exploits this feature of the medium to bestow an ethical ambiguity or undecidablity on the events he presents. For example, when Cary Grant coils his arm around Joan Fontaine at the end of *Suspicion* or the lodger kisses his bride at the end of *The Lodger* under the light of the neon sign that has accompanied the murder of the blonde show girls, do we witness an expression of love or the intent to kill? Or is the point that love *is* death? The figure of the birds and the bird-like human allows Hitchcock to weave this ambiguity into his very portrayal of the human.

To return to the opening scene of the movie: if the exchange between Mitch and Melanie suggests a romance and incipient attachment that counters the fear of the other, it does not suggest this unambiguously. It is in retrospect striking that Melanie does not wear the costume of a love-bird in this scene but the costume of a death-bird. In the first shot of the film she is framed on the sidewalk by the bird shop where she meets Mitch and buys the love-birds. A boy scout gives her a wolf whistle, and in the same gesture of returning his glance she turns her head skyward to look at the circling birds that will subsequently attack. The qualities that provoke desire and death cannot be readily discriminated. If her play-acting and banter with Mitch is indicative of romance, it could also connote a contentment with meretricious, superficial forms of human interaction that, as Wood points out, sustain human isolation.[22] Is this form of behavior a symptom of Melanie (and Mitch's) self-isolation or the road to a cure?

Other scenes only support our doubt. The rather sharp banter between Mitch and Melanie after her second visit to the Brenner house is accompanied by the screeching of the birds in a manner that suggests not simply the intrusion of Lydia's specter into the burgeoning love affair, but a destructive rather than a reparative aspect of the romance that is in some sense, constitutive of it. As Melanie swoops down to Bodega Bay in her sports car, she is not simply, it seems, a love-bird, but a bird of prey whose mechanical cry is heard in the screech of the car brakes that anticipate the squawking of the death-birds.[23] Consider, too, the shot in which Melanie purses her lips in pursuit of Mitch (fig. 19). As she ducks down coquettishly on the right of the screen, giving all the appearance of a love-bird, dominating screen left is the gigantic black head of the boat engine. Without any marks that identify the object as an engine it looks like a great blot or stain in the visual field that functions as an abstract figure of death, of the death-bird. Is this inert, obscene object the love-bird stripped of her appearance and agency? This oval black object is an exemplary instance of what Žižek has called the Hitchcockian Blot, an arbitrary element within the visual field that denatures what we see and draws us into Hitchcock's realm of supplementary, ironic, and deathly meanings.[24]

The bleak conclusion to be drawn from *The Birds* is that the monstrous in human nature is not something that is produced by, say, bad mothering that instinctive or natural forms of behavior can repair (as the therapeutic discourse of the film might suggest), but that it is impossible to distinguish the good nature from bad, authentic human behavior from the monstrous. This conclusion receives strong support in the way Hitchcock draws an analogy between children and the death-birds. In the therapeutic narrative of the film, children, as I have already suggested, embody the innocence and emotional openness that is threatening to the emotionally isolated adult, and runs counter to forces of destruction and death. However, in certain scenes the children are connected to the death-birds in a manner that suggests a humanity that is corrupted at its source. It is, after all, a school-house that doubles as the gigantic gothic bird-house from which the birds appear to emerge to attack the children and the parallel between the death-birds and the children is reinforced in several ways. The death-birds mass on the jungle gym, birds and children alike swarm, *en masse,* out of the gothic structure. The sounds of flapping wings resonate with the sounds of the children's stampede, and the screeching of the birds bleeds into the screams of the children. These are images of pure chaos that suggest, at least for their duration, that the human and the death-bird are each other's mirror image. The human is in perpetual, panicked flight from the other; the bird exhibits the relentless, indiscriminate fury of the other, but the flight and the fury it unleashes are ultimately one and the same.

It is in this context we can better understand the ironic, demonic quality to the depiction of Annie Hayworth, who as keeper of the school house is therefore also mother to the death-birds. Hitchcock inscribes Annie's demonic aspect quite masterfully in the image of her looking out after Melanie who has just departed (fig. 7). In terms of the narrative this image is quite insignificant, a throwaway, but it also carries an extraordinary symbolic weight. Although Annie nominally looks at Melanie, the image is held long enough for her gaze to seem like a blank stare, a stare that denies its object, the stare of the death-bird whose black-and-white-speckled costume she also wears, her black plumage blowing in the wind. The red sweater has an earthy quality to its texture and color that, together with the white picket fence and its climbing plant, links Annie to the garden and benign nature. However, in a context where the red sweater is juxtaposed with the bright red letter box that dominates the image against a white background, it becomes associated with threat and danger. Furthermore, the vertical lines of the white picket fence are graphically connected to the fence on the right of the character that inscribes Hitchcock's signature parallel diagonal lines motif. Trivially, the threat posed by Annie is to Melanie, for she is a rival to Mitch, but it has a universal resonance. The universality of the image is suggested in the background that picks up the black and white motif and juxtaposes the square gothic schoolhouse with the pointed spire of the church. Annie Hayworth, earth mother and figure of redemption, could also be the most monstrous, if to be human is to be like the death-bird.

In *The Birds* Hitchcock poses something of a double-bind. The hierarchy between human and natural orders that the birds threaten by their attacks can be restored only by separating out human and bird-like qualities, yet the positive qualities of romance and renewal embodied in the character of Melanie that are the source of such fascination and pleasure in the narrative depend on blurring the lines between the avian and the human. Brill has shown the way in which the trajectory of outsider status followed by personal renewal that results in social reintegration is a standard feature of romance narratives to which Hitchcock's films conform. However, in Hitchcock's films the kind of qualities of character that compel fascination are precisely qualities that cannot readily be squared with the reestablishment of convention other than ironically or at a cost. In *The Birds* the social order can be restored only if Melanie can be stripped of her otherness or bird-like qualities, and this happens in her final "rape" by the birds. Yet in losing her "bird-like" qualities, Melanie is threatened with the loss of precisely those qualities that define her. Stripped of her "nature" she loses her human identity as well.

In Hitchcock's later work, difference or "queerness" and conservatism are increasingly difficult to reconcile; the therapy required has the destructive and self-defeating force of violence. Mitch, a lawyer, cuts a very square and conventional figure in *The Birds* that is at odds with Melanie's wild nature, and she is finally tamed only by being reduced to a catatonic state. In this respect, *The Birds* anticipates the impossible romance of *Marnie*, where Mark Rutland (Sean Connery) is attracted to a woman whose identity, founded upon her hostility to men, must be destroyed for her relationship with Mark to be possible.

Yet here I wish to insist on the redemptive as opposed to the ironic aspect of *The Birds*, a quality that can be brought out by briefly comparing the film to Hitchcock's previous work to which it owes a great deal: *Psycho*. As a figuration of the monstrous within the human, *The Birds* rearticulates a complex analogy between bird and human that already exists in *Psycho* and is announced in the opening sequence of that film. Over the bird's-eye view of a city we read "Phoenix, Arizona." Shots of an hotel room where Marion (Janet Leigh) and Sam (John Gavin) are making love evoke the point of view of a bird who glides down, alights on the window ledge, and slips into the room. We spy on a pair of love-birds: Marion *Crane* and Sam *Loomis* (i.e., "is a diving bird").[25] Perched on the edge of the bed, they lean forward to kiss by craning their necks (fig. 26). Janet Leigh's prominent white (bra-covered) breast is thrust forward during their lovemaking in a manner that is echoed in the posture of Annie Hayworth when she greets Melanie Daniels in *The Birds* (fig. 25).

In contrast to the figure of the love-birds and the possibility they represent of mating and procreation lies the figure of the stuffed bird and the activity of stuffing birds in *Psycho*. Stuffing birds is the hobby of Norman Bates, the queerest character in Hitchcock's work. The activity of stuffing birds objectifies the absence of the inner that, as we have already seen, characterizes the figure of the bird. Norman, the bird-philosopher, well understands this. "I don't really know anything about birds," he tells Marion, referring explicitly to the habits of feathered animals and implicitly to women:

> My hobby is stuffing things. You know, taxidermy. I guess I'd just rather stuff birds because I hate the look of beasts when they're stuffed. You know, foxes and chimps. Some people even stuff dogs and cats but, oh, I can't do that. I think only birds look well stuffed, well, because they're kind of passive to begin with.

But Norman's hobby is far from innocent: his supreme creation is the stuffed bird he keeps in the attic, his mummy. This "stuffed bird" was created by the act of "stuffing a bird" in the sense that combines both a sexual act—the implied incest between Norman and his mother—and the act of killing. The monstrous figure of Norman's mummy is condemned endlessly to repeat this act.[26] Animated by Norman, Norman's mummy swoops down from the gigantic gothic birdhouse/fortress, endowed with a predatory agency of a singularly destructive kind. Accompanied by the bird-like screech of Bernard Herrmann's violins, Norman's mummy devours Marion in an act of sexual frenzy that is visually inscribed in the beak-like stabbing of the kitchen knife (fig. 27). Marion Crane ends up slumped like a bird with a broken neck on the bathroom floor, her blank, wide-eyed avian stare, the stare of death (fig. 28). The figure of Norman's mummy anticipates a defining creature of modern horror: the figure of the "living dead" that contains, within an emotionally numb exterior, an insatiable appetite for destroying the human.

In *Psycho*, as in *The Birds*, the human as love-bird is confronted with the human as death-bird, but the ambiguity that is thereby accorded the metaphor of human as bird receives a negative resolution in *Psycho*: there is no possibility of redemption through love. The opening scenes of the film unequivocally endow the activity of love-making with a sense of lack, alienation, and sordidness that prompts Marion into the act of stealing that leads her to the Bates Motel. When Marion arrives there and Norman invites her for a modest meal in his "parlor," the situation invokes a mating ritual, somewhere between a "call" and a "date." "You eat like a bird" remarks Norman, captivated, as Marion pecks at a piece of bread held deftly between her fingers (fig. 29). But Marion has no interest in Norman. Her avian qualities bespeak an emotional detachment that seems to justify Norman's reaction to her half-hearted attempt at therapy: "People always mean well. They cluck their thick tongues and shake their heads and suggest, oh so very delicately." In any case, Marion is too late to rescue Norman from his mother, for his own avian qualities betray his colonization by a predatory maternal super-ego. His wide eagle-eyed stare beneath the looming figures of the stuffed owl and raven is too intense for comfort (fig. 30). The earlier scene of lovemaking between Sam Loomis and Marion Crane is ironically echoed in the "perverse" scene of desire that immediately precedes Marion's murder, where Norman spies upon Marion, now clad in a black bra, through a peephole (figs. 31, 32). Furthermore, Hitchcock's camera, initially identified with the love-bird, now comes to occupy the gaze of the death-bird in a series of high-angled shots that accompany the murder of Marion Crane in the shower and when it rises to the position that would be occupied by one of Norman's stuffed birds as Norman's mummy swoops down to murder Arbogast on the landing of the gothic staircase.[27]

FIGURE 1

FIGURE 2

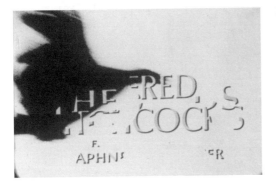

FIGURE 3

FIGURE 4

FIGURE 5

FIGURE 6

FIGURE 7

FIGURE 8

FIGURE 9

FIGURE 10

FIGURE 11

FIGURE 12

FIGURE 13

FIGURE 14

FIGURE 15

FIGURE 16

FIGURE 17

FIGURE 18

FIGURE 19

FIGURE 20

FIGURE 21

FIGURE 22

FIGURE 23

FIGURE 24

FIGURE 25

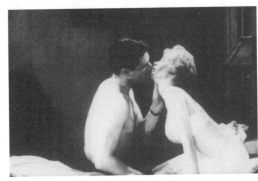

FIGURE 26

FIGURE 27

FIGURE 28

FIGURE 29

FIGURE 30

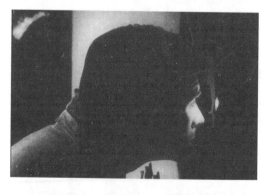

FIGURE 31

FIGURE 32

FIGURE 33

FIGURE 34

"We're all in our private traps. Clamped in them," Norman tells us, "And none of us can ever get out. We scratch and claw, but only at the air, only at each other. And for all of it, we never budge an inch." Norman's vision of the human condition where mutual acknowledgment and recognition of the other is impossible is realized in the images of human entrapment in *The Birds*, most notably in the shot at the end of the film where Melanie, psychologically scarred from her ordeal in the attic, claws helplessly at the air, at Mitch, and at the camera/spectator (fig. 33). However, in *The Birds*, in contrast to *Psycho*, the force that creates the condition of human isolation and entrapment is externalized in the figure of the birds; it is detached from human agency, even as it is metaphorically linked to it. While various characters in *The Birds*, and Lydia most of all, exhibit emotional numbness and are deemed to be like birds, no one manifests Norman's assimilation of avian identity. Also in *The Birds* in contrast to *Psycho*, the "death-bird" is not simply a figuration of the maternal super-ego or death-dealing femininity; the rage expressed by the birds is not reducible to Oedipal jealousy. As a consequence, *The Birds* affords a space for the redemptive aspects of femininity and for the benign aspects of human nature that are absent in *Psycho*. Whereas in *The Birds*, melodrama and horror, redemptive femininity and corrupting femininity are held in balance, in *Psycho* melodrama simply cedes to horror: the patriarchal social order undergoes catastrophic breakdown, and the restoration of the family is impossible. As a horror film, *The Birds*, like *Psycho*, evokes a human nature poisoned at its source to which Melanie, like Marion, is sacrificed. However, in the melodrama of *The Birds*, *Psycho*'s catastrophic Oedipal logic is checked by the redemptive, therapeutic narrative of the mother-daughter relationship; Melanie, as family therapist, uses her intuition, her contact with nature, to redeem the Brenner family from emotional isolation.

The final assault of the birds is vicious in the extreme and suggests the sexual frenzy of a rape in keeping with the Oedipal interpretation of the film, but the scene also marks the culmination of the psychotherapeutic narrative of *The Birds*. Symbolically substituting herself for Cathy, Melanie goes to Cathy's room upstairs, where she exposes herself to an attack of the birds, for there is a large hole in the roof. Melanie is retrieved from the room by Mitch as if brought down from the cross, and her sacrifice finally yields Lydia's look of acknowledgment as she nestles Melanie in a maternal embrace. Melanie's reciprocating smile, while tentative, does suggest that she is not completely lost to the world. By leaving their home, the embattled Brenner family undoubtedly expose themselves to further attack. Yet it is precisely because they abandon their isolated, fortress-like homestead and leave in Melanie's car, thereby rendering themselves vulnerable, that Lydia and hence Mitch open themselves to the possibility of acknowledging the other and overcoming their emotional isolation. Although the birds cackle and deliver a peck or two, their anger has abated. Blackbirds and seagulls, all mixed together in the final feverish attack on Melanie, have sorted themselves out somewhat (although not completely) into groups of black and white—suggesting at least the possibility of a newly constituted equilibrium that mirrors the tentative equilibrium of a new family, a new civilization, heralded by the dawn (fig. 34).

NOTES

1. Margaret Horwitz, "*The Birds:* A Mother's Love," in *A Hitchcock Reader*, ed. Marshall Deutelbaum and Leland Poague (Ames: Iowa State University Press, 1986), 281.

2. Slavoj Žižek, *Looking Awry: An Introduction to Jacques Lacan through Popular Culture* (Cambridge: MIT Press, 1992), 99.

3. Horwitz, "*The Birds:* A Mother's Love," 282.

4. The commingling of black and white can be understood as a universal, formal rendition of the conflation of logical categories that Noël Carroll finds to a central feature of the monstrous. See *The Philosophy of Horror or Paradoxes of the Heart* (New York: Routledge, 1991), 32.

5. Horwitz, to her credit, notes that the motivating stare is shared by all the characters, but she does not explain how this fact squares with her singular identification of the bird attacks with Lydia's maternal super-ego ("*The Birds:* A Mother's Love," 282).

6. See Robin Wood, *Hitchcock's Films Revisited* (New York: Columbia University Press, 1989), 152. My understanding of *The Birds* is indebted to Wood's interpretation, together with that of Donald Spoto, in *The Art of Alfred Hitchcock* (New York: Doubleday, 1976), 329–38.

7. This metaphor is noted by Horwitz, "*The Birds:* A Mother's Love," 284.

8. Donald Spoto discusses the importance of this dialogue in *The Dark Side of Genius: The Life of Alfred Hitchcock* (New York: Ballantine Books, 1983), 489–90.

9. It is, of course, Žižek who, via Lacan, has enabled us to understand the role of the returned gaze in Hitchcock's work.

10. Harry Guntrip, *Personality Structure and Human Interaction* (New York: International Universities Press, 1961).

11. Evan Hunter, "Me and Hitch," *Sight and Sound* 7, no. 6 (June 1997), 33.

12. Guntrip's own rather reductive contribution to object-relations theory is centered on the concept of the "regressed ego." This is a state of isolation and helplessness caused by bad mothering that expresses itself in a flight from genuine attachments and the establishment of conflictual and masochistic relationships with others as a defense against regression. When flight is paramount, the subject longs for death; where hope is fostered by the analyst/parent, the patient seeks a return to the womb and re-birth of a restored self. These ideas are less evident in *The Birds* but are clearly central to *Marnie*, whose heroine is in perpetual flight from an emotionally neglectful mother figure.

13. Horwitz, "*The Birds:* A Mother's Love," 282.

14. Brill does not discuss *The Birds* in detail in *The Hitchcock Romance* (Princeton: Princeton University Press, 1988).

15. See Raymond Bellour, *L'analyse du Film* (Paris: Editions de l'Albatros, 1979), 105.

16. Cavell's thoughts on the unknown woman are to be found in *Contesting Tears: The Hollywood Melodrama of the Unknown Woman* (Chicago; University of Chicago Press, 1996).

17. On queerness in *Marnie,* see Lucretia Knapp, "The Queer Voice in *Marnie,*" in Corey K. Creekmur and Alexander Doty, eds., *Out in Culture: Gay, Lesbian and Queer Essays on Popular Culture* (Durham: Duke University Press, 1995), 262–81. See also the other essays on queerness in Hitchcock in the same volume.

18. William Rothman, who was the first to draw attention to this motif, suggests other meanings that may be attached to it in *Hitchcock—The Murderous Gaze* (Cambridge: Harvard University Press, 1982), 33.

19. See Stanley Cavell, *The World Viewed: Reflections on the Ontology of Film* (Cambridge: Harvard University Press, 1979), 16–29. Stephen Mulhall provides an excellent gloss on Cavell's argument in *Stanley Cavell: Philosophy's Recounting of the Ordinary* (Oxford: Clarendon Press, 1994), 223–36.

20. My argument against the Bazin-Cavell line on realism is in "Looking at Motion Pictures," in Richard Allen and Murray Smith, eds., *Film Theory and Philosophy* (Oxford: Clarendon Press, 1997), 76–93.

21. See Gregory Currie, *Image and Mind: Film, Philosophy and Cognitive Science* (New York: Cambridge University Press, 1995), 79–112.

22. Wood, *Hitchcock's Films Revisited,* 155.

23. The aural association established between bird, human, and machine is analyzed by Elizabeth Weiss in *The Silent Scream* (London: Associated University Presses, 1982), 143–45.

24. See Žižek, *Looking Awry,* 88–106.

25. According to the *OED*, an obsolete meaning of "loom" is "penis."

26. Rothman makes related observations in *Hitchcock—The Murderous Gaze,* 335.

27. For further discussion of this sequence see Rothman, *Hitchcock—The Murderous Gaze,* 316.

There is no body in the family plot.
—Advertising slogan for *Family Plot*, 1976

ALFRED HITCHCOCK: REGISTRAR OF BIRTHS AND DEATHS

DAVID STERRITT

Throughout his career, the Master of Suspense was a Master of Ambiguity as well, in everything from narrative development to nuances of montage and *mise-en-scène*. Alfred Hitchcock had a clear distaste for self-enclosed discursive systems, and took a carnivalesque pleasure in disrupting traditional notions of what constitutes "correct" content and "proper" procedure in creating a cinematic text. This tendency marks the structures and stories of most of his major films, shining most brightly through deliberately transgressive works like *Rope* and *Psycho*. It also underlies the themes and subtexts he favored most. The celebrated "transference of guilt" and "knowledge equals danger" motifs, for instance, are ways of particularizing his disdain for rigid demarcations of innocence and culpability, power and vulnerability, good and evil. More to his liking are the shades of philosophical gray that signal ambivalence, interdeterminacy, and the paradoxicality he finds at the root of social and individual experience.

Hitchcock's last completed work, *Family Plot*, takes his characteristic ambiguity to extremes that are all the more surprising, given the tone of mild whimsy that typifies much of the movie's atmosphere. Even its title is multi-valent, suggesting several meanings, as Donald Spoto has observed.[1] While the film's profound ambivalence is partly the culmination of a set of dis-cursive positions Hitchcock had been refining for decades, it may also re-flect biographical factors, particularly as he found himself in the unique (for him) position of filming a death-related story while nearing the end of his own life. Slavoj Žižek notes that in his *Family Plot* cameo, Hitch-cock appears "as a shadow on the windowpane of the registry office, as if wishing to inform us that he is already close to death."[2] True, he was not on the way out just yet—he worked conscientiously, if fretfully at times, on both the planning and execution of the picture. Still, his physical and emotional capabilities swung drastically up and down during the process, and contemporaneous accounts portray him as edgy, irascible, and "more ambivalent about making this, his fifty-third feature film, than about any picture in years."[3] Although he still had a few years to live, he appears to have felt dispirited and disempowered by his clearly worsening health. While this situation might have weighed down a lesser artist's work, however, it may have deepened Hitchcock's accomplishment as he poured his fears, hopes, and uncertainties into detailed instructions on everything from dialogue to camera angles during the bursts of enthusiasm that intermittently energized his creativity. If a single formulation can sum up his impulses as he assem-bled the film with screenwriter Ernest Lehman and other collaborators, one might say he was searching for loopholes in the human condition—hitherto unnoticed signs pointing toward renewal and regeneration rather than fi-nality and closure. While the movie's cemetery represents a "dead end . . . dead and buried" for the George Lumley character, Hitchcock identifies with the Mrs. Mulroney figure, who barges into the story for a few vivid moments, crying, "Fake! Fake!" as she lustily kicks a bogus gravestone. As the strictest of all boundary lines between existential realms, death became a prime target for an artist who disliked determinacy to his bones—especially when this particular kind of determinacy was looming in his own imminent future.

This essay will employ biographical information about Hitchcock along with ideas from intertextual theory, Michel Chion's theorization of cine-matic sound, and Žižek's contribution to Lacanian psychoanalysis. Its goal is to suggest that Hitchcock's investment in religious thinking has a value in Hitchcockian hermeneutics far beyond its usual limited role in expli-cating religiously inclined films—like *I Confess* and *The Wrong Man*—and analyzing thematic concerns like guilt, confession, and what Eric Rohmer and Claude Chabrol call "a taint which contaminates the soul and then the body"⁴—a phrase that itself calls attention to Hitchcock's blurring of boundaries between material and spiritual realms.

One sign of Hitchcock's resistance to closure during the *Family Plot* period is the film's extraordinary wealth of allusions to a wide range of works from his earlier career. Such intertextuality surfaced in his work before *Family Plot*—there are many references to other Hitchcock films in *Marnie*, for instance—but here it acquires unprecedented force and frequency. Some allusions are fairly obvious, as when Lumley and Blanche Tyler have a wild automobile ride as darkly comical as Roger Thornhill's in *North by Northwest*; or when Lumley identifies himself as a lawyer with the (phony) firm of Ferguson, Ferguson, and McBride, recalling John "Scottie" Ferguson of *Vertigo*, who pursues an investigation with some resemblances to Lumley's own. Others are more ephemeral, as when Mulroney insists he's not a "sponger," a key word in *Blackmail*; or when *The Birds* is evoked by a hastily noted license-plate number and a dangerously lit match near a gasoline pump. An important allusion echoes *Shadow of a Doubt*, where a villain also receives an utterly misguided funeral oration. And a noteworthy number of references point directly to *Psycho*, perhaps the most self-consciously cyclical Hitchcock movie. Arthur Adamson waits for Frances near a street plainly identified as Bates Avenue; a tombstone reading "Mother" marks the foreground at the start of the big cemetery scene; the entire story is set in motion by a woman (the Rainbird dowager whose spirit Blanche claims to communicate with) exerting her influence from beyond the grave; there's a close-up of a toilet that recalls a key shot preceding Marion's death; and Lumley's search for Blanche recalls Lila's search for Marion in the Bates home, which also culminates in a small, dark chamber in the bowels of the house.

Such moments are an appropriate tool for Hitchcock's cultivation of ambiguity, since, like all intertextual references, they show how hazy the dividing lines must always be between related textual systems. More specifically, numerous Hitchcock movies from *The 39 Steps* and *The Lady Vanishes* to *Spellbound* and *Marnie* attest his belief that memory can defend against the future by reconjuring the past. It should not be surprising that the filmmaker's self-referential circuits worked overtime as he prepared his last picture knowing his powers were weakening in ways not likely to be reversed. Anecdotal evidence bears out the notion of a Hitchcockian flight into memory: Lehman told me in the late 1970s that his working sessions on *Family Plot* were so full of good-old-days storytelling by the director that getting down to business was often hard to do. Once again, though, the film marks this area with ambivalence. The first words we hear from Blanche's familiar spirit, Henry, are: "Too many memories, too much pain, too much sorrow."

Just as Hitchcock toys with the lines dividing supposedly separate texts in *Family Plot*, he takes a more complicated pleasure in muddling and partially erasing the boundaries between different identities, on the individual level of personality and the group level of gender. Notions of discrete, coherent personality are challenged largely through Hitchcock's characteristic use of performance as a narrative strategy and a thematic trope. Blanche begins the movie with her impersonation of a psychic in touch with the spirit world. Soon afterward we see dark, average-height Fran portray a tall, blond woman in the first kidnaping scene. Lumley is an actor pretending to be a cab driver. Adamson has been an imposter throughout his adult life, hiding his past as psychopathic Eddie Shoebridge by posing as Arthur the respectable jewel merchant.

Nor are these "performances" cleanly separable from the "real" persons who execute them. Blanche the "fake" medium may have "actual" psychic powers, as the movie's last scene ambiguously suggests; Adamson remains a habitual criminal in his new life; and Lumley earns his living as a cab driver even as he claims to be merely impersonating one. These personality confusions are compounded by gender confusions—some involving men, as when Lumley emerges from the car crash with Blanche's purse on his arm, but most centered on the ambiguously named Frances, whose first appearance is marked by much palaver about how sure the police were their kidnapper would be a male. And throughout all this, guilt and innocence are scrambled with Hitchcock's usual abandon. All four major characters are frauds accepted by the world as respectable persons; Fran and Adamson treat their kidnap victims with nurturing care; for all their perfidy, Lumley and Blanche seek only reward money and not the inheritance nor the diamonds that cross their path; even the murderous Mulroney has done enough good in his life to elicit the glowing eulogy spoken at his funeral; and the movie never clarifies his wife's role in the near-murder that leads to his demise.

Most powerful and poignant of the *Family Plot* ambiguities, however, are those that cut close to the intimations of mortality that burdened Hitchcock during this late phase of his life, inducing the mixture of confidence and melancholy that appears to have characterized his thoughts and moods. Many moments in Hitchcock's films take notice of religion in one way or another, from the climaxes of *The Lodger* and *The Wrong Man* to lighter gestures like the Tabernacle of the Sun scene in *The Man Who Knew Too Much* (1934) and the repeated resurrections in *The Trouble With Harry*, for just a few examples. But these moments are woven into narratives that deal, at least ostensibly, with very different subjects. Leaving aside the churchy

I Confess, there may be no Hitchcock film more replete than *Family Plot* with religious references and allusions to Christian imagery and language. This aspect of the movie—often decked with irreverence, but imposing nonetheless—is another sign of the resistance to closure that always typified Hitchcock, here shaped by the preoccupation with final things that makes this film unique. While commentary on Hitchcock has generally used his Roman Catholic background to explicate his fascination with earthly guilt, sin, and redemption, his vague but lingering religious notions also relate to fantasies of an afterlife that bound and rebound through his last film. "One never knows the ending," Spoto quotes him as saying not long before his death. "One has to die to know exactly what happens after death, although"—he added in a phrase as significant as it is revealing—"Catholics have their hopes."[5]

The story of *Family Plot* is launched by a character's claims of communication with the spirit world, signaling the movie's interest in blurring the most daunting of all boundaries confronting Hitchcock at this time—that between life and the facts of materiality on one hand, death and the possibilities of spirituality on the other. Although the character herself is (probably) a fake possessing no real entrée to the spirit realm, the film uses her appropriation of spiritualistic speech as the starting point for its own inquiries into the possible permeability of the line dividing earthly existence from whatever its alternatives may be. At once tentative in their philosophical tone, naive in their psychological transparency, and resonant in their aesthetic force, these queries reveal a Hitchcock more vulnerable and less guarded than usual.

This said, however, it's important to note that Hitchcock had long seen earthly existence in richly ambivalent terms— inextricably chained to the brute fact of materiality with all its imperfection, limitation, and decay, yet affording a measure of freedom and transcendence to those with sufficient resources of imagination, audacity, and mental energy. This does not imply much optimism in the habitually sardonic filmmaker, since such transcendence can take chilling, even horrifying forms—one thinks of the pyrrhic triumphs over reality achieved by Norman Bates and Rose Balestrero near the endings of *Psycho* and *The Wrong Man*, respectively. And even in more benign manifestations it may carry a disturbing sense of the uncanny, as when Scottie Ferguson makes his ghostly way through an increasingly derealized urban landscape. Still, the world for Hitchcock is not merely the vale of violence, treachery, and tears that his lifelong obsession with the thriller genre might suggest. Rather, the human condition is a deeply dialectical affair, equally invested in the mud below and the heavens above, forever hurtling toward death yet never quite stripped of hopes for regeneration and rebirth. William Rothman sees this paradoxical embrace of deadness and its opposite as an integral aspect of cinema itself—its images are "immortal" and "always already dead" at the same time—and uses the oxymoronic label "death-in-life" to describe the ultimate state of such characters as the Lodger, the vampire-like Uncle Charlie in *Shadow of a Doubt,* and of course Norman Bates in his final madness.[6] *Family Plot* deals with death-in-life from its first moment—a dialogue with the dead conducted by a most vivacious psychic—and goes on to build a narrative world in which brute facts of reality are consistently challenged by less rigorous alternatives.

The film's tentative rapprochement of matter and spirit is indicated near the beginning by two mentions of "crystal balls," referring not to the familiar tool of Blanche's trade but to Lumley's masculine anatomy. This reference plants *Family Plot* in territory that Mikhail Bakhtin would identify as ripely carnivalesque—full of laughter, affectionate regard for what he called the "material bodily lower stratum,"[7] and a richly ambiguous attitude toward the dialogic relationship between the metaphysical/aesthetic (crystal) and the physical/biological (balls). Hitchcock's love of Rabelaisian humor was a key component of his life and work, and it seems hardly to have dimmed in the *Family Plot* period. Faced with indecision over the film's title, for instance, he remarked at one point, "It will be called Alfred Hitchcock's 'Something'—perhaps Hitchcock's 'Wet Drawers.'"[8]

The movie's dialogic structure is inscribed more deeply in its major characters: two couples loosely identifiable as the dark pair (Adamson and Fran, both dark-haired and capable of dark, violent acts) and the light pair (Lumley and the aptly named Blanche, a blond whose dishonesty does no real harm). In typical Hitchcock fashion, neither couple seems wholly good or wholly evil. Not so typical are some of the means by which Hitchcock indicates their moral liminality. Fran, for instance, is a kidnapper and accomplice to a killer, yet she keeps her victims warm and comfortable in a womb-like room, nourishing them with food so carefully prepared they can't help commenting on it. Adamson is less ambiguous in his badness, yet the name he's chosen for himself—the son of Adam, hence an Everyman if ever there was one—suggests that his sins are natural parts of the (fallen) world in which we live. Lumley seems like a nice fellow, but his complicity with Blanche's con operation reveals an unscrupulous side to his persona.

Most interesting is Blanche, steadily associated with the film's most ethereal possibilities. It's she who responds to Lumley's expletive "Christ!" with a "Christ" of her own, then a request that he "stop blaspheming"—an unexpectedly heavy word, in this whimsical scene, conveying the suggestion that Hitchcock isn't kidding just now. This bit of business indicates that *Family Plot* will go beyond diffuse allusions to the otherworldly, taking pointedly Christian material as part of its natural territory. The film becomes charged with Christian references and iconography as it proceeds, reaching one high point during the abduction of a bishop in his own cathedral, depicted in a way that again conveys Hitchcock's deeply mixed feelings about both conventional religion and the afterlife to which it may or may not hold a key. The camera photographs the cathedral reverently, unveiling its majestic height with the sort of respectful care that *Blackmail* bestowed on the British Museum years earlier. Yet what takes place within the building is a travesty of church activity, with the godly master of ceremonies kidnaped before the eyes of a confounded flock that's too "religiously polite," in Adamson's words, to interfere or even comprehend what they're witnessing. The ambivalence here—respect and disrespect in a single narrative sequence—recalls Blanche's combined repetition and refutation of Lumley's mild blasphemy. Such moments might be explained as simple ironies on Hitchcock's part, but other scenes offer Christian allusions that don't contain their own contradictions—the presence of a crucifix in the stonemason's cemetery office, for instance, or the distinctly cruciform posture into which Blanche's body slumps when Adamson immobilizes her in preparation for her murder. While these are fleeting images, they are constructed with obvious care, making it hard for the film's mystical subtext to pass unnoticed.

What is most striking in these moments is not only the mystical allusion itself, however, but the copresence of a forcefully material element that restores the symmetry between physics and metaphysics, sustaining the ontological and epistemological ambivalence that Hitchcock so highly valued. The kidnaping in church would be mere farce if the cathedral had not been introduced with such visual majesty, just as the doping of Blanche would be mere melodrama if her body did not momentarily slouch into its symbolic shape. By the same token, the film could be seen as a heedless flight into Christian daydreaming if its religious signifiers weren't so finely balanced by earthbound elements.

The contrapuntal play of body and spirit reaches one of its most refined (and carnivalesque) expressions during the near-deadly automobile ride that provides one of the film's most exuberant set pieces. The scene immediately before this takes place in a tavern, where Lumley and Blanche await their rendezvous with Mulroney, not knowing he is murderously sabotaging their car at that very moment. Hitchcock here indulges his taste for

Rabelaisian humor again, but his vulgarity is far from gratuitous. Serving a round of beers to her time-killing customers, the waitress stands so that her ample backside almost fills the screen, nearly obscuring our view of the main characters. This evocation of the lower body is reinforced by a sign reading "Girls" on a restroom door just behind Lumley and Blanche. The two swill their beers for a while, then give up on Mulroney and head for their car—from which a close-up shows brake fluid leaking, in an amusing displacement of a bodily function one readily associates with beer-drinking and restrooms.

This blatant visual pun is typical of Hitchcock's humor—Hitchcock's "Wet Drawers" might have been a great title, after all—and in a different film it might have stood alone as a momentary joke. But in *Family Plot* it serves a deeper purpose, establishing the first portion of a body-spirit equation whose second (transcendent) portion follows immediately. Caught in the deathtrap Mulroney has made of their car, Lumley and Blanche careen down a winding road at ever-increasing speed, Blanche's limbs flailing so crazily that Lumley can barely see the road, much less control the steering wheel. Finally leaving the roadway and skittering along the adjacent hillside, the car crashes through a cross-shaped signpost before veering up a slope and flopping onto its side—whereupon the ride meant to kill the characters leads instead to their rebirth. This is pictured with striking clarity as Blanche climbs arduously out the top of the womb-like auto—a foot mashing her companion's face into the scrunched-up shape of a baby fresh from the birth canal—followed by Lumley, who lumbers from the bottom.

This portion of *Family Plot* thus anchors itself solidly in the material world—by equating human bodies with leaking, dangerous machines—then flies into a realm of symbolic transcendence complete with a Christian cross and a metaphorical rebirth. Then, connecting these contrasting tropes, it inflicts a symmetrical death on Mulroney by causing his own car to crash in flames—whereupon a teenage onlooker materializes from nowhere and squeals to his friends, "Let's get the hell out of here," underscoring the Biblical provenance of the fiery image. A little later, at Mulroney's funeral, his widow remarks that the phoenix-like Eddie Shoebridge "went up in smoke twenty-five years ago and came down in the city"—linking the destructive smoke of Mulroney's death with the creative smoke of Shoebridge's transformation. This cyclical pattern recalls the phoenix-like trajectory of *Psycho,* another film in which life, death, birth, and burial depart from their accustomed order with unsettling regularity.

Another marker of ambivalence in *Family Plot* is Hitchcock's treatment of sight and sound in the film and in the lives of its characters. It's likely that every Hitchcockian pundit has commented on the importance of seeing within his films, and visual operations play their usual strong role in *Family Plot*. Also typical is Hitchcock's treatment of sight as an invaluable aid in negotiating the business of life (consider Adamson assessing his jewels, or the crystalline clarity of the cemetery scene) and also as a duplicitous deceiver that shouldn't be relied on for much of anything (consider Fran's ease in changing her appearance, or Adamson's trick of hiding a sparkling gem in plain view).

If sight is deceptive, however, sound is downright diabolical—especially the human voice, wrapped up as it is with slippery substances like gender, personality, and identity. Voices can be hidden, as Fran's is when she refuses to speak during the first kidnaping scene. Their meanings are ephemeral, as Blanche and Lumley discover during their argument over whether he told her about Mrs. Rainbird's medications. Voices fall prey to interference, as when random noises threaten to drown out a conversation Adamson is straining to overhear. They're prone to ellipsis and elision, as when Blanche hesitates to say the word "bastard"—shades of Norman Bates and his "B word," bathroom—even though the term as applied to Adamson is as accurate as it is impolite. And voices are not very tightly stitched to the people who seem to own them. Some are actually "disembodied," or at least secondhand and mediated, like the ghostly voice the kidnap victims hear in the hidden room. Others have bodies that don't quite match them—the best example being Blanche, with the many voices that issue from her versatile mouth.

Of all the unmoored voices in *Family Plot*, the one nearest to Hitchcock's heart might be the most mysterious of all: that of Henry, the familiar who guides Blanche in her pseudo-excursions to the spirit world. His name recalls the irrepressible title character of *The Trouble With Harry*, one of the director's most personal works, and his liminal presence in the narrative could be called an extended aural parody of Hitchcock's trademarked cameo appearances.

But the Hitchcock character who most resembles Henry is probably Mrs. Bates in *Psycho*, since both are examples of what Chion calls an *acousmêtre*, a character who appears in a film as a voice without a body. It is appropriate for an *acousmêtre* to open the richly ambiguous *Family Plot*, since the relationship of such figures to the screen is marked by, in Chion's words, "a specific kind of ambiguity and oscillation . . . neither inside nor outside the image" yet "implicated in the action, constantly about to be part of it."[9] By nature, Chion notes, the *acousmêtre* "blur[s] the boundaries between onscreen and offscreen."[10] This makes the *acousmêtre* not only a fitting character in *Family Plot* but also a telling encapsulation of the ambivalence at the movie's core. Indeed, the very ambiguity of the *acousmêtre* is rendered ambiguous in this film. Calling the typical *acousmêtre* a gifted and powerful figure, Chion nonetheless states that it "can be instantly dispossessed of its mysterious powers . . . when it is *de-acousmatized,* when the film reveals the face that is the source of the voice," a process that generally goes "hand in hand with his descent into a human, ordinary, and vulnerable fate." Chion adds that de-acousmatization "can also be called embodiment: a sort of enclosing of the voice in the circumscribed limits of a body— which tames the voice and drains it of its power."[11] This never happens with Henry, whose independence of Blanche's body remains a distinct possibility when her clairvoyance in the final scene suggests that her contact with the spirit realm may have been more genuine than even she ever suspected. Neither embodied nor disembodied, neither definitively acousmatic—is it just Blanche's growling all along?—nor conclusively de-acousmatized, Henry is a boundary-blurrer par excellence, straddling the Hitchcockian border between reality and unreality as deftly as Norman's mother ever did, and with a much nicer attitude.

So nice that it may be Henry who guides Blanche to the purloined jewel hid in plain sight on the chandelier, providing her with the impossible knowledge that solves a mystery no one else in the movie could penetrate. "Impossible knowledge" is another paradox-producing phrase, this one taken from Žižek, who also uses it in connection with Hitchcock's cameo appearances—which reveal an awareness denied to all others in his films, as if he "were capable of assuming for an instant a position of pure metalanguage, of taking an 'objective look' at himself and locating himself in the picture."[12] Since the filmmaker addresses his audience from the screen at these moments, they are examples of what Žižek elsewhere describes as the picture looking back at its viewer, an action that scrambles cinema's usual comforting distinctions between objectivity and subjectivity.[13] This takes more than one form in Hitchcock's films. At times, objects within the diegesis appear to address characters pictured along with them, as when *Psycho* cuts between Lila's approach and the facade of the Bates house, the latter seeming almost as sentient as the former. At other, more elusive times, the picture-looking-back-at-its-viewer is the movie itself, confronting the audience's gaze with an image so complex and polysemic that it seems less a spectacle to be consumed than a consciousness to be engaged with. This creates a radical celebration of cinematic ambiguity by denying the boundary between diegetic object and spectatorial subject. Hitchcock's last movie ends with one of his most heroic erasures of this boundary as Blanche turns directly to the camera and bestows a knowing wink on her audience.

This is prompted by her discovery of the missing diamond, an object that might not seem important enough to catalyze such an extraordinary gesture—it is, after all, a mere "MacGuffin," one of those trifles that Hitchcock grudgingly allows into his movies so the characters will have something to fuss over while he pursues his deeper interests. Turning to psychoanalytic theory, however, the diamond seems a solid example of what Žižek, following Jacques Lacan, calls the "stain" within a scene: the implicitly phallic detail that "does not fit" with its environment but "denatures it, renders it uncanny."[14]

Bearing out the significance of the diamond is its frequent appearance—directly, metaphorically, or metonymically—during the course of the film. The movie's first image is Blanche's crystal ball, in which her face soon materializes, already prefiguring the last scene, which ends with close-ups of Blanche and the diamond. The shape of the diamond rhymes with the roundness of Blanche's eye—a resemblance that's underscored when we see Blanche through the peephole of the kidnappers' door, and again when Hitchcock cuts from Blanche's wink to the diamond hanging with its crystal look-alikes in the chandelier. Adamson has devoted his ostensibly honest career to the care and connoisseurship of gems, and Lumley's crystal balls have already been discussed.

These and other instances add up to a lengthy hermeneutic trail, consolidating the diamond and its doubles or displacements as more than the paltry MacGuffin one might at first expect, but rather a stain in the Lacanian sense, named after the anamorphic blot in Hans Holbein's painting of a seemingly life-affirming scene haunted by a subliminal specter of morbidity and death.[15] Žižek notes that the incongruity and uncanniness of a stain render all aspects of a picture suspicious and thus open up "the abyss of the search for a meaning"—figured in this film, I'd suggest, by images like Lumley in his Sherlock Holmes getup and Adamsom ravishing a diamond with his erect jeweler's loup. In this abyss of a search for meaning, Žižek observes, "nothing is what it seems to be, everything is to be interpreted, everything is supposed to possess some supplementary meaning. The ground of the established, familiar signification opens up; we find ourselves in a realm of total ambiguity."[16]

Within the fissure of undecidability thus opened by his signifying practices, Hitchcock finds a comforting space, charged with the multivalence and ambivalence that allow experience of the body to be supplemented by fantasies of transcendence and immortality. These culminate in the film's ethereal conclusion, when the camera floats upward in a small but touching ascension that, along with Blanche's wink and the luminescence of the impossibly discovered diamond, reassures the camera and the world that everything's going to be all right because Hitchcock is still in control, for the moment at least, and he will stave off deathly determinacy as long as he humanly can. In his *Family Plot* cameo, Hitchcock appears in profile behind a door in City Hall, flanked by an inscription—"Registrar of Births & Deaths"—that amusingly sums up the decades he spent inscribing the lives and determining the fates of the countless characters who strutted and fretted through his films. He presented himself as a silhouette partly for real health reasons—pain and cortisone had taken a visible toll on him—but in going through with this appearance he is not merely signaling his impending death, as Žižek claims. He is asserting one last time his lifelong desire to wield an authoritative hand over the worlds he constructs, and by extension over the world he inhabits. He is indeed a shadow on a windowpane, but many shadows—such as the figures crystallized on movie film—last longer than the bodies that produce them. He is above all what the words on his windowpane proclaim him to be: the Registrar of Births and Deaths, a god-like figure "playing as many practical jokes on human beings as he can," as Raymond Durgnat wrote in a different context, yet combining "poor taste" and even "cruelty" with "a dreamy, mischievous human pleasure."[17] Behind his fantasy is a longing for the impossible knowledge of what really lies beyond (the "hopes" of "Catholics" are no longer enough for him) and a profound investment in cinema's ability to counterpoint the bodily—fraught with the weakness, infirmity, and decay that burdened him in his late years—with the transcendent, which he refuses to define but succeeds in evoking, alluding to, and yearning for throughout his last remarkable film.

NOTES

1. Donald Spoto, *The Art of Alfred Hitchcock: Fifty Years of His Motion Pictures* (New York: Hopkinson and Blake, 1976), 448

2. Slavoj Žižek, *Looking Awry: An Introduction to Jacques Lacan through Popular Culture* (Cambridge: MIT Press, 1991), 180.

3. Donald Spoto, *The Dark Side of Genius: The Life of Alfred Hitchcock* (Boston: Little, Brown and Company, 1983), 531.

4. Eric Rohmer and Claude Chabrol, *Hitchcock: The First Forty-Four Films*, trans. Stanley Hochman (New York: Continuum, 1979), 98.

5. Spoto, *Dark Side of Genius*, 554–55.

6. William Rothman, *Hitchcock—The Murderous Gaze* (Cambridge: Harvard University Press, 1982), 341, 54, 235, 339.

7. For an extended discussion, see Mikhail Bakhtin, *Rabelais and His World*, trans. Hélène Iswolsky (Bloomington: Indiana University Press, 1984), 368–436.

8. Spoto, *Dark Side of Genius*, 534.

9. Michel Chion, *Audio-Vision: Sound on Screen*, trans. Claudia Gorbman (New York: Columbia University Press, 1994), 129.

10. Chion, *Audio-Vision*, 131.

11. Chion, *Audio-Vision*, 130–31.

12. Žižek, *Looking Awry*, 180.

13. Žižek, *Looking Awry*, 118.

14. Žižek, *Looking Awry*, 90.

15. See Jacques Lacan, *The Four Fundamental Concepts of Psycho-Analysis*, trans. Alan Sheridan (New York: W. W. Norton, 1978), 92.

16. Žižek, *Looking Awry*, 91.

17. Raymond Durgnat, *The Strange Case of Alfred Hitchcock, or, The Plain Man's Hitchcock* (Cambridge: MIT Press, 1974), 48.

HITCHCOCK AND HIS LEGACY

"A HERO FOR OUR TIMES": FOREIGN CORRESPONDENT, HERO, AND *THE BONFIRE OF THE VANITIES*

LESLEY BRILL

We usually discuss intertextuality in terms of evocation of traditions, homage, incorporation of ideas or moods, restatement of themes for variation, and so on. This critical practice stresses the influence of past works or artists upon later ones. Alternatively, we think of what we call postmodern pastiche, a paradoxical intertextuality that displays the inaccessibility of the past to the present. Works that affect our understanding of their predecessors, by contrast, participate in an intertextuality in which the present revises the past. The influence of later works upon earlier ones is less often observed than the opposite, but it occurs continuously as traditions develop, evolve, disappear, and give birth to new traditions. The best known theoretical statement about such intertextuality remains T. S. Eliot's "Tradition and the Individual Talent," in which he asserted that every new work alters retroactively the meaning of its tradition, and of the individual works that constitute it. "Whoever has approved this idea of order . . . will not find it preposterous that the past should be altered by the present as much as the present is directed by the past."[1]

Studying film, we are less accustomed to analyzing the ways in which current movies alter our experience of past ones than we are to taking note of influences, remakings, and decorative allusions acknowledging (or dismissing) artistic forebears. Such a critical practice has the unhappy effect of prematurely ossifying our conception of film history in general and of film genres in particular. A more fertile and accurate approach to relations between earlier films and later ones accounts for both progressive and retroactive influences; it treats film history as growing from its roots as well as its branches.

This essay examines an instance of intertextuality that is bi-directional in time. It looks at the correspondences among two recent films, Brian De Palma's *The Bonfire of the Vanities* (1990) and Stephen Frears's *Hero* (1992), and Alfred Hitchcock's *Foreign Correspondent* (1940). Frears's and De Palma's films at once allude to Hitchcock's and suggest a reinterpretation of it. The relationship between *Bonfire* and *Foreign Correspondent* has been only incidentally noted; similarities among *Hero* and the other two films have, so far as I know, gone unremarked. Understanding the relations among these three movies helps to clarify both the contemporary films and their predecessor.

Generally judged an uncharacteristically patriotic polemic reflecting the pressures of World War II and Hitchcock's concurrent removal from England to the United States, *Foreign Correspondent* has several memorable sequences, modest strength as a whole, and what is widely regarded as a clumsy, ill-fitting ending. Thomas Leitch offers a recent assessment: "This ending is a deliberate non-ending; . . . it addresses the complications of its plot not by resolving them within the frame of the story but by taking up a collection in order to forestall them."[2] The best remembered moments of *Foreign Correspondent* include a windmill that reverses the direction of its turning blades, the rush of water into the cockpit when an airliner crashes into the sea, and an overhead shot of open umbrellas that trace the flight of an assassin as twitching grasses trace a concealed snake.

Although *Bonfire* and *Hero* allude to specific sequences in *Foreign Correspondent* and to Hitchcock's work generally, it is the problematic ending of the earlier work that De Palma and Frears approach most significantly in articulating the complex textures that their own narratives require. The similarities of their concluding movements to the end of *Foreign Correspondent* also suggest an aesthetically recuperative understanding of the last sequence of Hitchcock's movie. We may discuss relations among Hitchcock's work, *Hero*, and *Bonfire* under three rubrics, in order of increasing specificity. First, the contemporary works have a general debt to broad themes and tendencies in Hitchcock's *oeuvre*. Second, there are specific parallels among the three films and allusions in the later two to *Foreign Correspondent*. Third, the ending of Hitchcock's spy thriller resonates with the denouements of the contemporary films; among the three, a reciprocity exists that affects our understanding of all of them.

Before continuing, a caveat may be in order. We will sometimes experience difficulty in ascertaining whether influences on the two later works come from Hitchcock's films or from genres, styles, themes, and modes predominant at the time of his early American period. *Foreign Correspondent*, *Bonfire*, and *Hero* all participate in well established sub-genres of narrative film, among them the reporter film, the film of political intrigue and exposé, and the film of an ordinary person more or less thrust into the role of hero. As examples of the last sub-genre, these three movies are notable for their refusal to simplify their worlds either by sentimentalizing their heroes or by reducing their societies to case studies in communal pathology.

Foreign Correspondent, *Bonfire*, and *Hero* all tell stories of reporters and news media. In accord with common conventions, they portray newspeople as idle, cynical, dissolute, and/or incompetent. The name of the main reporter of *Bonfire*, Peter Fallow (Bruce Willis), suggests as much and adds an equally conventional lechery. In *Foreign Correspondent* and *Bonfire*, inept reporters blunder into the stories that make them famous. By contrast, Gail Gayley (Geena Davis), the reporter/heroine of *Hero*, is shrewd and alert, but she too falls into her great story. All the reporters are pessimistic, hardened observers of human folly who, according to another venerable convention of the news movie, will delay, compromise, or suppress their stories for noble motives.

Of the broadly Hitchcockian debts in the two later films, the most obvious has to do with the not-wholly-deserved accusations leveled against their protagonists. The main characters of *Hero* and of *Bonfire* are, if not exactly innocent, less guilty than those who conspire against or judge them. As is well known, the majority of Hitchcock's heroes combat an unjust accusation, often while fleeing the police and trying to apprehend the true malefactor. Interestingly, that situation has only a tertiary importance in *Foreign Correspondent*, in the unjustified suspicion that Carol Fisher (Laraine Day) conceives about the amorous motives of Johnny Jones (Joel McCrea).

Bernie Laplante (Dustin Hoffman), the nasty little hero of *Hero*, is a convicted felon, a thief, ingrate, and liar—"not," as he observes, "a nice guy." But beneath his cynicism and self-absorption survives a loving father, a person capable despite himself of altruism in desperate circumstances, and someone who can acknowledge his responsibility for what he has become.

An "asshole" like everyone else, Laplante is also, unlike everyone else, a hero. The technical innocence of Sherman McCoy (Tom Hanks) is clearer than Bernie's, but his life and character remain disturbing. He collects stupefying sums of money in a role that he refuses to defend beyond the disclaimer that "I don't make the rules"; he persists in an affair that puts the happiness of his wife and daughter at risk; and, like Bernie, he lies. His crimes are venial, however, in comparison with those of other establishment figures in the film: the avaricious, race-baiting Reverend Bacon; the bigoted, politically ruthless District Attorney Weiss; and various self-serving media figures.

Further possible debts to Hitchcock include such familiar themes as contrasts between public accounts and private realities (*Notorious, I Confess, Easy Virtue,* and others) and the related issue of whether "truth" ever corresponds to the stories we tell ourselves about it. Parent/child understandings like those arrived at in the Frears and De Palma films form an intermittent motif throughout Hitchcock's work (*Young and Innocent,* via surrogates in *The Lady Vanishes* and *Spellbound, Foreign Correspondent, The Birds,* and *Marnie*). Other Hitchcockian touches in *Hero* and *Bonfire* include De Palma's version of a zoom/track shot when Sherman is confronted by "natives" in the North Bronx, a parade at the end of Frears's film that recalls those in *The 39 Steps* and *Rich and Strange,* and the close-up in *Hero* on another favorite Hitchcock image, a life-saving clasping of hands.

Certain details in *Bonfire* and *Hero* point us specifically toward *Foreign Correspondent.* As we might expect, De Palma's allusions are the more easily identifiable. Most obviously, he reassembled the components of a well-known Hitchcock sequence, which begins on a rainy day in Amsterdam with a high shot of reporters under open umbrellas on the steps of a public edifice. In her book on the filming of *Bonfire,* Julie Salamon writes, "De Palma decided to transform Sherman's descent into terror into something beautiful by taking a cue from a scene in Hitchcock's 'Foreign Correspondent.'"[3] In *Foreign Correspondent,* the gathering of newspeople is prelude to an apparent political assassination by a gunman disguised as a newspaper photographer; in *Bonfire,* the same sodden herd collects for a character assassination that is largely executed by a particular newsperson (Fallow), and that is equally political.

Other possible allusions to *Foreign Correspondent* may be found in the credit sequence and in the plot and characterization of *Bonfire.* In both films, the reporter shares a conveyance with the subject of his story—a cab in Hitchcock's, a subway in De Palma's. In both, public figures betray their trusts: Steven Fisher as president of "The Universal Peace Party" in the earlier film, and the District Attorney, the Reverend Bacon, and various lawyers and reporters in the later one. Johnny's idleness (we first see him making a paper cut-out at his desk) and his inclination toward strong drink is sharply exaggerated in the characterization of Fallow, but the categories endure. The final image of Hitchcock's movie is of a statuary eagle; the opening credits of *Bonfire* are set next to a monumental steel eagle overlooking Manhattan. *Bonfire* may thus be said to start imagistically where *Foreign Correspondent* left off. The credit sequence of *Bonfire*, incidentally, is also related by place and an implied theme of time to the opening credits of Hitchcock's film, which begins with a close-up of a turning globe atop a skyscraper from which the camera pulls back to reveal buildings in a city identified as New York. The obvious artificiality of the Hitchcock set is matched in De Palma's credit sequence by the artifice of time-lapse cinematography and the streaking lights that condense into the film's title.

The parallels to *Foreign Correspondent* in *Hero* are subtler than those in *Bonfire*, and more generic to the news film of the 1930s and 1940s, but they retain some specificity to Hitchcock's movie. In both, plane crashes provide the most notable occasion for heroism. Both have reporter/heroes with alliterating names, the absurdity of Gail Gayley's matching that assigned by his boss to Johnny Jones, "Huntley Haverstock." A Hitchcock composition in *Foreign Correspondent*, a high shot looking down on the exteriors of adjacent buildings, is matched by notably similar compositions in *Hero*, and in both films acrophobic action takes place on the ledges of the heroes' hotels. In several late scenes, Frears introduces exaggerated verbal and visual rhetoric and overdubbing of patriotic music that practically duplicates the tone and technique of the final broadcast of *Foreign Correspondent*.

Toward what conclusions about *Foreign Correspondent, Bonfire,* and *Hero* do these correspondences and allusions direct us? At the thematic center of all three films is heroism, and our understanding of that idea is crucially conditioned by their interconnections. According to Johnny, Fisher "died like a hero," and Johnny's own refusal to abandon his radio broadcast for a bomb shelter exemplifies stereotypical journalistic heroism. For Bernie, "heroism is stupidity," and for the television station manager (Chevy Chase) in the same film it amounts to "a crock of shit"; but neither of those attitudes prevails by the end of *Hero*. In the voice-over of *Bonfire*, Fallow assures us that Sherman is "the real hero of the evening" and "as close as we're likely to get to a hero these days." For all these films, the notion of heroism is complicated, even self-contradictory. Considered together, their shared conception of that virtue is no less complex, but it is easier to apprehend.

Let us review the last fifteen minutes of *Foreign Correspondent* briefly in order to recall the aesthetic and ethical problems that it appears to leave unresolved. Having learned that he will be arrested when the airplane on which he is a passenger reaches the United States, Fisher confesses his true identity to his daughter. "I'm just coated with an English accent," he declares, "a thin coat. I fought for my heart and my country in a very difficult way, because sometimes it's harder to fight dishonorably than nobly, in the open. And I've used my country's methods because I was born with them." Carol, although she is without sympathy for her father's cause, accepts his explanations. As Johnny disavows any intention to persecute his fiancée's father, the plane comes under fire and crashes into the ocean, the survivors clustering on a precariously floating wing. Carol's father sacrifices himself for the others by quietly slipping into enormous waves. Johnny futilely tries to rescue him, despite Carol's pleas that he come back. They and the other survivors are picked up by an American ship and the story surreptitiously transmitted to *The Globe*. The film then returns to London where "one of the soldiers of the press," Johnny as Huntley Haverstock, delivers a rousing political sermon:

> Hello, America. I've been watching a part of the world being blown to pieces. A part of the world as nice as Vermont, Ohio, Virginia, and California and Illinois [*air raid sirens sound in the background*] lies ripped up and bleeding like a steer in a slaughter house. And I've seen things that make the history of the savages read like Pollyanna legends. [*A station employee tells him that because of the air raid, the broadcast must be postponed. But Johnny and Carol continue, because "They're listening in America."*] I can't read the rest of the speech I have because the lights have gone out, so I'll just have to talk off the cuff. All that noise you hear isn't static, it's death, coming to London. Yes, they're coming here now; you can hear the bombs falling on the streets and the homes. Don't tune me out. Hang on a while; this is a big story and you're part of it. It's too late to do anything here now, except stand in the dark and let them come. As if the lights are all out everywhere, except in America. [*"The Star Spangled Banner," played by an orchestra, comes up on the sound track.*] Keep those lights burning, cover them with steel, ring them with guns, build a canopy of battleships and bombing planes around them. Hello, America, hang on to your lights. They're the only lights left in the world. [*Fade to black, then fade in on a stone eagle over which the end title runs as a chorus joins the orchestra, ". . . and the rockets red glare, the bombs bursting in air, gave proof*

through the night . . ." and so on to the end of the anthem, as the screen darkens.]

While this ending is consonant with the opening dedication to "those intrepid ones who went across the sea to be the eyes and ears of America . . . who early saw the clouds of war while many of us at home were seeing rainbows," it has left many commentators unsatisfied. Written by Ben Hecht (uncredited), its histrionic script and staging seem ill-matched to the more complex view of politics and human affairs that the film has dramatized.[4] "In war . . . one lives by half-truths," writes Northrop Frye. "Not only is the traitor the lowest of criminals, but it is indignantly denied that any traitor can be honestly motivated."[5] The end, and perhaps the beginning, of *Foreign Correspondent* seem to answer to Frye's description, but what transpires between those frames shows us a traitor who is honestly motivated, who loves his daughter, and who is loved by her even after he is exposed. If one omits the written overture and Johnny's broadcast, *Foreign Correspondent* reiterates Hitchcock's most characteristic attitude toward the politics of conflict. Films like *Notorious, North by Northwest,* and *Topaz* suggest that no one is innocent in war, hot or cold; escape or salvation can only be found away from politics in love. In addition to appearing un-Hitchcockian, the ending of *Foreign Correspondent* strikes many viewers as aesthetically crude and unconvincing. It is over-written, over-scored, over-staged; in every sense of the word, overwrought.

How do *Hero* and *Bonfire* interpret and use the conclusion of *Foreign Correspondent*? And how do the two later films alter our understanding of the earlier one? The sequences in *Hero* and *Bonfire* that most resemble the end of *Foreign Correspondent* are the inspirational broadcast and hotel ledge rescue in Frears's film—both further heated by sentimental soundtracks and visual special effects—and the notorious "decency speech" of Judge White (Morgan Freeman) in De Palma's (quoted below). But let us begin at the beginning, credits and first sequences, since these set the tone and pose the problems that the subsequent stories will address.

As already observed, Hitchcock inserted a written dedication between the credits and the beginning of the narrative. *Hero* begins, like *Foreign Correspondent,* by celebrating something; in Frears's movie we are never told what, but the images for its credit sequence consist of a ticker-tape parade in a succession of extreme telephoto shots, with grandiose dissolves and pans that compress the unnamed city in space much as the credit sequence of *Bonfire* compresses Manhattan in time.[6] What sounds like a marching band plays a rousing version of "Aulde Lang Syne." The arrangement of that melody, the use of vintage montage, waving flags, falling ticker-tape, soaring balloons, and a slightly dated crowd reinforce the suggestion that what we are about to see will be somehow relevant to good old days that we should not forget. At key moments during the narrative that follows, in particular during the long scene on the hotel ledge, Frears will reintroduce such old-fashioned conventions.

Degraded and small in comparison with the imagery of the credit sequence, the present enters in a courtroom where Bernie is being pronounced guilty of selling stolen property. While his attorney, a young woman just out of law school, argues for continuance of bail, the defendant confirms the prosecution's assessment of him as "a slippery little shit." He filches his lawyer's cash from her pocketbook, then gives her a little of her own money back as payment for what she has already loaned him. Nothing about Bernie appears remotely heroic; even the scale of his crimes is mean. The contrast between the credits and the courtroom sequence implies that each is typical of its era—the first of some happier time, the second of ours.

The opposition between the heroic and the degraded is similar in early sequences of *Bonfire*. Manhattan viewed from beside the eagle evokes an urban sublime that, like the credit sequence of *Hero*, is associated with a romantic conception of cities not much favored by current cinema. As the credits continue, a limousine pulls into an underground garage, a security man announces "Fallow arriving area A," and a bevy of staff rush to greet the celebrity. He emerges half-dressed and wholly drunk, then does a memorable imitation of a Yahoo: sucking at his whiskey bottle, exchanging it for a martini and tossing the glass into the wall, drunkenly pawing the daughter of an ambassador, scooping a handful of salmon mousse from an elaborately prepared platter, groping the rump of his next female guide with his slimy hand, and so on. In voice-over, this anthology of appetite and appalling manners identifies itself as "the man of the moment, the hero of the evening." So much, it would appear, for contemporary heroism.

But Fallow announces that the real hero of the evening is absent, and in flashback we see Sherman McCoy drag his dog into the rain so that he can use a public phone booth, despite "the existence of eleven telephones and seven different lines" in his extravagant apartment. En route he calls the doorman "Bill" and replies "whatever" when that person observes that his name is "Tony, sir. It's Tony." From the telephone booth he mistakenly calls his wife and asks for "Maria" (Melanie Griffith), his mistress. When he returns, his wife denounces him as "cheap, rotten, and a liar." Later his father observes about his profession, "In my day, there was some integrity to it [dealing in bonds]. . . . Now it isn't about anything, is it, except the money?" So Sherman, another representative of our bad times, appears to be an equally improbable hero.

From the start, then, *Bonfire* and *Hero* treat heroism as something that has either come down to us dreadfully diminished or has simply not survived at all. As *Hero* continues, the sentimental media exploitation of the "Angel of Flight 104" seems to support this jaundiced view. "Out of the darkness, out of the smoke and the fear," declaims Gayley over a television sound track of military drums and brass, "came a man with no name, no uniform, but an abundance of courage, a man who was thinking not about himself but about others [the music modulates into "The Battle Hymn of the Republic"], risking his own life for ours." The end of her piece is accompanied by typical television graphics, and the whole effort is emotional enough to make even the hardened station manager blow his nose. It is an apt imitation of television news, like much well-aimed parody hardly distinguishable from its originals. In its excesses of writing and music, it recalls the concluding broadcast of *Foreign Correspondent*.

Viewers' reflexes may be affected like Chevy Chase's, but we are unlikely to be convinced at a cerebral level of the divinity of The Angel of Flight 104. We have seen Bernie only grudgingly agree even to open the door of the airplane and then steal Gayley's wallet and "Silver Microphone" award when he goes inside. As to the benefits to him of his heroism, they come to less than nothing: he misses a night with his son, is excoriated by his ex-wife, loses his job, is arrested while trying to sell Gayley's credit cards, and suffers the final indignity of seeing John Bubber (Andy Garcia) collect the million dollar reward that Gayley's television station has offered the unknown Angel.

By the time the film arrives at the second of its emotionally amplified sequences, however, the skepticism that the first one invites has been very much undercut. Bubber is a brilliant success, inspiring a children's hospital where he is instrumental in reviving a comatose boy, assembling support for the homeless, and generally acting as a tonic to a society weary of human corruption and desperate for a hero without layers of weakness and scandal. Indeed, investigators discover that Bubber really is a hero, having saved the lives of fellow soldiers during combat in Viet Nam. What's more, the audience knows he has the profound guilt about his imposture that a genuinely decent person would feel.

Despite ironic complications, *Hero* reaches an inspiriting conclusion. Bubber will continue his vocation as public savior; Bernie will avoid jail and send his son to college; Gayley acknowledges Bernie's heroism, the rightness of Bubber's continuing in his role, and the happy truth that there is truth.

For it does not turn out "that there wasn't any truth, just stories." There are both, and both count. Bernie lectures his son that "what you learn as you get older is there ain't no truth; all there is is bullshit." But a few moments later he will be telling Joey "what really happened" when Flight 104 went down.

Hero closes with a Hitchcockian comic symmetry that plays like the kiss in front of the puzzled ticket-taker at the end of *Spellbound* or Guy's fleeing the clergyman at the end of *Strangers on a Train*. Early in the film, we saw Bernie with his son at the zoo, looking at a roaring tiger. "If you were in there with him he'd kill you, wouldn't he, Dad?" "Yeah, yeah, something like that," his father answers absent-mindedly. As the movie ends, they are again in the zoo. We hear a scream, "Please, please, my little girl she fell in the lions' cage! Help me please!" As grudgingly as he went to the aid of the wrecked airliner, Bernie sets off to another rescue. "Oh for Crissake," he mutters. Then, to his son, "Here, watch my shoes."

Bonfire has two endings.[7] First, the trial of Sherman culminates in Judge White's speech on decency, then the film returns to the present with Fallow's arrival at the civic reception in his honor. Each brings its story to an end and each contradicts, or at least deeply complicates, the thematic and emotional dominants of the other. Judge White's speech provides a moral conclusion that the film largely endorses, I think, albeit with ironic qualifications. Fallow's final sequence re-emphasizes the reservations that attach to idealistic notions of heroism, much as those notions are counterbalanced in *Hero* and in *Foreign Correspondent*.

When Maria testifies that her lover was driving the car that hit Henry Lamb, Fallow's voice-over declares, "And there it was, my friends, the end of Sherman McCoy. . . . My hero was gone, finished." But at this moment, a long panning shot that has ended by dollying to Fallow cuts to one that moves toward Sherman, who is taking a small speaker from his briefcase and smiling faintly. He plays the tape on which Maria declares that she was driving. Sherman then claims, falsely, that he recorded the conversation himself, and the Judge dismisses the indictment "in the interest of justice."

Stung by an accusation from one of the spectators that he is "a racist pig," Judge White delivers his impromptu oration on justice and decency. He speaks from a position of authority established by a set and camera angle that place him above his audience and by a biblical diction we have already heard: "I say unto you, what does it matter the color of a man's skin if witnesses perjure themselves, if a prosecutor enlist the perjurers, when a district attorney throws a man to the mob for political gain, and men of the cloth, men of God, take the prime cuts?" As he speaks, the camera alternates between upward-looking medium and close shots of the Judge and a series of close-ups of the malefactors he is describing, the grotesqueness of the last three emphasized by a wide angle lens. The Judge then steps down from the bench to the floor of the court. He descends at the same time to a less formal diction.

> I'll tell you what justice is. Justice is the law. And the law is man's feeble attempt to set down the principles of decency. Decency. And decency is not a deal; it isn't an angle, or a contract, or a hustle. Decency, decency is what your grandmother taught you. [*Brief shot of Sherman's parents as music starts to come up on the soundtrack.*] It's in your bones. Now you go home, go home and be decent people. Be decent. [*Triumphant fanfare on soundtrack.*] Mr. McCoy, you're free to go.

Coming at a point when the forces of opportunism, greed, and cynicism have finally lost a crucial battle, Judge White's speech carries a feeling of authoritative summation. The fact that we know him to be a realist as well as a just man gives his words still greater authority. He carries himself with a nobility unique among the important figures of the film. Despite its self-conscious corniness, his address to the courtroom returns the heroic overtones of the sculptural eagle, watchfully guarding the great city below. Behind the judge, prominent throughout the sequence, stands another old-fashioned symbol of strength, justice, and protection—an American flag.

But the audience is not allowed the satisfaction of a conclusive sermon, a summing-up that would perhaps have been finally unpersuasive. Instead, De Palma moves to his second conclusion, closing the present-tense narrative frame that takes the drunken Fallow from the hotel garage to the reception. Like *Hero*, *Bonfire* ends by reiterating themes of constructing stories, the complexities of heroism, and the intersections between public accounts and private realities. Fallow's voice-over continues as the image cuts from the courtroom: "And so we come to the end of our story. That was the last I saw of Sherman McCoy, the last anyone saw of him. He was gone in a blaze of glory. A hero for our times. Or as close as we're likely to get these days."

At this point, Fallow's voice-over is interrupted when he is introduced to a cheering crowd as "the man of the moment" by—astonishingly—District Attorney Weiss. The camera pans over the crowd, a shot that rhymes with previous pans in the courtroom. Although the setting and dress of the assembly are transformed, the featured principals remain familiar. Most of the cynics, cowards, and knaves are present and unabashed: besides Weiss,

we see such nemeses as Fallow's threatening boss; his daughter, the hereto-
fore scornful Caroline Heftshank; Sherman's lawyer; Weiss's chief assistant,
Geraldo; Assistant D.A. Kramer; the patronizing Albert Fox; and Reverend
Bacon, seizer of prime cuts.

How can these people be honoring Fallow, who tells a story in which
they play disgraceful roles? We can only guess that they have somehow
turned his book, like everything else, to their advantage. Or that the story
conveyed by Fallow to us may not be the one for which he won his prizes.
Or both, or neither. The film does not tell; it only shows in its second and
final ending that business goes on as usual among the ethically illiterate
brokers of power, money, lies, and influence. We can probably assume that
Fallow, their whore throughout the narrative, has continued to "take care
of" them and they of him. Absent, besides Sherman, are his wife, his parents,
Henry Lamb's mother, and Judge White. None of the real players or victims
of the events are present. The media flamens and the media-manipulating
politicians do not need them anymore.

The soirée of politicians, media entrepreneurs, and assorted lackeys
brings their story to an end with a self-celebration. Fallow exists, by his testimony, as an invention of the media: "unless you haven't read a newspaper
or seen a television in the last few months, you know exactly who I am."
Exactly. Fallow collaborates with initially hostile media to create an identity
defined by the applause he basks in as the film ends—like Rupert Pupkin in
Martin Scorsese's *The King of Comedy* (1983). If in the process of getting to
that point he has lost his soul, "ah, well, there are compensations."

But the conclusion of the reporter's story no more compendiates the
film than does Judge White's speech on justice and decency. Indeed, Fallow's
award-winning book at least partly serves the truth, despite its author's ve-
nal motives. *Bonfire* insists on its representations of self-contradictory people in an incoherent world. "You know," says Sherman's father to him before
the last trial sequence, "I have always been a great believer in the truth. . . .
I believe in the truth as an essential companion to a man of conscience,
a beacon in this vast and dark wasteland that is our modern world. And
yet . . . in this case, if the truth won't set you free, then lie." Sherman lies
to bring the truth to light. A tragic hero of less than heroic proportions, he
"lost everything. But he gained his soul."

The casting by Peter Gruber and De Palma of Tom Hanks as Sherman
McCoy was a decision as eccentric as it was right. This "Master of the Universe," the tragic hero who plunges from a great height, must not simply be
flawed, he must be common. Hanks does a superb job of portraying a person
who is, as Aristotle said, "like us." His eminence results from the station in

life that he inherits, not from oversized talents, energy, or ambition. He is exceptional only in that he is "insulated by wealth and power." As unreflecting and self-satisfied as most people, he falls and then rises into a consciousness of the world and himself; he gains his soul. Like the alternately grubby and glamorous protagonists of *Hero*, he answers to Bubber's self-description as an ordinary person caricatured by the media: "I'm just like the next person, full of frailty, with some courage, some decency mixed in."

Hero, Bonfire, and *Foreign Correspondent* share a paradoxically realistic idealism. Romantic, flawless heroes and heroism have limited plausibility in the self-doubting society that De Palma and Frears address in the 1990s, just as they must have sounded hollow in 1940 as humanity set about its second self-immolation in twenty-five years. Bernie, Bubber, and Gayley are all open to serious charges, as are McCoy, Fallow, and even Judge White, who at the beginning of *Bonfire* insists on a convenient plea bargain for a defendant who "pulled a knife on a seventy-year old lady, robbed her, raped her, and shoved her in a garbage can." Johnny Jones does not commit crimes against truth or his fellow creatures; but in his clumsiness and ignorance he doesn't look like much of a stay against the darkness, either. Even in what Van Meer calls "the poor, suffering world," however, good and heroism are imaginable, desirable, can really happen. If humankind is "full of frailty," ordinary people nonetheless have "some courage, some decency mixed in."

In the knotty textures of *Hero, Bonfire,* and *Foreign Correspondent,* we turn to, settle for, and celebrate unexceptional protagonists who do good deeds as well as foul ones. The simplicities of patriotic hoopla, tales of absolute virtue or absolute corruption, are empty calories, pure sucrose or pure roughage. They lack truth and therefore lack hope. Fabled good old days are as distant from *Foreign Correspondent* as they are from *Hero* and *Bonfire.* The same is true of the unrelieved depravity of bad new days.

Hitchcock's skepticism, like that of Frears and De Palma, targets the simplifications to which people try to reduce themselves and their worlds as much as it does their deliberate lies. Media news, unjust legal systems, and propaganda are objects of consternation in Hitchcock's films from early examples like *Easy Virtue,* through *Notorious* and *North by Northwest,* to the end of his career in *Frenzy.* Among Hitchcock's other political thrillers, *The 39 Steps* and *Saboteur,* with their unremarkable often clumsy heroes, are perhaps most like *Foreign Correspondent.* The successive endings of that movie, like those of the films of Frears and De Palma, bring to conclusion several not-always-congruent actions—the exposure of Fisher, the quest for a big story, the courtship of Carol and Johnny, the political polemics. The apparent inadequacy of patriotic clarity at the end of an earlier Hitchcock war movie, *Secret Agent,* anticipates that of *Foreign Correspondent* four years later.[8]

In their address to less desperate circumstances than those Hitchcock confronted in 1940, *Hero* and *Bonfire* come to precarious, qualified affirmations of diminutive champions and ambiguous values. The framing story of De Palma's film begins, after the opening image of Manhattan, with a suggestive shot. On a black screen two tiny lights appear in the far distance. They move toward the camera as the screen brightens to reveal the limousine carrying Peter Fallow to his exaltation. From one point of view, this image is ironic: the headlights do not herald the truth but a Prince of Darkness, a maker of lies and money. From another point of view, the irony is itself ironized and we are encouraged to return to a less subversive interpretation: both Fallow, "the man of the moment," and McCoy, "a hero for our time," cast some illumination on reality, however complicated it may be and however uninterested they may ultimately be in doing so. Gayley's reporting and the fragmentary heroism and nastiness or weakness of Bernie and Bubber in *Hero,* as we have seen, provide similarly double-faced data for dismay and reassurance. Neither viewpoint is entirely ascendant or discredited.

Fifty years after Hitchcock's film, the complex endings of De Palma's and Frears's movies and the multiple, unstable meanings that they generate allow us to see more clearly the analogous structures in the closing movements of *Foreign Correspondent.* In a balance of sentiment and irony, all three films find a rhetorical resting point that counsels at once against assurance and despair. Hitchcock's movie leaves us with something like the following. In a dark, confused world upon which catastrophe is settling, we find heroes to be ordinary persons and villains to be human beings, not monsters. But we should not confuse the better with the worse, nor embrace a sweeping pessimism. Such heroes as we can imagine may be frail or foolish, compromised and commonplace, but they are the best we have. Though the villains are no more demons than the heroes are demigods, they are still to be fought and their accounts of the world remain relatively untrue and dangerous.

De Palma's and Frears's films have the luxury of less appalling social situations and therefore make less urgent appeals, but their premises and the conclusions they draw are very much like those of *Foreign Correspondent.* All are self-consciously skeptical about the sentimental rhetoric that supports their affirmative proclamations—the overstated call to arms at the end of *Foreign Correspondent,* the media inflation of Bubber in *Hero,* the paean to decency of Judge White. As the movies turn out, however, their protagonists come "as close to a hero as we're likely to get these days" and their appeals to idealism, compromised as they are, are ultimately sympathetic. If they lead us to regret that we cannot expect idealized saviors greater and finer than ourselves, they offer us the consolation that we occasionally manage some heroism within our ordinary lives. In a world on the brink of global war (*Foreign Correspondent*), or one in which reality appears to be no more than weepy news stories constructed of "layers of bullshit" (*Hero*), or in a society ruled by hypocrites who enrich themselves by subverting truth and justice (*The Bonfire of the Vanities*), such consolations are considerable. They bring with them the conviction of films that refuse to simplify their understanding of life in the service of either fond wishes or facile cynicism.

NOTES

1. T. S. Eliot, *The Sacred Wood: Essays on Poetry and Criticism* (1920; rpt. London: Methuen, 1946), 50.

2. Thomas M. Leitch, *Find the Director and Other Games* (Athens: University of Georgia Press, 1991), 128. Critics like Sam Simone, who regards *Foreign Correspondent* as a work of unalloyed anti-Nazi propaganda, do not find the ending incongruous, but they are likely to leave uncommented the complications of earlier episodes. See *Hitchcock as Activist: Politics and the War Films* (Ann Arbor: UMI Research Press, 1985), 29–60.

3. Julie Salamon, *The Devil's Candy* (Boston: Houghton Mifflin, 1991), 144.

4. Charles T. Samuels asked Hitchcock about the end of the film: "*Foreign Correspondent* is very patriotic; it even ends with 'The Star-Spangled Banner.' Was that your idea?" The director answered, "That was Walter Wanger and Ben Hecht." See *Encountering Directors* (New York: Capricorn Books, 1972), 244.

5. Northrop Frye, *Anatomy of Criticism* (1957; rpt. New York: Atheneum, 1967), 347.

6. The Drake Hotel later reveals, to those who know where it is, that the city in which the action takes place is Chicago. It is not certain that the city in the credit sequence is the same, however. Nor does it seem that the audience is expected to identify the setting with any particular place, despite the identifiability of the Drake.

7. According to Salamon, until a late moment in its development, *Bonfire* also had a coda in which Henry Lamb quietly gets out of bed and leaves the hospital unobserved. The confusion of preview audiences seems to have persuaded the makers of the film and the executives of Warner Bros. to simplify the ending. See *The Devil's Candy*, 353–74.

8. I have discussed *Secret Agent* at more length in *The Hitchcock Romance* (Princeton: Princeton University Press, 1988), 184–86.

ECHOES OF ALFRED HITCHCOCK'S *VERTIGO*, *THE BIRDS*, AND *FRENZY* IN FRANÇOIS TRUFFAUT'S *STORY OF ADÈLE H.*

James M. Vest

The two year hiatus between *Day for Night* (1973) and *The Story of Adèle H.* (1975) was the longest in Truffaut's filmmaking career. While preparing this new project, which he had been toying with since 1969 and which would be very different in nature from his previous films, Truffaut was also thinking of Hitchcock and continuing to compile materials for an updated edition of his monumental work on his father figure and mentor.[1] Aware that Hitchcock was nearing the end of his career, Truffaut conducted a substantial interview with him at the Cannes Film Festival opening of *Frenzy* in 1972 and also saw him as often as he could in Hollywood during visits to California, which became increasingly frequent after 1973.[2] Thus during the pre-production and production stages of *Adèle H.* Truffaut was steeping himself in Hitchcock, both the man and his *oeuvre*. The two conceptual domains—that of Alfred H. and that of Adèle H.—grew together within him.

Based on the diaries of Victor Hugo's youngest daughter Adèle, Truffaut's film chronicles Adèle's trials as she travels to Nova Scotia and then to Barbados in search of her former lover, a British officer who is no longer interested in her. Although Hitchcockian allusions and influences are less obvious and less overarching here than in some of Truffaut's earlier works, still *The Story of Adèle H.* exhibits a discernible Hitchcockian imprint.[3] This essay will examine aspects of Truffaut's film that display that imprint most clearly—including the director's cameo appearance, scenes set in the bookstore and in a shelter for beggars, and scenes of Adèle's fitful sleep, as well as the sense of obsessive, vertiginous *kinesis* central to *The Story of Adèle H.* as a whole—which demonstrate not only Truffaut's homage to Hitchcock but also ways Truffaut managed to internalize and personalize Hitchcockian elements in his own filmmaking.

THE DIRECTOR'S CAMEO

François Truffaut may be seen in six of his own films. In three of them he is a principal protagonist: Dr. Jean Itard in *The Wild Child* (1970), the director Ferrand in *Day for Night* (1973), and Julien Davenne in *The Green Room* (1978). He also appears in silent parts in other films. He may be glimpsed with the young Antoine Doinel (Jean-Pierre Léaud) in the amusement park scene in *The 400 Blows* (1959). He has a two-second cameo as the father of Madeleine Doinel (played by his daughter Laura Truffaut) at the beginning of *Small Change* (1976) and a slightly longer scene as a British soldier in *Adèle H.*, one of the most historical and at the same time interiorized of his works, where questions of power and control are paramount.[4] His appearances tend to function within the story more diegetically than Hitchcock's, since Truffaut plays characters with a distinct role in the plot, whether major or minor.[5]

The cameo in *The Story of Adèle H.* occurs early in the film. Soon after arriving in Halifax, Adèle (Isabelle Adjani) is shown scouring the streets and ramparts of the port in search of her lover, a British officer, Lt. Pinson (Bruce Robinson). Adèle's encounter with the "wrong" soldier initiates the compulsive wandering pattern that will become the central motif of the film, establishing its parameters and modeling what is to come. Her *faux pas* represents an important step in her search for her lover, an early indication of her determination to leave no stone unturned in her obsessive quest to find him. It is literally and figuratively a turning point. As the camera circles about her at the end of this sequence, viewing her from on high, she raises her hand to her mouth. In that instant she is the picture of one facing the terrible realization that she could be wrong, that she herself is capable of not recognizing the one she loves, that the mistake lies within.

This scene occurs a quarter-hour into the film, after we have been exposed to claims to the film's factual accuracy, a rapid-fire historical prologue, and an opening sequence showing Adèle's arrival in Halifax through a ruse, her installation under an assumed name, her disturbed sleep, and the beginnings of her search for Lt. Pinson under multiple false pretenses.[6] We have learned that he refused to read a letter Adèle sent him, and we have seen him once leaving a bookstore, dressed in black cape and cap, accompanied by an attractive young woman who is carrying two wiggling dogs. With Adèle we have heard the bookstore owner, Mr. Whistler (Joseph Blatchley), say that although Pinson has been in town only a short time he has made a reputation for himself. Whistler chooses an expression that explicitly compares Pinson to a wolf—"il est déjà connu comme le loup blanc"[7]—and identifies him as one who purportedly accumulates debts. After these provisional introductions to Adèle and to her hussar, we are prepared for their paths to cross definitively.

The scene by the ramparts promises to bring the two together for the first time in the New World. This scene is entirely without dialogue, yet it is far from silent. The raucous cries of seagulls dominate the soundtrack. The camera follows Adèle along the ramparts as she passes numerous red-coated soldiers.[8] She and we glimpse an officer dressed in the same manner as Pinson at the bookstore, a darkly clad figure who brushes her sleeve as he moves between her and the camera. She pivots and follows him, and the camera tracks backward with her toward the soldier. She approaches him, arm outstretched, and in her haste to overtake him nearly outruns the camera. The sounds of the birds die down and the scene becomes eerily quiet as she moves toward him. This shift toward silence and visual privacy intensifies the emotional force of the moment, effectively shutting off stimuli from the outside world, emphasizing Adèle's subjective vision and anticipation. She touches the officer. He turns around. The face she and we discover is Truffaut's.

This scene is reminiscent of the opening of *The Birds* (1963), where gulls' cries fill the soundtrack from the credits into the scene where Melanie Daniels (Tippi Hedren) crosses a San Francisco street and enters a pet shop. As she goes through the door, she rubs shoulders with Hitchcock who is emerging from the shop. As this scene unfolds, the gull sounds diminish and then cease altogether, replaced by a wolf whistle from a youthful passerby, just before her path crosses that of the director.[9] Although Hitchcock's role serves no diegetic function, the scene has metaphorical significance within the context of the larger film. In *The Birds*, much of which is played in pantomime, the bird sounds increase the dramatic tension to such an extent that their absence becomes as ominous and unsettling as the noises themselves.[10]

In *The Story of Adèle H.* the effect of the scene with Truffaut is like that of the pet shop in *The Birds* in several respects. Both Melanie and Adèle are products of difficult family situations and looking for love that may not be possible on their terms. In their meetings with their directors, both actresses move obliquely, first from right to left, then swing about abruptly, suggesting the difficulty of direct movement through life, of direct contact, of meaningful communication. Adèle's gesture of covering her mouth with her gloved hand as she looks down and turns away reinforces this motif. This scene is an early indication of the trouble Adèle experiences communicating on the plane of reality: absorbed in her fantasy, she fails to recognize the object of her desires. When she finally meets the "right" man, her first gesture will be to cover his mouth with her hand, effectively cutting off exchange, and in her final scene with him she will ignore the real officer altogether in order to keep alive her illusions.

In both cases the director's cameo sets the tone for much of the symbolism and even the structure of films where human relations and communication are major concerns. Hitchcock is escorted out of the shop by two rambunctious dogs. He and his canine friends—two (somewhat) civilized wolves accompanying the "big bad wolf" *par excellence*— represent a puckish extension of the wolf whistle heard as the gull sounds subsided, inchoate natural sounds that lead to the first verbal exchanges in the film, exchanges that turn out to be disappointing, misleading, ultimately life-threatening. Thus, in its tongue-in-cheek manner, Hitchcock's appearance anticipates major themes of *The Birds*: nature run amok, the difficulty of verbal communication, human nature reduced to its non-linguistic minimum.[11]

Similarly in *The Story of Adèle H.* Lt. Pinson has already been identified by the book shop owner as lupine, "comme le loup blanc," and the expectation is that the wolf may well be revealed in the officer's clothing. The audience has been prepared to meet Lt. Pinson and to learn how he will react to seeing Adèle. Like her we are in a position to be pleasantly or unpleasantly surprised by this encounter, and like her we are anxious to see at close range the hidden face of this soldier. The encounter is prolonged for a few awkward seconds, limited contact is established, and the effect of the "shock of recognition" is accentuated. The grand irony is that at the very moment she discovers that she does not know him, we find ourselves in a position to discover that we do, as we recognize the officer's face as Truffaut's.

The director plays the part of a mistake that is, in actuality, no mistake at all.[12] His appearance is thus open to interpretation at two distinct levels.

In the context of the unfolding story he is an unwitting obstacle to Adèle's happiness, but in the viewers' world his appearance is planned. For her he represents a stranger, a stroke of bad luck, a blocking force unknowingly countering her desires; whereas for us his blocking is not only knowing but purposeful, cunning, ominous—anticipatory of other blockings and disappointments that Adèle must endure as she pursues her misguided dream. The two stare at each other blankly. Unmoved, he turns away. She covers her mouth and the camera turns slowly around her, viewing her from above. Within the narrative, we confront with Adèle a man who does not measure up to her expectations. Beyond the narrative, in the world of films and viewers, we are confronted by the spectacle of the filmmaker himself garbed in a uniform of one aspiring to authority, and left to wonder how well his work will measure up to our expectations. The dual effect is at once emotional and intellectual. We are invited simultaneously to sense the intensity of Adèle's initial disappointment and to distance ourselves from it, to participate with the director in his directorial games, to connive with him, to anticipate with him other blockings of Adèle's desires and plans, and perhaps of our own as well.

There is a double movement of rejection at the end of this scene: the officer turns away from her and she then looks down and turns in the opposite direction as the camera rotates about her. That haunting, destabilizing movement lingers like a specter throughout the film. This scene adumbrates a series of encounters that culminate in Adèle's last contact with the object of her affections when she walks past Pinson just as the officer played by Truffaut had walked past her, without recognition. There, in the depths of madness, she does not know Pinson, even when he turns back to catch up to her—reprising her movement in the earlier scene—and calls her by name.

Another Hitchcock cameo closely akin to Truffaut's walk-on part in *Adèle H.* is to be found in *Frenzy* (1972), where the director appears in a bowler hat, black suit, and flanged Eton collar.[13] Because of the high angle of the shot, he is visible only from the elbows up, as is the case with Truffaut in *Adèle H.* His hat, like Truffaut's cap, covers much of his face and accentuates movements of his head. In one of his most extended cameo appearances, Hitchcock is shown among a crowd, in attendance at the first major development in the plot, the discovery of a corpse floating in the Thames. Initially he distinguishes himself by refraining from joining in the general applause for a politician's remarks. Instead he stares impassively, keeping his own council. After the discovery of the body, he reappears, apparently listening to conversations in the crowd around him concerning the spate of necktie murders then under way in London.[14] Members of the crowd have eyes to see and ears to hear but do not understand, and here Hitchcock appears part of that limited understanding of events of which he, as director, is creator. Even one who should be in the know seems caught up, like the others, in the confusion, in the need to understand. Thus the director appears as an observer with limited knowledge whose presence in this context serves to sanction the destructive events portrayed, a role adopted by Truffaut in his unsettling contact with the self-destructing Adèle.

OTHER HITCHCOCKIAN ECHOES

Additional references to *Frenzy* and other Hitchcock films may be discerned throughout *The Story of Adèle H.* An allusion to *Frenzy* is apparent in the dormitory scene near the end of Truffaut's film. Destitute, Adèle is forced to take up lodging in a shelter for indigents. Events at the shelter are filmed in much the same way as a comparable scene in *Frenzy* where the outcast Dick Blaney (Jon Finch) spends the night in a Salvation Army shelter. In both instances, the person in the bed on the right makes a move to steal from the down-and-out protagonist, who successfully blocks the attempt. The lighting, spatial relationships, camera angle, rhythms, and progression of action in the two scenes are in many ways analogous; but the outcomes are quite different. Whereas Blaney dominates the situation, offering violent retribution to the offender, Adèle retreats, ending up on the floor under her bed clinging to her precious case full of writings. While Blaney emerges from the scene as a force to be reckoned with, Adèle is clearly no longer "une force qui va."[15]

The themes of nature and domesticity central to *The Birds* are also found in *Adèle H.* in conjunction with both birds and dogs. In *Adèle,* the two Pekinese are seen for a second time as they are unceremoniously run off by Pinson when he and his companion climb the stairs to the bedroom where Adèle will spy on them. In *The Birds,* the dogs are also portrayed as an impediment, tugging at the leash, seemingly propelling Hitchcock through the door. One of the West Highland terriers is shown starting to go the wrong way, prompting Spoto to note that Sarah the terrier may be the only performer in Hollywood who refused to take direction from Hitch.[16] In addition to their direct association with sexual longing in both films—specifically the temptation to intervene in the affairs of lovebirds—the dogs represent not only an element of levity but also the possibility for change of direction and the ultimate lack of human control.

This motif is underscored in *The Story of Adèle H.* when Pinson watches unperturbed as a large dog barks and bites at Adèle. As he looks on, it claws at her and tears her dress, then chases her off. In this chilling scene of complicity he is connected to the rending threat of incompletely domesticated instincts. Here the menacing dog represents not only the threat of scarcely masked wolfishness, but also those wild impulses that will tear Adèle apart, psychically and physically, before the film ends. [17]

Birds figure prominently at two other junctures in *Adèle H.* The first is in the account offered by Mr. Saunders (Reubin Dorey) of the officers' banquet as he recounts his attempt to deliver Adèle's letter to Pinson. According to Saunders, the meal was an elegant multi-course affair, conceived as a formal repast *à la française*, in stark contrast to the simple fare at the boarding house—and not unlike Mrs. Oxford's culinary attempts so vividly portrayed in *Frenzy*. Saunders' verbal picture of the banquet depicts Pinson telling jokes amid curried chicken and Scottish grouse in whiskey, a portrait indicating the hussar's abject lack of caring for Adèle. [18] Caught up in the festivities, he doesn't deign to open her letter: his frivolity cannot be interrupted for real contact, commitment, or compassion. In this context, birds are to be consumed or ignored, not loved, a thin mask for a crass lack of feeling and civility. Another avian scene depicts Adèle descending a stone stairway and hiding behind an arch so as not to be seen by a detail of soldiers, on her way to intervene in Pinson's affairs. Again, as in the cameo scene, the raucous cries of gulls suggest the wildness and impossibility of her mad venture. For Insdorf, Adèle is marked, emblematized by the cries of seagulls, particularly in her final scenes by the sea, where she "rises by the waves but makes a fearful sound." [19]

A bird's eye view characterizes some of the most effective camera work in all three films. The elevated camera in the cameo sequence in *The Story of Adèle H.* recalls the camera angles in the opening sequence showing Adèle coming ashore in Halifax. The privileged point of view in both instances is that of a bird or of an all-seeing narrator, a perspective reminiscent of *The Birds* and of the opening sequences in *Frenzy* where a long helicopter shot under the credits leads directly into a series of shots filmed from on high, including Hitchcock's cameos and the discovery of the floating body. Rather than long shots, Truffaut prefers more psychologically revealing medium shots and elevated close-ups which assist in the presentation and development of character. The high-angle photography contributes to that visualization of Adèle as a "woman who realizes herself in self-destruction," a "divided self." [20]

Nowhere is this more in evidence than in the five scenes where Adèle is shown sleeping or trying to sleep. These scenes punctuate the narrative and contribute to its form and thematic focus. In all of them, we look down on Adèle. We see her in bed in the first and final two scenes, tossing in troubled sleep. In the second and third scenes we stare into the depths of her dream, looking straight down into the face of a drowning Adèle who is sucked under the surface before our eyes. This recurrent nightmare represents Adèle's internalization of the drowning death of her sister Léopoldine, a death that traumatized both Adèle and her father and continued to shape their lives for decades.[21] This image is imposed over that of Adèle tossing in bed. These scenes, which vividly depict Adèle's subconscious identification with her sister and the pressing, disturbing sense of her own loss of identity, are reminiscent of Scottie's oneiric redefinition in *Vertigo* (1957). The inexorable process of loss is emblematized by the high-angle photography which casts protagonist and viewer alike adrift in an all-absorbing sea. Just as, eventually, Adèle will cease to recognize her hussar, so ultimately she will cease to recognize herself. Because of our angle of vision and distance, as in the worst of nightmares, we participate in her helplessness but can do nothing to stop it.

One of the most telling high-angle shots in Truffaut's film is that of the face of Adèle as she composes a letter to Pinson, the first of a series of falsehoods she commits to paper during the film. Viewed from on high her face is illuminated, but her dark clothing blends into surrounding darkness to make her visage seem disembodied. The intensity of the gaze, the strange vitality in the eyes, the inventiveness and patent falseness of the letter all give the scene a sense of detachment, mystery, and impassivity reminiscent of the woman's isolated face shown during the opening credits in *Vertigo* and of the dream sequences later in that film. Adèle's disconnected face reappears later, over water. Truffaut said that *Adèle H.* is "l'histoire d'un visage," the story of a face, and of "quelque chose de vertigineux," something vertiginous.[22] Although critics such as Insdorf, Colville, and Haskell have commented on similarities between Truffaut's film and *Vertigo* especially in the common theme of a compulsion to make another over into an idealized vision, insufficient attention has been given to other parallels, particularly the centrality of circuitous movement and the unusual role played by bookstores in both films.

As in *Vertigo*, vertiginous movements are recorded throughout *Adèle H.* and constitute the vital circuitry of the film. From beginning to end, the camera circles characters as if stalking them, viewing them as within a vortex. Shots looking down into water in the opening sequence and dream sequences as well as the elevated camera angle in the cameo sequence that ends with the camera circling Adèle—these devices set the tone for the central dynamic of the film which, as in *Vertigo*, is a protracted, wandering search for an illusion. This theme is reified in scenes at the book shop, where Adèle is first seen passing by, glancing in, reversing her direction, the better to stare through the window at a nattily dressed hussar in the shop. Convinced it must be Pinson, she moves out of sight to a position where she can watch him as he leaves the shop with the woman and her dogs. She then returns to the shop door and enters it, thus engaging the interior space recently occupied by Pinson. She quizzes the proprietor about the identity and character of the lieutenant, then buys some writing supplies and leaves. We view this whole scene from a somewhat elevated position, as from a perch. We are made privy to Adèle's comings and goings, her observations, lies, and demands, and her ultimate departure in a completely different direction, all from a slightly superior perspective. Since the action on the street is framed within the bookstore windows, as if on a stage or screen, we have the sensation of being provided first balcony seats, the best view in the house, over what is happening both on stage and also in the protected, yet histrionic space of this miniature theater that is the bookstore.[23]

The bookstore becomes a centerpiece in Truffaut's narrative. Until near the end of the film it is viewed exclusively from within, interiorizing its effect. Even when actions on the street are important, as when Adèle collapses in front of the shop, we remain within its dark warmth, viewing these events from inside. Since it is a stationer's shop as well as bookstore, it becomes the source of her writing materials and hence of her means for creating her story.[24] Like Pop Liebl's bookstore in *Vertigo,* this book shop is a privileged space where past and present merge, where the changing lights of the world beyond are filtered through a protective lens, where expansive windows provide a means of viewing that world and also a means of shutting it out in favor of an imaginative inner realm. Both represent a source of information about the domain outside the windows, but also a retreat from it: bound volumes reflecting heritage, tradition, and conventions seem stable, comforting, but also inadequate and challenging to those who perceive their own lives as "romanesque" stories in the making.[25] In both instances, a knowing proprietor supplies information about the legends and the potential of the area and also establishes disquieting links between the past and a personal, highly passionate present. The sun sets while Scottie (James Stewart) and Midge (Barbara Bel Geddes) are inside the bookstore; the couple depart into darkening night. Unescorted, Adèle leaves the darkness of the book shop's interior to enter the world beyond, which she attempts to force to correlate to her world of inner darkness. The last time we see the bookstore, we view it from the street; it is now only a window where the crazed Adèle's reflection appears beside Whistler's face. She has definitively renounced him and the safety of his shop for the world and its folly.

The book shop in Halifax plays a more sustained role than the one in San Francisco, serving as a locus for existential motifs characteristic of Truffaut. In *The Story of Adèle H.* it becomes an important unifying site for the developing action as well as a potential source for human contact, kindness, and understanding as its proprietor develops a personal interest in Adèle. It is from within this shop that we witness the beginnings of her wanderings— after learning about Pinson, she walks off in a different direction than her original course—and it is from this spot that we are allowed to monitor the progress of those wanderings as she returns for reinforcement in her mission in the form of stationery, books, and inspiration. The continuing contacts between the bookseller and Adèle suggest that when one leaves the safe confines of the shop, one risks loss or hurt, as when Adèle faints in the street or when Whistler ventures to the boarding house to offer her sympathy. That ill-fated visit prefigures a definitive rupture. When next we see them together he offers her a copy of her father's novel *Les misérables,* only to discover his good intentions rejected and rebuffed.

In this context the book shop represents a stark contrast with other sites in Halifax, notably the bank and Adèle's room at the Saunders' boarding house. At the bank Adèle is trapped in oppressive bureaucracy and paternal imprisonment through the letters she receives from her father and through the financial institution that serves as intermediary for their delivery and for the funds she needs in order to survive. Her room at the boarding house represents another extreme where she is in a world of her own invention, free to create herself and to worship at the shrine of "her" Pinson. The bookstore seems the one spot where she has the potential to establish some degree of equilibrium between the systematized, hierarchical outside world and the imaginative, yearning life within. Like Scottie in *Vertigo,* Adèle chooses to forego the relative safety and balance of the book shop to pursue destructive imbalance instead.

As in *Vertigo,* the trajectory of the principal character in *Adèle H.* is a circuitous one, consisting of wanderings and spyings, false starts, deceptive leads, contrived separations and unexpected reunitings. Adèle wanders the streets of Barbados at the close of the film just as she had done in Nova Scotia at its start. Waters serve as a visual and psychological correlative for these peripatetic maneuvers in *Adèle H.* as in *Vertigo.* Truffaut's visualization of the drowning scenes in which Léopoldine's experiences are relived by Adèle recalls both Judy/Madeleine's plunge into the Bay in *Vertigo* and

Scottie's own identification with her in his dream. The final image of Adèle's identity-asserting vision of herself by the sea evokes that of Judy/Madeleine at the California coast. In all these instances questions of selfhood and of incomplete identities seeking realignment are addressed and visually resolved through the use of water and a flexible, often elevated camera, devices that effectively portray the mechanisms by which Scottie and Adèle allow themselves to be mesmerized into seeking someone who exists primarily in their own imaginings.

CONCLUSION

While it would be audacious to claim a consistently Hitchcockian vision in *The Story of Adèle H.*, one can see in it evidence of Truffaut's tendency to recognize and reuse elements derived from Hitchcock, taking sustenance from them, adapting them for his own purposes. Always interested in character development, Truffaut resolves the dramatic situation in a personal and individual manner in keeping with Adèle's psychology and character, and with his own. Adèle's relationship to her father is in many ways comparable to Truffaut's relationship to Hitchcock. Her struggle to establish her identity over against that of "a genius . . . the most famous man in the world" is Truffaut's own struggle, *vis-à-vis* "the greatest director in the world" who would curtly criticize Truffaut's work.[26] Like Victor Hugo, Alfred Hitchcock represented both a cultural bastion and a forceful paternal figure to be recognized and reckoned with.

Although the story of a disintegrating self and some of the trappings in *Adèle H.* are reminiscent of Hitchcock, the resolution is distinctively Truffaut's. This is conveyed by his cameo role in which he presents himself as a self-possessed authority figure with limited knowledge. In the course of the narrative, Pinson, the soldier with whom Truffaut's character is confounded, is promoted from "place holder"(*lieu-tenant*) to "chief" (*capitaine*). In his masterful use of high-angle shots, circuitous movement, and telling silences Truffaut himself salutes Hitchcock with deference and with ingenuity while establishing a distinctive, highly personal aesthetic vision. With that vision came an assertion of his own future, which would become less overtly Hitchcockian thereafter. In *Small Change*, released the same year as Hitchcock's last film *Family Plot*, Truffaut appears as the first adult in a film where parents grow with their children and teachers learn with their pupils. The two strains of reverential memory and personal growth converge in *The Green Room*, where Truffaut plays a writer of obituaries who is obsessed with preserving the memory of the dead but who also learns sign language to communicate with his adopted son. Thus we find Truffaut coming to grips with the concentrated, vertiginous world of Adèle H. and Alfred H., and asserting in the end that growth and communication are possible after all, even in the shadow of parental figures such as Victor Hugo or Alfred Hitchcock.[27]

NOTES

1. First published as *Le cinéma selon Hitchcock* in 1966; English trans. by Helen G. Scott (New York: Simon and Schuster, 1967); French ed. reissued with a new introduction in 1975; rev. ed. 1978. Definitive ed., entitled *Hitchcock/Truffaut*: French ed. 1983, English trans. 1984. For complete bibliographic data, see Eugene P. Walz, *François Truffaut: A Guide to References and Resources* (Boston: G. K. Hall, 1982), 154–61. On Hitchcock as father figure to Truffaut, see Annette Insdorf, *François Truffaut*, rev. ed. (Cambridge: Cambridge University Press, 1994), 138, and Georgiana Colvile, "Pères perdus, pères retrouvés dans l'oeuvre de François Truffaut," *The French Review* 68 [2] (December 1994): 286–87. See also Truffaut, *Le cinéma selon François Truffaut*, ed. Anne Gillain (Paris: Flammarion, 1988), 329 (cited hereafter as *Cinéma*); Don Allen, *Finally Truffaut* (London: Secker and Warburg, 1985), 171–73; and Pauline Kael, "All for Love," *New Yorker* (October 27, 1975): 130. See also François Truffaut, *Correspondence 1954–1984* (New York: Cooper Square, 2000), 88, 166, 177–84, and Antoine de Baecque and Serge Toubiana, *Truffaut: A Biography* (New York: Knopf, 1999), 78.

2. For details see Gilles Cahoreau, *François Truffaut: 1932–1984* (Paris: Julliard, 1989), 291–93.

3. See Insdorf, *François Truffaut*, 39–67 and *passim*. For the text of the screenplay, see François Truffaut, "L'histoire d'Adèle H.," *L'Avant-Scène du Cinéma*, no. 165 (January 1976): 3–47; and *The Story of Adèle H.*, trans. by Helen G. Scott (New York: Grove Press, 1976).

4. "Une histoire réelle transformée en fiction [a true story transformed into fiction]" (Truffaut, *Cinéma*, 328).

5. Truffaut's anonymous role in the "Rotor [Centrifuge]" scene in *The 400 Blows*, is discussed by Colvile ("Pères perdus, pères retrouvés," 286). On Truffaut's roles as father-figures in his films see Colvile, 283–87; on the extent to which Hitchcock's appearances form a coherent part of his films, see Raymond Bellour and Guy Rosolato, "Dialogue: Remembering (this memory of) a Film," trans. Thomas Y. Levin, in *Psychoanalysis and Cinema*, ed. Ann Kaplan (New York: Routledge, 1990), 201–02; Colvile, 287; Maurice Yacowar, *Hitchcock's British Films* (Hamden: Archon

Books, 1977), 270–78; and Thomas M. Leitch, *Find the Director and Other Hitchcock Games* (Athens: University of Georgia Press, 1991), 8–11, 21.

6. Insdorf has commented on the framing devices used in this film (*François Truffaut*, 133–39), and Colvile has described the nesting structures with which it begins and ends: from historical frame to Adèle's arrival in Halifax at the outset, mirrored by her departure from Barbados to historical frame at the close ("Pères perdus, pères retrouvés," 289).

7. Literally, "he is already as well known as the white wolf," i.e., quite well known; although this expression (rendered in the subtitles as "a man about town") need not necessarily convey sexual overtones, in this Anglo-French context it may; in French culture wolves traditionally connote menacing aggression and danger, as in the folk tale of Little Red Riding Hood, La Fontaine's well-known fable of the Wolf and the Lamb, and nineteenth-century French preoccupation with werewolves.

8. On the color symbolism in *Adèle H.*, see Anne Gillain, *François Truffaut: le secret perdu* (Paris: Hatier, 1991), 222–23.

9. Robert E. Kapsis explains that this is an inside joke: Hitchcock first saw Hedren in a commercial for a diet drink in which she responded to a similar whistle; see "Hollywood Filmmaking and Reputation Building: Hitchcock's *The Birds*," *Journal of Popular Film and Television* 15, no. 1 (1987): 10.

10. In his initial attempts to persuade Hitchcock to consent to his five-hundred question interview, Truffaut expressed the opinion that Hitchcock was a masterful and effective director—indeed "the best director in the world"—in large part because of his profound understanding of silence as the essence of filmic art (letter to Hitchcock, 2 June 1962, rpt. in Cahoreau, *François Truffaut: 1932–1984*, 213–14). On the moral and emotional resonances of silence in *The Birds*, see Elisabeth Weis, *The Silent Scream: Alfred Hitchcock's Sound Track* (Rutherford: Fairleigh Dickinson University Press, 1982), 138–47; cf. Truffaut, *Hitchcock*, 292–97.

11. Yacowar sees Hitchcock in the role of a "complacent man whose relationship with the animal world is about to be upset" (*Hitchcock's British Films*, 275).

12. Truffaut: "Ce plan dans Adèle . . . ait une valeur symbolique. C'est une blague vaguement triste [This scene in *Adèle* . . . may have a symbolic value. It's a somewhat sad joke.]" (*Cinéma*, 332). Stills of two outtakes from this scene may be found in Molly Haskell, "*The Story of Adèle H.* Is a Tribute to an Experience," *Village Voice*, October 27, 1975, 144; and Allen, *Finally Truffaut*, 176.

13. See the cover photo on Donald Spoto, *The Dark Side of Genius: The Life of Alfred Hitchcock* (New York: Little, Brown, 1983), hardback edition.

14. On the content of the remarks in this scene and its importance to the symbolism of the film, see Dick Stromgren, " 'Now to the Banquet We Press': Hitchcock's Gourmet and Gourmand Offerings," in *Beyond the Stars III: The Material World in American Popular Film*, ed. Paul Loukides and Linda K. Fuller. Studies in American

Popular Film, 3 (Bowling Green, Ohio: Popular Press, 1993), 38–50. He also discusses Hitchcock's more active role in the discovery of *Frenzy*'s corpses in the trailer for the film (48–49).

15. "A vital force on the move" or "a force to contend with": the famous line applied to the hero in Victor Hugo's 1830 play *Hernani,* the play from which literary manuals usually date the onset of French romanticism; on Adèle as female Hernani, see Allen, *Finally Truffaut,* 176; cf. Insdorf, *François Truffaut,* 134.

16. Donald Spoto, *The Art of Alfred Hitchcock: Fifty Years of his Motion Pictures,* rev. ed. (New York: Anchor, 1992), 444.

17. The idea of the dog as incompletely domesticated wolf is firmly anchored in French school children's minds via Alfred de Vigny's poem "La mort du loup," a staple in French secondary education for over a century.

18. The reference to Scottish grouse in whiskey seems pointedly sardonic and triply applicable to Hitchcock.

19. Insdorf, *François Truffaut,* 140.

20. Kael, "All for Love," 130, 132. High-angle shots so dominate *Adèle H.* that Kael's sensation that she "wasn't aware of sky at any time during the movie" (132) is accurate.

21. On the thematic importance of these dream sequences, see Gillain, *François Truffaut: le secret perdu,* 223–25. Léopoldine was named for Victor Hugo's father, General Léopold Hugo, whom the poet viewed as a true hero and exemplar of generosity and courage (see, for example, Hugo's didactic poem "Après la Bataille," in which this case is made dramatically in a war scene where lessons are taught to a young hussar at considerable personal risk). Adèle was named for her mother. It was rumored that her father was not Hugo (Kael, "All for Love," 132). Léopoldine was favored by Victor Hugo, and her drowning death at age nineteen was commemorated in over 160 of his poems (see L. Cellier's introduction to *Les contemplations,* i–xxxviii, and the collection of pictures that precede it, as well as Allen, *Finally Truffaut,* 173).

22. Truffaut, *Cinéma,* 331, 325. "L'idée fixe [*d'Adèle H.*] a quelque chose de vertigineux et je crois que j'ai été entraîné dans ce vertige [The recurrent idea (of *Adèle H.*) has something vertiginous about it and I think I was caught up in that vertigo]" *(Cinéma,* 325).

23. Cf. the position occupied by Adèle herself when she spies on Pinson at the Music Hall.

24. On the importance of Adèle as writer, composing the story of her own (fictive) existence, see Insdorf, *François Truffaut,* 132, 180–81, 200–01, and Colvile, "Pères perdus, pères retrouvés," *passim.*

25. The term "romanesque" is invoked by Adèle early in the film when she solicits a notary's help in locating Pinson. Used to describe her imaginary niece,

the term is equally applicable to Adèle herself. Rendered as "too romantic" in the subtitles, it means fanciful in a specifically novelistic way, as in Arthurian romances or ancient romances such as *Daphnis and Chloe*. It was an excess of "romanesque" adventures that undid Flaubert's Emma Bovary; on Adèle as Emma's descendant and Truffaut's alter ego, see Colvile, "Pères perdus, pères retrouvés," 289, 291. "Je suis 100% en faveur du romanesque dans les films [I am 100% in favor of the "romanesque" in films]" (Truffaut, *Cinéma,* 328).

26. The first statements are from the doctor in *Adèle H.;* the last, from Truffaut's letter to Hitchcock, 2 June 1962, rpt. in Cahoreau, *François Truffaut: 1932–1984,* 213–14. For Hitchcock's critiques of the derivative nature of Truffaut's cinema, see Laurent Bouzereau, *The Alfred Hitchcock Quote Book* (Secaucus: Carol Publishing Group, 1993), 158, 160.

27. A version of this essay was presented at the March 1996 conference, "The Late Alfred Hitchcock: Re-viewing Alfred Hitchcock with Twenty-Twenty Vision," sponsored by the *Hitchcock Annual* and Baylor University. I am indebted to Richard Allen, Geo Presley-Brooks, Chris Caldwell, Brian Dixon, Jason Leawoods, and Nancy Vest for their assistance in the preparation of this essay.

THE MYTH OF APOCALYPSE
AND THE HORROR FILM:
THE PRIMACY OF *PSYCHO*
AND *THE BIRDS*

CHRISTOPHER SHARRETT

There is compelling evidence that the American cinema underwent a profound change in the late 1960s, one that indicated an accentuation of an apocalyptic spirit that has become central to discourse about contemporary culture.[1] Like its earlier manifestations, this apocalypticism prefers myth over historical consciousness, and consequently opts for radical destruction over radical change or even reform. This apocalypticism, in part a reactionary response to the Vietnam/Watergate epoch, in fact has its roots deep within American sensibility that is regularly manifest in the popular genres. For example, the Western, the genre most concerned with celebrating the American civilizing experience, gradually became extinct. Peckinpah's *The Wild Bunch* (1969), released at the close of the decade and at the height of the Vietnam War, has come to be regarded as the quintessential "last" Western for its summary statement on the end of a distinct period of American life. A key motif of *The Wild Bunch* is the setting sun; this, combined with the extreme violence of the film's ending, suggests that an older way of life (viewed with both cynicism and nostalgia) must be obliterated totally (taking the guilty and the innocent) since, it cannot be recuperated.[2] On a more modified level, Arthur Penn's *Bonnie and Clyde* (1967) shares similar assumptions. The nostalgia of this film is interwoven with the theme of the death of innocence and the failure of a rather vague ideal vision. Bonnie and Clyde are an attractive if misguided young couple brutally murdered by hidden gunmen as they drive down a country road; the parallels with the crushed ideals of the 1960s and with the paralyzing shock of such events as the JFK assassination are deliberately unmistakable.[3] The apocalypse of this film, like Peckinpah's, resides in its acceptance of the inevitability of defeat. *Bonnie and Clyde*'s success with the youth movement of the 1960s supports such a claim. *Bonnie and Clyde* helped advance both an apocalyptic and a political view of the nature of the opposition; the oppressed are necessarily victims, but the only solution in the face of an implacable enemy is death. Rather than opt for radical change, the film inevitably embraces an American ethic of total annihilation. The film projects a view of its characters as martyrs precisely because they must accede to this concept.

These films are significant because their apocalypticism stresses the inevitability of failure based on flaws inherent within American society. These flaws are not defined along traditional moral or religious lines, but instead represent a simple rejection of certain assumptions represented in earlier American cinema (Capra and Ford) about the value of the community. Still, these works are concerned more with misplaced dreams than the failure of capitalism or fundamental defects of human civilization. The total unrecuperability of society would be dealt with by the *fantastique,* and the precedents are without question Hitchcock's *Psycho* (1960) and *The Birds* (1963). A discussion of these works must be prefaced by a comment on the incipient apocalypticism long evident in the horror film.

Most students of horror and science-fiction would no doubt look to the latter for evidence of the apocalyptic sensibility and the "imagination of disaster."[4] Obviously many of the science-fiction films of the 1950s support that view, but in fact few if any of them address problems deeply rooted in human psychology or the constitution of civilization. Rather, the more famous "Armageddon movies" or monster epics of the post-war years (e.g., *War of the Worlds, Beast from 20,000 Fathoms, Godzilla*) are involved with the failure of technology or with concerns that could be explained with reference to the political/social milieu—*Invasion of the Body Snatchers* (1956), with its Cold War intertext, is a good example. What is significant here is that the crises befalling society as depicted in science-fiction are indeed *explainable* without penetrating analysis of social or economic systems. More important, society is most often depicted as recuperable in science-fiction, even after total devastation has taken place. This optimism places most of past science-fiction within the more comfortable mainstream of American genre cinema.

By contrast, the horror film has not only co-opted the role of science-fiction in responding to social concerns, but has done so with a critical eye focused on more than discrete issues of current society. The horror film has long since cut many of its ties to the Gothic novel, Romanticism, and the conventions of early horror films (e.g., those produced by Universal and Hammer) in order to assume this new posture. This transition is not unusual—the novel *Frankenstein* has, after all, been interpreted as a fore-runner of both horror and science-fiction.[5] At the same time the horror film has seldom been recognized as a genre annotating sweeping political/social problems.

Generally, the horror film is thought to deal with properties of the un-conscious mind, and to draw its power from marshaling nightmare imagery connecting to individual mental life.[6] Unlike art movements such as Surre-alism, however, the horror film's function in exposing the workings of the unconscious mind seldom served as overt social critique, largely because of the incredible nature of the genre's content (psychoanalytic or political readings of *Frankenstein* and *Dracula* have seldom been accessible to the mass audience). It is nonetheless obvious that the horror film has inher-ited the apocalyptic current of American literature that emphasizes collapse over the revelation of biblical mythology. It has also formed a critique of society using a multivalent textual apparatus. In brief, the horror film has begun a process of unmasking its own conventions while offering a pow-erful critique of fundamental assumptions of much American art, includ-ing concepts such as "human nature" heretofore treated as self-evident and sacrosanct by all genres. While undertaking this critique, the horror film has refused to adopt any programmatic response, to accept a critical method or admit to any system of causality in describing the apocalypse; although some films (the work of George Romero, for example) contain allegories of consumer culture or corporate evil, the chief concern of this apocalypse is with a collective failure that cannot be reversed.

Whereas the early horror film contained a "demon" (mummy, vam-pire, werewolf, ghoul) on whom violence could be displaced, the post-1960s genre has dispensed with most monsters in order to make the issue of pathology both transparent and transpsychical. The current device of psychopath-as-monster both turns the bourgeois subject into a model of explanation and upsets audience expectations about the localization and displacement of evil. The horror film's often conscious awareness of psychoanalysis has made its plots less concerned with terrible but discrete incidents and more involved in describing a general evil. To be sure, this characteristic is present in some allegorical features of early horror, including Edgar Ulmer's *The Black Cat* (1934), which relies on an expansive notion of evil arising out of social turmoil; in Ulmer's film a close equation is made between a decadent aristocracy and the ravages of war produced by a class system (the devil worshipper's chateau is built on the graves of World War I). With this work, however, the recuperability of society is still emphasized, even as hero and villain both descend into madness and barbarism.

In two pivotal works of the 1960s the belief in the recuperability of society begins to disappear. Cultural anthropology is relevant to the horror film's description of the presence of an evil age overtaking all experience; this evil age, present in various mythologies,[7] is relevant for its sense of an approaching apocalypse based on a recognizable disintegration within the human community rather than the capricious displeasure of a wrathful God. Although the landmark importance of *Psycho* to the apocalyptic horror film is deflated slightly by the intervention of the psychiatrist (repeating the role of the horror film's Van Helsing-style scientist) and the resultant closure this scene provides the film, almost every scene serves to subvert conventional notions of what American society is and what a work of art should represent.

II

Hitchcock's *Psycho* cannot be overemphasized as a prologue to the resurgence of the apocalyptic temperament in cinema, and to the privileged position of the horror film in furthering apocalypticism in the ensuing twenty years after this film's release. The first authentic horror film of Hitchcock's career (there is only one other—*The Birds*), *Psycho* can be viewed as a prelude to the cultural anxiety that grew with the political assassinations of the 1960s, escalating and seemingly random domestic violence, the Vietnam War, the Watergate affair and the adjacent breakdown of consensus that in turn engendered a new interest in cataclysm that quickly became evidenced in art. This way of viewing *Psycho*'s importance of course ignores an interpretation that would see the film as a repository not only of many existent genre conventions but of a number of various strains of cultural assumption that predated the film. Hitchcock's choice of a particular locale and time of the day for the film's establishing sequence ("Phoenix, Friday,

Dec. 11, 2:43 P.M.") and his decision to portray the Janet Leigh character as "a perfectly ordinary bourgeoise,"[8] suggests an attempt to unravel some principal assumptions of American middle-class life and to show a general psychopathology simmering underneath the superstructure of these assumptions.

The classic opening of the film, which selects the city of Phoenix and then a particular bedroom window to locate the narrative, has the function of instilling a sense of arbitrariness in the construction of the actual narrative that unfolds. This establishing shot, viewed in retrospect, has a metadocumentary, "you are there" quality suggesting that the pathology we eventually see in Norman Bates has its causes in the general American experience. While the swerve in the film's plot from a tale of stolen money and a woman's frustrated love life to one of psychological aberration and murder might still be viewed by audiences as simply a filmmaker's decision to upset genre conventions and audience expectations, there is no way one can avoid the ultimate recognition of the causal links between the two plots, and it would be foolish to assert that the "first" plot is simply a red herring to provide a premise for the "gimmick" of the famous shower sequence.

The difficult interconnections between the erotic drive, the Puritan ethic, and the demands of capitalism are established in *Psycho* in such a way as to form a sense of "desire" quite in keeping with psychoanalytic and structuralist cultural investigations. There is little overstatement here, since Hitchcock develops a narrative that continually reveals itself to be a systemic analysis of American life.[9]

The frustration and confinement that form the bleak atmosphere of the film are established in the furtive affair between Sam Loomis and Marion, the tenderness of which is quickly deflated by the puritanical constraints of Marion's life and the dismal financial legacy Sam inherits from his father. The pall of oppression/repression hangs heavy in this early scene, as Sam glumly humors Marion about her demand for "respectability" while at the same time complaining that he is "tired of sweating for people who aren't there" (just like Norman?). An equation is made between Sam's financial burdens (imposed not just by a dead father but by the absent presence of capitalist rule) and Marion's total acquiescence to the "respectable" sexual mores of patriarchy that have driven the couple into dank hotel rooms. We are immediately forced to recognize the burden of the past weighing down on all the characters of the film. The film does not propose specific causal ties between sexual frustration and crime, and it would no doubt be less successful if it attempted such connections. (Marion's precise reasons for the theft are not clearly established beyond her yearning for a "private island.")

It is precisely in the way in which the film shows people motivated by unconscious drives, unable to perceive the operation of ideology in personal interchange, that *Psycho* is a compelling depiction of middle-class existence. Film scholarship has already paid considerable attention to *Psycho's* reflexive aspect and its tendency to subvert not just audience expectations but audience assumptions that it remains distant from the implications of an art work. What has *not* been clearly established is that the film's attempt to incorporate the viewer as voyeur/victim cannot be read simply as a clever visual device or intellectual conceit, regardless of authorial intentionality: if we as spectators accept the role of voyeur along with Norman Bates, we accept the alienation associated with this pathology and the conclusions psychological/ideological criticism might draw not only about the nature of spectacle but about the social conditions that engender fascination. It is not misleading to suggest that *Psycho,* of all Hollywood films, aspires most to be a mirror of its audience.

The case of *Psycho* as a critique of an entire society is made stronger in retrospect by a study of the iconographic and textual links among all the characters. Marion's white brassiere, an early symbol of her frustrated desire (and a reminder of a restrictive production code) takes on amplified significance in describing the situation of the characters when we get to see the inside of Norman's house, with his mother's drab Victorian wardrobe, the bronze cast of folded hands on a dresser, and Norman's own bedroom, where male sexuality regresses to the infantile. The very structure of the Bates's house (whose style is actually termed California Gothic[10] and is unmistakably a reminder of a Puritan heritage and the burden of the old world), with its Bachelardian stratification (repression hidden in fruit cellar and attic), suggests the illness within American Gothic and the new pathology it gives rise to in the "total system" of the 1950s motel and automobile culture, the culture that affects Marion. We are forced at last to recognize Norman as an extreme but lawful consequence of behavior that continues universally in everyday life, an idea supported by the duplication—at some level or other—of many of Norman's actions by other characters early in the film in such a way as to preface almost all of his actions.

The statement by the overbearing Cassidy that Marion's boss "should air condition [her] up" has a deliberately erotic/sadistic tone underlined by Marion's cavalier treatment by Lowery and Cassidy. Cassidy's constant references to his "baby" (about to be married and become a propertied member of bourgeois culture) makes us aware of society's infantilization of both women and men as a way of conditioning them to authority. Cassidy's "baby" prefigures the monstrous infant Norman. And the fact that the secretaries' workspace does *not* have air conditioning unites the authority of capital with the condescension and degradation of patriarchy. Marion and Sam have a masochistic fixation on the gaze, born out of guilt, that is very similar to Norman's relationship to his wide-eyed stuffed owls, the ever-present dominance of the mother, and his need to turn his guilt into sadism. Sam snidely suggests that he and Marion "turn mother's picture to the wall" before they make love, a suggestion that upsets Marion, who is also dominated by the presence of a dead mother. Marion looks up with a certain contempt as Cassidy attempts to flirt with her from a perch slightly above her desk; Cassidy's brandishing of money as a weapon of authority with which he will buy happiness for his "little girl" helps Marion to commit her crime out of a feeling of resentment rather than greed. The sexual/economic dynamics and tensions of the Lowery/Cassidy scene are nicely preceded by the patter from Marion's colleague (Patricia Hitchcock). She offers Marion tranquilizers, which she claims she needed on her wedding night, even though "Teddy would be furious if he knew." When Marion asks if there were phone calls before she came to work, her coworker tells her "Teddy called, then mother called to see if Teddy called." The banality of this 1950s sitcom dialogue illuminates the oppressiveness of this culture, particularly the guilt that results from the paternalism and obsessive supervision of the young common to middle-class life.

As with Norman, Marion's guilt seems to propel her further into repetition, exaggerating both her self-importance and self-loathing to the point of narcissism, as when she imagines the vendetta Lowery and Cassidy are planning as she flees the scene of the crime, and when she panics on being discovered by the highway patrolman.

Marion and Norman Bates are tied together by a bond of guilt, and guilt along with a necessary divine retribution become characteristic of the apocalyptic cinema all the way to *Taxi Driver* (1976). The concept of the gaze, an element emphasized in various descriptions of Hitchcock, can be understood in the apocalyptic context.[11] The patrolman's one-way impenetrable gaze, the early shot of Marion supine under Sam's upright figure, Lowery and Cassidy watching Marion as she is seated in the office, even the shower head in the Bates Motel, all emphasize Marion's guilt and helplessness, feelings that precede her actual crime and continue after she acknowledges her crime as an attempt to escape to a "private island" (suggesting that the robbery was not meant to make possible a life with Sam but to permit a rejection of society). The notion of the private island recurs in Romero's *Dawn of the Dead* (1978) and *Day of the Dead* (1984), apocalyptic horror films explicitly about the idea that current society is beyond repair. If we read the shower head as another of the film's "eye motifs" (as William Rothman suggests[12]), some concentration must be focused on it as the last image Marion sees before her vicious murder. If it is the final hypostatization of her guilt, this eye of God produces the "great rain" of retribution not unlike that of Travis Bickle's self-abasing wish-fulfillment in *Taxi Driver*. Norman's guilt is an even more exaggerated extension of Marion's, with the all-seeing eyes of his stuffed birds prefiguring the furies of *The Birds* in their representation of a terror internalized that will burst forth not in purgation but self-destruction. The Bates's Gothic homestead towers in the background, actually an empty carcass, but for Norman a seat of divine power that dominates his every gesture. A good example is Norman running up to his house apparently to "tell off" his mother and assert his independence after his sex urge has been awakened by the sight of Marion's nudity. He stops short as he enters the house, standing alone, intimidated, at the bottom of the staircase, as if this were a stairway to a throne. It is not ironic that it is only when Marion confronts Norman, the most diseased (and most representative) member of the society in which she is involved, that she undergoes an *anagnorisis*. The fact that Marion is nonetheless murdered after her self-realization suggests that neither she nor the society that produced her is recuperable.

A more detailed analysis (and there have been many) of *Psycho*'s images can only develop this film's indictment of the American condition and the vaguely-hedged pessimism about the consequences of this condition. We notice that the action moves from Phoenix into Southern California, the borders of the frontier, and the sense of the now-limited expanses of the American landscape are evident at various points, e.g., the desert landscapes in Lowery's chintzy, sweltering outer office workspace for Marion and her coworker, and the general motif of flight, search, and rescue. A very drastic closing down of the frontier is visible in Lila's discovery of Mrs. Bates. A comparison to the Western must be modified: the movement of the film is steadily downward and inward, away from the feeling of daylight, abundance, and expanse (also evident at the start of *The Birds*) to a nightmarish claustrophobia that exteriorizes the unconscious mind. Lila's entry into the fruit cellar and her first sighting of Mrs. Bates are sequences more unnerving than the punchline of the mummified corpse itself. The cellar, bathed in the harsh, high-contrast light of a single naked bulb, seems apart from the rest of the dwelling, possibly because this is an image not comfortably associated with expectations of the middle-class home, even one that is a relic of the last century. The jugs, baskets, casks, shelves, and slat-work surrounding Mrs. Bates are as much part of a petrified history as the corpse in the antique chair. But what makes this setting so disturbing? The convention of the cellar in the Gothic genre is well-known, as is the cellar as architectural component corresponding to stratification in the unconscious mind (i.e., the cellar as repressed anxieties, the attic as stored dreams).[13] Other ideas circulate during Lila's exploration, however. The long black shelves to the left of the door recall concentration camp bunks so familiar from documentary footage,[14] and the black-and-white realization of this image and the rest of the Bates house isn't far from the TV version of "I Remember Mama" and the 1950s media presentation of the bourgeoisie (*Psycho* was first intended as a teleplay). So the film's expansiveness is also on the micro level, detailing the universality of pathology and societal collapse in the single image's capturing the interconnections of the film with a morbid history of repressive Western culture.

The expansiveness of the film's central concerns are evident also in the title: *Psycho* reflects the transmogrification of scientific language into a jargon that represents a certain pervasive distrust of psychoanalysis and the tendency to deny the existence of the unconscious mind. (It is noteworthy how popular genres of the 1960s and 1970s have established the "psycho" as demon and as member of a criminal class, although little or no attention is paid to the causative factors behind the appearance of a host of "crazies" in the popular consciousness that fosters this art.) It has already been established that the title, as jargon, seems deliberately unspecific in suggesting a reference to both a person and a general condition.

As suggested, Hitchcock's decision to conclude the film with the psychiatrist's speech has the effect of narrowing the scope of the work. On one level the speech might be seen as the introduction of the device of the *escolio* (such as in Borges) to expose the narrative and make it more self-reflexive. Certainly the speech makes the story much more obviously concerned with psychopathology, but at the same time it makes it more concerned with Norman Bates alone. Without this scene the film might be obscure to an audience (certainly less so for audiences of today), but with a less explanatory ending there would likely be a far stronger suggestion that the disease represented by Norman's case is not containable, and is actually overcoming the entire society. The final image of the film—the dissolve of Norman's death's head grin into the salvaging of Marion's car from the swamp—has a most devastating impact that subverts the neat closure of the psychiatrist's speech. The surfacing of the car from the mud undercuts the psychiatrist's glibness, and this bleak image is bolstered by the terminal state of Norman's illness; the latter is reinforced by the sophisticated integration of the last image of Norman with that of the car. The salvaging of the car may state, on a more literal level, the forced confrontation with the consequences of repression long since out of hand.

III

We must make a case for *Psycho* as an apocalyptic work at least because of the premises in the film relevant to a broad cinematic current to follow, and for the articulation of apocalypse recognizable in later films. The films of the 1960s and 1970s show that *Psycho* was the progenitor of a new apocalyptic tradition, a premise confirmed by the way the impulses of the film were given a more spectacular and devastating elaboration in Hitchcock's next project, *The Birds*.

After introducing psychoanalysis into the horror film to create a very expansive metaphor, Hitchcock subverts this in *The Birds* to rely on an allegorical apparatus that proposes the "cosmic" nature of social disaster and the failure of interchange. *The Birds* reflects, it would seem, a distrust of the empirical, scientific solutions evident in his earlier films. It might be a temptation to say that Hitchcock turned a corner with this film and that *The Birds* may force one to reevaluate his career. In fact, however, Hitchcock's later films were unremarkable and formulaic; it is not my purpose here to establish anything about the centrality of *Psycho* and *The Birds* to Hitchcock's career, but rather to suggest that these films embodied a moment of cultural change that became best represented in a particular genre.

The birds of Hitchcock's film are Furies that bring wrath (not justice) to a small-minded and hysterical community. Ironically, what ties *The Birds* to the apocalypticism of the modern horror film is its general dismissal of mystical/metaphysical elements of the genre while at the same time depending heavily on elements of myth and cultural ritual to signify society's disintegration. If psychoanalysis is the primary tool for understanding *Psycho*, the metalanguage of *The Birds* requires structural anthropology and mythopoeics to apprehend the film's assault on the empty belief systems of bourgeois society.

In iconology, birds have been interpreted as demons and predators and, in literary tradition and psychoanalytic criticism, the turbulent aspects of the unconscious mind.[15] In *The Birds,* the female principle is represented by the birds' attacks; the screeching, capricious, wildly destructive bird assaults are coordinated with evidence of the rapid collapse of a hysterical, largely matriarchal society that itself is a response to the arrogance and devastation wrought by patriarchy. The rather Jungian, reactionary nature of the bird symbolism complicates the film's ideology, but does not divert the film from its criticism of bourgeois life.

The action of the film is centered on three women—a possessive mother (Lydia Brenner), a spurned girlfriend (Annie Hayworth), and an unbalanced career girl (Melanie Daniels)—whose personal entanglements and feud over a man (Mitch Brenner) eventually reflect a kind of general disruption in the small community of Bodega Bay. As the narrative develops we understand that Bodega Bay is a microcosm of society. The action moves from a large, cosmopolitan city—San Francisco, perhaps the most liberal and sophisticated West Coast city—to a small, rural community, in the manner of *Psycho*. As in *Psycho*, the heroine's flight from the city suggests a form of escape, only with Melanie Daniels the flight involves more of a capricious escape from *ennui* than an act of desperation to secure love and peace of mind. *The Birds* reminds us, as did *Psycho*, that the American rural settlement was the original repository of frustration and neurosis before America closed its borders and built its cities. Unlike Norman Bates, Mitch Brenner is a healthy individual fully integrated into the community; he is seemingly able to live with his clinging mother and a sister not half his age without showing any lack of self-esteem or internalizing resentment. Yet his authority—the authority of the charismatic professional male—is undercut as Mitch's mother reminds him that the "real" male is absent ("If only your father were here!"). Mitch's integration in the community has the effect of disturbing it; as a well-to-do lawyer his presence suggests the "gentrification" of the town and the disruption of the simple values of a working class settlement. This is underscored with the arrival of Melanie Daniels, who in a short time provokes the xenophobia in the town. Marion Crane's paranoia is further developed in the character of Melanie; the hysterical mother in the seaside restaurant explicitly labels her as "evil" and the irrationality of her accusation, although decried by Mitch and the others, is apparent in almost all interaction. The eventual isolation of Melanie and the Brenner family confirms them as scapegoats, not quite arbitrarily selected, who help displace the evil of the town itself. The total breakdown of social consensus in the town is obvious in the restaurant scene. Mrs. Bundy, the bird expert who pooh-poohs the idea of the attacks, speaks with the authoritative voice of empirical reason, but as a representative of the intelligentsia she is viewed as a crackpot and curiosity. Sholes, the roughneck fisherman, is complacent about the attacks; his chief regard is bringing in his boats. Mitch says Sholes is "a man people listen to," but Sholes shrugs off the suggestion that he help organize Bodega Bay. This is *High Noon* (1952) continued, as the strong male opts for individual survival and abandons society. The middle-class businessman who orders a scotch has a solution: "Get yourself some guns, kill 'em all. . . . Messy animals." His rightist reaction and bravado are punctuated by a basic stupidity as he incinerates himself. Hitchcock relies on the convention of the fool for the word of truth; a Sean O'Casey-style drunk raises his glass and says, "It's the end of the world!"

The Birds is unique in its unqualified assault on causality, a tactic not taken up in the same way in the fantastic cinema until almost a decade later. What the audience is left to focus on is an atmosphere; the bird attacks are explained by a sense of the inevitable. The film begins, like Psycho, with an expansive shot of the city. We then see Melanie's nonchalant dismissal of her sighting of a large flock of gulls. By the end of the film Melanie's nonchalance, born out of wealth and position, dissolves as she is reduced to a near-catatonic state. Mitch's savoir faire also dissolves as he undergoes a subtle, then blatant humiliation under Lydia, Annie, and Melanie. He is demeaned and attacked outright by his mother, then forced to admit his impotence in fending off the bird attacks. Lydia, the clinging mother, separates herself from her children when she fears for her own life. Annie is killed by the birds at the point when she seems to be resolving her jealousy and developing a sympathetic (lesbian?) relationship with Melanie (Annie's prolonged gazes at Melanie suggest sympathic interest and longing as well as jealousy as Annie confronts a new rival). It is always tempting to say that the birds are a force of retribution, but repression is redressed rather than "evil." The murder of the chicken farmer fits well into a "political" reading of the film: the birds crashing kamikaze-like into his bedroom windows suggest the selfless solidarity of a warring, oppressed class. But this murder is counterbalanced by the attack on the school, for which there seems little plausible rationale outside of the sexual tensions brewing in the Melanie/Annie/Mitch relationship. It is noteworthy that the attack occurs after a very uneasy reconciliation between Melanie and Lydia; Melanie seems a bit testy about the errand of mercy she is performing and is even more disturbed by the errand being protracted by her rival Annie.

There can be no mistaking Melanie as the principal scapegoat in the narrative. Her scapegoating, as Girard suggests, represents the collapse of cohesion in the community.[16] Even the emblems of homespun common sense—the feed salesman and police chief—haven't a clue as to the reason for the birds' disruption of normalcy. The birds, if we are to regard them as Furies, do not really have the role of representing classical vengeance—only the force of repression/oppression unleashed. This is why there seems little direct connection between the bird attacks and any specific incident in the everyday, natural world in which the characters are involved. Because nothing apparently "happens" in the narrative beyond the soap-opera bickerings of the principal characters, the bird attacks are especially jolting and horrific. This is the most significant element conjoining *The Birds* to *Psycho*, demonstrating a continuity between the two films. One could assert in retrospect that Norman Bates was principally a metaphor for the bubbling-over tensions of Marion and her own "normal" middle-class circle, just as the bird attacks (which have the same jarring suddenness and staccato rhythm of Mrs. Bates's knife) evidence the tensions of Mitch's and Melanie's families and of Bodega Bay. Both Norman and the birds appear out of nowhere, at first dismissible issues having little relation to the central stories of the respective narratives. There are various structural similarities between the two films, most prominent of which are Marion's and Melanie's attempts to flee the frustrations of bourgeois life. The importance of *The Birds* is the use of the "monster" strictly as a metaphor of social crisis. Pathological repression is no longer localized; there is no scientist to explain the birds, no evidence of the unconscious surfacing.[17]

When a society cannot displace its evil in a systemic way, a disintegration into chaos must occur. An enormous amount of hate and suspicion is directed toward Melanie, but in an ambivalent manner that does not provide new cohesion. Her neuroses, fetishism, and sexual promiscuity might be seen, considering her eventual victimization, as repetition-compulsion brought on by the neglect by her mother and unhappy early life that she describes to Mitch (the description of which precedes an attack on the Brenner home). There is an equation of insanity with evil that is not quite medieval: it is supported by Melanie's rather conscious compulsions and her refusal to confront her unhappiness in an analytical manner, apparent in her flighty pursuit of Mitch. Her upper-class liberalism, including her involvement with orphan children and her linguistics classes at Berkeley, also speaks to this self-deceit.

The Birds presents apocalypse as a society's descent into primordial chaos, but it is a descent that is involuntary, a consequence of problems left unaddressed, and dissimilar to primitive rite. It occurs because a society has fallen out of contact with any common language and social contract; it seems evident that ideological and psychoanalytic readings of this situation (relative to *The Birds* and succeeding films of apocalypse) must subsume this point. Like traditional apocalyptic literature, *The Birds* is not strictly a cautionary tale; the state of crisis is accepted as a given and cannot be refused by analysis. The Brenners and Melanie seem to survive the disaster (at least temporarily), but unlike, for example, the story of Noah, there is no indication that their survival is the result of their fulfillment of any social or spiritual contract. At the same time there is no evidence to explain away the crisis in strictly social-psychological terms, since science is jettisoned (Mrs. Bundy).

IV

The importance of *Psycho* and *The Birds* is understood in light of the horror film's subsequent developments. Films as divergent as Romero's *Night of the Living Dead* and Jeff Lieberman's *Squirm* (1976) rely on the basic premise of *The Birds*: society is suddenly being overtaken by its own evil, now constituted as a mythic and unmanageable force. *The Texas Chainsaw Massacre, Eaten Alive, The Hills Have Eyes, Mother's Day, Don't Go in the House, Maniac, Frightmare, Friday the 13th, Nightmare on Elm Street,* and earlier films such as *Homicidal, Straitjacket,* and *Fanatic* are all in *Psycho*'s direct lineage. What distinguishes films like *The Texas Chainsaw Massacre* from *Psycho*'s immediate successors is not its concentration on horror-as-pathology as much as what is perceived as *Psycho*'s fundamental discovery. *The Texas Chainsaw Massacre* recreates many elements of *Psycho* chiefly by way of showing the universality of evil and how pathology ("evil" and the metaphysical disappear) has origins in commonplace features of the American middle-class experience. *The Texas Chainsaw Massacre* and its successors also rely on *The Birds* to replace *Psycho*'s "psychoanalysis" with a nihilistic reading steadily denying the recuperability of society.

There are some particular ways by which *Psycho* and especially *The Birds* contain a perspective toward apocalypse that is extremely modernist yet dependent on tradition, and in this schizophrenia reside basic characteristics of apocalypticism. The horror film, through its heritage in the metaphysical, frequently has been resistant to systems of rational causality; the current horror film amplifies the disappearance of causality by debunking the conventions of the supernatural, but also by deconstructing itself as a genre. While some current directors (e.g., David Cronenberg) tend to circumvent this process somewhat by a head-on rational analysis of mass psychopathology and by attempting to uncover "new myths" in the modern technological landscape, it is possible to attempt a unifying principle within the new apocalypticism only by recognizing the sense of the hopelessness of human intervention and the worthlessness of totalizing analytical or political systems.

It is worthwhile to view the continued impact of the perspective represented in *Psycho* and *The Birds* within one of the more recent and possibly least representative (at least from an aesthetics standpoint) works of the genre, William Lustig's *Maniac* (1981). This representative of the "slasher" film cycle may be dismissible on aesthetic or ideological grounds, but its attention to the inability of society to recover itself must be noted, along with a probably unconscious overlap of psychological and ideological issues touched on in *Psycho* and *The Birds* respectively. *Maniac* seems particularly significant in its debt to *Psycho*; it along with numerous slasher films (including the popular *Friday the 13th* series) is concerned with the subject of the oppressive role of the mother and, more specifically, child abuse. Child abuse, an important current topic for the exploration of patriarchy, finds an ironic locus for examination in the exploitation horror film. (The inclusion of such themes distinguishes the "slasher" film from what might seem logical progenitors—the gore films of William Castle and Hershell G. Lewis, which are for the most part unoriginal attempts to capitalize on the style and success of *Psycho*.) In the horror genre the theme of child abuse approaches the metaphysical; rather than a component of the operation of the family (implied in *Psycho*), it is viewed as a grotesque aberration, but one that is linked inexorably (but vaguely) to all sexual relationships and the deification of woman in religion and traditional art. There are instances where *Maniac*, like *Psycho*, attempts to trace some foundation for pathology; Frank Zito's mother is revealed to have been a prostitute, and her reduction to a commodity appears to have caused her to displace her rage in her son. But this line of reasoning is ultimately refused. *Maniac* does not attempt *Psycho*'s fairly systematic portrayal of a transpsychical illness. Rather, it ventures into a sense of cosmic evil and malaise that reminds us of the way *The Birds* refused the perspective of *Psycho*.

Maniac "answers" the themes it borrows from *Psycho* by an intertextual usage of responses to the upheaval and malaise found in other recent works. Frank Zito wears a military jacket and prowls an atmospheric New York in the manner of Travis Bickle in *Taxi Driver*; he murders a young woman with a bayonet in a lavatory where "apocalypse now" appears on a wall as graffiti. One helicopter flyover sequence and its concurrent soundtrack recall the opening of Coppola's film.[18]

Maniac acknowledges the centrality of Scorsese's and Coppola's films to the horror film's new wave as much as to the apocalyptic temperament of the 1970s and 1980s. By referring to *Taxi Driver* and the Vietnam War, the film deliberately relates the psychoses of Travis Bickle and Norman Bates, and suggests that Frank Zito is explainable by an understanding of the world of Scorsese's film as much as by a reading of *Psycho*. *Maniac* makes *Psycho* and *Taxi Driver* blur together, and by so doing refocuses analysis of the root cause of social disturbance. In short, *Maniac*'s fusion of *Psycho* with *Taxi*

Driver connects the pathology of the bourgeois family and community to state power and state crimes.

The citations of *Apocalypse Now* (1979) further compound the situation as apocalypse is constantly reasserted. In its usage by *Maniac, Apocalypse Now* seems more explainable by reference to *Totem and Taboo* than *The Golden Bough*. Like *Apocalypse Now, Maniac* paradoxically begins *in medias res* with death, that is, with an ending. What *Maniac* emphasizes about *Apocalypse Now* is not the mythic and literary references Coppola uses to explain his story, but the notion of a descent into hell, the pervasiveness of insanity, the irreducible nature of evil, and the link between insanity and evil that cannot be refused by interpretation. In short, *Apocalypse Now* is alluded to as a horror movie informing other horror movies. Frank, like Willard and Kurtz, "goes too far," but not for any overreaching mythical purpose. Frank's scalpings and mutilations of women, like Norman Bates's mummification of his parent, reduces primitive or ritual violence—that violence often lionized in folklore—to its pathological core. But this film, unlike *Psycho*, stops short of clinical definition since it assumes, much like *Apocalypse Now*, that the recognition of a transpsychical illness constitutes a perverse new mythology; psychopathology is fetishized.

Frank has a plethora of toys and gimcrack fetishes in his apartment, most of which are recent consumer products and invite us to understand pathology not solely in terms of Frank's regressive adherence to an early stage of development. While the viewer is shown far more immediately than in *Psycho* that the subject matter concerns psychosis, s/he is bombarded with evidence ostensibly aimed at explaining the nature of this psychosis in a way that complicates a systematic reading of the film: Is Frank a victim of child abuse or some sort of product of post-Vietnam social dysfunction? This is by no means to suggest that *Maniac* is unreadable (I doubt if a close reading is ultimately very profitable), but rather that it refuses the conventional sense of closure associated not just with horror but most commercial narrative film. One cannot say that films like *Maniac* are as representative of some of the dominant concerns of horror film apocalypticism as, say, the works of Tobe Hooper, George Romero, or David Cronenberg; the most subversive element of the slasher sub-genre is the attempt to assert and in some sense valorize the psychotic as a representative figure. But this valorization does not carry with it any redefinition of psychosis (such as might be offered by Foucault or Deleuze and Guattari) and its function in society. At the end of the film Frank's disturbance and guilt cause him to hallucinate himself suffering a revenge at the hands of his dead victims; the gratuitous nature of the episode is so designed to draw the spectator into identification with the revenge, while at the same time the text at that point reveals Frank as a pitiable wretch. Rather than use its landscape as a parodic backdrop for the failure of the American civilizing process (as in *The Texas Chainsaw Massacre*), *Maniac* assumes and exploits a general scoffing at all humanist impulses, at all critical interpretations of behavior. The ideological and psychological reasonings of crime are made to dissolve in a tacit consensus of disbelief in any human purpose.

Maniac may be representative only in its extreme pessimism, but, after all, few of the films described herein have any eschatological system attached to their visions of apocalypse. The exploitation film may be aesthetically and philosophically distant from the main current of apocalyptic sensibility we see in *The Birds*, but at least part of such films' success may reside in their general disavowal of causality, their assault on reason and liberalism, and their expressed contempt for the idea of the individual as social being that often surface as controlling factors of their apocalypse. As this expression asserts a view of apocalypse divergent from religious tradition (apocalypse as disaster rather than "revelation"), it should become apparent how the horror film's cataclysm intersects with the general world-view of works outside the genre that continue a critique of political and social assumptions.

NOTES

1. See, for example, Hal Foster, *Recodings: Art, Spectacle, Cultural Politics* (Port Townsend: Bay Press, 1985), 1. The apocalypticism of much postmodern discourse (particularly the work of Baudrillard and his followers), with its *fin de millenium* preoccupation, very much recapitulates the ideology of the Puritan jeremiads as recounted by such historiographers as Perry Miller. Foster notes that postmodern apocalypticism is "finally complicit with a repressive status quo." See also Jacques Derrida, "Of an Apocalyptic Tone Adopted in Recent Philosophy," *Oxford Literary Review* 6, no. 2 (1984): 20–21.

2. The most comprehensive writings on Peckinpah are Jim Kitses, *Horizons West: Anthony Mann, Budd Boetticher, Sam Peckinpah: Studies of Authorship within the Western* (Bloomington: Indiana University Press, 1969), and Paul Seydor, *Peckinpah: The Western Films* (Urbana: University of Illinois Press, 1980).

3. Arthur Penn has remarked: "We even had a piece of his [Warren Beatty's] head fly off, just like in the famous film of Kennedy being shot." See Curtis Lee Hanson, "An Interview with Arthur Penn," *Cinema* 3, no. 5 (summer 1967): 12.

4. See Susan Sontag, "The Imagination of Disaster," in *Against Interpretation* (New York: Delta Books, 1966), 209.

5. The importance of *Frankenstein* to both genres is demonstrated in Darko Suvin, *Metamorphoses of Science Fiction: On the Poetics and History of a Literary Genre* (New Haven: Yale University Press, 1979), and George Levine and U. C. Knoepflmacher, eds., *The Endurance of* Frankenstein: *Essays on Mary Shelley's Novel* (Berkeley: University of California Press, 1979).

6. Ernest Jones's *On The Nightmare* (London: Liveright Books, 1971) has become important in applications of psychoanalytic method to criticisms of the *fantastique*. The relationship of the horror film's apocalypse to psychoanalysis and a critique of capitalism is Robin Wood's definitive "An Introduction to the American Horror Film," in *The American Nightmare*, ed. Robin Wood and Richard Lippe (Toronto: Festival of Festivals, 1979).

7. See Mircea Eliade, *Cosmos and History: The Myth of the Eternal Return*, trans. Willard R. Trask (Princeton: Princeton University Press, 1965), 113–14, and *passim*. The concept of the evil age in relation to Western apocalypse is discussed in John R. May, *Toward a New Earth: Apocalypse in the American Novel* (Notre Dame: University of Notre Dame Press, 1970).

8. François Truffaut, *Hitchcock* (New York: Simon and Schuster, 1967), 211.

9. A good introduction is James Naremore, *Filmguide to* Psycho (Bloomington: Indiana University Press, 1973).

10. Truffaut, *Hitchcock,* 205.

11. See William Rothman, *Hitchcock—The Murderous Gaze* (Cambridge: Harvard University Press, 1982).

12. Rothman, *Hitchcock—The Murderous Gaze,* 280.

13. See Gaston Bachelard, *The Poetics of Space,* trans. Maria Jolas (Boston: Beacon Press, 1969), for the definitive exploration of such metaphors.

14. Robin Wood has suggested that *Psycho* is "a key work of our age" recognizable only after psychoanalysis on the one hand and the death camps on the other. See *Hitchcock's Films Revisited* (New York: Columbia University Press, 1989), 150.

15. See, for example, James Hillman, *The Dream and the Underworld* (New York: Harper and Row, 1979), 148, 150.

16. The concept of scapegoating is central to the investigation of myth and ritual in society in René Girard, *Violence and the Sacred,* trans. Patrick Gregory (Baltimore: Johns Hopkins University Press, 1977).

17. The Daphne du Maurier story that inspired the film does not help us understand the allegorical nature of Hitchcock's narrative as well as Gabriel García Márquez's "One Day After Saturday," in *No One Writes to the Colonel,* trans. J. S. Bernstein (New York: Harper and Row, 1968).

18. One musical composition for the score to *Maniac* by Jay Chattaway is entitled "Apocalypse N.Y." (Varese Sarabande STV 81143).

"SEE IT FROM THE BEGINNING": HITCHCOCK'S RECONSTRUCTION OF FILM HISTORY

JOAN HAWKINS

Surprisingly little U.S. film history has been written about the gradual disciplining of film audiences during the post-World War II era. While books like Douglas Gomery's excellent *Shared Pleasures* and Richard Maltby's more recent *Hollywood Cinema* chronicle everything from the rise and demise of the movie palace to the introduction of air-conditioning in neighborhood theaters, they say relatively little about the gradual introduction of a "come on time" policy for all films (not just blockbusters) and about the gradual training of the audience to see films from the beginning.[1] Indeed, as Linda Williams implies in her article on *Psycho,* the lack of hard historical data (or discussion) on the gradual disciplining of the audience has encouraged the growth of certain popular cinematic legends.[2] Thus, when I first studied film history, I learned that the dominant mode of film spectatorship changed in 1960, thanks to the forceful vision of one man working in the American film system, Alfred Hitchcock.[3] Prior to that time, I was told, unless the feature was a "special" presentation like Laurence Olivier's *Hamlet* (1948) or a blockbuster like *Gone with the Wind* (1939), movie audiences could walk into a movie theater more or less whenever they felt like it. This was the day of double and sometimes triple features, so viewers could come in during the middle of one show, watch the next show in its entirety, and then, usually, stay to see the beginning of the film whose end they'd already seen. (The phrase "this is where we came in" dates from this era).

Hitchcock's film *Psycho* changed that.[4] Nobody would be admitted to *Psycho,* Hitchcock decreed, once the film had started. And Hitchcock went to great lengths to ensure that what might seem like a showbiz gimmick to some theater owners was enforced at the local cinemas. As Williams documents, a whole series of promotional trailers designed to teach audiences *how* to watch *Psycho* were used to build up a certain viewer expectation about the kind of new cinema-going experience that the film seemed to promise. As Williams points out, "each trailer stresses the importance of special discipline: either 'please don't tell the ending, it's the only one we have,' or the need to arrive on time."[5] Some trailers had very little information about the movie itself, but only showed baffled patrons being instructed to come back at the beginning of the next screening, as if the important thing about *Psycho* was not the story, but the event—the experience of buying a ticket and waiting in line to be admitted.

In addition, a special theater manager training film, "The Care and Handling of *Psycho,*" sought to ensure that theater managers would know how to maximize the audience anticipation that Hitchcock had so carefully fostered. The film showed managers how to post the starting times for the movie, how to cordon off an area of the lobby for waiting ticket-holders, and, perhaps most important, how to play the special message from Hitch, which became a part of the pre-show entertainment. The taped message stressed the necessity of seeing the film from start to finish, and assured spectators that the wait would enhance their viewing pleasure. Many theaters set up outside loudspeakers, so that this taped message could be played to the patrons waiting to purchase their tickets (and, incidentally, to passersby who might be seduced into buying a ticket); and ticket holders were always stationed where they could see the lucky customers who had just seen *Psycho* as they exited the theater.

Now, there were explicit reasons why *Psycho* seemed to demand such a unique spectator policy. The film's break with many of the Hollywood conventions that made the "this is where we came in" mode of viewing possible at all (generally, you could come in during the middle of a film because generic conventions made the plot easy to pick up) was to some degree responsible for the policy.[6] Certainly the effect (and affect) of the shower scene hinges on the audience's sympathy for Marion Crane, built up over the first half of the picture. And, as Williams convincingly argues, the sexual horror that the film plays upon seems, in many ways, to have been reinforced by the patient waiting demanded of the audience lining up outside. But the new admittance policy also points up a duality in the film, a duality perhaps in Hitchcock's own perceptions of himself, which dovetails nicely with the kinds of theoretical debates raging at that time about what precisely cinema ought to be.

For all the carnivalesque, showbizzy, Hollywood elements of its implementation, the *Psycho* "arrive on time and don't tell the ending" rule seems, at this remove anyway, completely imbricated with the auteurist agenda fostered by *Cahiers du cinéma* and other journals. In insisting that audiences attend *Psycho*, a low-budget movie, in the same way that they attended theater (that is, from the beginning to the end, with no latecomers seated until the first intermission), Hitchcock seemed to be saying, along with Bazin, that cinema—even low-budget cinema—is an art form and, as such, deserves the same respect and attention traditionally paid to other high art forms.[7] Furthermore, the very look of the film itself—such a break from Hitchcock's lush color films of the 1950s—invites comparison with European art cinema, the *cinéma des auteurs*. So, as James Naremore argues, does the opening sequence showing Marion and Sam, semi-clad, in a hotel room.[8]

As Williams points out, the idea of forcing audiences to see *Psycho* from start to finish "supposedly came to [Hitchcock] during the editing."[9] "I suddenly startled my fellow-workers with a noisy vow that my frontwards-sidewards-and-inside-out labors on *Psycho* would not be in vain," Hitchcock told the *Motion Picture Herald*. "Everyone else would have to enjoy the fruits of my labor to the full by seeing the picture from beginning to end. This was the way the picture had been conceived—and this was how it had to be seen."[10] In point of fact, however, there's evidence that Hitchcock had been thinking if not about *Psycho*, at least about disciplining the audience, for some time. And he started thinking about it because a French director, whose work he knew very well, laid the groundwork.

Henri-Georges Clouzot's thriller *Les diaboliques* (also known as *Diabolique* and *The Fiends*) opened in Paris in January, 1955. It is a taut little film about two women, the wife and mistress of a bullying headmaster, who decide to take control of their lives by murdering the man who is persecuting them. Most of the film treats the psychological aftermath of the crime, showing how poorly prepared the wife, in particular, is for the anxiety and guilt that follows the deed. As if Catholic bad conscience weren't enough, she begins to suspect that she's being haunted—or, worse yet, that her husband isn't really dead. Children at the school where she works report that they've seen him; the suit he was wearing the night of his death mysteriously comes back from the cleaners. At the end of the film, she has a heart attack, literally scared to death by the return of her husband. The film has two trick endings. The first is that the whole murder-resurrection plot was a theatrical ruse, hatched by the husband and his mistress as an elaborate means of killing the wife (who, we learn, has a weak heart and lots of money); the second is that the murdered wife herself might still be alive.

The film was a great success, both in France and the U.S., and it established Clouzot as one of a long line of "French Hitchcocks."[11] In Clouzot's case, though, the title seems to have had particular resonance, since Clouzot and Hitchcock actually competed for the cinematic rights to various properties. In 1951, Donald Spoto tells us, Hitchcock was interested in directing *Le salaire de la peur* (*The Wages of Fear*), a thriller about a crew of men who must deliver a cargo of dangerous explosives. "But," Spoto writes, "the negotiations with the author and publisher failed under the burden of Parisian bureaucracy and the story was sold to director Henri-Georges Clouzot."[12] About a year later Hitchcock wished to secure the rights to a French novel, *Celle qui n'etait plus* (*The Woman Who Was No More*) by Pierre Boileau and Thomas Narcejac; the rights once again went to Clouzot. Hitchcock did manage to secure the rights to *D'entre les morts* (*From among the Dead*), another thriller by the same authors. Stephen Rebello situates these negotiations, too, within the context of the developing rivalry between Clouzot and Hitchcock. *Celle qui n'etait plus,* the novel bought by Clouzot, provided the basis for *Les diaboliques; D'entre les morts* was adapted by Hitchcock for *Vertigo.*

Rebello emphasizes what he sees as open rivalry between the two men. He even implies that *Psycho* was conceived out of a kind of Hitchcockian pique, a desire to get back at Clouzot for his success at Hitchcock's expense. While Rebello may be overstating the case here, it is clear that Clouzot's career throughout the fifties was on the rise, while Hitchcock's seemed to be in decline. And Clouzot's biggest successes were the films that Hitchcock had initially wished to direct. Clouzot's *Wages of Fear* (1953) won the British Academy of Film and Television Arts' Best Picture Award, while none of Hitchcock's brilliant work of the 1950s was rewarded by the American or British Academies.[13] *Les diaboliques* was a critical and financial success; *Vertigo,* when it was first released, was not.

Furthermore, the critics who reviewed *Les Diaboliques* inevitably compared Clouzot to Hitchcock, usually at Hitchcock's expense. The critic writing for the *Los Angeles Herald-Examiner* called Clouzot "the master of the suspense thriller today." "True," he wrote, "Hitchcock is suaver; but this Frenchman is joltier, a master of timing and building an almost unbearable suspense" (Rebello 21). And in France, the country that would later elevate Hitchcock to the status of "auteur," *Les diaboliques* was similarly received as a film that out-Hitched Hitch. Georges Sadoul wrote, for example, that *Les diaboliques* is an exercise in style, "which refuses the obviousness ["les gros sabots"] . . . of Hitchcock."[14]

I am not as convinced as Rebello that "Hitchcock had a score to settle with Clouzot" (20). But it is clear that Hitchcock watched *Les diaboliques* with special interest and, as Rebello notes, "appropriated"—or paid homage to—several scenes from the film (21). Rebello writes,

> Similarities between *Les diaboliques* and *Psycho* range from sur-
> face matters—black and white cinematography; the grubby mi-
> lieu of rented rooms and humdrum jobs; the merciless, despairing
> tone and careworn characters; the matching hairdos of Janet Leigh
> and Simone Signoret—to thematic, visual, and structural motifs."
> (167–68)

These motifs include the way both films are divided into two parts, the "Everyman" detective who emerges in the second part of each film, the swampy swimming pool in *Les diaboliques* where M. Delassalle's body is disposed and the actual swamp in *Psycho* where Norman hides Marion Crane, the closeups on bathroom drains and men's adam's apples, and both films' "surprise, twist" endings (167–68). Rebello mentions, in passing, that Hitchcock undoubtedly was relieved that "surprisingly few critics—even the French—commented upon the *obvious* debt that *Psycho* owed to *Les diaboliques*" (167, italics mine).

In fact, elements from *Les diaboliques* showed up in other Hitchcock films as well. The hotel room scene in *North by Northwest* (1959), where Roger Thornhill tries on George Kaplan's suit jacket, is remarkably similar to the hotel room scene in *Les diaboliques,* where Christina Delasalle finds her "deceased" husband's freshly laundered suit. And soon after the release of *Les diaboliques,* Hitchcock cast Charles Vanel, the actor who played In-spector Fichet in Clouzot's film, as Bertani in *To Catch a Thief* (1955).[15] The success of *Les diaboliques* may even have had something to do with Hitch-cock's reworking of *D'entre les morts* for *Vertigo.* In the novel, Judy is not revealed as Madeleine until the end of the story; the reader finds out her identity at the same time that Scotty does. For the film, Hitchcock changed this. Judy is revealed to the viewer as Madeleine long before Scotty finds out, and part of the suspense of the film derives from her need to keep this terrible secret. The film plays with viewer sympathies in much the same way that Les diaboliques does, in that it asks the spectator to identify with, or at least feel compassion for, a woman (Mme. Delasalle, Judy) who appears to be an accomplice to murder.

Most importantly for our purposes, however, Hitchcock seems to have been unusually interested in Les diaboliques' publicity campaign and the conditions under which the film was shown. When the film opened in Paris, Clouzot demanded that, contrary to the contemporary practice of allowing audience admittance at any time during the projection of a film, the doors of the theater were to be closed at the beginning of Les diaboliques. Wishing to maximize the shock value of the movie, Clouzot required audiences to see Les diaboliques from beginning to end. In addition, at the end of the film audiences were enjoined not to be diabolical themselves: "Don't spoil the film for your friends. Do not tell them what you have seen."[16] When the film opened at the Fine Arts Theater in New York on November 20, 1955, under the title Diabolique, the theater utilized the same publicity and end titles that had been so successful in France, to similarly successful effect. Variety was amazed at the box office popularity of what it termed "French product." Calling Diabolique the "Year's Surprise Import," the trade paper commented that "observers are somewhat at a loss to ascribe the success of the French thriller to any particular factor other than that its unusual and has been well-handled publicity-wise."[17]

The film, as Variety reported, was a tremendous crossover hit, "playing off in situations that ordinarily don't even touch foreign lingualers"; eventually it was dubbed for "regular [as opposed to art house] commercial runs."[18] Even during its "regular" U.S. commercial runs, however, the film's publicity gimmick remained the same. And if the "see it from the beginning; don't spoil the ending" rule was, as Variety suggests, the secret to this French lingualer's success, it also demonstrated the degree to which mainstream U.S. audiences were willing to abide by arthouse and blockbuster rules, even for a "regular" picture. As a successful low-budget, crossover thriller, Diabolique indicated that perhaps the time was ripe for a change.

According to Rebello, Hitchcock followed Diabolique's handling "publicity-wise" and Clouzot's stratagem for disciplining mainstream audiences with great interest. And it is within this context—the context of his own relationship with Clouzot, and the evolutionary strategy of the Euroamerican thriller—that his subsequent decision to regulate and discipline Psycho's audience must be seen. That is, the idea to force spectators to see Psycho from beginning to end may have come to Hitchcock, as he claimed, during editing. But it was an idea that, as Spanish horror director Jess Franco once said, was "in the air."[19]

If *Diabolique*'s marketing ploy interested Hitchcock, it interested other directors on both sides of the Atlantic, as well. The notion that audiences could be disciplined and that such discipline could be exploited to sell horror and thriller films was picked up by Warner Brothers as early as 1956. While not going nearly as far as either *Diabolique* or, later, *Psycho,* Mervyn LeRoy's *The Bad Seed* utilized an ad campaign that seems indebted to *Diabolique*'s successful admittance regulation policy. A double ad spread for the film in *Variety* (Sept 5, 1956) advised theater owners to give "A BRIEF 'CATCH YOUR BREATH' INTERMISSION AFTER EACH SHOWING," and to limit audience seating during the end of the film. "WE RECOMMEND: NO SEATING DURING THE LAST FIFTEEN MINUTES," the ad proclaimed. "WE RECOMMEND: TALK ALL YOU WANT ABOUT THE MAN AND THE WOMAN BUT *PLEASE DON'T TELL ABOUT THE GIRL!*"[20] The ad campaign was apparently successful. Two weeks after the double page ad appeared, *Variety* reported that Broadway first run theaters had been given a nice lift. "Standout newcomer is *Bad Seed*," the paper reports, "with a wow $49,000 or near for first week at the Astor."[21] And in 1960, the same year that audiences in the United States were being taught how to line up for *Psycho,* a British film utilizing a similar marketing strategy—*Peeping Tom*—was creating a stir in Europe. "Warning! " the ads for the film advised. "Don't see *Peeping Tom* unless you are prepared to see the screaming shock and raw terror in the faces of those marked for death." Interestingly enough, the "warning" obviously designed to attract a horror-loving audience, concludes with special instructions for prospective viewers. Those planning to see the film, the advertisement admonishes, should plan to "see it from the beginning."[22]

Despite Hitchcock's successful use of the "see it from the beginning" policy for *Psycho,* audience discipline remained something of a horror-show gimmick throughout the early 1960s. No less a showman than William Castle used it to market his 1964 film, *Strait-Jacket.* "WE URGE YOU TO SEE STRAIT-JACKET FROM THE BEGINNING," the ad copy reads, "IN ORDER TO BRACE YOURSELF FOR THE SURPRISE ENDING!"[23] The change in American spectators's viewing habits, then, apparently took place gradually over about a twelve year period (1955–67), the same period that Gomery identifies as the "apogee" of the distribution of international art cinema, the *cinéma des auteurs,* in the United States.[24]

Elsewhere I have discussed the similarity between the distribution, exhibition and reception of art films and that of horror/sci-fi/exploitation films in the U.S.[25] Denied the MPPDA (Motion Picture Producers and

Directors Association) seal, European art films were initially shown in the bump and grind houses that habitually featured exploitation and "educational" films.[26] In the late 1950s and early 1960s, the tradition of booking foreign films and exploitation films in the same venues persisted, as both art houses and exploitation theaters continued to feature both high "art" films and low horror films that fell outside mainstream consumption. Given the fact that the same theaters often showed both kinds of film, it is perhaps not surprising that both high art cinemas and low exploitation houses experimented with a regulated audience admittance policy throughout this period.

Small art theaters simply could not afford to stay open all day and run continuous screenings. Furthermore, they catered to a specialized, college-educated audience that had already been disciplined, through exposure to film journals and film theory, into seeing cinema as an art form, on a par with theater. While exploitation houses could, and often did, stay open all day, the 1950s saw the increased introduction of special theatrical exploitation "gimmicks" designed to attract spectators. And regulated audience admittance was one of these gimmicks. As Carlos Clarens notes, by the late 1950s it was clear that "an increased audience participation was in order if the horror film was to survive."[27] What this amounted to in practice was an increased theatricalization of film screenings. Movie theater employees dressed as nurses would take the blood pressure of people entering the theater to ensure that the patrons' hearts could withstand the shock of the picture. Other staff, dressed as creatures from the film, would wander the aisles, and try to catch unwary patrons off guard. And theaters routinely advertised technical-sounding special effects that were designed to make the movie literally leap off the screen. Embellishments like Psychorama, Hypnovista, and Emergo were frequently more ballyhoo than they were true innovations (Emergo, for example, consisted largely of a luminous skeleton strung on wires and suspended over the spectators). But they did provoke audience response, usually in the form of loud, excited screams, and they encouraged a kind of carnival atmosphere in the theater. Spectators talked, threw popcorn at the screen, and moved freely around the house. This was such an established feature of exploitation cinemas during this period that film critic Pauline Kael—who saw both *The Haunting* (Robert Wise, 1963) and *The Horror Chamber of Dr. Faustus* (Georges Franju, *Les yeux sans visage*, 1959, released in the U.S. in 1962) in such an atmosphere—complained in print that audiences didn't know how to watch movies anymore.[28]

While these gimmicks were introduced to revitalize audience interest in horror, they had the added effect of encouraging audiences to come to theaters at a specific time—before the movie started—and to watch movies from the beginning (John Waters has described, for example, how he went to the theater well before *The Tingler* was scheduled to start and checked all the seats in order to make sure that he got one wired for the "Percepto" experience). This was especially true in cases where Mr. Castle himself was scheduled to make an appearance or introduce the show. Fans eager to see the showman made sure they arrived on time. And as I argued earlier, the "come on time" rule could itself be used as a theatrical gimmick to bring in audiences.

Taken in this context, Hitchcock's showy implementation of Clouzot's "see it from the beginning" policy was both a means of introducing art cinema discipline to mainstream audiences and a masterful way of exploiting the theatrical gimmicks expected by the horror crowd (at the DeMille Theater in New York, for example, a Pinkerton man was on the premises to enforce the promotional imperatives). The loudspeakers and enforced waiting in line took the carnival atmosphere and put it "out front," outside the theater proper. The wait not only built anticipation by reinforcing the idea that the crowd was about to see something special, it helped to dissipate some of the crowd's energy (it's hard to maintain a consistent level of excitement while standing in line, particularly if you have to lower your voice in order to listen to periodic taped announcements); it helped to establish that this was a different kind of horror audience, one composed largely of adults.

By forcing spectators to see *Psycho* from beginning to end, Hitchcock effectively engaged both art cinema and horror conventions, and emphasized the film's status as art-horror—a status it still enjoys. In that sense, *Psycho* shares a cultural niche with Clouzot's *Diabolique* as "one of the few financially successful films which can defensibly be called [both] an art film, and a classic of the horror genre."[29]

I began this essay talking about film history, and that's the way I would like to end. It is interesting to read about the way directors get their ideas. But what is more important for us as scholars is to consider the way that history gets made and the way that directors themselves participate in the creation of certain legends surrounding their work. While Hitchcock was not nearly as self-aggrandizing as someone like D. W. Griffith (who took out newspaper ads claiming that he had invented close-ups, crosscutting, and just about every innovation in silent cinema), he did help to create the story that the idea of forcing audiences to see *Psycho* from the beginning came to him spontaneously while he was editing the film, and his claim—that he decided to force audiences to see *Psycho* from start to finish because the complex editing of the picture seemed to demand it—demonstrates perhaps his own desire to be seen as an auteur, as someone who controls every step of the creative process, including promotion and exhibition. But while Hitchcock's implementation of the "see it from the beginning" rule was innovative and inventive, the disciplining of the mainstream U.S. audience that the policy helped to promote needs to be seen within a broader historical and cultural context, as part of a cooperative effort between several cinéastes—from different cultures—working in the suspense/thriller/horror genre and art cinema mode.[30]

What Hitchcock did and did brilliantly was to take a strategy that had flourished predominantly in a specialized U.S. market (theatrical block-buster, art cinema, and horror) and turn it into a viable marketing ploy for mainstream cinema. In that sense, Hitchcock's implementation of the "see it from the beginning" rule was as much a "crossover" success story as *Psycho* itself. While *Psycho* initially won "only middling to hostile reaction" from the critics, who were irritated by the restrictive screening policy (and by the fact that Hitchcock didn't let them see it in an advance screening), it quickly became an "audience phenomenon" (Rebello 160, 161), fueled as much by stories about the implementation of Hitchcock's "see it from the beginning policy" as by the film itself.

And when it came to implementation of the "see it from the beginning" policy, Hitchcock definitely outmaneuvered Clouzot. One famous anecdote, for example, describes a near-riot that took place at the Woods Theater in Chicago. Caught offguard by a sudden Midwest summer downpour, patrons threatened to tear down the theater if the manager didn't let them into the lobby. Panic-stricken, the manager phoned Paramount and asked what he should do. Finally, Hitchcock himself intercepted the calls. "Buy them umbrellas," the director said. That's what the manager did, and the story made the front page of the newspaper the following day.

If *Les diaboliques* established Clouzot as the director who out-Hitched Hitch, *Psycho* definitely restored Hitchcock's reputation as the "master of shock" (Rebello 164). And if Hitchcock ever felt he suffered as a result of his competition with the French director, history and cultural amnesia have given him a kind of revenge. In his movie capsule review of the American remake of *Les diaboliques* (*Diabolique*, 1996) Indiana critic Michael Redman pans the American film's use of "scenes directly lifted from Hitch's movies."[31] These "scenes directly lifted" from Hitch, were of course the scenes that Hitch himself had borrowed from "French Hitchcock" Clouzot, from the original version of *Les diaboliques*.[32]

NOTES

1. Douglas Gomery, *Shared Pleasures: A History of Movie Presentation in the United States* (Madison: University of Wisconsin Press, 1992), and Richard Maltby, *Hollywood Cinema: An Introduction* (Cambridge, MA: Blackwell, 1995).

2. Linda Williams, "Learning to Scream," *Sight and Sound* 4, no. 12 (December 1994): 14–17. An expanded version of this essay appears as Linda Williams, "Discipline and Distraction: *Psycho*, Visual Culture and Postmodern Cinema" in *"Culture" and the Problem of Disciplines*, John Carlos Rowe, ed. (New York: Columbia University Press, 1998), 87–120.

3. The origins of this particular legend seem to come from two sources: a slightly overdetermined reading of Peter Bogdanovich's *The Cinema of Alfred Hitchcock* (New York: Museum of Modern Art Film Library/Doubleday, 1963), which doesn't really cover the role *Diabolique* played in inspiring *Psycho*'s screening strategy, and the personal experience of my professors, who remembered *Psycho* as the first popular American film they'd seen from the beginning.

To some degree, Williams repeats the legend giving Hitchcock credit for single-handedly disciplining the audience when she writes in "Learning to Scream": "In the larger sense, however, his [Hitchcock's] demand that the audience arrive on time would eventually lead to the set show times, closely spaced screenings, elimination of cartoon and short subjects and patient waits in line that are now standard procedure" (14).

4. I don't mean to suggest that no films prior to *Psycho* required audiences to come on time. As I mentioned earlier, exhibitors of *Gone with the Wind* (1939) were reminded to stress starting and intermission times "to ensure that audiences missed no part of the movie" (Maltby 37). And in some parts of the country Laurence Olivier's *Hamlet* (1948) was managed as though it were a stage play. In Twin Falls, Idaho, for example, the film was shown twice daily and patrons bought their tickets in advance. But *Psycho* is often credited for taking a practice that had applied only to special, "spectacular" films and extending it to popular features. I am indebted to Gary Kellard for the information about *Hamlet*.

5. Williams, "Learning to Scream," 16.

6. Killing off the main star before the picture was half over was just one of the Hollywood conventions that *Psycho* broke.

7. Hitchcock's relationship to his own auteur status is a curious one. On the one hand, as Robin Wood notes, Hitchcock was extremely "modest and unassuming" about his work, and made "no claim for his art outside the evidence of the films." On the other hand, as Wood also notes, Hitchcock was well aware of the auteur status that Truffaut, Chabrol, and other writers at *Cahiers* had given him. See Robin

Wood, *Hitchcock's Films Revisited* (New York: Columbia University Press, 1989), 61. And at times, as Anton Kaes pointed out to me, Hitchcock's public statements about his role in shaping his art and his stars seem wittingly or unwittingly designed to link him directly to an auteurist tradition. As I later argue, Hitchcock's claim that the decision to show *Psycho* from start to finish came to him while editing can be seen in this context. As Kaes reads them, Hitchcock's statements about discovering Tippi Hedren and turning her into a star can be seen as expressions of the director's wish to link himself to a European auteurist tradition. Kaes compares Hitchcock's claims about "making" Hedren to Von Sternberg's claims that he "made Marlene."

8. See James Naremore, *Filmguide to* Psycho (Bloomington: Indiana University Press, 1973). The film's look also derives in part from the low-budget horror films Hitchcock was studying at the time. As Stephen Rebello points out, Hitchcock had been tracking the box office figures of low-budget horror pictures, such as William Castle's *Macabre* (1958) and Albert Band's *I Bury the Living* (1958), turned out by Universal-International, American International, Allied Artists, Hammer Film Productions, and others. At the same time he began to "quiz his associates" as to "how profitable they thought a first-class, low-budget shocker might be." Associates dismissed these questions as more evidence of what Rebello calls Hitchcock's "puckish" side, but when the director began referring to his recent James Stewart and Cary Grant movies as "technicolor baubles," they knew something was up. See Stephen Rebello, *Alfred Hitchcock and the Making of* Psycho (New York: Dembner Books, 1990), 22. (Further references to this book are cited by page number only in the text of my essay.) *Psycho*'s own low budget, as well as its gory murder sequence also played a role (as they did in the low-budget horror films he'd been tracking). Hitchcock was worried about censorship: the shower murder could not have been shown, he felt, if he had shot the film in color.

9. Williams, "Learning to Scream," 15

10. Alfred Hitchcock, "A Lesson in PSYCHO-ology," *Motion Picture Herald,* August 6, 1960, 17–18; also quoted in Williams, "Learning to Scream," 15.

11. Claude Chabrol and Louis Malle were also periodically called "the French Hitchcock."

12. Donald Spoto, *The Dark Side of Genius* (New York: Ballantine, 1983), 355. The film, starring Yves Montand, was released in 1952.

13. In fact, the American Academy of Motion Picture Arts and Sciences' treatment of Hitchcock during this period often amounted to what might be considered a slap in the director's face. *To Catch a Thief* (1955), *Vertigo,* and *North by Northwest* (1959) were nominated for best art direction, not for best direction or for best picture.

14. Quoted in José-Louis Bocquet, en collaboration avec Marc Godin, *Henri-Georges Clouzot Cineaste* (Sèvres: La Sirène, 1993), 95.

15. Vanel also had a role in *Wages of Fear.*

16. "Ne soyez pas les diaboliques. Ne détruisez pas l'intérêt qui pouraient prendre vos amis à ce film. Ne leur racontez pas ce que vas avez vu" (Bocquet, 94; my translation). Asking the audience not to divulge the ending showed up in other pre-*Psycho* films as well: Billy Wilder's 1957 film, *Witness for the Prosecution,* also asks the audience not to give away the ending.

17. *Variety* 202 (April 4, 1956): 7.

18. *Variety* 202 (April 4, 1956): 7.

19. Franco said this by way of explaining why his film *Gritos en la noche* (*The Awful Dr. Orlof,* 1962) was so remarkably similar to Georges Franju's *Les yeux sans visage.* Denying that his film was a remake, he said, "so these things are around, in the air, you know. I remember when I made *The Awful Dr. Orlof,* at about the same time Georges Franju made *Les yeux sans visage.* There was no connection between us. It was impossible that he could know my story or for me to know Franju's story. And then the two films were very similar. So these things are in the air. I think the ideas are *there* you know. So, suddenly, you start to make the film, the connection with these ideas comes suddenly and you start to make the film even if you don't want to." Harvey Fenton and William Lustig, "A Different Point of View: The Jess Franco Interview," *Flesh and Blood* (London) 9 (1997): 35.

20. *Variety* 204 (Sept. 5, 1956): 8–9.

21. *Variety* 204 (Sept. 5, 1956): 9.

22. Reprinted in Michael Weldon, *The Psychotronic Encyclopedia of Film* (New York: Ballantine Books, 1983), 541.

23. Reprinted in Weldon, *The Psychotronic Encyclopedia of Film,* 661.

24. Gomery, *Shared Pleasures,* 189.

25. See my *Cutting Edge: Art—Horror and the Horrific Avant-garde* (Minneapolis: University of Minnesota Press, 2000), and "Sleaze-Mania, Euro-trash, and High Art: The Place of European Art Films in American Low Culture," *Film Quarterly* 53, no. 2 (winter 1999–2000): 14–29.

26. See Eric Schaefer, "Resisting Refinement: The Exploitation Film and Self-Censorship," *Film History* 6 (1994): 293–313.

27. Carlos Clarens, *An Illustrated History of the Horror Film* (New York: Capricorn Books, 1967).

28. Pauline Kael, "Zeitgeist and Poltergeist; or, Are Movies Going to Pieces," in *I Lost It at the Movies,* third edition (Boston: Little, Brown, 1965), 3–27.

29. Donald Spoto, *The Art of Alfred Hitchcock: Fifty Years of His Motion Pictures* (New York: Doubleday, 1976), 355.

30. See David Bordwell, "The Art Cinema as a Mode of Film Practice," *Film Quarterly* 4, no. 1 (fall 1979): 56–64. In Clouzot and Powell's case, the directors were working in both the horror thriller genre and art cinema mode simultaneously.

31. *Bloomington Voice*, 5, no. 13 (March 28–April 4, 1996): 11.

32. A much shorter version of this paper was presented at the European Cinemas, European Societies 1895–1995 Conference, held at Indiana University, Bloomington, Indiana, Sept. 28–Oct 1, 1995. I am indebted to Barbara Klinger, who read the first draft of the expanded paper and made suggestions for its revision into an article; to Jim Naremore, who urged me to submit it; and to Skip Hawkins, Gary Kellard, Oscar Kenshur, and the editors of the *Hitchcock Annual* for their help and suggestions.

REMAKING *PSYCHO*

James Naremore

Critical discussions of movie remakes have a good deal in common with discussions of literary adaptations. Both deal with the somewhat questionable idea of the original versus the copy, both value the unique work of art, and both treat the "precursor text" with a kind of deference. The typical essay on adaptation can be summed up by a *New Yorker* cartoon that Alfred Hitchcock once described to François Truffaut: two goats are eating a pile of film cans, and one goat says to the other, "Personally, I liked the book better." A roughly similar argument can be found in most writing about remakes, if only because classic Hollywood is now universally regarded as a respectable art form that created a large number of culturally treasured works, many of which are subject to recycling, updating, and retelling by contemporary producers.[1]

Certainly there is nothing new about the phenomenon of remakes, which sometimes result in good films. (Consider Hitchcock's *The Man Who Knew Too Much*.) Popular art and commercial entertainment have always depended upon the repetition of successful formulas. But audiences today have an unusual historical self-consciousness (many of them enjoy watching old movies on TV), and certain remade movies are more likely than others to be regarded with suspicion by cognoscenti. Some Hollywood films (*King Kong*, for instance) are especially suited to remaking because they are inherently spectacular and have an elemental, mythopoetic quality. Others resist the process, either because they require unique stars (The Marx Brothers, Astaire and Rogers), or because they belong to a particular period of entertainment that is difficult to "translate" into the present (the Freed-unit musicals at MGM). Still others (*Citizen Kane* is the preeminent example) have such artistic prestige and historical significance that remaking them, as opposed to quoting them or borrowing their ideas, seems crass and pointless. Among the esteemed pictures in this last category is Hitchcock's *Psycho*, and it comes as no surprise that director Gus Van Sant's 1998 attempt to reshoot that film in color with contemporary actors was treated by most critics as a travesty.

Van Sant is a respectable filmmaker with several fine pictures to his credit, including *Drugstore Cowboy, My Own Private Idaho,* and *To Die For.* In this case, however, he chose a project that was simply asking for bad reviews.[2] Perhaps he didn't care, but even if his aims were purely commercial, he failed miserably. Hitchcock's *Psycho* is one of the most profitable pictures ever made, whereas Van Sant's *Psycho* (backed by a heavy Universal Studios promotion campaign and a mail-order contest offering a grand prize of dinner for two at the Bates Motel on the studio lot) did only lukewarm business, at best helping to stimulate video rentals of the earlier film. And the reason for its box-office failure is fairly obvious: despite the fact that Van Sant reproduces many of Hitchcock's key sequences shot for shot, he seems unwilling or unable to generate even a modicum of the fear Hitchcock induced in his original audience.

Here I speak from direct knowledge, because my first viewing of Hitchcock's *Psycho* was during its initial theatrical release, at the Lowe's Theater in New Orleans, Louisiana, and it was one of the most carnivalistic events I've experienced at the movies. You could barely hear the film because of the hysterical shrieks and nervous laughter of the crowd, who had bought their tickets not for the sake of art but for the sake of a roller-coaster ride of primal emotion. The loudest screams came when Lila Crane started down into the cellar, and they continued straight through the unmasking of Norman, only to be followed by a barrage of jittery conversations that entirely covered up the psychiatrist's "explanation" at the end. For me at least, that viewing was unpleasantly raucous, and the film was galvanically terrifying—almost as disturbing as when my mother took me as a small child to see a re-release of

Disney's *Snow White and the Seven Dwarfs* (perhaps significantly, the witch in Snow White bears a certain resemblance to the corpse of Mrs. Bates in *Psycho*). In 1960 I was already a confirmed admirer of Hitchcock, and yet almost a decade went by before I could detach myself enough from my initial fright to recognize that this particular picture was not simply a brilliant piece of exploitation, but also an artistic masterpiece. When I was invited in 1973 to write a critical monograph on *Psycho*, I actually worried because I thought that repeated exposure to certain scenes would give me nightmares.[3]

By contrast, Van Sant's film strikes me as academic and not at all scary. On my personal fright meter, it registers far lower than any number of the movies that were clearly influenced by *Psycho*, including Polanski's *Repulsion*, Friedkin's *The Exorcist*, Spielberg's *Jaws*, and even De Palma's *Carrie* and *Dressed to Kill*. But this does not mean that it entirely lacks interest. On the contrary, it deserves at least a brief footnote to film history, if only because it is almost unique among movie remakes.

We should recall that Hitchcock himself was not averse to remaking *The Man Who Knew Too Much*, and that he wanted to make a sound version of *The Lodger*. Several of his films have been remade as average or downright bad pictures by other directors, including *The 39 Steps, The Lady Vanishes, Shadow of a Doubt, Dial M for Murder, Notorious*, and *Rear Window* (some of these were released under different titles, and the last two were produced as TV movies), and *Psycho* and *The Birds* have spawned sequels and a prequel. One could even argue that Hitchcock's very authorship, like that of a few other major directors in the classic period (Howard Hawks comes immediately to mind), lies in his ability to continually remake or recombine a basic repertory of narrative situations and cinematic techniques, thus creating a characteristic "world." None of these examples, however, is quite the same as Van Sant's *Psycho*, which appropriates most of the original film's script, decoupage, music, and design, sometimes duplicating the tiniest details of the *mise-en-scène* (such as the word "okay"printed at the top of a newspaper sticking out of Marion Crane's purse). It does all this, moreover, not with just any film, but with the picture that, more than any other, established Hitchcock as the major figure in the auteurist movement and the most influential director in Hollywood history.

In interviews at the time of the film's release, Van Sant claimed that movies were rather like theater pieces, and that there was no good reason why classic films shouldn't be restaged in the same way as classic plays. This argument is of course disingenuous, because movies have as much in common with novels as with theater, and because Van Sant's *Psycho* is not simply a re-filming of Joseph Stefano's script. More like a colorization or an elaborate quotation of things that were literally printed on another film, its closest analogue can be seen in a few sequences from Van Sant's earlier picture, *My Own Private Idaho,* which offer a replay of key episodes in Orson Welles's *Chimes at Midnight,* with all the actors dressed in contemporary costume. As far as I know, such a technique is peculiar to Van Sant, although in a general sense it seems fully symptomatic of our *fin-de-siècle* culture, which often succeeds less as straightforward entertainment or as thoughtful representation than as pastiche, quotation, and conceptual art. Surprisingly, given its large budget and wide commercial release, Van Sant's remake of *Psycho* resembles nothing so much as a museum installation. Its chief value is on the pedagogical or theoretical level, where it functions, intentionally or not, as a metafilm and reveals a good deal about Hitchcock's specific achievement.

The remake demonstrates that differences, not similarities, are important, and that even the small differences have enormous consequences. The credit sequence, for example, reproduces Saul Bass's original design (adapted by Pablo Ferro), but the lime green background spoils the stark graphic effect and seems inconsistent with what Bernard Herrmann himself once described as "black and white" title music. The opening view of Phoenix, Arizona is a Panavision, color image of today's skyline photographed from a helicopter; and when the camera moves toward an open window, a computer enhancement allows it to execute a showy trick effect, floating straight past the casement and into the room without an apparent cut. Inside the hotel room, the conversation between Sam and Marion not only involves new actors and a glimpse of male nudity, but also a different pattern of blocking, cuts, and camera movements (including a close-up insert of a house fly that foreshadows the one on Norman's hand at the end of the film). Even in the later scenes, which often adhere quite closely to Hitchcock's original, Van Sant introduces significant variations. For me at least, his film becomes less a horror movie than a purely intellectual exercise. I know what's going to happen next, and the only suspense (if that is the correct term) is in watching to see what sorts of glitzy alterations will be made to some of Hitchcock's best scenes.

As an indication of these alterations, here are a few notes on the formal systems of both pictures:

Script. In keeping with contemporary Hollywood, the 1998 film is more explicit: Norman masturbates as he watches Marion disrobe for a shower, and when Lila explores Norman's room, she discovers a pornographic magazine. The dialogue is subjected to a certain updating (bits of profanity and

contemporary slang), and the psychiatrist's speech at the end is greatly modified. Van Sant probably thought he was being more sophisticated by omit-
ting the pompous explanation of Norman's behavior (especially the line
about transvestites, which usually draws unwanted laughter at screenings
of the original film); but in my view, this change gives the psychiatrist more
authority than he deserves, and it places the blame too much on Mrs. Bates.
In Hitchcock's version, the ending is more ambiguous, and the contrast between the rational world and the mad world is more vivid. Who is really
speaking to us in the closing interior monologue of Hitchcock's picture? Has
Mrs. Bates "taken over," or is Norman simply regressing into his psychotic
fantasy of the dead woman and using her as a perverse rationale? Does it
make any sense to assign a coherent self or personality to the voice we hear
and the body we see? Some of this vertiginous mystery is lost in the new
version.

Casting and Acting. On the whole, Van Sant's cast is highly talented, and
in most cases they behave more naturalistically than the original players.
But only occasionally, in the minor roles, is there any improvement over
Hitchcock. Julianne Moore is a far more gifted actor than Vera Miles, and
Chad Everett is more effective than Frank Albertson as the smarmy, vaguely
threatening businessman in a cowboy hat who makes a pass at Marion
Crane. The major problem is with the leading players. Anne Heche conveys
almost nothing of Janet Leigh's hard-boiled intelligence and mounting neurosis, and the best thing one can say about Vince Vaughn is that he makes us
appreciate the greatness of Anthony Perkins. Vaughn's chief difficulty may
be that, in keeping with the overall approach of the film, he is required to
copy Perkins's performance almost gesture for gesture; the result is a stale
imitation, with nothing of the boyish humor, pathos, and sinister grace that
derived from Perkins himself. To make matters worse, Vaughn is a different
body type from Perkins, and he cannot evoke the subtle "doubling" one
senses everywhere in Hitchcock. In the original version, Norman sometimes looks feminine and avian (the double of Marion Crane), sometimes
like a dark-haired leading man (the double of Sam Loomis), and sometimes
like an angular stick figure (the double of Mrs. Bates's skeleton). These visual rhymes are completely missing in Van Sant's picture, which almost
entirely lacks the creepy wit of the original. In the climactic scenes, when
Sam and Norman battle in the cellar, Norman looks like a fullback wearing
a fright wig.

Sound. The 1998 film makes far greater use of ambient sound to comment on the images. In the opening scene, for example, we hear not only
street noises but also a strange muffled cry coming from elsewhere in

the hotel. During Norman's interior monologue at the end, we hear a muted chorus of babbling voices and echoes, representing the mind of a schizophrenic—a type of aural expressionism that seems to me far less effective than the "mad" lucidity of Hitchcock's version. I would also note that even though Van Sant has the benefit of Bernard Herrmann's original score (adapted by Danny Elfman and Steve Bartek), the music in his film seems less forceful, less fully present, than in Hitchcock. The reason why may have something to do with the orchestration and the distracting effect of the color photography; but it probably owes more to Van Sant's slight modification of the original relation between image and music—especially in the shower scene, which delays the start of the music, and in the film's closing shot, which overly prolongs the scene of the car emerging from the swamp and then segues into a long credit sequence overlaid with a modernized, electric-guitar rendition of Herrmann's theme music.

Photography. If Hitchcock had made *Psycho* in 1998, he would probably have used color, because black and white seems a bit too arty in contemporary films. His decision to avoid color in 1960 seems to have been motivated less by aesthetic than by economic concerns. He actually feared that *Psycho* might not be a success, and the completed film, photographed in noirish style by low-budget cameraman John Russell, is as close as Hitchcock came during his American career to making a B picture. No doubt Hitchcock was also worried about the censors, and he used black and white because he knew that it would make the scenes of bloody murder less explicit. By contrast, Van Sant has no reason to think his viewers will be repulsed by the sight of red blood running down a shower drain (countless Hitchcock imitators have already shown this), and he even shows the open red knife wounds in Marion Crane's back. He also employs photographer Christopher Doyle, who is one of the most talented exponents of color in the business. Doyle evokes some of the atmosphere of the original by using rich, deep blacks and cast shadows, but the overall effect of the new film at its best is rather like an eerie, surrealistic retouching of some of Hitchcock's most memorable images. Vivid notes of color—an orange dress and parasol, a blue sky, a flash of red neon—are introduced into the original compositions, as if the older film were being "dreamed." Unfortunately, the color slightly attenuates the force of Hitchcock's brilliant montage sequences, which were designed for black and white. Notice also that Doyle cannot achieve deep focus in the low-key scenes. During the crucial interview between Marion and Norman in the motel sitting room, we have very little sense of how characters are related to objects in the background.

Editing and Camera Movement. When Van Sant makes a fundamental change in any one of the film's formal elements, he affects all the others. He reproduces Hitchcock's editing of the famous murder scenes almost exactly, but the Panavision framing and color photography in the new film creates a kind of "noise" or extra layer of information that somewhat obscures the bold graphic conflicts and relatively abstract, geometric quality of Hitchcock's work. As if to compensate, Van Sant plays minor but obvious variations on these sequences, inserting a metaphoric images that briefly disorient viewers. (In the shower scene we glimpse a bank of storm clouds; when detective Arbogast is stabbed, we glimpse a woman wearing a G-string and a black mask, and a lonely cow on a wet road.) He also tries to "improve" on Hitchcock by using the latest camera technology; for example, he greatly exaggerates the spiral out from Marion's dead eye, rotating the image so dizzily that he spoils the mood of one of the most famous dissolves in movie history.

Mise-en-scène and Production Design. The clothing and set decorations in the new *Psycho* have been updated for the 1990s. Marion Crane wears a Wonder Bra, and her sister carries a back pack. Even the haunted house on the hill looks oddly and inexplicably modernized, rather like a kitschy mansion in the suburbs. But what does this updating actually involve? Americans today wear many of the styles they wore in the Eisenhower era, so that the differences between then and now are relatively trivial. Women's brassieres and the censorship codes may have changed, but in general we no longer create new fashions; we simply recycle and modify the old ones, just as we make movies that nostalgically return us to the pop culture of the 1940s, 1950s, or 1960s. Van Sant can therefore remake *Psycho* with very little alteration of its basic settings. Even so, he makes bad choices. In his version, the shower spigot in cabin one of the Bates motel is octagonal in shape, and we therefore lose one of the important graphic motifs of the murder scene. Also in his version, the painting Norman removes from the wall when he spies on Marion is a reproduction of Titian's *Venus with a Mirror*, which seems to suggest both feminine narcissism and rape, as if Marion were somehow responsible for what happens to her. In Hitchcock, the painting is more appropriate: a biblical scene depicting Susanna and the Elders. (Susanna is disrobing for her bath while a group of old men spy on her.)

I could go on, but further details of this sort seem unnecessary. Van Sant's film is ultimately an intriguing lesson in what not to do with a remake. It makes me think of a parable by Walter Benjamin, which I shall attempt to paraphrase:

An old and fabulously wealthy king who was about to die summoned his master chef to the throne room. "When I was a child," the king said to the chef, "our nation was invaded by my father's enemies, and he and I fled briefly into the northern provinces, where we took refuge in the snow-covered cabin of a peasant woman. While we were there, the woman cooked us the most delicious mulberry omelette I've ever eaten. The memory has stayed with me all my life. I want you to recreate that omelette now, so that I can taste it again before I die. But I warn you, it must be the exact same omelette. If you succeed, you will be rewarded with half my wealth; if you fail, you will be executed." The chef thought this problem over for a moment and then replied, "Sire, I know exactly how to prepare the omelette of which you speak. I know the bushes from which the mulberries must be gathered. I know the exact seasonings the peasant woman used. I even know that the eggs must be stirred with a wooden spoon in a counter-clockwise direction. But unfortunately I cannot recreate your omelette. Your boyhood fear, your journey to the north woods, and your warmth and comfort in the peasant cabin—none of these things are in my power to reproduce. My omelette will never taste the same as the one from your youth, and I have no choice but to go to the executioner."[4]

One implication of this parable is that works of art depend on their context, and that our experience of any given work of art changes over time. Thus, even if Van Sant had been completely faithful to Hitchcock (assuming such a thing was possible), he could never have recreated "my" *Psycho* or anyone else's. A better solution would have been to simply remaster the original 35mm print and exhibit it around the world. A new print of *Psycho* was in fact shown as part of the Hitchcock centennial celebration at NYU. But was that film the same one I experienced in my youth? I think not. For all its continuing interest, *Psycho* is no longer a cutting-edge horror film. Hitchcock's dark satire of American sex and money has entered into popular folklore and become part of the cinema's imaginary museum, but it is also of its time and place. Like all powerful works of art, it can be reinterpreted and reevaluated. It can produce new meanings, acquire new audiences, and inspire new films, but it shouldn't be slavishly imitated.

NOTES

1. For additional comments on adaptation in film, see my anthology, *Film Adaptation* (New Brunswick: Rutgers University Press, 2000). On remakes, see Andrew Horton and Stuart Y. McDougal, eds., *Play It Again, Sam: Retakes on Remakes*

(Berkeley: University of California Press, 1998). See also Thomas Leitch, "Twice-Told Tales: the Rhetoric of the Remake," *Literature/Film Quarterly* 18, no. 3 (1997): 138–49.

2. For negative reactions to the Van Sant film, see William Rothman, "Some Thoughts on Hitchcock's Authorship," in Richard Allen and S. Ishii Gonzales, eds., *Alfred Hitchcock Centenary Essays* (London: BFI, 1999), 29–44; Jonathan Rosenbaum, "Hack Job," *Chicago Reader* (1998), online at http://www.chireader.com/movies/archives/1998/1298/12258.html; and Constantine Santas, "The Remake of *Psycho:* Creativity or Cinematic Blasphemy?," *Senses of Cinema* (October 2000), online at http://www.sensesofcinema.com.au. It should be emphasized, however, that not everybody agrees with these views. For an interesting commentary on Van Sant's revisions of the gay subtext in Hitchcock's film, see Steven Jay Schneider, "A Tale of Two *Psychos:* Prelude to a Future Reassessment," *Senses of Cinema* (October 2000), online at http://www.sensesofcinema.com.au. At the 1999 Hitchcock centenary conference at NYU, Thomas M. Leitch delivered an intriguing paper about the remake, entitled "Hitchcock Without Hitchcock," which takes issue with some of the points I have made (a longer version of his paper is forthcoming in print). During the discussion after Leitch's presentation, Peter Wollen made the interesting suggestion that the Van Sant film could be thought of by analogy with the contemporary recording industry, where pop stars often perform "cover" versions of older songs. The analogy strikes me as in some ways appropriate, although it leaves aside the question of whether Van Sant's "cover" is of any particular merit.

3. James Naremore, *Filmguide to* Psycho (Bloomington: Indiana University Press, 1973).

4. My retelling of this story, like Van Sant's retelling of Hitchcock, is inferior to the original. For Benjamin's version, see "Food," in Walter Benjamin, *Selected Writings*, vol. 2 (Cambridge: Harvard University Press, 1999), 363–64.

CONTENTS OF
THE *HITCHCOCK ANNUAL,*
1992–2000

Essays contained in this collection are indicated by •

NOTES ON CONTRIBUTORS

Richard Allen is Associate Professor of Cinema Studies at New York University. He is author of *Projecting Illusion,* and co-editor of *Film Theory and Philosophy, Wittgenstein, Theory, and the Arts, Hitchcock: Centenary Essays,* and a forthcoming volume of papers from the Hitchcock Centennial Conference, which he directed. He is currently at work on a book about Hitchcock's films.

Sabrina Barton is an Assistant Professor of English at the University of Texas at Austin, where she teaches film and gender studies. She has published several articles on the topics mentioned in the title of her book project, "Look At It My Way: Competing Identities in Hitchcock, the Woman's Psychothriller, and Feminist Film Theory."

John A. Bertolini is Professor of English and Film at Middlebury College. He is the author of *The Playwrighting Self of Bernard Shaw* and editor of *Shaw and Other Playwrights.* He is currently at work on a book about Terence Rattigan's plays.

Lesley Brill is Professor of English and former Chair of the Department at Wayne State University. He is the author of *The Hitchcock Romance* and *John Huston's Filmmaking*.

Joseph Garncarz is Privatdozent in Film Studies at the University of Cologne in Germany. His dissertation on film versions was published as *Filmfassungen*. He has published numerous articles on German film history in English, American, and German journals and edited collections of film studies.

Sidney Gottlieb is Professor of English at Sacred Heart University, Fairfield, Connecticut. His publications include *Hitchcock on Hitchcock: Selected Writings and Interviews* and a forthcoming collection of interviews of Hitchcock.

Joan Hawkins is an Associate Professor in the Department of Communication and Culture at Indiana University, Bloomington. She is the author of *Cutting Edge: Art-Horror and the Horrific Avant-Garde.*

Thomas Hemmeter is Professor of English at Arcadia University. His essays on Hitchcock have appeared in *Journal of Film and Video, Hitchcock's Rereleased Films,* edited by Walter Raubicheck and Walter Srebnick, and *Literature and Film in the Historical Dimension,* edited by John Simons.

Thomas M. Leitch directs film studies at the University of Delaware. His publications include *Find the Director and Other Hitchcock Games* and, most recently, *Crime Films* and *The Alfred Hitchcock Encyclopedia.*

Frank M. Meola has published essays on Ralph Waldo Emerson and issues of friendship in the nineteenth century, and on Francis Parkman's myths of masculinity. These essays are part of a work-in-progress titled *Emerson's Alternative Nation*. He is also author of the novel *Blood Relations*. He received an MFA from Columbia and a Ph.D. from UCLA, and currently teaches at Polytechnic University in Brooklyn, New York.

Christopher Morris, Charles A. Dana Professor of English at Norwich University, has published articles on Hitchcock in the *Hitchcock Annual, Literature/Film Quarterly,* and *Cinema Journal*. He is the author of *Models of Misrepresentation: On the Fiction of E. L. Doctorow.* His book *The Hanging Figure: On Suspense and the Films of Alfred Hitchcock* will be published in 2002.

James Naremore is Chancellors' Professor of Communication and Culture at Indiana University and the author of several books on film, including, most recently, *More Than Night: Film Noir in Its Contexts*, which received the Kraszna Kraus Moving-Image Award.

Leland Poague teaches film and literary theory in the Department of English at Iowa State University. He is co-editor with Marshall Deutelbaum of *A Hitchcock Reader* and author of *Another Frank Capra*. His most recent book (co-authored with Kathy A. Parsons) is *Susan Sontag: An Annotated Bibliography 1948–1992*.

Christopher Sharrett is Professor of Communication at Seton Hall University. He has edited *Crisis Cinema: The Apocalyptic Idea in Postmodern Narrative Film* and *Mythologies of Violence in Postmodern Media*. His work has appeared in *Cineaste, Film Quarterly, Persistence of Vision, Journal of Popular Film and Television, CineAction, Canadian Journal of Political and Social Theory*, and other publications.

Charles L. P. Silet teaches courses in film and modern literature at Iowa State University. His recent books include *The Critical Response to Chester Himes, Talking Murder: Interviews with Twenty Crime and Mystery Writers*, and *Oliver Stone: Interviews*.

David Sterritt, film critic of the *Christian Science Monitor*, is Professor of Theater and Film at the C. W. Post Campus of Long Island University and a member of the Film Studies Faculty at Columbia University. His books include *The Films of Alfred Hitchcock* and his articles have appeared in many publications, including *Cineaste, Journal of Aesthetics and Art Criticism*, and *Film Comment*. He is co-chair of the Columbia University Seminar on Cinema and Interdisciplinary Interpretation.

Sarah Street is a Reader in Screen Studies at the University of Bristol. Her most recent books are *British National Cinema* and *British Cinema in Documents*. She has also contributed to John Belton, ed., *Alfred Hitchcock's* Rear Window.

James M. Vest is Professor of French at Rhodes College, where he teaches in the Interdisciplinary Humanities program. He is the author of several articles and books on French literature and culture. His essays on Hitchcock's

French connections have appeared in *Journal of the Midwest Modern Language Association* and *The French Review*. He is currently working on a book on Hitchcock and France.

INDEX

BOOKS IN THE CONTEMPORARY FILM AND TELEVISION SERIES